Tom Clancy is the author of *The Hunt for Red October, Red Storm Rising, Patriot Games, The Cardinal of the Kremlin, Clear and Present Danger, The Sum of All Fears, Without Remorse, Debt of Honor, Executive Orders,* and *Rainbow Six*. Besides *Into the Storm* and *Every Man a Tiger* in the Commanders Series, he is the author of *Submarine, Armored Cav, Fighter Wing, Marine, Airborne* and *Carrier* in the non-fiction Military Library Series, and is also the co-creator of the Op-Center, Power Plays and Net Force series. He lives in Maryland.

General Chuck Horner, now retired, held many field commands during his career, and served as Commander, Ninth Air Force; Commander, U.S. Central Command Air Forces; and Commander in Chief, SPACECOM. He has won dozens of honours from the United States and other countries, and currently writes, consults and lectures on a wide range of aviation and security matters. Born in Davenport, Iowa, he now lives with his wife, Mary Jo, in Shalimar, Florida.

Every Man a Tiger

TOM CLANCY

with

General Chuck Horner (ret.)

SIDGWICK & JACKSON

First published in the United States of America 1999 by
G. P. Putnam's Sons, a member of Penguin Putnam Inc.

This edition published 2000 by Sidgwick & Jackson
an imprint of Macmillan Publishers Limited
25 Eccleston Place, London SW1W 9NF
Basingstoke and Oxford
Associated companies throughout the world
www.macmillan.co.uk

ISBN 0 283 07281 4

All maps C. P. Commanders, Inc., by Laura DeNinno
Book design by Deborah Kerner

The right of Tom Clancy and Chuck Horner to be identified as
the authors of this work has been asserted by them in accordance
with the Copyright, Designs and Patents Act 1988.

3 5 7 9 8 6 4 2

A CIP catalogue record for this book is available
from the British Library.

Printed and bound in Great Britain by
Mackays of Chatham plc, Chatham, Kent

DEDICATION

Normally, a book like this would be dedicated to those who paid the ultimate price in the desert; but here a different view is in order. Those of us who deployed were proud to be there; it was an honor to be allowed to participate in the effort to free Kuwait. At the same time, we felt gratitude for the troops who didn't deploy and were supporting us with spare parts and doing the other things that needed to be done back home or at their bases overseas. We were also extremely grateful to the reservists who were activated to man our home bases—guarding the gate, or working in the hospitals, or taking care of our families. Most of all, we felt a deep sense of gratitude to the people who supported us so vigorously with mail, cookies, and encouragement. They didn't fully understand why we were in the desert; they sure were concerned about a war and its attendant casualties; but they gave us their love and prayers without reservations.

CONTENTS

I: Into the Wild Blue

II: Shield in the Sky

III: The Thousand-Hour War

INTRODUCTION

I once observed that fighter pilots are little boys who never really get past the stage of buzzing past little girls on their bikes. I still believe this to be true. But then how does one deal with a general of fighter pilots? All the more so, how does one deal with a professional warrior who has the most elegant and subtle intellectual disguise this side of Jeff Daniels in *Dumb and Dumber*?

Well, okay, you need a few things right off. To fly an F-16 fighter plane, you have to have the skills of a concert pianist—in fact, you need to know how to play two pianos at once, since all the buttons you use to fight the airplane (that's why it's called a fighter) and all the buttons that work the radar, guns, and missiles are located on the stick and throttle quadrant so that you can kill people without having to look down. So, there you are, flying an aircraft that looks and evidently acts like a Chevy Corvette (but in three dimensions), head up, eyes out of the cockpit, looking for some Bad Guy to give a Slammer (AIM-120 AMRAAM missile) to. . . . Well, just flying the damned airplane isn't all that easy—which is why, as anyone can tell you, one of the differences between a fighter pilot and an ape is that it doesn't cost $1,000,000 to train an ape.

There are numerous other such differences between fighter pilots and apes, of course—you can, for example, trust your wife around an ape. . . .

Anyway, where were we? Oh, yeah. There you are, at 20,000 feet with a highly expensive fighter plane strapped to your back, flying it with the sort of skill the average guy with perfect eyesight, the reflexes of a mongoose, and the killer instinct of Jack Dempsey after a few hard drinks can develop in, oh, ten or twenty years of practice. Right hand is on the stick, identifying the various weapons-control buttons by feeling with your fingertips, while your left hand is doing the same on the throttle quadrant. There are other people out there who want to kill you. Some in their own airplanes, others on the ground with surface-to-air missiles, which are like fighter planes, but dumber, though somewhat faster, and still others with various firearms ranging from the ubiquitous AK-47 7.62mm (.30 caliber) to 100 millimeter (four-inch, and these bullets explode when they hit or get close to you), because, amazingly enough, not everyone likes fighter pilots.

But, getting back to business, this fighter jock is a general officer. He isn't merely supposed to mount his gallant steed and tilt off against a willing foe on the field of honor. He's supposed to lead, and command others like himself, because all of this fighting stuff is supposed to make sense, because you're not merely a well-paid and highly-trained ape-substitute. You are, in fact, supposed to make a plan on how to use all those three-dimensional Corvettes that carry bombs and missiles with the purpose of enforcing your country's will on somebody who might not quite see things our way.

A fighter pilot is, when you get down to it, a warrior, a person who puts himself in harm's way, and does it all by himself. Such people are both the same as, and different from, other warriors. The differences are mainly technical. The fighter jock drives something sleek, neat, and expensive, and loves driving it (as the wife of a naval aviator once wrote: "I'm his mistress—he's married to the airplane") because it's what sets him apart. That's what makes him bigger than other men, and this is something the fighter jock never forgets. And so, in the tradition of armored knights of medieval times, there he is, up there for everyone to see, proud and alone, doing his job for his country.

They don't have to look like killers. We so often think all professional soldiers should look like John Wayne. A good and serious man, the Duke, but he got no closer to combat operations than the offensive line of USC's football team back in the 1930s. I mean, nobody will ever mistake Chuck Horner for Duke Wayne. This transplanted Iowa farm boy is so laid back that one sometimes wants to stick a needle in his arm to make sure he's still alive, but then you remember that we don't select fighter pilots or flag officers off park benches, and you look a little closer and try to penetrate the disguise. What's the difference between a fighter pilot and an ape? You don't entrust an ape with the safety of your country.

This overage farm boy has the eyesight of a gyrfalcon, and he can play two pianos at the same time. As a team member of Lockheed-Martin, he still has access to his beloved F-16. Along the way, he's picked up a few long tonnes of knowledge, and more than that, he's got a place inside his brain where he's systematized the science and application of air power in the same way that Isaac Newton once organized physics. It's not just longer-range artillery. It's a way to attack an enemy systematically—all over, all at the same time. And you can do real harm that way. Not just punching him in the nose. Not just twisting his arm. Going after every square inch at once: Hi, there, you are now at war, hope you enjoy the ride.

Horner also, to quote John Paul Jones, has something a professional officer must have: "the nicest sense of personal honor." Right and wrong are identifiable in Chuck's universe, and separate. In a community where a man's word is his life, Chuck Horner's word is found in gold lettering on an adamantine wall of granite. He is a man of the American Midwest, and he has all the values and qualities one associates with such an origin: honesty, fair play, respect for others who may look or talk a little differently. He is the shrewdest of observers, and he's a man who enjoyed being a Wild Weasel, a fighter jock tasked to finding and killing SAM sites—that is, eliminating the people and things whose job it was to eliminate him. Weaseldom was dangerous. Chuck Horner enjoyed the game.

For this reason, and others, Chuck Horner is regarded as a "fighter pilot's fighter pilot" by a friend of mine who went "downtown" over Baghdad a few times himself back in 1991. The combination of brains, skill, and pure physical talent kept him alive when other men were less fortunate. When the Air Force nearly collapsed in the 1970s, he was one of the men who saved it, and rebuilt it in the 1980s, not just fixing the broken parts, but defining what an air force is supposed to be. What such organizations do came largely from Chuck's mind. It's business for Chuck, and a serious one, in which at best the people who die wear the other sort of uniform, something General Horner keeps in mind.

Chuck's also a superb storyteller, as you are about to see, with a keen eye for detail, and he's blessed with a puckish sense of humor that shines over a glass of something adult in a comfortable corner of the local O-Club, while you also learn a lot of things, because he's a dazzlingly effective teacher. The short version is: Chuck Horner is a hero who has paid his dues many, many times. He's been there, done that, and he has the T-shirt to prove it. In the first war of smart bombs, computers, and high-performance aircraft flown by true professionals, Chuck led the winning side, proving that the difference between a fighter pilot and an ape is that the pilot is quite a bit smarter, and better to have on your side.

—TOM CLANCY

DESERT SHIELD / STORM TIMELINE

AUGUST 1990

2 Iraq invades Kuwait
6 U.S. forces gain permission to base operations in Saudi Arabia
7 F-15s depart for Persian Gulf
7 USS *Independence* battle group arrives south of Persian Gulf
8 1st TFW and 82nd Airborne arrive in Persian Gulf

NOVEMBER 1990

8   200,000 additional troops sent from United States
29 United Nations authorizes force against Iraq

JANUARY 1991

12 Congress approves offensive use of U.S. troops
15 United Nations withdrawal deadline passes
17 D day. Coalition launches airborne assault
18 Iraq launches Scud missiles at Israel and Saudi Arabia
25 Air Force begins attacking Iraqi aircraft shelters
26 Iraqi aircraft begin fleeing to Iran
29 Battle of Khafji begins. Airpower destroys Iraqi force

FEBRUARY 1991

24 G day. Start of 100-hour ground battle
26 Fleeing Iraqi forces destroyed along "Highway of Death"
28 Cease-fire becomes effective at 8 A.M. Kuwait time

PROLOGUE

3 AUGUST 1990

On Friday morning of the August week in 1990 when Iraq invaded Kuwait, Lieutenant General Chuck Horner was at 27,000 feet, cruising at .9 Mach (540 knots), and nearing the North Carolina coast. He was headed out to sea in the *Lady Ashley,* a recent-model Block 25 F-16C, tail number 216, that had been named after the daughter of his crew chief, Technical Sergeant José Santos. Horner's aide, Lieutenant Colonel Jim Hartinger, Jr., known as "Little Grr," was on Horner's left side, a mile out, slightly high. Horner and Hartinger were en route to a mock combat with a pair of F-15Cs out of the 1st Tactical Fighter Wing (TFW) at Langley Air Force Base in Tidewater Hampton, Virginia: a winner-take-all contest that would match wits and flying skills. After that, they were all scheduled to form up and return to Langley AFB as a flight of four aircraft.

It was a bright, clear day—a good day to be in the air. Horner felt the joy he always did when flying thousands of feet above the earth in a fast and nimble aircraft, an emotion that few others ever had the opportunity to experience. Part of it was the feeling of unity with his aircraft—the fighter was like an extension of his mind and body. The brain commanded and the aircraft responded, with no other conscious motions. In an air battle, a pilot had no time for unnecessary thoughts. He evaluated angle, range, and closure with his target, while keeping track of all the fast, nimble aircraft that were trying to drive him in flames out of the sky. He thought and the jet reacted.

It was Hartinger's turn to lead, to call how he and Horner would fly from takeoff to landing, and he had set up a two-versus-two air combat tactics mission—what fighter pilots call a 2v2 ACT—with the F-15s. Horner was looking forward to it. At Langley, he was scheduled to attend an aircraft accident briefing with his Air Force boss, General Bob Russ, commanding general of the Tactical Air Command. Accident briefings were never pleasant experiences, even when the accidents were proven to be unavoidable, so Horner was happy for the chance to "turn and burn" with the guys from Langley before he hit the painful part of the day.

His policy was to try to maintain his combat skills whenever he flew his F-16. Even when traveling to an administrative meeting such as the one at Langley, he liked to make the trip worthwhile. It was a good way to stay up-to-date with the younger—often much younger—pilots he might someday lead into real battle.

He was in his fifties, but he wasn't too old to go up against an enemy. He could hold his own with most U.S. fliers; and those fliers were better than 95 percent of anyone they might meet. What he'd lost in eyesight and physical stamina, he made up for with experience and brains. Experience atrophied with disuse, however, and he needed to know firsthand not only that his combat skills were current and credible, but also what the younger fighter jocks were doing, what they were practicing—their aerial, radio, and shooting discipline and tactics.

Fighter pilots are members of a very tiny, elite tribe, who also happen to be the most arrogant group on earth. Flying high-performance jets is a consummate art, and to be merely somewhere near the top of the food chain doesn't begin to make it. They want to be the top. If there's nobody around you left to beat, there's still yourself. That means if a commander does not remain credible, a pilot may be reluctant to obey his lead. In war, failure to obey in the strictest manner can get people killed. So Horner felt he owed the people he commanded the duty to remain up-to-date in the use of his equipment, in tactics, and in understanding the stresses they faced.

Since April 1987, Chuck Horner had been commander of Ninth Air Force, which supervised the Air Force's Active and Reserve Fighter Units east of the Mississippi River. In that position, he also served as the air component commander for the Central Command, the United States military organization responsible for national security interests in the Middle East and parts of East Africa (except for Israel, Syria, and Lebanon). In 1990, Central Command was led by Army General H. Norman Schwarzkopf. It was Horner's job as CENTAF Commander to work with his foreign counterparts in a region that stretched from Egypt to Pakistan and to plan military operations—air campaigns that might be needed should a crisis arise that endangered the interests of the United States. It was also his job to make sure that U.S. air units were combat-ready, and that the logistics were in place to support them during a rapid deployment in peacetime or war. And finally, it was his job to command air assets that had been deployed to the region—during the recent Iran–Iraq war, for instance, USAF E-3A AWACS radar aircraft had kept watch over Saudi Arabia in order to prevent the local conflict from spilling over the border. When Horner wasn't visiting his assigned bases in the United States, he was visiting the nations in the CENTCOM area of responsibility.

The job kept Horner in the air and away from home much of the time. Somewhat unexpectedly, he had discovered that he had a second home in the Gulf region. Over the years he had made many friends there, especially with other airmen, and as he'd grown more familiar with them, both professionally and as a guest in their homes, his respect for them had increased. He'd come to admire their ways, their differences from westerners, their pride in their own nations, and their reverence for God. In time he'd also come to love the nations that had given them birth, with their rich history, culture, and scenic beauty; he found himself devouring whatever books on them he could find.

When these friendships developed, he had no idea how valuable they'd turn out to be later.

★ The two hats Chuck Horner wore—as Ninth Air Force and CENTAF Commanders—derived from a generally little-known but far-reaching transformation in military structure brought about by the 1986 Goldwater-Nichols Defense Reorganization Act. Goldwater-Nichols revolutionized the way the United States military services operate.

Each of the military services has its own culture and traditions, its own sources of pride and ways of doing things, but these differences, in addition to the inevitable competition for resources and status, can easily get in the way of cooperation. Meanwhile, the speed—the tempo—of warfare grows ever faster; and war becomes more lethal. The U.S. military must be able to project massive, shattering force quickly from many directions—land, sea, air, and space—which means, among other things, that service parochialism is an expensive and dated luxury. The new military mantra is "jointness"—all the services must be able to work together as well and as comfortably as with members of their own organizations.

Goldwater-Nichols aimed to implement "jointness" by breaking the hold of individual services on their combat forces. All operational control was taken away and given to regional Commanders in Chief (Europe, Central, Pacific, Southern, and to some extent Atlantic, Korea, and Strategic) and functional Commanders in Chief (Transportation, Space, Special Operations, and to some extent Strategic and Atlantic Command). This meant that the services became responsible *only* for organizing, training, and equipping military forces. Once the forces were operationally ready, they were assigned to one of the Unified Commanders. Thus, a fighter wing in Germany no longer was controlled by the Air Force, but would logically be assigned to EUCOM, a destroyer off the coast of Japan to PACOM, a satellite to SPACECOM, and a stateside army division could be assigned to any of the unified commands.

As the Ninth Air Force Commander, Chuck Horner worked for Bob Russ, the TAC Commander, who in turn worked for Larry Welch, Chief of Staff of the Air Force. As CENTAF Commander, he worked for Norman Schwarzkopf, who worked directly for Secretary of Defense Dick Cheney. The Joint Chiefs of Staff could meet in Washington and advise Colin Powell, as Chairman of the Joint Chiefs, but neither Powell nor any of the service heads had direct operational authority over Schwarzkopf, unless Cheney wished it (as did, in fact, happen). Likewise, neither Bob Russ nor Larry Welch had operational authority over Horner in his role as CENTAF Commander.

The new system created by Goldwater-Nichols was not universally popular in the Pentagon, but the people in the field loved it.

★ Meanwhile, the first week of August had been a difficult—and strange—time for the CENTAF Commander. In late July, when the Iraqi Army had begun massing on the border with Kuwait, he had put on alert the 1st TFW's F-15C Eagles at Langley and the 363d TFW's F-16C Fighting Falcons at Shaw AFB in Sumter, South Carolina, where he himself was based. On the night of August 2, a Wednesday, Iraq had invaded Kuwait, such a blatant act of thuggery that Horner had expected an immediate U.S. response. With Kuwait in Saddam Hussein's bag, Saudi Arabia and the other oil-rich Gulf Arab states were very much at risk. Several divisions of Iraq's powerful Republican Guards were poised in an attack posture along the Saudi–Kuwait border. Horner could not imagine how the United States could allow Saddam further loot. If sabers were to be rattled, then Ninth Air Force was likely be the first one to get the call.

For the next two days, Horner expected to hear from General Schwarzkopf, his Unified Command boss, yet so far he had not heard a word either from him or from CENTCOM headquarters at MacDill AFB in Tampa. Since the Iraqi army had poured across the border to Kuwait, there had been a truly eerie silence. So he had just kept to his schedule for the week as planned. On Friday, he flew off toward Langley.

The radio broke Horner's thoughts. Grr was calling for a "G" warm-up exercise, a necessary precombat discipline in the very hot and quick F-16s. Pilots needed to know that their G suits and other protective systems were working, and that they themselves were ready for the rapid onset of G forces. Otherwise there was the danger of a blackout and an unpleasant encounter with the ground. He put himself through a ninety-degree turn to the left at 4 Gs, then 4.5 Gs, as he pulled back harder on the stick grip in his right hand. He ran through a mental checklist: G suit inflating properly; breathing not too fast, not too slow; as he strained to force the blood up into his brain. No dimness in vision—the small vessels in the eyes were the first warning signs that the brain cells were being denied oxygen-rich blood. All was going well. He rolled out, then lowered the nose, and throttled at full military power as his left hand pushed the power lever forward as far as it would go. He quickly rolled into a ninety-degree turn back to the left. Six Gs this time, again running through the checklist, pleased that his fifty-three-year-old body could handle the pain and strain of the heavy G forces. Meanwhile, even as it squeezed his thighs and calves—forcing blood into his upper body—the rock-hard, inflated G suit felt as if it were trying to pinch him in two. Once again everything was in order. He rolled out, checked for Grr on the left. Their formation was still good. Now they needed only to cruise out to the east end of the ACM practice area and wait for the 1st TFW Eagles to show up.

As they crossed the Atlantic coast, Horner's jet almost imperceptibly shuddered, as single-engine jets always seemed to do when a pilot got beyond sight of land. He instinctively checked the gauges . . . all of them were in the green.

Then the radio came alive.

"Teak One, this is Sea Lion. Your F-15s have canceled and Washington Center asks that you contact them immediately."

Sea Lion was the Navy radar station at Norfolk, Virginia, that kept track of military training airspace out over that part of the Atlantic. In an instant, Horner knew what was up—a recall to Shaw. Grr called them over to 272.7 MHz, the proper UHF channel to contact the center controller, checked Horner in, and gave Washington Center a call.

"Washington Center, Teak One. Understand you have words for us."

"Teak One, this is Washington Center. We have a request that you return to Shaw AFB immediately. Do you need direct routing?"

"Roger, Washington. We'd like to go present position direct Florence direct Shaw FL 320," that is to say, flight level—altitude—32,000 feet.

"Roger Teak, cleared as requested. Squawk 3203." Grr then dialed a setting into his onboard radar transponder, the transponder transmitted a code that was used to cue the ground controllers, and "3203" was displayed over their return blip on the Center's radar screen.

My God, Horner thought, stunned, as he and Grr turned back toward Shaw. *It's on. This has to be about the Iraqi invasion.* A million questions roared through his mind: *Have the Iraqis entered Saudi Arabia? How much force will we deploy? How fast can we get our Ninth Air Force squadrons in the air to rendezvous with the SAC tankers? How much heavy airlift is available to get our spares and maintenance people deployed to the Middle East? How do we get our pre-positioned tents, munitions, fuel, and medical equipment from their warehouses in Oman and Bahrain, and from the ships at anchor in the lagoon at Diego Garcia?* And inevitably, *How many young men and women will die?*

Thank God for Internal Look, Horner thought. Every second year the Commander in Chief of CENTCOM held an exercise in the United States in which his staff planned for a mock war. CENTCOM's forces were then brought into the field to execute that "war." The actual component commanders, such as Horner, John Yeosock of the Army, Walt Boomer of the Marines, and Schwarzkopf himself would deploy with their staffs and forces and conduct the kind of operations they might use in a real crisis. In the process, they learned to work with each other and to test the staff's and their own abilities, and the CINC was able to evaluate his team and learn how to use them and all of his forces to best advantage. In the intervening year the CINC would hold training exercises in the Middle East, where U.S. soldiers, sailors, marines, and airmen could experience life in the desert and serve side by side with their Arab counterparts.

In the early days after the founding of CENTCOM, it had been feared that the Russians would attack south through Iran, thus attempting to make real a long-standing, indeed, pre-Soviet dream. Early CENTCOM plans, consequently, had been aimed at stopping such a move. By November 1989, when General Schwarzkopf had taken over CENTCOM command, the Soviets were not about to attack anywhere, so CENT-COM had had to look for a new mission. They didn't have to look far. After the Iran–Iraq War, Iraq had been left with a huge, well-equipped, well-trained, and seasoned military force and an astronomical debt. *How do they pay off the debt?* Norman Schwarzkopf asked himself. *They go where the money is: south, into Kuwait, and if they are really ambitious, into Saudi Arabia.* As a result, General Schwarzkopf had directed that the 1990 Internal Look exercise take off from the premise that Country Orange (read: Iraq) had invaded some of its Gulf neighbors. Thus, early in August of 1990, when Iraq actually followed the Country Orange scenario, Schwarzkopf and his staff had a considerable head start on the planning needed for a U.S. military response to the invasion of Kuwait.

★ All these thoughts got shoved into the back of Horner's mind when Shaw AFB appeared under his nose. They were about 1,500 feet up; Grr guided their airplanes over the runway without slowing down. Horner took a quick glance at the airspeed displayed on the windshield's heads-up display; they were on the initial approach at a screaming 450 knots.

They were going to make a pitchout—a loop laid on its side—that would bring them down to runway level while they slowed down to landing speed. It was not an especially difficult maneuver if the pilot didn't mind pulling a lot of Gs and working to maintain the same altitude and spacing as the other aircraft in the flight as he rolled out in the landing pattern. It was something like driving down the street at 250 mph in formation with other cars going the same speed, then making the corner together. Of course, the leader wants to keep the maneuver tight, with the guys behind him in tight, so he doesn't want to make the turn too loose, or else everyone else in the flight will spread out, and the landing will be inelegant. Inelegance is not an option.

The downside to making the turn too tight is to spin out and crash.

Horner felt the extra Gs needed to slow down in the pitchout force him down into his seat, then he took a little extra spacing on Grr in the event Hartinger turned a wide base. He wanted to save enough room to cut inside of him if Grr got wide on final approach, but still not overrun his aircraft. As usual, though, Grr kept the base leg tight, just outside the runway overrun. Horner grinned, put the gear down, lowered the nose sharply, and pulled the F-16 around with the stall warning sounding a steady noise in his headset. It was about 11:00 A.M.

After they landed and parked, José Santos, their crew chief, approached the aircraft, a worried look on his face. He figured they'd returned because of a mechanical problem, which would be a slap in the face for him. José disappeared for a moment to insert the ground safety pin into the emergency hydrazine tank that powered the F-16's electrical systems and hydraulics if the engine failed. When he emerged, Horner gave him an OK sign, and his worried look changed into a relieved grin. After that, Horner ran through the engine shutdown checklist: inertial navigation system off, throttle off, and canopy up.

All about them, the ramp was silent. Shaw had been ready for two weeks to go to war, so local flying was at a minimum.

As soon as Horner climbed down the ladder, he told José to get the jet ready to go. He suspected he'd be on the ground only a short time. Meanwhile, Grr came running over. Horner told him to file a flight plan for MacDill; then he shrugged out of his G suit.

It's hard to look anything but rumpled when you shed a G suit, but this was not a problem for Chuck Horner. For him, rumpled was normal. He had a comfortable, but not pretty, bloodhound face, sandy, thinning hair, and a bulldog body. He looked nothing like Tom Cruise or Cary Grant, or any other Hollywood fighter-jock image. On the other hand, Horner moved with great verve and dash; he had an easy, infectious laugh and a wicked wit; and inside his bloodhound head was one of the sharpest, quickest minds inside the Air Force or out. He liked to play the Iowa farmboy, but he'd come a long way out of Iowa.

He walked over to his staff car, threw his G suit in the backseat, and drove to his office in the headquarters Ninth Air Force/CENTAF building just two blocks away.

Horner's secretary, Jean Barrineau, was waiting at the door of the outer office. A tall, slender, middle-aged woman with light brown hair who looked younger than her years, Jean was the Ninth Air Force Commander's brain. She ruled his schedule, yet she wielded her power lightly. Most of the time a visitor would find her with a twinkling face, her eyes shining with amusement, and a little-girl smile, as though she was playing some private joke on her boss—which she often did.

Today there were no tricks and no smiles. She was worried and all business. "General Schwarzkopf wants you to call him," she said, "secure."

He blew past her into the office.

The office was institutional but pleasant, with the inevitable government-issue big mahogany desk at one end and a small seating area at the other. The walls held the collection of "I love me" plaques and pictures a man accumulated in the military as he went from base to base. On one wall was a large painting of an F-15 with Horner's name painted on the canopy rail—a gift from the 2d Squadron at Tyndall AFB in Florida, where he'd served from 1983 to '85. On the coffee table in the seating area was a copy of the Holy Bible and the Holy Koran; the Bible came from the base chapel, the Koran from a friend in Saudi Arabia. Both were in English. Around the room on various end tables and bookcases were the odds and ends he had gathered while traveling around the world. A gold-colored dagger was a gift from the AWACS crews in Riyadh, a bronze block paperweight commemorating his time in TAC Headquarters as the deputy for Plans and Programs, and there were fighter squadron plaques from the Ninth Air Force units with whom Horner had flown training sorties during base visits. To the right of the back wall was a door that led to the toilet and washstand he shared with his deputy, Major General Tom Olsen. A large, computerlike telephone was located on a credenza under the office's rear window, directly behind the desk. It shared the space with a few books of the trade, including his F-16 Pilots Handbook and a copy of the United States Military Code of Justice. The phone looked like a computer, because in fact it was a computer, designed to scramble conversations, and it featured thirty or more hot-line buttons that connected with locations in the building and around the world.

Horner sat down behind his desk and punched the top right red switch hot-line button; it was marked "CINCCENT." Schwarzkopf's Master Chief answered after the first ring; she said the General would be on the line right away. A moment later, the gruff yet friendly voice of H. Norman Schwarzkopf came on the line. "Chuck, can you come down to MacDill?"

This wasn't a request. It was simply a civilized way to say, "Lieutenant General Horner, this is General Schwarzkopf. Get your ass in my office as soon as possible."

"Yes sir," Horner answered, in his best subservient military voice, then added, "Can you tell me what this is all about?"

General Schwarzkopf confided that he was flying up to Washington the next morning to brief the President on the situation in Kuwait, and about the options the President could consider should the Iraqi Army continue its advance into Saudi Arabia—a possibility that was worrying the President just then.

"I'll be right there," Horner responded quickly.

When he told Jean he'd be off for MacDill, she said that she had already called TAC Headquarters at Langley AFB, and told General Russ's secretary that he'd miss the accident brief. He smiled and headed out to his F-16. It was then about one o'clock. They'd be in Tampa about two.

It was Horner's time to lead the flight, and in the best of all possible worlds, he would have put together a low-level transit to Tampa; but they didn't have time to plan that. It was first things first; a potential air war got priority over training and fun.

The trip itself was a blur. His head was a swarm of thoughts and plans—deployment concepts, numbers of sorties, bombs, enemy fighters, data from a dozen exercises, hundreds of briefings, endless hours of planning over the past three years for a threat from the north. Yet he was in no way anxious. He knew he was ready, well trained, and well supported by a dedicated staff of men and women. Some of them, in fact, had been at Shaw AFB back in the early eighties when the then CENTAF Commander Larry Welch (later the Air Force Chief of Staff) had formed the first Air Force component of the Rapid Deployment Joint Task Force, before RDJTF had become CENTCOM about 1982.

The RDJTF had come about when U.S. political leaders realized that the industrial world's primary oil supply was located in one of the most dangerous neighborhoods on the globe, and that America's allies there did not have sufficient population to create a military force capable of protecting it. The RDJTF concept had been to create a hard-hitting strike force of Army, Navy, Marine Corps, and Air Force units capable of deploying halfway around the world on a moment's notice; hence the terms "Rapid Deployment" and "Joint." Unfortunately, when it had first started, it had been neither very rapid nor very joint. In the intervening years, successive leaders had honed the deployment skills of their units, and practiced fighting as an integrated team in numerous joint exercises in the California deserts.

Thus, Horner's Ninth Air Force team had been preparing to go to war in the Middle East for the past decade. Endless hours had been dedicated to intelligence workups of the region and its people. The operations and logistics staffs had fought many paper wars, using computers to evaluate their plans, strategies, and tactics. Now all that work, all that study, and all that planning was to be put to the test.

★ H. Norman Schwarzkopf was a big man, with an unusually large head and broad face—so broad that someone seemed to have stuck his small nose on as an afterthought. He was not simply big, he was imposing. When he was in a room, he was the room's focus; he didn't leave much oxygen for anyone else. When you worked for him, it wasn't hard to fall into awe of him. He thrived on confrontation. His temper was famously quick and violent, and he was notorious for verbally hanging, drawing, and quartering those who didn't reach his standards. The term for that was "CINC abuse."

The term would be used often in the coming months . . . but not by Chuck Horner. In the short ten months he and Schwarzkopf had served together, the two generals had forged a very different kind of relationship. For Horner, Schwarzkopf was not the screaming, tantrum-throwing prima donna others feared. He knew, first of all, that the CINC was very intelligent and amazingly softhearted, and, for him, Schwarzkopf's confrontational style of leadership was a plus. Horner also thrived on confrontation. If working for him was like an air-to-air battle, that was no problem. Horner was a fighter jock. That kind of competition was a joy. Horner always worked hard to enter engagements with the CINC prepared for any maneuvers he might throw at him; and as a result, their relationship was cordial and warm. Schwarzkopf had even learned to tolerate occasional jabs from Horner's sometimes wild sense of humor.

On this day, however, there would be no humor.

When Horner walked into Schwarzkopf's office, he saw that the General looked very tired. The CINC didn't waste any time: When he briefed the President and the cabinet the next morning (August 4) at Camp David, he said, he had a pretty good idea of the options the U.S. ground forces could employ to halt any Iraqi advance into Saudi Arabia, thanks to Internal Look, and he was confident he could give a clear, solid briefing to the President. But about the "Air" part of the briefing, he was much less secure.

If the Iraqis decided to move south into Saudi Arabia, the CENTCOM ground component was the XVIIIth Airborne Corps, which could be on the scene relatively speedily, some of it in days. Iraqi options were limited. Since the terrain became more and more difficult the farther west one got from the Gulf coast, and since the Israelis were in the extreme west watching any military moves in their direction, any Iraqi attack would probably come down the east coast. This was also where the oil was and most of the significant Saudi population centers, such as Jubail and Dhahran. If Riyadh was an Iraqi goal, they would probably come south and then turn right toward the capital. It was clear to Schwarzkopf what divisions he'd need and where they needed to go to stop such an attack.

Air, however, was another matter. Horner was aware that Schwarzkopf had no significant knowledge of that component, much less experience with it. The proper use of an air force was not then part of his mental equipment. Horner was also aware—though the CINC never said it explicitly—that Schwarzkopf was less than confident his planning staff would be able to prepare an air briefing for him that he could happily take to the President. That's why he wanted Chuck Horner at MacDill. After he'd explained to Horner that Air Force Major General Burt Moore's J-3 (CENTCOM Operations) shop was working the briefings, he asked if Horner could go down to the command center and give them some assistance. Moore was the chief reason Schwarzkopf was worried about his planning staff.

Moore had only recently taken over the CENTCOM J-3 slot after four years as the Air Force congressional liaison in Washington—hardly the best preparation for planning and operations. Not only was he new to the job and yet to prove himself, but he lacked both experience in the theater and current knowledge of airpower. Almost as bad: he was an Air Force officer, a segment of humanity that the CINC instinctively disliked and distrusted. "With Schwarzkopf," Horner reflects, "you had to out-tough him to be accepted. Once he'd concluded that you were smart, tough, and loyal, then he would accept you. If he didn't accept you and you were an Air Force officer, you were double dead meat." Schwarzkopf didn't accept Burt Moore.

Moments later, Horner was out of the serene yet intense office of the CINC, and into the noisy chaos of the CENTCOM command center. Burt Moore was under the gun, and a raft of Air Force, Army, and Marine lieutenant colonels and colonels were crowded into a small conference room, all of them very much on edge, building briefing slides to present to the CINC at the 1700 (5:00 P.M. EDT) conference. The urgency of their efforts was heightened by their fear of provoking a Schwarzkopf rage.

As soon as he walked into the conference room, Horner sensed that such an event was a very real possibility. Everyone there was more than a little confused and demoralized. Their efforts lacked order and focus, and they seemed to be missing essential details, such as basing, logistics, and sortie rates.

For their part, Moore and his people were neither delighted to see Horner nor eager to listen to his thoughts and suggestions—which he understood. Ordinarily it would have peeved him to be told to get out of their hair when he was sure he could help them, but they had obviously been working the problem for days, and they didn't need some outsider sticking his nose into their business. If they were going to be ripped apart by the CINC, at least it should be as the result of their own efforts, and not because of some unwanted advice from the Air Force component of the command. He was also well aware that rank had little importance among fighter pilots. He let the matter drop. If they needed his help, they would call him.

There was a spare office up on the second floor. If he liked, they told him, he could wait up there. He sighed, and retired to the solitude of the bare-bones office on the second floor.

It was now 3:00 P.M. He decided he might as well not waste his time, so as he sat, he pondered: *What would I tell the President of the United States if I were General Schwarzkopf?*

He'd tell him how much military force he could deploy; what types of units, how fast, where they would be based, and how they would be supported. They'd be broad summaries clearly based on intensive examination of thousands of details. Next, he'd show what amount of military coercive force this air armada could generate. Again, the summaries would capture the strength of modern airpower without boring the listener with the particulars. Here, too, the President would know these statements were supported by a thorough review of nuts-and-bolts detail. Finally he'd conclude with employment concepts—a strategy for employment of airpower to bring the invasion to a halt in preparation for an offensive air campaign that would throw the invading army out of Saudi Arabia *and* Kuwait, seize control of the air, interdict Iraqi fuel, munitions, food, and water, as well as command and control, and provide close support to the outnumbered ground forces. All of this would be enough to the point to let the President know that he, General H. Norman Schwarzkopf, U.S. Army, had his act together and was ready, capable, and in charge.

More specifically, Horner thought, *Schwarzkopf would want to pro-*

tect our own forces, so he'd want to put up a defensive air CAP—Combat Air Patrol—with AWACS, so he could keep the Iraqi Air Force from attacking us. This would also allow our forces maneuver space, and protect the cities and oil facilities. Once that was done, he'd worry about the Iraqi ground thrust. Where our ground forces were engaged, he'd provide air support. But the real aim of air in this situation would be to defeat the enemy's ability to sustain the attack, so he'd go after supply depots and lines of supply. That would likely mean he'd have to give up some ground in the opening battle, but as the enemy's supply routes became longer, the Iraqis would become increasingly vulnerable to air attack. In time we'd cause the attack to dry up, while forcing their ground forces into a posture that our ground forces could handle. Meanwhile, we would conduct operations against their infrastructure and their nation that would punish them for initiating the attack. How? By hitting specific targets with a specific number of sorties. In order to do it, we'd provide such and such a force, to be based here and here . . .

In order to fill in the blanks, Horner spent the rest of the afternoon on the phone to Shaw AFB, getting information from his Director of Operations, Colonel Jim Crigger, and his Director of Logistics, Colonel Bill Rider. Crigger looked up for him the sortie rates they'd used during the Internal Look exercises, as well as historical aircraft loss rates, readiness states of various fighter and bomber units, deployment schedules, and beddown locations—locations where units would have fuel, food, ammunition, housing, and everything they needed to function. Rider provided endless streams of data on munitions availability, spare parts, fuel supplies, and the beddown capacity of various bases—all the supporting factors that spelled the difference between victory and defeat.

★ Above all, Horner wanted to avoid the misconceptions that got tossed around all too easily in discussions of air planning and air operations— that there were such things as distinct "strategic" and "tactical" airpower. He knew that if they got bogged down in such distinctions, then the whole operation could be a disaster. He explains:

> *The use of the words "strategic" and "tactical" are a heritage from previous wars, where in general strategic attack was directed at an enemy's heartland, and tactical operations were directed at his military forces in the field or at sea. More recently, "strategic"*

has come to mean nuclear strikes against the Soviet Union, or other powerful enemies, and "tactical" all other forms of air warfare.

Meanwhile, the less lofty terms, "offensive" and "defensive," have long been associated with counter–air operations. Defensive sorties were ground alert, airborne alert, or scrambles launched against enemy aircraft attacking your territory or forces. Offensive sorties attacked enemy forces, usually over enemy territory or controlled seas.

I understand offensive and defensive; they have to do with where and when and situation. I don't understand tactical or strategic. The words have now become meaningless and dysfunctional. In fact, in modern military speech, they are more often used to divide people and frustrate efforts than to illuminate and facilitate. People use them loosely who don't know what they are talking about. So, for example, a B-52 is called a "strategic bomber." A strategic bomber? Then why was it doing close air support in the Gulf, a "tactical" operation?

In reality, the person most likely to call a B-52 a strategic bomber will be an airman from SAC headquarters trying to keep control of an asset he is responsible for in terms of organizing, training, and equipping. If that asset is engaged in non-nuclear operations and deployed to a theater other than CINCSAC's, it's an asset potentially lost to SAC. It's all thought of as a zero-sum game.

There is also a service-biased crowd that like to think of the USAF as made up of strategic or tactical elements—that is, either elements that attack the enemy heartland (as the Eighth Air Force did over Germany in World War II—the real Air Force) or tactical elements that are essentially mobile artillery for the army, and therefore not really Air Force. I call such people airheaded airmen. They don't realize that air can and will do whatever is necessary to get the job done. In fact, the real Air Force does not define the job as either "strategic" or "tactical." The job flows down from the President and the Unified Command. As an airman, my job is to tell the President and the Unified Commander what air can do to get that job done, either on its own or by supporting other forces.

This last explains in part why Goldwater-Nichols has had such a deep and far-reaching effect on our military. It is an effort to stomp out the desire of each service to think it is the end-all, and *the others are around just to support them. Thus, in the traditional Navy view of the world, it's "We like you all, but we are busy out here alone in the middle of the deep blue, so don't bother to write except to send tankers and AWACS overhead." The Air Force has those who see airpower as the only solution to all problems, but they want the Army to defend their bases and the Navy to make sure the JP-4 fuel tanker ships get to port. The Marines are most "joint" of all; they need the Navy to get them there, they can't survive without the Air Force's lift and heavy support (they don't have enough jets), and the Army is responsible for designing and acquiring their equipment. So the way they keep their bias alive is to make sure they always fight alone on some island somewhere without ever integrating into a larger picture.*

Some of the more doctrine-laden ground people also talk about the strategic, operational, and tactical levels of war, so they can think in bins or boxes: "strategic" means whatever the President thinks about and does, "operational" is what the CINC thinks about and does, "tactical" is component-level-and-below thinking and doing.

To an airman this is meaningless. My tactical fighter (tactical), flying to Baghdad (operational), kills Saddam Hussein (strategic).

So finally, in talking about air plans or air operations, I keep as far from these words as I can. Airpower is essentially very simple: aircraft can range very quickly over very wide areas and accurately hit targets very close to home or very far away. Nothing more. Nothing less.

★ These are the briefing elements Horner put together that afternoon at MacDill:

First came the basics:

- **Forces Available:** Under Goldwater-Nichols, CENTCOM was apportioned certain forces—primarily the 1st TFW (F-15s at Langley) and the 363d TFW (F-16s at Shaw). There were also F-111s, A-10s, C-130s, intelligence assets, ground radar units, a number of E-3 AWACS, a Red Horse engineering unit (for construction services), the Ninth Air Force staff and commander, and so forth. The CINC of CENTCOM could also obtain units apportioned to other CINCs, but for that he needed the approval of the Secretary of Defense. Thus, CENTCOM was later given the Army's VIIth Corps, which came from EUCOM and was an enormous addition to its ground forces; and CENTAF was also considerably augmented before the actual beginning of the war in January of '91. (All of these changes were several months in the future.) In August, Chuck Horner's position was to fight the forces that were already apportioned to CENTCOM. Since, as CENTAF Commander, Horner was not just the Central Command Air Force component commander, but also the joint force air component commander (JFACC), the forces available additionally included the fixed-wing aircraft that belonged to the Navy, Marine, and Army units assigned to CENTCOM. He looked at all of these forces day to day, to keep track of their readiness posture, so he knew what forces he could count on.

- **Types of Units:** Though all types of units make up an air force, the basic breakdown of roles are Air Superiority, Air Interdiction, Close Air Support, Reconnaissance, and Airlift. Some of the units were dedicated to one role. For example, the F-15s were used only in air-to-air missions*; the F-16s could do any role except Airlift; the A-10s were best used for Close Air Support (though they could do much more than that); and the C-130s hauled men and matériel, mostly Army, around the theater. However, C-130s had also been used in Vietnam to drop huge bombs to make helicopter landing pads in the jungle. So when Horner looked at an aircraft, he considered all its possible roles.

- **Speed of Deployment:** This issue had to be approached from three directions—need, tanker availability, and airlift availability. Horner's first job was to make sure he controlled the air and could protect the rest of the force arriving by air and sea. Thus, he needed F-15s (for air-to-air), AWACS (for radar), and Rivet Joint (for signals intelligence). Flying the large jets such as the AWACS to Saudi Arabia was not a problem, since they could cross the ocean without tanker support; but the smaller aircraft, such as F-15s, required tankers, meaning that his deployment tempo was limited by tanker availability. Next, only the C-130

---

*Later F-15 models could be used in other roles, as well.

units could self-deploy—that is, bring their own spare parts and people with them. In order to be operational when they arrived, the jets sent to Saudi Arabia would need a support airlift, or else they would have to be based with a like Saudi unit to allow Horner to support operations with Saudi parts and maintenance people until his own people and parts arrived. Thus, he initially based the 1st TFW's F-15s with Saudi F-15s at the Saudi base at Dhahran. Once these three basic elements were determined, he prioritized the lineup in terms of what he wanted to go first and how long he thought it would take, knowing that all active air force units must be capable of deploying in twenty-four hours, and all guard and reserve units in forty-eight hours.

- **Basing:** Over the years, Horner had done preliminary planning about what units and aircraft to base where, and in fact his people already had considerable basing experience in Saudi Arabia. Earlier that year (1990), for example, AWACS and tankers had come home from Riyadh air base, where they had been operating for the previous eight years, protecting Saudi Arabia and its oil from possible spillover from the Iran–Iraq War. Since there were already hangars, ramps, fuel, and all kinds of equipment and supplies available, and the unit knew where to set what up, it made sense to send AWACS to Riyadh. Again, like units went best with like units. After that it was a matter of available ramp space and a feel for the pluses and minuses of the bases themselves. From visits with his counterparts, Horner knew all the airfields in the region. He had walked the ramps and flown from their runways. He also knew which countries were likely to let the United States in and which ones might balk. (As it turned out, all of them were very cooperative.) In short, he had done his homework; basing would not be a problem.

- **Facing the Enemy:** Since the aim of all this activity was not movement or placement of assets, but (at least potentially), the generation of combat sorties, aircraft needed to be located where they would be available for the maximum number of sorties. Thus, Horner wanted to put the A-10s and Marine Harriers (short-range Vertical Take-Off and Landing aircraft) as near Kuwait as possible, because A-10s and Harriers were used primarily in close support roles. He also knew that the Marines liked to be near the sea. Conversely, he wanted the air CAP jets near the border, which meant placing them at Dhahran and Tabuk. On the other hand, since his tankers were nothing more than modified 707s and MD-11s, and since a 707 or MD-11 didn't know whether it belonged to United Air Lines or the United States Air Force, the tankers would fit best at international airports, where maintenance and ground-handling equipment were available for large commercial aircraft. He wanted to place aircraft carriers in waters as close to Iraq as he could persuade the Navy to put them. And he wanted B-52s near the theater, but in locations that were not vulnerable to Scud or air strikes.

Second, Schwarzkopf (and after him the President) would want to understand the amount of military coercive force this air armada could generate. Here, briefing slides would come in handy:

The first of these would picture a map of the Iraq, Kuwait, and Saudi Arabia region, a very simple map, just border outlines with a few symbols of major towns, highways, and rivers. On this map, a pair of large arrows would drop out of Kuwait, one aimed south along the coast, and a second aimed south but then bending to the west toward Riyadh. One of these two would be the probable Iraq course of attack. The map would then depict aircraft in orbit over central Saudi Arabia—AWACS and their CAPs to the north of them. It would also depict F-16s and A-10s attacking the lead elements of the Iraqi army, as well as the logistics bases and supply lines supporting the attack.

A second slide would list aircraft types down the left side. A middle column would list the number of aircraft expected to be based in theater and the expected sortie rate. So, for example, the sortie rate for the A-10 might be 3.5, and for the B-52 it might be .60. The right-hand column would multiply the number of aircraft by the sortie rate to give the number of sorties Horner would expect to fly per day. This would convey the level of effort he expected to sustain once the battle was joined.

★ How would these forces actually be used to defeat an Iraqi invasion of Saudi Arabia?

The basic strategy was to defeat the Iraqi invader by first cutting off his essential supplies and then by hitting his forces where they were causing problems with the U.S. ground forces. More specifically:

- **Seize control of the air:** Blind the centralized air defense system by knocking out their radars, and the command and control that directs them. Shoot down the Iraqi fighters brave and stupid enough to fly. Hit their airfields to limit the number of fighters they can put up to challenge you. Strike fear in the hearts of the radar-guided SAM operators by using Wild Weasels and HARM missiles to make them afraid to turn on their radars. And avoid the guns and shoulder-fired infrared (IR) missiles by flying at medium altitude.

- **Interdict Iraqi fuel, munitions, food, and water:** Armies have to set up dumps where their vehicles can go for gas and ammunition, so find the dumps and blow them up. Armies need fuel trucks to carry gas to their tanks and vehicles; and they need freighter trucks to carry their ammunition, so patrol the roads to the dump and strafe the trucks going and coming.

- **Attack command and control:** Find enemy headquarters—probably a group of tents or command-and-control vehicles (armored personnel carriers—APCs—loaded with antennas). This is an attacking army, so it has no bunkers. You find these headquarters by listening for them. They have to talk. They have to use radios or ground lines. Either way, you'll know it. Without communication, a commander can't control anything. (He can use runners or carrier pigeons, but the bandwidth on those is very low.) When you hear them talking, you can do four things: (1) listen but otherwise leave them alone, so you can disrupt their attack plan; (2) jam them and so deny communication; (3) voice over them and deliver the wrong communication ("Saddam Hussein here. I want you to change your direction of attack. Go north. Got that? North."); (4) or bomb them. Because you control the air, the enemy has none of these options (though he might try ground-based systems; the range of these is short, however, due to the earth's curvature).

- **Provide close air support to the outnumbered ground forces:** There were two issues here—providing close air support (CAS) for U.S. ground forces, a mission that had been practiced long and hard, and providing CAS for the Arab allies, which was more problematic because of language issues, and because it hadn't been practiced—at least adequately and routinely. However, even CAS for U.S. forces had some problematic elements, partly because of the differing needs (or perceived needs) of air and ground forces, and partly because of recent changes in the very nature of warfare itself.

An air force is in the ordnance-delivery business, just as an airline is in the seat-delivery business. A TWA jet is well used when it is in the air and all its seats are filled. An F-16 is well used when it is in the air delivering ordnance to a target. The needs of ground people are somewhat different. For one thing, they like to have friendly aircraft visibly overhead. It makes them feel good. If these aircraft are not in fact delivering ordnance, that is not terribly important to their feelings of well-being. For another, ground people like to schedule air strikes the way they like to schedule artillery—hours, sometimes days, in advance. However, modern warfare has changed so greatly, the tempo of war has speeded up so much, and a good modern army is so mobile (you don't know what you need because you don't know where you'll be fighting), that scheduling air strikes in the old way had become seriously counterproductive.

Very early on in their command relationship, Horner talked at length with Schwarzkopf about these issues, and convinced him then of a way of providing close air support that later came to be called Push CAS. That is, aircraft would be designated for CAS, but where, how, and when they would be used would be determined "on the run" by events in the field. If no one in the field had an immediate need for CAS, or if they were holding their own or winning, Horner would send the jets to the enemy rear area. Though the effects of these last strikes wouldn't show up immediately, when they did, they would prove dramatic. Push CAS required excellent communications and control and also good ways of identifying the precise locations of the targets, but it was not otherwise more difficult than earlier ways of operating. Schwarzkopf had bought into Push CAS in April during the Internal Look exercise, and Push CAS became a reality in February 1991.

The problem of providing CAS to Arab-only speakers was solved by asking the RSAF (Royal Saudi Air Force), all of whom were bilingual in English and Arabic, to provide CAS controllers. It also turned out that there were a few USAF fighter pilots who, by reason of family origin, spoke Arabic. However, neither of these solutions could be instantly implemented. There would have been real problems in August 1990 if the Iraqis had come south.

- **Once the Iraqi invasion has been brought to a halt, begin an offensive air campaign whose aim is to throw the invading army out of Saudi Arabia *and* Kuwait:** Though CENTCOM tasking in August was to focus on the defense of Saudi Arabia, nonetheless, no one could ignore the event that had started the crisis, the invasion of Kuwait. Thus, initial plans had to be made for attacks against key targets in Iraq—oil refineries, power-generation plants, major rail yards, large factories, interstate highways, bridges, and the like. The idea was to link the destruction of these targets essential to Iraq with a coherent strategy designed to gain a political objective, such as the removal of the Iraqis from Kuwait. In point of fact, Horner and Schwarzkopf had recently come from the Internal Look exercise in Florida, where their air planners had been selecting targets throughout Iraq in response to the exercise scenario. Most of the target materials used during the war had already been ordered from intelligence sources the previous spring (primarily the DIA) as part of the preparations for Internal Look.

By the time the 5:00 P.M. conference with the CINC had arrived, Horner was ready to step in, if necessary, and provide Schwarzkopf with the basics he'd need to take to Camp David. He grabbed his notes and headed down to the CINC's conference room to listen to the briefing proposed for the CINC by the J-3.

The small conference room was small and crowded, and the atmosphere was tense. The CINC was tired, the process of preparing the presidential briefing had not gone smoothly, and now time was running out. Fortunately, no one was allowed to smoke. Schwarzkopf's predecessor, Marine General George Crist, and many of his staff had been chain-smokers; CENTCOM meetings in those days had been agony to non-smokers.

The meeting started with a short update on the situation in Kuwait. It turned out that when the crisis had broken out in July, General Schwarzkopf had had a man in a hotel across the street from the American Embassy in Kuwait City. His name was John F. Feeley, and he was a major on the CENTCOM Intelligence staff. Feeley had been sent to

Kuwait with a briefcase full of top-secret photos to show the Kuwaiti leaders and had been caught there during the invasion. Now he was providing direct eyeball updates via a man-portable satellite phone. Horner didn't know this man, but he imagined he was operating at a high pitch of excitement, perched as he was in the middle of the Iraqi Army as they rounded up elements of the Kuwaiti Army and foreign visitors. The CINC was obviously pleased that he'd inserted a pair of eyes in the enemy camp. Horner wondered if the "pair of eyes" shared the CINC's joy.

The next part of the briefing took up the use of ground forces to counter an invasion of Saudi Arabia. Schwarzkopf asked few questions and made few comments; it was obvious this was his briefing and he had personally worked hard on it. The material was clear, understandable, and to the point; it addressed in detail the issues that constitute war on the ground—terrain, enemy forces, lines of communication, armor, tactics. For someone who could only guess at how events would unfold, it was quite reassuring.

The air part of the briefing was another thing; it turned out to be everything Horner had feared. As soon as it started, Horner could see a titanic disaster in the making. Burt Moore's people, for all their talent, had fallen into the trap of trying to give the boss what they thought he wanted, rather than what they knew he needed. The material was vague, airy, lightweight. It scarcely began to show comprehension of the myriad facts and details that a good briefer condensed and focused into a very few words.

It primarily contained a list of forces that would deploy according to the Time Phased Force Deployment List (TPFDL—which is the military's way of talking about moving things and people), as well as some discussion about where the forces would be located on the Saudi Arabian peninsula. This was interesting and important information as far as it went; but the point of any deployment was not the movement and placement of forces, but the way the forces could be brought to bear against a potential enemy. The briefing did not address that issue. It did not convey the combat power those aircraft were capable of bringing against the attacking Iraqi forces, nor did it point out where and when the aircraft would strike the Iraqi forces, nor the logistics factors (such as fuel and munitions availability) these combat operations would require, or how these would impact sortie rates.

In short, the briefing talked about *things,* the elements of airpower—

numbers of aircraft and bases—but did not talk about the application of force and how it would be used to frustrate the enemy and accomplish the CINC's military objectives. It described a horse without telling the listener how he intended to use the horse.

During the first two slides, the CINC showed amazing patience. "Perhaps he was hoping it would get better," Horner observes, "like the kid pawing through a pile of horse manure hoping to find a pony inside." Unfortunately, the briefing got worse, and so did Schwarzkopf's temper. As his questions and comments increased in volume and velocity, the room grew charged with electricity. Many hunkered down into the near-fetal position staff officers learn to achieve in an upright chair. Others gleefully anticipated the inevitable Schwarzkopf eruption.

For a second, Horner allowed himself a small, childish "I told you so" thought, but quickly switched it off. *Time's running out,* he told himself. *No need for any poor sons of bitches to suffer CINC abuse. And more to the point, it's not fair to Schwarzkopf to provide him less than our best efforts.*

He turned to the CINC and quietly suggested that perhaps the President just wanted to know how soon Air Force units could arrive in the theater, where they would be located, how they would be supported, what levels of effort could be sustained, and what type of jobs they could be expected to undertake to deter or defeat an Iraqi invasion. He could see that this part of the briefing had been troubling the CINC, and that he was looking for a way to convey this information to the President in as credible a manner as the ground piece of the briefing, which he had worked out so well.

Schwarzkopf agreed. In fact, Horner's suggestion was just what he wanted to hear just then. That being the case, he ordered the staff to turn out and help Horner put it together.

You could feel the relief in the room from everyone except Chuck Horner. In essence, he'd promised that he'd fix up everything himself. Now he had to perform perfectly, and fast; the CINC was due to depart for Washington and Camp David around midnight.

He returned to the command center, only this time he did not ask, "Can I help?" Horner told them what he wanted, and, to their credit, Burt Moore and his J-3 staff gave him their complete support.

What he needed first of all was a stack of overhead transparency slides. Since 1990 was already the day of desktop computers with dedicated software, he sat down next to a young, computer-literate staff member and his machine, and went to work. He'd draw a sketch of what he had in mind on a piece of typing paper, and then the kid would punch it into the computer to produce the finished slide. Quickly, the pile of slides began to grow—number charts, maps, diagrams. The various slides outlined a vast exercise in airpower, rapidly and easily deployed, hosted at a number of bases throughout the Gulf region. The operations were to be supported in large measure by over a billion dollars' worth of equipment, munitions, and supplies.

If Iraq continued its attack through Kuwait and into Saudi Arabia, land- and sea-based aircraft would immediately be on the scene to work with the Gulf allies. They would bring to bear an array of modern weapons targeted by a host of the latest intelligence-collection assets, directed by a theater-wide command-and-control element that could devastate the attacking Iraqi forces as their supply lines fanned out across the desert and along Saudi Arabia's highways. It would be a formidable challenge. It had to be. Iraq's air force was well trained and equipped. Its army was shielded by thousands of antiaircraft guns and surface-to-air missiles. Formidable as they were, however, they would encounter airpower beyond their ability to comprehend.

Horner threw himself into the briefing. With over thirty-two years of experience in the Air Force, and three years of working with the Gulf nations and their air forces, he knew he could put together a briefing that would make the pieces of the air plan clear to the President. No one knew more about threats, air war, and air operations in the Middle East than he did.

He was confident, and it showed when he went over the slides with General Schwarzkopf at 2300 (11:00 P.M. EDT) that Friday night.

But then his fighter pilot confidence wavered when General Schwarzkopf smiled and said, "Looks good, Chuck. Why don't *you* brief it? The aircraft leaves at 0200."

Horner sat stunned for a moment, then let out a puff of air. *They can kill me, but they can't eat me,* Horner told himself.

★ Later, after Schwarzkopf had left, he sat thinking. He couldn't screw this up. If he failed to transmit the right information, it could endanger the lives of many thousands, and the existence of a nation he respected deeply. This was not about war. In fact, if the military options were presented truthfully and executed skillfully, then war might be averted. But if war *was* in the cards . . . he let out another puff of air . . . then he would be the commander of the most powerful air attack in history.

He looked through his notes again, then through the slides, then he leaned back in his chair, thinking back to that day twenty-eight years before that was never far from his mind: the sand, the sky, the certainty that he was going to die. Was this what it had all been for? Was this what God had had in mind . . . ?

I
Into the
Wild Blue

1

EVERY MAN A TIGER

Fighter pilots know something of what Arabs know, and what few of us like to admit—that none of us is in control of our lives, that we're all in the hands of God.

In 1962, while he was stationed at Lakenheath, England, young Lieutenant Chuck Horner was in North Africa, at Wheelus, Libya, flying an F-100D Super Saber, training on the gunnery range that the Air Force had established in those days of friendship with the Libyan government of King Idris. The weather in Libya was better than anywhere in Europe; there were hundreds of miles of desert to spare for a gunnery range; and for recreation, the old walled town had a camel market, Roman ruins, decent Italian restaurants, and beaches nearby for relaxing on weekends. The officers' club rocked every night, and the pilots had plenty of time to drink and lie, two of their most pleasurable activities. It was fighter pilot heaven.

One day at Wheelus, Horner was number three in a group of four, flying strafe patterns. Imagine four lines in a square pattern on the ground whose corners are—very roughly—a mile apart. At each of these corners is an F-100. The target is located in one corner of this box. The airplane on the corner turning to head toward the target is rolling in to shoot at the target. The airplane behind him at the corner diagonally across the box is turning base leg; he is getting ready to shoot next. The airplane behind him is flying toward the base leg turning point. And the airplane coming off the target has just completed his gunnery pass and is trying to visually acquire the other three aircraft so he can space on them for his next turn at the target. It's extremely important to maintain that spacing. If the pilot puts the base leg too far out, then his dive angle is flat and he can pick up ricochets. If he gets it in too close, his dive angle's too steep, and he'll hit the ground while trying to pull up from his firing pass on the target.

That day there was a *ghibly* blowing—a sandstorm. Visibility was bad, less than a mile, which meant each pilot could see where he was in relation to the ground and could sometimes dimly spot the location of the aircraft ahead of him, but it was next to impossible to see the target itself or determine how the aircraft were spaced in relation to each other and the target. In other words, it was a day they shouldn't have been on the range.

According to the procedure they normally followed, when a pilot made a turn, he'd call it over the radio—"turning in," "turning off," "turning downwind," "turning base." Most of these calls were for the information of the other pilots, to let everyone know where he was. But the "turning base" call was more serious. That call let the safety observer in the tower know he was about to approach the target. When the observer heard that, he would be watching the aircraft ahead of the caller making his firing pass, which meant he was also ready to hear the next pilot's turning-in hot call. Then he would give the pilot, or deny him, clearance to fire. For instance, if another airplane was in the way, he would say, "Make a dry pass" or "You're not cleared." And then the pilot would break off his attack, fly through level, and resume the correct spacing.

At Wheelus was a nuclear target circle, next to the conventional bomb circle and strafe targets. This circle had a long run-in bulldozed in the desert that served as a guideline about where to fly when the fighters were in the strafe pattern. On the run-in line was a smaller bulldozed line, more like a short streak across it, that was located 13,000 feet out from the nuclear bomb bull's-eye. This mark was exactly the right place to start the turn to base leg to set up a pass at the strafe target. Normally, pilots making the gunnery run would turn base over that same streak. On this day, though, the pilot (number two) ahead of Horner got lost. Instead of turning base over the bulldozed lines in the desert, he kept flying away from the target and the proper place to begin his base leg turn.

Horner, meanwhile, was waiting for him to call base, as he himself was closing in on the base turning point. Finally, the call came, "Turning base." Meaning: Horner was looking for him on base to his left front, expecting him to be moving toward the final attack roll-in point. Of course, he wasn't anywhere near there; he was in front of Horner, far from the base leg and the target.

As Horner searched the roll-in point ahead, he had to watch his airspeed. If he got too fast, he would overrun the man he thought was ahead of him; and if he got too slow he wouldn't have the right airspeed (about 400 knots) for shooting his guns—the sight picture was based on airspeed and the angle of attack of the airplane. Still, he had no other choice; he slowed down, slowed down, slowed down . . . waiting for the other pilot to call "turn in." Finally, Horner turned base—since the other guy *had* to be pretty close to his turn in by then—and hit the power, still waiting for number two to call his turn in to the target. A moment later, at last, number two called, "Turning in." Horner scanned out toward the target, looking for him. *He's got to be shooting,* he thought. *He's got to be shooting.* By then, he'd reached the point where he himself had to turn in, still staring out left in the direction of the target. Out of the corner of his vision to his right, he saw something screaming toward him fast and close.

"Shit!" Horner cried out, instinctively pulling hard back on his stick; his F-100 went nose up and slowed—the way a hand does if held flat outside a car window with the wind slapping against it—and the other guy blasted through the space Horner's aircraft was about to occupy. There was Horner, mushing ahead with his nose high, his plane acting like a water skier when the towboat slows down too much. But that didn't last long, because the nose snapped through and the airplane flipped. Now he was staring at the ground, 3,500 feet below, his airplane in a stall.

Super Sabers were equipped with leading edge slats that worked by gravity; at slow airspeed they came out and gave the aircraft more lift. However, one of his slats had stuck—sand had clogged it—while the other one had deployed. As a result, one wing had a lot more lift than the other, which caused his aircraft to snap-roll and enter a fully stalled condition where there was insufficient airspeed to make the flight controls responsive. His aircraft had just become a metal anvil heading toward the earth. At normal flying speeds, the tail should have provided sufficient control to recover from the dive he had entered, but at his now-slow airspeed, the elevator surface in the tail was not effective.

He said to himself, *Okay, pull up.* The stick went all the way back to his lap. Nothing happened. The nose didn't move. He glanced over to the airspeed indicator, and it read close to zero—fifty knots. For all life-supporting purposes, that was zero. He said to himself, *Screw me. I'm out of here,* and reached over to grab the ejection handles. But then pride took over.

You know, he told himself, *if you eject from this airplane, you will never be able to drink with the guys in the bar again. You owe it to yourself to try and get it out. You always do.*

When a pilot breaks a stall, he puts the stick all the way forward in order to pick up airspeed, and that way get some control surfaces working for him.

Horner did that, then tried to bring the nose up . . . and nothing happened.

Meanwhile, all he could see was ground screaming up at him, surrounding him, all about him. It was too late to punch out with the ejection seat. And nothing he had done was bringing the plane under control.

At that moment, he went through the death experience. *I'm going to die,* he said to himself. *There is no way an airplane will recover from this shit. It's not capable of doing it. I'm going to die out here in the shitty, nowhere desert, splattered like roadkill on the ground, and I'm not going to get out of this.*

Two things happened then, both of them a normal consequence of the sudden onset of adrenaline pumping through one's system as death nears:

First, outrage. He was filled with fury that his wife Mary Jo was pregnant with their first child and he would never see it. Second, time slowed. The fire pulse—the adrenaline—was pushing him to high speed. The data in his head was spinning through like mad. Even so, he was preternaturally calm. It was like one of those old science fiction stories, in which somebody takes a potion that speeds time up. An hour in speeded-up time is a second in the world's time.

There he was, not far from the ground, certain he was about to die, feeling simultaneous outrage at dying and absolute peace and surrender, and time had slowed to a near stop. He had never felt so calm and serene in his life.

Somewhere in this timelessness, he somehow rose out of the top of his head and was suspended there, looking down at himself, sitting in the cockpit. As he stared down at himself, he thought, *What can I do to get out of this? I don't really want to die here.*

Meanwhile, the airplane was sinking to the ground, at something like 150 to 200 miles an hour. He tried again to pull the nose up, but the nose rose only a little bit, an inch at a time. He was still going to hit the ground.

A memory came to him. He was sitting in the coffee bar back at the squadron in Nellis AFB in Nevada, where he'd spent three months in top-off training and nuclear certification before assignment to a fighter wing. As he sat with his cup of coffee, two instructor pilots were talking about a student in an F-100 who'd been turning base to final on a landing approach. At 300 feet above the ground, he'd let the nose of his aircraft get above the horizon, thus producing adverse yaw, and the plane had snapped over. By then, of course, the airplane had used up all its energy, which meant there was not enough airspeed to recover.

"What about the afterburner?" the instructor in the back cockpit had asked himself, and instinctively slammed the throttle into it, knowing that was their only chance to live.

The F-100 engine was not supposed to light in afterburner at slow speeds; and ordinarily it wouldn't. Instead it would shoot about twenty feet of flame out the air intake in the front of the jet, and there'd be a violent explosion that would physically knock one's feet off the floor. This was called a compressor stall, which—though it might seem odd—didn't harm the engine. If a pilot happened to cause the engine to compressor-stall, he then pulled the throttle to clear the engine, then brought the throttle back up as he got more airspeed and more air going through the engine. Once he had these, he could try lighting the afterburner again.

Back at Nellis, when the instructor had thrown his throttle into afterburner, the engine shouldn't have lit. It should have experienced a compressor stall. But it hadn't. It *had* lit, and given him half again as much thrust. And that thrust had saved his life.

Remembering that, Horner said, "Let's try the afterburner." He moved the throttle up full, then pushed it outboard . . . and waited. He felt a shiver in the aircraft, and looked up. *Above him* were sand dunes to his right and to his left. But he was moving ahead; and he realized that he now had the airplane, the controls were responding; and the jet continued to respond as he made small inputs to level off above the ground. He was flying it carefully, carefully, carefully. . . . *If I screw this up one little bit,* he told himself, *then the aircraft is going to hit the ground.*

The afterburner had lit after all, and the nose was actually coming up, though of course the tail was now probably inches above the ground. Behind him, the increased thrust hitting the sand looked like a Texas tornado. Slowly, the airplane staggered up out of the desert.

About that time, the tower officer, sensing trouble, put in a call: "Three, are you having a problem?"

"No," Horner answered, "but I am returning to base." And he flew home.

★ Later, the events of that day hit him hard. He put the maneuver under his mind's microscope, and he realized that the numbers didn't compute. There was no way he could have recovered that airplane. It was physically impossible. The physics of the maneuver were such that it just wouldn't work.

If that's the way things are, he asked himself, *why did it happen? Why was I allowed to live?*

The answer wasn't long in coming. What he'd just experienced out there over the North African desert was a message from God. Horner didn't make a big issue of it, but he was a deeply religious man. God was saying to him, "Mister Fighter Pilot, you aren't in charge of your life. I have a purpose for you, even though you don't know what it is yet. So get on with your life and see what happens. And just remember: I'm the one in charge here. Any questions?"

It was as though God literally, physically, had kept his airplane from hitting the ground . . . at least that's how he saw it. He had no other explanation that fit the facts.

After that Chuck Horner had changed fundamentally. Here is how he describes it:

> *Every day of my life after that event has been a gift. I was killed in the desert in North Africa. I'm dead. From then on I had no ambition in terms of what course my life was going to take. That was up to God to decide. I'd go do the best I could. I'd enjoy whatever promotions, pay, money that came my way. Anything that came my way I'd enjoy and use, but I wouldn't live for it. I never wanted to be a general, for instance. I was proud when I made general; I was pleased; I liked the money; and I like people saying, "Yes sir," "No sir," and "You're really good-looking today," and all that. I loved all the lies and all that shit. Don't get me wrong. But the fact that I made general is no big deal. It's what God wanted me to do, not what I wanted to do. So I gave up me.*
>
> *Now Christians talk about rebirth. Some piss me off when they do. They go around holier than thou. "Well, I've got the word now, because I've been reborn in Jesus." Well, fine, okay.*

But if you really have all that, you don't need to tell me, I'll know.

In my case I know. I was reborn. Why? He wanted me to do something. . . . What? I don't know. He has never told me what He wanted me to do . . .

Whatever it was, I let go of my life and everything else in 1962. Sure, I fall into passion and lust and smallness. I'm still a human being. But when I really start getting upset about something, I just say, "Screw it, I'm dead, it doesn't matter."

That was the way it was twenty-eight years later, in August of 1990 when I was riding in an airplane going from Jeddah to Riyadh, temporarily in command of all U.S. forces in Saudi Arabia, and I said to myself, "What in the hell am I going to do? If they come south, I'm responsible. Well, shit, I don't know how to do that. I've never fought an invading army. We don't have any forces. What am I going to do? How am I going to do all this?" And then I realized it was what the Arabs call inshallah: *"It is not mine to do; it's mine to do the best I can; it's going to happen according to God's will."*

INTO THE SKY

The Divine purpose is rarely easy to discern, but it is safe to say the obvious in Chuck Horner's case: he was meant to be a fighter pilot. It might have come as a surprise, though, to anyone who had known him as a boy and young man, in Davenport, Iowa. They'd have had to look extremely close to see the few glimmers that showed before he fell into the Air Force ROTC during the course of slouching without much visible purpose through the University of Iowa.

When he'd gone away to college, he'd found classes a bore. He avoided most of them, and learned whatever he needed to keep a C average by picking the brains of anyone who actually attended. Otherwise, he worked at odd jobs, drank beer, sat around arguing with other students, and did his best to have a good time. Meanwhile, when the C average killed off what hopes he had of majoring in medicine, he needed to cast around for something to occupy his time after he graduated until he could figure out what he wanted to do with his life.

In those days, all male students at Iowa had to be enrolled in an ROTC program, and making the best of it, he'd opted for Air Force ROTC . . . they had fewer parades. As it turned out, he actually liked the experience, and even showed some leadership—he could drill the troops better than most, and he made marching fun for his guys by making it challenging rather than tedious. But the real pull of ROTC came to him almost out of the blue. He discovered flying.

Born on October 19, 1936, Chuck Horner was old enough for World War II to have made a strong impact on his young mind. The war had made aviation enthusiasts out of everyone, but for him it was more personal. His heroes were all pilots, especially his cousin, Bill Miles, the Jack Kennedy of the family—an all-state football player and straight-A student, tall and good-looking, with a winning smile, who always had time for little guys like Chuck. Everyone in the family looked up to Bill. When the war broke out, he'd joined the Army Air Corps and become a B-24 pilot.

One afternoon in 1944, when Chuck was eight years old, he came home from school to find his mother crying. Bill was dead, on a mission over Italy. A single 37mm antiaircraft artillery round had punched through the airplane's skin beneath his seat and killed him instantly, the only casualty on the mission. The news devastated the whole family; and it left an eerie association in Chuck—death, heroism, and flying.

Later on, Chuck lost a second pilot hero.

Like Bill Miles, John Towner was a man young boys idolized. Handsome and self-assured, John had also been an all-state football player in high school; and he'd gone on to play football at the university. In 1952, when Chuck was a sophomore in high school, John had graduated, married the youngest of Chuck's three older sisters, Pud,* entered the Air Force, and started fighter pilot training. Basic gunnery training was taught at Luke Air Force Base in Arizona. Shortly after Christmas of 1953, John was killed on the air-to-ground bombing range at Luke, when his F-84 aircraft failed to pull out of a dive-bomb pass. Once again, the family was devastated; and once again came the eerie association for Chuck of death, heroes, and flying.

It didn't turn him against flying, however. He already had the gift

---

*Born Margaret, but called Pud from childhood. Ellen and Mary Lou were the other sisters. Chuck was the only son.

possessed by every successful fighter pilot—the ability to put death in a box, and keep it separate.

It wasn't until Air Force ROTC, however, that he really got hooked. It was in ROTC that he first spent serious time in the air—first in a single-engine Ryan Navion piloted by one of his ROTC instructors (who, to Horner's delight, liked to push the normally staid executive aircraft into loops and rolls), and then in a little Aeronca Champion, in which he learned to fly solo. Flying captured him then—he was *good* at it. He was enthralled for life.

★ Chuck Horner had met Mary Jo Gitchell, two years his junior, when they'd both been in high school; and they'd continued dating, with some ups and downs, in college. Though they were not at all alike, he knew from the start that she was the right woman for him. He was shy; she loved to meet people. He hated to talk; she could spin words out of the simplest event into rich detail, bubbling over with enthusiasm.

By the time he left college, Chuck knew he wanted to make the Air Force his life, but he also knew that such a life involved hardships that could destroy even the most secure marriage. Before he left school, Horner discussed all this with her, and the two of them reached an agreement: she had to live with his airplanes; and she had to know that he cared for flying as much as he cared for her. She did *not* come second in his life—it was just that he wanted very badly to excel, and he didn't want her to grow jealous of his mistress. She needed to know ahead of time the sacrifices that would be expected of both of them. (There is a joke about the wife of a fighter pilot who complains, "You love the Air Force more than you love me," to which he replies, "Yes, but I love you more than the Army or the Navy.")

For her part of the bargain she got control of the family money, which at $222.00 a month, plus $100.00 flight pay, was not much of a victory. On the other hand, she knew Chuck pretty well by then; and he wasn't famous for a heavy supply of cash. When they'd started dating at the end of her freshman year in college, for instance, they'd had to tap her college money to pay for dinner at a pizza place on Sunday night. One time he'd bought her a birthday present, a small portable radio. When the check bounced, he'd had to borrow the money from her to make it good.

Their agreement about money still stands.

They were married on the twenty-second of December 1958, in the Congregational Church in Cresco, Iowa, Mary Jo's hometown.

★ Horner was commissioned in the Air Force Reserve* on Friday, June 13, 1958, just before his graduation from the University of Iowa. In October, he attended Preflight Training at Lackland AFB, San Antonio, Texas. And in November, he was sent to Spence Field in Moultrie, Georgia, to enter primary flying training in the T-34 and T-28 aircraft.

At that time, USAF flight training consisted of about 120 hours in T-34s (two-seat, prop planes still used today, with a turboprop engine, by the Navy), and T-28s (larger than T-34s, not unlike P-47s from World War II). This took about six months, and was followed by another six months in T-33 jets, after which the student pilots got their wings. Horner loved every minute.

The training was strenuous, and there were few active duty pilot places to fill—it was not unlike an entire college senior class showing up at NFL summer camp and vying for a position on the forty-man roster. At this time, the Air Force was capable of producing far more pilots than they needed. Their pilot factory had been constructed to satisfy the huge need for pilots during the Korean War, but now the Air Force was smaller and more stable, and thus the name of the game was to wash out anyone who showed a weakness. Instead of receiving additional instruction when he made a mistake, a student pilot entered a process designed to eliminate him from the program. He was gone, no second chances. That meant he never left blood in the water, or else the sharks would come to visit.

The overall washout rate from entry into preflight at Lackland to graduation from Basic Training was near 85 percent, with the vast majority coming from the aviation cadets, men who did not have a college degree. (Student officers tended to be older and more mature than the cadets; and they had additionally made it through college—itself a screening process—and had passed through the light-plane screening program.) Every day someone would be out-processing after being eliminated.

To make sure he was never in jeopardy, Horner studied as he had

---

*After he finished gunnery school, Horner intended to apply for a regular commission, the type academy graduates got; but before he could get his paperwork together, the Air Force changed the procedure. In the new dispensation, a board selected the ones they wanted instead of letting people apply directly. Later, while he was stationed at Lakenheath in England, Horner was called into his squadron commander's office one day and asked if he would accept a regular commission, since a board had selected him for one. "Sure," he answered. And so he was resworn into the Air Force in 1962.

never studied in college. He actually practiced the next day's flight maneuvers sitting at home in a chair, going over in his mind all the challenges he might run into the next day. The hard work paid off. He was soon headed to jet training at Laredo AFB and, if he made it, his wings.

The T-33 (T Bird) Horner would fly there was a two-seat training version of the F-80, one of the first jet fighters. F-80s had fought in Korea.

The T Bird was a good-looking aircraft, but old—most of them had been around for five or ten years; the T Bird's technology was from the 1940s. It was fully acrobatic, very honest to fly, reasonably fast, and could stay airborne for two and a half hours at high altitude, but since it was straight-winged, it was subsonic. The worst thing about the T Bird was the seat. Though there was a seat cushion, you sat on a bailout oxygen bottle, which was like sitting on an iron bar. Flying a T Bird meant you had "a one-hour ass." After you were in the jet that long, your tail hurt so bad you wanted to land.

In those days, the Air Force was still young and wild. Aircraft were underpowered and often poorly maintained, not nearly as safe as they are today. The leaders in the air were often veterans of World War II or Korea, where they had been rushed into combat with little training and a lot of attitude. Those who had survived were often indifferent to risk-taking that would make most people cringe. Low-level flying was *low*, often measured in a few feet above the ground, though as the old flyboy joke put it, the world's record for low flying was tied, with fatal results. If it had been tough in Georgia, where they eliminated half the class, it was going to be hell in Texas.

Yet for Horner, life was blessed. He loved his work, flying came easily to him, and he excelled in the academic courses. He learned instruments by flying under a hood in the backseat of a T Bird; he learned transition—takeoff and landing and acrobatic maneuvers—and he learned flying formation. He knew now that he wanted to be a fighter pilot.

His flight commander, Captain Jack Becko (he looked a little like Jack Palance and was a terror in the sky), had been an F-86 pilot in Korea and was a joy to fly with. Captain Becko loved flying and acrobatics and formation. Too many pilots were timid—they got nervous in close formation or joining up after takeoff—but Horner, who loved it all as much as Becko did, was very aggressive, very wild on the controls. The flight commander adored that; he howled with glee when he flew an instruction ride with Horner, and Horner slammed the throttle around and made the jet go where it needed to be to stay in formation. And then, after they'd gone through all the required maneuvers, Captain Becko showed him how to shoot down another jet.

Some of the more conservative instructors—the ones with multi-engine time—were less enthusiastic, but since Horner always flew well and was always in position, they kept quiet.

At Laredo, a table, little larger than a card table, was the "office" where an instructor briefed his students. The flight room had about ten of them along the walls. On them were maps and diagrams under Plexiglas, so you could draw on them with a grease pencil, to show the path over the ground during an instrument approach, the procedures needed to compensate for wind drift, and the like. Each IP would have from one to three students in his table.

Horner grew so proficient that one day the instructor for his table, First Lieutenant Art Chase, asked him to fly lead for another, much less skilled, student. That way, Chase could get in the other student's backseat and provide formation instruction.

When the other student lagged two ship lengths behind him, Horner saw a temptation it took him no time to give in to. He knew it was going to put him in deep trouble. It was not part of the training, it was not briefed, he was supposed to provide a stable platform for the other student to fly off of, and if he made a wrong move, they would collide and all three pilots would be killed. *But what the hell,* he thought, *you've got to go for it sometimes.*

He reefed back hard on the stick, kicked right rudder, rolled hard right, and slipped neatly in behind the other aircraft in a perfect guns tracking position. The instructor, in what had now become Horner's target, never even saw him disappear. Worried they had overrun him and were about to collide, Chase started shouting on the radio. At about that time, Horner was calling guns tracking and feeling like the biggest, meanest tiger in South Texas.

That feeling lasted about as long as it took Art Chase to order him firmly back in the lead.

He knew then that he was in for—and deserved—one huge ass-chewing. He knew he had taken unfair advantage of his friendship with Chase. Yet none of that mattered. He had joy in his heart. By executing a difficult and dangerous dogfighting maneuver, he had proved to himself that he was a fighter pilot.

He has never regretted doing that roll over the top that flushed Art Chase and his table mate out in front for a guns tracking pass.

When they landed, there was indeed hell to pay; Chase wanted Chuck Horner's hide, and he gave him the ultimate punishment, which was to be sent into the Flight Commander's office, where you were made to wonder if you would escape with your life, let alone stay in the program. There, Jack Becko gave Horner one of the finest dressings-down ever delivered. Then, as Horner was leaving the room—scared but not defeated—Becko gave him a wink. "Chuck, you're going to make one hell of a fighter pilot," he said.

At that moment Chuck Horner walked on clouds. *I'm going to be a fighter pilot!*

The only problem was: nobody was getting fighter assignments.

With the draw-down after the Korean War, if you wanted to be a fighter pilot, you could get assigned to either Air Defense Command or Tactical Air Command. By Chuck Horner's time, Air Defense Command was a dead-end job, flying obsolete planes. Since it was becoming obvious that ballistic missiles were about to replace the Soviet bomber threat, there wasn't going to be much need for fighter interceptors to knock out the bombers. Over time, the Air Force has gone from a hundred squadrons of fighter interceptors to about six or eight today.

If you were sent to Tactical Air Command, however, you would check out in F-84s, F-86s, or perhaps F-100s, and spend six to eight months in gunnery school.* Since the Air Force had no need for fighter pilots, however, you would probably then go to bomber school for another six to eight months and graduate as a Strategic Air Command B-47 copilot, or, if you were one of the top students, you might be asked to remain in Air Training Command and become an instructor pilot. There you would spend three years building flight time and teaching, but a lot of that flying would be in the backseat of the T Bird, a fate Chuck Horner did not relish. After that, if you wanted to fly fighters, you would probably get

---

*In World War I, World War II, and Korea—even though some fighters carried bombs—the fighter's primary weapon was its gun, and most fighter actions were gunnery actions: air-to-air, and strafe of ground targets. Hence, when a young pilot went to school to learn how to be a fighter pilot, he went to gunnery school. There he would also learn to drop bombs, even nuclear bombs, and shoot missiles.

assigned to gunnery school, and if you wanted to fly heavies, to bomber school, or to air transport school. There was in those days—and there is still—an informal screening system: people believed to be incapable of flying fighters were urged to fly, or were otherwise sent to, heavies.

Because Horner had graduated number one in his flight and was fighter-qualified, he was eligible either for instructor training or for one of the few gunnery school slots. The matter came to a head when the Group Commander, Lieutenant Colonel Jack Watkins, offered him a teaching spot at Laredo. When the offer was made, however, he gulped, refused, and somehow found himself picked for one of the few F-100 gunnery school slots. He figured you better follow your destiny, even if it might take him to B-47s. The main thing was that fighter flying was in his blood. Even if he got sent on to B-47s, he knew that somehow in the future he would find a way to fly fighters.

★ One of the proudest moments in Chuck Horner's life came on the day Mary Jo pinned a very tiny set of pilot wings on his uniform. The ceremony took place in Laredo, in a paint-peeling, run-down, non-air-conditioned base movie theater, straight out of World War II. He had never worked so hard for anything as he had for those wings.

It was also in Laredo that Horner was introduced to the tough side of military aviation, the missing-man formation flyby, to commemorate a pilot killed in an aircraft accident.

One day, he was sitting on the end of the runway in his T-33, awaiting takeoff clearance, when the aircraft ahead of him, as it was lifting off, rolled abruptly and flew into the ground. The ailerons—the movable surfaces on the aft part of the wing that enable a pilot either to keep his wings level or to roll the aircraft—were incorrectly rigged* so that both of them moved in the same direction. When the pilot made an input to level the wings, the aircraft rolled; the more he tried to level the wings, the more he kept rolling.

So there was Chuck Horner, a twenty-two-year-old kid with a fire-breathing jet strapped to him, staring at what just seconds before had been a silver jet, and was now billowing black smoke and orange flame.

---

*The mechanics had installed one of the pulley reels upside down, so both ailerons moved in the same direction. This made them flaps and not roll controls. And this made the rudder the only roll control the pilot had. His aircraft was going too slow, however, for it to generate the control moment he needed to use the rudder to keep the wings level.

The rescue helicopter and fire trucks roared onto the scene, and the flames were quickly extinguished. Then the pilot's remains were placed on the helicopter (there was no way anyone could survive that crash) and were just passing overhead on the way to the base hospital, with the charred legs of the pilot's body dangling out the door, when the tower cleared Horner for takeoff. He swallowed hard, closed the canopy, pushed the throttle forward, released the brakes, and prayed.

In the thirty-six years in the Air Force that followed, he learned to do that again and again. Too many times, he and Mary Jo went to church services that ended outside the chapel with four pilot buddies roaring overhead in formation, and then the number three man pulling abruptly up to disappear from sight heavenward.

★ If flying in training command was dangerous, gunnery training was several notches worse. Chuck Horner took to it immediately.

On January 5, 1960, he reported to Williams AFB, Arizona, for gunnery training and check-out in the supersonic F-100.

The Super Saber, which had replaced the venerable F-86 Saber, was the first USAF aircraft capable of exceeding Mach 1 in level flight. It was a swept-wing, single-seat, afterburner-equipped, single-engine fighter, and its mission was day-fighter air-to-air combat, though subsequent models were also modified to carry both conventional and nuclear bombs. For armament, it had four internal 20mm rapid-fire cannons and carried heat-seeking air-to-air missiles. The gun sight was primitive by today's standards, but sophisticated at the time. It was gyrostabilized, and a radar in the nose provided range to target for air-to-air gunnery. The F-100 was normally flown at 500 knots/hr and had reasonable range: with external drop tanks, it had about a 500-mile radius. For its day, it was reasonably maneuverable. Though older aircraft like the F-86 were more agile, the afterburner engine gave the F-100 an edge on acceleration and maintaining energy. Maintaining energy is a plus in air-to-air combat. When a pilot loses his energy all he can do is point the nose down and keep turning while the enemy figures out how to blow him away. F-100s were used in the Vietnam War, primarily in South Vietnam, for close air support, since by then the aircraft did not have the performance, speed, range, payload, and survivability to make it over North Vietnam. Those who flew it liked it: it was honest most of the time, and with it they got to do air-to-air as well as air-to-ground gunnery training.

The training of fighter pilots has always been dedicated to creating an individual capable of meeting an adversary in the sky who is flying an equally capable aircraft, and shooting him down. A pilot can't hold back or be timid. There is no room for self-doubt. He must know his limitations, but he must always believe that the better man will survive, and that man is him. When Chuck Horner was in the program, its unofficial title was "Every Man a Tiger," and the main emphasis, aside from flying and gunnery, was on the pilot's attitude and self-confidence.

Chuck Horner has never been short of self-confidence.

Meanwhile, for a lieutenant student, the training was tough, the flying and instructions in the air demanding, and the debriefings brutal. Many nights Horner rolled into bed exhausted from pulling Gs in the air while trying to keep track of other fighters in a swirling dogfight over the desert. Yet often he fell asleep with the light still on, as Mary Jo stayed up to finish her homework. In the morning, she usually left for classes before he woke up.

★ A superior fighter pilot is made up of one part skill, one part attitude, one part aggression, and one part madness. You have to be more than a little insane to take on tasks that will likely kill a man unless he performs them perfectly and with luck. The good ones perform those tasks regularly and successfully . . . most of the time.

One day when Horner was going through gunnery school, he was involved in a one-on-one air-to-air simulated combat engagement with an instructor pilot, Major Country Robinson. Horner was in a single-seat F-100C, and Robinson was flying an F-100F with another student sandbagging—along for the ride—in the backseat.

When two fairly equal pilots in equal jets get into a fight starting from a neutral setup—meaning neither has an initial advantage in speed, altitude, or nose position—then one of two predictable outcomes will come about. Either one of the pilots will make a mistake, allowing the other to get behind his adversary and achieve a guns tracking position, and the game is over with a clear winner. Or each pilot will fly his jet to its maximum performance, conserve energy appropriately, and correctly maneuver on his own and in response to the maneuvers of his adversary. In this case, neither pilot will achieve a position to kill his adversary, and both aircraft will wind up in a nose-low death spiral. In ordinary practice combat, one of the pilots must call this off, usually when they pass some minimum altitude such as 10,000 feet above the ground.

On this day, young Second Lieutenant Horner was matched against the wily, experienced IP Robinson, meaning the IP expected to wait for a green mistake, kill him, and then put him through a tough debriefing, so he wouldn't make the mistake again.

The problem was ego.

They flew out to the area north of Williams AFB, where they were based, turned away from each other, flew apart until nearly out of visual range, and turned back in, passing each other. "Fights on" was called, and they started the dance of death. Major Robinson was good, and he didn't make a mistake. Since his jet was a two-seater, it was a little heavier than Horner's, which made a slight difference in Horner's favor. At the same time, Horner had learned his lessons well up to this point and was holding his own. The result: no one was gaining clear advantage. They twisted, turned, and rolled, nose up to gain smaller turning radius, diving to gain speed for maneuvering, using afterburner, but sparingly (if either used too much, he'd exhaust his fuel and have to declare bingo and head for home, which meant the other pilot won). Finally they were canopy to canopy, each in a steep dive; for neither aircraft had enough airspeed to bring its nose back up without accelerating, which would place that aircraft ahead of the other—and it would lose. They passed 30,000 feet, then 20,000. The altimeter needles looked like stopwatches, they were unwinding so fast, and meanwhile the airspeed was approaching the minimum that allowed control of the aircraft.

Suddenly, the two-seat F-100F snapped uncontrollably and entered a flat spin, an unfortunate tendency of the two-seat F-100 at low speed. At that point, by the rules, Major Robinson should have made a "knock it off" call. In any event, he had to get on with the business of recovering his aircraft before passing 10,000 feet, or else begin to seriously consider ejecting from his fighter. But he was good. He was able to work the recovery and still keep the fight going. He was not going to lose . . . not to any damn second lieutenant student.

During all of this time, Horner was able to extend away from Robinson's jet and achieve sufficient airspeed to regain enough nose authority to bring his gun sight to bear on the spinning, falling instructor pilot's jet. But his own aircraft was in a full stall, falling toward the ground at about the same rate as Major Robinson's. No matter: he was on the radio calling, "Guns tracking kill," and he knew his gunnery film would show the F-100F slowly turning in front of him, nose, tail, nose, tail, nose, tail.

Got him!

He'd beaten his better . . . who was in the fascinating position of being about to die if he didn't take instant action. Horner had half a second advantage over his instructor, in that he could wait that long before he had to recover his jet. He put that half-second to the only possible use: he kept the pip of his gun sight on the other jet and felt the rush.

Finally, neither of them could stand it any longer; they broke off the mock combat and turned to recovering their aircraft—with each regaining control only a few feet above the yucca, palo verde, and mesquite, fractions of seconds before taking things too far and crashing.

Clearly each of them had failed to exercise good judgment, each had violated the rules that guided training, and each should have figured out a way to achieve a simulated kill before approaching the extreme they reached. But neither did any of these. They were both so deeply involved in the fight that everything else was secondary. They were both training with the intensity combat requires, except in combat no one would be so foolish as to allow the enemy to tie him up in such a tight-turning battle. They fell into that trap because they were flying nearly equal jets, and fighting with the same level of proficiency. In the end, it was simply a contest of wills, and neither flinched until the very last second.

That ability to push on to the margin and not crash is what a fighter pilot seeks. Sadly, the ability to judge the ultimate "knock it off" point escapes some pilots, and they die, or else they pad that point to allow for their own inadequacies, and find themselves constantly defeated.

Wise, *old* pilots look for an early, easy kill, relying on experience and knowledge; and they don't play fair. They pick a weak one from the pack they're fighting, go for a quick kill, and then blow through the fight. The young pilot fails to recognize the weak ones, so he moves in close and turns and burns. He is strong and quick, however, so he can get away with it. When a pilot's old, he tires faster, and he avoids the pain of lots of sustained Gs. He can still pull them—but why, if he can succeed with less effort and more brains?

★ At the end of the training, Horner received his first operational assignment: he'd be flying F-100Ds with the 48th Tactical Fighter Wing, RAF Lakenheath, England. His faith had paid off. Suddenly the Air Force needed fighter pilots again. He and his entire class had dodged the fate so many previous gunnery school graduates had suffered, condemnation to B-47s. They were going to join the fighter community worldwide.

Before he left the States, there was a short stint at Nellis AFB in Nevada for top-off training. There, Horner checked out in the F-100D, got training dropping live bombs, did day and night air-to-air refueling off a KB-29 tanker, fired a live AIM-9B heat-seeking missile, and planned and flew realistic combat missions.

Since the F-100D had a better nuclear bombing system than the F-100C they had trained in at Williams before coming to Nellis, and since the primary mission of the 48th TFW was to sit on alert with a nuclear weapon targeted for the evil empire, there was a great deal of emphasis on delivering nuclear weapons (their secondary mission was conventional weapons delivery). The training for that involved flying a single ship in at low level—between 50 and 1,000 feet above the ground—while navigating and making turn points and accurate timing at 360 knots. A pilot would arrive at an initial point at a specified time, accelerate to 480 knots, and by means of very accurate visual navigation, he'd arrive at a precomputed offset point (upwind) from a target. From there, he'd start an afterburner Immelmann,* so that at a precomputed angle (just over ninety degrees—almost straight up), a gyro would release a 2,000-pound nuclear shape (in training, filled with concrete). After release, he'd bring the nose below the horizon on his back, roll wings level upright, and make a high-speed escape away from the blast of the nuclear weapon. Meanwhile, the bomb was climbing to 30,000 feet. There it would run out of speed, swap ends, and fall to the ground. The time of flight of the weapon gave him the time needed to escape the blast.

Since it was not easy to do all this accurately, an instructor pilot would usually orbit the target to document release time and to score the hit: you can see the dust fly when 2,000 pounds of concrete going warp nine hits the desert. The SAC generals called this method of delivery "over the shoulder," but the pilots, who had no love for the nuclear tasking (if all you and your adversary are doing is deterring each other, you are both being stupid), had another name for it. They called it "Idiot Loops."

---

*An Immelmann is half a loop with a roll on the top. The roll allows you to return to level flight after you've reversed your direction. If you want to make the loop smaller, you pull more Gs in the climb, but that means your airspeed at the top is slower.

SQUADRONS AND WINGS

For all the impressive technology of its multirole aircraft, equipment, and weapons, for all the freedom of the environment in which it operates, the U.S. Air Force is structurally only a few degrees away from feudal. It is an organization of knights and squires. The knights are those who are rated (to fly), while the squires are all the others—the vast majority of the force—who keep the planes in the air and the bases running. In the air, only the knights—the rated—fight the enemy. Though the majority of the rated are officers,* rated enlisted members include flight engineers, load masters, gunners, and parachute jumpers, PJs—rescue men. PJs were among those most decorated during the Vietnam War.

The elitism of the rated is a given. The knights of the sky, by virtue of their position, are offered automatic respect (which they can, of course, forfeit). In practical terms, that means that the enlisted troops like to see their officers behaving like heroes; it increases their own stature as the people who keep the heroes in the air. On the other hand, officers who don't behave like proper knights of the sky get into big trouble: there are a million moving parts under the skin of an aircraft, and only the enlisted force knows what is working and what might get the pilot killed. Wise officers make sure their relationship with the enlisted force is respectful—both ways.

By contrast, the enlisted do most of the fighting and dying in traditional armies, and rank is all-important. In these organizations, nothing is left to chance, communication tends to be top-down, and command means telling a crowd of enlisted guys with loaded weapons who didn't ask to be there in the first place to go forth and charge up the hill, when even the most dense among them can figure out that about half of them are going to get killed or wounded.

In the Air Force, the transaction is far different when an officer strolls out to his jet and chats for a moment with his crew chief—a person who selected the Air Force in order to grow his (or her) technical expertise. The officer asks, "How is the jet?" and the enlisted man (or woman) answers, "The jet's ready to go. Good luck. Let me help you strap in. Go

---

*When Horner entered the Air Force, there were about 900,000 people on active duty, of which about 130,000 were officers, and about 70 percent of those were rated. Today there are about 350,000 in the Air Force, with about 70,000 officers, of whom about 20 percent are rated.

get one for me." Much is implied in this exchange. The crew chief knows that the officer, who is about to go risk his life for his nation, for his unit, and even for him or her, has entrusted his very life with his crew chief's talent and ability to take responsibility. The officer will die if his chief has forgotten to connect a fuel line or rig an ejection seat properly.

The mutual dependence between the rated and the enlisted in the Air Force is profound.

★ When Horner arrived at Lakenheath in the 1960s, this is how a squadron and a wing were set up.

In flight, the basic fighting element consists of two ships, but most fighter flights are made up of two elements—four ships. Two elements are more than enough aircraft for the flight leader to keep track of and manage. In a flight of four, the most experienced pilot is usually the flight lead, number one, and he usually flies in front, with number two on one side and number three on the other; number four flies on number three's wing opposite the flight leader. If you hold up your left hand, the middle finger is number one; the index finger is number two, a wingman; the ring finger is number three, the element lead; and the little finger is number four, another wingman.

The flight leader plans the mission, determines the goals to be achieved, briefs the flight, navigates, dictates the tactics, and in general works all the details.

The element lead, or deputy flight lead, backs him up and takes charge if for some reason the lead is unable to maintain the lead (if he loses his radio, crashes, aborts, or is shot down). He also keeps track of navigation, in case the leader gets lost; clears the sky behind numbers one and two aircraft; keeps track of his own wingman, to make sure he is doing his job; and thinks about what he would be doing better if he was the leader.

Number three and number one run the flight and make the decisions about how to attack, what formations to use, and whether or not to penetrate bad weather. It is their job to get the mission done and bring the wingmen home alive.

The wingmen, number two and number four, are the greenest flyers. They are expected to keep their mouths shut unless they are low on fuel, have an emergency, or see an enemy aircraft approaching the flight (especially from behind it)—but only after no one else has called it out.

Though watching over four aircraft is near the limit of any single leader's abilities, air-to-ground missions will sometimes contain up to sixteen aircraft. This is usually not a problem, as long as nothing goes amiss in the preplanned mission. However, if an enemy fighter somehow works into the middle of a sixteen-ship flight, it will be a chaotic mess, with airplanes all over the place trying to kill the enemy, stay alive, and regain order.

In determining who is to be the flight leader, rank in itself is not an issue. However, since flight leaders are usually the experienced pilots, they are more often than not captains and majors, or—higher still—lieutenant colonels, such as the squadron commander and the ops officer. In Vietnam, however, when the Air Force frequently used nonfighter pilots, the flight leader was often a young lieutenant with sixty to ninety missions under his belt leading around majors and lieutenant colonels who had come from bombers and thus weren't credible in fighters. (This was one of the many U.S. failures in Vietnam that resulted from the rotation policies: a pilot came home after 100 missions in the North or after a year in the South, and other pilots were rotated in for their chance at combat . . . whether or not they had been trained in fighters, or even—for that matter—in conventional war.)

All young jocks aspire to make leader. Most of the time, they do it by working their way up a complex training regime: first, check rides as element lead, then a few rides with an instructor on the wing as practice lead, and finally a flight-lead check ride. That system isn't always possible, however. At Lakenheath, for example, there was no established flight-lead check-out program. Instead, the squadron flight commander, operations officer, standardization and evaluation pilot, instructor pilot, or the commander flew with a pilot a few times, looked at his check rides, then just published orders making him a flight leader.

★ There are four flights in each squadron, with about six pilots in each flight. The primary work force of the squadron are the line pilots—that is, the combat-ready pilots. Flight commanders are always line pilots, while instructor pilots, functional test pilots, and standardization and evaluation pilots may or may not be; the ops officer and squadron commander are overhead pilots. The command chain runs from line pilots through the flight commander, who is the line pilot's first line supervisor, to the squadron commander (but the squadron operations officer has a great deal to say about each pilot's life, and he usually becomes the next squadron commander) up to the wing director of operations, and finally to the wing commander.

Flight commanders shepherd the five pilots assigned to them. They work with the ops officer's shop to schedule missions for their assigned pilots; they tell them when they are going on alert; what sorties they will fly and when, and when they will go on temporary duty (TDY) to places such as Wheelus or to Germany as a forward air controller (FAC)*; and, most important, they write their pilots' Officer Efficiency Reports (OER). That is to say, they chew their asses and pat them on the back.

The squadron commander runs the squadron; he tells everyone what to do based on what he is told at the wing staff meetings. The operations officer's job is to make sure the operation goes smoothly. Thus, he watches over the squadron's monthly schedule and makes sure it is workable. Then he makes sure that the flying schedule is going as planned; and he makes changes as pilots call in sick, aircraft break, the weather turns bad, or as someone needs a special, unanticipated training event. He also works with the other squadrons to coordinate missions and training. And finally, if the commander is flying or TDY, he backs him up by attending wing staff meetings and taking over other duties, as appropriate.

Other important members of the squadron staff:

Stan Eval (standardization and evaluation) pilots administer check rides and tests, inspect operations for compliance with regulations, and check on the personal equipment of the troops to make sure they are taking care of the pilots' masks and G suits. From Stan Eval pilots, line pilots get an instrument check (capability to fly on instruments), tactical check (capability to fly a combat mission), and flight-lead check (capability to lead other pilots around the sky).

Instructor pilots fly with the new pilots until their initial check ride, and also with pilots scheduled for upgrade (such as someone who is about to become a flight leader).

Weapons and Tactics pilots, usually fighter weapons school graduates, watch over bomb scores to make sure the squadron is doing a good job or if it needs extra training in bomb-delivery techniques; they keep track of the weapons-delivery systems, to make sure maintenance is keeping the guns harmonized with the gun sights and the release racks working prop-

---

*FACs work on the ground with Army units as liaison with close air support fighter-bombers.

erly (the release racks have to give the bombs a precise shove when the bomb shackles are blown open); they conduct training classes at bomb commanders school; and they keep the tactics manuals up-to-date and available for the line pilots to study in their free time.

Trainers keep watch over individual training records and make sure the flight commanders are scheduling their people for needed training programs.

Intelligence, usually a lieutenant, is nonrated. He keeps track of enemy threats, conducts classroom training on such things as SAMs and enemy aircraft, and helps in mission planning.

★ A typical squadron schedule at Lakenheath would usually start with the maintenance troops coming in at 0300 to get the jets ready. At around 4:00 A.M., the first pilots scheduled to fly would open the squadron and make the coffee; they will be on duty after 8:00 P.M., for a typical day of over twelve hours. Supervisors start arriving at 0500.

The flying schedule begins with three four-ship flights taking off at 0600, 0615, and 0630, for an hour-and-a-half mission; followed by three more four-ships at 1100, 1115, and 1130; followed by two more four-ships at 1600 and 1630. The first eight sorties would go to an air-to-ground range for bomb deliveries. The other four aircraft would be configured without external fuel tanks and bomb racks and would engage in two-versus-two air-to-air training in airspace off the coast. All of those aircraft would be "turned" to the same mission in the midday "go," and four of the bombers would drop off the schedule for the third "turn." Some pilots fly twice; others only once.

If few jets break during the day, then the aircraft set aside for spares will not be required, which might allow an add-on sortie or two. On the other hand, if the jets give a lot of trouble, the maintenance troops might work until midnight.

Also on the schedule are the pilots who are on alert, attending ground school, in the simulator flying practice instrument and emergency procedures missions, at the altitude chamber for their annual chamber ride, or who are TDY to the weapons ranges, to Germany as forward air controllers, or back in the States for fighter weapons school.

The schedule is roughed out monthly with range times, takeoff times, and number of sorties. Names are filled in weekly and changed daily, with the next day's schedule usually posted by 4:00 P.M., so each pilot can check it in time to go home and get some rest if he has to be back by 4:00 A.M. Starting in 1969 (and still in force, except during wartime), pilots were required to have twelve hours off before flying.

Also at work in the scheduling process is the law of supply and demand: if there is to be a workable schedule, a squadron needs so many flight leaders. For instance, if the daily schedule calls for four four-ship flights in the morning, four more in the afternoon, and three more later in the afternoon, that means a total of forty-four sorties (what they called "4 turn 4, turn 3"). Say a pilot can fly twice a day. Then about eleven four-ship flight leaders are needed, plus someone on the duty desk and in the tower. Since some of those forty-four sorties require an IP or check pilot, that means about fifteen flight leaders are actually needed.

There are about thirty pilots available in the squadron, plus a few overhead—the squadron operations officer (he may have an assistant) and the commander (who also has an adjutant, an intelligence officer, and a maintenance officer, who are not rated). However, four of the pilots are on alert, five are attending school in the United States, or are at Wheelus, Libya, for gunnery training, or are attending bomb commanders school, three are on leave, two are on Duties Not Include Flying (DNIF) with colds or sprained ankles from sports, two are processing out to return to the States, three are new pilots who just arrived and are looking for a house, and three more are in Germany on forward air controller duties. That means that twenty-two of the thirty pilots are not available. You can get some help from the five wing staff attached to the squadron for flying, but that still only makes thirteen pilots to fly, with fifteen flight leaders needed. . . . That kind of math went on all the time.

★ The wing commander is the senior commander on the base and has about 3,500 people under him. In the past, the wing commander was a colonel (as were his deputy and his vice commander), but now he is a brigadier general. Immediately under the wing commander comes the vice wing commander (usually a steady old hand whose job is primarily to help a young up-and-comer who will probably get promoted to general), who fills in when the wing CO is flying, TDY, or otherwise off-base. Under the vice comes the DCO, or deputy commander for operations, who runs the three flying squadrons (and who usually moves up to wing commander); the DCM Maintenance, who is responsible for all the aircraft maintenance (a big job which can make or break the wing; the DCR

Resources, who runs supply, finance, and the motor pool; and the base commander, who watches over civil engineers, services, security police, legal, public affairs, and personnel.

Above the base level (at the time Horner was in England) was a three-star numbered Air Force commander (in those days, most Air Force one- and two-stars worked in the Pentagon), then a four-star Air Force Command commander (commanding TAC, SAC, MAC, USAFE, or PACAF), then the Chief of Staff of the Air Force, the Secretary of Defense, and the President.

The Goldwater-Nichols Law of 1986 changed all of that, at least in terms of operational command, but that was twenty years into the future.

LAKENHEATH

In October 1960, after three months at Nellis, Chuck and Mary Jo Horner left for England. Their C-118 transport landed at RAF Milden- hall, and they boarded a bus for Lakenheath just a few miles away.

RAF Lakenheath was in Suffolk, just north of Cambridge, and about two hours' drive time northeast of London. Originally a World War II base, whose Quonset huts and brick tower looked like sets from *Twelve O'Clock High,* it had been closed after the war, but been reopened for B-47s, which for a time sat alert with nuclear weapons. There was a problem, though. A dip in the runway too often caused the big bombers to get airborne before they had enough speed to maintain flight. Most of the pilots would relax and let the aircraft settle back on the runway, but a few of them would struggle with the controls and try to fly. The aircraft would stall, fall off on a wing, and wind up a fireball.

A more accommodating airfield seemed like a good idea.

A replacement for the B-47s appeared in the late fifties, when Charles de Gaulle ordered U.S. fighters to leave France; and in 1960, the 48th Wing, then stationed at Chaumont Air Base east of Paris, pulled up stakes and moved to Lakenheath. In the process of the move, personnel who were close to the end of their overseas tours went home early. This in turn resulted in unusually large numbers of new people being assigned to the wing. This had a downside: every week six or seven lieutenants with the bare minimum of flying time showed up at each of the wing's three squadrons. Since Horner was in the first wave, he became a flight leader almost immediately. For a young pilot to become a flight lead is an honor and indicates rare confidence from the squadron leaders—or else it means there aren't any experienced pilots in the squadron and you use what you have and hope for the best. In Horner's case, it was the latter. The blind were leading the blind; and the accident rate proved it. In the first three months he was assigned to the wing, six aircraft and four pilots were lost (Horner didn't actually contribute to any of these accidents, but he came close). Since the tour was for three years, that meant he stood an excellent chance of going home early in a pine box. On the other hand, young Chuck Horner was having a very good time, and learning a great deal about flying fighter aircraft.

Second Lieutenant Horner got quite a shock, however, when he first walked into the squadron. He had 100 hours of F-100 time, had never flown in really bad weather (a daily occurrence in England), and expected to be led around by the hand for six months or so to learn the ropes. The ops officers smiled, got him a local area check-out and a Stan Eval check ride to certify he could sit alert, then stamped him flight leader and hoped he made it.

When Horner arrived at Lakenheath, among the first people he met was his new squadron commander, Major Skinny Innis—one of the wildest members of a profession that tries to corner the market on wildness. Innis, like many others, had gone off to World War II before he finished college. During that war, pilots of his age group had operated almost without rules—the name of the game had been to get the job done. The downside was that a lot of them had died in accidents and not as a result of enemy fire. Innis had survived that war, and Korea, by means of brains, energy, flying talent, and luck.

In the two worlds that make up the military—field and headquarters—Skinny Innis was at the far extreme of the field orientation. One earned points there for being outrageous, and Skinny had acquired just about as many outrageous points as it was possible to accumulate. All he wanted to do was fight wars and have fun in the downtime. He was profane, inelegant, not only un- but antidiplomatic, and often wrongheaded; but he deeply loved his nation, flying, and the Air Force; he made it fun to serve with him; and he kept his pilots looking at the enemy instead of worrying about their own careers.

Skinny hated to be supervised. In practice that meant that he and the wing director of operations, Colonel Bruce Hinton, (who was called "Balls" Hinton and had had several kills in Korea), often had fistfights when they had a difference of opinion. Since they had both served in World War II and Korea, lived with adjoining backyards, and were friends as well as antagonists, however, they tolerated each other's wild behavior.

Even though Skinny hated authority, he was loyal to senior commanders, which meant he worked their problems and did the mission they laid out for his squadron. He ran the squadron the way he wanted to, however, which today would not be politically acceptable, and he specialized in making flamboyant statements.

At the officers' club at Lakenheath, a large bell was mounted over the bar. When you walked in, you had to buy drinks for everyone at the bar if someone could ring the bell before you got your hat off. Skinny turned the game upside down. He bought bowler hats for all the 492d Squadron, declared them the Mad Hatters, and "ordered" them to wear their hats in the bar. If they didn't, they had to buy the bar a round. (The bowler rule was in effect only when you wore a civilian jacket and tie; uniform was excepted.)

Then Skinny decided that wasn't enough. His squadron also needed to be different from the other two squadrons at work, so he bought them glengarries, the traditional Scottish hats, to wear with their flight suits. When Bruce Hinton tried to stop this change in uniform (correctly judging it against the uniform rules), they had another fight, and Skinny won. Thus, for the three years Horner was at Lakenheath, everyone in Skinny's squadron wore a glengarry, with his rank on it, with his flying suit.

There was a serious point behind the apparent silliness. Skinny's goal was to create an elite unit, the 492d Tactical Fighter Squadron, within an elite unit, the 48th Tactical Fighter Wing. His methods probably went too far by today's practices; but back then, in the shadow of World War II and Korea, commanders had a great deal of latitude. During Vietnam, Horner and the other pilots at the bases at Korat and Ta Khli in Thailand wore nonregulation Aussie hats for the same reason.

Horner's initiation into the Skinny Innis leadership style came on the day of his first mission at Lakenheath.

That morning, he looked out the window at fog thick enough to cut with a knife. Believing that prudence was a wise course for junior officers, he reported to Major Innis in a military manner and calmly informed him that since he had never flown in actual weather, let alone the kind of fog they had outside, the major might consider finding someone else to take the mission. Major Innis looked up from the paper he was reading, glared at Horner, and snapped, "Get your ass in the air. You don't think I'm going to fly in shit like this, do you?"

It was a case of learn or die, and he learned.

As it turned out, after Horner had been in the squadron a couple of months and proved he could hack it, Skinny let him know that he had gone to high school in Iowa with his cousin Bill Miles and had been one of his closest friends. They had both joined the Air Corps together, and gone on to get their wings.

Years later, in 1964, Innis—now a colonel—was in Saigon flying old, broken-down B-26s over South Vietnam. In those days, the U.S. government was pretending that Innis and the other Air Force people in the country were "advising" the VNAF, though in fact, they were doing much of the fighting. Some of Skinny's friends loved being there, because that was where the action was, and when Chuck Horner heard about that, he did what he could to get himself into the war.

When he wrote Innis to ask for his help, however, Skinny advised him to stay as far away from Vietnam as he could. Even then, Innis realized the war was destined to collapse into disaster.

★ The mission of the 48th TFW was primarily nuclear strike, backed up by conventional air-to-ground and air-to-air. That meant that the pilots primarily trained in the delivery of nuclear weapons and sat alert in the European version of the SIOP (the Single Integrated Operations Plan for conducting a one-day nuclear war), just as SAC pilots did in bombers back in the States. In order to qualify in nuclear weapons delivery, they had to drop a certain number of practice bombs every six months and certify on their target. They also had to describe to a board how the weapon worked, talk through their mission, and know command and control cold—that is, they had to know who could release them to go on the mission, what procedures had to be followed in order to arm the bomb, what kind of code words they could expect, and so on.

Each training period, pilots also flew a few air-to-air and air-to-ground conventional-weapons training sorties, but they were only required to be familiar in those events—they didn't have to qualify by achieving a specific bomb score average.

★ This is how a typical nuclear delivery training sortie might go—a two-ship air-to-ground:

The lead and the wingman brief two hours before takeoff, check the weather and notices, suit up, and step to the jets about twenty minutes before start engine, which is twenty minutes before takeoff time (which is predicated on range time). After preflighting the jet and starting and checking out the systems, the two taxi to the arming area at the end of the runway. There the weapons troops take out the safety pins on the practice bomb dispenser and arm the guns by rotating a live round into the chamber and connecting the electrical plug that provides current to the bullet primer. From there the two taxi onto the runway and close the canopies. After a head nod, the brakes are released. After a second head nod, they light the afterburners and take off. A third head nod is the signal for gear up, followed by flaps up. They then turn out of traffic on the air traffic control frequency and fly a departure route, climbing to 1,000 feet on top (that is, in the clear on top of the overcast).

Since the lead planned a low level in France, they now head for the letdown point. In the meantime, the lead moves his wingman out to about 4,000 to 6,000 feet, meaning that the lead is not looking into the sun and he can clear his wingman's six o'clock (his tail) without himself having to squint into the light. After he reaches the let-down point, he rocks his wings, which signals the wingman to join up on his wing. The wingman lines up the light on the lead's wingtip with the star on the lead's fuselage in order to maintain forward and aft reference, and down the two go into the weather.

The lead breaks out at 1,000 feet above the ground and kicks his wingman out by fluttering the rudder. The wingman then takes up a chase position off to one side and slightly high, about 500 feet aft of the lead's jet. From there he can look through the lead to clear the air for other airplanes that might appear in his path. The lead's job, meanwhile, is to fly the route and arrive at the range at the scheduled range time.

The navigation is not easy. The lead must maintain the planned speed and heading, while using a map to locate an identifiable point on the ground. If it comes into view at the precise time and the precise place that had been planned, then they are not lost. (They must not try it the other way. That is, they must not find a point on the ground and then try to find it on the map. Doing that means they are lost.)

At the Initial Point (IP) to the range, the lead switches the flight over to range frequency and calls the range officer for clearance. The wingman now splits off and makes a 360-degree turn, which will leave him about two minutes spacing on the lead's aircraft for a nuclear over-the-shoulder delivery. Meanwhile, the lead arms his switches, gets clearance, pushes up to delivery speed, and heads toward the range.

What follows is a variation on what he practiced earlier at Nellis:

The bull's-eye is a set of concentric circles on the ground: the outer circle is 2,000 feet in radius, the next is 1,000 feet, the next is 500, and the smallest is 100. The lead's immediate task is to fly over a spot upwind from the bull's-eye. For example, if he has a wind from the northeast at 20 knots and he is heading north on the run-in, he lines up his jet over the ground to the right of the bull's-eye, waits until he is past the bull's-eye at the prescribed offset point, lights the afterburner, and presses the pickle (the bomb-release button on top of the stick). At that point, he starts an Immelmann. At a preset angle, nose up (which primarily depends on the outside temperature and wind velocity at release point), the bomb is automatically released. Sometimes this is a twenty-five-pound practice bomb, but often it is a 2,000-pound bomb shaped like a nuclear weapon (when he releases one, his aircraft bounds like a kangaroo). The bomb then climbs to more than 30,000 feet above the ground, runs out of speed, and turns around and heads to earth. When it strikes the ground, a shotgun shell filled with white phosphorus puts out a large puff of smoke. This allows the range crew to score the hit by referencing it to the circles. Since the pilot is dropping a simulated nuclear weapon, a satisfactory score is well over 1,000 feet.

Meanwhile, at release he calls, "Off on top wet," which means that a release light lit in his cockpit, and the bomb is in the air headed for the ground. He then rolls out so his wingman can start his run. As he comes off on top, they both enter the bombing and strafe pattern. After they expend all their bombs and bullets, they join up and start for home.

As they cross the Channel, the lead checks in with the British, so the cousins don't scramble a fighter on them, and enter the holding pattern at Hopton beacon on the English coast (which served as the initial fix for airfields in East Anglia), until the expected approach clearance time, EAC.

When control informs him that he is cleared to penetrate, the lead switches to the Lakenheath GCA frequency and contacts the controller, who talks him down. He breaks out into the fog at 300 feet above the ground a half mile off the end of the runway, touches down, deploys his drag chute, and gingerly steps on the brakes as the jet slips and slides on the always wet runway. He turns off on the end and jettisons his drag chute. The armorers then disconnect the gun plugs and put safety pins in any remaining bombs. About this time, the wingman lands. The lead waits for him to get safetied, and then he taxis back to the ramp in front of the squadron, shuts down the jet, climbs out, and stops by maintenance debriefing. Then he goes back to the squadron and stows his gear.

After that, he and his wingman spend maybe half an hour debriefing the flight: what went right, what went wrong, why the bombs were good or bad.

No small part of the discipline of a fighter pilot derives from the debriefings after a mission.

Since these can be brutal, the lead makes *very* sure that in the mission he follows the game plan, and if he's made a mistake during the mission, he had better be the first to admit it. If he doesn't, or if he wasn't aware that he had made a mistake, or if he tried to cover up his mistakes with self-serving excuses, he was probably dead meat in the debrief.

Debriefings in operational units often involve heated debate, for the stakes are incredibly high, and the participants have strong and differing opinions about what will survive and work in combat and what is just fanciful thinking. On the other hand, the debriefings in combat crew training units tend to be much more structured and much less heated. The students do not have the experience to know what is functional and dysfunctional, and the missions themselves are usually very structured. However, since every mission includes unexpected events, there is always room for differences of opinion.

The most respected pilots are the ones who can identify their own shortfalls and learn from them. And the best instructors are the ones who can tell them the root cause of their failures in the air and give them tools to avoid them—either new physical techniques or different thought processes.

★ Another typical mission out of Lakenheath was called a night MSQ. This was a single-ship mission in Germany. Ground radars with very accurate beams had been placed near the East German border, in order to direct a fighter in wartime to a point in space for bomb release of a nuclear weapon. The bomb would then fly a predictable route to the target.

On an MSQ mission, a pilot might take off single-ship near the end of the day and fly at 40,000 feet to a contact point on the East German border. At the contact point, he'd call in the blind; that is, he'd broadcast without receiving an answer. Meanwhile, in the upper-left-hand side of his instrument panel was a four-inch-round dial on which were a number of small symbols, windows, and icons. One arrow pointed to the left, another arrow to the right; one window said one minute, and another said thirty seconds; and at the top of the dial was a single red light. When that one lit, he knew the radar was locked on to his jet. Then he followed the instructions it was sending him, which were relayed through the arrows, windows, and icons on the dial. Most frequently, they sent you north along the western edge of the East German border. To be on the safe side, the pilot would also tune the low-frequency navigation set on the floor between his legs to a series of twenty-five-watt navigation beacons. These gave him a cross check to make sure he didn't stray over the border.

Meanwhile, in the darkening sky, he would see the contrails of a Russian fighter shadowing him, hoping the pilot would stray over the border so he could try to shoot him down.

Soon, the one-minute light would come on, meaning that the pilot had sixty seconds to release. At the same time, he would be getting left or right arrows, while maintaining his altitude and airspeed at the prebriefed values. Then the thirty-second light would come on, and thirty seconds later, he'd hit his bomb button. This would cause his radio to emit a tone, which the radar site would score. (Both the pilot and the radar site were given a score.)

Afterward, he'd turn away to the west and either return to the contact point for another run or head for home, hoping to hit his bed by midnight, because he had to be at work at 4:00 A.M. for a six o'clock take-off the next day.

★ Fighter pilots never get enough of air-to-air training—dogfights—yet, for some reason, probably having to do with the nuclear delivery mission, U.S. pilots in the late fifties and early sixties were given very little air combat training; and what they were allowed was rudimentary. As a result, they all went underground. They practiced against other NATO fighters that happened to be in the air at the same time they were.

So, for example, if a pilot was flying the nuclear delivery profile above, a Mirage fighter might well start a practice intercept run on him. When the pilot saw the Mirage, he tried to do what he would do in actual combat. He'd push the power up and turn into the attack. Then he and the

Mirage pilot would conduct a series of maneuvers aimed at foiling the other while winding up at his six o'clock for a heat-seeking missile or gun attack. All of this was unbriefed and there were no rules. In fact, it was illegal. Worse, you were often in a dangerous configuration, carrying, say, four external fuel tanks and a practice nuke bomb, which made the fighter apt to go out of control.

Those who did well in this school learned how to fly their aircraft on the edge of the envelope and how to fight a broad range of aircraft and pilots.

Mirages, for instance, tended to be more maneuverable than Super Sabers, because the F-100s usually carried external fuel tanks, but Mirage pilots often entered the fight in afterburner with speed brakes out, thus negating the advantage of either function. As a result, it was pretty easy to get them to overshoot initially. After that, a pilot had to be careful at slow speed because the Mirages could out-turn him. The British Hawker Hunter was a sweet jet and tough to beat, but U.S. aircraft had after-burners and Hunters did not. While F-100s could not out-turn them, they could use the vertical dimension (that is, they could climb faster) to gain some advantage over a less skilled pilot. On the other hand, the Javelin (also British) was heavy and underpowered, so it didn't take much to gain the advantage on it. The British Lightning had both superb turning ability and outstanding thrust, but didn't carry much fuel. So if a pilot got jumped by a Lightning, he'd just stay defensive and fend off his passes with hard turns, nose low to maintain energy, until the fight wound up on the deck and the pilot's turns now became level. Then he'd spend about ten pain-filled minutes looking over his own tail while the Lightning tried to get off a valid shot. Eventually, if he "survived," he'd see the Lightning level his wings and turn for home, meaning that his meager gas supply was about gone. Then the pilot would light afterburner, fly after him, and place his nose on his tail just so he got the message.

Fighter pilot ecstasy.

★ Combat units are tested periodically to see if they can do their mission. The Super Bowl of tests for Horner's wing was called an Operational Readiness Inspection, or ORI. Since for the 48th TFW the primary mission was to load their nuclear weapons and deliver them on the Soviet enemy situated throughout Eastern Europe, an ORI usually began when the wing received an alert message (plainly marked "Exercise Only") that warned of an impending crisis. Soon inspectors flew into the base, and the commander was briefed on the nature and rules of the exercise. Usually the wing was expected to break out the nuclear weapons, deliver them to each combat-ready aircraft, and get them uploaded in a specified number of hours. If all that took too long, or if there were any unsafe practices, the exercise was stopped and the wing flunked. This often resulted in the appointment of a new wing commander, followed by a period of months to practice, and a retest.

Meanwhile, as the weapons were loaded, the pilots were briefed on the flying phase of the exercise. This usually meant they were given simulated targets in France or Germany. After the weapons were all successfully loaded, they were then downloaded and returned to the secure storage area. Once that was done, dummy bombs—concrete shapes— were uploaded; the exercise clock was restarted; sorties were launched in accordance with the tasking from the IG team (often the IG team threw in disruptive events, such as an enemy air attack on the airfield, to complicate matters); and the pilots had to figure out in the air how to fly their route and reach the bombing range on time to make their assigned Time over Target (TOT). As the pilots flew their routes, the IG had people in France or Germany on the ground at various checkpoints, noting if the pilots passed by there and the time. When the pilots reached their bombing range, they got a single pass to release their weapon, and this was scored by the IG team.

Much could go wrong: the jet could break (pilots often took off with a mechanical failure and sweated it out until they released their bombs and could declare an emergency); or the bomb might not release during the over-the-shoulder delivery. If there was weather, as there often was in Europe, crafty pilots would reset the switches while upside down in the overcast, near a stall, do a loop on instruments, and jettison the bomb while heading back toward the ground. The IG on the ground would see only this ton of concrete and steel scream out of the clouds into which the plane had just climbed, and score the hit.

Other missions were less demanding. Pilots would simply fly to a simulated target and do a dry pass. No practice bomb would be released, but the IG team would score the pilot's time over target and whether he hit the proper offset point at the target.

ORIs were exhausting, and it was all too easy to fail. If a pilot didn't get a high percentage of his weapons to release on the range on time with a given Circular Error Probability, for example, he died . . . or at least the wing commander died, and he usually took others along with him.

Horner was called to make what turned out to be his last flight at the "Heath" because of a surprise ORI. It was supposed to have been his last day in England, and he hadn't expected to fly. Meanwhile, the Horner household goods were packed; Chuck and Mary Jo had moved into the officers' club guest house in Brandon Forest, and they were waiting for transport out.

About noon, the housekeeper came looking for him with an urgent request to call the squadron. Major Nogrowski, the operations officer (they called him Nogo), was desperate. The wing was being given an Operational Readiness Inspection; they were short on pilots; and they needed Horner to fly one more mission. As luck—and planning—would have it, Chuck's flying gear was stashed in his personal baggage. He'd gotten into that habit whenever he made a Permanent Change of Station move (PCS), so he'd be ready to start flying first thing at his new station.

"Okay," he said, "no problem." Then he kissed Mary Jo goodbye, caught a ride to the base, and checked into the 492d Fighter Squadron. Nogo briefed him at the duty desk. They needed to fly two more sorties to pass the ORI. Nogo had a new pilot he could send on one of them, but he'd run out of flight leaders.

"No problem."

Horner changed into his gear and briefed the new wingman: easy mission takeoff, climb out, and cruise over to France. Let down through the weather, fly low to an abandoned air base in northern France, and conduct a simulated attack. The Inspector General team did not have observers at that target, so the attack would not be scored. The weather was clear, and there was a full moon for their return to England in the early evening. As usual in those days, the wingman was inexperienced, a green lieutenant; but all he had to do was stay in formation, follow Horner's orders, and avoid the ground with his aircraft during the low-level navigation and target attack portions of the mission.

The first half of the mission proceeded without a hitch. But as they were climbing out from the target toward the setting sun, Horner's wingman called him on the radio—an unusual event, since new guys were to maintain strict radio discipline and speak only when spoken to.

"Blue Leader, this is Blue Two. The bottom of your aircraft is dark.

Request permission to join to close formation and take a look." Horner rolled his eyes in exasperation and cleared him in as they leveled off en route home.

But the next call really got his attention. "Sir"—Horner had just made captain—"there is a bunch of fluid all over the bottom of your aircraft." Horner scanned his cockpit gauges, and all was normal. The engine was running fine. Perhaps the setting sun, he thought, had caused a lighting condition that was playing tricks with the lieutenant's vision.

The wingman's next call, as they crossed the English Channel, was even more alarming. "Sir, you're streaming so much fluid it's making a vapor trail behind the aircraft."

Horner rolled the aircraft to the left, looked over his left shoulder, and saw a trail of white mist arcing out from the tail of his jet. As he wondered what could cause this, the darkening cockpit lit up with red and yellow warning lights. Much of his hydraulic systems had quit. The system needed to operate the flight controls remained, but the second flight-control system and a third system that lowered the landing gear and powered the wheel brakes registered zero hydraulic pressure. The fluid Horner and his wingman had observed was the hydraulic fluid from these systems leaking overboard.

Okay, no sweat, he thought, *I have good flight controls, at least enough to fly home and land, an emergency one-shot backup system—* to lower the landing gear—*and a backup electric motor-driven system,* for braking action. This and the drag chute (a parachute packed in the back end of the F-100 that was deployed after touchdown to slow the aircraft down and save wear and tear on tires and brakes) should permit the aircraft to stop safely on the runway. *Maintenance will have to tow the jet into the parking area, and I'll have to declare an emergency with the tower, which means extra paperwork; but what the hell, the weather's good*—rare in England—*and I'm in control.*

When they arrived at Hopton Radio Beacon on the East Anglia coast, Horner called the Tower at Lakenheath. "Lakenheath tower, this is Blue One at Hopton, I have an emergency. One has lost his primary flight control and utility hydraulic systems, and am bingo fuel." Meaning: he had only fuel enough to proceed to the field and land. He then informed them he would depart the fix (that is, from the radio beacon's location on the English coast) and fly to the field, and asked for a weather update.

The supervisor of flying (SOF) called back with unwelcome news: a fog bank was moving in, the ground-controlled intercept radar (GCI) was not in operation, and he was fixing to close the field and go home. Because the weather was supposed to be good enough for a nonradar approach, they had shut the GCI down for periodic maintenance. Because it was England, the fog had just come up unexpectedly. He directed Horner to fly back to France and land at a suitable base; there were several possibilities.

Horner looked at the clear night sky, then at his sick jet's flashing warning lights, and then at the fuel gauges, all seeming to read zero fuel left, and let the supervisor of flying know where he could go. "I can't make it to France," he went on. "I'm coming home, I have to land, and can you get the crash crew out?" He was thinking that the presence of the big fire truck with its yellow-suited firemen might come in handy in the event he couldn't get his landing gear down, or if it collapsed on landing, or if he lost heading control after landing because he didn't have nose wheel steering, or if his drag chute failed and he ran off the end of the runway and wound up in a fireball.

As the night sky grew dark and the moon started to slide above the horizon, he could make out wisps of white fog filling in the low spots in the English countryside.

As they let down into the night, he began to check in his mind all the things that could go wrong, then instructed the wingman how to react— that is, how to avoid getting caught up in the explosion of Blue Leader's jet. Meanwhile, to his credit, the SOF stayed cool (it occurred to Horner about that time that the SOF could afford to be cool, seeing as how his ass wasn't in a sick jet trying to get on the ground before the field became socked in). By then, Horner could make out the lights from villages and from cars on the roads shining up through the wisps of fog. He had flown into the field hundreds of times, in far worse weather, but always with the calm assuring voice of their British air traffic controllers guiding his actions as they observed his flight path toward the field. *Tonight,* he thought, *they're all drinking ale in some pub because the weather was supposed to be good and we were the last flight and the radar needed periodic routine maintenance.*

In the end, Horner found the field, dropped down to the treetops in the dark, and—using dimly lit references—found the runway. He landed, his drag chutes worked, and he gently used the emergency brakes to bring his wounded jet to a stop on the runway. By then, the fog was so thick that the fire truck that came racing down the runway almost col-

lided with his jet. He sat there, wet with sweat, hands shaking more from
fatigue than anything else, and realized one more time there was a God
who didn't want to talk with Chuck just yet. Just a routine day in the life
of a fighter pilot, cheating death and thinking he did it on his own, but
knowing in his heart it was divine intervention that let him beat the odds.

Chuck went home and picked up Mary Jo and their year-old daughter Susan, and they boarded the transport home to the United States.

SEYMOUR JOHNSON

Horner's next assignment (it was now 1963) was to the 335th Tactical
Fighter Squadron, 4th Tactical Fighter Wing, at Seymour Johnson AFB,
Goldsboro, North Carolina, where he would fly the famous, or infamous, F-105 Thunderchief. There his son, John Patrick Horner, would be
born, and from there he would go off to combat for the first time.

The Thud, as it was called—at first by its detractors, and then by
everyone else, after it proved to be the jet of choice if one was going to
be shot at—was big and spacious: a man could stand up under its wing,
and he needed a ladder to climb up into the cockpit. The cockpit was
roomy, and the instruments were as modern as one could get, with tapes
instead of dials, which made it a breeze to read while screaming down the
chute during a dive-bomb pass. The Thud was also solid; since fuel was
not stored in the wings, AAA could blow huge holes in them, and a pilot
could still come home without a problem. And it was fast—nothing could
touch it for top speed; it routinely exceeded twice the speed of sound,
Mach 2, on test flights. What made it fast was a huge gas-sucking engine
and very thin wings, so it flew faster in military power than most aircraft
did in afterburner. Unfortunately, this capability was achieved at the cost
of lift. The thin wings took forever to fly on takeoff. When a pilot had a
full load of fuel and bombs, he used the entire runway. Even then, the
Thud didn't want to fly; but rather than set a land speed record, the pilot
would pull the beast off the ground and stagger into the air, whacking off
branches of small trees with his aircraft until he was able to start a climb.

This same reluctance manifested itself when he wanted to turn in air-
to-air combat. The Thud would go fast, but it did not like to turn. Thus,
the preferred tactic in a fight was just to enter it, pick a target, scream in
for a shot, and then blow on through. A pilot didn't have to look back,
because no one was going to catch him.

Similar principles applied in bombing runs: just after a pilot released his bombs, he put both hands on the stick and pulled it back into his lap. He didn't have to worry about over-geeing the aircraft, because the Thud was so solid, it didn't seem to mind ten or twelve Gs. But if he didn't immediately begin the recovery, he was sure to hit the ground.

Early F-105s had two seriously bad habits: they had a tendency to blow up in the air; and if the pilot wasn't alert, they slammed into the ground.

They blew up because of a design problem. At times fuel got trapped between the hot section of the engine and the fuselage. After a while, a fire got going back there, which in time would melt through hydraulic lines (no flight controls then) or a fuel cell (a small fire instantly became a very big fire and the pilot was the marshmallow).

They hit the ground because of mistakes in Air Force tactics. In the erroneous belief that one would avoid enemy defenses that way, tactics in those days emphasized flying at low level; but the Thud, being slow to pull out on a dive-bomb pass, needed more air under it than those tactics wanted to give it.

Still, the pilots came to love flying the F-105, especially after the design and tactical flaws were fixed. It was an honest aircraft; a pilot loves a jet that obeys his commands, and a jet that makes it easier to put the bombs on target. And if he wanted to strafe a target, he had an M-60 Gatling gun. With that, much of the time, he could expect to put every round through the target, for a 100 percent score. Today, many of the attributes of the F-105—such as stability and accuracy—are found in the A-10. On the other hand, the A-10 turns, but it won't go fast. All things being equal, fighter pilots will tell you, "speed is life."

★ Horner had a good tour at Seymour Johnson. The 335th was a fine squadron, and there was a lot of excitement with firepower demonstrations and plans to attack Cuba—in those days there was well-justified fear that the Russians would install nuclear missiles on the island. On the other hand, the otherwise joyous squadron parties and deployments around the world were tempered by the F-105's bad habits, blowing up in the air or slamming into the ground, either of which meant somebody had to erase a name off the pilot board, empty a locker, and return the pilot's effects to his widow or parents.

That happened when Horner's flight commander "bit it"—another one of those expressions people use when they don't want to face the reality—when he flew into the water on the gunnery range off the coast of North Carolina. Parts of his body were recovered, and then came the ceremony of sitting with the grieving widow, taking care of the children, helping arrange for the funeral, and attending the memorial ceremony, with its missing-man flyby. . . . By now, all this was a familiar routine for Chuck Horner, except this time it all hit him on the head with a powerful new insight.

At that funeral, I guess I was beginning to grow up; for I started to notice something about our warrior culture that I hadn't really noticed before: the pain and agony of the widow.

Hey, fighter pilots are tough. When one of us died, we felt sad, got drunk, and made jokes, in an effort to laugh in the face of our own deaths. But without our knowing it, it was our wives who really suffered. Air Force wives are indoctrinated from the get-go, "Don't make a big issue over a death. Don't make a thing about the loss. Cover it over. Don't get your own pilot husband upset. He needs to be alert and to concentrate when he's flying his six-hundred-mile-an-hour jet." And they do cover it over. Meanwhile, the wives, and not the warriors, know the real horror.

Among the American Plains Indians (so the story came to me), when a warrior died in battle, everyone was happy (dying in battle was about as noble an act as you could imagine) . . . everyone except the warrior's widow. She tore her clothing, rubbed ashes in her hair, cut her arms with a knife, and wailed as though her soul had been torn out of her body. For the widow, it was more than losing her husband (Indian husbands not being famously loving, caring mates, anyway). Rather, with her husband dead, she no longer had standing as a human being in the tribe. Unless she remarried, she would cease to exist in the eyes of her former friends, and she would be left to fend for herself. When the tribe moved on to new hunting grounds, she'd fall behind, she'd have nothing to eat, and soon, she'd starve, or else weather or wolves would kill her. For the warrior's widow, in other words, the death of a warrior husband was a sentence condemning her to a death that was lonely, slow, and shameful.

Our warrior society, I began to see, isn't all that different. The husband would die. The widow would be comforted, food would be brought over, there'd be tears and shared memories and that missing-man flyby that chilled all of our souls. But Monday would roll around, the pilots would go back to their jet aircraft mistresses, the wives would go back to raising kids and bonding with one another, and the movers would be pulling up to the widow's house. She no longer qualified to live on the base; and her former pals, her inner circle, didn't want their own husbands hanging around her, lest she snag a new husband. Worse, none of our warriors, husbands or wives, wanted her reminder of the death that lived seconds away whenever we strapped on our jet and took to the wild blue yonder.

It hit me then that, daily, our wives had to contend with the unspoken horror of all that. Not only did they dread our death, but just as real was the knowledge that their lives, as members of an extremely close interdependent society, also hung in the balance. And I came to appreciate the steel in their unspoken and unacknowledged courage—as opposed to our own drunken ribaldry, which we pretended was "guts"—in the ever-present face of death. The pilots were scared children who used booze, offensive behavior, and profane language to hold the awareness of their fragile mortality at arm's length. But our women shared a gut-wrenching horror that someday the wing commander would show up at their front door to announce that they were now going to have to provide for and raise the children alone, that they were about to be turned out into the world to fend for themselves, and that their closest confidantes in the world would soon stare through them, lest they see what might be in store for themselves.

Service wives, especially fighter pilot wives, are the most underrated warriors in the world. Daily, they confront their own fears, staying home to change a dirty diaper and getting ready for the next move, while shoring up the inflated egos of their mates before they go off to chase around the sky. God bless and watch over them.

★ Death came personally to Chuck Horner during his time with the 4th TFW.

One of the 4th's missions was to deploy to Turkey and sit alert with a nuke on their F-105s. They flew gunnery training over the Mediterranean, air-to-ground at Koyna range in Turkey, and low level all over Turkey. While Horner was in Turkey around Christmas of 1964, his parents, his sister, Mary Lou Kendall, her husband Bill, and their three children were killed in a car accident in Iowa (Christmas was not a lucky time for the Horner clan; John Towner had been killed during the Christmas season of 1953–54).

Those deaths were terrible, and so was Horner's grief. Despite them, however, there was a fascinating side story that made, and still makes, the horror and grief a little more bearable.

When Chuck Horner came back to the States for the funeral, he was a nobody captain with a lot of pain, yet the USAF took care of him royally—actually, they treated him like a *warrior*. They arranged transport that brought him from Turkey to Des Moines before his sister from San Diego could get there. Colonel John Murphy, his wing commander, even had the TAC commander's personal T-39 transport meet Horner at McGuire AFB when he got off the military air transport system aircraft that brought him from Germany.

All of this cost a great deal of money. Nowadays, the media might even have a field day with the story of misuse of government jets. But the cost of that government jet that flew Chuck Horner from McGuire to Des Moines got paid back many times over during the next few years. There are some things you have to do for warriors.

After the 4th TFW, Horner's next move was into combat in Vietnam.

2

THE BIG LIE

In April of 1965, Chuck Horner was on TDY at McCoy AFB in Orlando at a gunnery workup, preparing for a weapons meet called Red Rio. Because it was a major meet, he had done a lot of flying to prepare for it—pure gunnery missions three times a day, bombing and strafing—and he was at the peak of his performance. One night at the bar, the ops officer fingered him. "You've got orders," he said. "Take a jet and get yourself back home to Seymour."

"I better wait until morning," Horner answered; he had a couple of drinks in him.

"No way," the Ops said. "Get your ass in the jet and go."

So Horner packed that night and flew home to Seymour Johnson, where he was met when he arrived. "You'll be leaving in the morning on a secret mission," he was told. "Pack for hot weather." He went home and kissed Mary Jo hello; the next morning a staff car arrived, and he kissed her goodbye.

Also in the car was Major Roger Myhrum, a friend from the 4th TFW, Seymour Johnson, who had joined the wing at about the same time in 1963 that Horner had. Myhrum was older than Horner and was in another squadron, the 333d, but they both flew F-105s and got along well. Now they were traveling together on commercial airline tickets to San Francisco, destination classified; they didn't have a clue about where they were going.

In San Francisco, a bus picked them up, along with some other pilots from McConnell AFB, Kansas, and took them to Travis AFB near Oakland. After the bus left them off, their destination began to grow clearer: somebody handed them an empty bag and sent them down a line. They filled the bag with soldiers' gear—rifle, pistol, mosquito netting, sleeping bag, poncho, helmet, mess kit, and web belt with canteen. In the military, they handed out that kind of gear when a man was about to go off to war, just in case he needed it. On the one hand, it was better to be safe than unprepared, but on the other hand, when a pilot gets handed a rifle and a poncho, he gets a bit edgy. It suggests that he's about to go and live with the Army in the field, directing air strikes. Horner wanted to fly jets, not stomp around on the ground. Fortunately, they also gave him a .38 pistol, which was a weapon you carried when you flew jets in combat, so that was reassuring. Well, time would tell.

Horner and Myhrum were then loaded onto a commercial jet contracted to the military and headed west. They landed in Bangkok, where they were told they would be going upcountry in a couple of days on the Klong Courier—that was the call sign of the C-130 that took people and supplies clockwise from Bangkok around to all the Thai bases in the morning, and counterclockwise in the afternoon. They were going to a base called Korat, in central Thailand, about a hundred miles northeast of Bangkok, where two squadrons of F-105s were located.

Korat was one of four bases—the others were Ta Khli, Ubon, and Udorn—the Air Force was then operating in Thailand, though the bases remained under the control of the Thai Air Force. The Air Force had been at these bases on and off for several years, training Thais. Early in 1965, F-105s from Korat raided North Vietnamese munitions storage areas supplying the Vietcong in the South. Even though more raids soon followed, the U.S. presence at the air bases in Thailand was kept very quiet, partly to keep it a secret from the enemy and partly to avoid embarrassing the Thai government.

Two days later, while Horner and Myhrum were waiting at the Bangkok airfield for the Klong Courier, Horner ran into a pilot from Korat whom he knew named Dick Pearson. Along with another pilot from Korat, Pearson was passing through on his way to Washington, D.C., where they were being sent to answer hard questions about an embarrassing incident over North Vietnam.

Horner was eager to pick Pearson's brain, for this was his first in-person conversation with anyone who had flown combat missions over North Vietnam. And it was here that he received the first of many lessons pointing out the gulf between reality and fantasy in the Vietnam War.

On April 6, during a strike at Vinh, in North Vietnam, two North Vietnamese MiG-17s had shot down two F-105s, numbers one and two in a flight of four.

The flight had been holding south of the target awaiting another flight to clear the area. As they waited, the flight leader let the formation get slow: the Thuds were loafing along at about 350 knots, and they were bomb-laden, and thus clumsy and vulnerable. To make matters worse, the two elements became separated by a couple of miles, though they were still in visual contact.

Dick Pearson, who had been number three in the flight, had looked up and watched in horror as the two MiGs slid in between the formations, and then each MiG blew an F-105 out of the air. He and his wingman immediately jettisoned their bombs and tanks and went after the MiGs, but they dove for the deck and escaped. Pearson and his wingman then returned to the scene of the shoot-down and started a RESCAP (Rescue CAP)—circling the area and looking for chutes or flares and listening for beepers.

What the commanders in Washington wanted to know was how a couple of ignorant Third World peasants flying two vintage MiGs could take out two supersonic, state-of-the-art American jets. The answer was no surprise to Horner, no more than to the two pilots who were about to get laid out on the carpet in Washington. However, it was not welcome information to the commanders in Washington: fighter pilot training during previous years had concentrated on nuclear delivery, and now the pilots were fighting a conventional war. Such incidents were bound to happen.

The MiG story, of course, came as a shock to Horner, but then he simply passed the North Vietnamese success off to a flight leader mistake. In fact, he was right up to a point. The flight leader *had* let his formation get too slow; and he *hadn't* made sure that everyone in the flight was alert to intruders. He had let himself fall into stateside gunnery range habits, where one tended to concentrate on spacing rather than combat alertness. On Horner's first mission, he remembers that his own pull-off from the target was not all that aggressive. Aggression came fast, however, when he noticed the orange golf balls passing his canopy and all the black puffs with orange centers of smoke between him and the number one aircraft.

More important, however, Chuck Horner was as naive as other Americans when he deployed to war for the first time. He was a believer. He thought he and the other American pilots would eat the enemy alive, that American jets were unstoppable, that American tactics were superb, that America's cause was just, and that American generals knew what they were doing. As for the actual leadership in Washington and the decisions they were making about the war in Vietnam, he didn't have a clue. As it turned out, neither did they.

KORAT—1965

In March 1965, a series of air strikes against ninety-six targets in North Vietnam called ROLLING THUNDER began, and a platform was needed from which to base the attacks. For this purpose, Thailand proved ideal. It was close to both countries; the Thai Air Force had very fine airfields with 10,000-foot runways that they were under-using; Thailand was secure (there was no insurgency there); and finally, Americans could keep a low profile (no press was allowed), which meant that the American military presence could be concealed.

Before ROLLING THUNDER, some of the strikes had been launched out of the bases in Thailand, but those were short-notice deployments in and out of the bases, and no real infrastructure had been needed. The U.S. Air Force had simply used the runways and ramps, and the pilots slept in hotels, tents, or U.S. training compounds. But in March and April, when the attacks against North Vietnam (and Laos) began in earnest, two F-105 squadrons were sent to Korat (which grew to four squadrons by the time Horner returned to Korat in 1967), and a wing infrastructure was now needed to operate the bases in Thailand. Horner and Myhrum were to become part of this infrastructure.

At Korat, the wing staff was headed by Bill Richie, who had earlier flown across the Atlantic, using British equipment and F-84s, to prove air-to-air refueling for deployments. Horner and Myhrum were to serve as duty officers in the Wing Tactical Operations Center—that is, they were to be staff officers, who would help plan the missions. There were no plans for them to fly.

★ And so there they were, in April 1965, standing for the first time on the aircraft parking ramp at Korat Air Base, the Klong Courier now on the next leg of its circuit.

Though it had a first-class runway with a tower, in those days Korat was at best a sparse place. On a ramp in front of the tower, the Thai Air Force had its trainer aircraft parked, and nearby was a parking ramp for the two squadrons of F-105s. The buildings were wood frame with tin roofs. The housing was in the same type of wood buildings, with screening and open boards, so the air could circulate.

Soon after they landed, Horner and Myhrum were met by a friend from McConnell AFB in Kansas, Major Pete Van Huss. Van Huss was the ops officer of the McConnell squadron at Korat; the other squadron came from Kadena AFB in Okinawa. They all piled into a jeep and drove to where the hooches were located, which was about a mile off the flight line where the jets were parked. Van Huss dropped them off in a dusty stand of grass. They set their bags down and watched a flock of Thai carpenters set to work nailing and sawing.

The Thais put up a hooch frame, nailed screening all around it, put up boards along the sides at an angle—to keep the rain out and let the air in—put on a tin roof, hammered on the doors, and then went to the next open space and started on another hooch. Horner and Myhrum walked in, dropped their bags, and set up the cots that services had left for them. Then they unpacked and slipped into flight suits to go over to the officers' club (a couple of hooches with a bar tacked together inside), run by hired Thais. Since they were the FNGs,* they kept their mouths shut, except to welcome old friends as they filed in back from flights or other duties. Since the fighter community is very closely knit, and Horner and Myhrum were experienced fighter pilots and had some reputation, it was easy for them to fit in.

They very quickly picked up a pretty good idea about what was going on at the base: who was there, the kinds of missions being flown—bombing targets in North Vietnam like ammo dumps and bridges—and what were the gripes and good deals. The bad news was that the pilots at Korat were not willing to let the new guys fly with them . . . at least not then. Horner and Myhrum were there as staff, and in those early days of ROLLING THUNDER, operational tempos were not active. There weren't enough sorties to go around.

That was to change a few weeks later as the flying tempo increased and some of the pilots got shot down. The resulting shortage meant that nobody could go on R & R unless Myhrum and Horner took up the slack in the flying schedule. But for the first couple of weeks it was very frustrating.

---

*The NG stands for "new guys."

★ When Horner arrived at Korat, the squadron from McConnell and the squadron from Kadena operated as independent units; the one from Kansas was owned by TAC, while the one from Okinawa was owned by PACAF (officially, Southeast Asia came under PACAF, which made the squadron from Kadena more equal, in an Orwellian sense, than the squadron from McConnell). The two had a common command post and shared a mess hall, where the food was just about inedible. Horner, Myhrum, and a few others (most of them nonrated—to take care of supply, motor pool, maintenance control, intelligence, civil engineering, and the like) had been brought in to set up a wing structure not only for Korat but also for Ubon, Udorn, and Takhli. However, that quickly proved impossible, for there were not enough people to handle it, nor were there sufficient communications. Consequently, provisional wing structures were set up at each field.

From the start, there was rivalry between the two squadrons. Both TAC and PACAF wanted their squadrons to get their noses in the war. On the face of it, Kadena, from PACAF, had first dibs, since it was PACAF's theater of operation. However, things weren't quite that simple. Because Kadena and Yokota (in Japan) had nuclear alert duties, PACAF needed augmentation, which meant that TAC deployed a squadron. That didn't mean that the TAC squadron was welcome, since PACAF didn't want to share the glory of fighting the North Vietnamese with a TAC squadron any more than TAC wanted to share the glory with a PACAF squadron. It was all very adolescent, and in the end, it all proved moot. There turned out to be plenty of war to go around.

The competition between the commands was obvious, even at base level. Though the pilots and maintenance crews were all perfectly friendly, the deployed commanders were often reluctant to help one another out; each was trying to hog the war for himself. For example, Kadena squadrons, unlike TAC squadrons, normally didn't deploy to other bases, and so didn't have available the extensive war reserve spares kits that the others did—metal boxes on wheels that contained what a squadron needed for the first thirty days until a supply line to the depot could be put in place. You'd think it would be easy for a mechanic from Kadena to get a part from the TAC deployed spares kit. Think again.

The rivalry was also evident in the makeup of the provisional staff. PACAF made sure that Kadena people filled all the important positions, no matter what their qualifications were. Another bone in the TAC people's craw was the rotation policies: the PACAF people rotated in and out on short notice, while the TAC people were there for as long as 120 days.

Leaving aside the command nonsense, life for the pilots in the spring of 1965 was relatively easy. They flew at most once a day, and planning the next day's mission might take a couple of hours. After that, their time was their own. As for the missions themselves, most of them were far from difficult: they'd fly in a two-ship team along a stretch of highway in south or central North Vietnam until they saw something worth shooting or bombing. If they hit bingo fuel before they found anything, they'd drop their bombs on a bridge. In those days there were very few big missions, such as the multi-flight attacks on a fixed target deep inside North Vietnam that later became more the norm; but there were a few (which typically did not go well). Wartime flying was in fact very much like peacetime flying . . . except that people were trying to kill you.

★ Meanwhile, Horner and Myhrum took up their jobs as duty officers in the one-room Wing Tactical Operations Center (though it had a divider that split it into something like two rooms). For security, it was surrounded with a barbed-wire fence. The security was necessary because that was where the Frag—the term for Fragmentary Order, now called the Air Tasking Order—was received from Saigon. The Frag order was a computer listing of all the data associated with the next day's air operations. It told pilots who would fly where, when, and drop what ordnance on what target, what tanker would be used and what off-load (that is, how many pounds of fuel each pilot would get from the tankers). It would also contain the call signs of the MiG CAP* and other information.

Each pilot, if he was any good, and certainly the lead pilot, would go through the pages of the Frag the way he might go through a telephone book and find his unit—say, the 388th Tac Ftr Wing (Provisional). There, listed by call sign, were all the sorties the 388th was expected to fly the

---

*If MiGs got into a bomber fight, the bombers would jettison their bombs and fight them. Even if the MiGs didn't shoot anyone down, the bombers still jettisoned the bombs . . . which meant they were ineffective. In order to counter this air-to-air fighter threat, the practice was to dedicate a few fighters to patrolling the area, so for insurance a few fighters were designated MiG CAP (Combat Air Patrol).

next day. After the call sign was further information: for example, Teak, 4 F-105s, Vinh Oil refinery BE12356778. This last was the bomb ency-clopedia number, or BE number. This told pilots where to look up infor-mation about each target (which in fact intelligence had already done for them, since they also got the Frag). The pilots would then go to intelli-gence, and be provided with whatever information intelligence had avail-able: this might be printouts of microfiche film of the target, drawings or maps, or only a verbal description. The pilots would certainly get latitude and longitude coordinates and probably DMIPs (Desired Mean Impact Point) and weapons-effects data: e.g., for 90 percent destruction, use this number of weapons of this type.

If intelligence had a photo of the target, the pilots would study it, so they could recognize it and know exactly where they should put their bombs, then they might divide up who targeted what. The flight would also plan the mission so that the debris from one aircraft's bombs would not obscure the target for those behind him. Usually first bombs were dropped downwind of the other aim point(s).

Maps and pictures were additionally used by the pilots to "go from big to little." Let's say they were hitting a power station, a small target that might be hidden by trees. First they would plan their ingress route, based on weather, enemy defenses, terrain, etc. Then they'd look for large visual reference points—a bend in the river, a rail line, a bridge. Once they had one or more of these, they'd start looking for other reference points, so they could walk their eyes onto the target. Thus, after the bend in the river comes a large triangular rice paddy, and then on the east corner of the paddy there is a small canal that runs north and south, with a patch of jungle just south, and then the power station is two football fields' dis-tance to the south of that on the east bank of the canal.

Many of the targets Horner's people were tasked to hit required this type of planning: they were so insignificant that they couldn't see them until just before they released their bombs at about 4,000 feet above the ground; and so they flew to where they knew the target was located, and when it appeared they had barely enough time to adjust their flight path. If they were good, it appeared under their pippers (the red dot in the gun sight) at the right altitude, airspeed, and dive angle for their bombs to hit the target. On the other hand, if they had a good target—such as a rail-yard full of boxcars—then advance planning didn't matter, since they could find the target from fifty miles away, and when they rolled in there was so much target that their pippers would be on something worth bombing regardless of their dive angle, airspeed, and altitude of release.

The Frag would also provide tanker information—that is, it told the pilot his air refueling contact time and which tanker track he'd be flying to—e.g., "Shell 30 at Orange anchor." And finally, the Frag would provide a Time on or over Target, which was the time the bombs were scheduled to hit the target (all the other aircraft involved in a mission—MiG CAP, RESCAP, radar surveillance aircraft, and later Wild Weasels and support jamming—planned their efforts based on a pilot making his TOT).

Working the Frag was harder for the flight leader than for the other pilots. First of all, he had to ask himself how long it would take to reach the target from the tanker drop-off point. He would then call the tanker unit and tell them where and when he wanted to be dropped off. Then he would figure out how long it would take to fly to the tanker and refuel, and that would tell him what his takeoff time would be. He would then give this to the wing ops center, who would pass the word over to maintenance and also "deconflict" his flight from the other flights taking off around that time, in order to avoid midair collisions.

Meanwhile, he would need to look up other information: Who was pulling RESCAP that day? What was the call sign and frequency? Were there special instructions (such as: avoid Phuc Yen airfield by ten miles . . . so as not to *really* disturb the enemy)? What were the flight call signs and targets being struck in the same time frame (so he'd know who was in the air when he was, where they were, and doing what)? And what were the code words for the day (such as for recall)? The better the flight leader, the more capable he was in reading the Frag, extracting all the relevant information, and then briefing the flight in such a way that a precise image of the coming reality was created and everyone could fly the mission in his mind before he set out. In that way, when he flew the mission he had already reduced the confusion and fog of war to the minimum.

★ Horner's and Myhrum's job was to break out the Frag order, and outline those items that applied to their base: missions, call signs, times for takeoff, refueling, and Time over Target. They would receive the Frag around 2200 at night (it would usually arrive on a T-39 executive jet that flew over from Saigon), with first takeoffs at 0600 in the morning.

In the beginning, the Frag was a nightmare to decode because the Frag team in Saigon would send the entire thing, which was a huge, complex document. Later the planners in Saigon separated out the information that didn't change (such as tanker tracks, radar control unit information, frequencies, and so forth) into a separate Frag that was kept in operations, and the daily Frag contained only information that was new.

Once they'd broken out the Frag, Horner and Myhrum would give the details to intelligence, so they could dig out target materials, and to maintenance, so they could load the jets with munitions and get them ready to fly.

Once these arrived, the two of them passed the info over to the squadron duty officers, who would wake up the flight leaders so they could plan the missions.

It didn't take them long to get into the groove of life at Korat.

During the day it was fiercely hot, but in the late afternoon or early evening, a thunderstorm would pass through and the air would cool off. That made sleeping at night very comfortable, and there was the squawking of the geckos—small, very loud lizards—to lull you to sleep. The roads were dirt, and red clay dust was everywhere. When it rained, they got muddy with red clay mud; but everything dried when the sun came out. They had common showers, where the maids also did the laundry and washed the sheets and clothing during the morning. And most had outdoor toilets.

For a swimming pool, they used a twenty-man life raft filled with rainwater. In the heat of the day, the pool water was cool and welcome. If you were flying and were sent on the early mission, you could find a place in the pool when you landed. But if you were flying a later mission, you had to wait until someone left the pool before you could sit in it.

★ After enduring a week of the confusion and frustration that goes with being in the military, Myhrum and Horner informed the two fighter squadrons at Korat that while they had been sent over to serve as staff officers and help plan missions, they still wanted to fly.

No one heard them. They kept getting the runaround: "Well, not today, but maybe tomorrow."

Fed up, finally, Myhrum gave a call to a friend at Ta Khli. "Sure," he told him, "we're looking for pilots. Come on over." Without telling any-

one in authority, the two men packed their flight gear, arranged for someone to cover them in the command post for a couple of days, and went
out to board the Klong Courier. But as they approached the ramp door
of the C-130, Major Pete Van Huss of the McConnell squadron ran out
to intercept them. "You can fly with us after all," he said. "You don't
need to go to Ta Khli." So they started flying. (Later, when the Mc-
Connell squadron rotated back to the States, they were handed off to the
new squadron, who needed their experience.)

Chuck Horner's first combat mission came in May 1965, when he
flew as number two in a flight of four F-105s, each loaded with eight
750-pound general-purpose bombs. They'd been sent to destroy a gasoline storage area and pumping station at Vinh, North Vietnam, which
was a hundred miles south of Hanoi. More eager than nervous, he accomplished what had become "the routine" of preparation, briefing, preflight, taxi, takeoff, aerial refueling, and formation flying to the target . . .
"routine," because as the duty officer breaking out the Frag, he had already helped plan many sorties and he had also planned and executed
practice missions for years.

It was early morning as they refueled over the Thai rice paddies, neat
brown and green squares waiting to be planted or harvested . . . a stark
contrast with Laos, which they crossed next. Laos was mostly mountainous jungle, wild and beautiful. Everywhere was a dark green canopy
of trees, and here and there were small mountain ridges and karst—lime-
stone mesas whose sides consisted of sheer cliffs thrusting sometimes a
thousand feet up from the jungle floor, their tops a dark green cap of jungle. Next they flew across the high, narrow, north–south-running mountain range that separated Laos from North Vietnam. Beyond lay North
Vietnam itself, a narrow strip of peaceful, beautifully green land, with the
mountains on the west, the sea on the east, and a scattering of islands
along the coast. Near the coast were numberless rice paddies, and near
the mountains were low foothills, usually covered with jungle. Several
rivers flowed from the mountains and snaked to the east and the ocean.
In the morning, the land was calm, with fog in the low spots. During the
day, rain clouds built up, especially over the mountains, and produced
much lightning and heavy rain until well into the evening. As the pilot approached the coast, he saw more roads, and more towns and villages.
These tended to be a cross between Oriental and French. Most buildings
were wooden, with tin roofs, and raised on stilts off the ground. More

solid structures, however, were occasionally left over from the French, usually large, made of white concrete, with red tile roofs.

According to the usual practice, they crossed North Vietnam at its narrowest around the finger-shaped lakes between Vinh and the South Vietnamese border (hence the name Finger Lakes), then flew out to sea and proceeded north until they returned inland to hit a target.

As they roared in from over the South China Sea, they could see the target from fifty miles, huge white petroleum storage tanks and a large pumping station to the west on the north bank of the river that ran out of the city toward the sea. They came in from the east at 15,000 feet above the ground. The air was crystal clear, and the sun was behind them. The leader rolled over to his right and pointed his Thud at the storage tanks.

Horner waited fifteen seconds and followed him down, offsetting to the west so he wouldn't get hit by enemy ground fire shot at the leader. It was absolutely calm as Horner watched the lead's bombs set off two of the storage tanks in a violent orange and black maelstrom. He eased his aircraft's nose to the right, checked his dive angle, airspeed, and altitude; and when his gun sight crept up on the huge pumping station, he depressed the bomb-release button on top of the control stick, then reefed back on the stick to keep from hitting the ground, and watched over his right shoulder as his bombs struck dead center on the mass of pipes and buildings that had once been a petroleum-pumping station.

With his head twisted completely around over his right shoulder and the nose of his jet now pointed toward the sky, he *somehow* saw red fireballs stream past on the left side of his canopy. *Someone is trying to kill me,* he thought abstractedly—the way we might think, *It's raining out.* Meanwhile, he racked his jet toward the sea and tried to see the lead, who was just fifteen seconds ahead. Then he realized that he couldn't see the leader because both of their jets were surrounded by greasy black smoke with orange centers making *whoomp whoomp* noises that rocked his jet. At that point, he put his jet into maximum afterburner, to get as much speed as possible, and started to dance around in the sky, to kill any tracking solutions the gunners might be working out.

It's just like the World War II and Korea veterans said it was, he thought, as he flew out over the sea. And instantly he was a veteran.

Later, AAA too became part of the routine. If he looked down at the ground, he could see the red flame from the barrels of the AAA as they shot up at him. He could tell when the big guns were shooting at him because of the black greasy puffs. The 57mm guns were arranged in a circle and would fire in salvo, so what he saw was a circle of fire. And then if he looked to the other side of the formation and above the flight, he could see the black smoke of projectiles exploding. The smaller-caliber weapons featured tracers that snaked up from the ground and then curved behind the flight. In reality, the tracers didn't curve; they appeared to because of the movement of his aircraft. Orange tracers were the sign of 37mm guns. The projectiles from these weapons exploded in gray-white smoke. . . . All in all, fascinating to look at.

After the excitement and skill of an attack and evading AAA, the trip home was easy—a thoughtful time. When a man is filled with adrenaline, he thinks fast, but on the way home he has time for meditating about what he has just done.

As he flew back to Korat that day—no longer a virgin—Horner realized that war is not the glamorous heady adventure described in song and story. He wondered what those gunners on the ground thought of him. He was pleased that they'd missed him, and glad that he'd frustrated them, but he took little joy that he and his companions had wrecked so much of their homeland and probably killed some of their countrymen.

As Horner accumulated missions—killing more people and destroying more property—he began to accumulate an abhorrence of war. For him, this abhorrence was a complex emotion:

He always felt the pain of the people he was attacking . . . but not enough for him to stop what he was doing. He hated the stupidity and immorality of war . . . but he loved being shot at and missed. He loved taking part in the struggle, the excitement, the high. He was afraid of being killed . . . yet unafraid (like most good fighter pilots, keeping his fears in a box). When he would sit in the arming area waiting for his flight to go, a little voice would whisper in his ear, "You are not coming back from this mission." Yet he would shrug it off and fly. Once he was on the mission, he was so busy that he didn't have time to be afraid. Afterward, sometimes, his hands would shake—probably, he claims, from fatigue as much as anything else.

"I love combat," he says. "I hate war. I don't understand it, but that's the way it is."

During the next two months, Horner flew forty-one combat missions. Most often the F-105s would fly in pairs into North Vietnam, conducting road reconnaissance—looking for trucks—with a fixed alternative target such as a bridge. They dropped a variety of munitions, most often 750-pound bombs; but they also carried antitank rockets and were sometimes Fragged to hit a bridge with them. These would punch small holes in the bridge floor, and repairs could be made in hours. The best missions were against stored petroleum, freight cars in rail yards, and big bridges. The worst were what they called "Whiplash Bango Alert," during which they'd sit on the ground in their Thuds and wait for orders to scramble in order to provide CAS for clandestine operations in Laos. When they finally scrambled, it was usually at the end of their vulnerability period—during the two hours from 1000 to 1200, they were "vulnerable" to a scramble; the jet was cocked, they had to wear G suits, and they sat around close to the jets so they could get airborne quickly—and the target was usually suspected troops in the jungle. Meaning: they bombed the jungle.

★ All the pilots soon came to realize that they were not fighting the war in the most efficient manner.

For the most part, the planning aim was to make it difficult for North Vietnam to help the Vietcong with logistical support, which was a reasonable goal. Within that aim, however, so many restrictions were placed on the pilots that very little of that aim was actually achievable. Robert McNamara's strategy was one called Graduated Pressure, and its aim was to *persuade* the North Vietnamese to give up rather than going all out to defeat them. As a result, the pilots were saddled with politically selected targets, rules of engagement, buffer zones, target exclusions, and all sorts of other counterproductive arrangements. Unlike the Army, the Air Force wasn't caught up in measuring success by counting bodies; however, the Air Force measures of merit, such as numbers of sorties flown, hardly made better sense. Any sortie might well have been useless, due to the lack of decent targeting or munitions; yet it was seen by headquarters as just as important as a sortie against a good target. Finally, the planning aim was to *avoid* gaining control of the air (for the sake of Graduated Pressure), and there was no serious thought given to destroying the enemy's capacity to make war and his will to fight.

When Horner first went to Korat, most pilots counted all of these oddities as a sign of the fits and starts and inexperience that goes with fighting a new war. Still, it was hard to overlook the inefficiencies, and not to ask why their efforts appeared to be so fragmentary, and without the conviction needed to win a war. It all seemed like such a *limp* way to hit the North Vietnamese. If you're going to hit them, then *hit* them.

In time the pilots came to realize that it wasn't just an efficiency problem; it was a stupidity problem. And then in time they came to realize that it was more than that, it was a matter of lies and betrayals. That realization—for Chuck Horner, anyhow—was not to come until later, but in the spring and summer of 1965, he could not fail to register oddities such as the following:

Early on, when they were short of munitions, he and other pilots would be sent over North Vietnam with a single bomb and their gun, their mission supposedly being to intimidate the North Vietnamese. Meanwhile, splendid targets, such as piers full of supplies and warehouses, were off-limits. Likewise, the airfields north of Hanoi were off-limits (allowing the MiGs a safe haven from which to launch attacks on our own aircraft). The enemy was allowed the use of his own government buildings, even as he was blowing up South Vietnamese government buildings in Saigon. And he was given buffer zones along the China border, in order for us to avoid "frightening" the Chinese. The enemy used this protected space wisely.

Orders like these flowed out of the bizarre rules of engagement. When the Frag came in at night with the targets the pilots were scheduled to hit, included would be a long list of ROEs, primarily telling them what they could *not* do. They could not hit any target of opportunity. In the beginning, they could not engage enemy forces unless fired upon (this changed). Areas such as Hanoi and Haiphong were off-limits. They could not attack SAM sites. And they could not attack airfields, even if a MiG was taking off to intercept them.

Pilots are realists and craftsmen. They want to get the job done, and to do it well. It didn't take them long to see that even their best efforts would not get the job done well.

What they didn't know was that, besides the policy of Graduated Pressure, the President and his Secretary of Defense wanted to maintain absolute control of the war for political reasons. On the one hand, they wanted to look strong in the United States and perhaps slap the North Vietnamese around enough to persuade them to give in. On the other hand, they didn't want the conflict to grow into a full-fledged war that would endanger the success of the President's domestic efforts, such as the Great Society.

In addition, the Secretary of Defense arrogantly believed in his own intellectual and moral superiority over his immediate military subordinates, the Joint Chiefs of Staff, and the Joint Chiefs passively accepted it. They were constitutionally responsible not only to the President but to the Congress, to tell the truth as they saw it, but they didn't. They *knew* the Johnson-McNamara policy would not work, and they were silent.

Meanwhile, in the skies over Southeast Asia, the frustration over the rules of engagement increased. The pilots sensed that they were constructed by men who did not have a feel for what was going on in the cockpits over the North. Their sense of fighter-bomber tactics and of the vulnerabilities of the F-105 was dim to nonexistent. Much worse, they had not the slightest vision of what they wanted done, and therefore they could not pass it on to the pilots.

If a pilot who is laying his life on the line is told to do a half-baked job, to perform less than credibly, even though he might die doing it, then you will soon have a problem maintaining military discipline and loyalty up the chain. The ROE orders made pilots perform tasks that were not credible . . . and so in time the orders were disobeyed and the pilots lied about it. In this way began the erosion of discipline and respect for authority that followed from the Vietnam experience.

★ Route Packages (so called because the mission was to interdict the supply of support to the Vietcong in South Vietnam) caused the pilots a somewhat different—though related—problem. The Route Packages themselves were simple enough. They offered a reasonable, though arbitrary, way to lay out North Vietnam into geographical areas.

The country was divided into seven zones, starting at the DMZ (the line separating the two parts of Vietnam) and looking north. Thus, from south to north, the Route Packages went RP I to RP IV. The part of the country that was mostly west of the Red River was called RP V, while the rest—including Hanoi and Haiphong—was VI. Phuc Yen and Hanoi were in VI A, the western part of VI, while Haiphong was in VI B, the eastern part of VI.

In practical terms, defenses in RP I and II were relatively light. In III and IV, defenses were heavier but still moderate (but with one or two real hot spots, such as the Than Hoa Bridge, which resulted in more shootdowns than any other single target). MiGs flew out of V, which was bad, but it also contained a lot of jungle where there were no SAMs or guns, which was good. VI was the worst, with the Red River Valley, MiG bases at Phuc Yen and Dong Ha, Hanoi and Haiphong, and the northeast rail-road.

The reason for Route Packages was to allow the U.S. Navy and the USAF to operate over North Vietnam without coordinating with each other. Each service could operate over its own designated zones, and in that way, each service could keep control of its own aircraft without having to place them under the control of a single air commander. Thus, the USAF got RPs I, II, V (V was farthest from the sea), and VI A, while the Navy got RPs III, IV, and VI B (VI B and IV were near the sea). In other words, the Navy got the midsection and the USAF got the top and bottom.

There were both benefits and drawbacks to Route Packages. The chief benefit was that the Navy and the Air Force kept out of each other's way and they could plan their operations apart from each other, so there was never a coordination problem. In those days, it was also likely that U.S. forces did not have the command and control that would have allowed Navy and Air Force aircraft to operate with each other in the same airspace. It was likely, too, that Air Force and Navy planes would have been intercepting one another and perhaps even taking shots at one another. The chief drawback, of course, was that U.S. forces were not mutually supportive, which meant that the enemy could easily take advantage of the split in U.S. forces, and contend with two weaker divided air efforts rather than one unified and coordinated force.

It also gave pilots another reason to act contrary to what they saw as stupid, wrong, and lacking in credibility.

For example, when the weather was bad in an Air Force Route Package, Air Force pilots were not allowed to hit an alternative target in the Navy's Route Packages.

Let's say that Horner was flying in RP VI A, going after a bridge on the northwest rail line to China, and the weather turned bad—thunderstorms. Logic would say he ought to fly over to the northeast rail line to China and drop on a bridge over there; but since that was in RP VI B, he was expected to weather-abort the mission and bring his bombs home.

Did he do that? No.

What he did was fly to wherever there looked to be a suitable target, drop on it, and then report 100 percent of ordnance in the original target area. He would not report any BDA (Battle Damage Assessment), since he knew that the original target had not been hit, while there was a smoking hole a hundred miles away that they could not correlate with any Frag, so they did not report it, even if photos showed it.

Meanwhile, Chuck Horner came to understand that both he and the enemy ultimately worked for people whose interests did not include either of them; they did not really care if he or they died. Their agenda involved some geopolitical goal, while his was to stay alive.

★ None of these realizations came in a flash. For Horner, some didn't hit him until after he returned to the United States. If, however, there was a Road to Damascus moment for Chuck Horner, it had to be on the July day in 1965 when the Thuds from Korat and Ta Khli made history. On that July 24, sixteen F-105s were sent to destroy a radar-guided SA-2 surface-to-air missile site located at the junction of the Red and Black Rivers in North Vietnam. This was the first-ever attack on a SAM site, and it turned into a ghastly fiasco.

Before that date, the Air Force and civilian authorities responsible for determining the course of the war had further determined that U.S. aircraft should not attack the SA-2 sites then being set up in North Vietnam. In that way, they reasoned, the United States wouldn't annoy the North Vietnamese enough to provoke them into using the SAMs. . . . "*Annoy* the North Vietnamese?" Chuck Horner observes. "Why would the North Vietnamese go to all the trouble of setting the SA-2s up if not to shoot at U.S. aircraft? And keep in mind that U.S. aircraft were already bombing their country, so they had plenty of reason to be annoyed. What we should have done is sink the boats bringing the SAMs from the USSR. We should have bombed the trains that brought them from China. If we missed them there, we should have bombed them the first time we saw them being taken out of the craft. And failing that, we should have bombed the very first sites they set up. Instead we put the sites off-limits in the 'hopes' that the North Vietnamese would not use this weapon against us, if we did not shoot at them. How dumb can you get?"

One day in July, the North Vietnamese shot down an RF-4C, an unarmed reconnaissance version of the McDonnell Douglas F-4 Phantom jet, with a SAM-2. In other words, the North Vietnamese had missed the subtle reasoning that would have had them install SAMs without actually using them, and now the United States had to teach them a lesson.

On the night of July 23, a warning order went out to Korat and Ta Khli to stand by, a retaliation mission against the North Vietnamese SA-

2 site was being planned; Frag to follow. At 11:00 P.M. the Frag arrived. It called for low-level tactics to defeat the SAMs, without thought of the many AAA guns that were defending the sites. To fool the North Vietnamese, the Thuds from Korat would let down in Laos just across the border, fly east down a deep valley in northern Laos that the Communist Pathet Lao used as their stronghold—without thought that the Pathet Lao might see them, or perhaps choose to take some target practice themselves—then turn north at the Black River and hit the target in the delta at the Black and Red Rivers junction. The Thuds from Ta Khli, meanwhile, would let down to the north and fly east until hitting the Red River, then come south—without thought to the midair-collision potential resulting from Korat flying up from the south and Ta Khli coming down from the north. They also Fragged the munitions. Since it was a low-level attack, the F-105s were given napalm and CBU-2s. These last were new munitions—tiny bomblets containing ball bearings carried in tubes under the wing. When you reached the target, you blew the ends of the tubes and the bomblets dropped out and fell to earth. When they exploded, the ball bearings inside were like bullets, scattering in all directions, punching holes in whatever they struck. (The bomblets also had the bad habit of colliding in midair behind the wing, detonating, and punching holes in the dispensing fighter aircraft, setting it on fire or destroying its fuel cells and hydraulic flight control lines.)

In all fairness to those who planned the mission, no one had experience against SAMs (other than the U-2 pilots who'd been shot down by SAMs over Russia and Cuba). There was, in fact, a general feeling that it was hopeless to fly against SAMs; they never missed. Finally, planning for the first-ever raid against SAMs was heady stuff—it was hard to step back and just look at the best way to do it—and so anybody in Saigon or Washington who had an opportunity to add a tweak to the plan did.

Was there a better way? In fact, yes. Higher command could have called down to the Wing and said, "If you can kill those SAM sites at such and such a location, please do so, and let me know what you learn." In other words, the Wing might well have had a more practical way to accomplish higher command's goal than higher command did. But that was not likely under the centralized system then in place.

Meanwhile, Horner and Myrhum, who were on duty handling the Frags, noted that the Dash-One pilot's handbook contained restrictions on using napalm. Specifically, the maximum speed for release of these weapons was 375 knots indicated airspeed. *Not smart,* they thought, *to go in against AAA that slow.* They passed that thought on to Saigon, and Saigon agreed. Another message came back at 2:00 A.M. that morning, saying, "OK, load up iron bombs and have at it." By that time, the munitions troops had already loaded the jets with napalm.

"Hey, wait a minute." Horner and Myrhum came running up. "Change in plans. Drop the napalm and CBUs and load up bombs."

"Okay, can do."

Then, around 5:00 A.M. the general in Saigon must have arrived at headquarters, because a new message quickly came in: "Load the napalm and the CBUs and go as ordered." So they went back to the hapless maintenance troops: "Hey, guys, there's been a change. Reload the napalm and CBUs. Sorry." It's because such things happen that maintenance troops have a low opinion of operations.

While all this was going on, the pilots who were about to fly the mission were doing what they could to sleep; but sleep wasn't likely, because this mission was a major operation. When the sun rose, the pilots assembled; and Horner and Myrhum delivered the mission data for the first-ever attack on a surface-to-air radar-guided-missile site, then prepared to grab breakfast and hit their beds.

As it happened, maintenance had a pair of extra aircraft loaded, in case someone aborted a primary jet. "Would you and Roger give those jets a hot preflight and start them up?" they asked. "If someone has to abort their primary aircraft, they can run over to yours, jump in, and take off on the mission."

"No problem," they answered.

"And would you please taxi them out to the arming area," they added, "in the event that one of the primary jets breaks out there?"

"Sure, no sweat," they answered. But because they had been up all night and they were tired, Horner was also thinking, *Let's get the show on the road so I can get some breakfast and sleep.*

Then the takeoff time was moved up, forcing Horner and Myrhum to go to the jets early (somebody brought them sandwiches from the club, but the meat was cold liver, which Horner hates, and he went hungry), climbed in the jet, started check-in, and then taxied to the landing area. All went well there, until Horner and Myrhum, who were sitting off to the side, heard two pilots in the first flight abort their takeoffs. Next the flight leader called to order them to take off and join him as numbers three and four. *Okay, no sweat,* Horner thought, *I can fly wing anywhere. All I have to do is put the light on the star* and stay in formation, refuel, and drop some napalm on whatever the flight leader puts in front of me. His flight plan will determine mine, since I am in formation with him.*

That was overhopeful.

After they refueled, but before they let down in Laos, numbers one and two decided they had to go home with aircraft problems. That left Roger Myhrum—who hadn't been briefed—to lead the whole show from Korat. On his wing was Chuck Horner. Other than what he could remember from the night before when he broke out the Frag, Horner was just as much in the dark about the mission as his friend. *Not to worry,* he thought. *We've faked it before, and anyway we know the area like the back of our hands from previous missions.*

When they let down in the valley in Laos, the Pathet Lao must have been caught unaware, because they scarcely shot at them. Soon they hit the river and turned north.

Suddenly the radio came alive: "Buick Leader is down in the river!" . . . "I'm hit and on fire!" . . . "Two, where are you?" All these messages came with automobile call signs, meaning Ta Khli was early in their attack. They were coming south down the river and getting shot at and hit.

Since it was not pleasant to have the enemy shooting at you at slow speeds, the Thuds from Korat pushed it up. Horner noticed Myhrum was doing a nice 550 knots and accelerating. *Good man,* he thought. *Hope the generals don't find out we're exceeding the 375-knot limit on the napalm.* He looked up then and saw Bobby Tastett's Thud rise up out of an area of dust and flames, with the whole underside of his jet on fire. He kept staring as Tastett's jet sank back into the dust and exploded against the ground.† Horner's next glance was over to the side, where he noticed the gun barrels of the AAA all lined up and shooting down the valley. They were flying so low the North Vietnamese couldn't depress their barrels enough to hit them. That meant the projectiles burst overhead, and most of the hits were on the topside of their jets. They were so

---

*That is, he set himself up with relation to the flight leader's plane so that the leader's wingtip light was on the star painted on the side of his jet. This means Horner was flying in the right position fore and aft and up and down. Then all you had to do to make sure the flight stayed in close formation was to hold this position and keep the same distance out, usually so his wings didn't overlap.

†Fortunately, Tastett bailed out and lived, then spent years in the Hanoi Hilton.

low that some of them came back with leaves stuck in underside doors and panels.

In a moment, Horner saw what looked like a SAM site, then dropped his munitions about the same time Myrhum did. Later they both admitted they weren't sure what they actually dropped them on, but since Saigon didn't want to hear that, they reported that 100 percent of the munitions were in the target area, and that made Saigon happy. Turning left and crossing the Red River, he heard Frank Tullo call to report he was punching out (ejecting). He was later recovered.

Then it was finished. When the guns stopped shooting at them, they checked each other over. Myrhum had a hung can of napalm, so they slowed down while he jettisoned it, then headed south across Laos back to Thailand.

En route, they listened in on the ops officer talking on the radio with a friend of Horner's, Bill Barthelmous. Bill had holes in his jet behind the canopy and asked the ops officer, Lieutenant Colonel Jack Farr, to check him over for fire, leaking fluid, or anything else. Sure enough, fluid was leaking. Suddenly Barthelmous' flight controls locked up from loss of hydraulic fluid, and he pitched up, smashing into Farr's jet, killing him. Barthelmous jumped out, but his chute streamered, and he was later found dead in a rice paddy with multiple broken bones and water in his lungs.

In the attack, Korat lost, in all, four jets and three pilots, one of whom turned up several years later as a POW, while Ta Khli lost two jets and two pilots. Bill Barthelmous and Jack Farr died; Bob Tastett and others checked into the Hanoi Hilton; and only Frank Tullo came back to fly north again from the hell of that day.

Afterward, poststrike reconnaissance film showed an untouched SAM site. But it turned out not really to matter that they missed it, since the site was fake. Its SA-2 Guideline missiles had been built out of telephone poles, with a dummy radar in the middle. They'd fallen for a very skillfully handled trap—a clever sting. That night, all the surviving pilots got roaring drunk and made a lot of noise celebrating being alive. In their hearts, though, they felt terrible, because they hadn't got the job done.

The next day, the PACAF Commander, General Hunter Harris, paid a visit in his 707. As the door opened, the local SAC base commander was standing there, dressed up in his blue uniform, waiting at the bottom of the stairs; the honor guard, with chrome helmets, was lined up on either side of the red carpet. Instead of General Hunter Harris standing in the door, however, there was Frank Tullo, his flight suit covered with blood, mud, and vomit. He had cut his head when he ejected, then he'd crawled around in the jungle mud trying to avoid detection by the North Vietnamese. After a few hours of this, Air America had picked him up and flown him to a forward site in Laos, where he got drunk on local Mekong whiskey, got sick, and vomited all over himself as he slept. When the pilots saw him, they all cheered, much to the annoyance of the SAC base commander, realizing as they did that General Harris had a sense of humor and knew what was important (even if he couldn't do anything about what they were being asked to do).*

★ The July 24 attack on the radar SAM site proved to be such a catastrophe that it served as an exemplary lesson in tactics and survival. The tactics were wrong on two counts: First, since it was thought that SAMs were 100 percent effective, it was concluded that aircraft had to underfly them. Second, from the Strategic Air Command commanders who were planning and running operations in Vietnam came bomber stream tactics—that is, large numbers of jets flying in trail over the target.

Both tactics derived from various historical and peacetime experiences—the bomber stream from World War II, and flying low level from lack of experience fighting against radar-guided SAMs.

Over Germany and Japan, the massed bomber formations would follow the same route into the target, the idea being to keep the wings level from Initial Point (IP) to target in order to get accurate bombing from level flight. The problem was that it gave the defense easy targets—ducks in a row.

In principle, flying low to defeat SAMs was far from unreasonable. The SA-2 radars the Air Force faced in Vietnam were limited to seeing targets at about 1,000+ feet above the ground, while the early-warning radars that fed them target information were limited to much higher altitudes. From that perspective, it made sense to come in low and fast. Unfortunately, the commanders failed to recognize that at low level, the guns were a much greater threat than a SAM. In point of fact—and ex-

---

*Roger Myrhum, we should mention, is now retired. After the war, he went on to fly with the F-5 squadron at Williams AFB training Saudis and Iranians, but after that Horner lost track of him.

perience was to bear this out—SAMs were not 100 percent effective. Even when they are flying within a SAM's range, and a missile is locked onto them, pilots have a chance. They can always acquire the SAM visually and outfly it, even if they don't have the Radar Warning Receivers, ECM pods, chaff, or flares that pilots now have.

Both tactics came out of the doctrine of centralized control—control from Washington and control from the Strategic Air Command. Washington has already been discussed. SAC's attachment to control derived from their approach to their primary mission, the Single Integrated Operations Plan. No deviation from the SIOP was allowed. Its timetable allowed no variation. Every sortie was fixed. Every warhead was to be exactly placed.

The same minds that made a religion out of the SIOP refused to change low-level and bomber stream tactics in Vietnam, even after these tactics had proved to be deadly.

★ The attack on the SA-2 site was a life-changing experience for Chuck Horner. His reaction to it, in fact, had a direct bearing on the success of the air war against Saddam Hussein in 1991. Here he is in his own words:

After we got back to Korat, we were treated like heroes and acted like fools. That night, as those of us who came home made ourselves gloriously drunk and loud, there burned a bitterness in me against the stupid generals who sent us in at low level, trying to sneak up on an enemy whom we had trained to be the world's best air defense experts.

Our generals were bad news. But later my bitterness grew to include the administration in Washington (the people who were ultimately responsible for the madness in Vietnam). They just did not know what they wanted to do or what they wanted military power to achieve. As a result, they came up with strategies almost on a day-by-day basis. Meaning: we had no real strategy in the air war over North Vietnam. Sometimes it looked as though we were trying to punish North Vietnam into coming to peace talks. Sometimes it looked as though we were trying to force North Vietnam to stop supplying the Vietcong. Sometimes it looked as though we were flying sorties just to impress the White House that we were flying sorties. It was like the game of crack the whip. A little jiggle in Washington resulted in a huge snapping of the end of the whip out in Southeast Asia.

That doesn't mean we didn't cause the North Vietnamese a lot of problems. We sure tried. However, in the overall analysis, I am also sure that we gave the North Vietnamese a lot of comfort. They had to have been greatly encouraged about the way we fought the war, about the way we parceled out airpower and didn't achieve dominance, about the way we ignored our own doctrine and failed to gain control of the air. As a result, we filled their POW camps with our pilots and littered their countryside with downed aircraft. We taught our enemy to endure air attacks, we taught our enemy how to best defend against the world's greatest air power, and we taught our enemy how to defeat us in the end.

In my heart, meanwhile, I knew that I would never again be a part of anything so insane and foolish. The name of the game is to get the mission done. That takes a combination of the fighter headquarters and the unit level leadership. It takes a team, not the teacher-student or parent-child relationship that we had with our SAC leaders. I vowed that if I ever got in charge, if I ever became the omnipresent "higher headquarters they," I would not let such madness reign.

In time my bitterness changed to hatred of them—the omnipresent them—everybody above my wing, all the Fighter Headquarters from Saigon on up (and later, too, the real culprits, primarily the President and the Secretary of Defense). I didn't hate them because they were dumb, I didn't hate them because they had spilled our blood for nothing, I hated them because of their arrogance . . . because they had convinced themselves that they actually knew what they were doing and that we were too minor to understand the "Big Picture." I hated my own generals, because they covered up their own gutless inability to stand up to the political masters in Washington and say, "Enough. This is bullshit. Either we fight or we go home." I hated them because they asked me to take other people's lives in a manner that dishonored both of us, me the killer and them the victim.

If you are going to kill someone, you better have a good reason for it. And if you have a good reason, then you better not play *around with the killing. We didn't seem to have the good reason, and we were playing around with the killing. Shame on all of us. If I had to be a killer, I wanted to know why I was killing; and the facts didn't match the rhetoric coming out of Washington.*

The rhetoric was that we were there to save South Vietnam for democracy and to keep the other Southeast Asia nations from falling into Communist slavery. Okay, I will buy that. But the way we fought was so inefficient that you wondered if the rhetoric was just a front we were putting up. Then there was the political situation in South Vietnam itself. It was bothersome that we were supposed to be defending a political realm that was so unstable and corrupt. You couldn't trust the elected government, and the elections we called for were rigged from the start. So in Vietnam there was hypocrisy. Next came the strong assurances from the President that he would fight the war to win and then he did nothing of the kind. Worst of all for me was coming home from the war in 1965, visiting my wife's hometown, Cresco, Iowa, and talking to the local Rotary luncheon. On the one hand, I was being told that we are out there on the frontier of freedom defending these people's interests, even eventually their freedom. On the other hand, these people had no idea what was going on in the war. They were supportive. But how much comfort can someone who is killing other humans take when the folks back home don't know what you are doing or why you are doing it?

What should we have done?

For starters, we should have actually taken control of the air. We should have taken down the MiG threat by attacking their airfields. We should have rooted out the air defense systems by attacking sector operations centers—even if they were in prohibited areas like Hanoi or Haiphong. We should have bombed any gun that shot at us on a priority basis. And we should have attacked the SAM storage areas.

How did I resolve these contradictions and confusions?

I returned to the United States in August of 1965, after maybe four months in the war, initially surprised that I wasn't kept in battle until the war was won. After all, isn't that how we do things in America? In 1965, I cared about winning. By 1967, I still wanted to win, but when I had a chance to go back to Korat as a

Wild Weasel, I'd concluded that since the President didn't really give a damn, and since the American people didn't understand what we were doing, then why should I worry about it? Since I knew the ropes by then, and that this would probably be the only war I'd ever be in, my goal was to get back to the war, do the best I could, and enjoy the thrill of combat, even though the war itself was a stupid, aimless, evil thing. My only disturbing thought then was the almost certain knowledge that as a Wild Weasel I ran an excellent chance of not coming home. But then, you never take counsel of your own fears.

To put it another way, I lied. Most of us did; and the folks above us wanted us to lie. I stripped myself of integrity. We lied about what we were doing in North Vietnam. We lied about what targets we hit: Say my Fragged target was a ford across a river. If I saw a better target—say, boxcars on a rail siding—I would miss my Fragged target and somehow my bombs would hit the boxcars. We lied about where we flew. For instance, I always tried to fly in the no-fly buffer zones on the Chinese border, because the North Vietnamese didn't have any guns on the ground there. They also knew about our buffer zones and figured we would follow orders.

When I went into North Vietnam, there was nobody from Washington up there, so I did what I felt was in the best interests of winning the war. If our leaders had no interest in winning, whatever that was, well, I did; and I was going to try to win, even if they didn't want to or were unwilling to really try. I loved the fighting. If they didn't care about the truth, then I would lie. If they didn't care about the killing and dying, then neither would I.

In war, of course, shit happens more often than at most other times. You are faced with the ever-present reality that you are out there killing other people, and that is very bothersome, especially if you really believe the stuff they taught you in church. You are stuck with a contradiction: "Thou shall not kill." But you are killing. The only way to resolve the contradiction is to try to do it as humanely as possible. That comes from knowing why you are at war, and then to fight it in such a way that it is over as quickly as possible and everyone can go home and live in peace . . . or at least until the next war.

So you do your best to hit the enemy where it hurts. For example, the North Vietnamese airfields were off-limits. Now, you tell

*me—you are a pilot over North Vietnam near Hanoi with your
head on a swivel, with Red Crown screaming out MiG warnings
and beepers going off as Air Force pilots are bailing out of their
jets, and there is an enemy airfield sitting there off to the right of
Thud Ridge waiting for you to drop some bombs on it, and the Big
Bosses send your bosses messages saying, "Do not bomb that airfield"—and you think,* You've got to be shitting me, *and you wonder how to get close enough to miss your Fragged target in order
to lay some ordnance on the airfield with a slightly long bomb.*

*What good did any of that do? I learned something. I learned
that you cannot trust America. And I tell my Arab friends that as
I point out to them that the once-upon-a-time capital of the last nation to put complete faith in American military might is now called
Ho Chi Minh City.*

NELLIS AFB–1965–1967

When Horner returned to the United States in August 1965, he and
Roger Myhrum went back to Seymour Johnson, where they worked in
the command post doing odd jobs and waiting for orders. The boredom
of all this was enlivened one day in October, when a parade was held at
Seymour Johnson, during the course of which Horner and Myrhum each
received an Air Medal for attacking the fake SA-2 SAM site that fateful
day in July. Horner was surprised; he hadn't expected it. And he was
proud: nobody else in his wing who'd entered the Air Force since the end
of the Korean war over a decade earlier had one of those blue and yellow ribbons on his chest.*

For the next two years Horner volunteered every chance he could to
return to the war, but was told by the TAC personnel assignments people that he was too valuable for that; his combat experience was needed
to train the rapidly growing pipeline feeding replacement aircrews into
the war. This meant a move to Nellis AFB as an instructor in the F-105
school, where they trained new and old pilots to fly the Thud in combat.

---

*For combat awards, the Air Medal stands below the DFC, but above the Air Force Commen-
dation Medal, which is usually given for excellence in job performance to company-grade officers. Though it isn't really a major award, at the time the Air Medal was highly respected. Since
the last war was Korea, by 1965 very few medals had been handed out since the early 1950s.*

During the time Horner was an instructor at Nellis, nearly all the experienced F-105 pilots had been or were being cycled through the war. By late 1966, that pool had been used up; those in it had either completed their tours (the normal tour for an F-105 pilot being 100 sorties, about four months) or had been shot down and killed or captured (the F-105 had the dubious honor of leading the pack in this category). This meant that the turnover rate in the F-105 (which flew only over North Vietnam or Laos) was at best four months. And this meant TAC had a tremendous training load in order to qualify replacement pilots. Since the pipeline could not feed the vacancies, the Air Force impressed non–fighter pilots, trained them in quickie courses, and shipped them off to war and near-certain death or capture. The term "There ain't no way" became common in the F-105 community about this time. It meant: "There's no way to make it to 100 sorties in the F-105, because you are going to get shot down before you reach 100."

Here is how the training at Nellis went:

An instructor was in a squadron with normally fifteen other instructors. Every six months he'd get a long-course class—second lieutenants just out of flying training with shiny new wings and shiny new attitudes, willing to learn. Every three months he'd get a short-course class—pilots who came from staff jobs or from flying other aircraft.

To both long and short, he'd teach classroom instruction on the systems in the F-105, as well as taking off and landing, flying in formation, and air-to-air and air-to-ground gunnery, weapons, and tactics. Even though these students were being sent off to Vietnam when they graduated, there was still considerable inertia in the Air Force, so he also taught nuclear weapons deliveries. But whenever he was teaching his students what they would actually use in war—bombing techniques, lookout procedures for MiGs and SAMs, and so on—he always made sure they got the message that this would be a test question administered in the sky over North Vietnam.

Predictably, Horner was best with pilots who were aggressive and quick to learn. If they were slow learners or incompetent, then he had no patience with them, and they suffered his verbal abuse. The long-course people, the real fighter pilots, were usually a joy to check out—a clean sheet of paper for what he could give them. All he had to do was tell them the function of the various switches and the unique aspects of the Thud.

However, the pilots who'd been flying heavies—the cannon fodder schooled in other ways of operating who were being packaged and sent off to war—resisted change and were difficult to teach. Though he could coax them through, and for the most part could make them safe in the Thuds, their minds did not move at the pace flying fighters required. They lacked good situational awareness. Most of them got by using checklists and rote procedures, but some—because they were behind the jet all the time—were dangerous. These he taught survival skills, such as: "Don't worry about hitting the target with your bombs. Worry about hitting the target with your airplane. Someday you'll get through all this and return to your C-118, where you are happiest."

Just as the conduct of the war in Vietnam was riddled with insanities, so also was the training for it: thus, instructors weren't allowed to wash anyone out of the program. While many pilots did not meet standards, they were graduated and sent off to war. However, in the case of those few who would clearly die if sent off to war in a Thud, instructors did their best to figure out ways to keep them from going.

Horner had a young heavy pilot who was so far behind the aircraft it was a sure thing that even if the enemy didn't get him, he would kill himself. One day, Horner learned that the young pilot had had a growth removed from his forearm. That was the excuse he needed. He had him sent to the squadron flight surgeon for an examination, and there it was "discovered" that this pilot's forearm was too weak to pull back on the stick of an F-105 and that he should be returned to transports. And so it came about . . . even though anyone who knows aircraft knows that pulling on the wheel of a transport requires a lot more strength than the hydraulically boosted controls of a modern fighter. Sometimes the only way to beat insanity is by canceling it out with another insanity.

★ All of this pointed up the deep flaws in the assignment of pilots into combat:

First, all military personnel sent to fight the war had to operate under an arcane accounting system that governed how long they would be exposed to combat. To CPAs and bean counters this made sense. To warriors this was madness. But it was the bean counters who were running the personnel system, and the personnel system was establishing the policy that drove the strategy.

Second, all pilots were to have an equal chance to gain combat experience, and no pilot was expected to spend more than one year in theater or 100 combat missions over North Vietnam. The constant injection into the F-4, F-100, and F-105 units of bomber and tanker pilots who were not experienced fighter pilots, but who were given a quickie checkout in fighter jets and sent to war, at least hurt and at times crippled the war effort. Often these people wound up in charge by virtue of their rank and tried to lead when they didn't know what they were doing. Some proved out, but most just muddled around until they finished their 100 missions or were shot down.*

This policy was obviously wrong on several counts, starting with the assumption that all pilots were of equal ability when it came to fighting. It further encouraged unusual tensions and risk avoidance, as pilots tried to stay alive for their 100 missions or their year rather than concentrate on the job of defeating the enemy. (Pilots with 90 missions would really get edgy.) Thus, it removed the primary incentive of a pilot for doing his combat duties to the best of his abilities, the goal of winning.

At Korat, one of the pilots was shot down after about 88 missions. He survived, came back to the base, and wanted to finish his tour flying with the Wild Weasels.

The job of the Wild Weasels was to locate and destroy SAM sites; and it was the job of the number one and three pilots in a Weasel flight of four aircraft to do that. The number two and four pilots were not Weasels; and they flew ordinary F-105Ds with bombs. Their job was to stick close and look out for MiGs while the other two were teasing the sites. If the one and three cornered a SAM site, two and four would drop regular bombs or CBUs on it.

This pilot figured that flying with the Weasels would be a soft touch, since the one and three often left their wingmen on the ridge in comparative safety, while they ventured out on the Red River valley floor to find the SAMs. They could maneuver a lot more aggressively if they didn't have to take care of a wingman.

As luck would have it, though, on his first mission with the Weasels, this pilot had sixteen SA-2 missiles shot at him. They all missed, but when he returned to base he couldn't even get drunk. His hands shook so much, he couldn't hold a glass.

To his credit, he finished his 100 missions, but he became a dip bomber and was never again effective.

---

*This was not always the case. When he returned to Korat in 1967, Horner served under an old-time fighter commander, Colonel, later Brigadier General, Bill Chairasell. Chairasell used his most experienced squadron commanders to lead, no matter what their rank—a practice of which Chuck Horner seriously approved.

A dip bomber was a pilot who went in at 15,000 feet, rolled in over the target, and at 14,000 feet dropped his bombs so they were sure to hit somewhere on the surface of the earth. He then immediately started a climb until he could rejoin the rest of the flight, who'd gone down to much lower altitudes to try to hit the target, even though it meant getting shot at. There were a number of dip bombers at Korat. Some, like this one, evoked sympathy; some were the object of scorn.

It's not hard to understand why pilots who'd been shot down became dip bombers. For a pilot the cockpit is an air-conditioned and familiar womb, but when he is about to go down and he blows the canopy, he's jerked out of the womb into the real world of wind blast, noise, and if he's flying at high speed, pain. The uncertainty as he floats down in his parachute quickly follows: *Will I get rescued? Will I get injured when I hit the ground? Will I get captured by civilians and beaten to death with hoes and stones? Will I be captured by the army and spend the rest of my life getting tortured in jail?* When your plane gets hit, you're scared. Chuck Horner's plane was never hit, but he has no doubt about how he would have reacted if it had been.

Why did the Air Force fall into this particular trap?

Partly for old-style ticket-punching reasons—to give every officer a chance for quality combat time in order to justify promotions. Worse, in Horner's view, the Air Force felt that since the war offered an opportunity to renew the combat experience of the force, they wanted to offer that experience to as many pilots as possible. Since it really didn't matter how good any of these pilots were, they could afford to send in the second team. In other words, playing the entire bench was more important than winning the game.

As far as Horner was concerned, the generals who led the Air Force should have resigned rather than put up with any of this.* Instead, they

---

*Horner himself stayed on at Korat beyond 100 sorties, because he enjoyed combat. Others stayed on beyond 100 sorties because they wanted to help the unit out. But by 1967, he wasn't aware of anyone who felt they were going to win this war. When I asked him what we could possibly have done to set up an acceptable end state, this was his answer: "Our overall strategic aim, as far as I can make out, was to devastate the North so badly that they would surrender any hopes of interfering in the South. Naïve. If we had really wanted to show the North Vietnamese we were serious, we probably should have shut down Haiphong and Hanoi, invaded below Haiphong, and cut the county in half lower down. In fact (though we didn't know it then), as it turned out, all we really had to do was befriend Ho. Seems he wasn't part of a monolithic Communist plot, and hated the Chinese more than anyone else. Since as it turns out we really didn't have any loyalty to the South Vietnamese people anyway, perhaps we could have brokered a deal after the French pulled out. But that is twenty-twenty hindsight on my part."

should have found the best pilots, put them in fighters, and sent them off to war with the warning: "Don't come home until you've won." They'd have figured out how to win. If they'd extended that policy all up and down the military line—as was done during Desert Storm—they'd have had a solid chance of victory.

The Israelis have devised a system that allows an air force to put its best pilots into the best planes. It wouldn't be at all difficult for the USAF to implement such a system. The Israeli Air Force has a ladder—a list naming the pilots: top of the ladder is the best and the bottom is the worst. The best pilots go to the best squadrons. There is also a ladder of squadrons: the best squadrons fly the top fighters, U.S.-made F-15s and F-16s. The next-best squadrons fly Mirages or F-4s, which are older fighters and cannot compete with the F-15s and F-16s. From time to time, the top of the ladder in the F-4 squadron will get orders to fly the F-16, and the bottom of the F-16 ladder will get orders to fly the F-4. Below the F-4s or Mirages are other, lesser aircraft, all the way down to multiengine and helicopters. Conceivably, an F-15 pilot who loses his nerve or concentration could free-fall all the way down to being a chopper pilot.

American personnel types don't like to hear about such a system, because it starts with the premise that some pilots are better than others, while the bureaucrats try to keep their own job simple by assuming that all pilots are round pegs for round holes, plug-and-play as the laws of supply and demand dictate.

WEASELING

Until the introduction into the war of the Wild Weasels and Electronic Counter Measures Pods (ECMs confused SAM radars), enemy SAMs had an easy time against U.S. jets. There was virtually no defense against them. The free ride ended in 1966, when the first combat Wild Weasel, a two-seat modified F-100F fighter, located an SA-2 site and killed it with rockets and cannon. This was the first confirmed kill of a SAM site. It meant the enemy manning them were no longer safe. When they went to work at their SAM site, they stood a chance of dying, just the same as the pilots they were shooting at.

Weaseling was fairly straightforward. A pilot teased and tempted the enemy enough to provoke him to try to kill the Weasel, and then the pilot dodged the bullets while he closed on the enemy's camouflaged position and stuck a knife in his heart. (The camouflage—nets over the radar and missiles—was quite effective, especially when a pilot was going 600 knots in a jet and trying to see all around him at once, looking for MiGs and missiles from other sites and tracking gunfire.) For Weaseling to be successful, the Weasel pilots had to have much better information than the strike aircraft about where the SAM radar was looking and the status of the SAM operator's attack on his target. Then, when SAMs were launched, the Weasels had to be able to see the best ways to maneuver in order to avoid being tracked or hit by them. In short, Weasel pilots needed better detection gear and better training than other strike pilots.

After a few months of Weasel attacks, the SAM radar operators were forced to limit their time on the air to just a few brief seconds, or else they would be located and killed. The combined effects of the Wild Weasels and the self-protection ECM Pods on the bombing aircraft meant that the SAM became a manageable threat. Now thousands of SAM missiles had to be fired before the enemy was able to knock one U.S. aircraft down. The growing ineffectiveness of the SAMs meant that attacking fighters could operate at medium altitude, out of the range of most of the AAA guns. The Weasels, by helping to solve the SAM problem, helped to solve the visually-aided-guns problem.

This success came at a price. Too many Wild Weasel aircraft and their crews were lost; the job was hazardous to your health.*

The inspiration for the Weasels came in 1965, shortly after the failed attempt to bomb the SAM site at the junction of the Black and Red rivers. After that failure, the Pentagon realized (to their credit) that it was time to take a hard look at electronic combat. The result was an acquisition process called QRP, for Quick Reaction Process, whereby the Pentagon sent queries out to industry about what could be done.

One suggestion was to mount electronic jamming pods under the wings of U.S. aircraft. The electronics in the pods put noise jamming on the SAM radarscopes, so the operators could not lock onto the target aircraft.

These pods led to a whole new way of flying bombing attacks. Instead of flying in at low level, where a pilot would be vulnerable to AAA, he'd come in at 15,000 or 20,000 feet in what was called a pod formation.

---

*The Wild Weasels amassed more medals per aircrew (pilot or his EWO) than any other unit in the war.

When the North Vietnamese tried to make out what their radars were picking up, all they could see was a blob—not an individual aircraft they could lock onto and attack. The Air Force liked this idea and implemented it. Before long, the pods began to have a good effect over the skies of Vietnam.

A second response, meanwhile, came from a small company in California, Applied Technology Incorporated. ATI suggested a radar signal receiver mounted on an aircraft that would allow the aircraft to locate SAM radars on the ground, then tell the pilot the radar's status—searching for a target, locking onto a potential target, preparing to fire, or just having fired a missile at a target—and it could tell the pilot if *he* was the target.

The Air Force also liked this idea, and ATI produced prototype black boxes for testing. Then they found a few experienced fighter pilots from TAC, such as Gary Willard and Al Lamb, and bomber EWOs (electronic weapons officers—the people who operate the black boxes) from SAC, such as Jack Donovan. (Most bomber EWOs had never been near a fighter, but they were schooled both in the ways of SAMs and of the black boxes that helped bombers penetrate Russian SAM defenses.) These people flew the black boxes in two-seat F-100s at Eglin AFB, Florida, and proved that they could find radars whenever they were turned on, no matter how much they were camouflaged.

The next step came in 1966, when black box–equipped F-100s were deployed to Southeast Asia and sent into North Vietnam. Al Lamb and Jack Donovan, flying one of these F-100s, killed the first SA-2 site (with rockets and strafing; later Weasels used a mix of Shrike radar-homing missiles, 20mm cannon, cluster bombs, general-purpose bombs, and sometimes, high-velocity rockets). Unfortunately, the F-100s were slow and vulnerable when flying in the heavy defenses over North Vietnam and took too many losses. As a result, this initial cadre of Wild Weasels returned to Nellis, and ATI built even newer black boxes for F-105s, which greatly improved their radar detection system. Since F-105s had a crude heads-up display, ATI could install antennas on the nose of the aircraft, and a red dot was projected on the pilot's gun sight that showed the location of the SAM radar on the ground. F-105s also carried more munitions, and they were faster and more survivable than the first F-100 Weasels.

★ At Nellis, meanwhile, Horner volunteered for a variety of test programs designed to introduce into the war the AT-37 Dragonfly (a T-37 jet trainer modified into an air-to-ground aircraft for counterinsurgency warfare; it was sold to several Third World nations) and F-5 Tiger Jet (a T-38 aircraft modified to act as a supersonic fighter; it was easy to fly and maintain, low in cost, and could be used by nations with small air forces; thousands of these aircraft are still flying today throughout the world). But he was turned down, just as he'd been turned down repeatedly for well over a year whenever he'd asked to return to Southeast Asia. He remained at Nellis.

One morning he was at Mobile Control, a small glass house between the runways, where one watched students in the traffic pattern, making sure they don't crash or land gear up. As it happened, Al Lamb, a captain like Horner, was also assigned to Mobile Control that morning. While he was there, he talked about his recent experience in Southeast Asia flying F-100 Wild Weasels, the new secret outfit designed to find and kill SAM sites. They were just starting up, he explained, and needed experienced pilots who were also volunteers. "I want in," Horner told him.

About an hour later, Lamb finished his tour in Mobile and left. Soon after he himself was relieved from Mobile that morning, Horner got a call from Gary Willard, a lieutenant colonel, who was commander of the new Weasel school. "Al told me you're a volunteer," he said to Horner.

"That's true," Horner answered, and by 11:00 A.M. that day he had orders to report to the Weasel squadron for extra training. The Air Force forgot the cold eye they had previously cast on his attempts to return to combat. They placed great importance on the Weasel program.

★ Horner entered Wild Weasel training together with his good friends, Billy Sparks and Jim Hartney (White Fang), whose father, a major, had been Eddie Rickenbacker's ops officer in World War I.* He also went through the training with a cool, somber electronics warfare officer named Dino Regalli, who had been an EWO on spy missions flown out of the Middle East to eavesdrop on the Russians.

The training itself emphasized the obvious, that Weaseling is like mak-

---

*Later, White Fang was shot down over North Vietnam and stoned to death by villagers. He and his EWO, Sam Fantle, were picked up by the Army and told to run for it across a field. If they were fast enough, the Army would protect them from the villagers. Fantle was fast enough to make it across the field. But White Fang was older than the rest of the Weasels (he had been a flight officer at the end of World War II) and didn't make it. He had a wife and son. His wife died years later from cancer.

ing love to a porcupine: you approach them and do your thing very carefully.

Practically, it consisted of a great deal of classified classroom instruction on SAM radars, SAM operations and limitations, and tactics for approaching a SAM site, as well as in-flight training. The ATI black box that allowed Weasels to see where they were in the enemy radar-tracking radar beams was called the ER-142. The Weasels also had a set of antennas that allowed them to see where the radar was located on the ground, even if it was hidden from visual view. Using these electronics, they were trained in the modes and tactics of the SA-2 radar. They were also trained to use the Shrike radar homing missile and to outmaneuver the SA-2 Guideline missiles.

★ In the spring of 1967, Horner, now a Wild Weasel, returned to Korat, Thailand.

Between 1965 and 1967, the base had expanded, and the facilities were much improved. There was now a large, new, air-conditioned officers' club with a swimming pool and all sorts of other amenities. (The 1965 club was being used to store soft drinks for the new BX.) There was also a two-story hospital and an air-conditioned church. The hooches were now two-man air-conditioned rooms in four-room suites. Each suite had a flush toilet and shower and a sitting area complete with refrigerator and chairs. Quite a change from the shacks where they lived and slept in 1965, and the rubber raft pool.

As a Wild Weasel, Horner flew both Wild Weasel missions and night radar bombing missions, a total of seventy in addition to the forty-one he'd flown in 1965.

The skies over Hanoi and Haiphong, meanwhile, and the surrounding Red River Delta, had become the most heavily defended real estate on earth. In the delta lowlands and the hills that ringed them had been placed more than 7,000 antiaircraft guns and as many as 180 well-camouflaged SAM launchers. By 1967, MiGs were also active, and doing surprisingly well against U.S. aircraft. At the start of the war, Air Force pilots had shot down four MiGs for every one of their own that was lost. Now the ratio was one to two. The Weasels and the ECM pods were badly needed.

A typical Weasel mission over Hanoi or Haiphong usually went something like this:

After takeoff, a pilot would proceed to the tanker in Thailand or over the Sea of China. After refueling, the package would form up. The Weasels would lead, followed by ingress MiG CAP F-4s, followed by twelve to sixteen bomb-laden F-105s, followed a little later (so they'd have fuel when the strikers were leaving the target area) by additional Wild Weasels and MiG CAP.

As he neared Little Thud Ridge, northeast of Hanoi, or Thud Ridge, running northwest of Hanoi parallel to the Red River, his MiG CAP would start down the ridge looking for any MiGs that might scramble, while the Weasels would fan out over the flats looking for SAM sites. (Pilots called it Dr. Pepper when a pilot was out on the flats with a SAM site at ten o'clock, two o'clock, and four o'clock locked onto him at the same time.) The Weasel's job was to play chicken with the SAM operators, to "encourage" them to turn off their radars. So he often turned into the site and flew toward it. When the radar operator saw him coming at him, he had two choices: he could fire a SAM at him from the ring of missiles that he operated, or he could shut down his radar, which was in the middle of the ring. If he fired, the booster on the Guideline missile kicked up a lot of dust and clearly marked his site, so all the pilot had to do was to dodge the missile(s) he fired, and turn in and kill him. But more than likely he shut down and waited for help from a nearby site. When that site came up on the pilot's electronics, he turned on him, and the dance went through another round. After a few minutes of this, the strike package had already gotten in and out and were back over the ridge. At that point, the egress Weasel flight would fly in to cover the pilot's exit back up to the ridge and the MiG CAP F-4s would wait around in case any MiGs showed up.

Throughout all this, there might be a Weasel or striker shot down, and this added to all the confusion of radar signals going off in the pilot's headset, of radio calls from his flight members about SAMs coming at him, of calls from the strikers trying to get their act together, of calls from the supporting command and control shouting out MiG warnings, of the constant junk chatter from the F-4s, and finally, of the ominous sound on guard channel of the beepers that are automatically activated when a pilot's parachute is opened.

When he crossed the coastline or the Red River (there were few guns or SAMs west of the river), he was flooded with relief. He knew then that he was alive for at least one more day.

★ Though not everyone bought the ECM concept, the ECM pods were also proving their worth. The people at Ta Khli Base, for example, were suspicious of them and were still flying low-level tactics, even after two years of deadly lessons to the contrary. (For a time, Ta Khli was bereft of Wild Weasels, all of them from that base having been shot down; the Weasels from Korat had to take over some of their work until more could be sent from the States.)

However, the wing commander at Korat, Brigadier General Bill Chairasell, decided that losses at low level were too high and ordered his pilots to try out the new pods and fly the required four-ship pod formation. Each aircraft had to fly so many feet from each other and so many feet above or below his leader, so the four ships filled a box of airspace about 4,000 feet across by 1,000 feet long and 1,500 feet deep. Though using the pods and flying in this formation left the North Vietnamese radar operators unable to discern individual aircraft on their radarscopes, and gave them insufficient accuracy in their systems to hit anything with the missiles they shot, that didn't stop them from trying. They sent up their missiles into the blobs on their screens. They came close, but they didn't hit. And this meant some jittery moments for the pilots up there, cruising along at 15,000 to 20,000 feet above the ground in their rigid formation, feeling naked to the SAMs, sweating it out if their pods would really work or not, only finding out when the missile would fly harmlessly by. Not only did flying the pod formation require extreme discipline, but flying it was a pure act of faith; yet it worked. Soon, because of Bill Chairasell's leadership and the use of pod formation and the Weasels, losses at Korat took a nosedive, and "There ain't no way" became "There is a way."

Did all of this make a real difference? In some ways, yes. Flying became safer for U.S. pilots. They had better targets—steel mills, bridges in Hanoi, SAM storage areas, and other targets in Hanoi and Haiphong. Later they had a few precision, laser-guided bombs, which also helped. Later still, Richard Nixon's Linebacker II campaign late in 1972 sent B-52s over Hanoi, and mined Haiphong Harbor. The B-52s put terror into the North Vietnamese as no previous U.S. effort had done, and gave notice to the Russians and Chinese that nothing in North Vietnam was immune to U.S. bombing.

But did any of this make a real difference? Obviously no.

LAST RITES

The war in Vietnam had many unexpected consequences, and many of them were surprisingly positive. Here, in his words, is how the war ended for Chuck Horner:

> In 1974, I traveled to Saigon and Australia, by then a lieutenant colonel in the Pentagon. While there, I had studied the 1973 Middle East war in detail. Based on this experience and my experience in Vietnam, I had put together a briefing (containing lots of Israeli gunnery film) on air-to-air combat for presentation to Congress. This briefing led to an invitation to a fighter symposium in Australia. As a courtesy, I visited the Vietnam squadrons flying the F-5 to provide them an update.
>
> Not much was going on in Vietnam in those days. The Vietcong, of course, had been wiped out during the Tet Offensive, and we had pretty much pulled out, though there were USAF units in Thailand that could defeat any major action. So the North Vietnamese just sat tight, concentrated on diplomacy, and waited for the United States to lose interest in the South Vietnamese.
>
> While I was in Saigon, the VNAF officers I was meeting knew we had pulled out for good and they were on their own. Therefore, having taken lessons from us for the past several years, they were putting their faith in hardware: if they had more, they would be OK. So they spent their time with me begging for matériel, radars, aircraft, bombs, transport, etc. By then I was aware that they weren't going to get most of what they were asking for. I also knew that the Congress had had enough of the war and that the next two squadrons of F-5Es scheduled to go to Vietnam were not going to be delivered. The Pentagon had already started action to use them in building an upgraded Aggressor squadrons force at Nellis.
>
> One day, I was scheduled to drive out in an embassy car with a driver to Bien Hoa Airfield to brief the squadron there (the same briefing I'd given the other VNAF squadrons), and a VNAF lieutenant colonel, Le Ba Hung, was assigned to escort me. Before I left for the air base, the escort officer called to ask if he could ride up in my car. I said sure, but was mildly surprised. Vietnamese officers normally didn't grab a ride with an American. They liked to

take their own cars. So by asking to ride with me, this Hung guy was giving up a little "face." He would have had more face if he had shown up at the squadron in his own car. Well, I went over to the VNAF side of the base. When he got in the car, he was wearing a flight suit, which was another surprise. "I've already heard your briefing," he told me. "So I'm going to get in a mission while you brief the squadron."

At once I liked this guy, which inspired me to ask him why he had decided to ride with me. He answered flat out that he'd had trouble finding gas for his jeep; and besides, any extra gas he could get, he used in his Ford Mustang convertible, which he used to haul around his French girlfriend. Now I really resonated with this guy. We were the same age, and he had been flying fighters since 1960. He had been shot down and Americans had rescued him. And when he was going through pilot training, he'd had an American girlfriend, but didn't feel he could get married due to the nature of his job. Now he was the F-5E Tiger II project officer on the VNAF Air Staff.

At that point he asked me point blank, "Are we going to get those other two squadrons of F-5E aircraft?"

"Do you want the truth?" I answered. He nodded, so I said, "No."

He looked down in disappointment, then asked me what I thought about that. As far as I could tell, I told him, the VNAF would not have to fight the MiGs. What his country needed, if North Vietnam invaded, was gas and artillery ammo. And he agreed . . . and surprised me again.

After I briefed the squadron, and he flew a combat sortie, we rode home together. In the car, he turned to me and asked what I thought of the squadron pilots. "They look awfully young and in-experienced," I told him uncomfortably. I was sure he didn't want to hear this. "Their appearance and their questions and comments don't give me a lot of confidence. If I were you, I'd be worried."

Then he looked me right in the eye and said, "Nixon's policy of Vietnamization won't work. My squadrons can't fight their way out of a wet paper bag. And no matter how much equipment you give us, no matter how many drunken alcoholic civilian technicians you send over to do the maintenance on the equipment you give us,

*we are going to lose the forthcoming war with North Vietnam."
Once that had a chance to sink in, he went on: "Go back to the
United States and tell your bosses what you've seen. Tell them that
we desperately need your airpower until we've had time to grow a
competent military force."*

I promised I would do that. And I did.

*When I got back to the Pentagon, I wrote a trip report that in-
cluded what I had observed. It said, among other things, that the
policy of Vietnamization was a sham and wasn't working, and
that we needed to somehow stay engaged in Vietnam. If nothing
more, we had to at least threaten to use our airpower if North
Vietnam invaded the south. That paper made it two levels above
me before it came back down with orders to destroy it and never
bring up the subject again.*

*Even to the end we refused to recognize the facts or tell the
truth about Vietnam.*

*After Saigon fell, I asked the intelligence guys to find Hung.
They located him a few days later in a hospital at Wake Island, suffering from exhaustion. I wrote him a letter, but didn't have any
further contact with him until later. During the last few days of the
war, he'd flown day and night, winding up in charge of the VNAF
when all the generals left the country. Finally, after his last F-5
mission, he taxied into Tan Son Nut, and there was no one left to
park his aircraft. Just about then, the North Vietnamese soldiers
were coming over the wall, but Nguyen Cao Ky, the flamboyant
fighter pilot who headed the South Vietnamese Air Force (and was
for a time prime minister), came by and picked him up in a helicopter. For a few hours they tried to rally the country; but when
mortars started falling on the Joint General Staff compound, they
climbed aboard Ky's Huey and flew to a carrier. There Hung collapsed.*

*Later, I tracked him to the United States Indiantown Gap
Refugee Center and drove up to see him, which delighted him. He
introduced me to Chan, his oldest sister, his mother, and Chan's
four children, one of whom had been born on Guam and was
therefore an American citizen. Chan's husband Coung, a lieutenant
colonel in the Army, had been ordered to stay behind to surrender*

the Army while his generals booked with the refugees who came out on the C-141s. But Hung had been able to use his Air Force contacts to get Chan and the children out. He'd called Colonel Marty Mahrt, an old F-105 buddy of mine, and Marty had arranged for Chan, the mother, and the three children to be evacuated on the next flight.

Then Hung went over to Chan's house and explained that she had to go, which was not what she wanted to hear. When Chan started crying and wailing, Hung took out his 9mm handgun and calmly told her that she had two choices. Either she, his mother, and the children would get on the airplane, or he would shoot them all and then kill himself. But he was not going to let them fall into the enemy hands. Chan knew Hung, and knew he meant it. So she packed a few things and they left for the airport.

En route, artillery fire sent them down in a ditch. But after it let up, they were able to make it to the airport, Hung and Marty were able to put them on a C-141, and Hung went back to trying to repel the invasion. To this day his Mustang convertible is probably parked in front of the squadron.

When I met them at Indiantown, I knew that they needed an American sponsor. (In order to leave the refugee center and settle in the United States, you either had to have a large amount of money showing you could support yourself, or else you needed an American sponsor, who could help you get settled—usually by giving you a job.) So when I asked Hung who was going to do that, he told me that he himself didn't need any help, since he had lived in the United States while attending various schools over the years and could easily find work and take care of himself. But it was going to be a problem for Chan and the others, because families who sponsored refugees wanted a family with a man in it who could earn money and help pay the expenses. "Okay, no problem," I told him. "We're on our way to Iowa for a vacation; but if no one comes forth in the meantime, they can come live with us."

And so on our way back, we picked up Ba, the grandmother; Chan; Bich, a thirteen-year-old daughter who was a year older than my oldest daughter; Lingh and Que, nine- and eleven-year-old sons (my son John was ten); and Ahn, the baby daughter, less than a year old. They lived with us for a year, and it was a wonderful experience. Every meal we ate rice with chopsticks. Mary Jo and Chan were like sisters. Ba took care of Ain and Nancy. The three boys roomed together and got along. Susan and Bich roomed together and acted like teenage sisters: they fought most of the time.

Hung, meanwhile, became the head manager at the Naval Academy Dining Room until the local mob ran him out of town because he tried to make them stop exploiting the Vietnamese who had replaced the Filipinos in the dining room. After Chan left us, she held good jobs and raised her family. Her oldest boy graduated from the Naval Academy with a degree in nuclear engineering. All the others excelled in school and are working citizens; Ain, the youngest, graduated from college and never received a grade below A in her life.

In November 1990, Chan's husband Coung was released from Vietnam. I was in Riyadh when I got the news and was overjoyed. Over the years after the evacuation of Saigon, he had been in re-education centers and had endured a great deal. Ba also died about that time; but her wish to be buried in the soil of Vietnam was never realized. Hung was married in Salem, Oregon, in 1979 to a wonderful and beautiful woman named Quin (who doesn't take any sass from him). His sons are named Viet and Nam, so he will never forget the country he once served so proudly.

3

THE VISION OF
BILL CREECH

Following Vietnam, the Air Force was in bad shape, but it was by no means only Vietnam that had caused it. The problems were systemic in nature; they were the consequences of the way the Air Force had been run for many years.

Ever since the heating up of the Cold War, it had been the nuclear mission, and those who were in charge of it, the SAC commanders, who had been running the Air Force. In doing so, the SAC commanders gave every other Air Force mission at best only partial attention. How could dropping a bomb on a bridge compare with destroying the Soviet Union? The SIOP became supreme, and, as Chuck Horner had discovered, other methods of training were either downplayed or forbidden.

Bomber generals like predictability, order, and control, and in World War II, the best guarantee of bombing success had involved sending one's bombers over the target in a specific line at a specific altitude. When the bomber generals became the SAC generals in the decades that followed, they ran the Air Force the way they already knew and already thought best—with order, centralized control, and intense micromanagement from above.

The authority of the SAC was further enhanced when Robert Mc-Namara became the Secretary of Defense, and instituted the Planning, Programming, Budgeting System (PPBS) used by the Pentagon to build the annual budget submission for Defense. PPBS made the USAF Nuclear Forces—SAC and Air Defense Command—into what were called the Major Force Program 1, MFP-1. Since MFP-1 programs supported the most important part of America's military strategy, they were to receive more DOD attention, and money, than other programs. Meanwhile, TAC and Conventional Forces were MFP-2—second class.

The SAC generals took the ball and ran with it. Their methods, their procedures, became the only ones allowable, and they refused to tolerate any deviations. They did their best to standardize everything for which they had responsibility, and manuals and directions became the order of the day.

For instance, Walter Sweeney, a SAC general who commanded TAC in the early sixties, devised a system for rating the wings using what was called "Management Computation System" (MCS). Each wing's activities were given a monthly score. These included not only measures of combat capability such as bomb scores and aircraft-in-commission rates, but also on-time payment of officers' club bills, the number of lawns that needed cutting in the base housing area, the number of DUIs (driving under the influence) ticketed to a wing, and the number of contributions to the Air Force Aid Society. From all this a composite score was computed. The wing with the top score was presumably the best wing in the Air Force, while the one with the lowest was the worst. If a wing had a bad record paying its club bills, that counted as much as anything else, and the wing commander would certainly be criticized, and might even lose his job.

It's no surprise that a system that measured uncut grass alongside bombing skill had no credibility with the troops. No surprise, either, was the result: the troops lied.

Take the case of a range officer at the bombing range at Poinsett, five miles south of Shaw AFB, at Sumter, South Carolina. An F-100 flight from Myrtle Beach was going to be on the range. The flight leader would give the range officer a call to tell him the kind of scores his squadron needed for their MCS points; and the range officer made sure that they got them. Consequently, if a pilot threw a bomb way off target, the score actually reported by the airmen became a no-spot (the smoke charge didn't function when the bomb struck the ground, so the airmen scoring the bombs couldn't tell where it hit). In short, there was no failure, and no loss of MCS points.

Another Sweeney game was to call from his office directly down to a squadron. Whoever picked up the phone was put to a test. Procedures that pilots were supposed to commit to memory were printed in the pilots' handbook in boldface letters, and the hapless man on the phone was asked to parrot the boldface for a given emergency in his type of aircraft. Sweeney, naturally, had the book open before him; and if the pilot on the other end of the phone missed a word, he got a vicious chewing-out. And Sweeney wanted it all exactly as written; it had to be "Throttle—Off," not "Throttle—Shut Down," even though they meant the same. The result, first, was that the boldface procedures were soon pasted to the wall over every telephone in every squadron in TAC. Second, when Sweeny asked for the pilot's name, he got an alias. Some of the names were very creative—Captain John Black, for instance, would become Captain George Suckfinger—yet the SAC general never caught on.

To the pilots, standardization and authority were important, but not this kind of mentality, and so the best of them fought back. They saw a vast gulf between the jobs they were being told to do and the jobs they felt needed to be done, and it seemed to them they had three options: they could crack under the strain, do a half-baked job, or fight by deceiving—lie and do the *real* job as much as they could swing it. Thus, integrity meant lying—not a good place to be, and the strains showed.

They showed in many ways—problems with drugs, alcohol, race, and sex. Too many crashed, too many were lost. They showed in smaller but equally telling ways, too: too many aircraft inoperable because there weren't enough parts, too many hangar floors filthy, too many NCOs in their offices instead of with their troops, too many troops without clean toilets or clean washrooms.

It wasn't until 1978 that a general named Bill Creech took command of the TAC, saw what needed doing, and did it, but that was several years in the future. In the meantime, men like Chuck Horner started laying the groundwork for reform.

When Chuck Horner returned from Vietnam in August 1967, he was primarily an operations man: he flew fighter planes, that's what he did. Now, while continuing his strong operational inclination, he found himself on a steep learning path. He needed to understand how to work the bureaucracy, needed the right kind of mentoring, needed to be shown how to get things done off the field as well as on. It was very lucky for him that his first major job offer after Vietnam put him in the heart of tactics development at Nellis AFB in Nevada.

NELLIS AFB

Nellis has long been, as it calls itself, the "Home of the Fighter Pilot." Because of the large-scale ranges and the free and open airspace, much of the USAF's fighter equipment and tactics development has been carried out there, and after Vietnam began to make its presence felt, and money was freed up to develop the new conventional systems needed to fight that war, it was a very busy place.

In the 1960s, two major functions were based at Nellis: a fighter wing that performed F-105 (and later F-111) qualification training; and the Fighter Weapons School (FWS), where top fighter pilots received (and still receive) advanced training in fighter pilot instruction—at first in the F-100 and F-105, and later in the F-4.

Fighter pilots with a great deal of experience (usually 1,000-plus hours) and credibility were selected both for their flying skills and their ability to instruct, and sent to the FWS for a six-month intensive training course—in effect, a doctoral degree in Fighter Operations. The academics were fiercely difficult, and there was nearly endless flying in which every move was graded in a laboratory environment on the ranges. Beyond that, FWS students learned how to be superb platform instructors, as well as how to work with maintenance to ensure that the bombing systems were working correctly and the munitions being maintained properly.

After leaving the FWS, graduates were called patch wearers: instead of their flying squadron patch, they wore on their right shoulder the FWS patch—gray with yellow circles and a bomb impacting this bull's-eye. After finishing the course, receiving their patch, and returning to their home base, patch wearers became the promoters of fighter excellence in their squadron or wings.

Graduates additionally received an "S" prefix on their Air Force Specialty code. Thus, AFSC A1115E signified the following: "S" meant FWS grad; "1115" meant pilot; and "E" meant F-105. When personnel people noticed the S on an AFSC, they knew this pilot needed to be handled specially, not only because of his special training, but also because of the Air Force's huge investment in him. For that reason, patch wearers were more likely to be assigned the good flying jobs.

★ In August 1967, Chuck Horner returned to Nellis to an assignment in the Combat Crew Training wing. This was not an appealing career move, since the wing was then converting from F-105s to F-111s, which was much more of a bomber than a fighter. After some finagling of dubious legality that kept him technically AWOL for six months but let him avoid his official assignment, he found himself flying as an instructor at the

Fighter Weapons School, where a friend, Gary Willard, was the commander. There Horner went to work teaching Wild Weaseling and Electronic Combat for pilots and electronic warfare officers. He also took on special projects, such as testing a new radar bombing system for the F-105 and new Wild Weasel black boxes. Meanwhile, after six months of less than official status, a friend in personnel took care of the paperwork that made Horner legal again.

In March 1968, Major Paul Kunichica asked Horner to join the team at the new Fighter Weapons Center at Nellis. Though the FWS had been set up to teach graduate-level fighter aviation, it soon found itself managing test projects, writing doctrine, and conducting advanced studies, all of which detracted from the quality of its principal mission, and so the center was created to take care of all those non-education functions, all the projects and functions that needed the expertise resident at Nellis. Instructors from the FWS populated the center, and though they still flew with the FWS, they now spent most of their time working on new bombs or writing requirement documents to guide the development of new aircraft.

Horner and Kunichica, a Japanese-American from Hawaii, had flown with each other a number of times and were friends. Kunichica worked for Colonel Dick Bond, who in turn worked for Brigadier General (soon to be Major General) Zack Taylor. Bond was very smart, below the zone (promoted to rank early), and liked cocky young men who enjoyed staying late at the office, while Taylor, a soft-spoken but tough-as-nails Virginia gentleman who'd been an ace in World War II, was the father of the Fighter Weapons Center, and a man of conspicuous integrity.

After he moved up to the Center, Horner still flew with the squadron and taught, but he spent most of his time on projects such as a study of F-111 bombing accuracy, and on concepts that defined the capabilities needed in the fighter aircraft destined to replace the F-105 and F-4. Out of these concepts came the FX and AX, which eventually turned into the F-15 and the tank-killing A-10.

More important personally, Horner began to understand what mentoring meant in the military, as the newly promoted Major General Taylor took him under his wing. "Bond and Taylor challenged me," Horner says now. Bond threw Horner into some of the General's pet projects, which meant that Horner and the General often found themselves on their hands and knees on the floor of the General's office, building charts that the General could use to brief his four-star boss, General Spike Momyer, at the time the TAC commander.

In young Captain Horner (promoted to major in 1969), Taylor saw a man who would see the problems through to a solution. Horner fought problems the way a dog worries a rag. He plunged into them and let fly. He loved making order out of chaos. When the smoke cleared, the floor would be covered with debris, but there'd also be the glimmers of a solution here and there, which Horner would gather up and present to his boss. During this process, he and Taylor would argue the concepts, push them and pull them, and in so doing Taylor often elevated Horner's sight picture, got him to aim better at the real target, propelled him toward working the right problem . . . often to stop thinking small. Taylor showed him how to think big.

This was Horner's first time really working the bureaucracy—an experience not too very different from combat, he quickly realized: a lot of men were gunning for him—not because he was arrogant, but because he wasn't afraid to stick his neck out and do the work at a pace they could not generate.

The largest question facing the Fighter Weapons Center had to do with its continued existence. After the Vietnam surge in weapons development ended, the various Tactical Centers had to be reorganized, and those that were no longer really useful or viable, eliminated. Besides Nellis, Shaw AFB had the Reconnaissance Center, Pope AFB the Airlift Center, Eglin AFB the Air Warfare Center, and Hurlburt AFB the Special Operations Center. Taylor involved Horner in a study to look at what they needed to do at Nellis. When it was done, Taylor took the briefing to Langley and his new boss, General Momyer, and even suggested that the F-100 test aircraft at Nellis could be retired, which would save much-needed funds. Momyer then ordered that all the Centers be studied, to determine if there could be additional assets cut or even if the Center was still needed. Taylor picked Horner to be the representative from Nellis on that study, as he had worked up the formulas that allowed Taylor to make the cuts there. Before Horner left, Taylor gave him some very simple but important advice. "Don't defend Nellis," he told him. "Do what is best for the nation and the Air Force." It was a magnificently empowering directive, for there was no hidden agenda. At the end of the day, Nellis's Fighter Center and Eglin's Air Warfare Center remained, but all the other Centers were shut down.

LANGLEY

When it was time for Horner to move on, General Taylor continued to take care of him—most important, by passing him on to Major General Gus Henry, the TAC planner, when Horner was assigned to Headquarters Tactical Air Command at Langley AFB, Hampton, Virginia. For the two years from 1970 to 1972, Horner was a staff officer, called the Action Officer (AO), in the office of the Deputy Chief of Plans in Plans in Studies and Analysis, under General Henry. There were five AOs, and for the most part they put together studies that aimed at answering questions such as how many fighter wings were needed, how best to use laser-guided bombs, and what the relative cost was of a sea-based attack sortie versus a land-based sortie (answer: ten times more expensive if you flew the sortie off a carrier).

At Langley, Horner learned the elementary lessons of what it takes to be a staff officer. It was a demanding job, filled with intrigues and battles, within both the TAC staff and the Air Force, and beyond, within the Army, Navy, and Marines. Horner's agenda was to push "tactical" as opposed to "strategic" aviation. Instead of funneling the bulk of the Air Force's efforts and budget into the nuclear war mission, he wanted to put the best equipment, training, doctrine, and tactics at the disposal of the people who might fight the actual wars.

The staffs themselves were war zones. At the TAC staff, the enemy was sometimes Strategic Command Headquarters, sometimes the Army, which was always trying to take control of the Air Force, sometimes another Deputy Chief of Staff who wanted his influence and power to grow at someone else's expense. Sometimes it was the "doctrine" of the other services.

Military doctrine is a conceptual statement, or even a philosophy, of how a service looks at its mission and intends to accomplish it. The essentials of Air Force doctrine can be stated simply: The first requirement of modern war is to gain and maintain control of the air. Airpower provides flexibility, range, and firepower. It can be adapted to a multitude of strategies, from attacking the enemy's capacity to sustain war to attacking the enemy's military forces directly.

The doctrines of the other services tended to be much more codified and specific, which presented problems for Horner. The other services' staff officers were better trained in their own doctrine than he was in the

Air Force's, which was more intuitive, so when he had an argument with the Army or Marines, they threw their doctrine at him from the rule book, while he had to make his points more with logic and enthusiasm. Landmen are lawyers; airmen are evangelists. Landmen think about defeating the enemy army; airmen think about defeating the enemy. Navy men fall in between: they look beyond defeating the enemy navy, but only think about defeating the enemy from the sea.

It soon became apparent that all the services advocated doctrines that optimized their own role in battle, but downplayed the overall role of joint operations. Fortunately, there were men in each branch, Chuck Horner among them, who felt differently. They were sickened both by interstaff and interservice parochial arguing, and the compulsion to defend service prerogatives and programs. They simply wanted to get the job done.

All through his career, Horner would run into people who had gone through the same catharsis, and when he did, they tended to get along, because of shared unspoken beliefs. They didn't lie to one another. If they thought someone had a dumb idea, they called him on it without attacking him as an individual, but if they thought he was being less then honest, they attacked him without remorse. They came to know whom they could trust, and it had nothing to do with the color of a uniform or with rank.

From the TAC staff at Langley, Horner moved on to the Armed Forces Staff College in Norfolk, Virginia, where he trained in planning for joint and combined air, land, and sea combat. During this period he was promoted to Lieutenant Colonel below the zone, in 1972. He then spent four months at the College of William and Mary, where he earned an MBA. And then it was on to the Pentagon, the Five-Faced Labyrinth, for a three-year tour.

THE FIVE-FACED LABYRINTH

As it turned out, Horner arrived at the Pentagon at just the right time. It was a heady period. The war was still ongoing, there was money in the defense budget, and the Air Force had started to acknowledge its shortcomings in training and equipment.

Once there, Horner joined a small basement office of unconstrained thinkers and freewheeling activists, which went under the name of

Weapons and Tactics, TAC Division of DCS Operations, under the leadership of Colonel Bill Kirk, a slow-talking, rumpled-uniform warrior who was an old friend of Horner's from Nellis.*

Their job was to make sure new equipment fit real-world tactics, and that the doctrine being written upstairs made sense to the operators who would have to follow it in combat. They produced studies and papers; briefed Congress about war in general and specific emerging programs such as the E-3 AWACS and new air-to-air missiles; pushed electronic-warfare systems and the laser-guided bomb programs; and when Israel fought the '73 war, they sent people over to study the tactics, and mistakes, and how the various USAF and Soviet systems had been used.

Most of all, they pushed to improve air-to-air training.

Dick Pearson's trip to Washington to explain how a pair of F-105s had been shot down by MiG-17s had had some effect on air-to-air training, but it was pretty tame. The problem was that F-105s fought like F-105s. One F-105 turned, accelerated, and climbed pretty much like another. As a consequence, pilots learned to estimate range against a big fighter, and learned to turn with another Thud, but they knew very little about exploiting the advantages of their fighter against an enemy aircraft of another type—like, say, a MiG-21. The Air Force needed dissimilar training.

The problem that put dissimilar training on the front burner was the exchange ratios in Vietnam—the number of U.S. aircraft lost compared with the number of enemy shot down. In Vietnam, exchange ratios were horrendously bad. In Korea, they had been something like six to one in favor of the United States. In Vietnam, owing to the limitations in the way the war was fought, they were often less than one to one—in other words, the North Vietnamese shot down more U.S. pilots than U.S. pilots shot down North Vietnamese. By 1972, when Horner was assigned

---

*Bill Kirk was a longtime fighter pilot, who is probably best known for his part in Operation Bolo: in 1967 the F-4s from Ubon tricked the North Vietnamese air force into thinking they were attacking F-105s. The F-4 wolf pack used the 105 call signs, and for the first time carried ECM pods and used radio discipline (something they were not noted for). Since the F-4s were the only friendly aircraft north of the Red River, they were allowed to use AIM-7 missiles beyond visual range, with just a radar lock on the target. As a result, they got face shots on MiG-21s out of the North Vietnamese base at Phuc Yen and shot a number of the North Vietnamese fighters before they could attack the force they thought was bomb-laden. The result was that the North Vietnamese MiG-21 force had to stand down for six months while they worked out what happened. It was a brilliantly planned event. Kirk eventually retired with four stars—after some trials and tribulations getting the first one.

to the Pentagon, more than 1,000 U.S. aircraft had been lost to MiGs, SAMs, and AAA. Very clearly, something serious had to change.

Thanks to the Fighter Mafia, it did.

THE FIGHTER MAFIA

In the late fifties and early sixties, a few Air Force, Navy, and Marine officers came to the conclusion that the dominance of strategic nuclear thinking was sucking the life out of *real* airpower, and gathered in an informal fraternity of fighter pilots and other like-minded types, which came to be called the Fighter Mafia. Some were veterans of Korea, and membership was not confined to fighter pilots or weapons systems officers. It was attitude that mattered—if a man could think outside the narrow SAC box. Early on, they began to make their presence felt, and they grew in influence as the Vietnam War progressed, and as people started to realize how ineffective U.S. training and weapons were for fighting a conventional war. They peaked in the early seventies, when Chuck Horner arrived at the Pentagon.

Inside the Pentagon, the bureaucratic path from a bright, shiny new idea to its implementation in an actual working program involved coordination throughout the staff. People like Horner and his colleagues in Bill Kirk's office would have to walk the idea through various duchies in the Labyrinth to obtain signatures of approval—approvals that many of the dukes were loath to give, since every good new idea meant the death of some preexisting idea. Much of the staff felt threatened by anything new. It was a zero-sum situation: you get budget money for your idea; I lose money for mine. As a result, it was important to have people you could turn to. If you knew a fighter pilot in the office in which you needed to get your package coordinated, you would work out with him how to push your idea through the office without running into known problem officers or potential problem officers—those too inept to make a decision, and who would therefore sit on your package.

This was the Mafia. They helped each other and schemed about ways to move the Air Force, and they grew very skilled. Their main value was as critics and as conceptual thinkers about warfare. They proclaimed early, for instance, the importance of timely action versus executing a preordained, changeless plan, such as the SIOP. They realized that any plan might be out of date when the time came to act on it, owing to enemy actions or changes in the environment. They also made conceptual inputs to aircraft design. The F-16 can trace its roots back to original Mafia work, because it was they who argued for lower-cost, small, and agile fighters.

They were not always right. For instance, the small jet they envisioned would not even have a radar. In those days, radars were big and complex, which meant building big and complex aircraft. This in turn drove up the cost, since every pound of radar on a jet required six additional pounds of structure, which meant larger engines to carry the added weight, which meant fuel to give the larger engines an effective range, which meant more structure to hold the fuel, and so on. In order to escape this spiral, they maintained, stop it at the beginning: don't put radar in the nose of the jet.

In fact, this kind of solution was foolish, because radar is simply too valuable not to have in combat. During the Gulf War, for example, the overwhelming number of air-to-air kills were achieved using a radar-guided missile. The better solution was to make radars smaller, which is what happened. Over time, advances in radar and missile technology have allowed the F-16, with its small and relatively low cost, to evolve into the premier fighter aircraft in the world.

The Fighter Mafia began to lose its punch as more and more conventional force people began to populate the leadership positions in the Air Force, and as mainstream Air Force thinking began to concentrate on air superiority and conventional bomb dropping. Later, when Bill Creech arrived on the scene, the old, original Fighter Mafia (by this time aging, pre-Vietnam rebels) tried to maintain their separateness and their control by continuing to rebel, but now there was nothing to rebel against, and Creech simply put them in their place.

During Chuck Horner's tour in the Pentagon, however, the Fighter Mafia was a godsend*—and he felt their influence immediately in the push for Aggressor Training.

---

*SAC is today called STRATCOM and it remains in the ICBM missile silos and missile subs, but it has lost its onetime clout. Though there is still a CINCSTRATCOM to execute the SIOP, no one believes the Russians and Americans will destroy the world. Meanwhile, the SAC forces were merged with TAC forces into a command called Air Combat Command, or ACC. Today, the ACC headquarters is located at Langley AFB, Virginia, where the TAC headquarters was once located, and is mostly commanded by former TAC personnel.

The ICBMs themselves later came under the Commander, Air Force Space Command, since

AGGRESSOR TRAINING

Horner made his first appearance at the Pentagon on a Wednesday morning, and the first thing his new boss, Bill Kirk, asked him was what he thought about starting up an Aggressors program—that is, a force that could visit the wings all over the world and give them realistic air-to-air training. The idea was that they'd buy MiG-21s from a Third World nation who'd been equipped by the Soviets, train a few really good fighter pilots in Soviet tactics, then study how to use our fighter force to its best advantage.

Horner was enthusiastic, and elaborated on why it needed to be done. When he'd finished, Kirk smiled and handed him a message from General Momyer to General Jack Ryan, the Chief of Staff of the Air Force and a SAC man, who had passed the note down the chain of command to Kirk. Momyer's note to Ryan said, "I'll be up to see you on Friday to talk about starting Aggressor training," and in passing the note to Kirk, General Ryan had implied: "You better have something good for me."

Kirk asked Horner to prepare a paper that outlined options for Ryan to use on Friday, and Horner immediately found an empty desk in the basement and started developing his thoughts about dissimilar air combat training. The paper discussed the kinds of aircraft needed to emulate the most likely enemy (the MiG-21); the organization of a Soviet-style Aggressor force, schooled in Soviet tactics and doctrine; and three optional force structure packages. After some rewriting at Kirk's direction, Kirk then called in a Mafia person from Forces Branch, who costed out Horner's options and helped him work out where to find the equipment and personnel to build this force. Together, they put together a package that recommended taking a small number of excess pilots, training them in T-38s (later F-5s), and assigning them to Nellis to form an initial Aggressor squadron. They further identified the source of money for the squadron and the types of training they would accomplish. The Aggres-

---

ICBM technology and space launcher technology are the same, while the strategic MFP-1 forces (nuclear missiles, boomer subs, and, when on alert, bombers) are now under the operational command of CINCSTRAT. The MFP-1 air defense forces are all now in the Air National Guard and come under CINCNORAD (one of Chuck Horner's last jobs on active duty) when on alert.

sors, like the Navy's Top Gun School in Miramar, California, would do air-to-air training, but they wouldn't do it only at one base, but would visit each fighter wing and give training over a two-week period.

By late that same Wednesday night, Horner had a package and a staff summary sheet ready to do battle for coordination. The next day, he took on the Pentagon. Horner and Jim Mirehouse, a Mafia lieutenant colonel who had flown Weasels with Horner, steered a tortuous course though the bosses and got the package coordinated through the variously reluctant offices. For instance, when the head of Air Force Programs, a lieutenant general, refused to sign off on the coordination, they waited until he went to lunch, so his deputy, a major general who despised him, could sign off on the package. There were other similar but lesser battles.

By 11:00 P.M. on Thursday, Horner had the package coordinated and delivered to the Chief of Staff's office; and the next morning, Momyer paid his visit. Afterward, the package was ready for pickup at the chief's front office. Attached to it was a two-inch-square piece of paper that said simply, "Do it. R."

The Air Force Chief of Staff had given the go-ahead for the Aggressors, despite his SAC prejudices. Later, when Horner appeared before General Hill so the general could program the aircraft into Nellis and authorize the money to man and operate the squadron, Hill flew into a towering rage. And yet, for all his shouts, he could not ignore that two-inch-square slip of paper that said, "Do it. R."

And so the Aggressors were born. It was a hugely successful program—as evidenced, for example, by the exchange ratios in Desert Storm.

RED FLAG

Red Flag came next. A vast scale-simulated combat exercise, based at Nellis and "fought" against Aggressors, it was primarily the creation of Moody Suter, a captain when he was at Nellis, and a major at the Pentagon. Suter, cocksure, irreverent, and boundlessly creative, had the face of a hunting hound, an overactive, not always orderly mind, and a brash confidence that never endeared him to the Air Force brass. Though all of his ideas were brilliant, many were too radical to be implemented. Either way, he worked and worried his ideas until they came to fruition . . . or else so enraged the senior leadership in the Air Force that he had to go into hiding until things calmed down.*

While Horner was still at Nellis, General Taylor had instigated a major study that envisaged an enormous training area using the combined Hill AFB and Nellis ranges. This area would include the airspace over the government land comprising half of the state of Utah and Nevada—enough room for a great many aircraft to maneuver with no interference from civilian airliners; enough room, also, to practice air refueling. The area would be open to supersonic flight and unrestricted military operations, from the ground up. It would have extensive radar coverage, including AWACS, so that pilots could debrief what went on during the simulated combat exercises. Live bombs would be dropped and missiles would be fired. There would be simulated SAM and AAA in the ground in the target areas. And the Aggressors who were not on the road giving training would be used to create an enemy air force.

After Horner left Nellis, Suter continued to work this program hard, developing the concept in operational details beyond the original engineering study. Later, in 1972, when Suter came to the Pentagon, Bill Kirk had him assigned to his office, and Suter brought this concept with him.

In October 1973, a new commander came to TAC, another SAC general named Bob Dixon, who was known as the Tidewater Alligator for his habit of tearing flesh from colonels and generals under his command (and from anyone else, for that matter; he was famous for indiscriminate hatred). Dixon had been in the Pentagon for years and was savvy about how to play the game there, and he was not about to let wild visionaries from Nellis sell him a pig with wings.

Before Suter and the others on the team wanted to take on Dixon, they built briefings aimed at selling the concept to the air staff. These came out of some telling creative analysis: at Korat and Ta Khli, the practice had been to give new pilots ten missions in the less dangerous southern parts of North Vietnam (in Route Packages I and II), where there were only a few SAMs and no MiGs. After gaining experience in those ten missions, they were ready to go "downtown"—to Route Package V, VIa, or VIb, which was Hanoi and its adjacent areas. When building the new Red Flag briefing team, the team used this experience to build a graph that showed

---

Suter died in 1997, but not before he was told that the Red Flag Complex at Nellis would be named in his honor.

loss rates and numbers of missions flown. What this graph said, in effect, was that the first ten missions a pilot flew were his most dangerous, and that if he could survive this without getting shot down, then his chance of survival significantly increased. "Why not give him the first ten combat missions over the Nellis-Hill ranges," the briefing went on to say, "where he can survive his mistakes and learn from his errors before the bullets and SAMs are real?"

Red Flag was taking shape conceptually. Meanwhile, however, it was running into bureaucratic problems. Though the Fighter Mafia had tried to push the idea up the chain at TAC, the support of colonels and generals leery of Dixon's temper was conspicuously absent.

It was time to pitch the concept to General Dixon. The job was to show him how this could be *his* idea.

At that point Moody Suter devised a scheme, which offered itself when the team received word that the Army's chief scientist was interested in battle lab training and emulation of combat to test Army systems. In other words, he was thinking about a land-warfare equivalent of what was becoming the Red Flag concept. (In time, the Army made this happen, with great success, at Fort Irwin in California.) Suter then slipped word to the scientist that the Air Force had been working on the exact concept he had in mind, and was busy developing a realistic training environment in the Nellis complex that would also be used for operational testing. Naturally, the scientist was very interested in learning more about the specifics of the Air Force program, and so he asked for a formal briefing. In point of fact, at that time they had no program, just a barebones concept that needed meat and structure. What they needed were slides, the chief props of a military briefing.

In due course, some graphics people who were also in the basement of the Pentagon began working with Suter and Horner to produce slides for the Army briefing. On the title slide, the head of the graphics section sketched a plain red flag, then used the logo on the subsequent slides. The "Red Flag" stuck, and so the program was named.

Now came the payoff to Suter's scheme: since Bill Kirk's team was going outside the Air Force to brief the Army, and since Nellis was owned by TAC (i.e., General Dixon), it was their duty to let General Dixon know what they were doing. This message implied much more than was stated: with the Army's "interest" in the proposed Red Flag program at Nellis came the implicit threat that the Army would want to start using

Nellis for their own battle lab, which could then grow to the Army own-
ing the base.

The result—and the whole point of the scheme—was that Dixon
asked to hear the briefing.

Suter put on his armor and took him on. Ferocious, but no fool,
Dixon clearly saw the merits of Red Flag. After the briefing, he told Suter
simply, "I've got it." Red Flag was airborne.

In its early days, Red Flag had predictable problems—too many
crashes, for instance. In time, however, everyone learned, the training
setup grew more realistic, and the young pilots realized they couldn't
take chances in combat. The safety record improved. It wasn't long before the Red Flag loss rate was lower than that of the normal home station training.

Over the years, range instrumentation also improved, and the Air
Force started to look at the integration of tactics and new equipment.
They discovered how to configure a strike package of bombers, fighter-
bombers, escorting fighters, rescue forces, Wild Weasels, and command
and control, which included AWACS, Rivet Joint (an EC-135 aircraft that
collected signals intelligence—"sigint"), and Compass Call (an EC-130
aircraft that not only collected sigint, but also jammed enemy signals between aircraft, their ground controllers, and their ground radar network).

In time, Red Flag also began to involve integrated flying operations
with Navy and Marine aircraft and with foreign air forces—French,
British, Korean, Saudi, Israeli, and German. Air Guard and Reserves also
flew in Red Flag, so that in the future, whenever a task force of USAF and
non-USAF fliers were brought together (whether in Desert Shield or some
Bright STAR exercise), they had no problem immediately integrating operations. Common terms and equipment were used, as were common
rules and tactics.

Desert Shield and Desert Storm went so easily in great part because
everyone had been there before. They had flown their first ten combat
sorties together and had already been indoctrinated as a team. It paid off,
not so much in terms of tactics development or even individual aircrew
training, but because the people had worked together and understood
one another.

★ It was while he was Assistant Deputy Commander for Operations to
the 4th Tactical Fighter Wing at Seymour Johnson in North Carolina

from 1976 to 1979 that Horner participated in his first Red Flag. Fresh from the Pentagon and a year at the National War College at Seymour Johnson, he worked for the DO, Colonel Harvey Kimsey, who worked for the wing commander, Colonel Bob Russ. It was a prime assignment, since it meant he was back flying, in F-4Es (then used in an air-to-air combat role). His job was to do whatever the DO didn't want to do. Since Kimsey was primarily interested in flying jets and didn't like paperwork, that left a great deal of work for his assistant, a situation that did not at all bother Horner, who was happy doing most of the jobs DOs do—looking after intelligence, tactics, standards/evaluation, plans, scheduling, and shops. The wing had three squadrons of twenty-four aircraft and thirty pilots, commanded by lieutenant colonels. Horner planned exercises and monitored flying, both by watching the schedule and by flying with each of the squadrons.

For his first Red Flag, Horner commanded two squadrons from his home base. General Hartinger,* Ninth Air Force Commander, also assigned him another job: he was to be the man responsible (officially: the Ninth Air Force Senior Representative). In other words, if there was an accident at Red Flag, then he expected Horner to explain it. As a result, while Horner commanded only the primary unit, the two squadrons from Seymour Johnson, he was responsible to the Ninth Air Force commander for everything that went on; and if anything went wrong, God help his career. Since the threat of hanging tends to focus one's attention, he made sure he sat in on the briefings and planning, spoke up if he sensed someone was going to do something stupid, and sent people home who didn't play by the rules. The result: everything went smoothly.

In time, Horner flew in more than his share of Red Flags, and he learned there many things. For instance, his long-held opinion about the absurdity of low-level penetration of enemy defenses was reinforced at first hand at a Red Flag in January 1977. His squadrons were playing the role of red air (enemy air) in F-4Es, while blue air F-111s were trying to sneak in on the deck. These particular F-4Es were equipped with TISEO, a TV telescope mounted on the left wing root that could be slaved to the radar. That way, on their radar screen, pilots could see a TV picture of the target they were locked into, which allowed visual ID of the target while it was still beyond eyeball range. Using TISEO, pilots could tell the

---

*Called "The Grr," and the father of "Little Grr," Horner's aide in 1990 when he was himself Ninth Air Force Commander.

type of aircraft they were facing at sufficient distance to launch an AIM-7 medium-range missile in a head-to-head engagement, closing at a total speed of 1,000 to 1,300 knots. The 111s themselves, with their distinctive, ungainly look, were easy to spot; and because they were flying close off the ground, visual acquisition was a snap. Then, for Horner's red team, it became just a matter of gaining sufficient smash (airspeed) to convert on them and film them with gun cameras. "It wasn't unlike shooting strafe at a banner," Horner remembers, "except in this case the target was moving at six hundred knots over the ground at fifty or a hundred feet. Just stay above the target and you won't hit the ground."

Pilots learned other basic lessons at Red Flags, as well: how to evaluate their situation in the confusion of combat (even as some people were talking too much on the radio, and others were talking too little); the necessity of looking after their wingmen and of herding a flight into the target and then into the return without soaking up fatal shots (even if they were only on video recorders); the necessity of using simple conservative tactics, so all can cope when the plan does not unfold as expected; the necessity of keeping situational awareness, even as hundreds of aircraft are swirling every which way at supersonic speeds; and the difficulty of finding the target and bombing accurately when a pilot's radar warning receiver is screaming in his ear that he is going to die in a few seconds unless he does something (most likely what he is already doing).

Though Red Flags did not totally replicate combat, they definitely caused pressures that resulted in the same adrenaline flow and the same cotton-mouthed feeling.

THE GCC SYSTEM

Finally, the GCC—Graduated Combat Capability—system, like Aggressor Training and Red Flag, was another way to train the way they planned to fight. To make this a reality on a day-to-day basis, standards were devised and an accounting system established: for a base to be combat-ready, so many sorties of a certain type had to be flown each quarter. For example, in an F-15 air-to-air wing, each pilot needed to fly X number of one-versus-one maneuvering, and Y number of multi-ship two-versus-two (or more) tactics missions. If a pilot then aimed for a higher level of readiness, he needed additional and more demanding missions.

The accounting system kept track of aircrew training activity and quality, in order to define the combat readiness of the force. More experienced pilots were given lower requirements. Thus there were A-, B-, C-, and D-level pilots, based on their total fighter time, and time in the current aircraft (a fighter pilot with 1,500 hours total time, of which 300 hours was in his current jet, might be an A-level pilot, whereas a new pilot with 800 hours of fighter time might need 750 in the current jet to reach A level). The pilots then operated at three levels of combat readiness—basic, advanced, and ultimate. A pilot at the ultimate level was so experienced, and was flying at such a high rate, that he was certified combat-ready in any mission the jet was capable of performing.

THE BILL CREECH REVOLUTION

All of this new training was wonderfully effective, but it still didn't address the root, systemic causes of the Air Force's problems with morale and discipline. The men could fly better, but the legacy of Vietnam had taken its toll on military institutions, and the old leaders followed styles of command—fear and intimidation—that had been in vogue during World War II and Korea but were useless today.

These problems were compounded, once again, by SAC's dominion over the Air Force. To a SAC general, all bombers and bomber crews were interchangeable. Fighter generals played the team according to the strengths and weaknesses of the individual pilots and their individual jets, but there weren't enough fighter generals to make an impact on the culture at TAC. As a result, midlevel TAC leadership of Chuck Horner's age group had for the most part either died in the war or left the service to avoid that fate.

Pilots, in particular, were leaving the Air Force in droves. The reasons were clear: they had joined the Air Force to serve their nation flying jet aircraft. Instead, they would come to work at 5:00 A.M. to brief for a 7:00 A.M. takeoff, wait until 9:00 A.M. until three of the four scheduled aircraft were reported by maintenance to be actually ready to fly, and finally mount up on these three planes, only to find after they started them up that one of them was in fact not capable of safe flight. Meanwhile, since the two planes that got airborne did not have working fire-control radars, the crews burned holes in the sky in a valiant effort to fly out the wing's assigned number of hours.

The situation grew worse daily, and so, monthly and yearly, the flying-hour program was revised downward, in the hope of discovering the minimum level of flying operations that was supportable. It wasn't anybody's fault. There was no money for spare parts; maintenance mechanics were not trained, owing to the hemorrhaging caused by the lack of experience personnel; readiness reports were shaded to look good, so higher headquarters felt justified in reporting to their boss in Washington that the Air Force was ready to carry out its wartime mission.

Experienced pilots were sick of the false reporting, the meaningless ground jobs (designed to keep them busy when there were no aircraft to fly), and the seemingly endless tragedies, as young, inexperienced, and noncurrent pilots died in needless aircraft accidents.

The drug problem was endemic in the nation, so it was no surprise that it affected the military, too. But it was one thing to be high on drugs at a party, and another to be high while guarding nuclear weapons or maintaining jets.

A case in point:

In 1977, while Horner was at Seymour Johnson, home of not only a TAC wing but a Strategic Air Command bomber wing, special agents from the Air Force's Office of Special Investigations discovered a drug problem on the base. One night after a change of the guard mount assigned to protect the weapons-storage area, the security policemen turned in their weapons and left the building, intending to go home or back to the barracks. Instead they entered a waiting phalanx of lawyers and OSI agents, who proceeded to read Miranda rights to 151 of a total of 225 policemen. They then charged all 151 with use or possession of illegal drugs (in this case marijuana).

Another night a year later, at Luke AFB, where Horner was wing commander, OSI agents boarded the van used on the wing's flight line to transport mechanics out to the various F-15 fighter aircraft that needed maintenance. They arrested not only the van's driver for dealing in illegal drugs, but seven technicians who just happened to be taking a "hit" before going to work in the vitals of a $30 million jet.

There was a race problem, too, but race was not as serious an issue in the Air Force as it was in the nation as a whole. Racial polarization in the Air Force setting was in reality a reflection of the alienation of the young from the officers and NCOs. A unit that had pride and discipline did not tolerate racial polarization, because they were a team. Unfortunately, there were all too few teams.

Chuck Horner takes up the story:

The lack of retention of trained mechanics and aircrews, the drugs, and the apparent lack of defense funding were the excuses. But the real reason we were on our ass was much simpler: we had lost the vision of who we were, what was important, and how to lead and how to follow, how to treat our people both with love and discipline and a sense of mission. In short, we had lost pride in ourselves. Pride is not arrogance. As Dizzy Dean said, "If you done it, it ain't bragging." Our "done it" was simply being ready to go to war, and in war to win.

Well, we weren't able to honestly claim we'd "done it." The result was we were living a lie and had lost our pride. Do not scoff at pride. For a military person, pride is vital. How else do you think we get people to work long days and weekends, leave their families at a moment's notice, endure living in tents and eating packaged food that no grocery store could sell, and do all that with minimum pay and the expectation that they might have to lay down their very lives? Military units live on pride, pride born of confidence in themselves and the man or woman on their left and right. Sure, they take pride in serving the nation, and they get goose bumps when they see its flag. But what really counts is pride in doing their job well, pride in their subordinates and leaders, and pride that their lives are spent serving a cause higher than themselves. After Vietnam, we tore pride down instead of building it. We lied about our readiness, we shortcut our maintenance, we chased our tails trying to fly more when in fact we flew less, our aircraft were dirty and broken and they looked broken, we dumped our people in housing that wasn't habitable, our pay was frozen (in an effort to halt inflation), and our troops worked in temporary buildings left over from World War II that would have embarrassed any Third World slum. Discipline along with pride had fallen by the wayside, so the good ones walked and the feeble ones turned to drugs. We had become a Communist nation within the very organization that was to protect our nation from the threat of communism.

★ Then, in 1978, General W. L. "Bill" Creech was appointed commander of TAC.

A onetime leader of the Skyblazers and Thunderbird acrobatic teams, Bill Creech was a consummately skilled and precise fighter pilot. After a tour as Director of Operations at the Nellis Fighter Weapons School, he'd served as the senior assistant to General Sweeney, the bomber pilot who then commanded TAC, and the author of those infamous impromptu phone calls. Though he never said an unkind word about General Sweeney, Creech took care never to emulate him. Above all, Bill Creech was a practical philosopher and psychologist. In analyzing problems, his philosophical side looked well beyond the obvious in a search for root causes; he then doggedly worked for ways to prevent things from going wrong again. As a psychologist, he was a student of human nature, seeking to understand why people made mistakes—not in order to rebuke them, but to find ways to change the environment that led to the failures.

He was eccentric, fastidious about his personal appearance, tireless in his search for excellence, and as demanding of himself as he was of others.

How did he begin to address the problems of the Air Force?

The essential Air Force vision has always remained the same: the application of force—quickly, precisely, violently, massively. Aircraft in the air doing whatever it takes to gain control of the air, putting weapons precisely on their targets, flying as safely as possible. Success in each of these areas can be measured. The data can be very precise. How many aircraft do you have flying (and not, for example, in the hangars being repaired)? How many hours are the pilots in the air learning their skills? How well are they learning those skills? How many bombs are on target? How many planes crashed per given period of time?

By any serious measure, the Air Force was not answering those questions satisfactorily, but why? What was preventing good, highly motivated people from doing the work that they passionately *wanted* to do?

The answer, Creech decided, was centralization, the top-down management structures so beloved of Robert McNamara and the SAC generals. Creech hated centralization, because it robbed the individual of ownership of his job, deprived him of responsibility, and destroyed his initiative. The people in the Air Force, he liked to say, had turned into

Russian workers: "We pretend to work and they pretend to pay us." For him, centralization was a fantasy based on the dream of a totally efficient institution, but it wrecked against the hard rocks of actual, everyday human personality and behavior. People simply didn't operate the way centralization expected and predicted they would.*

Every organization is made up of building blocks, and if the organization is running smoothly, these building blocks mesh smoothly together. The way centralization does it is to organize them from the top down, and functionally—that is, by functional specialty, and by the job done within that function. For instance, specialists are gathered together in centralized locations and sent to work on jobs as needed: electricians work together with other electricians, hydraulics specialists work with other hydraulics specialists, all parts are located in a centralized supply area, and so on.

Under this system, all jets and all the people who work on them are alike and interchangeable. The whole mass is rated, and individual success or failure is obscured. The basic rationale for this is "economies of scale": efficiency, cost savings, elimination of duplication.

When Bill Creech arrived at TAC Command, however, he found no hard data supporting any of these claims—in fact, quite the opposite. When all the electricians worked from a centralized shop, and were dispatched in trucks to service an entire wing's flight line (three squadrons of twenty-four aircraft apiece, a total of seventy-two fighters), there was a lot of travel, coordination, and paperwork involved. There were no economies of scale. With a centralized storage area, it took an average of three and a half hours from the time a part was ordered from the storage area to the time it was delivered to its customer. By then the technician who ordered it would have either moved on to another job, cooled his heels and drunk several cups of coffee with his buddies, perhaps lost interest in the job, or even conceivably forgotten the nature of the problem he was originally fixing. Out of the 4,000 TAC aircraft, 234 a day, on average, were what were called "hangar queens," those grounded for more than three weeks for supply or maintenance problems. Of those aircraft that broke in some way during a normal flight, only one out of five

---

*The following discussion very closely follows Bill Creech's analysis in his excellent book, The Five Pillars of TQM: How to Make Total Quality Management Work for You, Truman Talley Books/Dutton, 1994, pp. 126–138.

were flyable again on the day they broke. And overall mission-capable rates were at 50 percent or less. (By way of comparison, in the stress and high tempo of Desert Storm, mission-capable rates were at over 95 percent.)

The "functional fiefdoms" (as Creech called them) of electricians, supply, weapons specialists, and so on, were oriented, he discovered, *not* toward satisfying the needs of the primary product (the aircraft) and of the various subsidiary products and functions connected with keeping the aircraft in the air, but toward satisfying the needs of the organization. Also, because of the vertical orientation of these fiefdoms, they did not work easily or comfortably together with the other fiefdoms—they didn't mesh well with each other, as Creech put it.

> *"When's the last time you washed a* rental *car?"*
> —A SERGEANT IN CONVERSATION WITH BILL CREECH

What did Creech to do change TAC?

First he started an education campaign, and used hard data to persuade those who believed in centralized systems that they had failed. Meanwhile, he set up trial units as models of decentralization, and then he compared the two. Once the hard data had proved the superiority of decentralized systems, he began to put those systems in place throughout TAC.

He reshaped the basic building blocks from vertical to horizontal, and broke up the "functional fiefdoms." Flight line maintenance, for example, was organized and integrated into product-oriented squadron teams (and smaller), in which electricians, aircraft mechanics, and hydraulics specialists all worked together. Members of one specialty were given elementary training in other specialties, so they could help their colleagues out, when needed, and would also have a better sense of the *whole* problem. Now, instead of a centrally administered central supply complex, all supplies directly related to aircraft supply were moved to the flight line, together with "dedicated" supply specialists who were devoted only to their flight line customer. Small computers that kept track of inventories also helped.

The squadron teams each set their own goals and devised their own schedules. Each made its own decisions, all of them aimed at the final product—planes in the air.

Finally, each fighter aircraft now had a "dedicated crew chief," whose name was painted on the side of the aircraft. That aircraft was now "his" or "hers." They "owned" it. It was up to them to be responsible for decisions—including mistakes—rather than waiting for orders from headquarters. While they would surely help one another out if needed, and the various technical specialists within the squadron teams were available to help, their performance was judged on how their jet or flight or squadron unit performed. At the same time, they were given what they needed, including more training, to make their jet perform well.

In time, Creech's decentralizing led to real ownership and empowerment, real teamwork, clear-cut accountability (poor performance was now easy to track), and a system in which people were able to operate as humans and not as functions in some machine.

Problems began to be solved by the people closest to them, to be cut off at the source. The problem solvers were freed both to do it right and also to make mistakes. Mistakes *will* be made—the key is to try to prevent them from recurring, and the best way is to make sure they are self-correcting.

More practically, he attacked the root causes of TAC's lack of readiness: He closed sick units so there would be enough trained people and parts to make the better units healthy. He kicked the senior NCOs out of their air-conditioned offices, where they had migrated under the centralized style of management, and placed them out on the flight lines, where they were truly in charge. He expected combat flying proficiency from his colonels and generals, so confidence in combat leadership began to be restored among the warriors. He ruthlessly rooted out and destroyed procedures and processes designed to maintain control for its own sake. He dictated goals and standards, then built visible and understandable scorecards that rated what actually mattered (such as sorties flown or aircraft in commission). As he slowly moved to decentralized leadership, he raised the goals and standards ever higher, as each day the men and women who worked for him proved they could exceed even his expectations.

He also made sure these changes were built on a foundation of absolute truth. Lying, shading of the truth, and making excuses were completely unacceptable. To make that point clear throughout TAC, Creech made a number of highly visible "public executions."

Here is one example:

Before Creech, the great game among commanders was to tell higher headquarters they could accomplish what was asked of them, when in fact they knew they could not, either because they didn't have the training or the resources, or because the mission was impossible. In fact, any commander who told the truth was likely to be fired. Under these conditions, the best promised as little as they could get away with, and through their own individual efforts made their units perform adequately; and in that way they didn't have to shade the truth overly much. On the other hand, the worst commanders simply lied and juggled the books. Some commanders spoke up and told it like it actually was. If they were very intelligent and savvy, they were actually listened to, and some changes were made. Others, not so savvy, were fired for not being team players in what Chuck Horner calls "the grand hoax."

In the F-4D, for instance, there was a computer-based bomb-release system, called the Dive Toss System, that supposedly allowed the aircrews to drop bombs from high altitude and thus to stay out of most visually aimed ground fire. The problem was that the Dive Toss System didn't work.

Nevertheless, the training rules called for F-4D aircrews with this system to achieve bomb scores of a certain average—say, CEP (Circular Error Probable) of fifty feet. The aircrew would fly the aircraft out to a bombing range and drop a bomb using the Dive Toss System, the range crew would then score their bomb impacts, and that data would be amassed at the wing and reported to TAC. Unless a certain percentage of the crews achieved the desired CEP or higher, the wing was not judged combat-ready. Yet, achieving a satisfactory CEP was usually a gamble, either because crew training was often inadequate, or worse, because the bomb-release computer in the Dive Toss System was more often than not malfunctioning. That left the aircrews faced with a no-win situation: since the system was incapable of giving them a fifty-foot average CEP, everyone up to the wing commander had to lie, or else the wing commander would be fired (though sometimes the wing commander would fire the squadron commanders and the chief of maintenance instead).

That meant that a crew would roll in on the target and call the pass: "Two's in for a Dive Toss"; but they would set their switches for a manual release, get the proper sight picture for the dive angle, airspeed, and wind condition, then release the bomb and make an abrupt pull-up so their friend on the ground scoring the bombs would see a Dive Toss, and not a manual dive, maneuver. Often they would drop a bomb with an even smaller CEP, which made the wing look very, very good. The commander would duly be promoted. The only thing that suffered was integrity. The crews called the event Dive Cheat.

Meanwhile, the generals thought they had a superior combat capability in the Dive Toss System, a system that just got better and better the more it was used because as the crews dropped more and more manual bombs, they grew more and more accurate.

One day, one of the F-4D captains suffered an attack of conscience and sent an anonymous letter to Creech that described the Dive Cheat situation. As a result, Creech sent the TAC Director of Operations, Major General Larry Welch, to investigate.

When Welch arrived, everyone in the wing except the wing commander told the truth. However, the wing commander claimed he knew nothing about what was really going on, even though he was current in the jet, and knew how he was getting his own bomb scores and certainly how everyone else was getting theirs. Not only that, he tried to throw the blame on others. He might possibly have survived what followed if he'd at least said something like: "Yes, sir, General Creech, my guys cheated, and I cheated, but that is what you wanted us to do, and we hate you and ourselves for doing it." But he didn't. In consequence, Creech had him fired in view of all corners of TAC. Afterward, everyone got the message that there was a new way of doing business that depended on telling the truth, that bad news was acceptable if you had done your best and still failed, and that lying or shading the truth to look good were far worse than failing.

★ All of this restored pride. But that wasn't enough. Creech also insisted on raising standards of appearance. Pity the poor commander whose base was not clean and painted. If he had to, he went downtown and bought his own tools and paint. He paid attention to color—no Easter eggs, but earth tones pleasing to the eye, yet businesslike. He paid attention to military dress. Combat uniforms were fine, but they better be properly worn, neat, and clean (unless soiled from hard work). It wasn't just looks that a commander watched out for. He paid attention to his people, he moved among them and listened to them, learning from all ranks as they figured out how to do their jobs more efficiently and quickly. He paid attention to families, too (family support centers and child-care facilities, for instance), so that people could concentrate on their work. Most of all, he paid attention to discipline. Discipline is fundamental to the good order needed to succeed in combat, and fundamental to pride. Hard tests were given in the air, on the flight line, and in all the multitude of areas that are required to carry out wartime missions. There were no excuses: If you failed, it was because you needed training, and you got it. If you needed resources, they were found. If you were overextended, you were given time to grow. But if you lacked the necessary desire, leadership, or integrity to be in the new military, you were given the opportunity to succeed in civilian life.

RESULTS

Here are some of the before-and-after performance data of the Creech reforms at TAC:

- The on-average three and a half hours from the order of a part to its delivery shrank to eight minutes.
- Pilot training sorties were doubled, increasing pilot skills and readiness.
- The number of aircraft grounded for maintenance was reduced by 73 percent.
- Hangar queens were reduced from an average of 234 per day to only eight per day.
- Fighters that landed with problems were now fixed much more quickly. The rate of those repaired on the same day was improved by 270 percent. Where before one out of five were flyable again on the same day, now it was four out of five.
- The ability to generate sorties in combat more than doubled.

All of this was accomplished with ever more technically sophisticated aircraft, thus burying two myths: (1) that U.S. aircraft were *too* sophisticated, and (2) that technically sophisticated aircraft couldn't be kept in the air.

Chuck Horner takes up the story again:

What Creech did, what we did, was learn how to be an air force all over again. We learned first how to maintain aircraft and generate sorties, so our aircrews got enough quality training to be ready for combat. The average flying hours per month for our crews more than doubled, from less than ten to more than twenty. Pilots could now hit their targets, as bombing accuracy rose. And they could survive, as their aerial fighting skills were honed to levels previously considered unattainable. The equipment worked, because it was maintained with pride. Each crew chief was given ownership of his own jet, and his name was painted on the side along with the pilot's. It was his jet and he was responsible for its performance. If his jet wasn't ready to fly on time and in perfect condition, everyone knew who was responsible. So the crew chief would not accept excuses from the supply sergeant. If he couldn't get a part, he found a friend whose jet was down for scheduled maintenance and asked to borrow the part he needed. And he didn't have to ask the colonel's permission. The transaction was between the two owners of the jets (decentralization at work).

The base also had pride, as the hospital waiting rooms were neat and clean, and the dining hall was decorated tastefully, with plants and clean walls and floors. Our people were being treated the way they deserved, and they knew it and responded.

What you saw in Desert Storm was the legacy of Bill Creech. When F-16 squadrons of usually twenty-four aircraft flew over a hundred sorties in a single day, that was because his liberation of maintenance crews from idiotic rules created an environment where individual initiative counted. Each crew chief and his assistants brought to the Gulf pride of ownership of their own aircraft. Add the awareness that we were in a war for a worthy cause, and there was no stopping us. We had pride, productivity, purpose, and a sense of professional dedication.

Decentralization was the key. Each man and woman knew what was expected, and each in turn busted his or her ass not only to do their job, but to exceed our highest expectations. Bill Creech had shown us what we were capable of achieving, he had created an environment where failure was not even a factor, and he had given us back the pride we ourselves had given away in the turmoil of Vietnam. There is no doubt the technology you saw on the television screens during Desert Storm was impressive, but to under-

stand the victory, you have to understand the people who operated the bases, maintained the jets, and flew them into combat. You have to know the far-reaching fire Bill Creech lit in each and every one of us in the military services.

TRAINING IN LEADERSHIP

When the Creech Revolution began, Chuck Horner was a colonel. In those days, both his flying skills and his bureaucratic maneuvering skills were well developed; now it was as a leader, as a senior officer, that he had to grow and develop. The service academies, he likes to point out, educate and train top-flight lieutenants, but you learn—or fail to learn—how to be a general when you are a colonel. Only as a colonel do you have the responsibilities, the hard choices, the opportunities for success or failure, that can show you how to lead as a general.

In this stage of his life, Horner had help from a variety of officers senior to him—both good and bad—including, of course, Bill Creech himself.

His first wing commander at Seymour Johnson in 1976 was a good one, Colonel Bob Russ. Russ was hard to please, yet he wasn't reluctant to reward outstanding performance, while letting those who fell short know they'd done so. And his efforts didn't stop there; he devoted much of his time to training subordinates in what they needed to know to do their jobs, and ultimately to replace him. Though he was tough, he looked at each problem nonjudgmentally—"How did we get into this particular situation, how do we get out of it, and how do we prevent it from happening again?"—rather than looking for somebody to take the blame. When he could, he anticipated problems and fixed them before they occurred. Finally, because he let them bite off as much responsibility as they could swallow, people worked hard for him.

By contrast, at one point Horner was the vice commander to a brainy but thickheaded wing commander who treated his subordinates with contempt and built his career on the bodies of those he'd stabbed in the back, thus negating his very genuine intellectual gifts. Horner studied this man very carefully, and learned from him that most valuable lesson: how *not* to act. He did his best to handle people just the reverse of the way his boss did, and in doing so, he learned the even more important lesson: you've got to be yourself. If you are the commander, people don't care if you are tough, or mean, or kind, or gentle, but if you are tough one day and kind the next, they are miserable. If they don't know who you are going to be on any given day, then they don't know how to act.

Much of the rest of Chuck Horner's education in leadership came painfully . . . because it's painful to have your shortcomings pointed out, especially if you are a fighter pilot with a large ego. Beyond that, if you truly care about the consequences of your acts, then you feel miserable when you make a mistake. "Good people don't need to be screamed at," Horner observes now. "They feel far worse about their shortcomings than you can ever make them feel. On the other hand, the bad person doesn't care or understand, so screaming doesn't work there, either. And if you are wrong, the good subordinate will reject your leadership in the future. So you just point out the error, to make sure they've gotten it, then discuss how to present it in the future, to rebuild their self-confidence. And then, if they are worth training, you send them on their way to sin no more."

On one occasion, while he was at the 4th TFW, Horner led another aircraft from Seymour Johnson to Hill AFB in Utah to conduct low-level flying training. In North Carolina, fighter pilots were restricted to flying no lower than 500 feet above the ground, but since no one lived in the deserts south of the Great Salt Lake, they could drop down to fifty feet.

When they reached Hill, Horner's wingman flew with another flight leader who was already deployed there, and Horner flew with the other flight leader's wingman, who was qualified to fly at fifty feet. Their two-ship element took off first, and they proceeded along the low-level route, practicing formation flying and lookout at 480 to 540 knots and altitudes as low as the fifty-feet minimum. When they reached a mountain range southwest of Salt Lake City, they ran into weather, with clouds obscuring the mountain peaks, initiated a weather abort, climbed up through a hole in the clouds, and called the other element to let them know about the problem. "We'll meet you on the gunnery range en route home," they said as they signed off.

When the second two-ship element arrived in the mountains, the flight leader turned away from the wingman and started to climb. Unfortunately, he didn't climb rapidly enough, and the wingman, who was trying to keep the leader in sight, failed to maintain situational awareness and scraped a ridgeline in his flight path. The aircraft skipped off the ridge and barely impacted the ground, but hit hard enough to cause the aircraft to explode.

Later, Horner and members of a ground crew search party found the bodies and debris in a canyon about two miles away.

After the missing-man flyby, Lieutenant General Hartinger, the commander at Ninth Air Force, let Horner know that it was his negligence that had caused the accident. He had failed in his responsibility as the leader, and so had "murdered" the two crew members.

He was already feeling sorry for himself, loathing himself for his failure and for his part in the deaths. Hartinger's condemnation made it worse. "I'm working as hard as I can," he told himself. "And now this. This dumbass flight leader doesn't take care of his wingman. And, shit, that kills my career." But the self-pity only lasted until he realized that what "The Grr" had pasted on him was exactly right—an insight that was reinforced by Bill Kirk, who was the DO at Ninth Air Force at the time. Kirk gave it to him straight, and Horner had to agree, that he had flat-out failed, and that he could either give up, or pull himself up, admit his mistakes, and start over.

I was responsible for these deaths, for a variety of reasons, but mainly because I was the senior officer present. It's not the flight leader's fault. It's mine. I should have ordered the second element to abort the flight and climb when they were in the clear and not assume they'd know what to do when they hit the weather. I was at fault; I should not have made the mistake of passive leadership.

If you want responsibility, if you want the tough jobs, then you better be ready to stand up and take the criticism and all the anguish when things go wrong. If you can't take the blame—even for mistakes that are beyond your control—then you are not in a responsible job, no matter what the job title says. The big jobs involve risk of great personal criticism. The jobs worth having are the ones with the biggest downside, and if you don't admit your own mistakes, you are not worthy of the trust given to you.

I couldn't guarantee that I would never again fail. No one can. But I knew that to seek credit for a job well done while ducking the pain and disgrace of failure is not leadership. No more. I would not wear a hair shirt; that's not my way. But whenever someone

*under my command was hurt or killed, it was my fault and no ex-
cuses would be offered. They only atonement I could make was to
do my best to make sure we all learned why the accident occurred
and to prevent it from happening again. The only way to give
value to the sacrifice of a life either in combat or in peacetime
training, the only way to salvage some good out of such a terrible
loss, was to do everything in my power to see that it was never repeated.*

*I started to become a "hard" man about some things—espe-
cially about things that could get people hurt. I never minded risks
to myself, but I sure minded unnecessary risks to anyone who came
under my command. Others under my command died over the
years, but I blamed myself first and then searched for ways to keep
the same thing from happening again.*

I was learning to lead.

★ His next assignment was at Luke AFB (in Glendale, Arizona, near
Phoenix), in 1979, where he was Colonel Pete Kemp's vice commander
at the 58th Fighter Wing.

Horner met Bill Creech for the first time at Luke, and the two men
quickly discovered that they were both from Iowa—there are not too
many Iowans in the Air Force. Other than that, it's hard for Horner to
say why he caught Creech's notice. In fact, it's hard to imagine two more
different personalities. Creech is precise, careful, vain. Horner is wild,
outrageous, and sloppy. But notice him Creech did.

Chuck Horner takes up the thought:

*I have no idea what Creech liked about me. We were certainly
never what I would call friends, or even had very much in common, other than a love for flying and the Air Force (Creech loved
the joy of being a fighter pilot). So I avoided him as much as possible, and in the beginning, I even fought what he was trying to do.
But when I realized he was actually showing us how to succeed
and that is exactly what we wanted to do, I became one of his
biggest advocates.*

*For his part, he was often very hard on me (which was good for
me), and he was a giant pain in the ass (because he kept after details). Yet he gave me prime but challenging jobs, then made sure*

I worked my ass off. And in those jobs we did work hard to im-
prove things—to have better-looking jets, cleaner facilities, and to
take control of our own lives rather than ask for help without
doing anything to make things better on our own hook. As the
same time, I never tried to suck up to him and tried to be honest
and admit mistakes to him I did not need to reveal. Though I think
he liked that, I didn't actually do it to impress him. That is just my
way.

In the end, I think he judged me on the scorecard of our ac-
complishments, based on his awareness of what my NCOs thought
of how I was doing. But I will never know.

★ By the time Horner and Creech met, Creech was starting to make his
presence felt. One of Creech's notable qualities was his ability to know
virtually everything going on in his command. He was simply a powerful listener ("You've got to get your ear down at the other end of the
pipe," he liked to say); he was always on the phone, or taking trusted
sergeants and officers aside to get the straight story. His network of such
people was vast. Thus, he was well informed about the situation at the
58th Fighter Wing when Colonel Chuck Horner first arrived there.

The immediate challenge at the 58th was that the wing was so large,
encompassing F-104s, F-4s, F-15s, and F-5s, that it had to be split in two.
Horner was to be the commander of one of these new wings, which he
assumed would be the one containing F-4s and F-104s. Meanwhile, he assumed that the existing wing commander, Pete Kemp, who was current
in the F-15, would get the far more modern F-15/F-5 wing.

Since the F-4s and F-104s were far older than the F-5s and F15s and
needed better maintenance leadership, Horner worked hard to find the
best possible people for those aircraft. He wanted the best for his wing.

But then on the day before the split occurred, Pete Kemp was told
he was leaving for another job, and that Horner would command the
F-15/F-5 wing (now called the 405th Fighter Wing). After watching
Horner make all the right moves for the F-4s and F-104s, Creech had
moved him on to the challenge of making himself proficient in the more
up-to-date aircraft.

★ In 1980, Horner was sent again to Nellis AFB, but now as the wing
commander of the 474th TFW. In those days, the wing was equipped

with long-out-of-date F-4Ds, but in a few months it was scheduled to receive the newest F-16As. That meant that, once again, Creech was offering Horner a large challenge, as well as the chance to make himself proficient in still another up-to-date, top-of-the-line fighter. He was to become one of the handful of pilots proficient in both air-to-air and air-to-ground in the two finest fighter aircraft in the U.S. inventory.

Meanwhile, the 474th offered many additional challenges. Not only were they switching over to the F-16s, but they were also taking on the very demanding Rapid Reactor commitment, because they were pledged to NATO. They had to be ready to deploy hours quicker than any other wing in the Air Force; then they had to be certified in all the mission areas required for a wing stationed in Germany; and at the same time they had to maintain all the other worldwide capabilities of any other wing. The wing successfully handled the commitment, as well as the F-16 changeover, and then six months after taking on their first aircraft and pilots, they won the TAC F-16 gunnery title, while taking an Operational Readiness Inspection and a Nuclear Assurity Inspection. "The results that followed these huge efforts were because of the entire wing effort and were not just a Chuck Horner thing," Horner is quick to add. "I just had the privilege of being there at the time."

In fact, Horner was taking command—a process as natural to him as flying.

I like a big challenge. That's what motivates me. I like to be faced with a task that no one else can do—or at least do as well as I can in my own mind. On the other hand, I don't care a hoot about small tasks, tasks that strike me as mundane or trivial (even though I also understand that the mundane may be as important as anything else; Jonas Salk must have conducted millions of mundane tests and observations to create his vaccine for polio). So I would much rather be given command of a wing in transition than a wing where things are going smoothly, and my challenge would be to make it better (without having a lot of room to make that happen). For instance, I was always happier to command a wing that was transitioning out of an old, difficult-to-maintain aircraft, like the F-4D, into a modern aircraft.

What turns my key is fear of failure in the face of a great challenge. And what causes me to go into the idle mode is to be given something to do that really doesn't need much doing.

None of this means that I have any illusion that I am the reason the big job will get done. That's not my function: I am a cheerleader, a mender of faint souls; I'm the one who listens to contending views of the path, the method for the use of resources or the organization of effort, and then decides which way to go.

★ These facts were not lost on Bill Creech. In the Air Force, commands are doled out very selectively, and most higher officers get only one of them in their entire life. But Creech kept moving Horner: two wings, two air divisions, and an air defense weapons center—all command billets. Then, after two years on staff, he spent five and a half years commanding regular forces, and spent the last few years of his career as a unified commander.

As a commander, you only get things done through other people. You lead people, you manage things. And if you can't lead, you command. You order people to do what you want. Sometimes I had to order people; sometimes I just didn't have time to go through all the niceties that leadership demands and had to lay a little leather on somebody. But leadership is best.

When you lead, you have to create an environment where the leader is the chief server. That is to say, he is the one who makes it possible for everyone else to do their jobs. He provides the backup and the support. I saw command as an inverted pyramid. I was the lowest guy in the food chain and the airman was the highest guy in the food chain, and it was my job to make sure I was working for all those people as much as possible.

The environment you create as commander will also have other characteristics. For one thing, it has to suit your personality (so you don't go crazy); within it, you have to lay down realistic guidelines and goals (so people won't fall off the face of the earth and will know where they're going); yet it has to allow those under your command the freedom to do their best and most creative work. And then you have to trust yourself and everyone else to let all that happen.

★ For Horner, the leadership environment he liked to create tended to approach the edge of chaos . . . but a focused chaos. A "chaotic" style goes with the fighter-pilot ethos, partly because fighting in air-to-air battles is by definition chaotic; partly because a fighter pilot's quickness of mind thrives in situations where inputs are many and varied and come lightning-fast; and partly because fighter pilots are themselves notably chaotic.

Wherever I went, if I didn't find chaos, I made it. Or else I did outrageous things. Why? Because I was goddamned if I was going to let anybody control my life. And that was an outward sign of letting people know that this is an individual. It's a revenge against the uniformity of the military service.

★ Yet Horner brought chaos down to earth and made use of it.

If you impose control to bring about order, then you will snuff initiative. My job was to exploit professionals and to get them to produce their best. I had to focus them, while letting them be themselves. Sometimes this generated friction, conflicts, or even explosions. So be it. A little friction is the price you pay for getting everyone to feel free to act and to use their initiative and talents; and this was especially true of the highly spirited people I was usually lucky enough to command.

On the other hand, some kinds of friction can be nonproductive. So it's very important to create the kind of environment where people can dislike each other yet remain civil. You need an atmosphere where they can debate and where you can get the best arguments from them; yet you have to make sure they don't come to blows or fall into some kind of irrational rage. Sometimes my subordinates would gang up on me. And sometimes I'd arrange situations that would make that happen. When I saw people getting too diverted by personal differences, I would turn myself into the enemy—not by doing anything hostile, but normally by humor with a sting in it. . . . I had no plan here; it was just instinctive, situational; it was a gut thing.

I've learned to support my guts. I've learned to trust myself. Not that I always get it right. But you have to make decisions based on uncertainty. You have to make decisions when the evidence is not clear. The black-and-white decisions are easy to make; they're no-brainers. If what to do or where to go is so clear-cut that anybody can recognize what to do, then you don't need a leader to make a decision. The hard decisions are the ones where the results are fuzzy, and where there's no convincing rationale to tell you that one way is right and the other is wrong. What I learned is to go with my instincts, even when other people had equally valid arguments on the other side of the issue.

★ By the time he commanded the 47th TFW, Horner had come a long way toward internalizing and bringing to life these principles. He knew that he could create an environment where the NCOs and officers were permitted to tell the truth and give their unbiased opinion—and that his respect for them and trust in their judgment and integrity in those areas where they were experienced would lead them to make every effort to succeed and bring the unit along with them.

★ Horner's handling of his NCOs and officers was one of the most crucial aspects of his leadership.

Noncommissioned officers—sergeants—are the heart and soul of the Air Force. They run its day-to-day operations, and they are fiercely independent.

The NCO's job is to manage the enlisted force, lead and train the young airmen, and enforce discipline. Within that frame, they don't think a great deal about officers, except insofar as an officer can cause the NCO problems while he attempts to do his job. They love a good commander who gives them meaningful work to do, and they despise a commander who undermines the performance they are trying to enforce among the enlisted members of the wing. If a commander loses their respect, they'll dismiss him as useless and wait out his time in office in the hopes that a good commander will come along.

Pity the poor officer who loses their trust. They can kill an outfit's productivity and capacity just by doing little or nothing. They do not have to work against the commander, they only have to do the job as told . . . and the commander will not fly his sorties, pass his inspections, or win his war. On the other hand, the simple act of listening to their advice and their views pays huge dividends in gaining their respect and loyalty.

Another way to win their support is to fire the right NCO. It goes without saying that not all NCOs are good and productive. The NCOs know who is getting the job done and who is coasting, but they will never tell on a fellow NCO to an officer. Fortunately, good NCO leadership is easy to detect. The best NCO leader is usually so busy getting the job done that the commander can't even find him unless he scours the flight line or back shops. There he will find clues: a clean wheel and tire shop; a hangar floor so scrubbed you can eat dinner off it; an office filled with pride, military courtesy, and helpful airmen; a motor pool where the vehicles are in good operating condition and neatly parked in straight rows.

The NCO who tells you how to run the wing, or finds a thousand faults with the way his boss is doing the job, is likely to be one with weak leadership skills and a bad attitude, and he or she needs to go before it infects the rest of the organization. That is why it is important that a new wing commander fire the right NCO. If he targets the NCO who is not carrying his weight, and is an embarrassment to the other NCOs, that wing commander has it made; the NCO force will make sure he is a success. If the hapless new wing commander fires the NCO he should recognize as one of the unsung heroes, then the other NCOs will at best perform cautiously. Why should they try extra hard if their boss is too stupid to know the difference?

So when a commander sees a unit that's gone bad, he has to fire or reassign the leadership of the unit, firmly and without hysterics. It is the hardest thing to do in command, for he can never be certain that he has accurately identified the person truly responsible.

By way of illustration, Chuck Horner tells this story:

> When I took command of the 47th wing at Nellis, I made some immediate changes that upset a few people. For starters, I sent NCOs who had been sitting in air-conditioned offices out on the flight line, with instructions given in private, "You're going to do it right, or you're going to retire." Young airmen who'd been playing loose with how they wore their uniform, got their hair cut, or shined their shoes also came in for close scrutiny from the new wing commander; and if they needed to be sharpened, I stuck them verbally in the sharpener—to include also their NCO supervisors (in the event they had forgotten what we were all about).
>
> For a while, the wing went silent, while everyone decided if I was a good or bad commander. If I was to get their trust or loyalty, I had to earn it.

The first breakthrough came one day when one of the best NCOs in the unit pulled me aside and told me to keep it up. I asked what that meant, and he told me that I must be doing good, because of what he saw when he stopped for a beer in the Tiger Inn, the bar just outside the back gate at Nellis. While any of the NCOs might stop there for a beer en route home, it was a pretty wild place. The folks who usually hung out there were the malcontents and young men looking to get thrown in jail or out of the Air Force. So this good NCO told me that I must be doing it right because the walls of the bathroom cubicles were filled with graffiti about how much of a shit Colonel Horner was. "Colonel," my confidante said, "at least you are pissing off the right people."

To this day I am certain that I made mistakes. However, the wings I commanded all had measurably higher output, aircraft in commission rates, more sorties flown, and better inspection results, to name a few, so I must have been right more times than I was wrong. I know in my heart that at each base I had the NCO corps solidly behind me, making up for my lack of experience and providing the leadership I was not able to provide.

What I had was a deep desire to make the unit better. I walked the flight line that day and night. When I saw something that needed to be fixed, I made sure the person I gave the job to had the resources to get the job done. I used to lobby at the headquarters for construction supplies. I challenged my own maintenance people to fix their own work spaces so they were neat and clean. You'd be amazed how it makes people more productive if they have a shiny floor to work on in the hangar. The light is better under the aircraft, and people don't get oily when they have to go down on the floor. Same for dining halls, same for clubs, dorms, offices, every aspect of the work and housing area. You start at the flight line so everyone knows what is most important in the Air Force: getting the aircraft and pilots ready to go to war. But then you also pay attention to the toilets, so the troops have a decent place to relieve themselves. Ditto for the dorms; they have to be clean too, and we had a program to fix up the dorm rooms so they were not dingy, moldy, and overcrowded, with rusty showers, broken blinds, and missing fixtures and light covers. I expected very high perfor-

mance standards from the troops, but only because that is what they wanted from themselves.

I made sure I was their servant, and I made sure my officers felt the same way. It was a no-harm, no-foul environment. I listened to the NCOs, but was never afraid of them or unwilling to say, "Thank you very much for your view, I will take it under consideration. In the interim, get your ass out there and lead," and they did. All of us were working so hard to get the job done that we didn't worry about who was in charge. In reality, they were in charge, since they were the only ones who could bring about success.

Officers are different from NCOs in a lot of ways. First of all, they stand out more, so it's easier to see how they are performing, and then there are several classes of officers:

To start with, there are the young ones whom you're grooming, the lieutenants and the captains with a future in the Air Force. So you'll want them to be energetic. You want them to make mistakes, but you want to keep close supervision on them.

Then there are the career officers who rose up from NCO and who went to officers' training school. Though they might be smart and talented, their careers have time limits. They'll almost certainly never be promoted to command ranks, just because they don't have enough time. Even so, they're proud of being officers. It's a big deal for them, because they've done it on their own (nobody in their family ever went to college or had anything like a professional career). So if you treat them honorably and with great respect and encouragement, they'll give you fine, steady work. When they do screw up (or anyone else, for that matter), you chew their ass (I tried never to let a screwup go unpunished; letting them go creates apprehension and leaves things hanging out of balance).

Then you have the fast movers. You're hard as hell on them, because if they're worth a damn, they can withstand your withering blasts and profit from them. If they're not worth a damn, if they bullshit their way, you need to destroy them. You need to push them so hard that they fail, and fail totally. You want to get them the hell out of there, and they want to get the hell out of there and go someplace where they can suck up to somebody and get ahead.

★ By the time Chuck Horner was given his first command, the Horner family had grown to five: Susan had been born at RAF Mildenhall, in Suffolk, England; John at Seymour Johnson; and Nancy Jo came while Horner was serving in Washington. While the Air Force does not officially admit it, wives (and now spouses) are an integral part of their society. This is not a formal thing. Each wife is expected to find her own niche, and yet, even though the commanders' wives are not in charge, the younger ones tend to look to them for leadership. Life in the unit is much easier when the commander's spouse promotes harmony among the non-military side of the community.

Over the years that Chuck was growing as an Air Force officer, Mary Jo grew as an Air Force wife. During that time they'd frequently run into wives of senior officers who tried to wear their husbands' rank. That didn't work. Back when they came into the Air Force, there was still a stiff and formal relationship based on rank. Wives were expected to conform in such ways as wearing hats and gloves to the teas at the officers' club or to some senior wife's house when she was hosting a coffee. That pretty much died out during the sixties.

Mary Jo had a different approach. As they moved around from base to base to base, everyone liked her, because she was spontaneously enthusiastic and genuinely liked other people. She was strong enough not to put up with any guff from her commander—and later senior commander—husband, yet she was and remains a loving wife and capable mother. People came to bare their troubles to her, because they knew they wouldn't get the conventional response from her or a moralizing lecture. Often at night she would share their pain with Chuck—a husband got passed over for promotion, or Chuck had fired him, or the couple was facing a long separation because of a remote assignment. In a very real sense, they were in the job together, and each had a role to play.

Chuck Horner learned never to discount the role of the spouse in the military community. "You know immediately," he says, "when you have a dysfunctional spouse at work, especially if she is the wife of the commander. Common sense says you don't make a big deal of it, but you can't help but be aware. Sure, you always try to pick the best person for the job—man, woman, married, unmarried, working spouse, whatever.

Still, if you are choosing between two equal men to make a subordinate commander, and one has a wife who promotes harmony, and one has a wife who (for whatever reason) is constantly causing trouble, you may select the former, just because you have too much to do already and don't need any headaches caused by strife in the distaff side of the house."

GENERAL HORNER

Over the next years Horner commanded at four different bases, two air divisions, the Air Defense Weapons Center, and finally Ninth Air Force.

After commanding the 474th, he was promoted to brigadier general, and from 1981 to '83 he was a division commander over two wings at Holloman AFB in Alamogordo, New Mexico.

From Holloman, he moved to Tyndall AFB in Panama City, in the Florida Panhandle. There he commanded the Southeast Air Defense Regional Air Division. As division commander of the southeast region, he had responsibility for U.S. air defense from New Jersey to Texas. Active-duty and Air National Guard fighter squadrons under his command sat alert at bases along the coast from Houston to Cape May, while radar sites every two hundred miles or so were collocated with FAA radars and were netted to provide an air picture at the command headquarters in a large building in Tyndall.

Three months after starting the job at Tyndall, he was moved over to command of the Air Defense Weapons Center (also at Tyndall), a more interesting and important job. It involved transitioning the wing from F-106s to F-15s, operating the radar controllers school, operating the Gulf air-to-air missile testing ranges, conducting Red Flag–type air defense exercises, called Copper Flag, and operating a large fleet of T-33s for air targets and F-100/F-4 drones for shoot-down aerial targets.

Bill Creech retired during Horner's tour in that command, to be replaced by General Jerry O'Malley. Soon after he took over, however, O'Malley and his wife were killed in a plane crash, and Bob Russ became the new TAC commander.

Then, as a major general, Horner replaced Tony McPeak as the TAC Deputy Chief of Staff for Plans at Langley (where he had worked at TAC as a major). He was responsible for the beddown of the forces and for preparing input on such matters as the budget, manpower, doctrine, war plans, studies and analysis, and joint matters. He also worked closely with the Army at nearby Fort Monroe, where their doctrine effort was centered.

From there he moved to command of Ninth Air Force and CENTAF, where one bright day in August he was ordered out of the sky and to Shaw AFB, ready to begin the biggest challenge of his life. . . .

II
Shield
in the Sky

4

MISSION TO JEDDAH

Saturday, August 4th: it was time to fly to Camp David to brief President Bush and his chief advisers.

Well past midnight, Horner, Schwarzkopf, and the other Camp David pilgrims boarded a C-21 Learjet, the Air Force transport normally used by VIPs, for the flight to Andrews AFB. The trip was tense and uncomfortable. The seats were small and the jet was full, so legs cramped, necks and rear ends ached. Everyone was exhausted, on edge. Horner himself was anxious; the thought of briefing the President was unsettling . . . not because it frightened him, but because he wanted to get it right, and that made it difficult to relax.

The CINC eased his great bulk into the tiny seat and tried to sleep; he was so large, he seemed to take up the entire plane. Horner slipped into a backseat next to Admiral Grant Sharp, the CENTCOM J-5 (Director of Plans), and reviewed his slides.

Sharp, a tall, gentlemanly, naval surface officer with gray hair and glasses, was a quiet man who spoke in well-constructed, thought-out phrases. Though he was old Navy and loved the service (his father, also an admiral, had been the Commander in Chief, Pacific Forces), he seemed more academic than military, which put him at a disadvantage when dealing with the fiery and mercurial Schwarzkopf. Sharp liked order and thoughtful discourse and hated the CINC's tirades, while Schwarzkopf never warmed to scholarly types.

After a 4:00 A.M. touchdown at Andrews, they were driven across town to Wainwright Hall, the Distinguished Visitors Quarters at Fort Meyer on the Virginia side of the Potomac, and a five-minute drive from the Pentagon. At Wainwright, Horner grabbed a twenty-minute nap and a shower, which took away some of the cobwebs and grunge of the previous day and night.

Despite the antipathy of the ejection-seat technicians in the Life Support shop to storing clothes where they didn't belong, Horner habitually kept a shaving kit and blue, short-sleeve uniform tucked up in the canopy of his F-16. Pilots normally used an underwing baggage pod for carrying personal baggage, but the pod limited maneuvering to only three Gs; and since he'd set out Friday morning to fight F-15s, there was no way he was going to stand for that.

He took advantage of the kit and the uniform now and, looking as put together as circumstances allowed, everyone regrouped and got in the cars that were to take them to the helicopter pad on the south end of the Pentagon.

By the time they reached the pad, it was about 6:00 A.M. Shortly afterward, they were joined by the Chairman of the Joint Chiefs of Staff (and Horner's old National War College classmate), General Colin Powell, who radiated the warmth and humor that make everyone acquainted with him think of him as a best friend. After the greetings, Powell drew General Schwarzkopf aside for some last-minute coaching, to head off the chance that Secretary of Defense Richard Cheney or President Bush might reach conclusions at the briefing that he didn't approve.

In Chuck Horner's view, Colin Powell was a decent, honorable, intelligent, and genuinely likable man with unquestionable integrity who was also a brilliant schemer, manipulator, and political operator . . . and he had one serious flaw: he was Army through and through. He had never been able to admit the ascendancy of airpower. In Powell's mind, it all came down to a zero-sum game, expressed in a simple syllogism: if airpower was growing in importance, then land power must be decreasing. That was bad for the nation, however; consequently, he had to make sure that brakes were applied to the growth of airpower.

Secretary of Defense Dick Cheney, wearing cowboy boots, walked up to the pad a couple of minutes after General Powell, and immediately introduced himself to Horner with a warm handshake and a smile. The Secretary of Defense was of medium height and build, balding, neat, friendly, and, Horner quickly learned, a good listener. Until this morning, the two had never met.

As for Cheney, this was just another general, not even a slim or handsome one, whose shy Iowa mumblings were not likely to inspire a powerful first impression. "What do you call the Secretary of Defense?" Horner kept asking himself. "Mister Secretary? Boss? Dick? Your

Honor?" Yet, for his part, Horner liked what he saw: this man was smart, selfless, and straightforward.

Everyone soon piled into a fancy Marine helicopter for the trip to Camp David.

The low man on the totem pole has some advantages. For starters, he can observe; he doesn't have to show off who he is. So Horner relaxed in the helicopter and watched Schwarzkopf and Powell do a power dance together, as they worked to establish their territory and power base, and made sure that they were recognized for their expertise in military matters and that, in the meeting to come, the Defense Secretary wouldn't take off on his own. Though Cheney was in charge, the senior uniformed types (as always) did their best to keep the civilian leadership from making military decisions on their own.

Thus, Schwarzkopf's body language said to Powell, "You may be the Chairman, Colin, but the Middle East is my theater and I work for Secretary Cheney." Thanks to Goldwater-Nichols, the CINC had a direct, unmediated working connection with the Secretary of Defense, making the Chairman hardly more than an adviser—though an extremely powerful and influential one. Powell's body language, on the other hand, said to Schwarzkopf: "Norm, let me guide you through this political maze." And to Cheney: "Dick, don't reach any conclusions about using military force until I get a chance to convince you about what should be done. And for God's sake, don't go to Norm direct" . . . *despite* the chain of command. All the while, Horner wondered if his own body language said what he hoped it said: "Here's the Joe Cool fighter pilot delighted to have such a beautiful day to fly up and see George, Dan, and the boys in the cabinet. Hope they'll like Chuckie."

CAMP DAVID

Camp David turned out to be comfortable, but not luxurious—it had earth-tone colors, a musty odor (like a mostly vacant summer cabin), government-issue hardwood tables, overstuffed brown vinyl sofas, and brass lamps. Since the windows were small and looked out onto the surrounding forest, and their light was only partially supplemented by lamps on end tables, it was dim inside.

Soon after their arrival, Horner and Schwarzkopf went into the conference room to check it out before they had to perform—to reconnoiter the battlefield. As Horner remembers it, the room was wood-paneled, with a neutral-colored office-style carpet on the floor. The meeting table could hold about twenty to thirty people around it, and there were chairs along the walls for straphangers (like him). An overhead slide projector sat on a small table near the right forward edge of the main table, and a portable screen was parked a few feet away in a corner of the room.

While the CINC stepped out to find a breath mint (their mouths being in full rebellion against the previous night's coffee and stress), Horner was alone until the first attendee entered. He knew the face . . . it was remarkably youthful; the man looked to be about seventeen years old. True to his Iowa upbringing, Horner did as his mother taught, crossed the room, stuck out his hand, and said, "Hi, Dan, I'm Chuck," to the Vice President of the United States, Dan Quayle.

Even as his good humor and graciousness took hold, Quayle, like Cheney, probably figured, *I don't know who this odd general is, but I wonder how he made it past sergeant.* He shook Horner's hand, smiled warmly, and said, "Good to meet you, General," without adding, "Dumb shit," for which Horner mentally thanked him before retreating to a chair along the wall. He was soon joined there by Admiral Grant Sharp, who sat next to him.

Meanwhile, the rest of the high-level invitees entered the room—Secretary of State Jim Baker; CIA Director Judge William Webster; White House Chief of Staff John Sununu; National Security Adviser General Brent Scowcroft; Dick Cheney and his deputy, Paul Wolfowitz, who sat immediately behind him; and a few others.

Last came President George Bush, chatting with Generals Powell and Schwarzkopf. Bush was dressed in slacks and a windbreaker, looking young and refreshed for a man who carried the burden of the nation. When the President appeared, Horner searched carefully for what detractors called his "wimp" factor—the limp, willowy New England boarding-school boy with high-toned, squeaky voice and goofy gestures. Nothing of that showed. To the contrary: the man Horner saw was a commander in chief, cordial, polite, but in charge. *Not bad,* Horner thought, thinking over his initial impressions of both Cheney and the President. *If we have to go to war, the civilian leaders we'll be working for can do the job.* He also remembered that the President had himself been a fighter pilot in the Navy in World War II, and knew what it was like to get hit and shot down. He was not surprised when, later, the President approached the day's deliberations with the visceral knowledge that comes from being shot at and hit.

As he passed through the room, Bush walked past Horner's chair and graciously reached for his hand, and Horner managed with surprising clarity, "Good morning, Mr. President, I'm Chuck Horner."

He added to himself, *Hooray, I didn't screw that one up.*

Soon the President, Powell, and Schwarzkopf took seats at the table and the meeting began.

The first business was a brief run-through of the CIA's estimate of the situation in Kuwait and the Persian Gulf region, which was given by Judge Webster. Since Schwarzkopf had better and more recent firsthand information, based on the telephone calls to his major trapped in the hotel across from the American Embassy in Kuwait City, he jumped in with it, clearly loving the fact that he could one-up the CIA.

Score one for the CINC, Horner thought to himself. *But shit, is this a tennis match?* The obvious maneuvering left him cold.

Schwarzkopf was then officially introduced. As he started his briefing, Horner said two quick prayers: first, for the CINC, that his message would be accurate, accepted, and lead to the right actions. Second, that he himself would not doze off after two F-16 flights the previous day and a night without sleep.

The first prayer was answered when Schwarzkopf proved to be as effective as Horner expected, as he used map outlines to show the possible axes of Iraqi attack—most likely down the coastal highway toward Dhahran—and the ways ground forces could be employed to stop it.

And it didn't take God long to answer the second prayer. Horner was soon in front of the slide projector, walking his way though the air component briefing. Though he was nervous, years of briefing very difficult generals about his failure to keep jets from hitting the ground and killing their pilots made this one easy. First, he talked about the size of the force they'd need (as it turned out, this would be about 30 percent of the actual war power finally deployed or at their disposal).* Then he talked

---

In fact, the situation changed dramatically between the time of the briefings and when the war became a reality. The greatest benefit of the Camp David briefings was to reassure the President that his military leaders were capable of reasonable planning and thinking. As it turned out, none of what Schwarzkopf and Horner briefed at Camp David came about: the Iraqis didn't come into Saudi Arabia in any significant way, the forces available to Schwarzkopf, both on the ground and in the air, increased significantly, and the battlefield in January and February of 1991 was far different from the battlefield they might have fought on in August 1990.

about how long it would take them to reach the Gulf and how soon they'd be ready to fight, if it came to that: about thirty-six hours to put the force in place, and another day to take the munitions out of prepositioning storage or off of ships on the way to the Gulf from Diego Garcia. Following that, he discussed the types of missions that would be flown against which targets, in the event the Iraqi Army came across the Saudi border (including types and amounts of munitions, sortie rates, levels of success expected, and possible losses). There would be, of course, direct attacks against the lead elements of the Iraqi armored force, but the strategy was to trade space for time, and therefore to attack the logistical support of the attackers—the fuel, ammo, food, and water supplies. As a result, while U.S. forces might seem to be losing in head-on engagements on the ground, the Iraqi Army would be starving itself to death, and at some point—a week or two?—their attack would grind to a halt and U.S. air would then attrit the remnants in the desert wastes of Saudi Arabia.

Following the briefing, questions were asked—the kind where the questioner already knows the answer but wants to let everyone else around the table see that he's present and accounted for. For the most part, however, these questions were not relevant, or even intelligent. "How are you going to give close air support to the Arab allies?" Answer: "The same way we give close air support to anybody else." To Horner, the procedure was more interesting than the questions themselves. First, Horner gave Powell and Schwarzkopf a chance to field the question, while they in turn waited for Cheney. Horner felt he looked a little dense standing up there, waiting ten or twenty seconds for the senior leaders to finish their waltz.

The silliest, most shallow queries mostly came from Chief of Staff John Sununu—*What's this idiot doing here?* Horner asked himself—but later, while watching CNN, he saw that the same "dumb" questions were the ones the reporters were asking, and his respect for Sununu grew. Sununu had simply been doing his job.

Meanwhile, Horner could see that Colin Powell was growing nervous that Horner was making "too good" a case for airpower—he had always found Powell easy to read—but the Chairman had such control of the meeting that he never came right out and said it.

At the first break in the questions, Horner took the opportunity to return to his seat against the wall to watch the debate that followed, primarily between State and Defense, the real centers of gravity that morning. Between those two, there was considerable staking-out of positions and ill-concealed hostility:

STATE: "Let's not rush into overt action that might make matters worse. We need to know more about what is going on over there."
DEFENSE: "We better get involved and ready to take action *before* matters get worse."

All of this discussion was open, freewheeling, and acrimonious in ways that set Horner wondering. Such open conflicts would *never* occur in a military conference, in which everyone bows to the senior officer and to the position they feel the commander has in mind. Yet he liked it. He liked to see people looking at the problem from a variety of angles. *In the military,* he thought, *it's too easy for everyone to back what they think the commander wants. So if you guess wrong and the boss is stupid, you strike out on two counts.* Horner called such things "school solutions"— like giving an answer in a classroom because you know the teacher endorses it.

During the discussion, the President scarcely spoke. He seemed detached, even lost in deeper contemplation, as the talk whirled around the table. It was clear that he wanted to hear what people had to say and didn't want to cast his shadow over the examination of the issues.

When he finally began to speak, two overriding concerns emerged: first, how to use military force against the Iraqis while keeping down the loss of life, and second, how to bring in other nations to form a coalition against Iraq (and thus avoid the arrogance of Vietnam). Chuck Horner easily identified with both concerns. It would have been hard for anyone who'd fought in Vietnam not to.

When Bush began raising the loss-of-life issue, Horner could see in his face and body language that it wasn't perception, or spin, or bad headlines he was worried about. It was about people bleeding and suffering. His personal anguish over the killing was unmistakably visible, and it wasn't just a question of U.S. lives, but of everybody's—U.S., Allied, and even Iraqi.

Horner—already in tune with those feelings—was pretty sure that Schwarzkopf felt the same way, but the others in the room seemed inclined to discuss the issues from a more distant standpoint—the way one would talk about putting out a new product, or taking out a line of credit. "What's the impact on our stock? What are the chances of success in the marketplace? What's the price of failure?" But the President saw that the discussion was about human life, and while he seemed willing to go down that road, he knew at a gut level the real price that would have to be paid.

The President's second set of concerns increased Horner's growing respect for him, for they represented a departure from the traditional American views of the world. Instead of marching in as the all-knowing Yanks, the President was saying: "We're not alone in the world. We need help and advice. We all have a problem, and let's see if we can all find a consensus about fixing it." It made Chuck Horner want to stand up and cheer.

Next, Bush moved on to practicalities: "What are we going to do about the invasion of Kuwait and the threat to Saudi Arabia?"

Baker continued to take the line that the United States must move cautiously. Powell's thinking was similar: "We have to protect our interests in the region, but let's not get into water that's over our heads." Cheney was most hawklike, but never outspokenly aggressive. His position was in tension with Baker's, but without acrimony.

To Horner, it all seemed like a lot of posturing with very little plain talk. It was what he called the "staff two-step." Everyone danced around the fact that they didn't have the slightest notion about a course of action. All the smart, articulate presidential advisers, unable to give a meaningful answer, seemed more concerned about avoiding the perception of being wrong than about working the problems.

Once that became clear to the President, which didn't take long, he asked Baker to consult with other world leaders. Bush already knew what Margaret Thatcher, the tough-minded prime minister of England, advised—he had spoken with her earlier in the week in Aspen, Colorado. She was all for kicking the Iraqis out. He planned shortly to call the French president, François Mitterand, to find out his views. "But what about King Fahd?" he asked. "After all, he is the one most threatened at this point." Here he struck a dry hole. The President's advisers simply repeated the positions they'd been taking all morning.

Then he turned to Cheney. "Dick, I want you to fly to Jeddah and talk to King Fahd. Find out what he thinks should be done."

And that was it. The room was cleared of outsiders, so the principals could carry on in private. To pass the time, Horner took a short tour of Camp David with Deputy Secretary of Defense Paul Wolfowitz. The two immediately warmed to each other. Wolfowitz was a power in the Pentagon, an insider with the Secretary of Defense and extremely smart, but a humble, thoughtful, approachable, good-humored man, who was just as interested in touring Camp David as Horner was. They were like a couple of starstruck tourists: "Gee, so this is the gym . . ." "Gee, here's where they watch TV . . ."

About the time the tour finished, the meeting of the advisers broke up. Their errand done, Horner and the others in Schwarzkopf's party hopped into the helicopter back to the Pentagon, then out to Andrews AFB and aboard the C-21 back to MacDill AFB.

GOODBYES

By that time, it was late afternoon, and Schwarzkopf dismissed the visibly worn-out Horner at planeside, thinking that his air commander would fly back home to South Carolina. However, a trip home wasn't possible that day, since he was out of what the Air Force calls "crew rest": an unbreakable rule—outside of war—says a pilot must have twelve hours of rest before he can fly. So Horner checked on his F-16, which was ready to go as always, then caught a ride over to the Visiting Officers Quarters to get some sleep, planning to fly home first thing the next morning. He was in bed by 7:00 P.M.

The phone rang. It was the Shaw AFB command post.

"General Horner, General Schwarzkopf asks that you call him secure."

He asked for the number, then realized he didn't have a secure phone in the VOQ room. Since General Schwarzkopf's house was only two blocks away, just in back of the base officers' club, he got up, dressed, and walked over. When he rang the bell, "BeBe" Bell, the CINC's executive officer, answered the door.

The CINC was holding a minimum-size staff meeting in the living room, and his mouth gaped when Horner walked in, thinking Horner had reappeared at MacDill via some *Star Trek* transporter beam.

His message to Horner was brief. Tomorrow the CINC was going to Saudi Arabia for a couple of days, and he wanted these people with him: his Army ground component commander, and old Arab hand, Lieutenant

General John Yeosock; his Air Force air component commander, Chuck Horner; and his planner, Admiral Grant Sharp. The flight was leaving from Andrews about noon.

"No problem."

"Keep the trip confidential," Schwarzkopf added. "And bring one other person."

Horner excused himself, ran back to the VOQ, and called Shaw AFB to set up a C-21 to leave about 10:00 A.M., to get him to Andrews by 11:30. As usual, he didn't tell his wife. He knew that if he did, she would have to keep the secret, which was very difficult for such an open, friendly person, so he decided to keep the burden away from her.

Besides, he said to himself with a laugh, *she thinks I'm an insensitive lout anyway.*

★ The next morning at dawn, Chuck Horner's F-16C leapt off the ground and soared up just as the orange ball of the sun broke the horizon.

Joy!

No matter how troubled he was, no matter how fearful or anxious, flying put his mind right. He couldn't take his troubles with him in the jet. There was no time for extra thoughts, no room for distractions as he slipped past the tumbling bright clouds and shielded his eyes from the sun, feeling the incredible union with the beautiful, sleek jet to which he was strapped.

Shaw AFB was asleep when he landed. After the transit alert crew chocked the *Lady Ashley* and put her covers on, he gave her a parting glance, not knowing then that he'd never fly *Lady Ashley* again.* He threw his flight helmet, parachute harness, and G suit in the trunk of his staff car and left.

The drive home took him around the base golf course, where hackers were already out on the front nine. He could understand their eagerness. It was a beautiful South Carolina morning, and the course was lovely. *Will I really be leaving all of this?* he asked himself. *And leaving Mary Jo yet one more time?* He thought of the demands pilots asked of their

---

*When he came home in April 1991, the wing had converted to new Block 40 F-16s. So there was a much newer and more reliable Lady Ashley. He has no idea what became of the original; he suspects she is parked in the desert getting dusty.

wives: "Take care of the home, raise our children, and face the emergencies alone, while we chase around the world. And always be ready for the visit—you know the one."

Mary Jo knows what's going on in Kuwait, he thought. *She knows I'm likely to go if a war starts. But it's still not fair to her.*

When Mary Jo met Chuck at the door, the questions started, as they always did when they met after an absence. But Horner could give her no answers. He was returning from a chat with the President of the United States and was about to leave home for an undetermined amount of time in a strange and distant country, but he still couldn't talk about it. She was still asking questions as they kissed hello. He told her he needed to pack some things, and she helped him pack enough underwear and clothes for a two-day trip. Nine months later, when he returned, the shorts were worn out. As he packed, he whistled and sang the way he always did when he was about to go off and slay dragons. Mary Jo always hated it when he packed, because she knew that she was going to be left behind.

★ When General Schwarzkopf told Horner he could take one person on the trip to Saudi, he probably expected him to bring his aide, Jim Hartinger, or his executive officer, Colonel George Gitchell. But Chuck Horner's thought process was different. He said to himself, *If you're going to a war, and you can only take one person, who would you take?*

The answer was obvious—his logistician. There are three kinds of staff people who are never heroes, but without whom a commander is dead in wartime: his intelligence, communications, and logistics chiefs. He can limp along in peacetime with less than capable people in those slots, but he's dead if there is any weakness there when the shooting starts. There is great truth in the old adage that amateur warriors study tactics, and that professionals study logistics. So Horner called his own command's logie, Colonel Bill Rider, and told him to pack his bags for the Middle East, and to be prepared for the deployment and beddown of some fighter squadrons in the CENTCOM area of responsibility.

"Yes, sir," he answered, "I'll meet you at the plane."

★ The next morning, Chuck Horner woke up the way he had many times before, eager as a bird dog before a hunt.

His goodbye kiss with Mary Jo was as special as he could make it. She still didn't know he was leaving for war, and he wasn't sure himself; but he couldn't get out of his head the times when he'd left for Vietnam. Each time they'd both had serious doubts about whether they would see each other again. When he'd gone as a "Wild Weasel," the odds had been high that he'd be killed or captured, leaving her with two kids and rapidly receding support from her Air Force family.

This day, he knew, was another such moment of truth in their marriage.

A terrible moment, as always. "There's no justice when you marry a military person," he observes. "Words are useless. So you just embrace and kiss each other. The pilot's anxious, nervous, and raring to go; and she's jealous because of all that, yet she loves him anyway, just as he loves what he does. Tears are not permitted. He can't cry because he's never learned how, and she can't because it hurts too much. Besides, there will be plenty of time later during the dreary loneliness she'll endure. So it's an 'I Love You' kiss, then he's off to somewhere that he can't even tell her, and she's off to play the organ at the nine o'clock Protestant service. He climbs in the car with a prayer, 'God give me time in Heaven to be a loving husband, because I sure as hell have been a shit to her on earth.' "

★ This is getting to be a habit, Horner thought when the C-21 disgorged him and Bill Rider at Andrews AFB.

Waiting in the distinguished visitor lounge was Lieutenant General John Yeosock, commander of the United States Third Army, which was the Central Command ground component, known as ARCENT. He, too, had the hunting dog look.

Yeosock was a soldier other soldiers referred to as "a piece of work." He had an IQ of about 140 and a homely face; he was totally selfless and impossible not to like. His only vice was cigars, expensive ones that came in metal tubes. John and Betta Yeosock had been at the National War College with the Horners and the Powells, and they'd all remained friends afterward. Even today, Horner and Yeosock still call Colin Powell "Your Highness."

Soon they went out to meet Schwarzkopf's assigned VC-135, a military version of a Boeing 707, from the 89th Airlift Wing. Then the three of them piled into a car and headed for the Pentagon. During the ride, Horner learned that confusion had already set in. Who was going to

Saudi Arabia? What was the agenda? What authority did they have to negotiate agreements? They didn't even know whose airplane they would take. As he listened to all this, Horner kept silent, but it seemed a little disorganized for a military operation.

Since it was Sunday morning, the Pentagon was almost empty. They went directly to Secretary Cheney's office, where Powell was waiting. As usual, the Chairman charmed everyone, especially Yeosock and Horner, because of their time in school together. A ready laugh, a hug; the man knew no strangers.

Then the discussion started. At first, it was, "Cheney's going. No, Powell's going. No, Cheney's going."

Then, "We're going to take Schwarzkopf's airplane. No, Cheney's airplane."

Why was there all the confusion and changes of mind, especially after Camp David, when the President clearly seemed to want Cheney to talk to King Fahd? Horner had no idea.

As the powerful flew in and out of the office and talked on the phone, Horner and Yeosock chatted, mostly about how confused and screwed up the powerful seemed. They both wondered what the Saudis would think about all this, especially considering that Americans often accused them of being slow to reach a decision. They'd probably get a laugh out of watching the Americans run around in circles.

Since smoking in government buildings was prohibited, Yeosock spent some time in the bathroom. You can reasonably assume it was thick with blue cigar smoke before he left.

Finally, the powerful came out of Cheney's office and seemed to know what was going to happen: Cheney would lead, and they'd go on his airplane. Colin Powell wished all of them the best of luck and they were off.

The trip to Jeddah was long and uneventful. The jet was a standard Boeing 707 that had been reconfigured with a private, simulated-wood-paneled "office" for VIPs just behind the cockpit. It took up about a third of the cabin space, with a double door opening toward the aft two-thirds of the aircraft; an aisle along the side of the aircraft connected the aft cabin with the plane's entrance behind the cockpit. The VIP office had large leather chairs, a sofa that opened up into a bed, a small desk, and a telephone hooked up to the communications panels forward in the cockpit area. This let the VIPs talk with anyone in the world on encrypted telephones with the highest levels of security. The lesser lights were seated behind the office in rows of large, comfortable, business class–type airliner seats. Aft of that was a small galley where a host of stewards heated frozen TV dinners (worse, if you can imagine, than standard airline meals).

During the flight, General Schwarzkopf frequently disappeared into Cheney's stateroom, and these visits fascinated the ordinary mortals. From where Horner sat, he could see the CINC through the open double doors squatting down next to the Secretary's easy chair, talking with great animation and intensity. Whatever they were talking about, the CINC chose not to reveal it, so Horner and Yeosock just chatted, read, and tried to get some rest.

JEDDAH

They landed in Jeddah at 4:00 P.M. on Monday, August 6, and a blast of hot air hit them the minute the aircraft door came open. It was a not totally unwelcome reminder to Horner that he was in a country that he loved and among people that he loved. He was looking forward to seeing and working with his friends again.

Chuck Horner relates how his association with the Arab world first began:

> Though I'd met a good many Arabs before 1981, the first senior Arab Air Force officer I got friendly with was a tall, taciturn brigadier general named Ahmed Behery, who was then the base commander at Taif.* By 1990, Behery had become commander of the RSAF, the Saudi Air Force.
>
> In 1981, Behery was escorting an energetic, fast-talking prince, whose name was Bandar bin Sultan (then a colonel in the Saudi Air Force and a pretty fair F-15 pilot, and more recently the Saudi ambassador to the United States and a major player in the Gulf War), on a visit to Nellis AFB. Major General Bob Kelly, the Fighter Weapons Center commander, held a garden party in their honor,

---

*Taif is the large city south of Mecca, a major stop on the ancient trade route running from Damascus in the north, through Jeddah, and into Yemen in the south. Because it is situated at about 3,000 feet above sea level in high desert, it is cooler than nearby Jeddah on the coast. The air base is quite modern, with new hardened shelters.

and the wing commander of the tenant wing at Nellis, the 474th TFW, Colonel Chuck Horner and his wife Mary Jo, were invited. The generals and host wing commander clustered around Bandar, who is extremely charming, and so I felt it wise to converse with the equally tall and distinguished, but much quieter, commander from Taif. Mary Jo and I walked over to him and introduced ourselves.

Behery is extremely shy, but not because other people frighten him. He is just reluctant to meet and greet. We made small talk for a while, until Mary Jo, in her blunt Iowa manner, broke in with some gripes against Arab men that had long rankled her. A particular incident still burned: During the days I was the wing commander at Williams AFB, we used to go to the graduation dinners for the foreign military sales training classes in the F-5E. At one of these, Mary Jo tried to strike up a conversation with an Arab student, either Saudi or Jordanian. Mary Jo is so open and friendly, it's hard for her to grasp how anyone can fail to respond to her overtures. So when this one did—he was off-puttingly distant, stiff, and unfriendly—she took that as a characteristic of the people. I suspect the man was more concerned that she was the wing commander's wife than that he was talking to a woman without a veil. Nonetheless, she came away with the idea that Arab men patronize women.

When Mary Jo concluded, "So you see, General Behery, Arab men are stuck up and snooty when they talk to me, and that's why I don't like to talk to them," he actually beamed with amusement. And his good humor remained as he explained to both of us why Arab men are somewhat aloof when dealing with Western women (they are not used to the aggressive behavior of strangers, especially women). Then, becoming quite serious, he gave us a nutshell lecture about the differences between the Arab and the Western view of women.

What he had to say was no surprise—the usual line that in his culture women are held in high esteem, much as they were in our South before the Civil War. For that reason, it is considered important to protect the sanctity of women, and ill-mannered for a man to talk directly to another man's wife. That is the reason for the veils and flowing garments. They protect women, he told us, much as one protects honey from flies by placing a cloth over the bowl. And yet he didn't stop there. The time he had spent in the United States had made him familiar enough with our culture to be aware that our women resented the kind of protection Arab men and women take for granted. He knew that what was protection for an Arab woman was suppression for an American. And he had no problems with that. In fact, Behery saw both cultures for what there were: both had good and bad elements. Good people in each culture who did the right thing for the right reasons would make each culture work, while bad people would screw things up, no matter where they were.

The conversation, which went on for hours, was a little revelation—not because he'd told us anything new, but because he was truthful, open, sensitive, and fair. I loved his honesty, insight, and understanding. Or as Bill Creech used to say, "You only get one chance to make a first impression." In this case, the impression Behery made was decidedly favorable.

Break Break. It was now seven years later. I had been told I was going to replace Bill Kirk as Ninth Air Force commander, but it had not been announced. Bill Kirk was about to take our boss, Bob Russ, around the Middle East, so Bob could see how the TAC men and women were living and serving in those countries: Egypt, Saudi Arabia, Bahrain, Oman, and Pakistan. Since this would become my beat, Bob took me along. While I was in Saudi, I met Behery again, and was even more impressed when I saw him on his own turf.

Americans have a tendency to look down on other people (I've done that myself). But when we meet foreigners who exceed our rather low opinion of what they should be, we tend to go too far in the other direction and get overawed by them. Let me tell you, all the Arab leaders that I met, colonel and above, were very impressive, and not because I was overawed—Turki at Dhahran, Sudairy in Riyadh, Henadi at RSAF, on and on. These men are truly exceptional individuals, regardless of where they are from.

In my journeys around Saudi Arabia, I found a far different country from ours. It's quiet, for one thing—a quiet that comes from the isolation; there aren't many people there; so for a New

Yorker it must be hell on earth, but for an Iowan it is natural. The food is strange but good. And I love the exotic customs and traditions, the extremely handsome architecture, the smells of spice. The weather is hot and dry, to be sure, but I can take that. You don't miss our television; and besides, you get to hear prayer call now and then during the day, especially before sunup and at sunset. This is beautiful, even though you don't understand the words. And finally, the tradition of the desert demands that hosts honor guests; there is nothing that competes with the welcome provided by an Arab host; he is delighted to honor his guest. Truly all that he has is at your disposal. Your home is his home.

Saudi Arabia is not my land or my home, but I have loved it more than I could love many of the places where I've visited or lived in my own country. A binding and genuine friendship with the Saudi land and people has grown steadily over the years and has touched me deeply.

After I took over Ninth Air Force, I made regular visits to the Middle East to visit my troops and see to their needs, to work issues associated with the prepositioned materials in the region, and to forge relationships with the leaders of the various nations' air forces. Sometimes these negotiations were very difficult, yet they were always carried on with mutual respect. Each side knew the other was only trying to do the best for his country—certainly an honorable motive.

I sensed, too, that they held (and still hold) the USAF in high respect, and I made sure we did nothing to weaken that esteem. So when one of our people committed an unlawful act, I took quick action—not primarily to come down hard on whoever was responsible, but to make sure that the countries involved know that Americans respect their national sovereignty.

In time I began to read all I could about the region and came to appreciate the long and rich history that goes back well before Europeans were still clubbing supper and living in skin shelters. I studied Islam and discovered its similarities with Judaism and Christianity. There is a common heritage that is lost when the doctrinaire types feud over ideas that are human interpretations of what God is all about, not what God thinks he is all about. Most significantly, I discovered that Arabs respect Americans because we

*work hard, we honor our own religion (or at least most of us do),
and because we have for the most part dealt with them honorably.*

*On numerous occasions in those years, I negotiated with the
various nations in the region about cooperation in the event of a
crisis there. And we were involved in a number of major operations, such as protection of the oil fields and refineries during the
Iran–Iraq War and the tanker reflagging and escort of Kuwaiti
tankers down the Arabian Gulf and through the Strait of Hormuz
during the time when the Iranian Revolutionary Guard were attacking them. I also helped out where I could: I spoke in their war
colleges, I attended joint and combined exercises in the region,
and I visited their people in the United States . . . little things and
big things, because it was my job and because it was the right thing
to do.*

*I soon became sensitive to the way Arabs have been presented
to the American people. Not well. It's another zero-sum game. Because we're pro-Israel (and I have no quarrel with that), we look
down on the Arabs. When was the last time Chuck Norris fought
a terrorist who wasn't Asian or Arab? Ignorant terms like "Islamic
fundamentalist terrorist" fill our newspapers—as though all Muslims were fundamentalists and terrorists. Sure, I have met Arabs I
don't like or trust. And there are as many dumb son-of-a-bitch
Arabs as there are in any culture, but the Arab military officers I
have worked with have earned my respect, and I hope they hold
me in the same regard.*

*Trust takes time, but when you have it, you have a wonderful
gift. I cannot tell you how binding the emotions are between me
and my close Saudi and other Arab friends; it is genuine and deep.*

★ Jeddah is located on the Red Sea about midway down the Saudi coast.
It is a large city, the capital of the westernmost province of the kingdom,
and the port of entry for pilgrims to the holy city of Mecca. The airport
is vast, and during the hajj, millions of travelers pass through it from all
over the world to travel to Mecca. It is a beautiful, majestic city, old and
new, with blue sky, blue water, and blue hazy mountains to the east. Its
mosques are lovely, quiet, and splendid. There are grand parks along the
waterfront, palm trees, and old buildings built out of huge blocks of
coral cut from the sea, their balconies decorated with delicate carved

wooden screens. A giant water fountain shoots water high into the air. The same sailing ships Arab seamen have used for centuries fill the harbor.

Because of its long history as a port, codes aren't enforced as strictly in Jeddah (or in Dhahran, on the Gulf) as in the interior. For example, foreign women are not harassed when their hair is uncovered as much as they are in Riyadh. And because of its proximity to the sea and to more moderate weather, the summer palace is located there—actually beside the sea, in a grove of date palms.

The American party descended the aircraft ramp past the Saudi honor guard and the ever-present television cameras with their satellite hookups. As always, CNN was there, which got a laugh from Horner. He couldn't tell his wife where he was going, yet when she turned on the morning news, there'd be her husband in Jeddah walking down the steps behind Secretary Cheney.

Soon they were in the Saudi VOQ, which was inland about ten blocks from the palace. Like the palace, the VOQ was surrounded by date palms, which provided much-needed shade from the glaring sun and gave cool relief from the hot ride in from the airport. Hot *gaua* followed by hot sweet tea was offered. Chuck Horner was home.

The *gaua* service followed ancient Bedouin custom. In the past, the desert dweller would roast green coffee beans over a camel-dung fire, and then grind the roasted beans with cardamom seeds and brew a greenish, sweetish, heavily flavored coffee in a distinctive long-spouted brass pot. Since water is so scarce, the coffee is served in tiny cups without handles, small enough to hide in the palm of one's hand. Maybe two tablespoons of coffee are drained with great flourish down the twelve-inch-long spout into a cup. This is offered first to the senior personage, then other cups are offered to each guest according to rank and status. He downs the boiling hot fluid in one or two gulps and holds the cup out again for seconds or to be collected. Normally, he takes only one or two cups, signaling the server that he's had enough by tipping the cup slightly. After the coffee, the server will return with a silver tray filled with small mugs of steaming hot tea, sweetened with two or more lumps of sugar. The taste of the tea will vary from area to area, depending on the local custom. But invariably, it is flavored with spearmint.

No matter how long a man has traveled, no matter how mysterious or strange the desert nation may seem, this simple ceremony, repeated every time he meets his Arab host at the airport, in his home, or even in his office, becomes the familiar opening that lets him know he is a welcome and honored guest. He is truly home.

When you are hosted by the king, you never go hungry. Sodas, juice, and dates and nuts were available in the VOQ rooms; dinner was served about eight; and Horner could call room service at any hour for anything else he wanted.

Sometime toward midnight—for that's when business in Saudi Arabia normally takes place—the U.S. delegation made the short trip over to King Fahd's palace. During the day, just as in the West, a visitor meets with his Saudi counterpart and talks over whatever subject is on his agenda. After nightfall, when things have had a chance to cool off, he gets together late and drinks tea and juice, and sometimes has dinner. Then, around midnight, he gets down to serious business and decisions are reached.

The trip to the Palace of the Defender of the Two Holy Mosques was a first for Horner. He'd heard it was splendid, and he was eager to check it out.

It turned out to be every bit as lovely as its reputation—with the usual Arab features: curving arches; brown, tan, or reddish-brown adobe; earth tones that blended in with the color of the surrounding desert; brick stairs; flowered tiles; fountains; and a glorious profusion of roses. The Saudis are especially astute at creating serenity and comfort in the midst of the beautiful but harsh desert in which they live.

While Horner and John Yeosock waited in an outer room, General Schwarzkopf and Secretary Cheney met with the King, joined by Chas Freeman, the U.S. Ambassador to Saudi Arabia, and Major General Don Kaufman,* the top U.S. military officer residing in the kingdom.

During that session, King Fahd made one of the most courageous, far-sighted decisions ever made by an Arab leader. The situation was clear. Iraq was in Kuwait, and much of the Kuwaiti population was in various Saudi Arabian hotels. The Iraqi army was on the border, and while it had not threatened to attack, no one could forget that Saddam had promised

---

*Kaufman was the Chief of the United States Military Training Mission (USMTM) to the Kingdom of Saudi Arabia. His job was to oversee the large number of important Foreign Military Sales (FMS) programs that were being executed between the two nations. He had a staff in Riyadh and people (military and contractor) scattered throughout the kingdom.

not to attack Kuwait either. All of this was a good argument to invite the help of the Americans and other friends.

On the other hand, asking in the Americans presented the Saudis with serious problems—not, as some people think, because the Saudis feared and rejected America and the West. That wasn't true. The Saudis admired and respected the West. Inviting in the Americans was problematic because Saudi Arabia was the most deeply fundamental Islamic nation. To the Saudis, fundamental Islam required them to stay as close to the teaching of the Holy Prophet and the Holy Koran as possible, and this required them to reject the aspects of our culture that, in their view, were offensive to God, such as pornography, drunkenness, and the like. They had no wish to encourage the spread of these vices inside their country. Like it or not, many Arabs viewed the people of the United States (including the U.S. military) as drunken, pot-smoking skirt-chasers. The ghost of Vietnam haunting us again.

So here was the King of Saudi Arabia trying to work out what to do after an army of brother Arabs had successfully invaded a neighboring brother country. As he gazed upon that ghastly situation, he couldn't help but ask himself, "Will my Arab brother attack me?" even as the ruler of the attacking country assured him that his armies meant no harm. So should he trust the good intentions of his admittedly treacherous brother, or should he invite a foreign legion of godless drunks and rapists to defend his people? It was one hell of a choice!

For a long time, the debate continued in Arabic between the King and his brothers, with Cheney, Schwarzkopf, Freeman, Wolfowitz, and a few other American representatives still in the room (since Freeman spoke Arabic, the main points of the debate were later reported to the others). On and on, with no clear answers. Then, at last, the King articulated very simply what he had probably had in mind ever since it had become clear that the United States was willing to offer military help. . . . Horner wasn't to know what that was, however, until after the meeting broke up.

As the American delegation left the Palace of the Defender of the Two Holy Mosques, everyone seemed unusually calm and peaceful. Cool breezes were blowing off the Red Sea, fountains sang in the courtyard. The only other sound was the chirp the tires made, like sneakers on marble, as the staff cars glided over the polished tile driveway. The delegation filed into the cars without speaking, everyone deep in thought, heavily troubled by what lay ahead.

Horner and Paul Wolfowitz climbed into the backseat of the car they were sharing. As they drove out the massive gates of the palace grounds, Horner quietly asked him how things had gone in the inner sanctum. "The King has asked us to come in and help," he said, with some wonder in his voice. "He said I've seen this nation come too far to have it destroyed."

It was as simple as that. Yet it meant that Chuck Horner was about to embark on nine of the most intense months of his life.

Back at the guest quarters, Secretary Cheney held a short staff meeting to discuss what needed to be done right away. Then everyone turned in for some well-needed rest.

Even though Horner was worried that the change in time zones and the adrenaline racing through his veins might make sleep impossible, for some reason he enjoyed one of the best nights of sleep he'd ever had. The decision had been made. Now all he had to do was execute his end of the operation.

The following morning the Americans met with the King's younger brother, Prince Sultan, the Minister of Defense and Aviation, the Arab equivalent of Cheney. After everyone filed into the vast, luxurious reception room (there was a light scent of rose water in the air), Prince Sultan took a seat in the corner in a large upholstered chair, Cheney sat to his right, while Prince Bandar stood between them to translate. (By this time, Bandar was the Saudi Ambassador to the United States; smart and devastatingly charming, he was the equal to Colin Powell at political maneuvering.) Prince Sultan, Bandar's father, was fluent enough in English to conduct the meeting in that language, but this was not the time for misunderstandings. Each word had to be carefully weighed before it was spoken; and then it was up to the former F-15 fighter pilot, Prince Bandar bin Sultan bin Abdullah Aziz, to make sure everyone understood what each side was agreeing to. Meanwhile, various Saudi military and the rest of the U.S. delegation took other chairs. Except for Sultan, all the Saudi military chiefs were in Riyadh.

Those in the room were tense and uncertain. They were in the first moments of a singularly important marriage, and the bride and groom were not sure they could get along . . . though they were more than willing to try. John Yeosock's and Chuck Horner's long experience in that part of the world—only Ambassador Chas Freeman knew the Arabs better—made them probably the most relaxed Americans there. They were familiar enough with Arabic not to totally depend on the translator; and, more important, they could read the facial expressions and body language of the Arabs, which allowed them to understand the emotions behind much of what was going on.

This is what the two sides agreed to that morning: the Saudis would open their bases and ports to U.S. military forces, and pay for the lion's share of the huge undertaking upon which both nations were embarking. The U.S. representatives promised that their forces would respect Saudi laws and culture, and would leave immediately when requested by their hosts. The United States had learned from Vietnam.

Once all this was settled, another question came up: who'd be in charge while the CINC returned to the States to start the great enterprise that would become Desert Shield? Someone had to be appointed as the United States' forward commander, to stay in the capital in Riyadh to organize and run things as the units and supplies arrived in-country—and to be in command of U.S. forces, in the CINC's absence, in the event of an Iraqi attack. After some discussion, General Schwarzkopf, sitting next to Secretary Cheney, pointed across the room to Lieutenant General Chuck Horner, USAF.

Two feelings hit Horner as he learned that for the next few weeks he was to be "CENTCOM Forward." First the big head—"Gee, I'm going to be in charge!"—swiftly followed by the more chilling realization that what he was in charge of could become a tremendous, tragic disaster. He thanked God silently for the presence of John Yeosock, Grant Sharp, and Don Kaufman, who were sitting beside him in that grand but somber meeting hall. Another prayer, never far from his lips, also came. "Please, God, keep me from screwing things up."

By midafternoon, Cheney and the others returning to Washington were at Jeddah's international airport, delivering last-minute instructions to those who were to stay in Saudi Arabia. No one there guessed that in six short months, this huge complex, called Jeddah New, the primary entry point for Islamic pilgrims making the hajj to the two holy cities of Mecca and Medina, would be wall-to-wall with B-52 bombers and KC-135 tankers.

Meanwhile, over two dozen battle-hardened Iraqi divisions stood at the border. Horner had at his disposal exactly two armored-car companies of Saudi National Guards.

In the windy afternoon heat, amid the bustle of loading and goodbyes,

Schwarzkopf and Horner stood on the airport ramp, at the foot of the stairs leading up to Cheney's 707, and discussed what needed to be done.

Among the points they talked about was campaign planning. "Since your staff will be disrupted packing up and deploying," Schwarzkopf said, "I'm going to ask the Joint Staff"—the planning staff of the JCS in the Pentagon—"to start work on a strategic air campaign plan." (Later this became the USAF staff in the Pentagon.)

The phrase "strategic air campaign" rang like Easter bells in Chuck Horner's head. The CINC was acting like a CINC and not like an Army general. Instead of talking about a ground campaign to repel an Iraqi invasion or to evict the Iraqis from Kuwait, he was talking strategic* air campaign.

What did that mean?

Most air campaign plans are put together at the behest of the Army, and the purpose of the Army is to defeat the enemy army. To an army person, air planning means using airpower to support his own operations. That is not the way an airman looks at it. To the airman, his job is to defeat the *enemy*—a job that may or may not include defeating an enemy army. Therefore, the Air Force code for use of airpower aimed at the heart of the enemy, and not at his ground forces, is strategic air campaign.

Back in April 1990, Horner had briefed Schwarzkopf about the need for a strategic air campaign plan in preparation for the planned July Internal Look exercise. The scenario there had been army-against-army, but Horner had wanted to show airpower as something beyond a ground support role, to expose his new boss to ways of thinking that would allow Horner to exercise airpower in a more productive and effective way. At the briefing, Horner had talked ballistic missile defense, close air support, how to work with Allied air forces, and how to use airpower "strategically." Schwarzkopf had liked the briefing and, as always, was sensitive to expanding his concept of airpower to complement his already vast understanding of land power.

Thus, when Schwarzkopf started talking right from the start about the need for a strategic air campaign plan, he showed that he remembered that briefing back in April. More important, in Chuck Horner's view, he showed that he had grown up—and away from—his Army roots.

For a moment, Horner was thrilled. How could he not be?

_____

*That is, for Horner, an "offensive" or "attack" air campaign.

But then the sounds in his head changed from Easter bells to Klaxons, and the ghosts of Vietnam assaulted him. "Washington? . . . the Pentagon? . . . Shit!" As soon as it dawned on him that the CINC intended to have the plans made in Washington, Horner went ballistic and shouted, "Okay, but we ain't picking the goddamn targets in Washington!"

Though his air component commander's anger caught him off guard, Schwarzkopf smiled. "Look, Chuck," he said, "you're *my* air boss, with final veto authority over everything connected with air. Any air plans will be 'presented' to you. We're going to plan and execute this war in the theater." He, too, remembered Vietnam.

The Joint Staff has its virtues, Horner was thinking, as he heard these words. It's even good at a few things. But it's best at compromise between the Army, Navy, Air Force, and Marine Corps. Any plan that is the product of compromise is bound to be mediocre. And any air plan that is built by anyone other than airmen is bound to be a disaster. Horner trusted that Schwarzkopf knew this in his guts and would ensure that any work started in Washington would be delivered to the fliers who had to execute it and succeed. He proved true to his word.

After the VIPs boarded their aircraft and headed home to America, Grant Sharp and Paul Wolfowitz left to tour the Gulf allies to consult, seek agreements, and secure support for the U.S. forces, while Ambassador Freeman, John Yeosock, his aide, Major Fong, Don Kaufman, Bill Rider, and Horner boarded a small, twin-engine C-12 prop plane operated by an outfit known as "GUTS Airline" (Greater USMTM* Transportation System—Kaufman's guys). Flying in this fragile-looking aircraft didn't bother Horner, but the Ambassador and Major Fong looked a little worried as they bounced into the hot desert air. Horner sat back in his seat as the noise from the props drowned out attempts at conversation, and tried to work out what he had to do.

Earlier, he had already started to unleash the flood of aerial reinforcements by notifying Bob Russ at TAC to get the 1st Tactical Fighter Wing F-15Cs headed east to supplement the Royal Saudi Air Force F-15s and Saudi AWACS who had been guarding the skies around the clock since the invasion.

The 1st Fighter Wing would be assigned the air-to-air missions, while the other wing, the 363d Fighter Wing, would be assigned primarily to

United States Military Training Mission.

do air-to-ground missions with their F-16C swing fighters. These were the two Ninth Air Force wings Horner had put on alert in July at the start of the crisis. For this, he had taken some heat from his bosses in the Air Force who were not in the CENTCOM chain of command. He also had the other Ninth Air Force units leaning forward.

Meanwhile, the Navy had a carrier task force headed for the Gulf, and Marines embarked on transports were also en route, as was Horner's good friend, Lieutenant General Gary Luck, with the lead elements of the XVIII Airborne Corps, primarily the paratroopers of the 82d Airborne Division.*

He then ran over where they would unload the Army and Marine Corps, as well as where to beddown the forces. *How do we house and feed them?* he asked himself, with the memory of the Beirut barracks bombing, where hundreds of Marines had lost their lives, still fresh in his mind. While Saudi Arabia was the safest nation in the world, some there would still side with Saddam Hussein. *What could they do to our forces as they deployed into the airfields and ports?* he asked himself. *And then as they moved to the bases and into the desert?* No matter how good the Saudi or U.S. forces were that were tasked to provide security, a single well-placed bomb could wipe out the deploying CENTCOM staff. Riyadh hotels were also an inviting target, vulnerable to a well-trained Iraqi special forces team.

If the threat of air or terrorist attack, or just plain accident (as in the crash of a troop-filled aircraft) weren't enough to give him pause, there were the growing numbers of Iraqi tanks and troops just over the border to the north. Consequently, the single most important question Horner had to ask himself in those dark days before his own forces were in place was *What will we do if the Iraqis come across the border tonight?* That particular night, any effective response would have been tough, since there wasn't much standing between the Iraqis and Riyadh but the Saudi Air Force and hundreds of miles of desert. If they'd come toward Riyadh

---

*Paratroopers are like fighter pilots, with a similar élan. And paratrooper generals have to jump out of perfectly good airplanes, just like sergeants. More practically, the commanders of the XVIII Airborne Corps and the Ninth Air Force have traditionally worked closely together. The Airborne headquarters at Fort Bragg is three hours up the road from Shaw AFB; assigned wings from Shaw provide airborne divisions with the jets they use for training (at Blue Flag and at CENTCOM exercises); and since the Airborne Corps is light, they depend on the Air Force for survival on the battlefield. Going through all of this together, Gary Luck and Chuck Horner had come to like and respect each other.

that night, Horner planned to drive to Jeddah and rent a boat. Each night thereafter, new and stronger forces were available to resist the invasion that never came.

Added to those questions were the more complex everyday problems of gaining the enthusiastic cooperation of all the host nations—not only Saudi Arabia but Bahrain, Qatar, the United Arab Emirates, Oman, and Egypt.

When one is doing business in the Middle East, the first requirement is patience. The American way is to focus on the heart of a problem, define a course of action, and implement the solution. In the Arab world, business is done more *gently*. Since personal relationships are all-important, business is conducted with a leisurely civility. A promise is given only after great deliberation, for once one's word is given, it *must* be kept. The Arab way is to discuss, consider, and avoid mistakes made in haste. The Arab way is to take time to understand all aspects of a situation; they have a deep aversion to making mistakes that could cause hard feelings between individuals, tribes, or nations. So Horner knew that all he needed was a couple of years to discuss how to beddown the oncoming troops, how to organize command arrangements, and who should accomplish which tasks, where, and when, in order make the deployment a success.

Time. Time was the real enemy. The desert summer of the Arabian Peninsula was a killer, and Iraqi intentions were unknown.

Sitting there in his aircraft seat, winging toward Riyadh, a hollow feeling came over him; fearful thoughts slithered through his brain. *I can't do it,* he told himself. *I'm not adequate. I won't get it right. No one's capable of meeting these challenges.*

Until it came to him, "I *don't have to succeed. John Yeosock, Bill Rider, and a host of others are here. I'm not alone. More important, none of us is alone. God's always present. So I'll trust in God.* Inshallah."

5

CENTCOM FORWARD

When they arrived at Riyadh Air Base, on the afternoon of Tuesday the seventh of August, Chuck Horner and the other Americans were greeted by Major General Harawi, the base commander and a friend of Horner's since his initial visit to the Kingdom in 1987. In their three years working together, he and Harawi had learned to solve issues "offline" that might have gotten stuck in both countries' bureaucracies if they'd been handled more formally. Meanwhile, Harawi spread the word that Horner could be trusted, which helped cement Horner's already growing friendship with General Behery, the RSAF chief, and a close friend of Harawi's. Among Arabs, friendship is everything.

The air base, now perched on the northeast corner of the city, had once served as the international airport, but modern hotels, apartment buildings, and shops spreading out of the old city center had crowded it, requiring the construction of a huge new facility, King Khalid International Airport, out in the desert well to the north.

General Harawi's base housed the Saudi Air Force E-3 AWACS aircraft, a C-130 squadron, and the Air Force academy, with its collocated flight training school. For almost ten years it had also hosted the USAF ELF-1 AWACS aircraft and tankers that flew out of Riyadh twenty four hours a day, and had provided early-warning radar coverage for the Saudi's eastern province during the Iran–Iraq War and the oil tanker convoy operation in 1988 and 1989.

During those years, Harawi had cared for a TDY family of about 1,000 U.S. Air Force men and women. If any of them had a run-in with the police or the *Mutawa*, the religious police force, Harawi got them out of it and sent back to the United States. Alternatively, if the hotel contractor tried to skimp on food or room services, Harawi paid him a call to remind him that the Saudi government was spending a great deal of money to make sure the USAF AWACS people were well taken care of during their stay in the kingdom. He had a major operation at Riyadh, and owing to its proximity to town, many VIPs used it, yet he looked after the American troops as if they were his own sons and daughters.*

Yeosock, Kaufman, Horner, and Harawi sat down in the elegant VIP reception lounge, with its cool, scented air, easeful light, splendid chandelier, and what seemed to be acres of blue-and-white Persian rug, while a tall, impassive Sudanese steward served *gaua* and sweet tea. In the coming months, the presidents and prime ministers, congressmen and parliamentarians who flocked to the Gulf to cheer and be seen with the troops of the coalition would all pass through this same impressive space. There they'd be served *gaua* and tea by the same impassive steward and be given the opportunity to make the transition from the rushed intensity of the West to the more measured pace of Saudi Arabia.

After a decent interval for small talk, Harawi probed Horner about events in occupied Kuwait and the other countries (many of them unfriendly) that bordered the Kingdom. What was happening in occupied Kuwait? Who'd gotten out and who'd gotten killed? What were the Iraqi forces doing? Would they attack or not attack? What was going to happen in Yemen and Sudan? On the adjacent seas? Like most Saudis, Harawi's primary source of information was rumors; the entire Kingdom lived on rumor. Information there was on very close hold, which meant that accurate information was *truly* valuable, and having such information gave the possessor great power. Even a two-star general such as Harawi was not in the top-level information loop, which meant that he had access to more rumors than news.

News was particularly important, because, unlike Americans, who think of threats from far away, Saudis thought of threats from a tight, immediate circle—Iraq, Iran, Yemen, or even Sudan. Their sensitivity was very acute, their fears very immediate.

Practically, in his capacity as Saudi AWACS commander, Harawi needed an accurate assessment of Iraqi intentions. His AWACS aircraft were maintaining twenty-four-hour coverage over the northeast. His immediate problem was that the single E-3 they had airborne (out of the five

---

*Because he was close to retirement and in fragile health (he was a diabetic), Harawi was replaced early in the crisis by General Iroky.

they owned*) could cover only a small sector at any one time (approximately one-fourth of the border), and the border between Iraq and Saudi Arabia was very long. This left gaps in the low-level radar coverage. If the Iraqi air force came south anywhere but in the east, the RSAF would have to depend on ground-based radar to pick up the attack. Harawi was worried that the Iraqis would take advantage of this weakness and make an attack on the kingdom—and Riyadh Air Base was a prime target.

After Horner had filled him in as best he could, and assured him that enough E-3s were on the way to fill his gap, the two friends said their goodbyes; then Kaufman, Yeosock, and Horner packed into a waiting car for the trip to MODA (the Ministry of Defense and Aviation) and a meeting with the heads of the Saudi military forces and their chairman, General Muhammad al-Hamad. Hamad, the Kingdom's only active-duty four-star general, was Colin Powell's counterpart.

Horner had known the tough but amiable soldier for well over three years, and made sure to call on him first thing whenever he visited the Kingdom. Their previous encounters had always been friendly, yet challenging. He wondered how this one would turn out.

Unlike Horner's counterparts, Behery and Harawi, who'd worked closely with him to solve practical, military cooperation problems, the job of the head of the Saudi military was to work the larger political-military picture. Specifically, he had to raise a modern military in a part of the world where there were real, immediate threats. For that, he needed U.S. help, though he was not always comfortable admitting it, or rather, he needed to be able to buy up-to-date American military equipment and training. Since the U.S. government had traditionally been acutely sensitive to the wishes of those who saw U.S. cooperation with Saudi Arabia as inimical to the best interests of Israel, the history of U.S.–Saudi military cooperation at Hamad's level had not been rosy.

As a result, whenever Hamad and Horner met, Hamad would welcome the American three-star warmly in English, a language he spoke perfectly. *Gaua* and tea, and talk of family and friends, would follow. Then he would switch to Arabic, to make sure his words were accurate, and, through a translator, give Horner a savage tongue-lashing—usually because the Congress was not acting on a military case of vital interest to Saudi Arabia. After the chewing-out, the talks would resume in Eng-

---

*A force of five allows one E-3 to be kept in the air at a time.

lish, with the tough Arab soldier wearing a broad smile and a twinkle in his eye. He would then wish Horner well and send him on his way. The routine never varied. Though he was dead serious, it was not personal. It was role-playing.

Why did he take shots at Horner? Because he was the closest American just then; and in the American setup you never knew who could really get things done. Hamad didn't know Horner from Adam in those prewar days, but he did know Horner outranked the two-star he had in his building who was the USMTM commander.

The car carrying the Americans passed through the air base's main gate, beyond which was a traffic circle. In the center of the circle was a large fountain. At one time the water had flowed out of the lip of a huge *gaua* pot, with four smaller *gaua* pots on the sides, and it thus became known as Teapot Circle. In 1989, the Saudis had torn the *gaua* pots down and put in a tiered water fountain with spray shooting out of the top—but it was still called Teapot Circle.

After swinging around the circle, the car headed south down Airport Boulevard toward the old city. Along this major artery was a complex of buildings that housed the Saudi military headquarters. Two blocks from the base was the MODA officers' club—rooms for guests, dining areas, athletic fields, and gyms for men and women. Although it was much larger than its American counterparts, it had all the features an American military officer might expect to find, save one. There was no bar.

Next to the MODA club was the United States Military Training Mission (USMTM) compound. This covered a city block, and was walled. Within the walls were offices, a club (also no bar), a soccer field, some small houses, and two high-rise apartment buildings where John Yeosock and Chuck Horner would room together for the next nine months. The job of USMTM was to administer the various foreign military sales contracts the United States had established with Saudi Arabia. There were Army, Navy, and Air Force sections, each with staffs ranging up to two hundred people, including those who instructed the Saudi military in the use of the equipment or in setting up the training programs they had purchased from the United States. For example, at the AWACS wing, there was a USAF cadre who lived in Saudi Arabia for a year or two and trained their Saudi counterparts in the operation and maintenance of the E-3 AWACS. The two-star commander of USMTM worked for the commander in chief of Central Command.

A few blocks down from the USMTM compound was the beautiful brown-and-blue marble headquarters of the Royal Saudi Air Force. Horner would make his office here after General Schwarzkopf arrived. Along the way were hotels and upscale shops, including a Holiday Inn just past Suicide Circle, the roundabout immediately south of the RSAF headquarters, and so called because to enter it was to take one's life in one's hands, and many old buildings in the process of being torn down. Farther down Airport Boulevard were the buildings that housed the Royal Saudi Land Forces (RSLF) and the Royal Saudi Naval Forces (RSNF). At last, the gleaming white MODA facility rose up on the right, about two and a half miles from the air base. It was a seven-story office building, with a high wall around it and a single square tower rising up in front. A much larger, three-winged building extended back from the street, and was backed by a five-tiered parking lot.

At about 3:00 P.M., the car carrying the American party turned in past the guards and into the parking garage in the rear. From there, they were escorted to General Hamad's office, where Hamad and the Saudi chiefs of services—land, sea, air, and air defense—were waiting.

During the walk through the lovely, spacious MODA complex, Don Kaufman offered a few suggestions:

First: the MODA building would be a good place for CENTCOM Headquarters.

A terrific idea, it instantly flashed on Horner. In that way, CENTCOM could be collocated with the Saudi JCS equivalent . . . and in so doing they'd be going a long way toward avoiding some of the major mistakes of Vietnam, where—except for some showcase "combined headquarters" and "liaison groups"—the Americans had remained apart from the South Vietnamese. Horner wanted everyone acting as one team: all equals, no "big brother come to save your ass" act.

Second: there was a newly completed underground command center at MODA; Horner should ask General Hamad to let CENTCOM use it.

Third: Horner would be welcome to use USMTM staff's small suite of rooms at MODA for his advance headquarters.

All three sounded so right to Horner that he enlisted Kaufman on the spot as his chief of staff.*

---

*Don Kaufman and his USMTM staff of military and civil service people played a vital role in getting U.S. efforts off the ground during these early days of Desert Shield. None of them are

A few moments later, they were shown into Hamad's conference room. Since the start of the crisis, Hamad had been meeting daily with his service chiefs; the Americans were now to be part of such a meeting. Around the large table sat Horner's closest Saudi friend, Lieutenant General Behery, head of the Royal Saudi Air Force. Next to him sat the Saudi land force commander, Lieutenant General Josuf Rashid, and the commander of the Saudi naval forces, Vice Admiral Talil Salem Al-Mofadhi. Also present was the head of MODA Plans and Operations, Major General Jousif Madani. And finally, to General Hamad's left, was a man Horner didn't yet know, Lieutenant General Khaled bin Sultan, who at the time was the commander of the Royal Saudi Air Defense Forces, and was soon to become the Saudi military commander and Schwarzkopf's coalition equal.

Khaled, another, older son of Prince Sultan, was a big man, well over six feet tall and weighing two hundred-plus pounds, with a black mustache and dark hair combed straight back. He'd attended Sandhurst, Great Britain's West Point, and spoke English and French fluently.

Khaled (as Horner was to learn very shortly) was a forceful man— probably due to his Sandhurst training. Instead of the bobbing-and-weaving style of most Arabs—who were so polite you couldn't tell what they were for or against—he was direct. With Khaled, you knew where you stood, which made it much easier to work with him than with most Arabs.

Everyone shook hands all around, and after some polite remarks, got down to business. Two or three people on the USMTM staff gave the group the same briefings Cheney had given the King, including intelligence photos. There wasn't much new there: the Iraqis were in Kuwait, much of Kuwait was in Saudi Arabia, and there were scarcely any serious military forces to stop the twenty-seven Iraqi divisions then in Kuwait from swinging south. For now, however, these seemed to be digging in on the border. The implication was that they weren't planning an immediate attack. On the other hand, a military person plans to counter capa-

---

even cited in the various postwar analyses, or otherwise recognized for their selfless service. Though torn away from their jobs of administering foreign military sales of United States training and equipment to Saudi military forces, they turned without complaint to feeding, housing, and supporting the onrushing tide of coalition forces. If they had not been in place throughout the kingdom, if they had not been trusted counterparts to the Saudi military leadership, the initial U.S. efforts would have failed.

bility and takes little solace in intent. The military has been fooled too often.

Horner then gave to the assembled Saudis a brief rundown of the visit to Jeddah—the reason for it, Bush's instruction to find out the King's needs and wishes, as well as some insight into what had taken place at the meeting with Sultan that morning and what was likely to happen during the next few weeks:

As a result of the King's invitation to U.S. military forces, U.S. Marines from the 7th Marine Expeditionary Brigade would soon be arriving in Jubail; meanwhile, the 82d Airborne would be moving into Dhahran, followed by the 24th Mechanized Infantry Division and the 101st Air Assault Division. Fighter squadrons would be going to every major Saudi air base. The 1st TFW F-15Cs and 552d AWCW E-3 AWACS aircraft were already en route. The Kingdom was about to receive hundreds of thousands of Americans: an urgent response to the military threat, but also an unwanted disruption to a culture vastly different from that of the United States.

Most of these generals had attended U.S. higher military schools at Fort Leavenworth or Maxwell AFB, so they understood the enormity of this deployment. However, none of them there—including Chuck Horner—had ever experienced such a movement in real life. He was ready for mass confusion, and he was not surprised when it hit full force.

At that point, the *number one* Saudi concern reared up. General Hamad broached it as if he were reading a script.

"Chuck, you're not going to deploy women, are you?"

It was more a plea than a question.

"General Hamad," Horner answered, "you know our services are totally integrated, that women make up ten to twenty percent of the units, and that even if we decided to prevent women from coming to the Kingdom, we couldn't do it because it would make our units combat-ineffective."

Hamad knew all this, and Horner knew he knew. They had worked this issue for the past ten years, as women assigned to AWACS had deployed to Saudi Arabia.

"Well, Chuck," General Hamad pleaded earnestly, "I know you are not going to let your women drive."

Here he was also well aware that women assigned to AWACS drove when they were on duty, in uniform, if their job required it. Sure, there were occasions when women drove while off duty or not in a uniform, but Horner had never heard about it, and therefore, in the logic of the Saudis, it didn't happen.

"General Hamad," Horner spoke softly, "these women will be leaving their homes, and in many cases their children, to come to the aid of your nation. Some of them may very well shed their blood, give up their lives in the defense of the Kingdom. If their military duties require them to drive, then of course they will drive."

For a time they were at an impasse, until the Land Force Commander, Josuf Rashid, came to the rescue. He asked some questions, his face stern but not angry. It was no time for warmth. There was too much to be done and too little time.

"Chuck, let me get this straight. You intend to deploy women as part of your forces?"

"Yes, sir," Horner replied.

"These women may have military duties that require them to drive cars and trucks?"

"Yes, sir."

"Will these women drive cars and trucks when off duty?"

Seeing where he was going, Horner replied immediately, "Of course not! Your laws and customs do not permit women to drive in the Kingdom, and we are sworn to obey your laws and respect your customs."

"Will these women wear uniforms when on duty?" he continued, apparently satisfied.

"Of course they will."

He smiled broadly. It was as if a curtain had parted. "General Hamad," he said, "you don't have a problem. Chuck is going to deploy women with the American units. They will respect our laws about driving. During the military duties, they may have to drive; but they will be in uniform, so they are not women, they are *soldiers.*"

Everyone nodded at this wisdom, and relief filled the room. The first crisis of the new alliance had been avoided.

On to the next crisis—this one instigated by Chuck Horner.

"General Hamad," he said, "I think we should collocate our military headquarters." He quickly added, "Could we look at your new command center in the basement as a place to set up the central combined headquarters?"

Discussing combined command arrangements this soon was very difficult for the Saudis to handle, but even more bothersome was the prospect of hundreds of American men and women in their new head-quarters building. Both Horner and Hamad were on uncertain ground . . . except that Horner was charging ahead, while Hamad was wondering how much he could agree to.

At that moment, the meeting switched to what Americans had come to call "Channel Two." When Arabs changed from English to Arabic, they were going to "Channel Two." Since Horner and the other Americans already had some experience in the Kingdom and knew some elements of the language, most of them could understand the general drift of a Channel Two discussion. This one seemed to go back and forth over two questions: whether to combine headquarters and whether to let the Americans in the building, especially the secret Command Center.

General Hamad picked up the phone and made a call, probably, Horner guessed, to check with his boss, Prince Sultan. A few brief words in Arabic indicated that General Hamad could not get through to His Royal Highness. Back to English and those at the table.

"Chuck," he said, "I don't know about using the command center. You see, it's brand new, and not all the phones and communication equipment are installed."

In Saudi Arabia, you seldom get a direct no. It is considered impolite. Instead, you hear excellent reasons why it is not possible at this time to reach a decision.

Just then, the man Horner had never met, the head of the Royal Saudi Arabian Air Defense Forces, Lieutenant General Khaled, went to Channel Two and delivered an outburst in Arabic to General Hamad. Horner roughly translates it as something like this:

"Boss, this is bullshit. The Iraqis are on the border, and we're fencing words about using one stupid command center. We need to get off our asses, and, with all due respect, sir, I'm going to see what can be done."

He then threw his notepad onto the table and charged out of the conference-room door. The room grew quiet, and for a while everyone talked about more mundane matters. But everyone around the table, including Horner, was more than a little dumbfounded by the force of his departure. Saudi Arabia is a most polite society, and the Arabs are extremely deferential toward officers of senior rank. In a second, Khaled went from a three-star general to a prince. And it took some time for everyone else to note the title change. When he reappeared and sat down, he was a subordinate general once more, but the prince had obviously made a phone call to put the train back on the track.

Next, as if by magic, General Hamad's phone rang. The conversation that followed took some time, and it was, at least on this end, very respectful. When Hamad hung up, he smiled and turned to Horner.

"Why don't we adjourn and go down and look at the command center?" he said.

Within minutes, the group was headed down the elevator to the two-story underground complex Horner would soon set up for General Schwarzkopf and his staff. Though he had no way of knowing it then, he would visit this command center every night he was in Riyadh, for the next very long nine months.

★ It goes without saying, that this meeting was important. It set the stage for Horner's own relations with the Saudis as Commander before General Schwarzkopf's arrival and as CENTAF Commander; and of course it had a large effect on the dynamic of U.S.-Saudi relations throughout the Gulf crisis. Even though the themes touched on that afternoon were few—women soldiers and use of the MODA Command Center—the consequences were large.

These themes, in fact, by metonymy, spoke for much, much more. They were focal points for a thousand other themes—telephones, rental cars, hotel rooms, basing, training ranges, port facility access, ramp space, airspace, storage areas, sharing of ammunition, on and on. Not the least of these issues was what military people call status of forces*—something never explicitly discussed but always in the back of everyone's minds. Fortunately, the USAF had been in the Kingdom for the past ten years, and the Air Force people had behaved themselves in an admirable manner. This trust built up over a decade made it possible for both parties to start the relationship without formal agreements, just the verbal agreements reached in Jeddah.

Nonetheless, there was real concern about all these Western troops barging into a deeply religious nation, a nation where customs changed very slowly and where no outside military force had been stationed

---

*Status of forces defines the legal relationship between forces deployed in a foreign country and the host government. It covers jurisdiction in legal matters, limits on carrying loaded weapons, obedience to local laws and customs, and the like.

since the overthrow of the Ottoman Empire. The women soldiers issue stood in for all that. It was, in reality, a status of forces agreement, and it said, "We will respect your laws, but you must understand that we are a force that recognizes a different role for women than your culture does."

The ground was broken. At that first meeting, the Americans and the Saudis tackled the tough issues with prudence and sensitivity, and that—along with the forceful leadership of General Khaled bin Sultan—enabled all that followed. If Horner had gone into that meeting and asked for 5,000 international telephone lines, 50,000 rental cars, and food for 500,000 troops, the Saudis would have gone into shock. Moreover, he had no idea then what he actually needed, and no one then could have estimated the final size of the force that deployed to conduct the liberation of Kuwait.

The command center issue was slightly different. Horner and his American colleagues worked that as an entrée to establishing a combined headquarters. If he had asked the Saudis to establish a combined command, they would have rejected the idea. Instead, he'd asked if he could move his headquarters in where theirs was. This de facto established a combined headquarters, without the direct request to do so.

SHEPHERDING CHAOS

The next few days were frantic.

Major Fong, John Yeosock's aide, moved Yeosock's and Horner's gear into the top floor of one of the buildings in the USMTM compound. Bill Rider, Horner's logistics chief, moved into the Saudi Air Force Headquarters and began to set up the air headquarters with the support of his RSAF counterpart, Major General Henadi, a man of great intellect and energy.*

Nothing went smoothly, yet everyone made do, and somehow forced everything to work.

One small example: the club manager at the USMTM compound went from serving thirty lunches a day to serving three thousand, all in a mat-

---

*General Henadi was also a devout Muslim, and he has spent many hours over the years (when there's time) instructing Horner in Islam, the Koran, and the teachings of the Prophet Mohammed.

ter of days. Everyone ate on paper plates and sat on the floor, but they survived.

Anyone walking into Horner's cramped offices in MODA in those difficult days would have gazed on what looked like absolute confusion, but that wasn't quite the reality. Confusion arises when you don't know what you are doing, and they did. There was simply so much to do, however, that everyone was always busy.

Meanwhile, the difficulties of deploying thousands of troops with their equipment were immense, even while speed was vital—the intentions of the Iraqis on the northern side of the Saudi border were still unknown. There was no time for rest, and twenty-hour days became the norm, with naps whenever possible.

In the meantime, Schwarzkopf was directing the sequence of deployments from his headquarters in Tampa, Florida. The thousands of miles between the United States and the Middle East were quickly spanned by an air bridge of immense capacity. Back home, they called it "the Aluminum Bridge." Around the clock, C-5 Galaxy and C-141 Starlifter aircraft were loading and taking off at bases all around the country. C-130 Hercules medium transports were beginning to head across the Atlantic, to distribute throughout Saudi Arabia, and the other countries of the Gulf Cooperation Council, all of the supplies and people that were being sent. The main hub was Riyadh, but the routes covered Saudi Arabia, Bahrain, the UAE, Qatar, Oman, and Egypt. It was not unlike the Klong Courier in Thailand. One "line," the Blue Ball Express, carried passengers, while the Red Ball Express carried cargo.

Despite everyone's best efforts, the next few days were utter chaos. The units back in the States were loading the equipment and supplies that they believed would be the most important, but their reporting system could not tell the people on the receiving end what would be dumped on the airport ramp or dockside in the Middle East; and no one knew where to send it to unload. In other words, the strategic airlift delivered their shipments to the wrong bases, and God only knew where equipment and supplies might be found.

Thus, a C-141 might take off from Pope AFB with 82d Airborne Division equipment on pallets. It would land in Spain or Germany to be unloaded, then part of the shipment would be loaded on a C-5, which would land at Riyadh. Meanwhile, the 82d was in Dhahran, in the northeast. So now the troops there were looking for their gear—which was sitting in a mountain of containers on the base at Riyadh—and Transportation Command was listing it as being en route. Try that times ten thousand, and at a growing rate, and you get an idea of what was going on.

(The C-130s turned out to be invaluable in straightening out the strategic airlift mess. Bill Rider just had the loads dumped in theater, then, while people there straightened things out, he sent the big jets back for more.)

In addition, every day people would arrive with no idea of the location of their unit. Thousands of men and women would land, starved for sleep, half-frozen from the long airplane ride, only to emerge in the blistering hot desert, given bottles of water, and asked, "Who are you and where do you want to go?" Most did not have a clue (in which case, if you couldn't find your unit, you found someone who could use you until things got sorted out).

The pain and suffering the troops endured during the early deployment was beyond belief. At some locations, there was triple bunking—three people sharing a single bed or cot in eight-hour shifts. Later, more people were added to the schedule by making room for sleeping under the bed. The Arab hosts in Saudi Arabia, Egypt, Bahrain, Qatar, the United Arab Emirates, and Oman opened up their bases, schools, hangars, and homes to help out. Americans were being housed everywhere.

Yet there was caution. After the 1983 murder of 241 Marines in Beirut by a suicide bomber, hotels were seen as risky (especially by General Schwarzkopf, who had a mania against hotels, because of his fear of terrorists). Often a person would arrive late at night, get bused to a beautiful hotel, enjoy the luxury of a bath with a fine meal and television in an air-conditioned room, only to get dumped in the desert the next day. There were thousands of stories like this.

And there were many snafus—at customs checkpoints, for instance, where vital munitions convoys would be held up at a border by bureaucratic agents. Customs people in every country feel they work for nobody, and that everyone is a smuggler, but this is especially true in countries that forbid the drinking of alcohol and consider bra ads pornography. Better to be slow than to take any risks. A shipment of munitions? Those papers had better be in order.

Then there were the communications shortfalls. Americans are used to telephones and communications access. Now a soldier was deployed to a nation where he needed permission for an international telephone line. He landed and went to the nearest telephone, perhaps a few miles away, so he could call home. But he couldn't get an operator who knew who he was and where he was trying to call. His frustration level was instantly sky-high . . . even as he recalled what they'd told him when he'd boarded the aircraft about being ready to fight the minute he hit the ground.

★ One of the first deploying USAF units was a support group from the 363d Tactical Fighter Wing at Shaw AFB, South Carolina, who had been on alert to deploy since the crisis had begun. After their F-16s had roared off into the night, the maintenance teams had been loaded onto C-141s en route to who knew where. Hours later—all spent in the hold of a cramped, freezing cargo plane—they landed at midnight somewhere in the Arabian Gulf.

As it happened, their F-16s were at Al Dhafra, and this C-14 had landed at the old military base in Abu Dhabi, about ten miles away, because the ramp at Al Dhafra was full and could not accept them. Nobody in the airplane knew that.

Peering out the aircraft's door, the thirty men and women from the 363d found only a dark, empty parking ramp, with hellishly hot desert air blasting them in the face. In the distance, they could see the lights of a city.

They climbed down the boarding stairs, and somebody thrust bottled water at them. Not knowing what else to do, they stowed it somewhere, then turned their attention to unloading the equipment they carried on board—spare aircraft engines, toolboxes, weapons, and spare parts. Airpower, as the United States practices it, brings it all—enough for thirty days of fighting until the supply lifeline can be built.

Meanwhile, all around them were guys in white robes and scarves over their heads: pleasant guys, as it happened, who spoke excellent English, though not the drawling southern dialect these folks from South Carolina were used to.

Before long they learned that they'd landed in the Emirate of Abu Dhabi and were to be bused to Al Dhafra, the military air base near Abu Dhabi, the capital of the emirate with that name. They were quickly packed into a small but clean bus. Then they headed out on a multilane freeway into the desert night—away from the city! Unaccustomed to the

110°F nighttime heat (it was even hotter during the day, and more humid), they began to drink the bottled water that had been thrust at them earlier, grateful for the relief.

The bus driver, a nice fellow, was from Ethiopia and spoke very little English. After a time, he turned off the highway and onto a dirt road that quickly became part of the vast desert. Up and down they bounced, over sand dunes and rock-strewn waste, until finally the bus came to a halt. "All out here," the driver ordered. The miserable band, loaded down with duffel bags and personal weapons, straggled out of the bus and assembled somewhere in the hot desert nowhere. Then off went the bus.

At that point, the lieutenant in charge, a young man named Tom Barth, took charge. Charge of what? Charge of whom? Where? Going where? It was pitch black, and the questions from the others started coming. But no answers were apparent.

Soon wild desert dogs began to circle the group, attracted to the smell of food from a few MREs (Meals Ready to Eat—field rations of questionable taste) and leftover in-flight meals. The big question was who was most afraid of whom, but the people did a better job of bluffing, so the wild dogs kept their distance.

Later, from the direction of the city lights they could still see over the horizon, a white cloud started to form. Was it a gas attack from invading Iraqi forces?

Actually, no.

Though this hearty band didn't know it, they were in fact hundreds of miles south of Kuwait, just a few miles from the UAE coast, and they were observing the sea fog roll in. But just to be on the safe side, the lieutenant had everyone check their gas masks. Though their full chemical protection suits were loaded on the cargo pallets on the ramp next to the aircraft, they all carried a gas mask for just the threat that now seemed to be confronting them.

The fog did not reach them, but in the distance a new terror appeared—the lights of an oncoming car, bouncing from dune to dune. Up drove a dark Mercedes with tinted windows. Terrorists? It stopped, and the electric window slid noiselessly down. Tom Barth, fully aware that it was his responsibility to keep this band alive, ordered security policemen in the group to be ready to shoot, but to aim for the legs, in case this visitor wasn't *really* a terrorist. Gathering up all his courage, Barth stepped forward to the open window and peered in. There he found a swarthy man with a large black mustache and cold dark eyes, and wearing one of those white robes.

The driver looked at him. "Are you Lieutenant Barth?" he asked politely.

"Yes, I am. Why?" Barth answered, in his most manly manner, greatly relieved.

The driver brushed off his questions and handed Barth a cellular phone.

Composing himself, he spoke into it. "Hello, Lieutenant Barth."

Rapidly, an American on the other end replied, "Tom, where the *hell* are you?"

Though Barth had no clue, he did his best to explain. Finally, it was decided. They would just stay put, and someone would come and get them in the morning. Without a word, the Arab (just somebody from the UAE who was told to find the lost Americans) retrieved the phone, closed the tinted window, and drove off into the night, never knowing how close he came to being kneecapped by a terrified American Air Force lieutenant.

The next few hours passed slowly. There were complaints about how fucked up things were—and questions about where the women could go to the bathroom, because not all the bottled water turned into sweat. But then daybreak came, and all of a sudden, up drove the bus and the hugely smiling driver that had left them there the night before. He took the hearty band to a huge air base farther out in the desert, where they would spend the next few days sleeping on a hangar floor and eating MREs until Bill Rider could send tents and field kitchens to them.

They had plenty to do, as the F-16s from Shaw AFB needed to be turned around for combat air patrols or put on alert with air-to-ground munitions.

Everywhere it was the same—chaos—with everyone pitching in to help each other survive, build housing, and somehow come up with all the necessary comforts that Americans normally take for granted.

In those early days, only the locals—such as the Ethiopian bus driver—seemed to know what they were doing, though their reasons often mystified the Americans. Faced with the end of a long day and a craving to go home, he'd simply dropped his passengers off in the desert where he knew they couldn't get hurt or in trouble. When his duty day had ended—at midnight, in this case—he'd gone home to get a good night's sleep, picked them up the next morning, and taken them to the air base as instructed. *He* really didn't understand those strange Americans.

★ Most of the arriving troops came into Dhahran, a huge Saudi Air Force base on the eastern coast. Its commander, Brigadier General Turki bin Nassar, an RSAF F-15 fighter pilot, held a master's degree in business administration from Troy State University, and was a graduate from the USAF Air University at Maxwell AFB. Prince Turki had hosted a small detachment of Chuck Horner's people from CENTAF during ELF-1 and EARNEST WILL. Turki was also responsible for the air defense of Saudi Arabia's vital eastern province, with its vast oil refineries, oil storage, and transshipment points. And then, in August 1990, he had a huge additional job dumped on him.

The 1st Tactical Fighter Wing, commanded by Colonel (later Major General) "Boomer" McBroom, arrived first. Even before all of the forty-eight F-15C fighters had arrived, they were moving to help out Turki's force of RSAF F-15Cs and Tornado F-2 Air Defense Variant (ADV) fighters in patrolling the skies along the Iraqi and Kuwaiti borders.

Meanwhile, thousands of Army troops from the 82d Airborne Division's alert brigade were also unloading at Dhahran. Turki's men opened every facility they had in order to beddown and process the arriving troops as they streamed though the air base en route to their camps in the desert. British and French troops and aircraft also arrived, and Turki found them homes, too.

He and McBroom formed quite a team. Since Turki was the host base commander, for most practical purposes McBroom worked for him, and together they solved a thousand problems every day: where to construct munitions storage areas, how to divide up ramp space, and the like. Cross support of RSAF and USAF F-15s became a daily occurrence, including the sharing of parts. Frequently, one would see USAF and RSAF repair teams helping one another, even if it meant that the two sergeants repairing the jet were a bearded Saudi and a fresh-faced American woman.

Throughout the Kingdom, the emirates, and the other host nations of what was already becoming known as "the Coalition," other examples of cooperation were going on—from generals and admirals, to sergeants and seamen. Day in, day out, trust, confidence, and cooperation grew as they all turned to defense of the Kingdom.

While all of this was happening, Major General Tom Olsen formed up the Air Force's Tactical Air Control Center (TACC) in the RSAF headquarters. The TACC was a vital part of what was to happen in the next nine months; the USAF could not have functioned without it. From there each day, Brigadier General Ahmed Sudairy and Colonel Jim Crigger and their staffs published an Air Tasking Order (ATO) for the growing Coalition air force. The ATO is the key document for running air operations in a theater—the sheet music that the aerial orchestra must use in order to play together. It covers everything from fighter and transport flights, to surface-to-air engagement envelopes and artillery fire. Anything that flies through the air needs to be in the ATO if it is to be safe, both for itself and others. In those early days, the ATOs out of the TACC were designed to execute the air defense of the Kingdom and the emirates, and to place aircraft on alert to repel a potential Iraqi invasion.

LINE IN THE SAND

The defense of the Kingdom was the other main driver during the "beddown of troops" period of Desert Shield. Every day, U.S. capabilities to defend Saudi Arabia against Iraqi aggression grew, which meant that new plans for that defense needed to be formed on an almost hour-to-hour basis.

On one of their first nights in-country, Horner asked John Yeosock what he had that night to fight with if the Iraqis decided to attack into northern Saudi Arabia. Yeosock reached into his pocket, pulled out a penknife, and opened its two-inch blade. "That's it," he said.

He wasn't far from wrong.

From the start, air defense was the first order of business. Fortunately, much of this defense was already in place, owing to some congressmen who had weathered criticism in order to support the sale of F-15s and E-3 AWACS to Saudi Arabia. These very aircraft now made possible the safe passage of the giant USAF transports vital to the rapid buildup of U.S. forces.

The first deploying forces were USAF F-15 fighters and E-3 AWACS aircraft, to flesh out the Saudis who had been flying combat air patrols since the beginning of the crisis. Next came the U.S. Navy aircraft carriers, USS *Independence* and USS *Dwight D. Eisenhower,* with their attendant battle groups. Then came the first USAF air-to-ground attack aircraft, F-16s from the 363d TFW at Shaw AFB in the States, and others from Europe. A-10 tank busters, known affectionately as "Warthogs," arrived from England AFB, Louisiana, and Myrtle Beach AFB, South Carolina. All of this was designed to provide enough airpower to blunt an Iraqi thrust, and to devastate their supply lifelines. Horner told Schwarzkopf what air units he wanted in what order, though there were also units that had not been anticipated—such as the F-111s from Europe or the F-117s—since they were not apportioned to CENTAF in the war plans.

Shortly after this, U.S. Marines aboard an Amphibious Ready Group (ARG) arrived offshore, followed by the larger and more powerful 7th MEB (Marine Expeditionary Battalion) from Twenty-nine Palms in California. These units drew their equipment from a just-arrived squadron of pre-positioned ships based in the Indian Ocean at Diego Garcia. With them came a Marine air wing of fighters, attack aircraft, tankers, and helicopters to support their efforts. Then 82d Airborne Division began to land in Dhahran.

All these forces deployed along the east coast, the high-speed avenue of attack, to protect the strategic assets there—the oil facilities and the desalinization plants, which supplied water to the interior as well as to the ports, towns, and airports in the eastern province. The forces were small and light, without much of the armored muscle that would be required to stop an Iraqi advance if it came.

The fundamental job during this time was to find places to put all the people and equipment as they arrived, and to do it as fast as possible.

The USAF units were bedded down by Bill Rider and the CENTAF staff, who set up shop in the RSAF headquarters, and were working the USAF beddown right from the start. At Horner's direction, the F-15s and AWACS went side by side their counterparts in the RSAF. The F-16s went to the UAE, because they had the range to cover Saudi Arabia, and this way they were based pretty much out of harm's way from either ground, air, or missile attack. The A-10s went into Fahd Air Base, ten miles west of Dhahran, since they would be vital to stopping an Iraqi tank attack—though in all likelihood they would have had to fall back in the actual event of an Iraqi attack. The F-111s and U-2s went to Taif, near Mecca, and the F-117s went to Khamis Mushayt, south of Taif and about thirty miles north of the Yemen border.

Grant Sharp did most of the Navy work. Since he already had a standing command afloat in the Gulf, the initial actions were to expand that command. Air tasking for the carriers would come out of the RSAF head-quarters, while surface actions would come out of Rear Admiral Bill Fogerty (until Vice Admiral Hank Mauz arrived to take over at NAV-CENT).

John Yeosock was in charge of the land forces, with Lieutenant General Walt Boomer, the Marine commander, and Lieutenant General Gary Luck, the XVIIIth Airborne Corps commander, working together imme-diately under him.

The 82d Airborne Division was the first on the ground, but there was no way to move them around except in the limited vehicles they had brought with them and the trucks and rental cars that could be scrounged from civilians. Owing to their lack of mobility, not much else could be done with them except to move them out from Dhahran into the desert near the air base, though some elements moved up toward the Kuwait border in position to fight delaying actions.

Defenses were dreadfully thin.

In those days, just in case, John Yeosock and Chuck Horner always kept their staff cars filled with gas, with a case of water in the trunk, and in the glove compartment a map of the road to Jeddah—if all else failed, the last-ditch fallback.

Most of the direst predictions did not envision a retreat that far, in-stead projecting the loss of the east coast down to Qatar or the UAE bor-ders. In that event, the plan was to take refuge in Bahrain by blowing the causeway to Dhahran, an island.

There would eventually be bright spots, like the arrival of the 24th Mechanized Infantry Division with its M1A1 heavy tanks and M2/3 Bradley fighting vehicles, or the rapid movement of the French ground forces from the port of Yanbu on the Red Sea across Saudi Arabia to the Eastern Province. But those events were weeks ahead, at the end of Au-gust and early September. For most of August, things were really hairy.

In the event of an invasion, the plan was for the 82d Airborne to act as "speed bumps." They'd move forward and blow the bridges through the sepkas and then fight until dislodged. Sepkas were swamplike low spots near the coast, where the salt water lay just under the desert crust, making them impassable for vehicles. The 82d would then melt into the desert, escape down the highway . . . or be captured or killed. They'd do this over and over.

If the Iraqis tried an attack down the Wadi al Batin, the Saudi forces in King Khalid Military City would place a large roadblock across it and try to halt the invaders. If they failed, not much lay between the Iraqis and Riyadh, except some very difficult terrain and airpower.

Such an attack remained unlikely, since the Iraqis' best avenue of attack would have been to race down the coastal road in the east, then make a right turn at Dhahran and come east toward the capital. But again, distance worked against them: the farther they attacked, the closer they came to the U.S. air based in Bahrain, Qatar, the UAE, and southwestern and western Saudi Arabia. Additionally, the Iraqis did not have the means to sweep the Arabian Gulf clear of the U.S. surface navy. Thus, the farther south they came, the more they exposed their flank to naval gunfire and air attack from the carriers. To cap it off, there was an aggressive disinformation campaign to inform the Iraqis of a planned U.S. amphibious landing in Kuwait City—the worst-kept secret since the story that D Day was going to take place at the Pas de Calais.

★ Of course, there were other problems, as well.

Working out corps boundaries between the USMC and the XVIIIth Airborne Corps, for instance, might seem easy enough—draw a few lines on a map; you stay on this side; you stay on that—but it wasn't. The corps had to be placed carefully so that the enemy couldn't take advantage of the terrain.

The basic situation was this: Khaled's Arabs (the EAC—Eastern Area Command) were on the coast; the Army's XVIIIth Corps was on the left; and the USMC was in between. The problem was that significant avenues of attack had to be properly covered, and could not be split between different units. For example, the north–south highway needed to be entirely in one corps area, if for no other reason than simplified traffic control, but since there were curves in the highway, the corps that owned it had considerable area to defend. To make matters more difficult, the sepkas caused chokepoints, and these chokepoints funneled the enemy back and forth from one corps area to another.

Since it was vital for Walt Boomer and Gary Luck to work out these issues together, from time to time Horner called on one or the other to make sure everything was going well. Though they didn't always reach full agreement, they achieved reasonable cooperation.

There were also disagreements about the placement of EAC forces—two separate issues, really, though they were related.

First: Khaled insisted that if the Iraqis attacked, Arabs had to be the first casualties. Horner understood the significance of that position, and he did not disagree. That meant placing Khaled's forces close to the border—too close, as it turned out. They were within Iraqi artillery range, which gave the Iraqis the opportunity to inflict easy casualties. In time, Khaled's objections were overcome, and the EAC and the SANG (Saudi Arabian National Guard, a small, elite force whose normal function was to protect the two principal holy places, Mecca and Medina) pulled back from the border. (This jammed them into the USMC coming out of Jubail, but that problem was also solved.)

Second: Khaled had orders from the King not to give up Saudi land. This was all well and good, but unfortunately, in those early days, the Coalition did not have sufficient land forces to execute that strategy, and even if they had, they'd have incurred large numbers of casualties. Though Khaled was truly caught in the middle between Horner and his King, he played his cards adroitly: even as he cooperated with the mobile defense concept the Coalition was faced with implementing, he extracted promises that U.S. forces would do their best to join with their Saudi allies to contain an attack on Saudi Arabia.

KHALED

Working out corps boundaries wasn't the only hurdle Walt Boomer and Gary Luck faced. More serious for both men was logistics—food, water, housing, latrines, and gunnery ranges. The last item became a problem when the Bedouins who had herds grazing in the parts of the desert that were to be given over for ranges declared that they didn't want to vacate them. Prince Khaled had to fix that.

Then congestion in the port at Al Damman became a problem. John Yeosock's port masters couldn't find anyone in charge. They would go to one agency, only to be told that some other agency worked the problem, and when they went to that one, they were sent to another. No one was responsible, yet everyone could cause delays or raise obstacles.

After a visit from Horner and Yeosock, Khaled stepped in. He put one of his people in charge, with full responsibility, and that was that. Then, when it was clear that there were not enough trucks to carry the stuff off the piers, it was Khaled who found more trucks.

His Royal Highness, Khaled bin Sultan, got things done. Another instance came with the problem of where to put the tens of thousands of

Americans pouring into the nation. They had to be housed in a place where they'd be both comfortable and safe—and where Saudi society could be protected from so many antithetical cultural and religious customs.

Khaled came up with the answer. Eskan Village, a huge housing complex on the southeast side of the city, became home to most of the U.S. forces stationed in or near Riyadh. It had been originally built as military housing, but then the base it had been designed to support was delayed, so this huge compound had been mothballed.

Horner and the CENTCOM J-4 (logistics chief), Major General Dane Starling, took a tour of Eskan Village to see if it would meet their needs. They found hundreds of villas, each with three bedrooms and three bathrooms. There were also high-rise apartments, schools, swimming pools, and recreational areas—a complete village just waiting for power and water to be hooked up. It was perfect.

Still, Khaled could not solve every problem. He could find housing for 30,000 people and open seaports, but when Chuck Horner asked him for a television and videocassette player for each villa at Eskan, he balked and grew evasive. Horner was amazed. It was such a simple request. Only a few thousand TVs and video players, so the troops could watch Armed Forces Television and play videotapes from home.

One day, over a cup of cappuccino in his office in the MODA building, Horner pressed the issue, and the reason for Khaled's refusal came clear. His people didn't know where to buy thousands of TVs and video playback units.

"If I can get them," Horner asked, "will you pay for them?"

"No problem!"

So Dane Starling phoned in the order to some lucky electronics dealer in Atlanta, and in a few weeks, the troops had their TVs.

SHEPHERDING COMMANDERS

Probably the most difficult issue for Horner as "CENTCOM Forward" was the determining of command relationships. At that time, command relationships between United States forces were not always easily understood or conducted. No one doubted General Schwarzkopf's authority, as defined by Goldwater-Nichols, but several areas needed work.

For example, there were air component and naval component commanders in CENTCOM, but there was no separate and distinct land component commander, which raised a number of nagging questions.

On the ground, Lieutenant General John Yeosock commanded the U.S. Third Army, which was in those days composed of one corps, XVIIIth Airborne Corps, commanded by Lieutenant General Gary Luck (later Lieutenant General Fred Franks's VIIth Corps would be added to Third Army). There was also a United States Marine Corps component, MARCENT, commanded by Lieutenant General Walt Boomer, with his 1st Marine Expeditionary Force (1st MEF). 1st MEF was initially composed of the 7th MEB, with their attached MAW and support elements, about 20,000 personnel; but eventually it grew to more than two divisions ashore, with over 90,000 Marines.

In the best of worlds, a ground component commander would have coordinated the various land forces, but for various political and practical reasons—primarily to keep the Army and Marine chauvinists in the Pentagon from going to war over the issue of which service was in charge, and to make sure that he himself was the focal point of the ground war, his area of expertise—General Schwarzkopf decided to retain the authority of land component commander for himself. The result was that when Schwarzkopf was wearing his CINC hat, he commanded the air, navy, *and* land components, but when he was wearing his land component hat, he was merely the equal of the air and navy commanders. So who was talking when? Things never got out of hand, but the situation was murky.

Meanwhile, Khaled and John Yeosock devised an organization between them to coordinate their efforts, one that would integrate the land forces of the host nations with the land forces of the non–host nations, principally those of the United States, France, and Great Britain. They named the organization C3IC—an acronym that meant nothing at all. The idea was to fuzz things up, to let the name mean all things to all people. A precise definition would have started debates about command and control between the nations. By keeping its nature amorphous, everyone was able to work together without the need for rigid guidelines telling who had to do what to whom.

C3IC was located in a large space with a two-story-high ceiling on the main floor of the MODA command bunker. It was there mainly because Horner and Khaled knew that General Schwarzkopf would eventually make his headquarters at MODA, and he was going to be the U.S. land component commander. John Yeosock brought a superb officer, Major General Paul Schwartz, to head the U.S. side of C3IC, while Khaled provided an equally talented Saudi Army general, Brigadier General Abab Al-Aziz, al-Shaikh.

Also on the main floor was the CENTCOM J-2 intelligence shop, and the CENTCOM J-3 operations shop in the hall. Schwarzkopf's command center, where evening meetings were held, was located in a small conference room near the command center. On the other side of the command center wall was a small amphitheater, where larger staff meetings were held until the air war started in January. Then all meetings migrated to the command center. On the floor above were offices manned by Saudi officers working with the Americans. There was also a main conference room with windows that looked down on the C3IC room.

★ As time went on, it did not prove practical to integrate every command, though C3IC remained. In the beginning, all commands were fully integrated; but over time, Third Army staff outgrew the Royal Saudi Land Forces headquarters, where the land commanders had originally set themselves up. So John Yeosock and the other land commanders found it more useful to maintain separate locations, and Yeosock moved Third Army headquarters to Eskan Village.

On the other hand, air planning and execution were fully integrated throughout the war. Integration is easier with air than ground. Once there's an Air Tasking Order, then the individual wings retain command of the units: Americans work for an American wing commander, though on a Saudi or UAE base; and the flight leader of a Saudi flight is Saudi, even though the flight might be part of a larger package commanded by a British flight leader.

Major General Jousif Madani, RSLF, the J-3 for the MODA staff, was a quiet, thoughtful man, who was charged by Hamad to sit down with Horner and work out the command and control issues; and Horner spent considerable time with him. Horner's problem was that he could go only so far without Schwarzkopf's approval. Though the CINC had empowered him during those days to do what he thought best, he didn't want to handcuff Schwarzkopf with any arrangements the CINC would have to change later. So, for once, it was the Americans and not the Saudis who were moving glacially.

However, Horner and Madani reached a general agreement that

Khaled and Schwarzkopf would serve on an equal footing, which would also place Hamad and Powell on the same level. This equality issue was of some concern to the Saudis, because it was important to them to make sure they were respected by the Americans.

All of this activity provided a framework for the buildup of forces that were beginning to flow into the region, but it in no way anticipated the eventual size of the Coalition force that would go to war some six months later. Time and events would severely strain these early arrangements, but for the time being, they had to do.

★ As air component commander, Horner had to solve a few other command relationship problems, as well.

According to Goldwater-Nichols, the various services still organized, trained, and equipped their forces, and they still watched over promotions, but U.S. forces did not "belong" operationally to them. Operationally, U.S. forces belong to the unified commander. Goldwater-Nichols further stated that the unified commander could organize his force any way he saw fit. In other words, neither service doctrine nor the service chiefs (nor even the Joint Chiefs of Staff) could make him use or organize his force in a way he did not want.

Meanwhile, service doctrine favored service commands—Central Command Air Forces, Army Central Command, Naval Forces Central Command, and Marine Central Command—while the unified CINCs tended to find functional command arrangements more to their liking— land, sea, air, and now space—since that allowed for better coordination and unity of effort. The passage of Goldwater-Nichols inevitably led to struggles between the CINCs and service doctrines and the service chiefs.

Like most CINCs, Norman Schwarzkopf favored functional command arrangements. Thus, all CENTCOM air was integrated under one commander, called JFACC (Joint Forces Air Component Commander). The CENTCOM JFACC was Chuck Horner. Though integrating functions made sense both philosophically and operationally, it wasn't always easy in practice. The Goldwater-Nichols command structures had never in fact been tried in wartime.

According to Marine doctrine, Marine air was intended for close air support of Marine ground units; it was a substitute for the heavy artillery they didn't normally carry with them. Marine doctrine or no, however, the air component commander in Desert Shield/Desert Storm was ferociously opposed to splitting airpower into separate duchies, and he fought to keep it from happening. Some accounts of the war tell a different story: that Horner and Boomer worked out a deal that gave Horner command of Marine air until it was directly needed for close air support of Marine ground units. These stories are not true.

What happened was that soon after Boomer arrived in-theater, he and Horner met in Riyadh, and Horner said: "Look, Walt, I don't want your air. But, by God, we are not going to fragment airpower. So your planes are going to come under me, and you will get everything you need."

To which Boomer said, "Okay by me."

And that was that.

Meanwhile, Boomer's air commander, Major General Royal Moore, who felt that a higher power than Goldwater-Nichols had ordained him to be in charge of the Marine air, tried everything possible to undermine the centralized tasking that placed Marine air under Horner. Before the war started, he tried to pull Marine air out of the Air Tasking Order, but he ran into the brick wall that was the air component commander. Later, during the war, he continued to play games, but in fact it didn't bother Horner. Moore was generating sorties to hit the enemy, and that is all Horner wanted him to do. The bottom line was that Horner, not Moore, was in charge.

In Horner's words, "If an Army unit had needed that air, I would have sent it to them and told Moore to piss up a rope. But it never came to that. In fact, just the opposite. Schwarzkopf shortchanged the Marines. Not on purpose. He was just fixated on the Republican Guard and the VIIth Corps attack against them. So when it became apparent by sortie count that Boomer's and the EAC's guys were not getting as much air as the VIIth Corps and that they had more enemy to attack, we shifted air over the eastern sector. This was the right thing to do, and it paid off, as evidenced by the collapse of the Iraqis in the face of the initial attacks in the east [before VIIth Corps took off]."

★ Like the Marines, the Navy was also protective of its own air.

Admiral Hank Mauz, who was NAVCENT when Rear Admiral Bill Fogerty took over, and then Vice Admiral Stan Arthur, was not an airman, so he was not aware of some of the issues that had burned in pilots' souls ever since Vietnam, such as "Route Packages." Air Force pilots had hated the practice of dividing up sections so that only Navy planes flew in one, and Air Force planes in another, but thinking it was a convenient way to keep his carrier admirals happy, Admiral Mauz suggested dividing Iraq up into sections, so the Air Force and the Navy could conduct their operations without getting in each other's way.

He was more than a little surprised when Horner gave him a withering look and told him, "Hell no. I'll retire before we try anything as stupid as that."

Mauz got the message.

THE CNN EFFECT

An invasion of sorts did occur in Saudi Arabia in August of 1990: not the Iraqis, the reporters.

The phenomenon of twenty-four-hour news network programming—instant and live—has fundamentally changed the way military professionals conduct war. Chuck Horner calls this phenomenon the CNN Effect.

War is by definition bad news. People are killed; homes and workspaces destroyed; money thrown away in obscene amounts. And now the TV camera provided people back home with instant access to it all. Unlike print, the TV camera sees what it sees. It's *there*. The tape can be edited, but, basically, the camera is not held hostage to the credibility and adroitness of the reporter's use of language. Whether he liked it or not, the presence of TV on the battlefield, on both sides of the lines, had a profound impact on how the military did business.

Chuck Horner elaborates:

> As soon as the folks at home see on TV part of a battle, part of
> a battle space, or even a major player walking down an aircraft
> boarding stairs in some faraway country (signaling major league
> interest in the place), there's a serious impact. Folks worry. They're
> relieved. They're angry. They form opinions about how you are
> doing that job. They may agree with what you are trying to do but
> disagree with the way you are doing it. The effect of a military de-
> cision is not only felt on the battlefield, it is felt immediately *back*
> home. And the impact of that can find its way back to the battle-
> field within hours. In a democratic society, of course, the effects of
> well-done planning are immediately available, while the effects of

poor execution or misguided adventures may take some time to discern.

When a military leader thinks through what he is doing and how he is doing it, part of that mental process damn well better include the impact of his choices back home and in the rest of the world. If not, he's likely to be in for surprises on the battlefield.

The Saudis were aware of the CNN Effect from the start (they carefully watch over their press, screening it for offensive material). So when Secretary of Defense Cheney walked down the airplane stairs in Jeddah on the sixth of August, 1990, the press was there because the King wanted them there. Why? I suspect he wanted to tell the Iraqis to keep out of here, because the powerful United States had sent its Secretary of Defense to offer its help.

Did Grant figure into his campaign the impact of widespread instant communication of the battlefield to all the world? You bet he didn't. But it sure happened to us in the Gulf War, and it was a driver in everything we did.

It affected the way we targeted (and I don't regret any of this): We did our best to avoid civilian casualties. We planned attack headings to avoid civilian areas. We accounted for the failures of precision munitions to guide properly. We did not shred Iraqi soldiers by dropping cluster bombs from B-52s. We did not drop bombs when we could not positively identify the target. We did our best to advertise the evils the Iraqis were committing inside occupied Kuwait.

And we screwed things up badly a few times: by hitting a command facility that was also being used as an air raid shelter, by demonizing Saddam Hussein instead of the occupation of Kuwait, and by allowing the wreckage on the road out of Kuwait City to be perceived back home as the highway of death, when there was very little death—though lots of destruction. (I am also sure the U.S. Army doesn't like people seeing what airpower can do to an army . . . to anyone's army.)

Thank God Saddam screwed up his own TV ops worse, time and again. Remember the burning oil fields of Kuwait? Remember the hostages? Remember the English hostage boy who was brought in as a "guest" of the great leader? When the President of Iraq came close to pat his little friend on the head, the boy froze with fear. All in glorious color. Saddam, old buddy, get a kid actor to stand in and stage the scene so he greets you with a kiss and a smile.

We in the West are stuck with a free press. It's not always easy for us in the military to deal with our press, yet the press is our ultimate blessing and our lasting glory. When we are wrong, we will (sooner rather than later) be shown as wrong. When we are right and our actions are good, that will also come out. Sure, we can try to manipulate the press, and the press can attempt to manipulate the truth; but in the end there is enough integrity in both the military and the media to make sure most of the truth gets out to the world. The old boys will try to tell you we lost Vietnam because the evening news showed American boys burning villages and shooting old people. Get a grip. We lost in Vietnam because we were wandering in the wilderness of goals, mission, and policy; and in the process we came to believe that burning villages and shooting old people was good. The CNN Effect means that God's looking over your shoulder all the time, and I think it is a blessing. It is not pleasant, and you take hits, but in the end it brings out the best in mankind when he is out doing his worst, waging war.

Here is how Horner made his own peace with the television invasion of Saudi Arabia in the summer of 1990:

Boomer and Turki at Dhahran became the stars in the eastern part of the country. I got the job of talking to the press in Riyadh, a job I had very little preparation for. Sure, I'd done local interviews and TV spots as the commander of various stateside bases. But Christ, these were the big boys. How was I going to handle questions I couldn't answer because the answers were classified? Worse, how was I going to handle questions I didn't know the answer to, which would make me look like a dumbshit? (Sure, I'm a dumbshit, but I don't want the whole world getting their jollies watching me prove it on TV.)

Well, I survived the first hits; and I learned a little.

As I gained experience, I learned to talk plain English to the press, to tell as much as I could of the truth, to try not to cover my own ass, and to hell with them if they didn't like an answer. That

*approach seemed to make sense to them, and we learned to trust
each other. Most of them did their best to report what I said as accurately as they could, and I did my best to give them what I knew.
If I didn't know, I would tell them so; usually they didn't know either and were just fishing.*

*In time, I also learned how to listen to a question and figure out
the questioner's story line. So if I thought some reporter was
headed down a blind alley, or had the wrong slant, I would tell him
so. Often this generated more useful, and more honest, questions.*

*Soon after I was appointed CENTCOM Forward, a Depart-
ment of Defense press pool was formed, with Carl Roschelle from
CNN as the designated leader. Carl was great to work with. But I
soon learned that the news business is one of the most competitive
in the world. A "can you top this" race between individual reporters, networks, and papers broke out.*

*The folks in the business are all trying to make a living involv-
ing extreme pressures to gather information and meet deadlines.
They all want their own organizations to succeed, and that means
getting the best, most exciting, most insightful information into the
world's TV sets before any of their competitors do.*

*This form of combat was brought home to me when ABC's
Sam Donaldson and NBC's Tom Brokaw showed up at my
doorstep in Riyadh. Each wanted an interview for that evening's
news in the United States. They flipped a coin to see who would go
first, and Brokaw won. Unfortunately, his crew's equipment, camera, and lights hadn't arrived on the airplane with him. But when
I suggested we set up with Donaldson's crew and let the NBC team
use that camera, it got very quiet in the room, and it instantly became apparent that Donaldson would do his interview, and if
Brokaw wanted to videotape, his guys would have to go out and
beg a camera.*

*As it worked out, we found a Saudi Military Public Affairs cam-
era, so both interviews were done in time to send a satellite feed
back to the states.*

*Our military often fails to understand the dog-eat-dog nature of
the news business, or that each form of media has different time
lines and communications requirements back to editors or studios.
As a result, we often fail to assist and facilitate the media in ways*

that would be useful for both of us. Thus, the always cynical media personalities often lash out against the military, rail against what they perceive as news management, and complain bitterly that they are being censored. Sure, media guys have a lingering fear of the military, another hangover from Vietnam. But in reality, the fault is a simple misunderstanding on the part of the military about how to best support the unique requirements of different media.

One of the toughest interviewers for me was Michael Gordon of The New York Times.* He came on with all the warmth of a cobra; his questions were well thought out, difficult to answer, and tough; he clearly thought I was hiding things from him—specifically, that our situation was much worse than I was letting on, and I was an idiot who really didn't have a grip on what was happening. (He was partially right on the last point.) Yet after reading his stories, I came to a different conclusion about Gordon than his interviews led me to. Media people, I realized, just like the military, live or die on their integrity. If a reporter deliberately strays from the truth, he or she is dead meat among their peers and editorial masters. Even though I might not like the particular story line he was creating, for all his flaws, Michael Gordon reported my words accurately.

During this period, a lot was going on, to say the least. While much of this had to be kept from the Iraqi intelligence-gathering system, it was important to provide reporters with a wide and deep background understanding of the current situation, so their reports were accurate and made sense. That meant they would inevitably learn data that, if reported, could endanger American lives or success on the battlefield. At the same time, we in the military prefer that some stories don't appear in the media—because they make us look stupid. Or we think we have to keep information secret that's in fact widely known back home. Trying to keep all of that in balance makes working with reporters a delicate operation.

From Michael Gordon's New York Times teammate, Eric

**And coauthor, with retired Marine General Bernard E. Trainor, of* The Generals' War *(Little Brown, 1995), a solidly researched and readable but opinionated view of the Gulf War (which it looks at through Marine eyes).*

Schmidt, I learned you can trust the media. Schmidt has a dogged investigative streak. He finds out more about what's going on than anyone I've ever met. But if the information he finds is truly classified—in order to protect lives or success in battle—you can depend on him to withhold it. Snow jobs will not work on Schmidt, so if you're stupid, expect to read all about it under his byline. But if it truly needs to be protected, you can trust him. The same holds for 95 percent of the media, to whom integrity is job one.

Fear of the media seems to go with the job description of soldier, sailor, or airman. Why? God only knows. When you think about it, if you can trust the press and the TV commentator to tell the truth, and I do, then it's not the media we fear but the American people . . . a sad commentary on our military mind-set.

Sometimes you . . . we . . . all of us do asinine things. If you are doing something stupid, pursuing a poor policy, or wasting taxpayers' dollars, and the press or television paints you in an embarrassing light, that is probably a good thing. In the long run, the exposure, no matter how painful, is good for the military and the nation. If, on the other hand, you are getting the job done skillfully, pursuing a noble cause, or managing a military operation with efficiency (how rare that is!), then you have much to gain from media exposure. The American people are quite capable of judging good and bad for themselves.

I guess the bottom line is we have little to fear if we trust the judgment of the folks who pay the bills.

ON AND ON

All the while, more units arrived daily, which meant that Horner and his staff would be neck deep sorting out additional difficulties, problems, and dilemmas, mostly about where to get more—more phones, more cars, more rooms, more food, more water, more everything.

Horner usually met with Khaled daily, often several times a day, mostly to work on logistical support to cover the beddown on incoming units. He also talked to Schwarzkopf two or three times a day. Since the CINC still felt strongly about not putting troops in hotels, these conversations were often strained. Unfortunately, there was simply nothing else to do. In those early days, until tent cities could be erected for the Army, or pre-positioned shelters for the Air Force, there was no other place to put people. Since the Navy and the embarked Marines slept on their ships, this was less of a problem for them.

Every night, Horner and his staff met with the Saudis to make sure everyone had the same intelligence view of the Iraqis and to sort out problems at the highest level. Then he and his people went over the day's confusions and crises, after which they discussed how the various land, sea, and air forces were deployed and the amount of military power they could assemble if attacked.

About 10:00 P.M., the rumors would start. On at least three nights, there was reliable information that the Iraqis had attacked. Horner kept cool and waited out each report, looking for corroborating intelligence. It never came.

By 3:00 A.M., they'd have things pretty well nailed down for the night; and then it was off to bed for at least three hours of sleep.

Then the whole drill began again.

15 AUGUST 1990

This is the way a typical day went for Chuck Horner during his time as CENTCOM Forward, as he reconstructs it:

> *0520   I wake up at the sound of the first prayer call in the apartment I share with John Yeosock. It's still dark outside. A few moments later, in the shower, I can smell the desert through the open bathroom window.*
>
> *0535   I eat breakfast with John Yeosock, Grr, my aide, and Major Fong, Yeosock's aide. I have a fried-egg sandwich and or-ange juice from a can. Even before Fong fixes John's breakfast, John is already through his first cigar of the day. We drink coffee in the living room and watch the evening news from the United States via the Armed Forces Radio and Television Service Satellite over the Mediterranean. There are no commercials, but there are spot announcements about how great it is to serve in Europe and enjoy the local culture.*
>
> *0600   I drive with Grr to the Ministry of Defense and Avi-ation five blocks south along Airport Boulevard.*
>
> *0620   We enter the rear of MODA, pass through a guard*

checkpoint before entering the garage, and park on the fourth floor of the parking garage in a reserved spot just to the right of the rear entrance. I have a Saudi security badge with my picture on it and all sorts of Arabic writing and stamps that lets me go anywhere in the MODA building. A similar one does the same for RSAF Headquarters. I don't have any badges for U.S. areas, though, since the only place I would not be in a Saudi facility would be on the USMTM compound, where we have set up a SCIF (Special Category Intelligence Facility) with a guarded entry point, and they all know what I look like.

0625   I enter Major General Don Kaufman's suite of offices on the fourth floor of MODA, two halls down from Khaled's office and four halls down from Hamad's, which is in the front of the building. The night shift is still at work; the changeover to the day shift is at 0700. Meanwhile, the day shift (mostly USMTM NCOs who handle message traffic) is starting to come on duty (the message center is located on the USMTM compound where our apartment is located). Since Bill Rider has already moved to the RSAF headquarters, the only officers now in the suite are all U.S.: Kaufman, Yeosock, Grr, Fong, and me. John and I sit down in our separate offices to start through the read file—all the messages that came in that night, a stack of paper about two to five inches thick. I read them quickly, look at the top lines for who sent the message, who it was intended for (usually one or more addressees are listed), and the message subjects; and then I scan the message to take what I want from it. Many of the messages cover what is currently being airlifted from the States, but there is also much intelligence information about the Iraqi army in Kuwait. On those messages where I want action taken, I will write on the side of the message. Here's an example:

On a message from the Joint Communications Support Element in Tampa that's addressed to their detachment in Riyadh (busy trying to plug U.S. comms into the MODA bunker, so CENTCOM Headquarters could talk secure to Washington), I might put something like this: "J-6, Make sure we can integrate with the Saudi secure comm. net. H." Though my note is addressed to the CENTCOM J-6, a major general USAF communicator, it actually goes to his rep in the MODA, only days in-country and still trying to figure out what's going on and what he should do. The point of my note is to inform him that we are going to operate as a coalition and that if he creates a U.S.-only comm system, that is a nonstarter.

Later in the day, he appears in my office to rant and rave about how our systems are incompatible with the Saudis' and so he can't do what I asked; and even if he could, doing it would give foreign nationals access to our crypto gear . . . and on and on.

"If you can't find a solution," I tell him, "then the Saudis will talk over unprotected circuits to their forces, and the Iraqis will be the foreign nationals who will have access to our secrets. So please get out of my office and figure how to rig it so we can talk secure (encrypted) to the Saudis and they can talk to their own units secure."

Dealing with messages will go on for an hour or so. But there will be interruptions when people stick their heads into the room to ask a question or to talk about some incident that occurred during the night they think I should be aware of (either because they want me to know they have things under control or because it will come up when Schwarzkopf calls or when I meet with the Saudis). I drink about four cups of coffee and eat some strange pastry from a local store. There is a cup to collect coffee and pastry money.

0900   John, Don, and I go down to a small conference room for the morning stand-up with the rest of the CENTCOM and component representatives. In some cases, these are dual-hatted. So, for example, Grant Sharp represents both the CENTCOM J-5 Plans and the naval component (currently a Navy two-star on the La Salle, *which is tied up in Bahrain, but will soon be a Navy three-star now en route to Riyadh and about to move the two-star out of his bunk aboard the* La Salle). *Tom Olsen, the acting Commander of CENTAF (until the CINC returns to the theater and I can go back to my old job), represents CENTAF. John Yeosock represents ARCENT, while Don Kaufman acts as the temporary CENTCOM chief of staff (and takes notes and directs actions that come out of the meeting).*

The meeting starts with an intelligence briefing, which updates the Iraqi deployment on the Saudi border, but may also include news items, such as events in Europe or the (not yet former) Soviet Union that relate to the crisis. There is a short weather briefing from the USAF briefer, who's come down from the RSAF Head-quarters with Tom Olsen. After these briefings, we go around the table and discuss matters that are of concern to all who are present, or that need to be resolved.

It might come up, for example, that Dhahran is overrun with incoming troops, that the army people do not have anywhere to stay and are already triple hot-bunking it: three eight-hour sleep shifts per day for two people per shift, one on the bed and one on the floor under the bed; you swap every other day, meaning that six people can sleep per day per cot. There is also much talk about fouled-up deliveries—people at one place and their equipment at another (especially a problem with the army units).

Later, John Yeosock goes over the ground defense for the day, and then Jim Crigger or Tom Olsen does the same for the air de-fense set-up. This is followed by what-ifs regarding an attack by Iraq on Saudi Arabia, update plans for evacuation of civilians, where we would resist and with what, and so on. None of this is pretty early on; but it gets better every day as more planes and troops arrive.

We break as soon as possible, so everyone can get back to work. (Long staff meetings are bad. They should start on time and we get them over with as soon as possible. They should take no longer than an hour, and thirty-five to forty minutes is better.)

1000   I wander down the hall to Khaled's office and have a cup of cappuccino with him. Among Arabs, you never jump into business, so at first we make small talk about unimportant things, such as how Americans are coping with the weather, or else he talks about Saudi history and old stories about the Kingdom. Even-tually we get around to real issues, such as the new demands for support that the buildup of forces is making on the Saudi hosts. The buck stops with Khaled, and he listens carefully. I am careful not to make outlandish requests, and I tell him often that my need for a thousand telephone lines is not crazy, but in fact I will likely be coming back to him in a few days asking for a thousand more. This in a nation where the king has to approve installation of all international phone lines.

We also talk about conversations I might have had with Schwarzkopf the previous night.

Finally, if Khaled has any complaints, he brings them up and I make notes for Don Kaufman (sometimes Don accompanies me and makes the notes); we will take action on everything, no matter how small. We intend to be good guests, especially since the Saudis are bending over backward to be good hosts. Our meeting may last an hour.

1100   I take the elevator to the first floor on my way to the underground bunker. On my way, I pass the mosque. If I do this during prayer time, the mosque will be full of military personnel, their shoes lining the hall and spilling out into the atrium. I walk quietly behind the prostrate worshipers and watch the imam on the stage leading them in prayer. On Friday he will give a sermon; and at all times the prayers and the Friday sermon are piped throughout the building, so those who cannot leave their workplace can still pray. Only the guards around the various guard posts are not prostrate.

A separate elevator takes me down six stories into an underground two-story bunker. On the lowest floor, CENTCOM people are busy stringing com wires, putting up maps and information boards on the walls, and working on plans. Grant Sharp already has set up an office and is working on a conference room for Schwarzkopf.

Often I'll climb the stairs up to the floor above and stop by Yousef Madinee's office to discuss command and control. Madinee is a Saudi Army two-star (and well thought of because of his heroic service during a previous crisis when Egypt's Nasser involved his Army in a nasty revolution in Yemen). Since I must leave the door open for Schwarzkopf to do what he wants when he arrives later in the month, it is hard for me to come to any real agreements with Madinee. This is frustrating for both of us, but we make progress simply because we are discussing command relationships.

After a while, I go back up to the USMTM suite.

1145   I catch up on messages that have come while I was out, and I may have a visitor.

A French delegation, for example, comes to call on the Saudi leadership. They stop first with, say, Prince Sultan. Sultan doesn't see them but passes them to a deputy. Then they do see General Hamad, who listens to them closely and then dismisses them with warm handshakes and no information or decisions. Now frustrated, they stop by to see the American in charge, both as a courtesy call and because they are scared that they cannot get their forces into this war, and if they do they will come under U.S. command and control, which they don't want. (Eventually it works out that French forces do come into the war, and under American command and control—but with allowances for French fears.) There is lots of cagey diplomatic talk, as they probe for concessions and try not to offer anything in return. As I listen, I resist the urge to stick in the needle about their NATO participation. That is, if they had been better allies in NATO, then we would not be having these "getting to know you" sessions in Riyadh. I play good guy without committing to anything but a warm welcome and assurances that their national sovereignty will be respected, and as a sovereign nation they will be equal partners. . . . Of course, after the war they will want to be superior partners when it comes to selling military equipment to the Arab nations (to include Iraq).

This all takes twenty to forty-five minutes, after which we part amicably. But by then they'll know that even though they would have preferred to come in as the big brother to the Saudis, they will have to work with the Americans if they want in the game. It is hard to be the big brother when the three-hundred-pound Yankee is around and you weigh 120 pounds.

Time for lunch.

1230   Grr and I jump in the car and head back to the USMTM compound to eat at the club. Before the crisis, it used to serve maybe thirty people at lunchtime and had a good menu at reasonable prices, hamburger and fries with a diet Coke being a good choice. Now it serves two thousand people with a buffet [chow] line set up in the entrance, and you eat chili or spaghetti or beef stew off a paper plate and get a paper cup of Kool-Aid. There are not enough tables, and I've made sure there are no longer reserved tables for the general officers, as was the case before the crisis. All are equal and first come first serve, so you either stand holding your food until someone leaves, or you find a place to sit on the floor or in the small movie theater where the USMTM fam-

ilies used to go for entertainment. People are considerate and eat fast, and they give up their seats ASAP.

Troops I run into at lunch ask me what is going on, and I pretend to know and give them the best update I can.

1300   I go to my apartment, take the elevator up to the fifth floor, and lie down for a twenty-minute power nap. After I wake up, I change into my flight suit from desert fatigues. Grr is waiting downstairs. We head out to Riyadh Air Base five blocks to the north along Airport Boulevard to go flying.

1345   We arrive at the jets, two F-16s parked together with the RSAF PC-9 trainer aircraft on the east ramp, about seven hundred yards from where our AWACS are parked. The jets are from Al Dhafra in the UAE; the crews come up to work a duty shift of a week in the TACC, and the pilots they replace will take the jets home after Grr and I get our flight in.

1400   Grr and I take off for Dhahran AB in the eastern province. We check in with AWACS (the normal thing to do), and they provide air traffic control services for us. Though we may fly a low-level navigation mission, we'll probably do Dissimilar Air Combat Tactics against F-15Cs. The mission will have been planned by Grr while I was at work that morning. After about an hour in the air, we land at Dhahran. We taxi up to the ramp where the 1st Wing has their jets parked, where we are met by Colonel John McBroom, the wing commander, who may have been in the flight we fought coming in.

1515   After a short debriefing on the training flight, I get in a car with Boomer McBroom to go visit the troops.

First we'll meet with the maintenance troops. We'll listen to their needs and answer their questions. Most of the time, these are about when are we going to go after "him" (Saddam). Morale is always high, and while working conditions are tough, they keep the jets in commission at very high rates. What the hell, they don't have anything else to do. It's amazing how much time families, drinking, and sex take from our day. When you are without, you are much more productive and do not get into nearly as much trouble. Yet all of this, too, has its limits.

1600   We have been out to the weapons-storage area, and then we visit the school where the USAF reserve nurses are being *housed. This last includes walking through sleeping areas where several nurses are in various stages of undress. They seem unconcerned about that, but I am embarrassed; and I talk to them with averted eyes, wishing I had guts enough to glance at their bra-clad chests. It's the shits when you have to be on public display and on your best behavior. Afterward, we stop by the mail room, since it is a hot spot, and I make sure they have all they need to move the huge amounts of mail out to the troops in a timely manner. Next, we stop by an RSAF Tornado squadron to meet with Brigadier General Turki, the base commander, and his wing commander, Brigadier General Mansour. We talk about their preparations for war and the ongoing Combat Air Patrols we are flying together in the air defense of the Kingdom role. After that, we pass through the integrated USAF and RSAF engine shop to see how our two maintenance forces are integrating and working together. Saudi NCOs and our men and women are working side by side there, but it seems to be working out. . . . Even though some of our women are visibly female under their T-shirts, this seems to have pretty much the same effects on all the males, whether Islamic or south Georgian.*

We will end up at one of the USAF squadrons and talk to Intel, pilots, etc., and answer questions, perhaps in a short pilots' meeting. The pilots are worried about screwing up in combat and tired of flying from midnight till dawn in the "CAP FROM HELL" (so called because you do it late at night, you are tired and bored, but you have to stay alert).

1700   Grr and I climb in our jets. I lead this time, and we fly along the Iraqi border to check out the ground forces that have moved in and to check in with any of the attached Tactical Air Control parties that may be in place. Grr coordinated with these while I was touring with Boomer. Lead elements of the 82d Airborne are north of Dhahran, and we do some dry CAS with their Battalion ALO; but there is not much else in the desert. By the time we land at Riyadh and the crews going back to the UAE take the jets from us, it is starting to get dark. I am tired from flying and fall asleep in the car as we drive back to MODA.

1900   In MODA, I read stacks of messages and make the usual notes on the margins. Don Kaufman has a list of things that have come up, and we run through them. I call Schwarzkopf to give him an update and listen as he anguishes about the problems he is facing getting combat power over ahead of headquarters (since headquarters doesn't fight the enemy). John Yeosock is also in the suite after an afternoon of visiting with arriving units (he gets around in a C-12 light aircraft or a helicopter); and we compare notes about what we will do if the Iraqis attack that night. As we talk, we eat some french fries and swarmas, which are Saudi sandwiches—pita bread with grilled slices of lamb and mayonnaise.

Later, I may have a visitor from one of the arriving coalition forces, and we chat about their plans—e.g.: what forces they are bringing, where they would like to beddown, what support they might need, and the command-and-control lash-up. I put them at ease about the logistics concerns and promise to help with any special needs. For example, the airmen all want to know how their squadrons will receive the Air Tasking Order, and I explain that we will either have them collocate with a CAFMS*-equipped U.S. squadron or I will get them a CAFMS terminal of their own. If the visitor is a high-ranking officer (which might be a major, if that is high ranking for that air force/army/navy), then I will invite him to the evening meeting.

2100   John, Don, and I go downstairs to the MODA bunker for the evening meeting with our Saudi counterparts. General Hamad and I will cochair the meeting, but Khaled will also be important. That is to say, if anything is to be decided afterward, it will be done in private with Khaled. John and his counterpart, Yousef Rahsid, Tom Olsen and Behery, Grant Sharp and Admiral Talil will all sit with one another. I am always diffident at this meeting, because I am simply filling in for Schwarzkopf and do not want to make any waves. Still, we need some structure for working together and addressing any problems that come up. We do not spend a lot of time working strategy, as I am not sure the American ground forces want to fight in an integrated manner with their Saudi counterparts, and besides they are just getting unloaded from the ships and planes and don't know how to find the bathrooms

---

*Computer-Aided Force Management System—a computer setup that is used to build and execute the Air Tasking Order.

yet. All the same, we must have some interaction. (The air forces, we quickly find, are already well integrated after years of training together and because of our AWACS operations during the Iran–Iraq War.)

The meeting will start off with an intelligence update: One night the United States will supply the briefers, the next night the Saudis will brief. After about twenty minutes of briefing, other briefers describe ongoing operations—who is flying what CAPs where, the status of forces in terms of buildup, and where they are deploying in the desert. Hamad says little, and the individual Saudi chiefs are reluctant to talk too much in front of him, probably because they wish to keep their own prerogatives and enjoy working with their U.S. counterparts. Thus, the RSAF and USAF work well together, while the RSAF and RSLF, though friendly and polite, do not have a history of close cooperation.

2230   I'm back upstairs putting out fires. There's a telephone call from a civilian contractor at one of the U.S. compounds asking if it is true that the Iraqis had launched an attack and that poison gas had been used. "It's not true to my knowledge," I tell him, "but I will check into it." A quick check of headquarters (the TACC in the RSAF) shows that all is quiet as far as AWACS can tell. RSLF listening posts on the border have not reported anything unusual. I get back to the contractor and calm him down, or else I have Don do it if I am busy with something else.

Now callers begin stopping by the office. You can never forget that most serious business in the Arab world is done between 11:00 P.M. and 3:00 A.M. A couple of print newsmen spend fifteen to thirty minutes asking me questions. Since it's too early in the deployment for a Public Affairs Officer to be in theater, I use my best judgment and depend on their honesty and willingness not to make me look like a fool. (I never really had a problem except with Jack Anderson, who was writing reports back in the States that gave the impression he was in Riyadh; he even "quoted" me. The man has no integrity.)

Midnight   I am really getting tired and fall asleep reading messages. My eyes start burning and watering, so I put some ice cubes on them, which gives some relief. I still doze off from time to time.

Even this late, there is lots of activity, and the phones are ring-
ing off the wall (it's daytime at CENTCOM Rear in Tampa and in
Washington). I avoid most of the calls, and John Yeosock and Don
Kaufman do most of the talking to important people, while the
small stuff is handled by Grr. I do talk to Schwarzkopf if he calls,
but he seldom does this late. And I also may talk with USAF gen-
erals, but I usually refer them to Tom Olsen at RSAF rather than
try to do both jobs. There will be plenty of time to command the
air forces when Schwarzkopf comes, and for now the people need
a commander for all the theater.

Later, John comes in, and we sit and talk. Others join in, and
we go over what we can do if the attack comes at first light or any-
time tomorrow. I may call Tom Olsen, Gary Luck, or Walt
Boomer if I have something to say to them, but I usually don't, as
their forces are just getting settled in and mating up with their
equipment on a very piecemeal basis. When I talk to them, I do a
lot of listening as to what they think and are planning, and I give
suggestions based on what John and I have discussed. But for the
most part, John Yeosock is in charge of organizing whatever
ground forces we can muster, and Tom Olsen has the air forces
along with Ahmed Sudairy, the RSAF/DO, who is an incredibly
brilliant and take-charge airman.

0300   Things seem to be settling down. The night shift peo-
ple are slowing down and starting to sit around and talk over cof-
fee. But they will still be organizing reports, answering questions,
or directing activities (such as rerouting an incoming C-5 so it
lands at Dhahran and not at Jeddah). By now I am pretty much
useless, due to fatigue; and John and I reluctantly head for the
sack.

On some days, like Friday (Islamic Sunday), we might sleep in
till 8:00 A.M. On some nights, just as we crawl into bed, the phone
will ring with someone from the States calling one or the other of
us. The idiot, not realizing the time in Riyadh, is trying to get a
problem solved or a question answered before he leaves the office.
They usually start off with, "Did I bother you? By the way, what
time is it where you are?" Both questions mark him as an idiot.

6

PLANNING THE STORM

It was time to start formulating the Plan.

War is essentially chaos, and the line between control and sickening confusion is paper-thin. If one takes care, the violence applied can be focused with precision, yet even when care is taken, it can easily degenerate into wild and formless mayhem. Look at Bosnia, Cambodia, and Rwanda.

It is no surprise that commanders devote much of their best effort to reducing chaos. One of the major means to that end is the Plan.

Planning in the U.S. military starts with the national command authorities—the President, aided by his chief advisers—who articulate the political objectives and overall goals to be achieved by the use of military force. The ball is then passed to the CINC in whose Area of Responsibility the force is to be used, and he determines how to put together and marshal the forces available to him in order to bring them to bear on his nation's adversaries with the maximum focus and effect (and thus with the minimum of disorder and chaos). It is then the responsibility of the various component commanders to construct a plan to achieve the CINC's objectives—a campaign.

★ That all sounds simple enough, but the reality is more complicated. To begin with, it is easy to assume too much for the capabilities of military force. What can military force actually do? What is its capacity to achieve a goal? The answer is: not very much, and very little well. At best, a specific goal can be more or less precisely matched with a specific use of military force—evicting the Iraqi army from Kuwait, for instance. But no amount of force could bring democracy to Iraq.

It is equally easy to assume too much, or too little, for an air campaign. The doctrinaire advocates of airpower believe, as an article of faith, that destroying the "controlling centers" of an enemy nation will render the enemy impotent and helpless, no matter how powerful his forces in the field. The doctrinaire advocates of land power conceive of air only as flexible, longer-range artillery, really useful only against those same enemy forces in the field. The reality does not so much lie in between as it varies with the demands of each situation.

There is further debate among airpower intelligentsia about whether the attack should be aimed at destroying an enemy's means (his military forces and the various facilities that allow him to make war) or his will (his determination to resist). The extremists on both sides hold that if you do one, then you don't need to do the other. Both are wrong. Attacking an enemy's will can pay big dividends, but it is hard to know exactly how to do it. Bombing cities into dust sometimes works, as does targeting his military capabilities, but both are costly and have many drawbacks; so the theorists can debate in their ivory towers until they run out of words.

Meanwhile, the men and women in the field have to select the best of both as they apply to their given situation, and sometimes they don't get the mix right. This was one area, in fact, where airpower failed in the Gulf War.

In Desert Storm, Coalition air forces attempted to destroy the will of Iraq by bombing leadership targets in Baghdad, but these attacks failed miserably to degrade Iraq's determination to resist. Why? Because Coalition air commanders did not know what constituted the sources and strength of Saddam's will. As Chuck Horner is the first to admit, he had the means to destroy Saddam's will but didn't know how to do it.

In contrast, when the Coalition attacked the means of the Iraqi Army in the field, it also destroyed that army's will. Thus, when Coalition land forces engaged forty-two Iraqi divisions, the result after four days was 88,000 Iraqi POWs and only 150 U.S. ground force deaths (half of which were accidentally inflicted by U.S. forces).

What went wrong? The first problem was with intelligence. U.S. intelligence operatives have not been trained to think in terms of the effects of military force on a given enemy. As a result, instead of risking judgments, they behave like accountants (with numbers, there is little risk). Intelligence operatives like to count enemy airplanes rather than determine the effect of killing an ace pilot.

The second problem was with the Plan. The Plan is not chiseled in stone. It is a script, and no performance ever goes according to script. After the first bomb drops, the enemy changes. Perhaps he is stronger than before, perhaps he is weaker. But changed. So the theorist is right at the opening moment of the war, and wrong ever after.

We'll be discussing both problems in more depth later on.

WHAT IS AN AIR CAMPAIGN?

An air campaign is a series of military actions that employs air vehicles in order to achieve a political goal. It may be a phase in an overall campaign that also uses land, sea, and space vehicles, or it may be a phase that uses air vehicles primarily. (Air is the area above the surface of land or sea and below the vacuum of space. The edge of space is currently reckoned to be about 90,000 feet above mean sea level, but in the future it will probably rise to about 350,000 feet above MSL.) A commander has a wide range of missions, available to him as part of those actions— air superiority, air interdiction, air reconnaissance, airlift, and close air support.

In addition, an air campaign (in fact, any campaign) has to address a specific situation—in this case, the invasion south by Iraq into Kuwait and, potentially, Saudi Arabia.

Once the objectives and the actual situation have been determined, how does a commander build an air campaign?

He starts by using his available intelligence information to decide on an overall plan, which contains all the elements he thinks are needed. Then he examines the contributions airpower can make and decides how it will be used. This last is primarily a list of functions, such as: "I want to gain control of the air and keep the Iraqi Army from inflicting casualties on our ground forces." This, in turn, leads to target selection, such as, for example: "I'll want to bomb a particular Sector Air Defense Operations Center." Or, "AWACS sees a MiG-23 flying south. We need to stop it." Or, "We need to destroy tanks and artillery in order to keep our own losses on the ground low." Once the targets have been determined (and the target list will always be changing), he aligns the targets with the attack forces he has available. He then overlays all the other support elements needed to get the job done—intelligence, command-and-control measures, refueling, search and rescue, AWACS, electronic countermeasures, Wild Weasels, communication codes—and lists them in the daily

Air Tasking Order (called the Frag in Vietnam). This is the control document that tells virtually everything that flies what to do in the air, where to be, and when (including where *not* to be—"airspace deconfliction").

We'll discuss the ATO in depth in a little while. Before that, however, Horner had a much bigger task in front of him as he began to figure out his air campaign.

THE PLAN AND THE CINC

Plans are not made in the abstract. They are addressed to specific commanders, and though this is primarily to satisfy the commander's expressed needs, it is also inevitably tailored to the commander's personality. As the various plans that eventually grew into the actual plan of attack in Desert Storm were created and developed, Chuck Horner was sensitive to both the needs and to the personality of H. Norman Schwarzkopf.

He was aware, first of all, that Schwarzkopf was a landman, not an airman. As a result, from the beginning of their relationship in CENT-COM, he had tried to elevate the CINC's sights into thinking about the importance of airpower to devastate the enemy in ways that were not directly connected to land warfare. He feared that Schwarzkopf would fall into the land-centric error that too many land officers made: thinking that war was *only* the battlefield meeting of two land armies. Those officers understood that you bombed the enemy homeland, government, and infrastructure, but they were never sure why or what relevance that had to *real* war, which to them meant surviving on a battlefield and destroying the enemy soldiers. Next to these, all else was of limited relevance.

Horner wanted the CINC to consider the use of airpower to achieve goals that were not about destroying the enemy army. And in fact, he succeeded.

As it turned out, Schwarzkopf wished to be the kind of CINC who approached warfare from a much broader perspective than is usually the case with land-centric thinkers. He wanted Goldwater-Nichols to work. The proof of it was in the way he created a theater leadership capable of blending the best of land, sea, air, space, and special operations activities and capabilities.

Horner didn't know that yet, however. This is the way he saw him at the time.

First of all, Schwarzkopf was extremely intelligent. It never took him long to grasp what he was being told.

Like Bradley, he deeply loved ground troops. He cared passionately about their safety.

Like Patton, he believed in his own destiny. This meant that he feared history would not remember him as the heroic man of destiny he considered himself to be . . . or rather, that others would foul things up for him and prevent him from achieving his historic destiny.

Finally, his ego was enormous, yet he was enormously insecure.

His insecurity was the key to his famous rages. For instance, Schwarzkopf could never handle well being put on the spot; and when he was put on a spot, his tendency was to lash out and bully or to throw blame on someone else. For this reason, Horner learned never, never to put him on the spot. He never confronted him in public, but always in his office, when they were alone or with another person the CINC trusted. This not only protected the CINC from himself and his insecurities; but when the CINC was nervous and insecure, he sometimes made wrong decisions, which might require a lot of work to undo.

To have constructed any kind of war plan without taking consideration of these and other personality and character issues would have been far worse than unwise.

INTERNAL LOOK AND THE EVOLUTION OF THE PLAN

Norman Schwarzkopf took command of CENTCOM on November 23, 1989. Chuck Horner took the first major opportunity he could to talk to him about airpower.

This came during the preparations for the Internal Look exercise planned for July 1990 in which Country Orange invaded Kuwait and Saudi Arabia. In April 1990, Horner gave General Schwarzkopf a briefing that covered his planned use of airpower in Internal Look—a briefing that came to have important consequences for Desert Storm, both in the way air was actually used operationally and in the way it added to General Schwarzkopf's understanding of airpower.

The briefing made a number of key points:

First, it showed the new CINC the deployment priorities for airpower in the Middle East region. The immediate need it foresaw was to build up air defenses (with fighters, AWACS aircraft, and SAMs), so that all the other component forces could deploy under a defensive umbrella covering Saudi airports and seaports. Next, attack and bomber aircraft would deploy to deter invasion, or (if an invasion occurred) to slow the invading forces until sufficient friendly ground forces could be put in place. Then came a whole basket of airpower capabilities most people did not appreciate: command-and-control aircraft to manage and facilitate air support of a ground battle, intelligence-collection aircraft, and vital support systems such as intertheater airlift. These were followed by discussions of mundane but essential issues such as how and where the air forces would be bedded down, supported logistically, and tied together with communications networks. Horner also described how his people would take over the air traffic control system and manage the airspace over the area of responsibility.

During all of this, the CINC listened closely and appeared to appreciate the important details.

Now came a discussion of actual operations. Here Horner described how they would manage intelligence assets and collection; air defense CAPs (Combat Air Patrols) and AWACS coverage; employment of Patriot missiles to defend against Scud attacks, and counter–air attacks on Iraqi airfields, radars, and SAM sites; as well as the overall command-and-control system networking them together. He covered interdiction of Country Orange (Iraqi) forces in Kuwait and Saudi Arabia (if those countries had been invaded), and cutting them off from resupply. He described how they would provide close air support (CAS) to ground forces, using the tactical air control system, and ways to provide that same support to potential Arab allies. And he covered possible nuclear, biological, and chemical (NBC) weapons targets.

Several elements from this Internal Look briefing remained months later in the plans eventually used in the air attacks on Iraq and its military. These included the first use of Patriot missiles in the ballistic defense mode; the integration of U.S. Marine air into CENTAF plans and operations; Push CAS; and perhaps most important, trust between the CINC and his air commander.

Patriot Missiles
Patriots, it should be noted, were originally developed for the Army as air defense systems (they were, therefore, Army missiles). Later, a ballistic missile defense capability was added, and that was how Chuck Horner

wanted to use them in the Gulf, as a defense against Iraqi Scuds, and not as air defense (other systems could handle that task better than adequately).

Some in the Army wanted to use Patriots as both air defense and ballistic defense, which would have located the Patriots in less than optimum sites for ballistic defense and would have involved procedures that would have jeopardized the interception of missiles. Horner, therefore, decided to take early action to ensure that the Patriots would be used in the most effective way.

What happened next is convoluted, but in its twists it shows some of the practical side of Goldwater-Nichols. It's also a good place to offer a brief primer on the way the various commands interacted.

★ As previously discussed, a service—whether Army, Navy, Air Force, or Marine Corps—organized, trained, and equipped forces to conduct military operations, and these forces were apportioned to unified commanders, who could organize their forces for battle in any way they felt was appropriate.

One such way might be to use them as a functional command. For instance, all fixed-wing air from both the Air Force and Navy were assigned to a joint force air component commander—which was Chuck Horner, who was also the CENTCOM Air Force service commander. This dual role wasn't unusual. As service commander, he had provided the major portion of the forces, and so it was appropriate that he be JFACC. If the Navy had provided the bulk of them, its service commander, Stan Arthur, would have had the position.

Disputes between functional elements in Desert Shield/Desert Storm were ultimately resolved by the CINC. If, let's say, a Marine air commander wanted to use F-16s to patrol a road instead of his Harriers, then the JFACC would arbitrate. If the former were not satisfied, he could always go to his service commander, who would go to the unified commander. So, in Desert Storm, Walt Boomer of the Marines could go to Schwarzkopf and complain. If the CINC found his arguments had merit, then he could ask the JFACC to justify or reconsider his decision, or he could override it entirely.

Disputes involving another Coalition partner were more complicated. If the United Arab Emirate Air Force representative at headquarters did not agree with the JFACC on the employment of his Mirage aircraft, then he could appeal to his Air Force commander, who was supposed to go to the UAE national authority, who would talk to the UAE ambassador in Washington, who would talk to the Secretary of Defense, who would talk to the President, who would talk to the Secretary of Defense, who would talk to Schwarzkopf. Since that was obviously clumsy and slow, the UAE commander more than likely went directly to Schwarzkopf and asked for help with Horner.

The relationship between the service and the functional commanders depended on the way the services' men and equipment were being used by the functional commander. Though on first glance there might seem to be potential for dispute here, in fact there was rarely a problem, since the functional commander used members of that service to plan how that service's force would be used.

The functional commander might also ask the service commander about the military readiness of the forces he was using. So, for example, Chuck Horner might say to Walt Boomer, "Hey, Walt, would you please ask the USMC to ship your deployed air wing more anti-radiation missiles?" Similar relationships developed among the air forces of the various Coalition nations. So, for example, even though the JFACC had ordered the U.S. and Coalition air forces to make their bombing runs at medium altitude, the RAF might still want to conduct their attacks at low level. "Okay, Bill," Chuck Horner would say to Bill Wratten, the RAF commander, "since your munitions can only be delivered at low altitude, go ahead." Adding to himself, *I hope they don't get their asses shot away in the process.*

As for the relationship between the component commander and the unified headquarters, George Crist, a former CINC of CENTCOM, summed it up this way, "The role of the Unified command is to create the environment needed for the component commands to fight the war." The Unified command creates the proper environment by defining the overall objectives, apportioning forces, ensuring that services or nations share people and material so everybody can fight, and by determining priorities for the employment of the various forces. The Unified command must serve as the connection between those who conduct the politics of war and those who do the fighting.

The problems that develop most often result when the Unified staff decide they'd rather run the war than devote themselves to the less exciting and prestigious job of creating a good working environment for the component commanders. Unfortunately for the staff, the component commanders have a direct link in the chain of command with the CINC. Commanders like commanders more than they like staff, for commanders are the ones who must lay it on the line, and who must be responsible for their decisions and actions. Staffs merely advise and coordinate. So when the truth is difficult to discern, or when the issue has two reasonable alternatives, the CINC will normally side with his subordinate commander rather than a subordinate staff member. He loves and treasures his staff, but he understands the role of command and the importance of trusting his subordinate commander (and showing that trust).

★ *As the JFACC,* Chuck Horner concludes, *I had to live or die by the quality of my ATO planning and execution. And while I looked for assistance from any source, in the end I had to satisfy the other component commanders, and ultimately the CINC, if I was to keep my job. Yet I could disagree with any of these and survive if my work was unassailable in terms of common sense and support to the overall campaign plan. If I failed to do that, it really didn't matter whether or not I pleased or angered any of the various staffs, components, or authorities with their agendas. I always listened, but always kept my own counsel and did what I thought was best. And in the end, I did what I was trained to do, command. The ATO was the expression of that command.*

★ We return now to April 1990, and the question of the Patriot missiles. Before his briefing to Schwarzkopf, Horner stopped into Third Army Headquarters in Atlanta to give John Yeosock (the Third Army commander, and CENTCOM's Army service commander, or ARCENT) a briefing of his own, since, as CENTCOM's area air defense commander (AAADC), that was also one of the JFACC's responsibilities.

Since Horner was the area air defense commander, the Patriots (by virtue of the declaration of air defenses states and the rules of engagement) came under his tactical control; but because the missiles were apportioned to ARCENT, either the Army or Horner could position them. Thus, in meeting with Yeosock, the two men simply needed to reach understanding about how to use them. Placement would logically follow. If Horner, as ADC, could not guarantee the Army that they would not be attacked by the Iraqi Air Force, then he would have had a very hard time obtaining agreement about placement of the Patriots. On the other hand, if he and the Army agreed that the ballistic missiles posed a greater threat than air attacks, then there would be no problem deciding where to put them. And this was what happened: Yeosock, the service component commander, said to Horner, "Good idea, you got them."

After Horner gave his briefing to the land component commander (Schwarzkopf), Schwarzkopf said the same thing, "Good idea, you got them." Since the air component commander and the land component commander had agreed, there was no need to raise the issue with the CINC for resolution. Horner simply informed him (Schwarzkopf) at the same time that he was convincing the land component commander (Schwarzkopf).

Thus, the Patriots were to be used in their ballistic defense mode during Internal Look . . . and of course later during Desert Storm.

Integration of Marine Air

Another issue Horner anticipated and headed off was an attempt by the U.S. Marine Corps to carve out their own space (as ground forces tend to do with land space). Marines like to run their own show, so they bring radars and air controllers to the fight, and are fully capable of controlling the airspace above their portion of the battlefield. Nevertheless, the JFACC is the airspace coordination authority under the CINC, and for him to cede a block of airspace to the USMC component would not only be inappropriate (a functional commander giving responsibility to a service commander) but would not provide for optimum management of the theater airspace.

Though it was not an issue with Walter Boomer, a few Marine officers did have a hidden agenda during the Gulf War: some Marines do not like functional commands—especially when another service will be commanding Marine forces. Since they are in essence a land force, and since the U.S. Army usually provides the major portion of the land forces, the Marines almost always work for the Army, and they don't like that. For that reason, they resist any efforts to strip off their forces—aircraft working for the JFACC, for instance.

And for *that* reason, in the part of the Internal Look briefing in which he discussed airspace management, Horner made clear to the CINC that U.S. efforts should be integrated with the in-place system of the host nation, and that all airspace should then be coordinated under JFACC, who knew how to do that better than anyone else, and who would not anger the host nation (which would have been the CINC's problem, but Horner's undoing).

Schwarzkopf agreed.

Though some Marines were not happy with this decision (as had been the case in every previous exercise), he had confidence in Horner, and little further came of this problem. (During Desert Shield/Desert Storm there were attempts by Marine officers to go their own way, but Walter Boomer set these people straight.)

Push CAS

Land forces require close air support.

But how much do they need? And when? Is air best used here and now, striking enemy tanks and artillery, or somewhere else—say, striking his fuel depots and tanker trucks? These questions aren't always easy to answer, unless enemy tanks are about to overrun friendly positions.

As a young pilot, both in war and in countless exercises, Horner had watched airpower's potential squandered by assigning it to support the Army. He was determined not to let that happen again.

Airmen and landmen see CAS from different perspectives.

The airman sees it as answering the question, "How do I keep from hurting my guys on the ground?" In other words, he sees CAS as a system to hit the enemy in close proximity to friendly ground forces. His worry is not so much about hitting the enemy as about *not* hitting his own troops on the ground.

Through the eyes of the soldier on the ground, however, "CAS is airpower attacking the enemy that is killing me." He sees it as powerful artillery. Sure, there must be measures to keep it from killing his own people, but the real issue is, "How do I get those jets to hit what is bothering me?"

These twin issues have been traditionally handled by means of the tactical air control party (TACP)—which is usually composed of a forward air controller (historically a fighter pilot in a helmet, with a rifle) and a radio operator who also drives the Air Force vehicle containing their radios and fixes broken equipment (radios, Humvees, or tents). The role of these two is to be assigned to a battalion (at the brigade and corps level, FACs are called ALOs, air liaison officers). The Army uses the FAC/ALO teams to communicate what it wants airpower to do, by means of preplanned processes. For example, the FAC/ALO may transmit a tasking directly to the TACC/AOC: "We need to hit the enemy machine gun bunker at 0300 two days from now in conjunction with an attack planned for 0330." That tasking would go into the ATO as a "preplanned CAS sortie," and forces would be assigned against that task.

Since the Army rarely knows what kind of air support they will need within the ATO cycle (two days), they put their requests for CAS in terms of "I will need ten CAS sorties sometime between 0300 and 0600 hours two days from now." And this is translated into "air or ground alert CAS sorties." Sometimes an aircraft that was intended to strike another target is diverted to support the ground forces because of a dire situation or an opportunity to do greater damage to the enemy. This is called "CAS Divert." There will also be a CAS CAP, if the fighters must come from a great distance or if the need for the air is expected to be sudden and dire.

"Push CAS" is a planned concept wherein the sorties are spaced so as to fly over the friendly ground forces throughout the twenty-four-hour period. Meanwhile, there is in place a command-and-control lash-up that can access any of these sorties if it is reasonable to do so.

There are several ways for the aircraft to be sent into a particular area: the pilot may have been tasked to go there before takeoff, or he may have been sent there by Joint STARS, AWACS, or, in the past, a system called Air Borne Command Control Communications (ABCCC*).

Once the aircraft arrives in the area of the FAC, the FAC tells the flight leader what needs to be attacked, where the friendly ground forces are located (including himself), and special information, such as enemy defenses in the area and perhaps a required attack heading, in which he amplifies target location data: "Look 100 meters to the north of the bombed-out schoolhouse at the crossroads east of the small hill in the bend in the river." This information is called a nine-line report, for it consists of nine items that must be briefed by the FAC (even if some elements are not required).†

---

*Called "AB triple C"—a C-130 carrying a joint army/air force team, and lots of radios. It served as the means for the FAC to talk with people who could talk to many aircraft.
†Now (in Bosnia, for example), the FAC uses a GPS Receiver and Laser Range Finder (that has a keypad and a radio). The FAC looks at the target with an optical device aligned with the laser. This both tells him the exact range to the target from his position and gives him the target's location in terms of GPS coordinates. Once he has the target's location, he types in other information, such as target description and the other elements in the nine-line format. Then he

Airpower must be used to support land forces—this is an absolute—
but only when appropriate. In Chuck Horner's view, land forces have too
often confused trust with ownership. Trust is the knowledge that they will
get the support they need. Ownership is the conviction that they *are*
guaranteed the support *they* believe they need.

Before Push CAS, the system used to provide CAS was both arcane
and obsolete. In theory, the CINC apportioned a percentage of the air effort to the land commander, who would then parcel it out to the various
subordinate commanders. They would then use this as an element of
their planning for the fight that was to take place in the future. Unfortunately, the subordinates rarely needed what they asked for (having been
trained to "ask for too much" in order to ensure they'd get something
close to their actual needs). Likewise, land commanders have often been
unwilling to turn back air they didn't need (unless a friend in dire straits
needed it more). Few land commanders willingly part from anything they
own.

Not all land commanders fell into this school. Some belonged to what
Chuck Horner calls the "trust school": "If we need it, it will come to us.
If we don't need it, let it be used efficiently against our common enemy."

In the April 1990 briefing, Horner convinced Schwarzkopf of that
position. And Push CAS was its expression: "We'll provide CAS where
and when it's needed."

Chuck Horner takes up the story:

> *In this briefing, I had two advantages: First, John Yeosock*
> *agreed with the Push CAS concept; and second, the land compo-*
> *nent commander knew he was responsible for all land forces and*
> *would have no problems apportioning the air effort to where it was*
> *needed. If lots of CAS was needed, he, Schwarzkopf (the JFLCC),*
> *would be able to convince the CINC (Schwarzkopf) to give him*
> *what he needed.*
>
> *I was also sure he was confident that his JFACC could work out*
> *for him how much airpower to place in the CAS role, because he,*

---

data-compresses the information and data-bursts it to an F-16 equipped with an improved data
modem (IDM) that receives the transmission and displays the information on the pilot's heads-
up display. When the pilot flies toward the target, and it is within the HUD's field of view, the
target designator box overlays the target on the HUD. In all of this operation, there are no ver-
bal transmissions, which are easily garbled (and the enemy cannot intercept what is going on).

Schwarzkopf (the CINC), had no idea how to determine how much airpower should be apportioned to CAS and how much to other roles, such as, say, Air Superiority or Air Interdiction. If Horner got it wrong, he could have him shot and find someone else. That way, if anything went wrong, Horner would get the blame. If things went well, then the man Horner worked for would get the glory.

Trust

Other issues raised at that briefing let the CINC know that Horner was thinking about fighting Schwarzkopf's war in Horner's part of the world and that he could have confidence that Horner was a team player working Schwarzkopf's concerns. For this reason, Horner showed him how he planned to work with the host nations (by merging air defense forces, by providing CAS to Arabs who didn't have tactical air control parties and didn't speak English, and by operating the Civil Airspace Control during time of war), and how he was ready to provide his air forces with sufficient logistical support and to take care of his people (with food, shelter, beds, and water).

Trust between and among commanders is essential. And it has to be earned. Horner earned Schwarzkopf's trust.

In Horner's words:

> *The bottom line was that I was telling him, "I know you are in charge. I am not going to be an Air Force prick, but I know more about airpower than you ever will, and you need to trust me and let me do my thing, so you will be a hero."*
>
> *In air-to-air engagements, if you can "lead turn" a jet flying directly toward you, and he fails to see what you are doing, you will have an advantage when you pass, in that you have already started to turn toward his tail. If he discerns you have started a lead turn, he can negate it by passing as close to your jet as possible. Then each of you have to make up the 180-degree offset in the ensuing maneuvers. If he doesn't and you have similar performing jets, then the one who lead-turns wins.*
>
> *At the April 1990 briefing, I was lead-turning the issues that had been a problem in the past: failure of the Marines to fight jointly, ignorant attempts by the Army to own the air forces, and*

failure of land force–trained CINCs to understand how to fight air-power. The briefing was a great success for me, for Schwarzkopf, and eventually the country.

I had Schwarzkopf's confidence, and I got that the old-fashioned way: I earned it. So when he would call me in the middle of the night in the TACC from his war room and say, "Chuck, I am looking at a Joint STARS picture, and I see thirty trucks at XYZ, can you get them?" I could reply, "I will certainly try, but if they are not there because the picture you have is too old, I will send the force to where it was originally scheduled to go." And he would reply, "Okay."

★ All the planning and the thousands of actions that go on in war depend on faith and trust. No single commander can know all that needs to be known, can be everywhere to make every decision that needs to be made, or can direct every action that is taken.

The Strategic Plan

The briefing ended with a discussion of what Horner labeled for Schwarzkopf a "strategic air campaign plan" (much to his later regret). What he meant was "targets strategic to Iraq"—that is to say, high-value targets, such as oil production and electrical distribution facilities, that could be held hostage in case Iraq used mass-destruction weapons.

Again, he was talking in the context of the essentially defensive Internal Look Scenario. Thus, the strategic campaign Horner was proposing then was only peripherally related to the plan of attack that later was to emerge in August and September of 1990. Unfortunately, the word *strategic* carries great magic, especially for commanders, and that day the word worked its magic on General Schwarzkopf. Ever after, he called the plan of air attack against Iraq the "strategic" air campaign, when, in reality, it was an *offensive* air campaign, a means to achieve the political objectives of the President and the Coalition, should diplomatic efforts and the embargo on Iraq fail.

This confusion was to resurface in August on the tarmac in Jeddah when the CINC asserted his desire for a "strategic" air campaign . . . and yet again in the plan proposed by Colonel John Warden and his CHECK-MATE team, about which there will be more to come.

THE D DAY ATO

Deterrence is effected by having a strong military force in place that is ready to fight and capable of winning.

We will probably never know why Saddam Hussein did not attack Saudi Arabia in August. He may well have had that intention, yet was deterred by the rapid buildup of airpower and the U.S. ability to conduct a sustained air campaign within hours of the initial deployment.

Meanwhile, though the military commanders on scene did not know Saddam's intentions, they had to be ready to counter the very real threat posed by twenty-seven Iraqi divisions on the border.

If Saudi Arabia were to be attacked, the following strategy was foreseen:

- First of all—and most important—air defense would be maintained, so Iraq could not use its own air forces to devastate the cities, ports, and airports in Saudi Arabia and Bahrain.
- There would be direct attacks on the attacking elements of the invading force.
- However, the greater concentration of attacks would be on the logistics lifelines of the Iraqis as they fanned out across the desert.
- Finally, Chuck Horner also asked for attack options against "strategic" targets inside Iraq. In this case, "strategic" attack meant strikes against targets not directly related to Iraqi military forces in the field.

This strategy was translated into what became the "D Day Plan" or "D Day ATO." This is a good place to discuss just what an ATO is.

Air is a *task-organized* force—that is, each airplane is tasked to go somewhere and do something that will benefit the overall effort to attain a campaign objective as part of the overall theater strategy to support national objectives. The air commander plans tasks and allocates forces to do those tasks, based on the characteristics of the force elements. So, for example, on January 25, 1991, from 1000 to 1030, the USAF tasked A-10s to patrol a particular road in Kuwait and kill vehicles, using its gun and Maverick missiles. The way this tasking was transmitted to the people who would have to execute it was by means of an Air Tasking Order. In Desert Shield/Desert Storm, the planning that went into the preparation of the ATO was centralized at the headquarters of the JFACC and was done by representatives of all the functional elements (A-10 pilots, F-16 pilots, AWACS pilots, etc.) and nations represented (the United Arab Emirates Air Force, the RAF, etc).

The ATO is a statement of marshaled resources that is based on the best available information and the best available guidance at the time it is prepared. Each day, the commander will have a new appreciation of what needs to be done. Perhaps the enduring objective he sought to achieve has also been modified by new realities (definitely the case for the side that is losing).

That is to say, when constructing the plan and its expression in the ATO, the commander can never forget that the situation is fluid, that chaos is always a close neighbor, and that terrific opportunities may arise in an instant. This is especially true in war, where aircraft move about in the battlespace in minutes or seconds, and information about new situations and alignments of forces arrive in real time and must be acted on instantly. Even though the commander must have principles to hang on to, as time passes, his objectives may become modified, and he will certainly gain more information about the reality of his situation.

To make all this more complicated: The ATO itself is like a moving train. If someone suddenly changes one element, he must consider the ripple effect on other elements. Sometimes the effect is minimal. For example, Tiger Flight is scheduled to hit target X at Y time, but new intelligence comes in that says target X has moved five kilometers north. No problem. The new target coordinates are inserted, the change is added, and the ATO is hardly affected. But suppose that Y time becomes two hours later. Then there's a serious problem. The new time may well drastically affect the aircraft generation schedule at the base. It may well affect tanker availability. It may well affect airspace deconfliction. And it may well affect the intelligence-collection efforts associated with that strike. For these reasons, it is sometimes better to freeze the ATO early and make up for the changes in the chaos that reigns in the current operations efforts during the day of execution.

Thus, an ATO is the marshaling of available resources against a series of tasks as they are best known when the plan is created. But the day that plan is executed, there will be more information that may in fact require reordering of priorities and tasks.

That means that the old paradigm—ready, aim, fire—has changed. In modern war, you ready, fire, and then aim. The deployment and sustaining of the force, a service responsibility, is the *ready;* the launch of the force against a preconceived schedule is the *fire;* while the command and control associated with the operations is the *aim.* That is, one now often loads up his aircraft, puts them in the air, and then decides what target to hit, based on real-time intelligence.

The plan, again, is not a sacred document. A commander has to be prepared to change it on the fly, and he has to have machinery in place to transmit the changes instantly to the people affected by them. For this reason, during Desert Storm, ATOs were built two and a half days—no more than that—before they were put into operation (since this was the minimum time for necessary preparations). This made it hard for the planners who made ATOs, but it ensured that changes would be more easily and quickly accommodated.

Chuck Horner imposed this two-and-a-half-day limit because he didn't want his forces to be constrained by planning that went on days or even weeks before the war started. He wanted planners to be forced to evaluate the first day's efforts and results, and then to plan what to do on day three. To make things easier, he gave them a half-day start. Then, as the days proceeded, they needed to make plans completely from scratch, using what they'd learned as previous days unfolded. "Of course, they had target lists hidden in their pockets," Horner adds. "I expected that. But I wanted to force them into thinking about where we were at a given time and then planning from that, instead of building an entire air campaign and then just modifying it here and there. Chaos reigns and Huns like me revel in it."

Likewise—as we've pointed out before—the commander can't allow himself (or herself) to be a slave to seemingly potent doctrinaire concepts such as "strategic," "tactical," or "operational."

Chuck Horner takes up the thought:

> *I have often said in the past that "strategic," "operational,"
> and "tactical" are confusing words. And if you try to link strategy,
> operations, and tactics with the first three, you have a real mess,
> where people are talking past one another. I can make a strategy
> of tactical operations using unique tactics in order to attain a se-
> ries of tactical goals to achieve an operational-level objective which
> turns out to be the strategic center of gravity. Take tank plinking.*

It was a strategy—to deny the enemy the use of his killing machines. It had tactical goals—to destroy one hundred to two hundred tanks a night. It had an operational-level objective—to deny the enemy the effective use of his ground forces against our invading army. It had unique tactics—medium-altitude air attacks using laser-guided bombs with infrared sensors. And it destroyed a strategic center of gravity—since Saddam's goal was to win a victory or stalemate by inflicting casualties on our forces. You have to be specific when talking about war. But unfortunately many are lost in the heady sense of destiny and all that bullshit, so they use powerful-seeming words like "strategic" when they don't really know what they are talking about.

★ The D Day ATO tasked the air forces assembled in Saudi Arabia and the other Gulf nations, as well as those aboard the Navy aircraft carriers in adjacent waters, where and when to strike attacking Iraqi forces. It was modest at first, but as more and more aircraft deployed into the AOR, and as more and more planners from the Coalition allies came aboard, the daily ATO (updated daily and stored on floppy disks ready for immediate execution) grew in size and complexity. Meanwhile, as strength on the ground grew with the arrival of more and stronger ground forces, the targeting emphasis changed to reflect new overall campaign strategies.

★ Three people watched over the development of the D Day Plan—Major General Tom Olsen (Chuck Horner's deputy), Colonel Jim Crigger (Horner's Director of Operations), and Lieutenant Colonel Sam Baptiste from the CENTAF operations staff.

It would be hard to imagine a more suitable deputy than the silver-haired, grandfatherly, commonsensical A-10 pilot Major General Tom Olsen: Olsen was loyal; thoughtful when Horner tended to be rash; nonegotistical (so he worked Horner's agenda, not his); and he made decisions Horner could easily live with. Olsen, in Horner's absence, was the senior commander who approved or disapproved the ATOs and other efforts.

Colonel Jim Crigger was more directly the driving force behind the setting up of the TACC and its processes to produce the ATOs. Crigger had been the last commander of the 474th TFW at Nellis (the wing was phased out in 1989) and then, when he didn't make General because of the drawdown resulting from the end of the Cold War, he became available for the Director of Operations job at Ninth Air Force/CENTAF. Crigger was intensely quiet, modest, and self-effacing, yet exceptionally smart (both in intellect and common sense), very tough, and deeply compassionate. After Horner hired him, he very quickly established his credibility with the hard-nosed staff (no small challenge, as they were the world experts in building an ATO and fighting war in the Middle East, having been together for over six years). The staff loved working for him; he coaxed their best efforts without driving them. Not only was his work as DO first class (he asked for guidance only when he needed it), he kept his mouth shut, and let the actions of his staff take the credit—always putting his people in front of himself when laurels were handed out, while taking the shots personally when things went wrong. Instead of ranting and raving at mistakes, he quietly dealt with them (including his boss's) in private with constructive criticism. It wasn't just his staff work that was exceptional; he was the point of contact with the deployed wing commanders, the man on the staff who, because he had himself just left wing command, could understand both their comments about ATOs and their needs, but could be counted on for good advice. The result was excellent chemistry with his commander.

Sam Baptiste had been operations officer for a squadron deployed in Iceland when a pilot had been killed in a crash and the blame laid on him, thus effectively ending his Air Force career. Afterward, Horner arranged to have him assigned to Ninth Air Force. Despite the cloud he was under, few people had his knowledge of fighter operations and intelligence. In the early days of Desert Shield, Baptiste handled the operations staff that determined which units would do which tasks if the Iraqis attacked; and in general, he laid out the details (such as CAPs) for Crigger. Later in the war, he joined Army Lieutenant Colonel Bill Welch in the more important job of planning the Kuwait Theater of Operations (KTO) portion of the daily ATO.

On August 8, 1990, when Olsen and the elements of the CENTAF planning staff arrived in Riyadh, Horner turned over to him command of CENTAF while he himself was occupied as CENTCOM Forward. Olsen quickly set up a warm working relationship with the RSAF commander, Lieutenant General Ahmed Behery.

Almost immediately, Jim Crigger and his staff had joined with the RSAF operations staff, and were conducting the appointment and guidance meetings that initiate the ATO planning cycle. Shortly after this, they were publishing a daily ATO. At first, these only coordinated combined air defense sorties, though they quickly grew to cover all the combined and coalition operational and exercise flying in the AOR. (This system was in place by August 13.)

On August 10, longer-range planning was begun. And on August 12, as the acting CINC, Horner asked Olsen to build a preplanned ATO that would rapidly respond to an Iraqi attack on Saudi Arabia—the "D Day ATO."

Though (thankfully) the D Day Plan was never put into effect, it served as a springboard to subsequent planning for an offensive air campaign—not, interestingly, because of the planning itself, but as a training device. Training became an issue when the planning staff was augmented with many new people who were familiar with combat, fighters, and bombers, but who had never built an ATO. Putting together the D Day ATO gave these people on-the-job experience in the reasoning processes and the integration that needs to be considered—such as airspace deconfliction, tanker tracks, command-and-control agencies, radio procedures, and code words.

Meanwhile, communication of the ATOs between the TACC and operational units was soon accomplished by means of the Computer-Aided Force Management System (CAFMS)—best understood as a combination of word processor and e-mail. In the CAFMS computers were preprogrammed forms (spreadsheets and text). When these were filled out by the planners they became the ATO. These forms were then accessed by the wings that had communication links with the TACC in Riyadh.

The CAFMS terminals were also used to execute the ATO. At each duty position in the TACC current operations room, the duty officers monitored and communicated with the bases via CAFMS. So, for example, takeoff times would be sent from the wings to the TACC, which meant that the TACC operators knew who was en route to the tankers or their targets and could divert them to other targets if they wished. The TACC would also receive flight abort information, which allowed them to divert other missions against those targets they really wanted to hit.

CAFMS had several limitations. For one thing, the Navy carriers were not equipped with the SHF antennas needed to receive it, which meant that floppy disks containing the next day's ATO had to be flown out to the carriers each night. (The foreign air forces that did not have a CAFMS terminal went to the USAF unit collocated with them and picked up the ATO there.) There were also systemic limitations. For example, because it was limited to word processor and e-mail functions, CAFMS was not able to show the effects of upstream changes downstream. Thus, if the TACC operators wanted to change a strike, the computer was not able to show how this change would impact on tanker off-loads and other such data.

JOHN WARDEN AND CHECKMATE

As Tom Olsen, Jim Crigger, and their staffs were setting up the planning and operational machinery required in theater, General Schwarzkopf was making good on his undertaking to Chuck Horner in Jeddah on August 7 to ask the Joint Staff to start the planning process for a strategic air campaign.

Recall that Horner had several reservations about the CINC's plan. He was, first of all, dead set against Washington making strike plans for the forces in-theater to execute (as in Vietnam). Schwarzkopf assured him that wouldn't happen. Horner was also worried that the CINC, and by extension the planners in Washington, would misinterpret the aims latent in the term "strategic."

On the other hand, on the ramp in Jeddah, Schwarzkopf raised the issue of a possible offensive air campaign should hostilities erupt immediately (either because of an Iraqi attack south or because the Coalition decided to initiate an attack north in the near future). He was thinking offense even while the immediate need was for defense. To Horner (as to any airman), such a campaign was mother's milk. This kind of campaign, every airman knows, would require striking the enemy as a system, not necessarily at his deployed military forces, but at what have come to be known as a nation's "centers of gravity" (a term from Clausewitz: "The point at which all energies should be directed"), such as its communications systems, power systems, oil refineries, industrial basis, centers of government, and in general, its means to sustain war.

When General Schwarzkopf returned home to MacDill AFB, he talked with Colin Powell, and later to the Vice Chief of the Air Force Staff, Lieutenant General Mike Loh, about development of an air campaign. Loh then called on a small planning cell, called CHECKMATE, to do the initial work. Formed in the late seventies to examine the strengths and weaknesses of U.S. and Soviet military forces and to create simulations, in 1990 CHECKMATE was headed by Colonel John Warden, a brilliant airpower theorist. While at the National Defense University, Warden had published what many considered a groundbreaking study of the subject, *The Air Campaign: Planning for Combat,* as well as several articles on the employment of air forces.*

Warden was the kind of airpower enthusiast who saw air strikes as the decisive influence on conflict, while other supporting arms, such as the Navy and ground forces, had become superfluous and obsolete. People have been preaching the virtues of airpower pretty much from the time of the Wright Brothers, and some of these sermons have had considerable impact. The problem for airpower enthusiasts was that hundreds of thousands of bombs had been dropped, but aircraft had yet to deliver the decisive blow in a war (leaving aside the atomic weapons dropped on Japan in 1945).

John Warden was different from earlier enthusiasts in that, for him, it was not the material shortcomings of airpower (i.e., aircraft and weapons) that had failed to deliver the decisive blow, but its ineffective organization and application. In other words, if the violence was applied quickly, precisely, and in the right places, the desired results would inevitably follow.

It is no surprise, then, that Warden embraced with enthusiasm the task of developing a plan to force Iraq out of Kuwait by using airpower to destroy Iraq's centers of gravity as defined by his Five Rings theory. For him, this task was the culmination of his military experience and of his search for new truths about the decisive potential of aerial attack.

---

*Warden argued that fielded military forces were merely the shell that protected the fragile nation. He then argued that the aim of air attack was to wage war from the "inside out." That is, in his view, air should attack not the shell but the center of the state. He fleshed out this idea in what he called his "Five Strategic Rings" theory, according to which air would attack violently and simultaneously an enemy nation's leadership (the central ring: the bull's-eye), its key production centers (the next ring: power, oil refineries, etc.), infrastructure (the next ring: transportation, roads, rail, etc.), a population's support for the government (the next ring: hearts and minds), and finally the outer shell, the military. All of this, of course, was premised on attaining air superiority.

Warden and his team immediately turned to this planning effort with great zeal and initiative.

The plan that came out of CHECKMATE was essentially a series of proposed targets to be attacked over a total of six days* (after which, presumably, the Iraqi leadership would give up and the war would be over). Attacking these targets would punish the leadership of the Iraqi government until it was driven into them that continuation of their land grab in Kuwait was futile:

- According to the CHECKMATE plan, Iraqi power and communications grids, command-and-control bunkers and facilities, and infrastructure like transportation and bridges, would be attacked.
- The plan also aimed strikes at Iraq's emerging capabilities to produce weapons of mass destruction (NBC) and their delivery systems, such as missiles—like Scuds—and aircraft.
- Significantly, the CHECKMATE plan took into account the importance of minimizing civilian casualties, primarily through the use of precision-guided munitions (PGMs). This campaign was to be nothing like the city-busting, population-punishing bombing of World War II (which was not only morally suspect but ineffective: it only made people fight harder).
- Key to making all this happen was to be the concerted effort (called SEAD—Suppression of Enemy Air Defense), in the earliest stages of the campaign, to wreck the Iraqi air defense system (called KARI—Iraq spelled backwards in French†), so that U.S. losses would be minimized and aircrews and planners would have the freedom to make most effective use of the new PGMs and delivery systems that had come into the Air Force inventory during the past decade.
- Finally, though there were some plans to attack the Iraqi military in the field (i.e., in Kuwait), these were relatively modest as compared with the rest of the effort. . . . The CHECKMATE plan did, however, produce some unintended benefits in that direction. There is no doubt, for instance, that it influenced favorably the

*The six-days plan was predicated on a force of thirty-five squadrons, roughly double the strength then available to CENTCOM.
†The system was designed and produced by French aerospace firms.

capabilities of the deployed forces; and because of it, the force that finally deployed was far more capable than the original force allocated to CENTCOM. For example, at Warden's behest, the air staff deployed the laser and electro-optical-guided bomb-capable F-111Fs from the 48th TFW at Lakenheath (the F-111Fs were later used to great effect in tank plinking) rather than the apportioned F-111Ds from Cannon AFB (which weren't so equipped). Though no one had any notion of the eventual success of tank plinking until the idea was evaluated in the Night Camel exercises in October and November, the F-111Fs were nevertheless much more valuable than the F-111Ds.

The CHECKMATE team worked hard on their plan, fine-tuning it with every computer model at their disposal. And through their excellent contacts at the various intelligence agencies around Washington, D.C., they were able to assemble a much larger and more refined target list than was initially in the field in Saudi Arabia (probably their most useful offering to Chuck Horner and his own planners). They also called in representatives of the other services to get their ideas and comments, all of which made valuable inputs to the plan. In particular, the U.S. Navy's SPEAR team, which had done first-class analytical work in examining KARI as a system, made valuable contributions to the SEAD portion of the plan (around which so much else depended). The SPEAR work gave planners a road map as to where and when to stick the knife into KARI (eventually giving rise to what became known as Puba's Party, which knocked out Iraq's air defenses on the first night of the war).

By the time it was done, the CHECKMATE campaign plan, called INSTANT THUNDER (with reference to the failed, gradualist, Vietnam War ROLLING THUNDER air campaign), ran to over two hundred pages. Given the time constraints levied on the CHECKMATE team, it was a dazzling effort. Now it was time to deliver the product to the customer, and that meant briefing it to senior leaders.

Warden flew twice to MacDill AFB to brief INSTANT THUNDER to Schwarzkopf, and both briefings were well received by the CINC. Warden's offensively oriented thinking (he liked to compare his plan, for Schwarzkopf's benefit, to the Schlieffen Plan and to Inchon) fit exactly into General Schwarzkopf's need to define an offensive strategy to free Kuwait. It also provided for options to respond to any Iraqi atrocity perpetrated against Western hostages then held in Iraq, or trapped in Western embassies in Kuwait City.*

One aspect of the campaign plan did bother Schwarzkopf. He found not nearly enough emphasis on reducing Iraqi ground forces, particularly the heavy armored units of the Republican Guards. By way of advice, the CINC mentioned this lack to Warden. It was advice Warden would later regret not taking.

After Schwarzkopf, Warden briefed Colin Powell, who also voiced his support for the INSTANT THUNDER plan. Now it was time to brief the CENTAF staff and Chuck Horner.

On August 19, a CHECKMATE team arrived in Riyadh and initially briefed Tom Olsen and the CENTAF staff. The team was headed personally by Colonel Warden, and with him were three of his key lieutenant colonels: Dave Deptula, Bernard Harvey, and Ronnie Stanfill. (Horner had known Deptula at Tyndall AFB, Florida, and thought very highly of him, both as an officer and as a fighter pilot.)

At the time of Warden's arrival, Chuck Horner needed a chief planner for the air campaign; and on paper, John Warden was the perfect man for the job, with every intellectual skill needed to craft a plan that could be executed by Horner's air forces, and which would drive the Iraqi armed forces to the edge of disaster.

But all that changed as soon as the two men met. To put it mildly, they didn't hit it off. The problem was in part personal (which could have been solved; Horner worked all the time with difficult personalities—including the man he eventually made his planning chief) and in part professional: they had irreconcilable views about constructing an offensive air campaign against Iraq.

Here is Horner's recollection of their encounter:

John Warden's briefing to Tom Olsen and the staff was well received, especially because of the outstanding targeting materials and attack options it contained. (I later learned this data came from Major General Jim Clapper, the head of Air Force Intelli-

---

At the start of the war, hundreds of westerners in Iraq and Kuwait were rounded up and placed in detention. Many of these were kept at strategic sites, as human shields. When the war started, Saddam Hussein removed the human shields—an act that, paradoxically, ensured the destruction of the strategic sites.

gence, whose people worked tirelessly in support of CHECKMATE.)
*After the briefing, Tom Olsen told me about the accomplishments
of Warden and his team, and suggested that I hear the briefing as
soon as possible. According to Tom,* INSTANT THUNDER *went well
beyond anything produced by the intelligence teams that had so far
passed through Riyadh peddling their wares.*

*Since I was anxious to hear what John Warden had to say, I
made a spot for him on my next day's schedule. And at 1300 on
August 20, I arrived in the RSAF Headquarters small conference
room, where the CENTAF staff chiefs and the* CHECKMATE *team
had assembled.*

*The briefing, unfortunately, started off poorly, the problem
being that Colonel Warden had built it for a different audience
than those like me who have been studying the Persian Gulf theater for years and airpower for decades. He had prepared the briefing as a stand-alone presentation for people at the JCS and CINC
level, who had no idea of how Iraq as a country, or airpower as a
tool, worked. That meant there was a lot of boilerplate up front,
to bring the audience up to speed and to lay the groundwork for
his subsequent points. Patience is not my long suit, and I don't like
being talked down to, so I waved Warden off from this preparatory
material and told him to get on with his main points.*

*Though he seemed a little shaken by my sharp words, he
quickly turned to his target listing. And here John Warden had the
real thing. No doubt about it. I could not fault him for the glitter-
ing listing of targets he laid out then. Not only did he have access
to target materials we had never seen before, but he had a good understanding of target systems, such as the relationship of the communications networks and the KARI air defense system. Most of
all, he had a way to rack and stack the targets so we could relate
their importance to overall political objectives. It was a solid piece
of work, and he and his team could rightfully take pride in it.*

*But then, after some discussion, I began asking questions, and
the wheels started to come off.*

*Keep in mind that the event had two aims. The briefing itself
was important. But I was also conducting a job interview. If John
Warden handled himself well—as I had every reason to expect he
would—he'd become my planning chief.*

So I had questions for him about the briefing and the CHECK-
MATE *plan—more or less factual questions (but which would at the
same time show me how well he thought and judged); and I also
had questions aimed at discovering his thought processes. I wanted
to know how his mind worked and how he solved problems. To
this second end, I threw a number of questions at him that would
give him the opportunity to reveal the depth of his knowledge.*

*For example, I asked him, "Do you think we direct too much
effort toward gaining control of the air?" Now, there is no right or
wrong answer to a question like that, but an answer would show
his reasoning process in building his plan. However, instead of
grabbing the opportunity to show how his mental machinery
worked, he simply dropped something like, "No, it's about right,"
telling me that he either knew it all and did not want to share it
with me, or else he didn't have a clue about gaining control of the
air and had just filled the "control of the air" bin with some sorties because he needed to fill the square.*

*His responses to the more factually directed questions were sim-
ilar. He danced around them—either because he didn't know the
answers (easy to understand; there was more plan than any less-
than-divine mind could easily comprehend), or else because he
didn't want me to be screwing around with his efforts. I suspect it
was a little of both.*

*Thus, when I tossed at him a question dealing with my broad
concerns about the emphasis on targets in the Baghdad metroplex,
he dodged it. To explain: any attack within an urban area carries
with it the almost certain guarantee of damage to civilian property,
and civilian casualties. But worse, because of its historical and cultural significance among Arabs, the devastation of the ancient city
of Baghdad by Western airpower could engender a hatred for the
West lasting well beyond the immediate postwar period. It would
be an Arab grievance and incitement to revenge for centuries into
the future.*

*But, as I recall, he had no real answer for this, except perhaps
to repeat his confidence in PGMs. Well, okay, I thought.* But what
if PGMs don't work as well as we hope? What then? *At that point,
Warden, as ever, got fuzzy. (In the event, PGMs performed superbly.)*

The truth is, by letting go of a little bit of control over the brief-ing, he could have easily provided me with useful answers. The plan was the work of many people. If he didn't know the answer to some question or other, it would have been simple enough to turn to the subordinate on the staff who handled such matters and ask him. He could have easily said to Dave Deptula, for instance, "Dave, you built the air control part of the plan. Can you tell Gen-eral Horner its basis, your assumptions, any limitations you see, and any possible holes in it?" While doing that would have brought risks, if in fact his subordinates had done their work, it would have been a mark of confidence and trust for him to let them answer. And of course, he could have corrected them as he saw fit. As it was, he was either too proud or too dense to try that solution.

There were also a number of other issues where we disagreed.

First, Warden's plan envisioned pulverizing Iraqi air bases and their command-and-control structure. Though that is good air-power doctrine, I didn't feel that going that far was either neces-sary or productive. It seemed to me that if we could render the KARI air defense network ineffective, then we could put the rest of the bombing sorties to better use. If an existing system is no longer going to be used effectively against you, what's the gain in de-stroying it?

Second, I had serious doubts about the way his plan allocated targets by area: some to the U.S. Navy, others to the U.S. Air Force. Though his reasons made some sense (he did it because of the physical constraints of the various aircraft types' payload and range), he unfortunately ran up against the personal experience of those who'd been frustrated, as I had, by the Route Package sys-tem in Vietnam. Now here was an Air Force colonel creating a concept that would easily lead to Route Packages once more. That wasn't about to happen on my beat.

But what I really choked on came next.

The six days of attacks, foreseen by INSTANT THUNDER, *were to be directed primarily against vital targets throughout Iraq, and principally on targets in the Baghdad area. That meant, for the most part, that Iraqi forces deployed in Kuwait and on the Saudi border would not be hit.*

Warden's reasons for this emphasis were straightforward: Airpower properly applied against the Iraqi centers of gravity would cause that nation's leaders to surrender and withdraw their forces from Kuwait. In his view, Iraqi land forces were actually a detriment, a drain, less a threat than a hungry mass that had to be fed and supplied. Therefore, once we had removed the core national strengths, the Iraqi Army would simply go home.

Though I admired Warden's singleness of purpose and his love of what airpower could accomplish, he was not the air commander. I was. More pressingly important, I was the on-scene CINC, and had other matters to consider, the most serious of these being the Iraqi divisions still poised just north of the Saudi boarder in Kuwait. At that moment, we had very few land forces in place to stop them.

First, while Colonel Warden held that because of our devastating strength in the air, the Iraqi land forces could not succeed in a ground attack, I was not in such a position to hope for the best. I knew that if we started the INSTANT THUNDER operation with only weak forces on the ground, our bases in northern Saudi Arabia might very well be overrun by the Iraqi army. That makes it very difficult to rearm and refuel aircraft.

Second, though Warden was certainly correct in his assertion that airpower would play the major role in any forthcoming conflict, I did not consider, as he did, that Iraqi ground forces—or our own ground forces, for that matter—were unimportant. But when I pressed him on these issues, the debate went further downhill.

Where I had expected intelligence (and Warden was certainly intelligent), I was getting a university academic teaching a 101 class. At every question I asked that dealt with the Iraqi ground forces, he would dismiss my concerns as unimportant. Even if he was right (which I greatly doubt), he would have been wise to forgo the temptation to treat me like a boob. The commander on the scene may well have been a boob, but he doesn't like to be treated like one. Warden's problem, I've come to realize, was partly due to personal arrogance. He doesn't easily suffer those who disagree with him. But it was also due to his absolute conviction that the entire package he was presenting was perfect. To question it, much less to doubt it, much less to consider changing it, was for him unthinkable.

Still, because I was much impressed with the excellence of his overall effort, I kept my patience, a rare thing, and continued to ask questions. "Humor me, John, just for the sake of discussion, what if the Iraqi army attacks? . . ." But each time, he seemed certain I was too stupid to grasp his central concept and gave me a patronizing "If you could only understand what I'm trying to tell you" answer.

Soon, as the discussions became increasingly disjointed, the room grew tense. One thing was clear: John Warden and I looked at the problem of air campaign planning differently. He viewed it as an almost Newtonian science, with the targeting list being an end unto itself, while for me, air warfare revolves around the ATO, logistics, joint service and allied agreements, and the million and one little things that he never had to worry about back in the Pentagon. For me, the campaign plan and the targeting list are just the starting point. They are the place where the real work on an air war begins.

The more he talked, the more I realized that the major flaw in his plan was more than the piece he had left off about the Iraqi Army. The major flaw was that he did not have an executable document. He had no idea of the processes used to integrate the air war and all that is involved. He says, "Hit this and that target." Fine, but where is the tanker schedule and the airspace deconfliction plan? Where are the rules of engagement, code words, IFF [Identification Friend or Foe] procedures, Coalition forces, radar coverage and orbits, and on and on? He skimmed through the details for a few days' effort, and ignored the problems he didn't want to or couldn't deal with. He saw war in terms of the SIOP: execute this plan and the enemy is defeated. Well, good. But what if he decides not to be defeated? What do we do then?

In the end, it took weeks to build the first offensive air campaign plan. Much of Warden's work was in it, but it went far, far beyond his work.

Sadly, I realized that his brilliance as a thinker would not carry through working with the team in Riyadh. Though I would have liked to use his efforts and his team to build an offensive air cam-

paign, John Warden was too much in love with his own thinking, and too prickly to handle the give-and-take—the communicating— that Riyadh required. I decided he was better off away from the Gulf theater. I did keep the lieutenant colonels he brought with him, to help form the nucleus of the planning cell that we would create.

John Warden went home, where he did continue to support us by sending forward a flow of valuable planning and targeting information. But as far as I was concerned, he was out of the war.

BUSTER GLOSSON AND THE BLACK HOLE

The forced departure of John Warden left Chuck Horner in a bind. He had to take the remains of the CHECKMATE effort, the Internal Look plans, and the discussions with the CINC, and meld these with the thousands of other details needed to build a campaign plan that fit into the CINC's intentions and, later, his overall plan for the liberation of Kuwait. This included the mundane aspects of logistics, communications, and day-to-day priorities. But more than all that, Horner needed a living, breathing plan that could adapt to the chaos of war, and not a set-piece, preordained effort that would lock him into a battle plan that was based on how *his* people conceived the world.* He needed an air strategy that could unfold in an ever-changing struggle, reacting to the enemy, maintaining the initiative and flexibility that airpower—and only airpower—could provide in this conflict.

Who could he put in charge of the plan? He needed the job filled *now*—August 20. He looked over his options:

Jim Crigger could do the job, but he was tied up running day-to-day operations. These were enormous, and getting bigger by the minute, as more reinforcements flowed into the AOR. Tom Olsen could also do it, but CENTAF needed a commander, and Schwarzkopf was still days away from coming into theater, meaning that Olsen had to continue as Horner's stand-in for the time being. Brigadier General Larry "Puba"

---

*The great mistake among military planners is not so much planning to fight the last war as planning to fight an enemy who is one's own mirror image. The enemy almost always has agendas planners are not aware of. Thus the need for superior intelligence collection. Sadly, Intel people tend to avoid these areas. They are fuzzy, mistakes are always possible, and Intel people don't like to risk being wrong.

Henry had arrived the day before, on loan until October from General Bob Russ, who had sent him to provide planning expertise on electronic combat operations (Henry had been an electronic-warfare officer—EWO). Few nonpilots make general, and none get to command fighter wings. Henry had done both. He was that good, and that smart. He would have been perfect as planning chief, but Horner needed his full efforts on the electronic-warfare elements of the plan, and besides he was only there on loan. His continued presence wasn't guaranteed. Brigadier General Pat Caruana was also a possibility (he'd been sent to work the bomber/tanker force), but Horner didn't know him, so he was out.*

"I was in a fog about who to pick," Horner recalls now. "Then, just like in cartoons when the lightbulb comes on over somebody's head, it hit me. Buster Glosson!"

Brigadier General Buster Glosson was already in-theater. In June of 1990, he had been exiled (for reasons lost to Chuck Horner) to work for Rear Admiral Bill Fogerty (aboard the USS *LaSalle* docked in Manamah, Bahrain) as deputy commander, Joint Task Force Middle East (JTFME), a job given to the Air Force in recognition of the important role the AWACS radar aircraft and air refueling tankers played in Operation EARNEST WILL (escorting Kuwaiti oil tankers down the Arabian Gulf and through the Straits of Hormuz). When Horner had arrived in Riyadh, Glosson had flown up to brief him on the KC-135 tanker deployment to the United Arab Emirates during July of 1990, which had been the opening U.S. response to Saddam's threats prior to the invasion of Kuwait. During the meeting, Buster had asked Horner to keep him in mind if he could be of any use.

"Yes," Chuck Horner told himself on August 20. "Now I can use Buster."

Buster Glosson was a South Carolina patrician—silver-haired, stocky, extremely intelligent, a smooth talker, quick to laugh . . . also complex, mercurial, and flamboyant. And very political; he was always working an agenda with great skill†; he was always intriguing; and he was extremely

---

*Afterward, Horner got to know Caruana, and when the chance came to pick a major general to be his three-star deputy at the U.S. Space Command, he was Horner's first choice. But in August of 1990, he had little knowledge of Caruana's tremendous talents.

†Before his exile to Bahrain, he was the Air Force's chief legislative liaison with Congress, a job he handled superbly.

competitive, extremely combative, abrupt, a bulldog: for him, like Vince Lombardi, winning was the only thing. If you were not on his team, then you must be the enemy—an attitude that inevitably caused friction in the staff. In some quarters he was (and is) despised.

Because he was himself an innovative thinker and doer, and liked aggressive innovators around him, he was a good leader for people with thick skins and daring. But he inflicted deep distress on those with an accountant's view of the world, or even on those seeking order and quiet.

Because he liked public praise, he was easy to motivate: praise him publicly and privately point out his shortcomings, and he would work harder than ever. And yet he was for the most part indifferent to what other people thought of him; he marched to his own drum.

Because he was usually decisive, he had to be reined in now and again, but for Chuck Horner, this was no sin. He would much rather have someone who took action, even if wrong, than someone who stood around waiting to be told what to do.

Chuck Horner had known Buster Glosson for years, and their relationship had sometimes been stormy, yet Glosson was obviously the one to head the planning effort. It wouldn't be fun or pretty, but he would get results. He would form a team, and he would seek feedback from the troops who might have to execute the offensive air campaign that he would be tasked to draft.

Horner called him that night (the twentieth) and ordered him to Riyadh. He was in Horner's office in the MODA building the next day.

Horner's instructions to Glosson were simple: Take the CHECKMATE effort and build an executable air campaign. To begin with, he had to build a team. He could have the CHECKMATE group that remained in Riyadh, he could have Larry Henry, he could raid deployed wings and bring over anyone else he wanted from the States; but since Horner could not spare many from the small CENTAFF staff, he was on his own. Second, Horner wanted to keep the effort U.S.-only, until they had a handle on the details of who was going to be joining in the effort. At the same time, he wanted to open up the effort to the Coalition partners as soon as possible. Third, Glosson's team needed to get their act together fast; the CINC would arrive in-theater within the week, and Horner didn't yet know when he would need an air campaign plan. Fourth, his guidance to Glosson was to prepare an ATO for the first two and a half days of the war and then, starting at day three, to be ready to build a new ATO every day until the enemy was defeated. Finally, above all else, Glosson needed to keep very close hold on security. Horner had been led to understand this last point was paramount, not only from the standpoint of operations security, but also because all the Coalition nations were doing their best to persuade Saddam to leave Kuwait peacefully. It would not help negotiations if he found out that that the United States intended to destroy him if he didn't leave.

Glosson went straight to work. In his usual, brusque fashion, he commandeered everything in sight, including the small conference room adjacent to Tom Olsen's office on the third floor of RSAF headquarters, as well as a number of CENTAF staff Horner had specifically told him *not* to touch. He also stole every high-quality person who showed up to augment Jim Crigger's CENTAF staff. Glosson would grab them, take them into his conference room, and tell them they were going to win the war by themselves, and if they told anyone what they were doing, he would personally rip their lips off their faces. Glosson was such a difficult person to deal with, not everyone was eager to join him, yet once they did, they adored it. The team he forged was tight-knit, and it was an exciting place to work.

The secrecy of the work, plus the fact that Glosson's people worked sixteen to eighteen hours a day, meant that a new person who came to Riyadh simply disappeared if he shanghaied them for his team. It was as if they had been sucked up by a black hole. And so Buster Glosson's area came to be known as "The Black Hole."

Late in August, after the D Day plan came to be more or less routine, Horner decided it was a good moment to mix some of the D Day experience and thinking into Glosson's team (most of Glosson's group were newcomers, while most of the D Day planners were Ninth Air Force staff who had been around a long time). Thus it was decided to beef up the "Black Hole" shop with a few of the D Day planners—a plan that was somewhat complicated by the secrecy associated with offensive operations: The D Day planners and the Black Hole planners could neither work together nor talk to each other.

One of the early D Day additions to the Black Hole group was Sam Baptiste. Though he was at first unwilling to work for Glosson (he liked working for Crigger—a preference many shared: Crigger led, Glosson drove), at Horner's insistence, he came around and agreed to work for Glosson. Baptiste and Army Lieutenant Colonel Bill Welch, a member of

Battlefield Coordination Element (BCE) team, became the key planners in building the Kuwait Theater target lists.*

Glosson and the Black Hole gang worked day and night, and as the hours grew longer, tempers grew shorter. Glosson didn't have much patience with slow learners or foot-draggers. And when a few of the original CHECKMATE team proved unable to adapt their thinking, they had to return to the States. Others, like Dave Deptula, excelled; the harder it got, the more they flourished.

The biggest of their problems was the moving-train aspect of planning. As soon as they'd have some piece of it set up, another unit would arrive and have to be accommodated in the plan; and this, in turn, could change everything else. Or else someone would gain a new insight into a better way to conduct an attack or defeat a system, and that would turn the whole plan upside down. Or else they'd outline a course of action, only to get bogged down in a shortage of aerial refueling tracks or of appropriate types and numbers of munitions. Each day was more confusion than order and light, yet they just steady, hard–worked their way through it.

★ On August 23, General Schwarzkopf arrived in Riyadh.

As soon as possible, Horner left him with all the diplomatic problems and organizational worries and hurried back to CENTAF, sharing an office in RSAF headquarters with Tom Olsen. Next door, the Black Hole gang was in full swing, with Buster Glosson constantly rushing in and out, trying out new ideas and sharing progress reports with Horner and Olsen. It was a heady time.

On August 26, Glosson emerged from the Black Hole to brief his offensive air campaign to Horner. This did not turn out to be one of Buster Glosson's shining moments. Though the plan itself was splendid, the briefing was a disaster. And Horner made his disappointment loudly apparent. When a crestfallen Buster Glosson returned to the Black Hole, and the others there asked him how it went, he summarized Horner's crit-

---

*The BCE was a hundred-person element that represented the ground effort in the air effort headquarters (TACC). Their team kept the air commander up to speed about what was happening on the ground, about what the ground commanders thought needed to be done, and about intelligence the ground forces were generating about enemy ground forces. Also, the BCE gave feedback to the ground forces about what the air was doing, how they were progressing, and any problems the air was having with the ground forces.

icisms this way: "The briefing," he told them with searing honesty, "was (1) ill-prepared, (2) poorly presented, and (3) violently received." They needed to go back to work.

The issue for Horner was not about the quality of the plan. He already saw that was shaping up just fine. The issue was that once Horner had signed off on it, the briefing would go to General Schwarzkopf. And the CINC would not only have to understand the plan, he would also have to buy into it as his own; and then he would also have to be prepared to defend this plan before General Powell, Secretary Cheney, and the President. Since the CINC's greatest fear was to lose his reputation, it was important to make sure that nothing happened that might embarrass him. That meant he had to comprehend what Horner and Glosson were telling him in sufficient detail that he was *certain* not to fail to answer any question Powell, Cheney, or Bush might ask him. And that meant Horner had to give him something he could comprehend (and alter if he so desired); but most of all, it had to be something that made him feel comfortable.

However, the briefing was so fuzzy, poorly organized, and broad that it was difficult for a listener to understand—especially if he was not an airman. It gave the impression that the Air Force didn't have a strong focus on its battle aims; it showed no understanding of the sequential effects of its plan of attack. Instead, they just seemed to be running around blowing things up in a helter-skelter fashion.

Later, Horner and Glosson got together to work out what needed to be done. Here, as throughout the planning process, Buster Glosson did the basic planning brainwork, while Horner made the plan intelligible to other people—and especially to non-airmen. He coached, he was a cheerleader and a sounding board, but he tried to stay out of the details. He was quick with pats on the back when the planning showed promise and innovation, and a frowner and barb-tosser when it did not.

During their discussion, Horner hit on the idea to turn Schwarzkopf's briefing into something like a movie that would tell the unfolding story of how they planned to use airpower. The "movie briefing" would work something like this:

First, they would talk about the weeks preceding the strike, when extra sorties would be flown every night, to get the Iraqis used to seeing activity. Likewise, in the days preceding the strike, tankers would begin to move forward with the fighter packages. And then in the opening scene of the "movie," the jets would take off late at night in minimum moonlight, to reduce the chance an Iraqi fighter could find the F-117 contingent visually as they slipped across the border at altitude. The scene would unfold with the nonstealth aircraft flying beneath the coverage of the long-range Iraqi radar. Then Special Operations helicopters would lead in the Army Apaches, which struck the first blow when they fired Hellfire missiles against a pair of border radars. (This was actually a later change, made after Schwarzkopf realized that Special Operations was going to strike the first blow. Since Schwarzkopf was famously suspicious of Special Forces, it was decided that the U.S. Army Apaches would strike the first blow, all of which helped sell the plan.) The rest of the briefing-movie scenes would follow:

The F-117s would hit Baghdad and the communications centers. F-111s would hit the Sector Operations Centers for KARI. F-15Es would hit fixed Scud sites. F-18s/F-16s/A-10s/AV-8s would hit Iraq Army units. A host of allied aircraft would also be doing their part: RAF Tornadoes would hit airfields; RAF Jaguars would hit the Iraqi Army; RSAF F-5s would hit airfields in the western parts of Iraq; Special Operations helicopters would be infiltrating to pick up downed airmen; there were tankers, AWACS, F-15 and Tornado ADV (Air Defense Variant) CAPs; there was Rivet Joint on the Voice Product Network (a secure, encrypted voice network that allowed the intelligence technicians on the Rivet Joint to relay vital information to the AWACS controller, who would then pass it on to the fighter in unclassified form). It was the full panoply of all that would unfold in the opening days of the war. And it would give a clear indication of what would continue. That is, the Iraqi Army would be so worn down that the land war to come would feature very few casualties.

To make all this work, Horner had Glosson build a series of plastic overlays with symbols showing where the various aircraft would be at various times, together with the targets they were planning to strike. Thus, the 0300 overlay showed F-117s near Baghdad, while the tankers with assorted fighters were well to the south, and the Rivet Joint and AWACS were in the orbits they usually occupied. Then the 0400 overlay showed explosion symbols on the targets being struck, together with the next wave of attackers. This overlay also showed the MiG CAPS over Iraq and not Saudi Arabia, as they had been all during Desert Shield. The movie unwound before the viewer not unlike a primitive jerky cartoon. Even so, anybody watching would get a sense of the timing, the enormity, the integration, and the sequence of attacks and how they related to taking down the air defenses, and hitting critical time-sensitive targets.

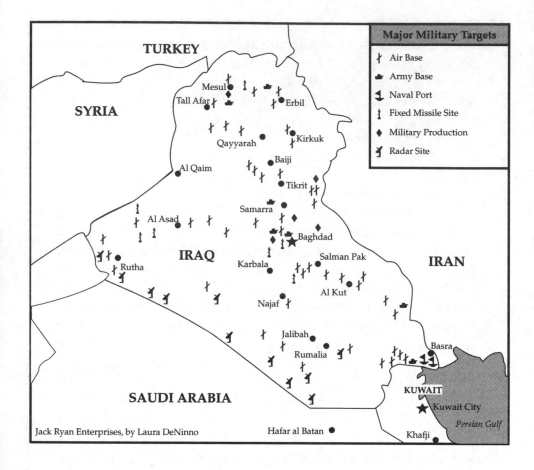

Major Military Targets

⊥ Air Base
🛥 Army Base
⚓ Naval Port
⬧ Fixed Missile Site
♦ Military Production
✗ Radar Site

Jack Ryan Enterprises, by Laura DeNinno

Owing to the CINC's anxieties about the Republican Guard, one significant element was added by Schwarzkopf to the plan, and to the briefing. Provisions had to be made to attack the elite Iraqi force early and
often. The problem for him was this: Colin Powell had decreed that success involved killing the Republican Guard, which for him was the Iraqis'
strategic military center of gravity. Thus, Schwarzkopf did not want the
loss of the Republican Guard to take place on his watch, and so he feared
that when the bombing started, the Republican Guard would pull up
stakes and head for Baghdad, and he would be judged a failure. In order
to ease the CINC's ever-growing anxieties, a large part of the air campaign was given over to preventing the Republican Guards from leaving
the battlefield. They were bombed heavily, with more B-52 sorties added
later. (In fact, Horner always doubted that the Republican Guards would

Battle Theater in Comparison to the Eastern United States

IRAQ

Baghdad

Columbus OH

As-Samawah

An-Nasiriyah

375 Km

355 Km

345 Km

Basra

Washington DC

133 km

Kuwait City

SAUDI ARABIA

King Khalid Military City

Knoxville TN

VII Corps Staging

Persian

400 Km

522 Km

Ad-Dammam

Raleigh NC

440 Km

400 Km

Augusta GA

Riyadh

0 _____ 400 km

Jack Ryan Enterprises, by Laura DeNinno

leave the field. First of all, it would have put them on the roads, where they would have been easy pickings. And second, if Saddam's strategy remained as it appeared then—that is, to plunge Coalition forces into the defensive arrangements he had worked so hard to erect along the border—then it didn't make sense to remove his strongest forces from the battle. In this, Horner later proved to be right.)

After Horner and Glosson worked through this "movie briefing," Glosson went back into his office, and a few hours later he emerged with the plastic overlay briefing that was to be his until the war started in January (though updated and fine-tuned constantly). This briefing in its various evolutions was given many times to General Schwarzkopf (who liked it enough to instantly make it his own), to Colin Powell on his September 12 visit to Riyadh, and to the Secretary of Defense and the President in Washington, D.C., a month later.

One change Horner added to the early briefing was to have a chart made that showed the fight taking place in phases. By phases he meant that various objectives would be emphasized at various times—that is to say, the four phases did not actually indicate separate actions, one beginning as the last ended, but levels of focus. They offered a way to communicate airman talk to non-airmen, and they were basically simple, the first phase being to gain control of the air, and the last to prepare the battlefield and support the land attack.

So:

- PHASE I—STRATEGIC AIR CAMPAIGN. To gain control of the air and hit the Iraqi leadership, NBC, Scuds, and electric and oil infrastructure. The idea was to deny Saddam supplies but not necessarily to destroy his heavy industry. That is, power and fuel would be attacked, but in such a way that facilities could be reconstituted relatively easily after the war—e.g., grids would be hit instead of generators.
- PHASE II—AIR SUPERIORITY IN THE KTO. This idea came from General Schwarzkopf, who was thinking like an army general, in terms of land area and lines on maps. Even though this phase was redundant (gaining control of the air would happen simultaneously over Iraq and over Kuwait), Horner didn't fight him on it. It gave him buy-in to the plan (as in, "I thought of that"), so why argue with him?
- PHASE III—PREPARATION OF THE BATTLEFIELD. This included iso-

lating the battlefield, killing tanks and artillery, and destroying morale. It was at this point that Horner and Glosson introduced into the plan the important (and later well-known) goal of destroying 50 percent of Iraqi tanks, APCs (armored personnel carriers), and artillery.

According to Army doctrine, when a land unit's effectiveness has been reduced to 50 percent or less, then it is no longer combat-useful. At the end of the planned air campaign, the Iraqi Army would be reduced by 50 percent. Hence, in essence, when the air effort was over, the war would be over, and little would remain to be done save collecting prisoners.

To understand this goal, it is important to remember that Norman Schwarzkopf genuinely loved his troops. Their safety and ultimate survival was one of his chief passions. Thus, any air plan that ignored the troops on the ground would be dead if presented to the CINC. It is also important to understand that Schwarzkopf did not insist on a ground campaign. On the contrary, he would have been delighted if the Iraqis had surrendered before his land forces went into battle. All the same, he knew there was a 95 percent chance of land war, and he wanted to make sure air operations were conducted to maximize the survival of the men and women of his land forces. Thus, the air plan talked about "preparation of the battlefield" and attriting "50 percent" of the Iraqi armor and artillery.

Why "preparation" instead of just bombing the Iraqis into the Stone Age? Because "preparation of the battlefield" has special doctrinal meaning to the U.S. Army. If a battlefield is well prepared, few U.S. soldiers have to die. Ergo, the more thoroughly the Air Force can prepare the battlefield, the happier Norman Schwarzkopf would be.

Airmen are too often perceived as fighting some war other than the land commanders' war. This war would be different. It would be the CINC's war. Though it would *primarily* be an air campaign, to sell that campaign, Horner had to get the approval of General Schwarzkopf the land commander, before he got it from General Schwarzkopf the CINC.

The CINC bought this idea, and even thought it was his. (By the by, if the Air Force actually achieved this goal, they would clearly demonstrate airpower's decisive effect on the battlefield—perhaps for the first time. Did matters unfold that way? We shall see.)

- PHASE IV—THE GROUND WAR.

How long would the campaign take?

The truth was, no one knew, and so estimates changed and varied. When the air staff ran the original ATO through the computer, the estimate was about a week. This seemed ridiculously hopeful to Buster Glosson, and so the time grew to three weeks. By November, it was thought that the planned First Phase would be pretty well achieved in less than a week (five to six days); Phase II in two days; Phase III in two weeks; and Phase IV would take up to three weeks. Later still, in a December briefing, Horner told Secretary Cheney that the computer models showed the war lasting from one to three weeks, but that he himself thought it would last at least six weeks. (This guess actually proved substantially correct.)

As it turned out, Phase I took from ten minutes to three days, depending on how success is measured. Phase II happened during Phase I. Phase III took five-plus weeks. And Phase IV took four-plus days.

WAR DURATION IN DAYS: DECEMBER ESTIMATE VERSUS REALITY

Time Required	I	II	III	IV
CENTAF Est. Dec 90	6	2	14	21
20-20 Hindsight	3	0	38	4

The numbers of days do not total. For example, the thirty-eight days of Phase III include strikes conducted during the three days of Phase I. The message is that the impact of airpower on the enemy was underestimated, and the ability of airpower to destroy a deployed enemy was overestimated. The airman is always too optimistic, while the landman is too pessimistic.

★ Finally, it would be useful to compare the changes that took place in the air campaign from John Warden's INSTANT THUNDER, to the September iteration of Buster Glosson's briefing, and then to the ATO when the war started. Here are some numbers:*

---

*Gulf War Air Power Survey, *Volume I, p. 185.*

Target Growth by Category

Target Type	INST THUN	13 Sep	15 Jan
Air Defense	10	21	58
NBC	8	20	23
Scuds	a	a	43
Leadership	5	15	33
CCC	19	26	59
Electricity	10	14	17
Oil	6	8	12
Rail and Bridges	3	12	33
Airfields	7	13	31
Naval and Ports	1	4	19
Military Support	15	41	62
Republican Guard	0	b	37
Breaching	0	0	6
SAMs	0	0	43
TOTALS	84	174	476

[a]Scuds included in NBC category
[b]Republican Guard included in Military Support category

This chart (a counting of the targets of targets to be struck in the first two and one half days) illustrates that while the first effort by CHECKMATE was commendable, it was out of date shortly thereafter. The number of targets doubled between INSTANT THUNDER and mid-September. And then the 174 targets in September grew to 218 in October, to 262 in December, and to 476 by war's start. And as the war itself unfolded, the number of targets grew to thousands.

INSIDE THE BLACK HOLE

The Black Hole started out in the conference room adjacent to the Olsen/Horner office on the third floor of the RSAF headquarters. In November, it was moved into the basement complex of that building. In that complex was also housed the TACC Current Operations Center, the computer room, the RSAF Command Post, and other offices. A long hall connected these; the TACC Current Ops occupied the far (or south) end of the hall, while the Black Hole was at the north end. The RSAF Current Operations Center was on the left, about halfway down the hall from the TACC to the Black Hole. On the right and across the hall from the RSAF Current Ops was the Computer Center, a large room (perhaps sixty feet by fifty feet) filled with computers. There were many CAFMS terminals, all fed by the single large computer that was used to pull the ATO together. Between the large computer and the CAFMS terminals was a laptop that translated the input from the large computer into data the CAFMS terminals could display and manipulate. At the end of the hall, and straight ahead, was a stairs that led down to the RSAF Peace Shield bunker (another hundred or so feet below ground). Though it was still under construction, it was used as an air raid shelter during the first few Scud strikes on Riyadh.

Just before these stairs, and a ninety-degree turn to the right, was the entrance to the Black Hole. Up until the war started in January, this door was closely guarded (what lay beyond being top secret). After the war started, the door was simply left open.

The conference room the Black Hole occupied was about thirty feet wide by fifty feet deep. Immediately inside the room and on the right there was a small administrative section. Straight ahead was a small office shared by Buster Glosson and his excellent deputy, Tony Tolin (who had recently given up command of the F-117 wing and was in line to be promoted to brigadier general). To the left was a room with maps on the wall and a bank of televisions. In this room, Dave Deptula led the group that worked the targets in and around Baghdad. (The televisions were supposed to display target information, but they never worked and weren't used.)

Down a small hall (created by plywood sheets) and to the right was a small room occupied by the Scud targeting section. Inside, pictures of fixed Scud launch sites were pinned to the wall. Also on the wall were maps showing Scud storage areas, Scud support facilities, factories, and the plants where Scud fuel was manufactured.

Because the missiles were moved out before the war started, once the fixed sites and the storage and production facilities were hit, there was nothing more to do but allocate sorties to Scud-hunting (A-10s by day, and F-15Es and LANTIRN Pod–equipped F-16s at night). As a result, the Scud targeting section turned out to be only partially useful.

A side story: Scud fuel was stable for only a limited time, and once it became unstable, it couldn't be used. The Black Hole planners therefore figured that if the fuel production factory was destroyed, the Iraqis would have to stop shooting Scuds roughly three to four weeks afterward. In due course, the factory was bombed in the opening days of the war; but it appears the Iraqis didn't follow the technical data, because they fired Scuds for the next six weeks.

Across the hall was the KTO (Kuwait Theater of Operations) Room, also containing many maps. Here Sam Baptiste and Bill Welch put together the effort to hit the Iraqi Army.

Behind it was the room occupied by the Air Superiority section, headed by Glenn Profitt, where Wild Weasel schedules and EF-111/EA-6 support were planned and put into the ATO (Profitt had taken over from Lenny Henry in October). As it turned out, once the war started, air superiority was attained faster than expected. And so work in this section, as in the Scud section, soon became routine, and the team became quickly unemployed.

Lastly, there should have been an "interdiction section" (that is to say, an "isolating the battlefield" section). To Chuck Horner's later regret, there wasn't. The reason not deserves an explanation. Let's let him give it:

> In our doctrine, we assign air to attack targets. When these targets are associated with the enemy air defense, our missions are called counter air. When these targets are in close proximity to our friendly ground forces, our missions are called CAS. When these targets are associated with whatever supplies the war effort, our missions are called air interdiction (that is, using air to interdict fielded forces from their support, logistics, command and control, reinforcements, movement, letters home, etc.). Other doctrinal missions include air superiority and nuclear strike (there is not a doctrinal mission called "strategic attack").
>
> Now, what do we call bombing a secret police headquarters that supports the evil regime? It isn't counter air. It isn't CAS. It isn't interdiction (although we have to file it under that mission area now). So what is it?
>
> What we need is a category of effort that addresses missions that are designed to defeat an enemy through means other than attacking his military forces. That is, once we have gained control of

the air and hit the various fixed targets, our main effort has to be to isolate the battlefield. In Vietnam we hit the North for two reasons: (a) to interdict supplies coming south; and (b) to punish the North Vietnamese into stopping their support of the insurgency in the south. This latter category (b) really needs a name. Some would call it strategic, but strategic technically means either attacking a nation's vitals or nuclear operations. Take your pick. I like the term offensive airpower, as this indicates you are doing something over enemy territory that is neither air superiority, air interdiction, nor CAS.

★ The Plan, of course, is only a step toward the war. Once the planning process was under way, there remained the millions of necessary actions, operations, procedures, problems solved, and just plain acts of sweaty labor that translated the Plan into focused violence.

7

BAND OF BROTHERS
AND SISTERS

By the time General Schwarzkopf returned to Saudi Arabia on the twenty-third of August, the offensive air plan had been hammered into workable shape, and Chuck Horner had come to realize that the United States would almost certainly have to fight Iraq. Says Horner:

> By then I had no doubts that at some point we would have to go on the offensive. It was just a question of when—sooner if the Iraqis launched an attack, later if we did. I hoped that my convictions were wrong and that perhaps diplomacy would work, but the fortifications rising in Kuwait made it very evident that diplomacy was going to fail. That would leave us with the job of throwing the Iraqis out of Kuwait. Though I was convinced this would mean hard work for us, I also felt the fight would go fast. As events unfolded, I was pretty much right.
>
> One option open to Saddam that may have saved him from war (and, thank God, he was probably too proud or too stupid to take it) was for him to have pulled out of Kuwait City and simply remained in occupation of the oil fields in North Kuwait and the islands at the mouth of the Tigris and Euphrates Rivers. Doing that would have posed a terrible dilemma for us: To stay and not fight? To declare victory and go home? Or to fight, even though Saddam had given up the greater part of his spoils? If we went home, then Saddam could continue to threaten his neighbors with an intact army. If we stayed without fighting, we would not only risk looking like an army of occupation, but it was a hard land and climate for our troops. But then, would an offensive to eject Saddam be justified?

*Saddam, it turned out, was a lucky adversary for us. He could
have made life much harder for us than he did.*

The actual military situation had changed very little during the CINC's
absence. There was as yet nothing much standing between Saddam Hussein's divisions on the Kuwaiti border and the Saudi heartland. The relatively thin Islamic Peninsula Shield forces were centered in the west in
King Khalid Military City,* while elements of the XVIIIth Airborne
Corps and the U.S. Marines were just getting off the boats and airplanes
at Dhahran.

The ground defense plan remained for small unit resistance along the
coast road, if the Iraqis had attacked that way. And if they had attacked
inland, where there were no roads, air would have stopped them. Since
the early U.S. defensive force consisted primarily of elements of the 82d
Airborne division, and the 82d has no armor (after they drop into battle, they walk), what effectively blocked Saddam from Riyadh was 82d
Airborne "speed bumps."

It would have been a repeat of Korea in 1950—that is, fight where
possible, but pull back. Trade land for time. Sting the enemy at every opportunity, but keep U.S. and friendly losses to a minimum. And use air
to sap the enemy's strength until he had exhausted his force, and friendly
forces could be built up for a counterattack.

All of this began to change when the 82d Airborne division began to
be augmented by the armored punch of the 24th Mechanized Infantry division and their Abrams tanks. At that point, Saddam had a lot more
than "speed bumps" to worry about if he moved south.

Meanwhile, Horner was eager to shed the hat he wore as CENTCOM Forward and get back to his *real* work as CENTAF commander.
Working the essentially political job of looking out for General
Schwarzkopf's interests (making sure that when the CINC returned to
Saudi Arabia, he could pick up where he would have been if he had not
left Jeddah nearly three weeks earlier) was not a grievous burden for
Horner; it was an honor that Schwarzkopf had entrusted him with the re-

---

*The nations of the Gulf Cooperation Council formed a military pact like NATO, but less formal. An expression of this alliance was a Coalition land force with elements from each GCC
nation that was stationed at the huge military base at King Khalid Military City near the
Saudi–Iraq border.*

sponsibility. But he was doing the CINC's work and not his own, and he wanted to get on with his own work—planning for and employing airpower. He wanted to be with his own troops. And he wanted to get into the details he'd had to relinquish to Tom Olsen. Though Olsen had handled things in his usual exemplary way while he himself was occupied with the CINC's business, Horner did not like being a spectator.

So there was no one happier than Chuck Horner when General Schwarzkopf's plane touched down on August 23.

★ Meanwhile, after much blood, sweat, and tears, the Black Hole team had created a complete, executable plan—that is, a plan that could be translated into a series of Air Tasking Orders that munitions and maintenance troops could use to load and marshal the jets, and that the pilots and crews could use to navigate and bomb. It met the CINC's guidance about political objectives, and it was a living document that would flex in response to changes in the coming battle.

Buster Glosson had been a difficult boss, yet that had had little impact on the morale of the people assigned to the Black Hole. They simply had had so much important work to do that they'd been too challenged and busy to be much bothered by him.

The toughest element in creating an ATO is its open-ended character: it can always be made better, but when one piece is moved, all the other pieces shift—some only a little, others a lot. Though a perfect ATO might exist in some dream (or textbook), it has never existed in fact; and each day the Black Hole crew worked on the offensive air campaign, they discovered things that needed to be done to make it better . . . and at first to make it executable.

In late August, the plan was little more than a briefing, covering the highlights that the ATO would in time cover in detail, but it was a briefing that carried much on its shoulders, for it was tasked with conveying the plans and intentions of Chuck Horner and his staff to those who had to approve them—Schwarzkopf, Cheney, and Bush. Later, the President would also bring approval of the United Nations and Congress along with him. Specifically, the briefing had to convey the mental images of thousands of airplanes in a nearly three-day-long ballet.

Why only three days? Even though Horner knew the air campaign might go on for several months, he was convinced that no plan would last more than a couple of days before events caused it to be taken apart and put back together, so he allowed Glosson and his team to lay out the first three daily ATOs and nothing else. The general planning went on, of course, but Horner did not want his people to lock into specifics beyond that time.

When the plan was presented to Schwarzkopf, he approved it with little change.

The only detail that bothered him was the use of Special Operations Forces (SOF) helicopters during the opening moments of the war to lead Task Force NORMANDY, a planned strike on Iraqi early-warning radars located on the border with Saudi Arabia. The issue came up during the third run-through of the briefing. As Chuck Horner tells the story:

The CINC's concern, and that's a polite term for an 8.0 outburst on the Richter Scale, was that the Special Forces were going to start their own little war up there. And when they got in trouble, as he feared they would (he had his own ghosts from Vietnam to deal with, remember), he would have to bail them out with regular Army troops. In response, Buster carefully pointed out that the MH-53 PAVE LOW helicopters of the SOFs had to lead the way because they were equipped with the new, accurate NAVISTAR global positioning satellite (GPS) navigation systems needed to find the radars. He further reported that the actual shooting would be done by regular Army AH-64A Apache attack helicopters of the 101st Air Assault division. He then added that the PAVE LOWs would also provide up-to-the-minute satellite communications, as well as provide a combat search and rescue (CSAR) capability, if it was needed.

This idea of Army helicopters striking the first blow of the war really appealed to the CINC and greatly worked in our favor. To wit, even though the F-117 Stealth fighters were approaching Baghdad, and the air- and sea-launched cruise missiles were on their way, the first actual ordnance on target in the war would be delivered by the regular forces of the U.S. Army. It's sort of like locating your Navy base in South Carolina when Mendel Rivers was in Congress. Though you could build the base at just about any harbor, it sure was going to be a lot smoother if you put it in Charleston, South Carolina. In our case, while anyone could drop the first bomb to hit a target, it made sense to use the Apaches. And it sure made the briefing with the CINC go a lot smoother!

CENTAF COMMANDER

Here, meanwhile, are Chuck Horner's reflections on the responsibilities he faced as he got back into the saddle:

I had several jobs, so I guess I didn't have to worry about boredom.

Planning for the offensive while maintaining the defense was job one.

Related to that was job two, which was to make sure we were ready at all times to go to war.

Job three was to be the leader without giving the impression of wanting to be in charge.

In this regard, I had to be especially sensitive in my approach to the contingents from the other nations in the Coalition. They expected me to lead, yet it was important for me to respect their inputs and concerns. In other words, I had to create the trust that would make them want to come to me for ideas, help, and coordination. On the other hand, if I needed anything from them, I had to be very careful how I approached them. And when putting together my guidance to U.S. airmen of all services, I had to make sure it was sound, not only for the sake of my own people, but for the sake of the Coalition partners. If they could agree with it, then they would nod and say, "That sounds good to me."

I worked very hard to create an environment of openness, respect, and trust. There were no secrets, no special friends; all of us were equal and important, regardless of service or nation.

This attitude sometimes rankled my people, but they soon caught on and operated in the same mode (except for the majors from the USAF and the USMC; they always kept a wary eye on one another).

Job four was to be the spiritual leader of the airmen, primarily of the USAF, but (in a more understated role) of units from the allies as well.

What do I mean? First of all, I visited each unit as often as possible to make sure they had what they needed (to the extent that I could get it for them). They needed a lot: In some places, the folks lived in tents. Others in the early days had abysmal food (some meat they got had hair and teeth). Others had trouble getting mail, intelligence products, or weapons. And from time to time there were small problems with the host nation that I was able to nip with a friendly word to the local commander.

A big part of doing this job was just being seen. This means a lot to the troops living in uncertainty (How long are we going to be here? When is the war going to start?) and in difficult conditions (where the temperature is 110 degrees Fahrenheit, and they live in tents, without cold beer, far away from home).

At the same time, the commanders knew when I was coming and that I would be asking about how the troops were being taken care of. Although they all knocked themselves out to take care of their own troops, it helped when they could go the local host commander and say, "You know about those gym privileges you were going to give my women on Wednesday nights? Well, General Horner is coming tomorrow, and I know he is going to beat me up about that. So can you help me out?" And General Mohammed (not a real name), who had been avoiding the issue, since he did not want women in his gym on Wednesday nights because his own troops couldn't use it then, would say something like, "Yes, I think it is a wise thing for the women to have use of the gym one night a week. But you must make sure that the doors are guarded and that no men are allowed to see them in their sports clothing." (By men, he of course meant his own men, some of whom would have been offended at the sight and might have complained to the local religious police.) But his real message was more like, "Okay, you got me, because your request is reasonable and I am your host. And besides, I don't want you to tell Horner that I am not helping you out, because he might go back to Behery and then I'd get chewed out."

To sum up, my job in Riyadh was to serve the CINC and form the Coalition. My job as a commander was to care for the troops. And my job as the JFACC was to provide for vision and esprit de corps.

Just about everything I watched over was of course the responsibility of someone in the staff. For example, Bill Rider in logistics, Randy Witt in communications, and Randy Randolph, the surgeon, had specific responsibilities in areas such as fuel, muni-

tions, spare parts for Rider; lines of communication, message traf-
fic flow, equipment status for Witt; and public health, hospitals,
and medical evacuation plans for Randolph. I didn't know any-
thing about these matters—all of which are pass/fail in war—but
I knew enough to know when they had all the bases covered; and
I could help them get what they needed when they were having
problems with their counterparts back in the States.

Though rank is not that big a deal in the Air Force, and we are
taught that getting the job done is more important, still, each of
these deputies was a colonel, while their counterparts in the States
were two- or three-star generals. Thus, there was friction now and
then. The folks in Europe and the States busted their asses to help
us, but sometimes they had a different appreciation for what we
needed than we did. Sometimes, in honest differences of opinion,
a general tends to think he is more right than the colonel way out
there in Riyadh. Well, if I sided with my colonel, then the guy back
in the States had no choice but to give in; for ours was the only
show in town, and the Chief of Staff of the Air Force was not only
my dear friend, but he sure didn't want Schwarzkopf telling Pow-
ell that the Air Force was not supporting their troops in the field.
Keep in mind that I did not throw my weight around, but I was
well aware of the power I had, and I didn't hesitate to indicate a
willingness to use it when it was appropriate to do so. In the
process I hurt a few feelings, but only those that needed to be hurt.

THE MIKE DUGAN FIASCO

General Mike Dugan became Chief of Staff of the Air Force in August 1990, taking over from General Larry Welch. The two men could not have been more different. Welch was shy, retiring, and shunned publicity, while Dugan was outgoing, flamboyant, and courted the press. He was also blazingly candid, and had a striking aptitude for putting his foot in his mouth.

In September, Dugan made a trip to Riyadh during the same week Colin Powell was in the Kingdom for update briefings (as Chief of Staff, Dugan's relationship to CENTAF was at best indirect, and thus the reason for the visit was of tenuous validity). The Chairman arrived on the scene quietly, bringing with him only an aide. Dugan arrived with an entourage, including several press people. Both the trip and the entourage were probably innocuous in themselves, though General Powell no doubt noticed and disapproved. Later events would cast them in a somewhat more sinister light.

In fairness to General Dugan, we should point out that he felt General Welch's inaccessibility had prevented the Air Force from gaining its fair share of press coverage. His own aim, therefore, was to build the Air Force's credibility with the media. And he had courageously set out to present the USAF as it was—good, bad, and ugly. Looking later at the events of September, Chuck Horner is convinced that Dugan brought reporters along on his visit not for the sake of polishing his own ego, but to give the press an opportunity to see and highlight the men and women of the Air Force in the desert.

In preparation for the visit, Horner asked General Schwarzkopf if Buster Glosson could brief the air campaign to General Dugan. The answer was a surprising no, owing to the CINC's deep concerns about security. This was not intended as a slight. Security *was* (and had to be) tight. So, for example, when Powell was briefed, Lieutenant General Tom Kelly, the J-3 of the joint staff, was left out. Because he was not cleared, he was not told about the plan. Schwarzkopf undoubtedly was also far from eager to have Washington brass second-guessing him or trying to run his war—certainly well-founded concerns.

Nevertheless, Horner insisted. "After all," he told the CINC, "this is the Air Force leader and a member of the Joint Chiefs of Staff. And it will mostly be Air Force people who execute this plan."

And Schwarzkopf finally relented.

The briefing itself pleased Dugan. In fact, it would have been hard for him not to like it. The information held no surprises for an airman, and indicated that Horner, Glosson, and the Black Hole gang had developed a thoughtful, executable plan.

During the flight back to Washington, however, the affair began to turn messy. General Dugan (undoubtedly in an expansive mood following his successful visit) discussed with members of his press entourage what might happen if an air campaign were to be launched against Iraq. The remarks were generalized and broad. He simply described how any airman would have conducted war against Iraq at this time and place, information every airman knows as well as he knows his own skin. In the process of describing the upcoming battle, it was clear that the Army would play second string behind the Air Force's lead (another act that was later given a somewhat sinister interpretation in some camps, though in the event it turned out to be correct).

Unfortunately, there is only one really good way to conduct an air campaign, which meant Dugan was guilty of giving away secrets. And there is no doubt that Dugan gave out information that had been outlined in specific detail in the air campaign plan briefing; and that he had made inferences and remarks which could have been taken as disrespectful to the Army, Navy, and Israel. There is also no doubt that keeping Saddam Hussein ignorant of U.S. war strategy made absolute sense; to do otherwise jeopardized the lives of pilots.

So in telling the airpower story, he gave away secrets, put down the Army, and was crucified for it. As the old children's joke has it, "Open mouth, insert foot."

On Sunday, September 16, the story broke in the *Washington Post*. An outraged Colin Powell called Schwarzkopf and Cheney. An outraged General Schwarzkopf called Chuck Horner, who shared his boss's outrage. And the next day Secretary Cheney called Mike Dugan to fire him. He had paid for his foolishness by being relieved from duty.

The official reason for the public execution of General Dugan was his revelation of secrets, and it is true, he was guilty of that. However, a case can be made that his real crime was insensitivity to the role of the CINC. It was Norman Schwarzkopf's responsibility, not Mike Dugan's, to describe how the air campaign in the Gulf Theater would be conducted. Dugan failed to appreciate that. Even his trip to Saudi Arabia was of doubtful wisdom from the point of view of his command responsibility. Yes, he was Chief of Staff of the Air Force; but he was also out of the direct command loop of CENTCOM.

Chuck Horner says in summary:

> I can tell you that while I love Mike Dugan as a close friend, I was hurt by his interview. First, even though both of us hate ego people (and granting that I am one myself), I felt he was on an ego trip. Second, I felt he had betrayed the trust I had put in him when I'd persuaded Schwarzkopf to let us brief him. But then, third, after I got my ruffled feathers back in place, I felt sorry for Dugan. I was surprised he didn't act smarter. Why not? I believe he had been suckered in by his own enthusiasm and the euphoria and

*false expectations you get when you become a high muckety-muck,
like the Chief of Staff of the Air Force, with everyone congratulat-
ing you and telling you how smart you are and how pretty. The line
between self-confidence and inflated ego is very fine, and generals
too easily slip over to the inflated side of the line. I know I've done
that, and it is likely that Mike Dugan did this time, and paid for it.*

BRIEFINGS IN WASHINGTON

Even as Buster Glosson and his Black Hole team were pounding out the
air campaign, a select group of Army planners had been developing a
ground campaign. The team, called the Jedi Knights, was led by Lieutenant Colonel Joe Purvis from the Army's School of Advanced Military
Studies at Fort Leavenworth. The Jedi Knights had developed a ground
campaign plan that called for a single U.S. Army Corps, U.S. Marine
Corps, British, and Islamic force attack into Kuwait.

Bear in mind that they were looking to attack an Army twice the size
of theirs—half a million men, including the elite Republican Guards,
with their up-to-date Soviet armor and equipment—and that the Iraqis
had been busily fortifying the Saudi–Kuwait border with artillery, mines,
trenches, barbed wire, fire ditches (ditches that would be filled with oil
and then ignited), and other obstacles to invasion.

By October 6, Purvis's planners had developed several options. The
most desirable of these involved an enveloping flank attack to the west
of the Iraq–Kuwait border (which lay along the Wadi al Batin, the dry
riverbed that slanted north and east from the southwest corner of
Kuwait). However, there were initial problems with this choice (which,
of course, was the plan that was eventually adopted): Primarily, it was
thought that not enough forces were available to effect the envelopment,
keep the pressure on Iraqi forces along the Saudi–Kuwait border, and
maintain a sufficient reserve. Army doctrine requires certain force ratios—that is, friendly-to-enemy ratios; and the forces then available to
CENTCOM didn't satisfy these numbers. Secondarily, no one knew
whether the desert west of Kuwait could support armor. How hard was
the ground? No one knew for sure.

What options were then open to Schwarzkopf? None of his other
choices was appealing. The best of them seemed to be to focus his attack
into the western sector of Kuwait, drive north to the heights near Mut-

laa Pass (west of Kuwait City), and hope that counterattacking Republican Guards could be taken out by air. And if that somehow didn't go as planned? . . . Well, they'd improvise.

Predictably, Schwarzkopf was set against this. That he never liked attacking into the heart of Iraqi defenses was always clear to Chuck Horner; that he liked armor was also clear: the lightly armored XVIIIth Airborne Corps was never his favorite attacking force against armor. And in fact, he didn't have far to look: he had the "Left Hook"—the envelopment west of the Wadi. For that, however, he would need another heavy corps. How was he going to get it? He would present what he had to President Bush, Secretary Cheney, and General Powell—with all of its limitations. When they saw how risky this was, they would realize he needed more, and they would give him the extra corps he required for the Left Hook.

In hindsight, we now know that the Army planners never sufficiently took into account the ultimate effect of the air campaign on the Iraqi Army, though in all fairness, no one—not even the most optimistic airpower advocate—anticipated how seriously air attacks would damage the Iraqi Army prior to the ground campaign. If this success *had* been taken into account, the Left Hook would have been executable with pre–VIIth Corps Coalition forces.

★ On October 9, Buster Glosson and a team from CENTCOM left for Washington to brief the air campaign to General Powell (on October 10) and to the President and his chief advisers (on October 11). Heading the team was Major General Bob Johnston, the CENTCOM chief of staff. The other Army briefer was Lieutenant Colonel Joe Purvis.

Before the briefers left Riyadh, Schwarzkopf made it forcefully clear to Johnston that he was not recommending any of the ground schemes Purvis was going to brief. His aim was to generate the question "What do you need to develop an acceptable ground campaign?" With the expected answer being "A heavy corps."

En route to President Bush, the briefings went through the usual reviews, which agreed that while the air campaign was well constructed and credible, the focus of the land campaign on sending forces directly into the teeth of the Iraqi defenses appeared unimaginative. Of course, it was not a lack of imagination that had given birth to this unhappy situation, it was a lack of friendly forces.

The briefing to the President had mixed results. The air briefing delivered by Buster Glosson was generally accepted, though not without questions about the plan's assumptions of success. It simply *looked too good*. It was hard to accept its claims.

It's worth looking at what lay behind these doubts—an outdated mind-set that did not yet understand the full impact and capabilities of modern airpower. Let's examine a pair of facts:

First, the reputation of airpower had been created long before by air campaigns whose success had at best been mixed—the P-40s at Kassarine Pass, the B-17s over Germany, the F-100s bombing the Vietnam jungle. If such actions were paradigms for all air campaigns, then President Bush and his advisers had good reason to throw hard questions at Buster Glosson. How could any human endeavor go as well as he promised?

Second, technology had outrun conventional perceptions. In the years after Vietnam, airpower had taken a technological leap comparable to the shift from cannonballs to rifled shells. Now there were laser-guided bombs on Stealth aircraft, A-10s with Maverick missiles, and 30mm cannon shooting up tanks and APCs in the desert. The air campaign *would* go that well.

In the event, despite attempts to poke holes in it, the air briefing stood up.

The Army briefing didn't fare so happily. For reasons unknown to Chuck Horner, it was never made clear that General Schwarzkopf had intended all along to offer Joe Purvis's plan as a straw man that would justify the extra corps the CINC wanted very badly. To the best of Horner's knowledge, Schwarzkopf had told Colin Powell time and again, "This plan is not what I want, but I can't do what needs to be done without another corps at the minimum." So Joe Purvis, courageously, stood up and got pummeled (and by implication, Norman Schwarzkopf got pummeled with him). The Army plan was called unimaginative, timid, risky. There were jokes about it: "Hey, diddle diddle, right up the middle." All the while, Joe Purvis stood up time and again and absorbed the hits that led people to come to the hard conclusion that more ground forces would be needed if offensive operations were to be initiated. Though he never got much credit for it, he turned out to be a key factor in the success of Desert Storm.

And in the end, General Schwarzkopf got his second corps.

TRAINING

As the plan of attack was being developed and briefed, the Coalition air armada was being deployed to the Gulf and trained to fight.

What did this take?

Deployability is a major part of the normal, necessary business of the U.S. Air Force. Units are graded according to their ability to deploy quickly, and are often tasked to deploy to an isolated area on their own base, from which they fly sorties at surge rates* to make sure they have brought the correct amount of spares and other equipment. Deployment to the Gulf was made additionally easy for the USAF because of pre-positioned stores and Coalition equipment at collocated bases.

The U.S. Navy and Marine Corps had different methods of achieving the same results. Primarily, the Navy and embarked Marine jets were already in deployed status when their carrier left the United States, while the Marines had spares kits (containing thirty days' supply of line-replaceable units, such as radios or altimeters) just like the USAF.

Though NATO units practiced deployment, it was usually not to the same intensity as U.S. services. However, since they were closer to home, they could use C-130s to ferry spares or equipment rapidly. Some units arrived with nothing more than aircrews and aircraft, but these were collocated with U.S. units that used the same equipment. If they needed a part, they could borrow one until another one could be flown from home. Special ground-support equipment and maintenance personnel were also shared as required. "One Team, One Fight," as the slogan has it. In this case, it was true.

★ Though the six-month span between the initial deployment and the start of the war certainly helped, air forces train the way they fight (and by assigning to the enemy their own capabilities, the U.S. Air Force makes peacetime training more difficult than any war they are likely to fight). Thus, when the Coalition units arrived in the Gulf, they already knew how to go to war. The next steps would bring everyone to the next level,

---

*At surge rates, the jets are flown at a much higher than normal sortie rate. The benefit is the amount of ordnance that can be placed on the enemy in a short time. The downside is the build-up of a maintenance backlog on the fleet. This must be taken care of in the future by standing down the flying schedule or by increasing the numbers of maintenance troops.

where a large, diverse force would be integrated, even as new approaches and methods (such as the Night Camel exercise, which we will look at more closely) were tried and practiced.

The focus of the training, in other words, was directed toward harmony among the various units, using the ATO as a score. Each pilot played a different instrument: the F-15C was used air-to-air; the F-15E, F-16, Mirage, or F-18 was used air-to-ground; and the Wild Weasel, the Joint STARS, the Compass Call, and the AWACS had their parts to play. If the music was written to exploit each unique sound, and if the tempo was the same for all, then it all would come together.

Everyone there was already a competent musician on his own instrument. The planners knew how to write a playable score. Chuck Horner's job—as builder of teams and teamwork—was to wave his baton to keep the beat and to cue in specific sections of the orchestra. As in an orchestra, the musicians knew if they were making beautiful music; they knew when they were playing as one, and they enjoyed the confidence that engendered.

To these ends, Jim Crigger's and Ahmed Sudairy's operations staffs planned and tasked units to exercise together, most of whom had never flown with each other. A practice strike on a target on a gunnery range in the UAE involved Saudi, Italian, British, U.S., and UAE aircraft, for example. Or one or more units from non-U.S. forces would act as red air and intercept U.S. attackers to give the MiG CAPs a workout. Or there would be launch rehearsals, during which several sorties would take off in quick succession. Additionally, everyone received training in large-scale tanker operations, during which sixteen fighters would take off, join up, fly to a group of tankers and refuel, and then drop off at the right place and time to form up with other aircraft so they could hit a target at a given time.

Such exercises accustomed everyone to using the ATO and other common procedures and documents; listening to a Saudi AWACS controller; using code words and radio discipline; and thinking about integrated packages of strike aircraft, CAP aircraft, and support aircraft (Wild Weasels, Rivet Joints, EF-111 jamming aircraft, and AWACS).

Such harmony was most difficult for the Islamic allies. Though the USAF and USN had experience working with Arab air forces (in Bright Star exercises; Red Flags; and as a function of the training detachments associated with foreign military sales programs), the Arab air forces, culturally reluctant to fail in public, rarely trained together (training always involves learning how to overcome mistakes). Though there was surely some nervousness among the Arab allies before they let their pilots fly in Crigger's exercises, there was an immediate imperative—war around the corner—that made these much more important than the cultural fear of public mistakes.

★ A more worrisome problem was aircraft accidents. There were far too many of them, though in Chuck Horner's view, no aircraft accident was ever necessary.

One involved an ANG RF-4C (a reconnaissance version of the Phantom jet) practicing low-level gun jinks—that is, flying at low level to avoid radar-guided SAMs while maneuvering so AAA guns could not track them. Another involved an F-111 flying at low level on a gunnery range at night. Both pilots flew too low and paid for the error with their lives. Later, a young pilot in a two-seat F-15E strike aircraft decided to "play" air-to-air against an RAF Jaguar, despite strict orders against making air intercepts (unless he was actually attacked). His job was to carry bombs. The problem was that F-15E pilots wanted to be F-15C pilots, for the F-15Cs had the air-to-air mission, the mission with all the glamour.

This young pilot took off on a single-ship training mission at maximum gross weight in his F-15E (it was equipped with conformal tanks, which made it much heavier than the F-15C). Before coming to the Gulf, he had had an exchange tour with an RAF unit in Scotland. As it happened, the two units were now based together, which allowed the young pilot to conduct an intercept with an RAF squadron buddy, who was also flying in the local area on a training mission—the RAF Jaguar fighter at 100 feet above the ground and the F-15E at 10,000 to 15,000 feet. Since the F-15E's radar could easily see the Jaguar, the young USAF pilot and his WSO attempted a stern conversion. In that maneuver, the pilot flies head-on to the target, then rolls on his back and pulls down until he can roll out behind his target, trading altitude for airspeed and G force for turn radius.

He almost made the final turn to pull out a few feet above the ground, but his tail scraped the ground three hundred feet before the final impact scattered the F-15E into thousands of burning pieces. The bodies were found in the wreckage and the final maneuver was observed and reported by the RAF pilot.

Horner was very upset with the wing commander, Hal Hornberg,* because he had specifically told him no air-to-air. If he had found out that Hornberg had winked at the ban on air-to-air training, or that he was running a lax operation in which others were winking at these restrictions (which many thought unreasonable), then Horner was going to find another wing commander. To find out the truth, Horner brought in from the States one of the most honest men he knew, Colonel Bill Van Meter, and sent him to investigate. In due course, it was determined that the old relationship with the RAF squadron, and not the squadron and wing commanders, was to blame. Horner further believes that if Hornberg had himself found that this tragedy had resulted from his own inattention or lack of leadership, he would have asked to be fired.

The year before deploying for Desert Shield, one of Horner's wing commanders actually did that after he had lost three aircraft (his wing had gotten infected before his arrival, and he had to reap the rewards of his predecessor's failures). "Fire me, boss, and put me out of my misery," he had said to Horner, whose answer was, "I'm too mad at you right now for these accidents, and so I am going to leave you in the job just so you bear the pain while you put a stop to this nonsense." He fixed the wing and went on to be a two-star; he was always an excellent leader.

In October, Horner called all the wing commanders to Riyadh for a let-it-all-hang-out meeting. The topic was not flying safety, it was preserving the force, and it got results. There was no screaming and shouting. There was no blame. Those wing commanders who'd had accidents felt worse than anyone else could make them feel ("If they didn't feel that way," Horner observes, "they shouldn't have been commanders"). The ones who had not had accidents knew that "but for the grace of God there go I." So each man gave his views about what he was doing right and what he was doing wrong, and about whatever he had discovered that led to accidents.

Everyone bared their souls, as they would at a mission debriefing, but with even greater intensity, brainstormed the potential pitfalls, and shared anguish for the organizational failures that had caused the deaths in the desert.

The actual reason for most of the accidents was not hard to discern: the crews were training too hard, pushing their aircraft, pushing the

---

Now a three-star who commands Ninth Air Force.

rules, and flying tactics far too risky for the situation. When pilots deploy away from home, constraints are lessened. And when they deploy in anticipation of war, the lure to go beyond the limits seems justified. As a result they often exceed their own capabilities and create situations that saturate their capacity to cope; they put their aircraft in positions that defy the laws of physics and are unable to recover.

Most of those at the meeting agreed that everyone needed some time off. Many of the pilots had been in the desert for over sixty days, living in crowded quarters, often with painfully uncomfortable sleeping arrangements, working twelve to fifteen hours a day, seven days a week. The troops were tired.

As luck would have it, living conditions were already getting better. Some of the units were now taking a weekly day off. As more tents became available, the number assigned to each tent was decreased. Recreation facilities were being established. But greater efforts were taken to lessen the stress.

★ The October meeting in Riyadh marked an important turning point in the period leading up to the war: Though other accidents happened, the curve went down. The dangerous trend was over. More important, the meeting marked the moment of truth when all the commanders realized they were going into the war in an orderly fashion, and that pilots must fly more conservatively in wartime than in peacetime. In peacetime they practice against a threat—SAMs, MiGs, AAA—that is perfect and omnipresent, while in an actual war they fly against an enemy operator, pilot, or gunner who is scared, tired, and working with equipment that cannot be well maintained and operated twenty-four hours a day. Very few accidents occur in combat. In combat, pilots avoid undue risks and keep everything as simple as they can. If an enemy kills you, that's a tough break, but no one wants to be killed by his own dumb mistake.

ROTATION POLICY

In the midst of the training and deployment, Horner had a serious disagreement with the generals and lieutenant generals in Washington over rotation policy. They wanted to rotate troops back to the States; he didn't.

He could not forget Vietnam, with its one year or 100 missions over the North, a policy that had robbed the deployed force of its commitment to success. He was going to have nothing like that in the Gulf . . . or he would go down swinging.

There were phone calls from General Russ, seeking Horner's views about such a policy. "Chuck," he asked, "what do you think about this—120 days in the AOR, and then we rotate the individual but not the unit?"

Horner's reply was close to an ultimatum: "Respectfully, General, there's no way I'll ever agree to a rotation policy."

"See here, Chuck," General Russ answered, disturbed by Horner's attitude. "This isn't a discussion of whether or not we are going to have a policy. It's a given that we are. Rather, it is a chance for you to give us your views about what policy we should implement. We can't keep those people in the desert forever."

To which Horner replied, "General, I respect what you are trying to do and appreciate your concern, but I will never agree to a rotation policy. We have been sent over here to do a job. When we get the Iraqis out of Kuwait, then bring us home. We are here until victory."

These were brave words . . . and maybe foolhardy ones, Horner told himself, and sometimes he didn't think he could make them stick. Yet he felt that this was one of those issues he needed to get fired over if it went the wrong way.

Fortunately, General Schwarzkopf felt as he did (probably as a consequence of his own Vietnam experience, though Horner can't say this for sure), and so Horner's policy stood—even in the face of higher-ups in Washington.

After that, Horner had to convey this hard message to the troops.

I found, he says, *that if I told them the truth, they understood: that in fact I didn't know when we would go home, that I didn't know when the war might start, but that in Vietnam we had a rotation policy which made it our goal not to win but to stay alive until we rotated, and that I wasn't going to be caught in that trap again.*

I also told them that I wanted to be home as much as they did, and while I had better living conditions than theirs, I understood their frustrations.

"We came to do a job," I went on to say, "and it's a worthwhile job. So as far as I'm concerned, we all stay until that job gets done. Sorry, but none of us can go home until the Iraqis are out of Kuwait, and the murder, rape, and robbery stop. It is my decision to make, and that is the decision I have made. If I get fired, then the new guy can do whatever he wants, but for us today it is here until victory."

Certainly, we let people with special circumstances go home, and we had to let some of the reserve forces rotate their people, because they were on active duty for only a limited time. As for everyone else, morale was sky-high; people understood the contract and they had a stake in the outcome. They were committed to it, so let's get on with it. A far cry from Vietnam.

THE AGONY OF KUWAIT AND THE HOME FRONT

Every day, the commanders in Riyadh and their staffs received reports of the Kuwaitis trapped in their occupied country—firsthand accounts of brutal acts of murder, torture, rape, and looting. At their best, the Iraqis in Kuwait City were a gang of thugs, stripping cars and houses. At their worst, they were beasts, executing children in front of their parents, decapitating with power saws men suspected of being resistance fighters, gang-raping foreign women once employed as domestic servants in wealthy homes.

Meanwhile, there was governmental and U.N. uncertainty about how best to remove Iraq from Kuwait, including considerable talk of alternatives to fighting. Most Americans wanted to avoid war, while many in and out of government—highly respected people such as Senator Sam Nunn and General Colin Powell—were counting on diplomatic initiatives and the U.N. embargo imposed soon after the invasion of Kuwait.

Others felt that the United States should not rush into a war where thousands of Americans might be killed, simply to secure Kuwait's oil— or as some op-ed wag put it: Would the United States have risked so much of its wealth and so many of its young warriors if the chief export of Kuwait had been broccoli? (President Bush famously disliked broccoli.)

The view in the Gulf was vastly different. Proximity to the suffering in Kuwait made war seem increasingly better than waiting for the always doubtful success of the embargo or other initiatives.

All the talk of delay, along with the confusion of aims among their leaders, disheartened the families of those who were deployed, and left them in a conceptual bind. Without the appreciation of events in the Gulf afforded by firsthand knowledge, they were reduced to whatever information was provided by the U.S. media—a perplexing variety of views about what should be done to end the crisis in the Gulf. The families at home saw at best a vague end in sight to the crisis—and what appeared to be an ever-longer separation from their loved ones.

Yet—as always with service families—they bore up under the stress of separation in always inventive and heartening ways.

The spouses, most often wives, began to call themselves "the left-behinds." The support they gave and received was a lifesaver, not only for their overall morale but also for their success in coping with everyday problems.

The yards in Sumter, South Carolina, near Shaw AFB, never looked so good, as neighbors turned out to mow and edge the lawns of families whose husbands had deployed to the desert.

The "left-behinds" began to bond together. Meetings were held to squash rumors, find out who needed help, and provide communication for those families living in unusual isolation. The wives got together for social functions, for a chance to just plain bitch to one another, and to take pride in not having to endure their terrible loneliness and pain on their own.

The shared sacrifice helped ease the panic and tears that came stealing into them when they were alone at night, wondering not only "when" but more importantly "if ever again" they would see their mates. Those in the desert had knowledge (though always sketchy and imperfect); they were busy; they were involved in a great and noble act; while the "left-behinds" worked to make their faithful, lonely lives seem normal at a time of almost unbearable abnormality. They did it because it was expected of them, because they had no other choice, and because of their courage and selflessness. They were real heroes of Desert Shield and Desert Storm.

★ On October 24, Chuck Horner at long last answered what had been Mary Jo's constant question: "When are you coming home?"

I don't know when we are coming home, he wrote her—with added comments—*but for sure it will be after we fight Iraq. So the question is when are we going to fight? The answer is pick one of the following:*

1. *After the '90 election.* (Generals always try to sound politically aware.)

2. *After the U.S. Embassy in Kuwait runs out of food and water.* (We had plans to rescue the trapped staff, if their lives appeared to be in danger.)

3. *After another 100,000 troops arrive.* (More than 200,000 additional troops actually came.)

4. *Before Ramadan begins.* (The Islamic period of fasting and holy days, due to start in March.)

5. *Before next summer.* (I didn't think we could survive the heat one more time.)

6. *After next summer.* (My attempt at humor.)

7. *After Iraq attacks us.*

8. *Before Saddam starts killing the hostages.*

9. *Whenever President Bush and the other leaders say so.*

10. *Whenever the U.N. says to do it.*

As it turned out, number ten, U.N. approval, occurred in late November, when the Security Council ordered a January 15, 1991, deadline for an Iraqi pullout from Kuwait, and number nine came with the President's approval of the air campaign briefing. This decision grew stronger with the November decision to deploy the VIIth Corps from Germany and to double our naval and air forces, and was cast in stone with the congressional approval of military action in January of 1991.

My advice to Mary Jo was simple: "Just listen to President Bush. He is telling you the truth, and he is telling you what we are going to do."

As for me, I had inside information. I knew that unless Saddam Hussein made an uncharacteristic change in his strategy, we were going to fight. In November, talk of rotation policy died, to be replaced by a growing sense of urgency, a clearer perception of what lay ahead, and an increasing awareness that, sometime after the first of the year, we were going to war.

BUILDUP

The first signs of the end of uncertainty came quickly. In November, the President's approval of the additional corps began to take visible effect when the heavy VIIth Corps began to deploy from Germany to Saudi Arabia. In Germany, VIIth Corps had defended the strategic Fulda Gap in the face of the now rapidly disintegrating Warsaw Pact; in the Gulf, their mission was to be the armored fist of Schwarzkopf's flanking attack aimed at the armored divisions of the Republican Guard, now based near the northwest corner of Kuwait.

Early that month, General Schwarzkopf called a commander's conference at the "Desert Inn," a military dining facility at Dhahran Air Base, to outline his plan for those who were new to CENTCOM, Lieutenant General Fred Franks and his VIIth Corps commanders, who had just flown down from Germany for an initial look-around.

The old CENTCOM hands, like Yeosock, Boomer, Luck, and Horner, were already familiar with what the CINC would be telling them. They'd come to the Dhahran conference essentially to meet and greet. Though they were more than happy to have VIIth Corps and its Abrams tanks and Bradley fighting vehicles, the old hands had their brown desert camos and suntans, and their close comradeship developed in the desert, and to them the new men looked just a little out of place and edgy in their pale skins and forest-green camouflage fatigues. The new people would fit in—that's what they were all trained and paid for—but there would be many tough moments in the weeks ahead.

In his briefing, the CINC covered what air was going to do, what the USMC, the XVIIIth Airborne Corps, and the Islamic Corps were going to do, and what he expected VIIth Corps to do. The Marines and the Islamic forces would attack the heart of the Iraqi defenses in Kuwait. XVIIIth Corps and the French would move into Iraq in the west, where they would support the flank of the main, VIIth Corps attack. When XVIIIth Corps reached the Euphrates River, they'd turn east and join the attack against the Republican Guards.

The CINC's final message was simple: Hit them hard. Hit them fast. Never let up. Never slow down. "We are going to move out fast," he told his commanders. "If you have commanders who are going to worry about outrunning their logistic tails, or about having their flanks exposed, don't bring them to this fight. This attack will slam into an Army that has been greatly weakened from weeks of air attack; and I want you to start out running and keep running until we surround them and destroy them as a fighting force."

★ The buildup that followed was spectacular. There had been nothing like it since the buildup in the south of England in the spring of 1944. In November alone, CENTAF's force grew by close to 40 percent, and that was only the beginning. Here is a snapshot of what was going on:*

MATERIAL BUILDUP

Aircraft	Planned	1 Nov	16 Jan '91
A-10	72	96	132
B-52	14	20	21
F-4G Wild Weasel	24	36	48
F-15E	0	24	48
F-16	144	120	210
F-111F	0	32	64
F-117	0	18	36
N.B.: There was little buildup of F-15Cs.			
USMC Fixed Wing	—	146	242

PEOPLE BUILDUP

	17 Oct	14 Nov	19 Dec	16 Jan
CENTAF	31,459	30,981	35,062	48,679
ARCENT	100,429	128,617	167,218	247,637
NAVCENT	34,001	32,775	32,978	67,851
MARCENT	41,923	39,037	48,239	85,447
SOCCENT	(There was little buildup.)			
CENTCOM	687	741	874	1,030

*These figures are taken from the Gulf War Air Power Survey.

USAF Air Power Buildup

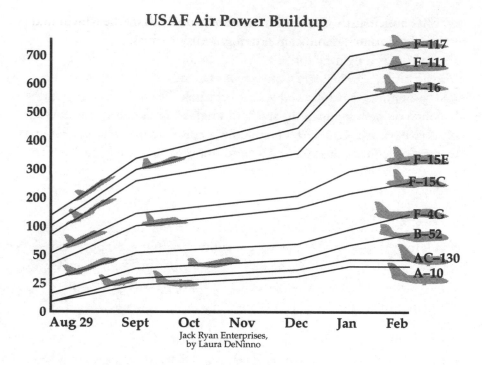

Jack Ryan Enterprises,
by Laura DeNinno

Much of the USN buildup was additional carriers.

The buildup posed many problems.

For Chuck Horner himself, the pace of his own planning grew ever more frantic. Each day he had to ask himself yet again: "What has changed? What new force can we accommodate? How can we support it? At what location? How will we introduce them into the existing ATO?"

At Horner's level, planning meant anticipating potential problems, then working out in advance how to avoid them, or solve them if they could not be avoided. It was his job to foresee everything that might happen, then to bring about the good outcomes and to head off the bad ones.

While the staff were up to their necks working immediate issues, he looked beyond what they were wrestling with to anticipate the next issues they needed to address when they finished what they were doing.

In this he was mostly successful, he now believes, for the war brought few surprises, while a thousand prepared-for events didn't happen. His two chief anticipatory lapses were the impact of Scuds on the Israelis and the Khafji invasion—significant errors, yet easy to miss.

★ Meanwhile, there were many countless practical and immediate buildup-related problems:

Command arrangements had to be both spread out and strengthened. On December 5, Horner decided that his span of control was too large. He therefore put the fighters under Buster Glosson (officially, he became the fighter division commander); the bombers and tankers under Pat Caruana; the electronic assets under Profitt; and the airlifters under Ed Tenoso.

The constant arrival of new intelligence led to changes in the offensive ATO. However, now that there were more strike and support forces, more targets could be hit, so the ATO grew larger and more complex.

The best use of the new Joint STARS had to be worked out (it arrived for the first time only a day before the war started).

New players such as VIIth Corps had to be accommodated.

The airlift west of XVIIIth and VIIth Corps had to be worked out, once ground movements had been finalized (during their move west to attack positions, the only land artery, the Tapline Road, was paved with trucks. The intratheater airlift created an airbridge that relieved some of that pressure).

More tent cities had to be built, to accommodate the increased numbers of personnel.

There had to be ample munitions at each base. The plan was to have a sixty-day supply on hand; but when the new aircraft arrived, it went down to thirty days. Yet within a few weeks, Bill Rider and his logistics team, with enormous support from the logistics organizations in Europe and the United States, brought munitions up to the required sixty-day supply. Saddam Hussein, constantly underestimating airpower, had told his troops openly that the Coalition would run out of bombs after a few days. He was wrong yet again. Not only did Horner have sixty days' worth of bombs and missiles on hand when the war started, but they would keep that level day in and day out as the war progressed.

Communications had to be built up, both to support the added forces and to execute offensive operations. Though there were more communications per person in this war than in any other, the miracles performed by Colonel Randy Witt and his communicators were never enough. The TACC could not get timely intelligence from Washington, and then they could never move it fast enough down to the wings. The link providing the AWACS air picture to the air defense command centers and the ships at sea was very fragile. The deployment into the desert of hundreds of thousands of troops with their small satellite terminals drained away vital communication links. And once the bombs started falling, the Air Tasking Order grew geometrically, yet still needed to be distributed on time.

All the while, the basics had to be attended to—such as air defense, in case the Iraqis tried a conventional air attack. AWACS orbits were set up and integrated with the Saudi Air Defense systems, providing complete radar coverage of southern Iraq and northern Saudi Arabia. Twenty-four-hour airborne CAPs were manned with USAF and RSAF F-15s and RAF and RSAF Tornado Air Defense Variants. Occasionally, an Iraqi would fly south at high speed as though planning to cross the border, but would turn back when the airborne CAPs, vectored by AWACS, maneuvered to intercept him. Sometimes they tried to lure Coalition fighters into elaborate ambushes in Iraq, but this never worked, because the AWACS saw the Iraqi ambush aircraft.

Finally, the existing air bases had to be enlarged, or in some cases new ones created.

First, each base was surveyed to see how much more it could accommodate. At some—such as Khamis Mushyat, where the F-117s were based—not much had to be done, since there were only a few more available to deploy. Other bases required much more.

Often, additional munitions storage areas had to be built. At Al Dhafra, in the UAE, one of these was dug in a small hill near a wadi. When it rained, the place filled up with water. The bombs weren't harmed, but the dunnage and fuse boxes were set afloat.

Even before the buildup, some bases were short of fuel storage. The added aircraft just made the problem worse, and increasing fuel storage was not possible (adding fuel bladders might give a base a day's additional supply). Bill Rider solved that problem by increasing the flow of fuel to the bases—that is, he increased the number of Saudi tanker trucks moving between fuel-processing facilities and bases. At Al Kharj and other bases, the flying depended on a constant stream of fuel trucks from the fuel-processing facility (in the case of Al Kharj, from Riyadh, about thirty miles north).

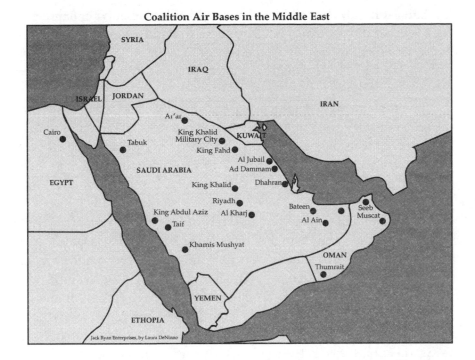

Coalition Air Bases in the Middle East

Fuel storage at Al Kharj was a problem because it didn't start out as an air base; it started out as a runway/parking apron—and nothing else—surrounded by sand.

In Desert Shield, the F-15Es had been deployed initially to Thumrait, Oman. Thumrait was a fighter base, it had the fuel and munitions storage required, and much of the Air Force's pre-position housing was stored there. The F-15E was a long-range attack aircraft, so the nearly eight-hundred-mile one-way trip to the (projected) battlefield (near the Kuwait–Saudi border) was not a problem. In fact, this distance was desirable if the battle started to move south and the Iraqis overran the more northern airfields. However, now that the projected battlefield was about to move north, the long round trip became a big disadvantage. It was therefore decided to move them five hundred miles north to the runway/parking apron the RSAF had built at Al Kharj. This move would put them an hour closer to the war.

Colonel Ray Davies and the 823 Red Horse Squadron, the Air Force's heavy construction battalion, having just finished building ramps at Al

Minhad in the UAE, and taxiways and parking at Sheikh Isa in Bahrain,* were sent north by Colonel Hal Hornberg to build a base and a host of living facilities throughout the desert for Air Force, Army, and Navy troops. The Red Horse would raise a city for over five thousand people in a matter of days.

The problems were daunting. For starters, the sand would not hold the tie-down stakes for the Air Force's temper tents—air-conditioned and heated desert tents that were the envy of their army brothers. Red Horse's answer was to lay down a deep base of clay over the sand. The clay hardened like cement and gave the camp a stable base. It's easy when you can think big.

They found and dug out ton after ton of clay, then overlaid miles of desert where they wanted to set down the tents. The next problem was no water or fuel. Their solution was to bring huge rubber bladders from pre-positioned stocks in Oman and Bahrain. Hangars for the airplanes were also up in hours, again from pre-positioned supplies. Munitions storage areas, dining halls, shops, a chapel, operations, even a sand golf course, all rose in weeks. By December, the base was ready to receive two F-15E squadrons, two F-16 squadrons, an F-15C squadron, and a C-130 airlift squadron.

★ The creation of the quick-turn base at KKMC was even harder.

Quick-turn is a simple concept: The great reliability of modern American military aircraft allows them to make several sorties a day, like airliners, lugging bombs instead of passengers. It therefore made sense to locate a base close to Iraq, where the aircraft could be quickly refueled and reloaded, and the pilot could be given target information for a new mission. In that way, they could strike the enemy four or five times a day—in a tempo that would leave the Iraqis reeling.

Though it had drawbacks, the choice for this base fell on KKMC, less than fifty miles from the border with Iraq. As with Al Kharj before the Red Horse, it contained a runway and taxiways, and little else. More

---

*Minhad is a UAE fighter base south of Dubai where Horner had placed F-16s. Sheikh Isa, the air base on the south side of Bahrain, is named after the island nation's head of state. It is home to two Bahraini squadrons, one of F-16s and another of F-5s. Horner put the USMC F-18s and A-6s on the main ramp, the Bahraini jets at the north end of the field, and the USAF Wild Weasels in the south end of the field in revetments and parking pads built by Red Horse (this was a huge task, as the parking pads and taxiways had to be carved out of coral, one of the hardest substances on earth).

worrying, it could be a prime target for enemy artillery. For that reason, no aircraft would be assigned there. The birds would only come to refresh.

Now Horner needed someone to build a tent city, munitions and fuel storage, and an operations area, and set up intelligence, air traffic control, and maintenance services . . . all in two weeks—no excuses. To bring off that miracle, he brought in Colonel Bill Van Meter to be the wing commander at the quick-turn base.

On December 21, Van Meter appeared in Horner's office, still groggy from his rush trip to Saudi Arabia. His challenge: to build a base at the end of the supply line, working his people day and night in an extremely new and isolated environment, while preparing them to survive missile or artillery attack and perhaps be overrun by an armor thrust.

With a rueful smile, he left to talk with Bill Rider and George Summers, the logisticians. Six days later, Horner flew up to KKMC. What he found there amazed him. The base was far from finished, but bulldozers were carving munitions storage berms out of the desert; pipes were being laid for the fuel farm that would enable the fighters to refuel and rearm without shutting down their engines; and a tent city was rising in the desert between the town and the base.

As they toured the base, Van Meter told Horner about a young female airman who had just arrived, disoriented and tired. During his briefing to the newcomers about their mission and responsibilities, she had sat calmly, but when he had touched on the possibility of enemy attacks, it had hit her that she just might die. And tears ran down her cheeks.

Flash forward to the days when Scuds were falling and pilots were beginning to die in shot-up jets. That same young woman proved to be one of the strongest combat leaders at KKMC.

COMMAND AND CONTROL

Managing the vast aerial armada called for an immense, intricately connected command-and-control system. Here are some of its more notable elements:

- TACC Current Ops—Located in Riyadh, the Tactical Air Command Center was the central node for the planning and execution of the air war. Chuck Horner maintained his headquarters there.

- AWACS—A Boeing 707 command-and-control aircraft with a large, long-range radar that could see aerial targets at all altitudes, provided they had a velocity over the ground relative to the AWACS aircraft. Though this number was adjustable, it was usually set at speeds greater than seventy knots, so cars would not show up as aircraft. The AWACS provided an air picture to all the theater, and the AWACS air controllers provided navigation assistance and controlled aircraft from pretanker rendezvous to poststrike refueling, as needed. F-15s and F-16s, with their powerful air-to-air radars, did not need such help; other aircraft often did.
- ACE Team—A small command-and-control node—usually a planner/executor, an intelligence person, and one or two duty officers—located on board the AWACS and operating in parallel with the TACC current ops. Because it was closer to the fight, and more aware of what was going on than the TACC staff, the ACE Team had the authority to divert sorties. Normally, though, they kept in close contact with the TACC directors. They could also have acted as a temporary backup if a Scud hit had closed down the TACC.
- ABCCC (Airborne Command, Control, and Communications; pronounced "AB triple C")—A C-130 aircraft used primarily for command and control of close air support. A command-and-control module in the cargo compartment held about fifteen people, half of whom were likely to be Army or Marines after the ground forces were engaged. The Marine ABCCC was called the Airborne Direct Air Support Center, or DASC.
- Compass Call—An EC-130H configured to jam communications, such as Iraqi military communications.
- Commando Solo—An EC-130 configured to conduct psychological operations by broadcasting television and radio.
- Rivet Joint (RC-135)—A special reconnaissance version of the Boeing 707 that provided data on enemy air defense systems and other intelligence information.
- Joint STARS (E-8A)—A modified Boeing 707, equipped with a large radar that provided Moving Target Information (MTI) and Synthetic Aperture Radar (SAR) images of surface targets. This information was presented to air controllers on the air-

craft, who tracked, identified, and directed strikes against enemy ground targets. Because the E-8 was still undergoing testing, it was largely crewed by Northrop Grumman civilian engineers who had volunteered for the war. The Joint STARS radar and air controllers proved to be of immense value in halting the Iraqi ground attack into Saudi Arabia at El-Khafji in late January.

- Killer Scouts—F-16 fighters assigned to patrol kill boxes (twenty-mile-square areas in Iraq and Kuwait) and locate Iraqi army units visually or by radar. They provided target information to flights of attack aircraft fed into their kill box area by ABCCC, AWACS, Joint STARS, or the TACC.

After the ground war started:

- Air Liaison Officers (ALOs) and Ground Forward Air Controllers (FACs)*—Both connected ground units with air and handled close air support. The difference lay in their rank and the level of army units to which they were assigned. FACs were usually junior officers assigned at battalion level or below. ALOs were usually majors or above and assigned to brigade or above. For example, a colonel would be the ALO at corps level, a lieutenant colonel at division. The ALO role emphasized senior-level experience and thus made the ALO the air adviser to the Army commander. While the ALO could control a strike, most often strikes were controlled by FACs, who were closer to the battle.
- Air Operations Support Center—A mini-headquarters, usually a corps ALO, heavily equipped with communications and computers. It was to the corps headquarters, or Army group headquarters, what the BCE was to the TACC. The Marine equivalent was called a Direct Air Support Center.

Other elements in the system:

- Control and Reporting Center (CRC)—A ground-based van that could also include one or more TPS-75 radars to provide an air

---

*Also called Tactical Air Control Parties (TACPs).

picture. CRC controllers backed up AWACS controllers when the AWACS was too busy or not available—though they could not do the job as well as AWACS, because ground-based radar could not see airborne targets at low altitude due to ground clutter and the curvature of the earth. Other elements in the command-and-control systems with a similar function included U.S. Aegis cruisers and the Sector Operations Centers, operated by the Saudi Air Defense system and co-manned primarily by the RSAF and USAF. CRC displays were also linked into the AWACS and other radar nets, and provided the AWACS picture to those who didn't otherwise have it. Thus, a CRC was set up at KKMC to give the Syrians and Egyptians an input into the air picture.

- Control and Reporting Posts (CRP)—Individual ground radar units that performed essentially the same functions as the CRC or AWACS, but were smaller and depended heavily on the other two for a comprehensive air picture. They were also called gap fillers.
- Wing/Squadron Command Posts—This was the primary hub linking the squadron, wing, or base with the TACC current ops. Each base would have a main command post, but its size and complexity varied with the base's size and activity level. At a base with just a few jets, like Arar, the CP might be a tent with a telephone, a CAFMS terminal, and a table with maps used for planning. At a big operation like Dhahran, the CP might have air defense displays with the AWACS picture, intelligence computers to display updated threats, and a wealth of duty officers and cells to coordinate operations.
- Flying Squadron Operations—Here pilots planned the missions and got intelligence not provided by wing operations, briefing rooms, and scheduling boards. The ATO came from the TACC Plans to Wing Operations, where it was broken out and parceled out to the squadrons to execute.
- The Air Traffic Control System—This included towers, departure and approach control, and air traffic aids—TACAN, VOR, ILS, ADF, runway lights, Air Base Operations, GCI, and GPS.
- And a number of support elements such as maintenance control; security police operations; civil engineer operations (who

watched over runway shutdowns); fire operations; bomb disposal; and hospital operations.

The center of it all, the TACC (pronounced "T-A-C-C"), had two functions: current plans and current operations. Plans—the Black Hole, current plans, and the computer room (which was part of current plans)—built the ATO; Operations executed it. However in normal conversation, the TACC meant Operations, which was much larger than Plans, and more was going on there.

The Operations section *changed* the ATO.

In a perfect world, where nothing unforeseen happens, no plan goes amiss. In the real world, where the ATO was already forty-eight hours old when it was executed, a system was required that could change the ATO *quickly,* based on new intelligence, weather changes, unforeseen enemy actions, new opportunities, or even relatively small mishaps, such as a KC-10 tanker aborting a takeoff. The jets that tanker was scheduled to refuel had to somehow find fuel, and one of the teams in the TACC Ops section had to find a way to provide it. Likewise, if the weather was bad in the ATO target area, one of the TACC teams would likely change the scheduled flight from its preplanned route to a new target area.

During the war, the closest that planning came to perfection was perhaps 50 percent, and on some days virtually every sortie was altered.

★ When the Ninth Air Force came to the Gulf, they brought their command center with them, originally housed in an inflatable building (called "the rubber duck"), which was set up in the parking lot behind the RSAF building in Riyadh. It soon became evident, however, that a better site was needed. For one thing, the American airmen needed to adapt their operation to the immediate situation. Since they were in Saudi Arabia, the appropriate site for the control center was with the air force of the host nation. For another, the rubber duck—based on an outdated vision that placed the Air Force out in the countryside with the Army—was obsolete and only marginally functional. It was too small, too dark, and most of its technology came from the fifties (though some systems, like CAFMS, were newer). The 150-plus members of the TACC staff needed a more efficient layout—and hard walls to shield against the Scud threat.

The obvious site was in the basement of RSAF headquarters. In December, Operations took over a fifty-by-seventy-five-foot room previously used by the RSAF to teach computer operators. Power generators, communications vans, and satellite dishes, however, remained in the parking lot, and their cables were rerouted into the new TACC.

A TOUR OF THE TACC

At the front of the Ops room was a small open space. Down the room's large center section were ranks of tables, covered with phones and computer terminals. Beyond a pair of side aisles were desks, most facing the center.

The right front wall contained BCE maps with plastic overlays depicting the strength and position of allied and enemy ground forces. To their left were a pair of large screens displaying the AWACS air picture and intelligence data, such as Scud launch and impact areas, active Iraqi radars, or data about airfields, transportation networks, or any other data loaded into the intelligence systems computer.

The commanders' table was at the front center.

Seated at its far right (facing forward) was a Kuwaiti Air Force officer, Lieutenant Colonel Abdullah Al-Samdan. On leave in Jordan when the war broke out, Al-Samdan had left his wife and children there, leapt into his car, driven to Riyadh, and set himself up as the Kuwaiti Air Force representative at RSAF headquarters. He was at the commanders' table because he held a special place of honor: it was his country they were there to free. But he also "paid his keep" by providing access to the resistance leaders in occupied Kuwait (they risked their lives daily by using their satellite phones to relay target data to him*) and by flying missions during the war. His parents, brothers, and sisters remained trapped in Kuwait City.

The RSAF leader, General Behery, sat on Al-Samdan's left, with Horner next to him, and either Major General Tom Olsen or Major General John Corder next to Horner (Olsen generally worked days, Horner

---

*They provided excellent target information—e.g., places where the Iraqis were conducting torture, or places where the Iraqi army was being billeted. Most notably, they reported a meeting of Iraqi generals in a private home. On the day of the meeting, with the house surrounded by Mercedes-Benz cars stolen by the Iraqis and used as staff cars for their generals, the Air Force put four bombs through the roof—and destroyed the cars.

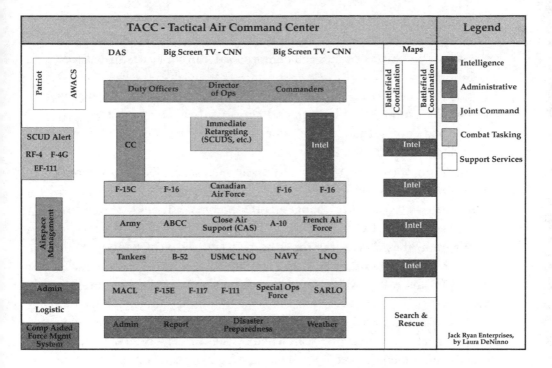

TACC - Tactical Air Command Center							Legend	

Jack Ryan Enterprises, by Laura DeNinno

worked nights, and Corder, it seemed, worked all the time). Horner had brought his old friend Corder onto the team as a general officer director of operations. Though Jim Crigger had been performing splendidly in the DO role, he had no stars on his collars and so was not taken seriously in high-level meetings with other services. The intense, intellectual,* selfless Corder could handle the point man role superbly, and allow Crigger full time to run daily operations.

The last two chairs were occupied by the TACC Directors—Jim Crigger and Al Doman (Mike Reavy and Charlie Harr worked the night shift). Their job was to run current operations—that is, to execute the air war. When a change was made to the ATO, they were the approval authority, ensuring that all the pertinent people were informed and coordinated.

Behind the commanders' table was a square table with a large map of Iraq under Plexiglas, around which sat the national leaders of the coalition air partners—Major General Claude Solnet from France, Major

---

The Ready, Fire, Aim concept was his.

General Mario Alpino from Italy, Lieutenant Colonel John McNeil from Canada, and RAF Air Vice Marshal William Wratten, RAF, who was also the deputy to Great Britain's top military leader in the Gulf, Sir Peter de la Billiere.

On their left sat the people who actually ran the TACC, primarily Lieutenant Colonels Bill Keenan and Hans Pfeiffer. They saw to it that people and equipment stayed in working order (they were the TACC's "building superintendents").

Duty officers—liaison officers from the various bases, air forces, and services—occupied the rows of tables down the center of the room*; their job was to organize changes to the preplanned ATO. Since most changes occurred after a flight was airborne, they were usually passed to the flights by the AWACS; but the airborne command element aboard one of the AWACS aircraft, or another command-and-control element, such as ABCCC aircraft or Killer Scouts, were also sometimes pressed into service.

The system also required a number of support and liaison elements, such as weather, intelligence, search and rescue, air defense, AWACS, airspace management (to keep objects from occupying the same place at the same time), electronic warfare, special operations, and the BCE (the liaison between the Air Force and the Army).

All of these elements were important. A few deserve more explanation:

The air is the Air Force's sea, so weather was obviously important— far more important than knowing whether or not it was going to rain. The decision to load TV-guided Maverick missiles, for instance, depended on the forecast of optical slant ranges: Could the pilot see through the haze with his Maverick so he could lock the missile onto the target? The current operations weather section (supported by Colonel Jerry Riley's larger weather shop across from the Black Hole down the hall) answered such questions and kept everyone in the TACC advised about weather in the target areas, refueling tracks, and airbases.

The large intelligence section in Current Operations received data from several sources: national intelligence sources (such as the DIA); units flying missions (their intelligence shops would debrief the pilots

---

*The term is used generically in the military for people who man a given station. For example, the officer who sits at the Security Police headquarters for an 8–12-hour shift is the duty officer.

and call in anything hot); and analysts in tents on the soccer field in the USMTM compound next to the RSAF headquarters. The soccer field also sent target materials to the wings and made studies of the Iraqis (which went, for example, to the Black Hole, so the findings could be incorporated into the targeting process).

In the rear corner of the operations room was the search-and-rescue cell, led by Colonel Joe Stillwell. His team initiated, coordinated, and tracked rescues. For this they could call upon any available asset—navy ships, army helicopters, or Special Operations infiltration capabilities. Because search and rescue required joint resources, the SAR team in the TACC worked officially for the CINC and not for Chuck Horner. However, since search and rescue efforts were directed primarily toward downed aircrew in territory that was accessible only to air, and since the first indication of a loss, as well as its location, came from the AWACS picture, the team was located in the air operations center in the TACC.

Each morning that Horner entered the TACC, his first stop was at this cell, to check on losses and rescue efforts. As he saw it, there was no more fitting way for a commander in wartime to start the day than to be reminded of the cost of his mistakes.

NIGHT CAMEL

Airmen are always experimenting with better ways to fight.

During Desert Shield, 48th Wing F-111F aircrews flying over the Saudi desert discovered somewhat unexpectedly that friendly tanks were visible on their PAVE TAC screens, even when the tanks were dug into revetments in the sand.

The PAVE TAC pod was located under the F-111F fuselage. This pod housed an infrared scanner that gave a fuzzy television picture of the ground 10,000 to 15,000 feet beneath the aircraft. Since the metal in the tanks heated and cooled more rapidly than the surrounding desert, the tanks showed up brightly when the aircraft pointed its sensor in their direction. Once they got a glimpse of a hot or cold spot, they'd lock the sensor onto the target, and it would track the target as the aircraft moved overhead. The sensor was quite sensitive and could present an excellent picture of anything in its field of view; but there was a trade-off. The field of view was very narrow. For the aircrew, it was like looking through a soda straw at objects three to five miles away.

Also in the pod turret was a laser slaved to the IR sensor. After the aircrew had found a tank and locked the sensor in a track mode, they would confirm the sighting with their cockpit television scope. The weapons system officer would then illuminate the tank with the laser and send a laser-guided bomb homing in on the laser reflection (F-15Es and F-16s equipped with LANTIRN Pods achieved similar results).

These tactics and procedures, practiced and refined during the Night Camel exercises in November and December, became tank plinking in Desert Storm. At the height of the Storm, the 48th Wing were killing over a hundred tanks a night.

Plinking had unintended effects. Soon after the campaign began in mid-January, reconnaissance photos began to show slit trenches some distance away from the parked tanks. During the war with Iran, Iraqi tankers had gotten into the habit of sleeping in their tanks—tanks being on the whole safer than the surrounding desert. Tank plinking ended that haven.

Later, during the ground war, U.S. tankers always seemed to get off the first shot against Iraqi dug-in tanks; and as the battles progressed, enemy tank fire was often sparse. Later analysis showed that when U.S. ground forces approached, the Iraqis were not in their tanks, and then as the first shots hit the Iraqis, the Iraqi tankers concluded they were under air attack and went into bunkers. By the time the truth hit them, it was too late. Though the bravest tried to crawl back to their tanks, they were often cut down by U.S. machine guns; and those who reached their tanks successfully were too confused to fight effectively.

Night Camel not only seriously weakened the Iraqi Army, it had a major impact on the ground war.

DECEMBER BRIEFING

In December, General Schwarzkopf called a command performance for his component commanders on the twentieth of the month to brief Secretary Cheney, General Powell, and Assistant Secretary Paul Wolfowitz at his headquarters at MODA. This was to be the last major war council before the proposed January U.N. deadline.

Though all the components were scheduled to participate, discussion of Army plans was to be minimal. Because the only war in the immediate, post–January 15 period would be the air war, the air campaign was to be the central focus. It was also Schwarzkopf's intention (Horner suspects) to limit the land force briefing to logistical matters, in order to avoid premature judgments about the tactical details of the proposed ground attack. There would be time for that after the progress of the air war could be analyzed.

The Navy and Marine discussion would also be kept to a minimum. Though the Navy was handling the embargo of Iraqi shipping in their usual solid, professional way, there was little to be said about that. There were, however, potential questions about a Marine amphibious operation into Kuwait, which a few Marine leaders in Washington were pressing for—though enthusiasm for such an operation died the closer one came to Riyadh (neither Schwarzkopf nor Boomer wanted one). The defenses the Iraqis were setting up on the shores of Kuwait looked murderous. In the end, an amphibious deception was part of the final ground plan, and it tied down several Iraqi divisions during the land phase of the war.

The briefing was held in Schwarzkopf's war room at MODA, and it was scheduled to last an hour, of which Horner had been allotted fifteen minutes; but since air would be the major topic, he prepared a fifty-viewgraph update of the briefing Buster Glosson had presented to the Secretary in October. That briefing had laid out a picture of the first three days of the war and a general look at the activities beyond that. Now Horner would explain in detail how all that would be accomplished, how long it would take, how the Air Force planned to fight as part of a coalition, and how they were going to support the ground forces when they came up at bat. Finally, he had been warned by Cheney's military assistant that the Secretary was especially concerned about Iraq's ballistic-missile and germ-warfare threats (in Horner's shorthand, Scuds and Bugs), and for that reason, he had prepared two separate briefings about his plans to handle them.

Horner expected to be candid and straightforward, and to tell the Secretary honestly what airpower could and couldn't do. For instance, he expected efficiency to drop for a time after the first three days. There would be an unavoidable lag until intelligence could be exploited and aircraft directed onto new targets (though this new targeting would be done in a matter of minutes). During the briefing, the Secretary seemed to welcome the candor, and in retrospect, it is clear that he would not have accepted a slick presentation that promised smooth and easy success.

When Horner made his presentation, he stood in front of a table where Cheney was sitting, with Schwarzkopf on Cheney's left, Powell on his right, and Wolfowitz on Powell's right. The other key component commanders were seated in the back, and the lights were low. As far as Horner was concerned, there were just five people in the room. Nobody else mattered. Though Cheney, Powell, and Wolfowitz did not expect him to fail, and they were not there to score debating points, their questions and comments were intense and probing; they intended to examine their concerns in detail.

The results, though, were rewarding. After it was all over, it was clear that the Secretary fully understood Horner's intentions and accepted his inability to answer every question as one of the prices of honesty.

Schwarzkopf made few initial comments. He seemed to be waiting to see how Horner made out before he took sides.

As it turned out, hopes for an hourlong briefing were misplaced. It went three hours that day, and continued into the next.

The first hard questions addressed the destruction of Iraqi forces in the Kuwaiti theater of operations—specifically, how long would it take to destroy 50 percent of Iraqi armor and artillery. Because different studies gave different answers, Horner walked Cheney through the analytical effort that provided the basis for his own estimate.

A Pentagon air staff study had claimed the 50 percent goal would be achieved in less than a week, but that just didn't pass the common-sense test, so Buster Glosson had asked the Plans and Analysis people to change their assumptions and fine-tune the data. Their new study expanded the campaign to three weeks—still unrealistic, in Horner's view. In his best judgment, it would take up to six weeks of air combat to prepare the battlefield.

Cheney gave a nod to indicate that this made sense to him, and the briefing continued (the six weeks figure turned out to be substantially accurate).

The two hardest issues concerned Scuds and biological weapons. Though chemical weapons were also discussed, these were expected to be delivered by artillery shells and used primarily against military targets. Since the military had protection against these weapons,* Cheney was not greatly worried about them.

---

*They could use antichemical suits and bomb forward storage areas (though the Iraqis had so many chemical munitions that Horner could not target all of them with any hope of success).

The "Bugs" were another thing. Not only could biological agents be spread in Israel and the populated areas of Saudi Arabia with relative ease, but there were no effective antidotes against them.

Earlier that month, Saddam Hussein had test-fired his homebuilt, "improved" version of the Soviet Scud missiles. To double the range of his Scuds, Saddam had to cut his warhead in half. Moreover, the Scud was already terribly inaccurate. To a military person like Horner, this meant the weapon was insignificant. To a civilian, however, a wildly inaccurate, seemingly unstoppable weapon capable of randomly destroying your house and family was very significant. As was demonstrated by the V-2 attacks in World War II and the Scud attacks in the 1980s War of the Cities between Iran and Iraq, even inaccurate ballistic missiles can terrorize civilian populations. Horner missed the point about the Scuds. Dick Cheney did not. He was a lot closer to the voters.

Horner outlined for the Secretary how his bombers would attack the fixed Scud erector launchers in western Iraq during the first hours of the air campaign. This was followed by a description of the strikes planned for Scud production, storage, fuel production, and repair facilities (although he believed most of these would be empty of the Scuds and their mobile launchers). Finally came the words Cheney was not eager to hear: "There is no way I can stop the Iraqis from launching Scuds at Saudi Arabia, Bahrain, and Israel from their fleet of mobile launchers." When the Secretary pressed further, Horner wanted to assure him that the problem would be temporary and the solution was at hand; but there was no way he could honestly claim that. At best he could only describe their measures to suppress Scud launches, or, failing that, to defend against them with Patriot batteries once they were launched. Stopping the Scuds, Horner had to admit, was hopeless.

This did not please Cheney, but he was a realist. He understood that if Horner had possessed a bullet—magic or otherwise—that prevented Scuds from falling on Israel or Saudi Arabia, he would have used it.

★ Saddam Hussein's use of poison gas on his own people and during the Iran–Iraq War was widely known. Less was known about Iraqi research and production of germ-warfare weapons. That meant there were a number of "what-ifs" to consider long before the Cheney briefing, all posing a number of dilemmas. The first problem was to isolate the Iraqi capabilities to produce, store, and deliver biological weapons.

Though intelligence information pointed to a number of laboratories capable of producing such agents, targeting production facilities was difficult, since very little was required to grow the agents—especially for people indifferent to protecting their work force from inadvertent exposure. To manufacture biological agents, no special chemicals (as in the case of most poison gases) or special equipment (as in the case of nuclear weapons) were required. Every hospital has a laboratory capable of producing biological agents, and food-production facilities can be changed into germ factories without difficulty.

If production facilities were hard to counter, delivery was even harder. Biological agents can be distributed to their intended victims any number of ways.

Against military forces, these were the choices:

The most effective delivery system would have been an aerosol-fogging machine (like those used for mosquito control) pulled behind a car or truck; but driving such a device into Israel or Saudi Arabia presented obvious problems. A helicopter equipped with spray bars could also have worked, but given the effectiveness of U.S.–Saudi air defenses, its potential for harm was limited. The agents could have been shot in artillery shells, placed in missile warheads, or dropped in bombs, but in each of these cases, dispersal patterns are small, and any explosion used to break open the projectile case would have proved fatal to some of its payload. In short, delivering biological agents against Coalition troops in the field would not have been efficient, especially since those forces were already prepared to endure attack from chemical weapons. The suit and mask designed to protect the soldier from gas attack also provided a measure of protection from biological weapons.

Biological agents could possibly have damaged Coalition armies and even terrorized many of the troops, but they would have been far more effective in terrorizing and killing civilians in large cities. In cities are herded men, women, and children who don't have available the gas masks and impregnated clothing needed to counter harmful agents. Because people are packed closely, small numbers of weapons offer effective coverage. Because the diseases can take several days to harm their victims, terror and confusion have ample time to get out of control. And because cities are usually dependent on centralized sources of fresh food and water, these sources are easy to contaminate. One scenario imagined Iraqi infiltrators entering Saudi Arabia and the other Gulf countries and releasing anthrax or botulism spores into water supplies.

Though air defenses and counter–ballistic missile operations could shield against most aircraft or missile-dispersed biological agents,* and Saudi border guards were doing a superb job picking up Iraqi infiltrators, such measures could only suppress delivery of biological agents. Total prevention could not be guaranteed.

That left storage as the best place to attack. And Intelligence information pointed to Salman Park, just south of Baghdad, where botulism and anthrax spores were stored in Teflon containers in massive, well-constructed, environmentally controlled bunkers.

Yet bombing these bunkers posed a dilemma for Horner and his planners. Would that destroy the spores, or would it release them into the atmosphere, where they could spread and contaminate the entire Arabian Peninsula? The choice then was this: To blow up the bunkers and kill every living thing on the Arabian Peninsula—a position given authoritative voice in a pair of scientific white papers published in England and the United States.† Or to let Saddam Hussein release the spores himself, which might also kill every living thing on the Arabian Peninsula.

As he was currently stationed on the Arabian Peninsula, Horner took the warning seriously, and there was no clear answer about the best course of action.

A solution to the dilemma came from an unexpected source.

One day in early December, an Army major, a biological-warfare expert from Fort Meade, Maryland, appeared at Horner's door and presented his credentials (Horner never actually learned his name). "I understand you are concerned about Iraqi biological agents," he said. Interested, Horner listened:

"While the white papers often lead readers to conclude that any minute exposure to anthrax or botulism will be lethal," he explained, "anthrax and botulism spores are not in fact as deadly as many so-called experts fear. In fact," he noted, "we are often exposed to anthrax, perhaps every day; the spores live for years in the soil. Exposure itself is not a problem. It is the amount of exposure that constitutes the danger. And it takes a lot. Or," he bluntly put it, "the best way to die from anthrax is

---

*One serious problem: Patriot missiles would only disperse the payload of a biological-tipped Scud overhead.

†There were glaring errors in the papers. For example, the authors always had the agents spreading equidistant in all directions from the bombed bunkers. Any pilot who has dropped a practice bomb knows the marking smoke always goes downwind.

to kiss a sick sheep." He then pointed out that while heat, sunlight, and water—especially chlorinated water—killed the spores, these were no guarantees. Therefore, at the risk of fallout (primarily in Iraq), the most reasonable course was to destroy the agents and deny the enemy their use.

That seemed like a good idea to Chuck Horner.

Already, plans for the destruction of the bunkers had been made to minimize fallout. The idea was to crack open the bunkers when the wind was calm just before first light, then put cluster-bomb units on the stored agents to create the maximum heat with the minimum blast. For good measure, the attack would be ended by dropping randomly exploding land mines, in order to prevent the Iraqis from scavenging undamaged Teflon bottles of agents.

★ "Chuck," Secretary Cheney asked, with deceptive simplicity, "what about attacks against the biological weapons storage areas?"

Horner described the target, summarized the Army major's position, and then described the attack sequence proposed by his planners and weaponeers.

While Schwarzkopf kept silent and Cheney asked questions to better understand the issues, Powell and Wolfowitz offered counterarguments, citing the white papers condemning such attacks.

It was difficult for Horner to argue with Colin Powell, his military superior, in front of Powell's superior, the Secretary of Defense, even when he believed he was correct. Nevertheless (diplomacy not being one of Horner's strong suits), he set forth his reasons, and Powell and Wolfowitz disagreed. For a time there wasn't much progress, since Cheney was withholding judgment, and Schwarzkopf continued to maintain his silence (though Horner remembers a gleam in his eye that said he enjoyed watching the Air Force general sweat).

The impasse continued until Horner recalled the larger issues. "Yes," he told himself, "this is a war against aggression. But it is also a war against the proliferation of weapons of mass destruction. And while our calculations may be in error, and some innocent Iraqi civilians may die from the fallout resulting from our attack, that would serve a useful purpose. The contamination of Iraq would send a signal, provide a lesson, to any nation contemplating building and storing those horrible weapons." It didn't take Horner long to lay out this new line of reasoning. Paul Wolfowitz quickly picked it up, and now began to find reasons to attack the storage bunkers.

As support for Horner's position waxed, Powell's opposition waned, until Cheney finally turned to Schwarzkopf and asked, "Norm, what do you think?"

"I think we ought to do it," Schwarzkopf answered.

Nothing more was said, and the bunkers remained on the target list.

As it turned out, they proved to be a difficult nut to crack, buried as they were under extensive layers of dirt and concrete. The munition selected for the job was the I-2000 bomb (Mark 84 bomb class), which was designed for that kind of job. The I-2000 Mark 84 had a steel nose that would not fracture when it hit reinforced concrete, and its time-delay fuse was in the tail, so the bomb could penetrate before it exploded. Finally, unlike most bombs, which are dropped on a slant, the I-2000 was dropped from medium altitude (which gave the bomb enough kinetic energy to penetrate the reinforced concrete and its earth overburden) directly over the target (which allowed its laser to guide it to a near-vertical angle). The force this generated was sufficient to penetrate most reinforced bunkers.

In the event, when the I-2000 penetrated the biobunker, its explosion touched off an enormous secondary explosion, with a vast fireball and prodigious quantities of billowing smoke. What was stored in that bunker will probably never be known, but it turned night into day.

After the war, Horner researched the available sources to see if there was evidence of fallout of biological agents. Though he found reports of Iraqi guards killed during the bombing attacks, no evidence of deaths from biological fallout appeared (there have been reports of postwar civilian deaths due to disease, but these cannot be connected to the bunker attacks).

After the bunker issue was settled, Horner's briefing was over, and he returned to his seat between John Yeosock and Stan Arthur at the back of the room. The meeting ended with a brief discussion of ground operations.

COUNTDOWN

The final weeks were a jumble. The buildup and beddown, as well as plans and training, were proceeding satisfactorily, though with lurches and hang-ups. To ensure that the executors of the plan had a say in its planning, Buster Glosson took the ATO around to the bases, briefed the commanders and crews, and ran one last sanity check on the tactics, the timing, and the force packages of various bomb droppers and electronic-combat support aircraft. Anything that looked unworkable was changed on the spot. Horner continued working his role as cheerleader and team builder, visiting the bases and the units, giving encouragement, laying on hands. Yet he always managed to find time to keep up his own flying skills, by combining visits to the bases with training sorties (he averaged four to six F-16 sorties per week).

Surprisingly, not every second was filled with demands. During free moments, he read military history (provided by Dr. Dick Hallion, the USAF historian) to see how others had done the job he was now doing. Two he especially remembers were *The Sky Over Baghdad,* about the RAF in post–World War I Iraq, and *Eagle Against the Sun,* about the war with Japan. He learned there that MacArthur's relationship with his air chief, Kenney, was very like his own with Schwarzkopf (both CINCs knew the importance of air to their overall combat plan, and both trusted their airman to carry out the right air strategy).

Finally, there was a round of official dinners with cabinet ministers, princes, heads of state, near heads of state, and other high-level people—somewhat daunting for a boy from Iowa, yet also a source of pride and a visible sign that he was moving up in the world. And in truth, important work was accomplished:

A dinner at the Crown Prince's palace found Horner seated between the Saudi Ministers of Petroleum and Finance, both men educated in U.S. business schools, both extremely personable, both working hard to keep the wheels of the Coalition turning; and Horner needed help from them. In August, the Saudi government had agreed to pay for jet fuel, but no one in August had envisioned how large U.S. forces would grow. Later, the Ministry of Finance was reluctant to fund the rapidly increasing fuel bills from the Ministry of Petroleum; and the Ministry of Petroleum was therefore reluctant to refine and ship the jet fuel Horner's increasingly large air forces were using. It was already costing $20 million a day to keep up air defense CAPs and conduct rehearsal training, and the costs were only going to grow. Over dinner, at Horner's urging, the Minister of Finance agreed to send the money to the Minister of Petroleum, so he would send the jet fuel to Horner's bases. (During Desert Storm, Saudi Arabia became a net importer of jet fuel, with an average of forty tanker ships per day inbound to the kingdom.)

Horner had another problem persuading the Saudis to allow the staging of B-52s at Jeddah (where facilities were large and modern enough to handle them).

Saudi leaders were reluctant to allow large bombers—especially large bombers whose original function was to deliver nuclear weapons—to be based on their territory . . . and worse, *near* Mecca. Fighter-bombers and transports were another thing. The Saudis were used to fighters and transports taking off and landing at their bases.

At Prince Sultan's horse farm about a mile across the highway from the international airport, Horner was able to engage Khaled on this issue.

Always sensitive to the likely Saudi reaction, he crafted his request carefully: "I know you don't want to do this because of the impact it can have on your people," he told the Prince, "but I need to base the B-52s closer to the enemy, so I can get more sorties out of them than if they have to fly all the way from England or Diego Garcia. If you'll let me put them at Jeddah the first night of the war, and operate them out of there afterward, I will redeploy them out the day after the war ends. And besides," he offered, "during the war there will be so much going on, the people won't notice them."

Prince Khaled bought this argument, and he and Horner reached an agreement. The bombers would land at Jeddah after their first combat sortie, then fly the rest of their combat missions into the KTO from General Mansour's military facilities at King Abdullah Aziz Air Base (the military part of Jeddah New). And Horner kept his side of the deal: the big bombers departed immediately after hostilities concluded.

Each dinner was different. Some were in embassies, some were in desert tents, some were in palaces. At some there were women; at others they were absent. Some went very late; others broke up early. At all of them, Horner drank orange juice, even though at embassy dinners there were normally liquids not readily available in the Kingdom.

And for Horner, not all of his performances were shining.

At an American Embassy reception—trying to play the slick insider—Horner suggested to the AT & T regional manager that the telecommunications infrastructure in Iraq and Kuwait might sustain damage if war broke out, and he might want to think about shipping switching equipment, cable, and other equipment to replace it. "Actually," the regional manager informed him (punching a large hole in his vanity), "the replacement equipment is already stored in warehouses around the region, awaiting installation after the war."

★ In December, Horner had to sweat. Tony McPeak, the new Air Force Chief of Staff, nominated him for the job of DCINC, or Schwarzkopf's deputy, to replace USAF Lieutenant General Craven C. "Buck" Rogers (Rogers, who was scheduled to retire in the fall of 1990, did not deploy to Riyadh).

When a joint position like DCINC came open, the service chiefs were asked to nominate one of their generals for the job. McPeak knew that Schwarzkopf liked Horner, that they worked well together, and that the current DCINC was an Air Force general. If Horner was the DCINC, he reasoned, he could then put another general in CENTAF, which would leave the Air Force well represented in CENTCOM.

"Bad thinking," Horner reasoned. "Worse, it's crazy. Nobody in his right mind wants to be deputy. The deputy handles all the issues the CINC doesn't want to fool with: he's the one who gives boring speeches, hosts minor guests at headquarters, attends all the meaningless meetings. And in meetings when the CINC is present, the DCINC is supposed to sit there and say nothing. When the CINC is out of town, he runs things, but God help him if he makes a decision not previously discussed with the CINC."

And so Horner pleaded with McPeak. "Don't do this to me, General," he told him. "It's a thankless job. You are not in charge of anything, and can only influence the CINC in private, which I'm already doing as CENTAF. And look—I know this sounds like big ego—but I don't know where you're going to find anyone better prepared to command CENTAF. I'm more operationally astute than most, I have more command experience than any of my contemporaries, I know the Middle East and the Arab military leaders, I've been working war in the Middle East since 1987; and the CINC is not likely to give a new guy the confidence that I have built up over the months."

McPeak, a hardheaded man, resisted these pleas, but to Horner's immense relief, Schwarzkopf agreed with him; and Colin Powell wanted his own man, Lieutenant General Cal Waller, in the job. Waller, a big, easygoing man, known for his common touch, would be a counterweight, some thought, to the far more imperial Schwarzkopf.

And so Schwarzkopf kept Horner as his air commander, and Waller became DCINC . . . and immediately stepped on a media land mine, after the manner of Mike Dugan.

Current plans called for the massive relocation west of VIIth Corps and XVIIIth Corps for Schwarzkopf's left hook—but only *after* the start of the air campaign, to prevent Iraqi reconnaissance aircraft from discovering the surprise Schwarzkopf had in store for them.

After reviewing these plans, including detailed analysis of the difficulties the corps faced in moving, Waller concluded that the two corps would not be in position to attack for several weeks after the air war started.

This led to the following exchange:

"Will the Army be ready to fight on the U.N.'s, and now President Bush's January fifteenth deadline?" a reporter asked.

"What's so important about being ready to fight on the fifteenth?" Waller answered.

He was technically correct. It was not important for the Army to be ready to fight on the fifteenth, it was important for them to be ready to move west, so they could fight where and when the CINC decided.

Unfortunately for Waller, his response implied that President Bush's deadline for Iraqi withdrawal from Kuwait was a sham.

Needless to say, there was little joy in Washington when the headline broke: "CENTCOM DCINC ASKED, 'WHAT'S SO IMPORTANT ABOUT THE 15TH?' "

Afterward, General Schwarzkopf took heavy—and hardly welcome—hits from his superiors, and Cal Waller never really regained the CINC's confidence, or had much influence in the upper circles in Riyadh. The resulting fallout ended Waller's shot at a fourth star.

One good result of the flap was the cancellation of media interviews. Horner had better things to do.

★ Christmas came and went—or C+140, as it was jokingly called in the desert. If C day was the first day of the Desert Shield deployment, then C+1 was the day after that, C+2 the next, and so on until C+140—December 25. In the event, it was a lonely, miserable time for American servicemen and servicewomen in the Gulf. They desperately missed their families. "Have a merry C+140" didn't quite do it. The good news was that everyone knew the climax was coming very soon.

New Year's Day followed. And for Horner, the rest of January was a blur.

By the end of the first week in January, people were leaving Riyadh, the normally bustling traffic-clogged streets were almost deserted, and weather over Southwest Asia was worsening. It would prove to be the hardest winter in years.

Horner reflects:

As the war drew near, I could see the change in the pilots. Now when I visited, they seemed more mature, more sober in their outlook. No more whining questions. They'd had their innocence baked out of them in the hot sun, dulled by the night combat air patrols, scared out of them by night practices and by large-scale rehearsal missions in the increasingly bad weather. They knew now they were going to war—an event they'd trained for all their professional lives and feared they'd never experience. They were going from the practice field to the Super Bowl. Some would not make it, yet they were not afraid. Neither was there much joy (though there was laughter)—a condition caused not by the threat of war but by loneliness and separation from loved ones.

No longer were we carefree, fun-loving fighter pilots.

On 15 January, I wrote my wife,

"This may be my last letter for some time. My mental attitude will likely be such you won't want to hear from me anyway. Some days lately I could puke. There are so many people who have no clue about air, people who are jealous because we have the predominant act in this circus. They spend all their time trying to get their two cents in at the expense of getting the job done.

I try to keep our operations stable and work to stay above the petty crises, because I know that when the shooting starts, the nervous Nellies will run away.

Forgive such a shitty letter, but we are entering a big game and I have a thousand details to attend to. Perhaps when the rest get doing their wartime thing, I'll have more time. Till then, know in your deepest secret place, I love you so very much."

III

The
Thousand-
Hour War

8

STORM!

Chuck Horner tells what happened next:

I arrived in the TACC shortly after 0100 on the seventeenth of January 1991. The war, scheduled to start at 0300, Riyadh time, was moments away.

The January 15 U.N. deadline had come and gone. Even the added teeth of President Bush's threat—"Evacuate Kuwait or face military action"—had produced no concrete results (though there'd been a flurry of diplomatic activity). This didn't surprise me. I was sure Saddam wouldn't back down, if for no other reason than he had dug too many trenches, piled too many sandbags, and poured too much concrete in the desert. He must have figured he held a winning hand, which had me worried about an ace up his sleeve. *Yet how could he,* I'd asked myself over and over, *when we hold all four aces?*

President Bush had sent a message to General Schwarzkopf: the start of the liberation of Kuwait is up to you, but make it as soon after the fifteenth as possible. The CINC had in turn delegated that responsibility to me. And I had chosen the early hours of January 17 as the best moment to launch the aerial assault.

This plan was based on a single factor. On that date would occur the least possible illumination in the night sky—no moonlight. Our F-117s were virtually invisible to radar, but they were visible to Iraqi fighter pilots; and they were particularly visible against the backdrop of a moonlit sky. They were attacking the toughest, most heavily defended target ever struck from the air—Baghdad. We were going to give them every possible advantage.

★ Knowing that I'd get very little sleep in the next days, I'd gone home to the USMTM compound next door at about 2100 that evening to try to sleep . . . until midnight, anyway. But sleep did not come. I was too keyed up, too tense. I lay there in the empty apartment (Yeosock and Fong were working at ARCENT and my aide Hoot Gibson had gone to Al Dahfra to fly in combat), trying to get some rest, wondering what I had forgotten, wondering what I had missed that would cost the life of a pilot. Sure, I knew some would die, but I wanted to be certain I had not made the mistake that cost them their lives.

There had been no last-minute phone calls to General Schwarzkopf, or to anyone else. These would not have been appropriate. We didn't want an increase in communications traffic to tip off the enemy that something big was in the works, though I am sure they expected something after the fifteenth.

Shortly after the deadline passed, wheels had been set in motion. And on January 16, B-52s from the 2d Bombardment Wing of the Mighty Eighth Air Force, armed with conventional air-launched cruise missiles (CALCMs), had departed Barksdale AFB, Louisiana (an event duly reported on CNN). The Mighty Eighth would go to war once more, this time under command of the Ninth Air Force. Quite a turnaround from the days of SAC rule. Seven B-52s were to fly a round trip of 14,000 miles in thirty-five hours (the longest combat mission in history) and fire thirty-five CALCMs at eight targets—military communications sites and power-generation and transmission facilities.

Why send B-52s all the way from Louisiana?

In any war, there were many time-sensitive targets, that is, targets we wanted to hit early—command-and-control nodes, Scud storage areas, airfields, and so on—all of which we wanted to close down quickly so we could hit our other targets more efficiently as assets (fighter-bombers) became available after turnaround. Therefore, it made sense to plan the opening moments of the war to include as many strikes as possible, as quickly as possible; and cruise missiles, though expensive, gave us the ability to hit many targets simultaneously.

In this war, cruise missiles were fired not only from B-52s but from battleships and submarines (thus showcasing the Navy). The Air Force's B-52s and their cruise missiles were the first to take off and the first to fire a shot in anger (thus showcasing the Air Force's emerging Global Reach Global Power doctrine). Ordnance from Army Apaches was the first to explode. And Air Force F-117s were the first to penetrate the airspace of Iraq. Lots of firsts for everybody.

Our tankers, AWACS, and fighters flying the air defense combat Air Patrols and training sorties had been flying near the Iraq border every day and night since August 6 (and the RSAF had been doing that alone before we got there). These flights had been carefully increased over the past weeks, so Iraqi radar operators looking across into Saudi Arabia would not be alarmed at the large numbers of radar returns. What they didn't see were hundreds of aircraft, primarily tankers and bomb-laden fighters, orbiting farther back from the border at altitudes below the Iraqi radar's line of sight over the horizon.

The first wave of these were deep-penetrating aircraft—F-111s, F-15Es, Tornadoes, F-16s, A-6s, and more F-117s. These had the range and large bomb loads needed to hit Iraqi command-and-control bunkers, Scud launch pads and storage areas, telecommunications and radio facilities, and airfields. They were complemented by F-15Cs, F-14s, and air defense Tornadoes, which would orbit above Iraqi airfields, waiting for Saddam's Air Force to rise to the defense of its country.

Also prowling over Iraq were a host of vital support aircraft—EF-111s to electronically blind Iraqi radar, Wild Weasels and Navy A-7s, equipped with high-speed radiation missiles to physically blind surface-to-air missile radar, and Special Operations helicopters, waiting near Baghdad to conduct pickup of downed aircrew. Throughout the night and next day, RF-4, U-2, RF-5, and TARPS-configured Navy/Marine aircraft flew reconnaissance and provided battle damage assessment of our opening strikes.

Backing up all of this were countless KC-135, KC-10, KC-130, and A-6 refueling tankers orbiting ever closer to the Iraqi border as the first wave of fuel-thirsty fighters and bombers returned from deep inside Iraq.

While airpower was striking the heart of Iraq, its army in the KTO did not go unnoticed. Waves of B-52s from England, Spain, and Diego Garcia began an unceasing avalanche of flaming iron upon the Republican Guard and other Iraqi troops. The rising sun brought another form of terror, as deadly A-10s dove down with their Maverick missiles, 30mm guns and bombs on tanks, armored personnel carriers, trucks, artillery, supply depots, and air defense SAMs and AAA guns.

Worse was to come, from thousands of other aircraft—versatile F-16s, often quickly turned around at KKMC airport, switching in moments from deep striker to hits on Iraqi Army targets minutes north of the bor-

Number of Fighter, Attack, and Bomber Aircraft

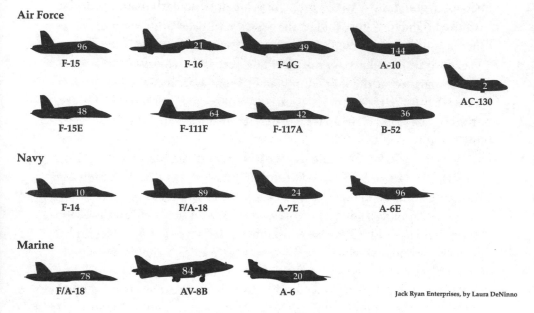

Air Force

F-15 — 96

F-16 — 21

F-4G — 49

A-10 — 144

AC-130 — 2

F-15E — 48

F-111F — 64

F-117A — 42

B-52 — 36

Navy

F-14 — 10

F/A-18 — 89

A-7E — 24

A-6E — 96

Marine

F/A-18 — 78

AV-8B — 84

A-6 — 20

Jack Ryan Enterprises, by Laura DeNinno

der; F/A-18s from the Navy and Marine Corps; allied Jaguars, Mirages, A-4s, F-5s, and F-16s; and waves of bombers and fighters from Incirlik Air Base in Turkey.*

All of these aircraft were waiting for the moment they would start the massive rush across the border that would open the aerial pounding of Iraq, which would go on unabated for the next 1,000 hours. What you don't know *can* hurt you.

Meanwhile, the first BGM-109 Tomahawk missiles were launched by Navy ships, aimed at vital targets in Baghdad, our first act that could not be recalled. When those missiles left their launch tubes and cells aboard the battleship *Wisconsin,* we were committed to war.

Even while the Tomahawks and F-117A Stealth fighters were streaming toward Baghdad, the first blow of the war was struck in Iraq's western desert, as Task Force NORMANDY—a pair of Special Operations

---

The Turkish government had given permission for us to use their Incirlik base to support the Coalition attack.

MH-53J PAVE LOW helicopters guiding a force of eight AH-64A Apache helicopter gunships—was approaching air defense early-warning radar sites near the Saudi border. The destruction of these sites would blow a hole in Iraqi's radar "fence" and buy time for ingressing F-111Fs, F-15Es, and Tornado GR-1s tasked to strike air defense and Scud targets in central and western Iraq. The closer these aircraft came to their targets before the Iraqi air defense radars and ground observers alerted their defenses, the greater the odds they would hit their targets successfully and return home. A lot of folks were depending on those soldiers in their Apaches, as well as the Air Force airmen in the PAVE LOWs, whose elaborate navigation and targeting sensors were leading the Apaches through the dark night.

When the time came, the Apaches launched their Hellfire missiles, and moments later we had our fence hole.

Meanwhile, as the world would soon see on CNN, thousands of guns and surface-to-air guided missiles defended the Iraqi capital city. Airfields ringing the city bristled with some of the most modern air defense interceptors, their pilots eager to get their first kill. The entire network of defenses was tied together with the ultrasophisticated French-built KARI command-and-control system. Though we didn't know it yet, KARI was about to commit hari-kari, by getting in the way of a bunch of grimly determined airmen.

We *truly* didn't know.

How soon would our strikes silence the command and control? How soon would they spark terror in the gunners, SAM operators, and fighter pilots? How many golden BBs (wildly fired stray bullets) would strike our aircraft? How good were our F-117s? Sure, we had all the test data, all the exercise results, and all the theory; but this was the first time this revolutionary aircraft would play in a big game. (Their debut in Panama had been against undefended targets where the goal was to confuse some sleeping soldiers.) Well, the F-117 team had left the practice fields behind them. Tonight they would receive the air warfare equivalent of a Super Bowl kickoff. Not only did they have to penetrate those intense defenses, they had to hit their targets without fail, since all the rest of the crews behind them were depending on the F-117As to devastate the Iraqi air defenses. They had to hit the system's eyes and brain—radars, command bunkers, communication sites—with never-before-demanded accuracy, and with no collateral damage.

★ At 0100, when I joined our team in the front row of the TACC, almost everyone was there (except for those scheduled to come on the day shift at 0700), watching the growing numbers of radar returns displayed by the AWACS data link on the huge TV screens on the front wall.

One screen gave the AWACS picture. On it, lines showed the boundaries of Saudi Arabia, Iraq, Iran, Israel, Syria, Jordan, and Turkey, as well as the northern ends of the Red Sea and the Arabian Gulf. Baghdad was at the center, Riyadh just off the bottom edge of the screen, Incirlik, Turkey, just off the top, the Mediterranean Sea just off the left, and Tehran just off the right. On the screen were red, yellow, or greenish-blue icons. Red was the enemy, yellow unknown, and the others friendly. Beside each icon was a series of four numbers, indicating the track number given by AWACS to the blip they were receiving on their radar.

The AWACS picture was a composite taken from four or five RSAF/USAF E-3 aircraft. This picture was augmented by U.S. Navy E-2 AWACS aircraft flying over the Navy ships, as well as by specially equipped ships, like the Aegis class, whose radars could be integrated into this picture. AWACS was also linked with the Rivet Joint Signals Intelligence Aircraft. Rivet Joint gave the AWACS controllers information about the ships that helped them more accurately identify them. An aircraft got a blue icon because it squawked on IFF (identification friend or foe) the mode and codes assigned them in the ATO. These told the AWACS who they were, the type, call sign, mission, target, time, tanker, and so on. It was our goal to make sure red returns got minimum flying time and whenever possible to terminate that status with extreme violence. For example, "splash two MiG-23s."

The other large TV box displayed intelligence information. ELINT data coming from a variety of sources was combined and displayed as symbols. For example, Scud launches observed by an infrared-equipped satellite and encoded into coordinates by Colorado Springs would be first displayed as a line on the map emanating from the Scud's launch point. This was quickly followed by a fan shape showing the area it was capable of reaching. The whole thing looked like a broom, with the top of the handle being the launch point, and the bristles showing the area where the warhead might fall.

To the right of the TV displays was a small movie screen used to show viewgraphs during shift change or special Intel briefings; and leaning up against the wall was the two-by-three-foot piece of cardboard listing all our airfields and the current weather at that base. (After the first night, we added a TV set tuned to CNN, so we could watch the war.)

★ When I came in at 0100, the TACC was quiet. What was there to say? You could only wait. It was going to be hell watching the war unfold without being in the cockpit.

As I sat down, I was still kicking myself for failing to sleep when I had the chance. But I had not been totally stupid. I'd made sure to put on a clean uniform; it would be some time before I got a chance to shower and change. Still, the air in the TACC was sure to get rank from the coffee and cottonmouth breath and nervous sweat. Yeah, I was neat and clean, but we all felt like hell.

Those minutes waiting for the war to start, waiting for our plan to unfold, were the worst minutes of my life.

We talked in low voices, as though we were afraid someone would notice us. At one point, Buster Glosson asked me, "How many aircraft are we going to lose before this is all over?"—a question that touched the heart of our collective anxiety.

There had been a number of estimates, ranging from a hundred to three hundred–plus. I checked with my guts, then wrote "42" on a piece of paper, folded it, and passed it to Buster.

My number turned out to be a good guess. But I had meant 42 USAF only, so I can't take much credit for accuracy.

Actual losses were USAF 14, USN 6, USMC 7, RSAF 2, RAF 7, Italy 1, and Kuwait 1, for a total of 38.

Buster's question hit us all where we were raw, because we were about to embark on actions that would take many lives. We would send our own friends and allies on missions from which they would never return. The death of friends and enemies alike hung over our heads.

I knew how tough it was to climb the ladder into your jet and fly to where folks were doing their best to kill you, even as you tried your best to wreck their homeland. And yet, as tough as that was, as terrifying as that was, there is a real up-close personal involvement that justifies what you do. When you fly over an enemy target, and the red golf balls are streaming up, and the black mushrooms with orange centers burst all around you, and the SAM missiles streaking toward you once in a while quit moving (meaning, they are homing in on you), and you hear MiG calls in your headset (meaning that those hard-to-see supersonic jets are trying to launch a missile at your jet), when all of that is going on, you develop a personal relationship with the enemy. Then you don't mind killing him; in fact, it seems like a good idea.

No, that doesn't justify killing the enemy, nor does it soften your concern about their attempts to kill you, but there is balance, there is some sort of justification for the horrible things you do. Sitting in the TACC, setting the killing in motion, you carry a lot more responsibility, a lot more feeling of dread. It was a burden I'd been carrying around since I'd signed the orders that would start all of this carnage in motion. It was the understanding that someday I would probably have to explain my actions to God, and there was no suitable explanation. When men are imperfect—and God knows we are—then there better be a forgiving God.

Well, it was time to suck it up and go to work. And that's just what we all did.

★ As we were waiting in the TACC, Mary Jo was eating dinner with her mother, who was visiting from Cresco, Iowa. Sean Cullivan, our aide, came in and announced, "Mrs. Horner, the war has started." Like many others, she and her mother left the dinner table and went into the family room to watch television. Like many others, they stayed glued to the TV for the next six weeks, morning, noon, and night. The "CNN Effect" bloomed into full flower during this war. (Interestingly, CNN became a major source of intelligence for us in the TACC.)

★ The radar display showed our strikers creep, at 500 to 600 knots, toward their targets. As we watched, someone announced that CNN's Bernard Shaw was reporting live from Baghdad that the guided missiles were beginning to land on their targets. In my office on the third floor was a television with a CNN hookup. Meanwhile, the critical F-117 strike against the telecommunications building in Baghdad that was the core of Iraqi command and control was about to occur. We called it the AT & T building. Bernie Shaw's reports were relayed to the United States over Iraqi telephone commercial circuits that passed through this building.

I asked Major Buck Rogers, one of the key Black Hole planners, to go upstairs and turn on my TV and let me know what happened.

The critical bomb impact time over target was to occur at 0302. As the second hand of the big clock on the wall swept toward the designated TOT, I talked to Buck on the hot line that connected my position in the TACC to my office on the third floor. The success or failure of this one F-117 mission, this one bomb, would tell a lot about how our air campaign would fare. If Iraqi telecommunications were destroyed, the air superiority battle became manageable: blind the enemy air defense system, and isolate the elements from the brain, and it is no longer a "system" but individual weapons operating in the dark.

Now we were hearing of the gunfire over Baghdad, intense and seemingly endless streams of bullets and missiles rising from atop every building and open area of the capital. I prayed for the F-117 pilots.

And then, just as the second hand swept past the twelve on the clock, Buck reported, "CNN just went off the air." That was it. The AT & T building had taken a mortal blow. The report of our success flew across the somber-quiet TACC, and as it did, all of us came out of our shells of silence. Everywhere there was backslapping and boisterous talk. We had gone from the pits of anxiety to the heights of self-confident self-congratulations. (To me it had been close to despair. Fighter pilots are control freaks. When we are not in control, we feel hopeless.) It was a wonderful moment.

Yes, we had a long way to go before the ordeal would be over. But we were off to a good start.

Report after report of mission success began to roll in. It was like putting a puzzle together; as the pieces came together, a picture began to take shape. Each target destroyed added to the picture we had been imagining.

More important, all the aircraft, save a Navy F-18, on a suppression of enemy air defense mission, returned to their bases.

It wasn't all smooth that night: Some of our 160 tankers ran out of fuel for off-load, and thirsty fighters had to find someone else to give them jet fuel. And the base at Taif, just south of Mecca (home to the F-111 fleet, all airborne striking vital targets across Iraq), was closed due to dense fog.

I was on the point of giving out commands, and then stopped. I needed to have faith in the commanders, in the AWACS crews, and most of all in the aircrews in each fighter. They knew how to figure out what needed to be done and then do it. If I got involved that would only add to the confusion and create dependency. Sure, I'd stay on top of the situation, but I had to let others make the decisions I dearly wanted to make. I had to delegate to others, watch them wrestle with problems that my experience made easy for me, and then watch in amazement when they found solutions I never even considered.

The air-to-air engagements were especially hard to stay out of.

Think about it. You're a pilot who loves the complex ballet of an aerial engagement. You've trained for thousands of hours. Every cell in your body knows how to detect the enemy, bring your aircraft and your flight's aircraft into the fight, engage the enemy aircraft with your weapons, and herd your team safely out of the fight toward home or into another engagement.

Now you are sitting in a room where a large display shows every aircraft in the battle (except F-117s). You see the friendly fighters going about their appointed rounds, delivering bombs or searching for Iraqi interceptors. All at once new blips appear, as a pair of Iraqi fighters scramble from their airfields. A microphone on the table in front of you connects you to AWACS and then to the fighters. You know almost as much as the AWACS knows. It would be so easy to pick up that microphone and direct, "Have Eagle flight kill the two fighters that just took off from Baland"—a fighter base in Iraq near Baghdad. All I had to do was say it, and it would be done. Even though it's a no-brainer for the AWACS controller and the F-15 flight leader to handle it, yet I feel good. I even feel important. And we win.

But no. I'm not going to do it the Soviet way, which is the Iraqi way, with the general sitting in a bunker somewhere and telling the pilot where to fly and when to shoot.

The microphone stayed on the table. And Aim 7 missiles, illuminated by F-15 radar, homed in on the Iraqi fighters and blew them out of the sky. Pennzoil 63 and Citgo 65, Captains Kelk and Grater from the 33d Fighter Wing's 58th Squadron, got kills on the opening night of the war, shooting down a MiG-29 and a Mirage F-1. As the Iraqi blips faded from the screen, the AWACS control team on my left called out, "Splash two," to a cheering crowd.

★ The plan unfolding that first night had worked, and all of us were uplifted. In retrospect, I think all the folks at home were also uplifted in those early days, as the reports of success vastly outnumbered the painful reports of casualties or mission failures. After the war, people who do not understand or take time to study this part of the battle, thought it was easy, that we easily seized control over Iraq. I will admit our people made it look easy, but it wasn't, not by any stretch of the imagination.

Meanwhile, my immediate concern now was to keep our folks from losing their intensity.

At the 0730 shift change, even as I congratulated those who were going off duty and brought the oncoming day shift up to speed, I admonished both shifts not to let up. We had a long, hard battle ahead, and they needed to remain grimly determined. "Our job now is to worry," I told them. "Our job now is to work longer and harder than ever, to be disciplined, be hard-nosed. Do not let the Iraqis up off the floor. Kick the shit out of them." Then I tried to put a smile on their faces with the inane blessing, "Have a good day."

And it was.

★ During the first twenty-four hours, we flew 2,775 sorties. We hit thirty-seven targets in the Baghdad area, of which most (about fifteen) were designed to sever communications used by the Iraqi military. The rest hit targets such as the electrical grid and the national headquarters of intelligence, the military, the secret police, and other leadership targets. We had about 200 sorties against airfields, 175 against Scud targets, 750 interdiction sorties against the Iraqi Army and its supplies, 436 CAP or defensive counter-air sorties, 652 offensive counter-air (these included the Wild Weasels and airfield attacks), and 432 tanker sorties. (The USMC called their AV-8 sorties close air support, but by definition that was impossible, since CAS takes place within the FSCL, and their sorties flew beyond the FSCL, which was the Saudi border.)

Our biggest day was February 23, when we flew 3,254 sorties, one-third of which (995) were interdiction in the KTO. Overall, we flew 44,000 sorties against the Iraqi Army, 24,000 sorties to get and maintain control of the air and protect our forces from Iraqi air attack, 16,000 refueling sorties, and 5,000 electronics warfare and command-and-control sorties.

The opening moments of the war demonstrated that we were able to get to our targets and destroy them and for the most part return safely. We had some air-to-air kills, and probably no losses to enemy fighters on our side. That boded well. Though I expected good results over time, I really didn't expect such good results so soon. Even if we had lost two or three aircraft, I would have marked the opening night as a success.

Still, I knew we were in for a long haul. We had trained for a fifteen-round fight, and I figured it would go the full fifteen—or, as I had told Secretary Cheney, six weeks. So I didn't read too much into our early success.

★ Like a fool, I stayed in the TACC, fascinated by the unfolding events, and neglecting sleep. I had admonished all the others to rest so they could hold up under the long haul, but neglected to follow my own orders. I was operating on caffeine and adrenaline, the "breakfast of champions" for a fighter pilot.

Meanwhile, the F-117s and F-111s were tearing Iraqi command and control to pieces. The strikes against key airfields and munitions production facilities were going as planned. The B-52s, A-10s, F-16s, Jaguars, FA-18s, and AV-8s were hard at work on the Iraqi Army deployed in the desert.

When we bombed the Iraqi Army with B-52s, we were primarily using them for effect. And they had quite an effect. One POW was asked which aircraft he feared the most, and he said, "The B-52." He was then asked to describe the experience. To which he replied, "I was never bombed by a B-52; but I visited a friend who had been, and I saw and heard what it was like, and so I feared the B-52 more than anything else."

After the war, another Iraqi was asked why he had surrendered so quickly. "It was the bombs," he said, pointing to pictures of B-52s and A-10s. "It was the bombs."

Little did he realize that he had most likely survived because we had targeted those aircraft to minimize Iraqi deaths. We did that because it was the right thing to do, and because we wanted to exploit the already low morale of the Iraqi soldier in his unholy occupation of a Muslim neighbor. If I had wanted to kill Iraqi soldiers, we could have loaded the B-52 "buffs" with wall-to-wall antipersonnel munitions; and, today, unexploded submunitions (ready to detonate if disturbed) would probably have left Kuwait and southern Iraq uninhabitable.

What we dropped were regular bombs. They made a lot of noise and tore up the desert for miles; and if one hit a bunker, the folks inside died. That couldn't be called an accident, but if by some miracle we had hit no

Iraqi soldiers, and they had all surrendered without fighting, I would not have been unhappy.

★ Before the middle of February, I actually paid little attention to the specifics of the war. I listened to all the BDA bullshit, but only to the extent that it told me what else needed to be done. I was trying not to rest on our laurels. Or, as Bill Creech told us, "Don't read your own press clippings." What was important was what was coming next. So I paid attention to what we had done only when it helped me with that. Each day we learned more about the Iraqis, and the thoughts about what that new information meant were my most important thoughts.

You don't really know about war until you engage in it against a specific enemy in a specific environment. Sure, you can make general assumptions that will in all likelihood hold up when the shooting starts, but you have to be careful about relying on these. It's like preparing for a boxing match. You study previously demonstrated tendencies, strengths, and weaknesses, but when the bout starts, that has only a limited value. Now you are concerned with your opponent's punches and openings. Strategies change because of many factors, such as fatigue or injury, that can only be known during the fight.

CONTROL OF THE AIR

Air superiority is not a precise concept. And the process of gaining it is no less fuzzy. What do you mean by air superiority, and how do you know when you've got it? There is no handy chart that lets you plot the x- and y-axis and find where the two lines cross.

What I wanted was to operate freely over Iraq and not lose too many aircraft. Okay, what does that mean? What is too many? I don't know exactly, but I guess I will know if it is too many. Later in the war, too many A-10s targeted against the Republican Guards were getting shot up. Because they were suffering too many casualties, I ordered them to other targets. Were there any specific numbers involved in this decision? No. It was a gut call.

Free operation over Iraq raises other issues. For starters, not every aircraft could be expected to go everywhere. Or if it could go everywhere, it might not do that all the time. The F-117s could go anywhere, but when the Iraqi Air Force was flying they could only go at night. (Again, we wanted to fly the F-117s in conditions where they wouldn't be seen.) The A-10s, on the other hand, were never sent to Baghdad, even after we controlled the air.

In other words, control of the air is a complex issue, filled with variables.

To take the question a step farther, I considered that I had air superiority when I could do what I wanted to within the strengths and limitations of my force, and when I could hold the Iraqi targets at risk while employing all my air assets as appropriate. That meant, for example, that my strike aircraft did not have to jettison their payload due to Iraqi defenses such as fighter interceptors.

I knew we would have aircraft losses throughout the war, but I wanted those losses to be the lowest possible until the ground war started. Then I expected the aircraft doing close air support would be taking greater risks, flying lower to identify the target or to get under the smoke and weather in order to support our engaged coalition ground forces.

An air commander manages loss rates. If you have time, and the target is not urgent (either in time or in priority), then you back off from great risk (on those occasions, for example, when the weather will make it difficult to visually acquire SAM missiles and outmaneuver them). On the other hand, if the situation is dire—if, say, a ground unit is being overrun—then you order the force into greater danger. At Khafji, we lost an AC-130 who stayed too long over the battlefield. Day came, and the sky grew light enough for an Iraqi shoulder-fired SAM gunner to visually acquire him and shoot his missile. Our pilot was not reckless. He elected to err on the unsafe side because there were lots of high-priority targets for him to shoot. It was a bad judgment, but that's how airmen think and evaluate risk. If the target had been more ordinary and he had been facing the same risk, he'd have gone somewhere else and hit an easier target.

Because I absolutely had to knock out the Iraqi air defense command and control, I risked sending all the F-117s to Baghdad (I didn't realize then how good Stealth was). However, if I had the same appreciation of Stealth that I had during the opening moments of the war, and the target was the Baath Party headquarters, I would not have sent the F-117s. That target wasn't worth the gamble.

To me, the goals of the air superiority campaign were threefold:

(1) To render the Iraqi fighters inoperable. We would blind them by

cutting off their command and control, terrorize them by shooting down anything that flew, and make life difficult by bombing airfields and radar sites.

(2) To render the radar-guided surface-to-air missiles impotent. We would attack command and control and use support jamming EA-6Bs and EF-111s, in order to force each piece of the system into autonomous operations (in that way they had to radiate with their own radars to find a target, making them more vulnerable to HARM attacks). We would terrorize the operators to induce them not to use their radars. We would kill them on a priority basis, using Wild Weasels and USN HARM-equipped aircraft. We would self-protect by using ECM pods, and by flying in VFR conditions, so aircraft could see the radar-guided SAMs and out-maneuver them.

(3) To render guns and shoulder-fired IR SAMs useless. We would fly at medium altitude; keep the time at low altitude (such as at the bottom of a dive bomb pass) at a minimum; and—the age-old lesson we always relearn in combat—we would not make multiple passes on the same target.

From the start, General Schwarzkopf was always asking when we would have air superiority, but I would never tell him. I knew we would be able to do anything we wanted to from the start, yet I also knew the Iraqis would contest control of the air as long as Saddam could fire his pistol toward the sky (as he often did in newsreels). The CINC wanted some magic number. I knew there was no such thing. I knew the answer lay in Chuck Horner's gut, and it was determined by my gut feelings about the losses and efficiency of the operation.

That is why my first stop every day was at the search-and-rescue cell to talk over losses. How did they happen and what was the status of the crews? That stop had many purposes: one, to keep reminding me that war is about death and killing and that our guys were dying, just as the enemy was; two, to keep the faith with the aircrews (we were honor bound to do our best to rescue them if they got shot down); three, to learn what was working and what was failing so that I could crank that information into my targeting, rules, advice, and strategy.

So when did we get air superiority?

We had it before the war began, because we had the means to get it—equipment, intelligence, training, and the courage of the aircrews. We had it the minute Bernard Shaw went off the air, because that told me the central nervous system of the Iraqi air defense system had been severed. We had it when it became clear that Iraqi fighters, their most potent weapon, were being shot down and our fighters were not. We had it when it was clear that Iraqi SAM radar operators were not turning on their radar, even as they shot missiles blindly into the sky. We had it when RAF Tornadoes finally stopped flying at low altitude.

About three days into the war, General Schwarzkopf announced that we had air superiority. This information did not come from me. He just went ahead and said it, I suppose because it was "good news from the front" sort of thing. Later he announced that we had air supremacy. Again, I never told him that, but I guess it provided him a means to show progress. Did I mind? No, of course not. My job was to plan and employ airpower operations against an enemy and to do that as efficiently as possible (realizing that war is about the most inefficient thing man does . . . and the most stupid). His job was to handle the bigger picture.

★ Here's how we did all this.

I'll say it again, the Iraqi air defenses were massive. One had only to tune in to CNN and watch the night sky over Baghdad to get some idea of what our aircraft confronted throughout the war. What you did not see were the Iraqi fighters and surface-to-air missiles.

Our plan to control the air was complex. First, we would blind the Iraqis by destroying communication links between the air defense search radars, the commanders who dispatched interceptor aircraft or assigned targets to individual SAM batteries, and the pilots who would be given vectors toward their target. Second, we would strike fear in the minds of the Iraqi Air Force pilots, SAM radar operators, and antiaircraft artillery gunners. Our goal was to make them hate to come to work. We wanted them convinced that if they tried to engage our aircraft they would die. Nothing subtle, no nuances, just fear. Finally, we would avoid as many defenses as possible.

★ There is a new buzzword going around nowadays—"information war."

When people talk about it, they usually mean putting viruses in a computer or making networks crash. Information war can do that, but it is really a lot more.

The key concept involves getting inside your enemy's decision cycle.

That is, you know what is going on faster and better than he does, and can therefore make and implement decisions faster. This permits you to take and maintain the initiative, and causes him to lose control.

At Khafji, for example, Joint STARS told me where and when the enemy was moving—which of course told me nothing about his intentions. Nevertheless, I attacked his movement, and as a result destroyed his attack before it started. He could not form up his attacking forces or mass for the attack, because when he tried, his convoys en route to the battle or invasion were destroyed. Perhaps this is stretching a point, but you could make the case that my information superiority and my increased capacity to analyze and decide what that information meant gave me the means to thwart an attack before I even knew I was being attacked.

Information war, then, is primarily a function of the increased pace and accuracy of data now yielded by computers, sensors, and communication systems.

The analysis of the KARI command control and communication system, as well as the subsequent disruption and dismemberment of its elements, was information warfare pure and simple. Our selection of targets was the product of this analysis—who was in charge of which sectors, which kinds of sensors, whether a radar site or a man out in the desert with binoculars and a telephone. We were counting on the Iraqi reliance on centralized control. Once it was gone, the air defense system would be disorganized.

Attacking the KARI computers and links was the divide-and-conquer concept on a massive scale. Our strategy meant the "AT & T" telephone exchange had to go, and it did. Communication cables in the desert and under bridges had to go, and they did. Microwave antennas located throughout the country had to go, and they did. Some of the links were off-limits, owing to their location in hotels or near religious buildings, and so they survived. But in the first forty-eight hours of attacks, we got enough to cripple KARI. After that, individual elements—fighter aircraft, radars, SAM sites, and AAA batteries—had to fight alone and uncoordinated, acting on their own initiative and judgment; and they had not been trained to do that.

★ Meanwhile, I had no doubt that the Iraqi defenders were as intelligent and courageous as any soldiers. I also had no doubt that they loved their country, and were willing to die in its defense, no matter how much they loved or despised Saddam Hussein and his gang. My conclusion: after weakening their systems of defense, we had to weaken their spirit of defense.

To that end, we conducted a campaign to strike fear in their hearts. I knew they would man their radars, fire their SAMs, and shoot their guns at our aircraft. They would do this, first, in defense of their people and their nation, but perhaps more important, to avoid being arrested and executed by their military superiors. I wanted thousands of Iraqi gunners who felt good about shooting (they would under most circumstances) but didn't feel bad about missing. You know, shoot your SAM missile, especially when the major is around, but don't bother to turn on the tracking radar needed to guide the SAM to the coalition aircraft. Bluntly, we were going to bribe the Iraqi air defenders by using their own lives as the payment.

The main target of the intimidation campaign was surface-to-air radar operations. This was nothing new. In Vietnam, we had learned the hard way that the SAM is a tough nut to crack. Now we had a war with lots of SAMs, most of which were more deadly than Vietnam's SA-2s. We also had F-4G Wild Weasels that were equipped with the new AGM-88 high-speed anti-radiation missile (HARM), a radar-killing weapon more accurate and easier to employ than anything we'd used in Vietnam. Though the F-4Gs were oldsters next to their F-16 wingmen, they were much more capable than the Vietnam-era F-105G Thunderchiefs I had flown. Most of all, we had a host of Wild Weasel aircrews who had benefited from superb electronic training at monthly Red Flag exercises at Nellis AFB in Nevada. The Air Force, Marines, Navy, and allied crews who had flown in Red Flag knew what these Weasels could do. The F-4G "Rhinos" were old and ugly, but now we were at war the first thing the F-16 flight leaders wanted to know was "Where will the Weasels be during our next mission?"

But first, we had to light up the minds of the SAM operators with fear. And to do this, we staged a party—"Puba's Party."

General Larry Henry ("Puba") had come to me in August to work in the "Black Hole" developing our offensive air campaign. His experience as an electronic-warfare officer in Wild Weasels, and his generally twisted mind, created the party we threw for the Iraqi radar operators.

His script was simple to build but difficult to execute. First, BGM-109 Tomahawk missiles and F-117As would arrive unannounced over Baghdad, their exploding bombs and warheads ensuring that Iraqi defenders who were not awake would get up and report to their units. At that point, the air defenses would be on full alert and fully manned, eager for the forthcoming battle. Puba would then send over Baghdad a host of small unmanned drone aircraft (ground-launched Northrop BQM-74s) that were designed to look like full-size manned aircraft on SAM radarscopes. Immediately behind the drones would be HARM-laden Air Force and Navy fighter aircraft. As the drones entered the SAM-defended areas over Baghdad, the SAM radars would radiate and the Iraqi operators would track their targets and fire their missiles. What they would not see was almost a hundred HARM missiles being launched from just outside their radar coverage.

And so it happened on the first night of the war. The Iraqi SAM operators succeeded in downing nearly all of the drones, and in so doing they provided dozens of targets for the incoming anti-radiation missiles.

The results had to be horrible. And from the horror came fear.

After Puba's Party, the number of SAM missile firings remained high, while the number of coalition aircraft shot down remained very low. As we had hoped, the guidance radars were not turned on. This was the feedback that told us Puba's Party was a stunning success. It was not easy, and it wasn't cheap (the drones and HARMs cost a bundle!), but it made possible all the efficiencies of precision munitions delivered from medium to high altitude that shortened the war and reduced the loss of life.

It was Puba's Party that gave us the vital medium altitude sanctuary. Sure, some continued to try low-level tactics to escape the radar SAMs, but as our losses at low altitude mounted, the message became very plain: get up to altitude and rely on the electronic battle now being directed by General Glenn Proffit, Larry Henry's replacement.

This lesson did not come easy. During Desert Shield, I had laid down the law to the wing commanders at the bases: no low-level tactics or training unless they could explain to me why they wanted their aircrews to do it. I expected a great gnashing of teeth, wails, and moans (low level keeps coming back, like a monster at the end of a horror movie). In the event, however, only two commanders came forward to argue for low-altitude tactics—Colonels Hal Hornberg of the F-15E wing and Tom Lennon of the F-111 wing. Because I'd promised the wing commanders they could run their own show in areas like tactics, I let them return to low-level attack tactics. But after a few days of real combat, real bullets,

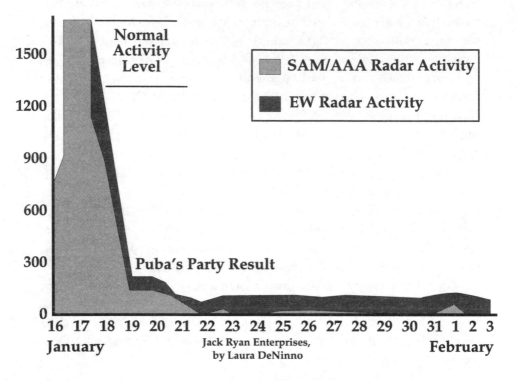

Iraqi Air Defense Radar Activity

Normal Activity Level

SAM/AAA Radar Activity

EW Radar Activity

Puba's Party Result

1500
1200
900
600
300
0

16 17 18 19 20 21 22 23 24 25 26 27 28 29 30 31 1 2 3

January

Jack Ryan Enterprises,
by Laura DeNinno

February

and unfortunately, real losses, both wings pitched out low-level operations and joined their friends at medium altitude.

When I asked the F-16 and A-10 wing commanders why they didn't ask to go back to flying among the rocks, their answer was simple: "We want to survive this war." Why, then, did the F-111s and F-15Es have to find out the hard way? I thought about that long and hard after the war. It couldn't have been peacetime training. No one spends more time flying at low altitude than the A-10s. Their slower speed permits the Warthogs to fly legally almost anywhere in the United States at low altitude. And yet, even with the protection of their titanium armor, the A-10s didn't want to tool around the Iraqis at low altitude. Why F-111s and F-15Es? The answer was twofold, I reasoned. First, except for the infrared sensor, their systems were optimized for low altitude. Their attack radars worked best at the low grazing angles afforded by low-altitude ingress. Most important, in my view, one half of the crew of these two-place fighters—the weapon system operator—earned his living telling the pilot where to go. If you were at low altitude without GPS (and only the F-16s had GPS), the pilot relied on the WSO for navigational assistance. When it came to attack, the WSO was the king; but if they didn't go low-level, the rest of the trip could be pretty meaningless.

Italian and British Tornadoes also suffered losses—all, save one, the result of low-level, low-altitude tactics. In fact, in the first two days of the war, approximately two-thirds of our losses were suffered by aircraft flying low-level tactics, even as the majority of our sorties were being flown at medium altitude.

Because they were taking on the most difficult, most well-defended targets outside of Baghdad, the RAF GR-1 Tornadoes were especially hard hit. Saudi and British Tornadoes were equipped with a munition designed to shut down airfields, the JP-233, which had to be delivered at low altitude. But the airfields bristled with defenses, especially AAA guns, which continued to take a discouraging toll of Tornadoes well after the F-111s and F-15Es got back up to medium altitude. The Tornadoes had few good alternatives to flying low altitude. And I had no alternative but to let them do it. If I was loath to dictate tactics to USAF wings, I was definitely not going to do it to an ally. But if I could find an opening to introduce the subject, I would.

One night at a gathering of national air commanders, I said, "We've gotten some experience in this war. This looks like a good place to take a look at what we are doing right and wrong. I suggest we form a multinational tactics team to evaluate our operations and suggest changes they think appropriate."

Without hesitation, Air Vice Marshal Bill Wratten spoke up: "I think that's a good idea, and I'd like to lead the effort." I couldn't have been more pleased. Bill, like all the rest of us, had been in anguish over the losses. Even though there had been all sorts of speculation about the causes and the possible fixes, we needed an experienced airman close to the scene of the action to give us an objective view. Bill Wratten was just the man, and with the support of Air Chief Marshall Patty Hine, we were able to stop losses due to low-altitude tactics.

Here are some facts and figures:

We lost twelve GR-1s (of which one was Italian and two were RSAF). Nine were shot down or crashed doing low-level attacks, two were lost at medium altitude, and one ran out of fuel. The GR-1 loss rate was significantly higher than other aircraft:

Aircraft type	Losses	Missions	Missions/Loss
RAF GR-1	9	1,644	183—Low level stopped after loss number 8
IAF GR-1	1	224	224—Low level stopped after first loss
RSAF	2	667	334—Low level stopped after first night
F-16	8	13,087	1,636
A/OA-10	7	8,084	1,155

The Tornado, which flew more low-level tactics than any other aircraft, had a loss rate nine times the F-16s and over six times the fairly slow A-10s.

★ AAA and SAMs were dangerous, but the most lethal threat to our attack was the enemy's interceptor aircraft.

Why?

Ground-based defenses stayed in one place and could be avoided by flying around them, if we knew where they were (and we usually did), or by high- or medium-altitude attack. If a SAM site shot at you, you could evade the missile and distance yourself from the site at 600 to 800 knots. A MiG, on the other hand, could encounter you anywhere over Iraq. If he jumped you, you might not be able to disengage; and since he was as fast as you, he could take a missile or gun shot if you turned tail to run.

I had studied the Iraqi Air Force for years, and had found many strengths, including a number of first-rate aircraft equipped with adequate missiles, a comprehensive command-and-control structure, and a few excellent pilots. Its single greatest weakness was its reliance on centralized command and control; but the training its pilots received was not uniformly good, and the logistics support was shaky.

To have had a chance against us, the Iraqis needed innovative tactics and an awareness of the air situation. They had neither.

In the hands of a good pilot, virtually any interceptor can badly hurt an attacking air force. Iraq had some excellent aircraft, especially their MiG-29s and Mirage F-1s, as well as an inventory of older aircraft, principally MiG-21s and MiG-23s. Though the older aircraft weren't much of a threat on their own, if they'd been used in conjunction with the newer Russian and French models, they could have caused us serious problems. Their best tactics would have been to engage our air-to-air fighters with their top-of-the-line fighters, then run the older MiGs in on the bomb-laden aircraft using high-speed hit-and-run tactics. Even if they were unable to achieve a kill, their supersonic bounce would have forced our bombers to jettison their air-to-ground ordnance (externally stored bombs and missiles cause drag and have to be dropped).

The weapons carried by these fighters, on the other hand, were not nearly as good as our radar and heat-seeking missiles. Nevertheless, they were more than adequate if the enemy pilot could put his aircraft in a position to shoot them.

★ I had never been impressed with Iraqi pilots, but that didn't mean we could always count on running into bad ones. Among the youth of every nation in the world you'll find a few "aces"—young men, and now women, capable of winning aerial engagements time after time. The traits found in those who consistently shoot down other fighters are found everywhere—though never in abundant supply. Good eyesight doesn't hurt, but some of our greatest had poor eyesight (they'd purposely select wingmen with good eyes). Courage is required, but that is easy enough to come by in air-to-air combat, where you either fight or die. The trait I most admire in great pilots is "situational awareness." It is the ability to keep track of what is going on around you and to project that awareness into an accurate mental image of what is about to happen during the next few moments; and it is extremely rare. It's an ability that has little to do with IQ. Some of our best fighter pilots do not appear outwardly intelligent. On the ground they will do the dumbest things, or get into serious trouble; but in an engagement they process data at speeds and complexities that would defeat our fastest, most powerful computers. Out there in every nation there are a few—very few—individuals with the inborn talent to process supersonic motion and project it in three dimensions. If properly trained and equipped, these people duel with the best in the sky.

During the Iran–Iraq War, our AWACS had maintained a close watch on the aircraft of both countries, and their aerial engagements had been analyzed and briefed by our CENTAF operations/intelligence team. I had also analyzed the few encounters between Iranians and Saudis (which gave me a good benchmark; I was familiar with the great competence of Saudi pilots). The Iranians had excellent, though aging, fighters—F-5s, F-14s, and F-4s—but it was apparent from their lack of success against the Saudis that their aircraft radars were inoperative, or at least poorly tuned. The Iranian pilots, while eager, had obviously suffered as a result of the fundamentalist revolution. When Iranian aircraft challenged Saudi air defenses, they were promptly intercepted and either shot down or driven back.

On the other hand, when Iraqi fighters engaged Iranians—either in defense of Baghdad or supporting air attacks on Iranian targets—they were, to be charitable, ineffective. The engagements were pure Keystone Kops. The Iranian and Iraqi aircraft would be vectored toward one another by ground-based radars. They would close to within a mile, then circle aimlessly, apparently unable to locate each other and shoot their weapons. This "ballet of the blind" occurred time after time. I had no doubt that all the pilots were willing, but they were overly dependent on ground-based radar vectors—once again pointing out the superiority of our F-14, F-15, F-16, and F-18 on-board target-acquisition systems.

★ Iraqi pilot training came from three sources: France, Pakistan, and the former Soviet Union. Lucky for us, Soviet training proved dominant, with their emphasis on rigid rules, strict command arrangements, and standardized tactics. Coupled with this centralized approach, the Soviets were suspicious of non-Russians and disliked Arabs. The Iraqi students were taught to take off and land their aircraft safely, but otherwise their training was so basic, so lacking in advanced tactics, as to be useless.

There was, however, a wild card. Not all Iraqi training came from the Russians.

Iraqi pilots were trained well by their French and Pakistani instructors.

The French training was evidenced by Iraqi attacks on Iranian shipping and the USS *Stark*. And Iraqi air-to-ground operations against Iran's oil facilities at Kharg Island and near Bandar Abbas were model operations, worthy of study by all airmen.

Pakistan has one of the best, most combat-ready air forces in the world. They have to; their neighbor to the east is huge, and the two nations have a long history of hostility. For Indian war planners, the Pakistani Air Force is their worst fear. Pakistani pilots are respected throughout the world, especially the Islamic world, because they know how to fly and fight.

On one or two occasions, I had the opportunity to talk with Pakistani instructor pilots who had served in Iraq. These discussions didn't give me great cause to worry. The Russian domination of training prevented the Pakistanis from having any real influence on the Iraqi aircrew training program.

Still, there had to be a few Iraqi pilots who'd observed and listened to their mentors from France and Pakistan and the useless guidance of their inept leaders. It was those few I was concerned about—the ones with great situational awareness and good eyesight, who had figured out how to effectively use their aircraft and its weapons to defend their nation.

If those gifted Iraqi pilots existed, and I'm certain they did, they probably died on 17, 19, and 24 January. We went after them so hard and so thoroughly that they never had a chance to show that they were respectable.

Our fundamental strategy was simple. Blind them and beat the tar out of them as they groped about. We were going to stomp the Iraqi Air Force into submission. Not fair, not pretty, not poetic. Our goal was to be as vicious and unrelenting as possible. To do otherwise would just prolong the suffering and death.

To blind the Iraqi Air Force, our first bombers fell on its eyes and brains—radars, command bunkers, and communication sites. Of equal importance was the forward movement of our interceptor fighters into Iraq. We put twenty-four-hour CAPs over each of the Iraqi fighter bases.* Forward fighters were positioned to intercept the Iraqi jets almost as soon as they broke ground. Our hopes for the Iraqi fighter pilot were very simple: take off and blow up.

For the most part, our hopes became reality. After the first three days of the war, we had seized control of the air over Iraq and Kuwait.

Three days may seem short, and the Iraqi Air Force may look like a pushover. But do not get the idea that gaining control of the air was easy. It was not a "macho," "no sweat" operation. What turned into a turkey

---

*These CAPs were maintained even after the air-to-air threat was eliminated. Since the F-15Cs, the F-14s, and the Tornado ADV (Air Defense Version) were only capable of carrying air-to-air weapons, I could not use them for other missions. RSAF F-15Cs had the software for air-to-ground, so when we no longer needed them for CAPs over Iraq, we configured them with bombs and used them against the Iraqi army.

shoot in late January and February started out as a bitter struggle; those first few days were the hardest-fought, most critical aspect of the entire war.

Meanwhile, when the bombs began to fall on Baghdad, Iraqi pilots ran to their planes and took off. I'm sure they sent their best and brightest, and I know they tried their hardest; but in air-to-air combat, it's win, lose, or get out of town. There is no second place. The Iraqis lost at least eight times on the seventeenth of January. They tried again two days later and lost six more times. Their last try (and their only effort to attack our forces on the ground with aircraft) was on the twenty-fourth, when two Mirage F-1s attempted to penetrate Saudi Arabia for an air-to-ground strike. An RSAF F-15C shot them both down just out to sea in the Arabian Gulf.

After that, they tried to hide in their heavily defended aircraft shelters, also to no avail, when we picked off the shelters, one at a time, with 2,000-pound hard-case, laser-guided bombs.

They were then left with the "get out of town" option. We had actually anticipated that, but felt their destination would be Iraq's Arab neighbor and sometime friend, Jordan. Wrong. They went to Iran, leaving our carefully placed barrier CAP aircraft orbiting between Baghdad and Jordan in the desert.

On the first night of the exodus, the burning question was whether or not the jets were defecting. Because they were fleeing to an old enemy, that was a possible inference. But when they did it again the next night, I was pretty sure it was organized and not defection.

In order to find out what was really going on, I called Mary Jo, in Sumter, South Carolina. No, she doesn't operate a spy network; but we had an Iranian-born friend who shared our passion for Persian carpets and whose father was well placed back home. She called our friend, and he called his father, who reported that an Iraqi general had shown up in Iran a few days before and negotiated safe haven for the Iraqi Air Force. The Iranians, justifying their reputation as "bazzaris," or traders, carefully responded, "We will keep your aircraft for you"; and so, it seems, they have. The aircraft are still there.

Once the exodus started, the Iraqis ceased operating as a fighting force; it was a panic rush to the exits. They'd wait for gaps in our CAP coverage, then bolt in groups for Iran, hoping that if they avoided our fighters, they'd have enough fuel to find an Iranian airfield. The pilots who didn't had to eject.

BRIEFINGS

We don't like briefings, because we don't like to sit around in meetings. But we have to have briefings, because they offer the most efficient way to keep vital information flowing to the largest variety of people. There were three that really mattered every day—the two at our TACC changeover, and the evening briefing at MODA for the CINC.

Since we had two teams, each working twelve hours a day, the changeover briefings occurred twice a day, morning and evening. Here there was no attempt at depth, or to make speculative projections (these came in the meeting that followed). For the most part, the presenters laid out facts and made reasonable projections of trends needed to plan ATOs and bring the staff up-to-date. Intel briefers, for example, would touch on the status of the Iraqi transportation system, the bridges he or she was recommending for strike, the reasons why the Iraqi Air Force was flying to Iran, or possible Scud hiding places. And there was also plenty of BDA, target systems, and current information.

When the incoming staff arrived, they'd gather around, while each section—Intelligence, Weather, Plans, Operations, BCE, Naval Liaison, and Marine Liaison—covered anything they wanted everyone to hear. Though the briefing was directed at me and the other senior leaders of the national air forces, it also allowed the staff coming on duty to get up to speed and to talk about the coming period and beyond. Anyone could ask questions (though few did). Then, at the end, I would make brief remarks designed to keep the staff focused on what I believed important. Most of the time I kept these remarks general, but on a few occasions I outlined specific tasks for the next twelve to twenty-four hours.

After this briefing, I would turn my chair around and face the back of the room, and the senior leaders from the U.S. Navy, Army, Marines, and the Coalition air forces, along with my senior staff—Tom Olsen, Randy Witt, Buster Glosson, John Corder, Bill Rider, Pat Caruana, Ed Tonoso, Glenn Profitt, and especially the four colonels, Crigger, Doman, Reavy, and Harr (two coming on and two going off duty)—would receive a purely speculative intelligence briefing from Chris Christon. (The briefing was not exclusive; anyone could stand around and listen; but as a rule, the duty officers had to get to work, now that the previous person manning their workstation had left for food and rest.)

Here Chris would let his imagination roam and give a far more hypothetical assessment of what we were about to face than was appropriate during the changeover briefing. I wanted him to really guess. Why? Because I had to think ahead. I had to make decisions. And if I used the usual intelligence data, I didn't have much to go on.

Our peacetime-trained intelligence organizations are taught never to be wrong. They like numbers, and don't like to talk about what the other guy is thinking. They don't predict, they just give you the rundown, like TV news anchors. Yet, as a commander, I had to think about what the other guy was thinking. I needed to get inside the other guy in order to find ways to spoil his plans and make his worst fears come true. That meant Chris had to speculate, stimulate our thinking, and provoke the questions we needed to ask. Sure, he might be way off base, but that was expected. And of course, having reviewed all the intelligence derived from our own operations (pilot reports and intelligence reports published by his staff) and from other organizations, he always explained the reasons for his projections.

In addition to providing insight into the enemy, these meetings expanded our collective thinking. For that reason, discussions always followed Chris Christon's predictions, and these wandered wherever the various leaders wanted. Obviously, there were cultural differences that dictated how and when a particular commander spoke. The Europeans, for instance, were comfortable speaking openly, and they all felt free to take any position on any issue. The Arabs, on the other hand, were more reticent and circumspect. Nonetheless, if they thought we were missing anything important—especially if it concerned the Arab mentality of our enemy—they spoke up.

Inevitably, issues came up that we discussed at length yet never really got a handle on. Some of these, like Scuds, came up frequently.

Finally, these meetings made us a team. Our U.S. Air Force people were already working hard for harmony, side by side, throughout the TACC and at the various bases, on the ground and in the air. I wanted all the national air force leaders to have the same feelings of trust, respect, and unity of effort. That is why it was important for me not to act in charge; and that is why it was important for me to listen to them and actively seek their views. It also didn't hurt to learn something new, and gain their perceptions, experience, and insights.

We were fortunate in this conflict in that if we failed to accurately gauge the enemy, our strength was so overwhelming that we would still prevail. Nonetheless, our mistakes could cost the lives of aircrew, or later, the lives of airmen and soldiers on the ground. That is why so many people worked so hard at thinking about the enemy, our plan to fight, and our actual minute-by-minute engagement with him.

"It all starts and ends with intelligence," I like to say. In war, your intelligence has to be the departure point for your thinking or planning. And then, after you execute your actions, your intelligence estimates the results and the effects on the enemy, so you can plan the next move.

War is not unlike chess. But in war, you do not have a clear view of the other side of the board.

★ Just before 2000 each evening, I left the operation to Tom Olsen and headed for the CINC's meeting at the MODA building bunker. As I ran up the stairs, I usually heard Buster Glosson doing the same thing; he, too, had been busy getting ready, for it was his job to brief the next ATO. We'd both hit the glass doors and race out into the cold night to an armored Mercedes sedan, the back doors open and the motor running. Behind the wheel was Technical Sergeant Mike Brickert, a six-foot-three deputy sheriff from Chelan County, Washington, who was an air policeman in the Air National Guard and an Olympic-class marksman and athlete. His job was to get Buster and me safely and quickly to the MODA so I could be in my seat before General Schwarzkopf called the meeting together. En route, Buster and I would review his briefing.

Most days, I had gone over this new ATO during the morning, when I would wander down to the Black Hole and discuss the infant plan. Buster and his people would then massage it the rest of the day, and from this would emerge a Master Attack Plan, which listed the primary targets we intended to strike. In the car, Buster and I would make changes based on how we felt the CINC would react to comments or targets. The key was to challenge him a little bit but keep him from overreacting. So we were careful to justify each target nomination.

The one area we could not judge accurately—and didn't really have to—was the number of sorties we needed to apply to the individual Iraqi divisions in the KTO. (All we knew for certain was that the Republican Guard was going to get more attention than conscript infantry units.) In the end, we were going to get them all, so the answer didn't really matter. Each day we used Sam Baptiste's and Bill Welch's best guess (based on ground force inputs) about which units to hit, and then we distributed the rest, based on ARCENT estimates of unit strengths. Every evening, as was his privilege as CINC and land force component commander, Schwarzkopf modified this part of the plan.

My strategy session with Buster usually ended as we hit the front door of MODA and ran to the elevator that took us to the underground command post. We were never late, but we were often in the hall only steps ahead of the CINC.

The meeting that followed (like the changeover briefing we had just left) covered the weather, intelligence updates, the progress of the war, and logistics, communication, and overall support updates provided by the CENTCOM staff. Then came the main order of business—the plans for the day after tomorrow. For the first five weeks of Desert Storm, virtually the only subject discussed was the air war—in other words, Buster Glosson's briefing. Though the daily plans tended to be an expansion of the previous day's efforts, each also had to be coherent in and of itself and address any interim changes.

When he came "on stage," Buster would take out his rolled Plexiglas sheets with the proposed targets outlined and notes written in grease pencil. For example, there might be a circle, with the number 50 inside it, over the general location of the 18th Iraqi Armored Division in Kuwait—meaning that two days from now we intended to task fifty attack sorties against that division (the exact time of each strike would depend on details too numerous to brief, and was anyhow of little importance in the current phase of attriting the Iraqi army before the ground battle started). Or there might be a green triangle overlaid on a series of bridges, showing how the effort to isolate the battlefield would continue. Or there might be red triangles overlaid on a nuclear research center, a tank repair depot, and a suspected Scud storage area.

Buster would quickly, but in detail, explain the nature of each target and how its destruction fit in the overall campaign plan. Once that was done, he would briefly cover the AWACS tracks, CAPs, Scud patrols, and electronic-warfare packages. The discussion of army targets was left for last. At that point, Buster and I would take out our pencils, ready for the CINC to break in, point to a list of Iraqi divisions posted on the wall, and rattle off the divisions he wanted struck. He always did.

It was the same night after night, never acrimonious, always professional and easy to follow.

Afterward, Buster would roll up his charts and leave. He needed to hurry back to the Black Hole to input the latest guidance into the ATO (which was already starting to run late).

The CINC would then poll the U.S. and Coalition commanders or their representatives to see if they had any pressing concerns, and if the CINC had any special guidance, he gave it out. After the meeting broke up, Schwarzkopf would call Khaled bin Sultan with his update, while I rushed back to the TACC for the evening follies.

BAGHDAD BILLY . . . AND SOME WINS

The confusion of war breeds endless myths. Some bring laughs, others bring deaths. Ours, sadly, was the tragic kind. It was called "Baghdad Billy"—the Iraqi interceptor from hell.

Soon after the start of air operations over Iraq, pilots flying the EF-111 electronic jamming aircraft began to report interceptions by Iraqi fighters, even when there was no evidence of airborne Iraqis. They claimed they'd seen Iraqi fighter radar signals on their warning scopes, spotlights from Iraqi interceptor aircraft, or even tracers and missiles being fired at them. Yet in no case could intelligence sources or AWACS confirm these sightings. Much of the time, there were no indications that Iraqi aircraft were even airborne. There was one constant: F-15s had been in the vicinity of the EF-111s during their mysterious sightings.

In short, they were imagining things. We called their phantom "Baghdad Billy."

But that was headquarters wisdom. The crews knew what they'd seen with their own eyes; they knew that they had narrowly escaped death at the hands of an Iraqi fighter pilot.

The sides were drawn. The fat-assed generals in Riyadh who didn't believe the crew reports, versus the pilots and weapons systems operators who were out there night after night risking their lives.

You don't enter an argument like this and expect logic to prevail. But these were fighter pilots, and it was all good fun until somebody got hurt. That happened the night of February 13.

Ratchet-75, an EF-111A tasked to support-jam Iraqi radars, was the third aircraft in a flight of three EF-111s crossing the border between Saudi Arabia and Iraq in the vicinity of Arar, a town in northwestern Saudi Arabia. At 1109 Saudi time, Ratchet-75 should have passed Arar at 21,000 feet, four minutes behind the leader, Ratchet-73, and two minutes behind number two, Ratchet-74. At 1128, Ratchet-75 should have been ten minutes south of his jamming orbit, which was located due west of Baghdad halfway to the Jordanian border. He never got there. At 1129, two F-15Es heading south over southern Iraq at 31,000 feet saw an aircraft below them ejecting eight to ten flares. The night sky was lit up by the flares and the blaze of afterburners, as the aircraft rolled out of a hard left turn and began a series of "S-turns" as it descended sharply. Twenty seconds later, the F-15s saw the aircraft eject three more flares, soon followed by a huge fireball as the aircraft hit the ground. The lead F-15E, Pontiac-47, began an orbit over the crash site, while his wingman, Pontiac-48, went to the tanker track to refuel. A little over three hours later, a Special Operations helicopter, Sierra-43, arrived on scene and the rescue team examined the wreckage. They confirmed the loss of the EF-111, its pilot, and the WSO.

Though we will never know what happened, it was reasonable to conclude that the crew of the EF-111, like other -111 crews, had radar warning signals or visual sightings that indicated an Iraqi interceptor approaching for a kill. Once again, the AWACS picture was clean of enemy aircraft, and once again, F-15 aircraft were in the immediate vicinity.

It seemed that Baghdad Billy had finally achieved a shoot-down.

Everyone in the TACC was upset; and—not surprisingly—there was blaming and finger-pointing.

In the hall the next morning, Buster Glosson lit into Chris Christon, whose intelligence shop had passed unedited reports of the phantom interceptor to all the aircrews, thereby giving the story credibility. Chris fought back. As he saw it, his job was to get the word out. If the EF-111 aircrews had observed something, he reported it to the other units. And it was then the job of the local commanders to make sure the aircrews didn't do anything extreme, like a low-altitude jink-out at night.

Both Buster and Chris were right. It was Chris's job to get the word out. And it was Buster's job as the fighter division commander to worry about the lives of his aircrews.

But the real blame was mine. I should have been more forceful about dispelling the Baghdad Billy myth right from the start. I should have seen that a crew would get so engrossed with defeating the apparently real threat that they succumbed to the ever-present killer, the ground. My failure meant two needless deaths and bitter tears for the families of the crew of Ratchet-75.

The message went out to knock off defensive reactions to Baghdad Billy.

The incident wasn't a total loss. It inspired a song:

BALLAD OF THE F-111 JOCK
   BY MAJ. ROGER KRAPF
I'm an F-111 Jock, and I'm here to tell
of Baghdad Billy and his jet from hell.
We were well protected with Eagles in tight
but that didn't stop the man with the light.
RJ and AWACS, they didn't see,
as BAGHDAD BILLY snuck up on me.
Then I found a spotlight shining at my six
and my Whoozoo said, "HOOLLYY SHEEIT."
I popped some chaff and I popped a flare
but the Iraqi bandit, he didn't care.
I had tracers on my left, and tracers on my right,
with a load of bombs, I had to run from the fight.
I rolled my VARK over and took her down
into the darkness and finally lost the clown.
When I landed back at Taif and gave this rap,
CENTAF said I was full of crap.
I'm here to tell you the God's own truth.
That Iraqi bandit, he ain't no spoof.
You don't have to worry, there is no way
you'll see Baghdad Billy if you fly in the day.
But listen to me, son, for I am right.
Watch out for BILLY if you fly at night!!!

There were other—far less tragic—confusions and mix-ups.

On one occasion, an F-15 pilot from our base at Incirlik in Turkey was lined up on an Iraqi jet ready to squeeze the trigger, when an air-to-air missile flew in from the side, turned the corner behind the Iraqi, and blew the target out of the sky. Chalk up one for the 33d TFW from Tabuk. Not the least bothered, the Incirlik-based F-15 turned his attention to the Iraqi's wingman and fired an AIM-7 radar-guided missile. It zeroed in on its target and exploded; but much to the amazement of our pilot, the Iraqi jet emerged serenely from the fireball. The intrepid American then fired a heat-seeking AIM-9, which again engulfed the Iraqi in a fireball; and again the Iraqi emerged and flew across the border into Iran. Our pilot may have been luckier than he thought, however. The Iraqi aircraft was either damaged or it ran out of fuel, and the pilot ejected shortly after escaping.

But more often the wins were clear-cut.

Not all our potential aces flew air-to-air fighters. In February, the A-10s at King Fahd bagged a couple of Iraqi helicopters while looking to bomb Iraqi tanks and artillery. Captain Swain, on the sixth of February, and Captain Sheehy, nine days later, observed Iraqi helicopters flying very close to the earth. Bad tactic, helicopters close to the ground stand out clearly to a fighter pilot. Both A-10s used their 30mm guns to dispatch their targets. Up until then, it was normal for the Warthog community to take cheap shots from their interceptor brethren in F-15s. No more. To flag the change, sometime around the middle of February, the A-10 wing commander, Colonel Sandy Sharpe, called the F-15 wing commander at Dhahran, Colonel John McBroom, to offer his A-10s to fly top cover for the F-15s, in case they wanted to do some bombing. After all, it only made sense, now that the A-10s had two kills to the F-15 wing's single victory. Boomer McBroom was not amused, but hundreds of A-10 pilots howled with glee.

The last kills of the war took out Iraqis flying combat sorties against their own people. In late March, an Iraqi Sukhoi jet fighter and a Swiss Platus propeller-driven PC-9 trainer, pressed into dropping bombs, were flying in eastern Iraq, in violation of the Iraqi no-fly agreement reached at the end of the war. AWACS vectored two F-15s against the aircraft. The flight leader, Captain Dietz, rolled out behind the Sukhoi, fired his AIM-9, and blew the target out of the sky. It was Dietz's third kill (he'd bagged a pair of MiG-21s in early February). His wingman, Lieutenant Hohemann, also with two aerial victories (he got them the same day Dietz got his), rolled out behind the PC-9. Though our rules discouraged shoot-down of trainers or cargo/passenger aircraft, and the PC-9 was a trainer-type aircraft, it had just completed a bombing mission against Iraqi civilians and wasn't supposed to be in the air anyway. *Should I shoot or not?* Hohemann asked himself. While the lieutenant's conscience wrestled with this question, the Iraqi pilot ejected! After seeing his leader blow up, the Iraqi wingman wasn't going to wait around and take his chances. After jinking to avoid the Iraqi's deploying parachute, Hohe-

Coalition Aerial Victories by Unit

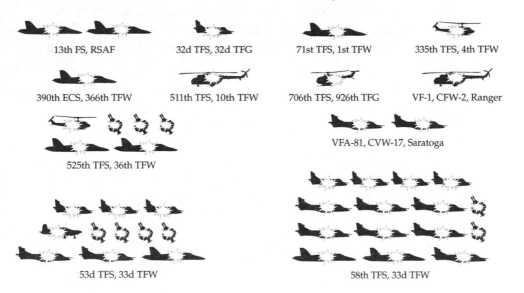

13th FS, RSAF

32d TFS, 32d TFG

71st TFS, 1st TFW

335th TFS, 4th TFW

390th ECS, 366th TFW

511th TFS, 10th TFW

706th TFS, 926th TFG

VF-1, CFW-2, Ranger

VFA-81, CVW-17, Saratoga

525th TFS, 36th TFW

53d TFS, 33d TFW

58th TFS, 33d TFW

Jack Ryan Enterprises, by Laura DeNinno

mann reached a decision: "It's a fighter, not a trainer." But just as he was about to shoot it down, the PC-9 rolled over and smashed into the ground.

Afterward, Jim Crigger awarded Hohemann credit for the kill, which brought his total to three victories, the closest anyone in the Gulf came to the five needed to become an Ace.

The first and last kill scored by the CENTAF staff was racked up by Colonel John Turk from the Black Hole. A longtime fighter pilot, John had been one of our top F-15 instructor pilots at Luke and Tyndall. But to his great disappointment, he'd sat out this war in the Black Hole, hard work and no glory. After the shooting had stopped, Turk hitched a ride up to Tallil AB in southern Iraq. As he was touring the airfield, Turk found a MiG fighter parked on a road. Though U.S. Army troops had destroyed the cockpit, the jet was otherwise fully armed and fueled. Like every fighter pilot, Turk was always looking for a kill. Making sure no one was around watching him, he fired a shot from his 9mm pistol into the MiG's drop tank, hoping for a fire. Fuel streamed out but failed to ignite. Undaunted, Turk took out a cigarette lighter and applied a flame to the jet fuel. A second later, it occurred to him that he was standing next to a fully fueled, munition-laden jet that was moments from erupting into a huge fireball. I don't know the world's record for the 440-yard dash in combat boots, but I'm sure John Turk set it that day at Tallil.

9

HITS AND MISSES

Chuck Horner continues:

During the first three days of the war, we were euphoric, and so were the folks at home. We were winning. The home team had scored time after time. And our touchdowns had been faithfully transmitted back to the States—amazing pictures of laser-guided bombs slaying doors of bunkers, airshafts of buildings, and the tops of aircraft shelters. For the first time since World War II, generals had become popular—Schwarzkopf with his energy, intensity, and focus, standing up and glaring at dumb questions; Powell with his warmth, intelligence, and smooth confidence.

Even I had a brief moment of fame. During a press conference, we ran a video of the Iraqi Air Force headquarters taken by one of our aircraft. I pointed at the display with my government-issue ballpoint pen. "This is my counterpart's headquarters," I announced as the building exploded. I wish I could take credit for the nice line. But the truth was I'd forgotten the name of the target, and it was all I could think of. Sometimes you get lucky; the incident landed on national TV.

It's just as well that I spent very little time in front of the cameras. I wasn't eager to press my luck under the glare of the lights when I needed to put all my energy into running the air war.

Most of my time, in fact, was spent urging on the team, deciding what needed to be done next, and trying to bring order to chaos.

Since we had no clear idea of what the enemy was doing, we had to guess. We'd take those guesses—officially called intelligence estimates or analysis—and try to deliver violence in such a way that the enemy could not do what we thought he was trying to do. That was working far better than we had dreamed.

Meanwhile—as in every war I'd seen—the Air Tasking Order was getting out late. Some problems are inevitable. Bad weather over targets required changes in the target lists, and there'd always be computer hiccups. Other problems were less forgivable: planners lust after the perfect plan, and generals like to general; both often pay more attention to doing their own thing than to taking care of the needs of the troops who are getting shot at.

There will never be a perfect plan until the intelligence that drives planning touches perfection. Don't hold your breath. Yet planners obsessively fiddled and tinkered with the daily plan, trying to squeeze every drop of efficiency out of it . . . as though it were a work of art and not a rough script. When we stopped the presses to make small changes affecting only a few units, we risked delaying the ATO for everyone. And that risked increasing confusion or, worse, chaos.

Generals don't feel like generals unless they make their presence felt. Fair enough, when they know where they are going and keep a light hand on the reins. That's leadership. Too often, though, they don't know where they are going, yet pretend they do (in the absence of virtue, the appearance of virtue is better than nothing); and then get the staff to plan the trip. Once the staff plan is prepared, the general will inevitably make lots of changes. General-induced changes make big ripples in the planning cycle. In our ATO planning process, we had lots of general-created tidal waves, including too many from me.

Despite the screwups, we gradually brought order to this confusion and speeded up the planning process in an orderly way that allowed humans to accommodate to them. Very early in the war, we learned to make changes early in the ATO, not by stopping the presses, but by sending change sheets directly to the units involved. We'd tell them something like: "When you get the ATO tonight, your F-16s are targeted against Target X. Disregard that and go to target Y." At first the new systems confused the wings, but they caught on rapidly.

After the war, the armchair generals had their say about speed-

ing up the planning process. "We've got to get the ATO cycle time down," they'd assert. "Two days is too long." They were right, we had to speed up the process; but they were blaming the wrong villain. The two-day cycle wasn't hurting us. You must give people some reasonable planning horizon, and two days is short but manageable. What needs to be worked on is the change cycle—the cycle of gaining intelligence about what you want to do and then implementing the required changes. In other words, we'd use the two-day plan to head the troops in the right general direction, and then we'd fine-tune as needed. For example, because the Iraqi Army units moved daily, we were never able to pinpoint their location in the two-day cycle. At first, we tried to update the ATO. But this only left the ATO in constant flux and therefore late to the customers. Instead, we put the F-16 killer scouts over the Iraqi army, then sent forth hordes of A-10s, F-16s, and F-18s in a well-planned orderly stream. When they arrived on scene, the killer scouts pointed out targets, and the fighter-bombers dropped their loads and returned home for more.

The timeline we had shortened was the time needed to bring intelligence to the attackers. Because the killer scouts' eyes were the intelligence collectors, the intelligence was only seconds old when the attacking aircraft acted on it.

For generals who liked being generals, this was not a happy situation; it put them out of the loop. Captains and majors were picking the targets . . . and it worked. We in Riyadh had succeeded in seizing from Washington the responsibility to pick targets, only to cede it to F-16 pilots over the battlefield. Sure, Washington still provided broad guidance; and sure, the generals in Riyadh told the killer scouts what divisions to orbit over and gave them the rules needed to prevent them from killing one another or breaking international laws; but in large measure, this war now belonged to the folks who were getting shot at.

CUTTING OFF THE SERPENT'S HEAD

In the most efficient of worlds, the centralized, totalitarian dictatorship should be most vulnerable to an efficient shot to the head—a bullet through the presidential window, followed by the quick elimination of presidential cronies, henchmen, military leaders, and possibly family; and then, for thoroughness' sake, the removal of the party chiefs, the heads of the secret police, and the top people in intelligence. Finally, one cuts off the physical connections between capital and country—the networks of communications, roads, rail, and air. Now headless, the oppressed people ought to rise up to remove and replace the remaining causes of their misery.

Sadly, the world is not so easy to manage. Totalitarian systems are rarely smart and efficient. More often, they are stupid and clumsy and overcomplicated, and therefore not especially vulnerable to neat solutions.

That, at any rate, was one of the lessons of the Gulf War.

The original CHECKMATE offensive plans centered on a strategy of destroying Iraqi leadership. With this accomplished, it was asserted, all other goals—such as the Iraqi withdrawal from occupied Kuwait—would be achieved. The concept was to kill Saddam Hussein, or at least to discredit him, so he could not rule the nation; and a more rational leader or leaders could emerge, probably from the Iraqi Army.

When the CHECKMATE briefing was presented to Chuck Horner in Riyadh, he found this line of thinking intriguing; yet he did not feel he could afford to throw the kind of effort CHECKMATE envisaged into a hunt for Saddam Hussein, or, more broadly, into a campaign to incite an overthrow of his government. Certainly a good case could be made for killing Saddam. He was, after all, the head of Iraqi military forces, he devised its military strategy, and he gave orders about the disposition of forces. Therefore, while President Saddam Hussein was not directly targeted, it is safe to conclude that the Black Hole's target lists included all the military command centers where Field Marshal Hussein might have been directing his forces.

In their initial plans, the Pentagon planners selected thirty-seven targets associated with Saddam's hold on Iraq. Some strikes were aimed specifically at the Iraqi leader, others at the tools or symbols of his rule, and some at targets (such as electrical power grids) whose loss would damage both the military capability of the nation and the political power of its leaders. By the start of the war, Black Hole planners had identified an additional 105 "leadership" targets, making a total of 142.

Because most of them were in Baghdad, however, the 142 targets covered a broader range than leadership. Many, such as the attack on the

"AT & T building," served to advance other strategic goals as well. The elimination of the telecommunications center not only hindered Saddam's ability to issue political and military orders, but prevented Iraqi air defense centers from coordinating air defense.

During the first hours of the air campaign, F-117s and cruise missiles targeted command, control, and communications sites. Two-thousand-pound laser-guided bombs destroyed five major telephone exchange facilities, including the "AT & T building" and its adjacent antenna mast. Telephone switching posts were destroyed, as were bridges over the Tigris River (in order to sever fiber-optic communication cables bolted under the roadway).

Command-and-control bunkers in the presidential palaces were struck, as were command centers for the Republican Guard, the intelligence services, the secret police, the Ministry of Propaganda, and Baath Party headquarters. Most of these targets provided capabilities needed to execute military operations, and General Hussein might also have been on duty at one of them; but, more generally, they represented Saddam's means of controlling the people of Iraq. Likewise, command post bunkers for the Iraqi Air Force and for air defense operations were attacked, both in an effort to gain control of the air and also because General Hussein might be inside directing the air defense of his nation. A number of such targets were struck in the opening moments of the war, and attacks continued throughout the war.

Did these leadership attacks hurt the Iraqis?

Yes, up to a point, and sometimes very directly: At the primary presidential palace was a hardened concrete bunker, deeply buried under a garden that came to be called the "Rose Garden," a target so difficult it could not be destroyed by ordinary bombs. Therefore, a pair of laser bombs dug a pit in the earth that covered the concrete shelter. These were followed by a third bomb, with a hardened steel shell and a delayed fuse, which was precisely guided into the crater dug by the first bombs. Because this third bomb did not have to fight its way through tons of earth, it easily penetrated the reinforced concrete roof and exploded inside the shelter. Very bad news for anyone inside.

The attacks also made it difficult for military leaders in Baghdad to communicate with the forces in the field (which might have been a mixed blessing, given the overall foolishness of Iraqi military leadership).

Was the leadership campaign successful?

No. It failed miserably.

American planners like to measure the enemy in numbers of tanks, ships, and aircraft, and shy away from measuring him in less certain terms, such as his morale, military training, or motivation. Yet—for good reasons—American planners endow adversaries with the same intelligence and efficiency as they themselves possess. They tend to attack enemies as though they were housed in some foreign version of Washington, D.C. They "mirror-image" the enemy.

The Iraqis are as intelligent as any people, but, as it turned out, when it came to Saddam's system of maintaining political and physical control, intelligence and efficiency were beside the point. The Baathists maintained control of the country by creating an Orwellian climate of mistrust. Iraqis not only feared the president and the secret police, they feared each other. Husbands were careful what they told their wives, in case their thoughts were relayed to the secret police. Parents could not trust their children, since the young were raised to inform even on their own fathers and mothers. If a friend confided to you a criticism of Saddam Hussein, you immediately reported it to the secret police, in case the friend had been induced to test your reliability.

And so, all the leadership targets were struck, and the leader stayed in power. The American planners failed to change the government of Iraq, because they did not understand how that government operated, and therefore how to attack it. They did not understand that Saddam stayed in power by creating an aura of crisis that caused his people to need him more than they needed change. The fear that motivated the average Iraqi citizen's loyalty to Saddam was beyond their comprehension, because they had never experienced life under a repressive regime. They did not understand that they needed to target the fear, and they did not have either the smarts or the intelligence analysis to destroy the hold of fear on the Iraqi people. They did not understand that the bombing of Iraq ensured that hold was increased and not decreased.

And yet, since Iraqi troops in the field had little reason to love their dictator, many were persuaded to surrender without a fight. Thus, the fear by which Saddam maintained control over his nation worked for rather than against the Coalition's battlefield success. In other words, killing Saddam may have turned out to be a serious mistake.

Likewise, in his paranoia, Saddam often had his top generals executed. The threat of execution sometimes concentrates the mind, but more often it leads to paralysis. This weakening of his military leadership could only benefit the Coalition. And finally, as General Schwarzkopf pointed out after the war, Saddam was a lousy strategist, and thus a good man to have in charge of Iraqi armed forces, under the circumstances.

NBC

In the eyes of tinpot dictators and other insecure regimes, nuclear, biological, and chemical weapons—especially when mated with ballistic missiles—are the visible symbols that make small nations into big players on the world's stage. The Iraqis have spent billions of dollars in research and development of such weapons.

The potential for large-scale tragedy is obvious, and tinpot dictators are indifferent by nature to the crucial insight that major powers long ago took to heart: that NBC weapons are not weapons of war but weapons of terror. What goes around comes around. You hit me; I hit you. To add to this unsettling thought, Saddam Hussein had already proved willing to use weapons of mass destruction both in foreign wars and against his own people.

Fortunately, the most fearsome of these weapons, the nuclear, are the hardest to make, and the programs to make them are the easiest to discover. The manufacture of nuclear weapons requires skilled engineers and scientists, a vast array of high-technology facilities, weapons-grade nuclear material, and other rare ingredients. Few of these are easily available to nations such as Iraq; and all of them can be protected and tracked. This requires more vigilance than is currently the case, but it can be done.

Unfortunately, the Iraqis have proved to be extremely skilled at avoiding existing protections, and brilliant at shell-game hiding of the pieces of their nuclear program (likewise of their biological and chemical program)—thus exemplifying the uses of paranoia.

Ten years before the 1990 Gulf crisis, the Israelis bombed Iraqi nuclear research laboratories. This delayed but did not stop the nuclear program (and may have encouraged them to greater efforts at concealment).

After the war, United Nations inspection teams uncovered large caches of technical and historical records of Saddam's nuclear program. These records indicated that U.S. intelligence organizations had been aware of only a portion of the Iraqi nuclear weapons efforts. Though prediction in this area is risky, some estimates claimed that Saddam's scientists were

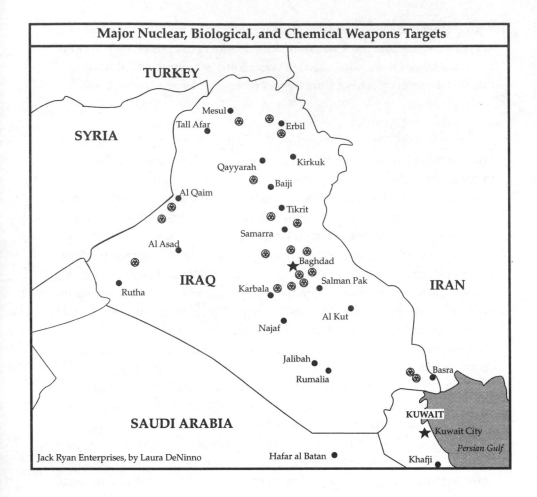

Major Nuclear, Biological, and Chemical Weapons Targets

TURKEY

SYRIA

Mesul

Tall Afar

Erbil

Qayyarah

Kirkuk

Baiji

Al Qaim

Tikrit

Al Asad

Samarra

Baghdad

IRAQ

Karbala

Salman Pak

IRAN

Rutha

Al Kut

Najaf

Jalibah

Rumalia

Basra

SAUDI ARABIA

KUWAIT

Jack Ryan Enterprises, by Laura DeNinno

Hafar al Batan

Kuwait City

Persian Gulf

Khafji

within months of producing a workable nuclear device. Whether this could have been mated to the warhead of a Scud missile is another matter, and it is doubtful that Iraqi fighter-bomber aircraft could have penetrated the air defenses of Israel or Saudi Arabia.

Still, no matter how close Iraqi scientists were to building deliverable weapons, it was a no-brainer for Iraqi NBC programs to top Black Hole target lists. These facilities were going to be hit, and hit early. The risks were too great.

Precision munitions were dropped on the Baghdad Nuclear Weapons Research Center on the first three days of the war, though to what effect it was hard to say, except by counting holes in buildings and bunkers. Later, a mass raid against the Al Qaim nuclear facility failed. The forty

F-16s found it defended by large numbers of AAA and SAM sites and ob-scured by smoke generators, and then the bombs from the first two air-craft raised so much dust that it was impossible for the remaining thirty-eight pilots to identify their aim points. The facility was later hit by a surprise F-117 night attack, which obliterated every assigned target.

But the fox, it turned out, had fled.

After the war, United Nations inspection teams learned that the Iraqis had already removed vital equipment from these locations and buried it in the desert (not a practice recommended for the sensitive, highly cali-brated electronic devices used in nuclear research). In other words, from the Iraqi point of view, the cure may have been no better than the disease. If that was the case, then God was once again on the side of the good guys. Either way, the air attacks delayed the Iraqi quest for nuclear weapons for a few more years.

★ In an earlier chapter the problem of preventing biological attack was discussed. There is little to add to that here.

Because production facilities for biological weapons are difficult to identify, intelligence and planning concentrated on storage facilities, usu-ally in air-conditioned concrete earth-covered bunkers. Attacking these sites, however, remained a dilemma, owing to the possible spread of toxic agents in the dust and debris resulting from bomb explosions.

Despite this risk, the cross-shaped bunkers at the Salman Pak Biolog-ical Warfare Center were hit on the first night of the war by the same one-two punch that destroyed the presidential Rose Garden bunker. And, as previously mentioned, the resulting explosion was spectacular. Aircrews reported that heat from the secondary explosions went thousands of feet into the air.

In the event, attacking bio-weapons storage may have been just as fu-tile as attacking nuclear production—though for different reasons. After the war, credible reports (from Saddam's sons-in-law, later murdered) indicated that the Iraqis were just as worried as Americans that biologi-cal agents could infect the entire region, and had therefore destroyed their anthrax and botulism spores before the aerial onslaught risked spreading them. If this was true—and Chuck Horner believes it was likely (due to the absence of cases of either disease during the war)—then greater effort should have been aimed at identifying and targeting bio-logical research and production facilities.

★ Though chemical weapons are far from precision munitions, they pose less of a danger to attackers than biological agents, and their effects on an enemy are more immediate. Saddam possessed lots of them. U.S. intelligence sources indicated that large numbers of artillery shells and rockets were available for delivery of nerve and mustard gas.

The problem: though U.S. intelligence had located the manufacturing facilities for these weapons, there were so many of them, there wasn't enough time for Chuck Horner's bombers to destroy them all.

The initial attacks hit the largest of these facilities, at Samarra and Al-Habbanilyah near Baghdad, as well as chemical weapons, bombs, artillery, and missile warheads located in close proximity to delivery systems. For example, bunkers at Tallil Airfield were targeted the first night. And throughout the war, any indication of chemical weapons near Iraqi units that could face Coalition ground forces brought quick attack.

Just as with biological agents, the unintended release of chemical agents as a by-product of air attacks brought potential problems. Fortunately, the fallout of poisonous chemical debris had fewer long-term effects, since the hot dry desert air quickly degraded the potency of chemical agents, even in winter months.

THE GREAT SCUD HUNT

Finding and killing Scuds was part of the anti-NBC effort. No one in the Coalition or in Israel was eager to witness the successful mating of a weapon of mass destruction to a ballistic missile launched at Riyadh or Tel Aviv. In the event, finding and killing mobile Scuds proved to be a nightmare.

During the War of the Cities phase of the Iran–Iraq War of the 1980s, both nations tossed Scuds at each other's capital. To military analysts, not much was achieved by this seemingly senseless expenditure of obsolete ballistic missiles. To civilians in Tehran and Baghdad, however, it was a very significant event indeed when an Iraqi or Iranian missile slammed into some neighborhood they knew. Later, Chuck Horner made himself familiar with that war (since it was waged in a part of the world he was expected to know well), yet these missile attacks did not greatly concern him. As he quickly came to learn in the early weeks of 1991, however, the people living near Iran and Iraq were not so sanguine. After the War of the Cities, Saudi Arabia had acquired very expensive long-range ballistic missiles, to deter its neighbors to the north and east. Israel also had missiles—and very likely the nuclear weapons to go with them.

No one had any doubt that Saddam expected to use his Scuds, and in October, his threats couldn't have been more emphatic. "In the event of war," he announced, "I'll attack Saudi Arabia and Israel with long-range missiles. . . . And I'll burn Israel." In December, he had test-fired his modified, longer-range Scuds. (This had a consequence he did not foresee: it gave U.S. space forces an invaluable opportunity to check out the space-based warning satellites and communication link from the U.S. Space command in Colorado Springs, Colorado. Now they could read out the infrared signals sent by the satellites, and from the template they put together after the December tests, they could tell with reasonable certainty whether or not a Scud had been launched.)

Chuck Horner's team was ready.

Plans called for preemptive attacks against Scud production facilities and storage areas (including missile fuel tanks). All the fixed launch pads painstakingly erected in Iraq's western desert were bombed in the opening moments of the war. And on day two, multiple attacks were made on the Latifiyah rocket-fuel plants and on rocket-motor production facilities at Shahiyat, all near Baghdad. Because the fuel the Scuds used was unstable, it could be stored for only perhaps four to six weeks. Therefore, fuel-production facilities were bombed, with the expectation that Scud attacks would stop when the "good" fuel was used up. Unfortunately, the Iraqis didn't follow this script, either because the Coalition failed to destroy all the Scud fuel-production facilities, or because the Iraqis failed to read the instructions that told them not to use old fuel. They were able to fire the missiles well into the last nights of the war.

Meanwhile, billions of dollars of satellites over Iraq searched for the hot flash of a launching Scud and predicted the warhead's target. There were civil defense warning systems. And there was the Patriot. In September, the antiballistic missile version, the PAC-2s, had been rushed to the region and deployed near airports and seaports, in order to protect entryways for forces deploying into the Arabian peninsula.

What was lacking, as Horner had informed Secretary Cheney, was the means to locate and kill the mobile Scud launchers.

The first of Saddam's Scud launches were directed at Israel on the afternoon of January 17. Early next morning, Scuds fell on Dhahran and Riyadh.

Phone calls from Washington quickly followed: "Do whatever you need to to shut down the Scuds." The great Scud hunt had begun.

From the first, Horner's planners had expected to hunt mobile Scuds, even though there was never great confidence that they would find them all. Still, until the hunt was on, no one realized the resources they would have to commit, even less how little the hunt would succeed. The day after the first attacks, A-10s, F-16s, F-15s, and an AC-130 gunship were deployed to search the deserts of Iraq, day and night.

First reports looked encouraging: A-10s in south central Iraq attacked a convoy of trucks that appeared to be carrying Scuds. However, it quickly became evident that if the trucks had in fact carried missiles, and if the missiles were Scuds (and not, say, shorter-range FROG 6s), the attack had had little effect on Scud launches, as missiles continued to rain down on Israel and Saudi Arabia.

Night after night missiles came down, five or more per night, and as Scuds fell, more and more scarce air assets were dedicated to hunting them: flights of four F-15Es were sent to orbit likely launch boxes in western Iraq. Any vehicle on the Baghdad-to-Amman interstate highway was attacked, much to the distress of fuel-truck drivers smuggling fuel to Jordan.

In Riyadh, the pressure for action was strong; in Tel Aviv, it was explosive. The Scud attacks had filled Israeli civilians with terror and outrage. They wanted revenge. Traditionally, Israelis did not delegate military action, and their traditional strategy was an eye for an eye. At the minimum, they expected to send their excellent air force against the Scuds. More dangerously, there was a real possibility that they would retaliate with nuclear weapons.

Hoping to put a lid on all this, Horner sent a delegation to Tel Aviv— including his deputy, Major General Tom Olsen, and one of the four TACC operations directors, Colonel Mike Reavy—to explain how Americans were working to suppress the Scuds. He also wanted high-level people there to consult in the event of an Israeli attack. If the Israelis weighed in, tangles between Israeli and Coalition air forces would have been very possible, and would have only helped the enemy. Washington wanted Coalition forces out of their way. Meanwhile, Washington was putting full diplomatic pressure into preventing Israeli action.

Chuck Horner observes:

Israeli retaliation would have been a terrible political mistake, and its chances of military success were not high, either.

Though Israeli pilots were among the best in the world, they were less well-equipped than we were to hunt mobile Scuds. Consequently, their only real contribution to the war would have been to boost the morale of their own people. Far more important, however, the Coalition was always a very fragile thing. Any Israeli retaliation on an Arab state—especially nuclear retaliation—no matter how justified, would have at best weakened the Coalition. At worst, it would have destroyed it. Though it is my belief that the Chief of the Israeli Air Force, General Ben-Nun (a dear friend and first-rate F-15 pilot), understood all this, he was under pressure to act. So planning went on day and night in Tel Aviv.

Relief in Tel Aviv came with the arrival of the U.S. Army's Patriot missiles. Though many will claim that the Patriots failed to stop the Scuds, the question about their success is really beside the point. The Scuds themselves failed to perform well, except to bring terror. By bringing relief from terror to the people in Israel, the Patriots succeeded magnificently. The relief was important enough to allow the release of Tom Olsen and Mike Reavy to come back to run the air war, where they were sorely needed.

On the downside, Israeli worries meant pressure on Schwarzkopf from Washington to start a ground war in the west just to shut down Scud attacks on Israel. This also would have been a terrible mistake, and a logistical horror.

★ Though efforts to halt Scud launches were never completely successful, neither were they futile. Flights of F-15Es and F-16s at night, and A-10s during the days, combed the desert Scud boxes (areas where Scuds could be successfully launched against a particular target, such as Tel Aviv). Though confirmed kills were few—and for the A-10s there were none—their pressure kept launches down. In time, the Iraqis risked their Scuds only when skies were overcast and U.S. aircraft couldn't see them. January 25, when ten were launched, was the high-water mark for Scuds. After that, the average fell to about one per day (though during the last days of the war, Saddam used up his reserves, and launches increased).

The A-10 search in the western desert was far from a total loss, for they discovered there an enormous unprotected storage area—munitions bunkers, tanks, APCs, and many other vehicles. What all that equipment was doing out there is a good question. Was Saddam preparing for an invasion to the west through Jordan into Israel? Or was this his idea of the best way to prepare for an Israeli attack against Baghdad? At any rate, the A-10s named the cache they'd found the "Target of God" and quickly turned it into a giant scrap heap. After the war, a high-ranking Iraqi confided to a Russian friend that 1,800 of Iraq's 2,400 tanks were destroyed by air before the Desert Storm ground war. How much of that was destroyed by A-10s in the western desert is hard to say, yet it gives a sense of the enormity of Iraq's war machine.

Meanwhile, it was not U.S. aircraft, but Lieutenant General Sir Peter de la Billiere's British special forces teams that had the greatest impact on Scud launches. Sir Peter had a long career in Special Operations, including service in the Middle East. His taciturn, calm, well-mannered demeanor masked a warrior ready to rip an enemy's throat with a large knife.

As de la Billiere was well aware, General Schwarzkopf had serious concerns about using special forces behind enemy lines, where they risked trouble that would require rescue by regular army forces (and perhaps start an unwanted battle). After somehow persuading the CINC that his worries were misplaced, Sir Peter approved several British Special Air Service Scud-hunting missions behind enemy lines.

Chuck Horner never actually received a formal briefing about this operation. The Brits simply implemented it. One day an SAS officer showed up in the TACC and, without fanfare or cloak-and-dagger secrecy, started working with Horner's people to coordinate the planning. "I'm going to send some lads up into western Iraq," he explained. "How's the best way for us to cooperate?"

"That's easy," Horner's planners said. "But aren't you worried that our Scud-hunting aircraft might attack your guys by mistake?"

"Actually, no," he said. "My lads have to hide from the Iraqis. That's far harder than hiding from a few high-flying jets. So if your folks find them, my folks are fair game."

The procedures they worked out were simple: his "lads" on the ground used handheld aircrew survival radios to communicate with U.S. aircraft—a very dicey business, because the Iraqis monitored the radio frequencies used by these radios and had extensive direction-finding equipment.

As with aircraft, hard evidence of their Scud-killing success is slim, but

Scud launches diminished; and the SAS troops certainly helped U.S. air-craft find launchers, as one data-recording videotape from an F-15E tes-tifies: the world viewed on CNN a laser-guided bomb hitting what certainly seemed to be a Scud on a transporter erector vehicle. What CNN didn't broadcast was the audio portion of that tape, in which a British SAS officer talked the fighter aircrew onto a Scud target. As he calmly directed the F-15, its crew spotted a missile much nearer his lo-cation than the one he'd seen, and they proceeded to put a 2,000-pound laser-guided bomb on the target. The resulting fireball was close enough to the Brit to singe his hair. The audio of their radio communication went something like this:

SAS: "I say, Eagle II, I have a Scud located at the following coordi-nates," which he read.

Eagle II pilot: "Roger. Am one minute out, approaching your position from the south."

SAS: "Understand you will be making your run from south to north. The target is in a small wadi, running southwest by northeast. And I can hear you approaching the target."

Eagle II pilot: "Roger. We have the target and have bombs away."

Soon the aircraft's laser was pointed at what appeared to be either a Scud or a tank truck filled with fuel just south of the SAS man. Then a very large bomb was headed through the air at near supersonic speeds. Just prior to impact, the SAS officer came on the air and said: "Under-stand you are bombs away. I'm observing some activity on the road just—"

At that moment, the bomb hit, the fireball of the secondary explosion rolled over the SAS man, and the loudest "JESUS CHRIST!" ever trans-mitted on the airways interrupted what had been a cool, professional conversation. Fortunately, he was not injured, and the tape delivered more than a good laugh to the commanders in Riyadh. For Horner, it showed they were making progress in an otherwise frustrating job. For Schwarzkopf, this evidence of success took off some of the heat from Washington to start a ground war in the west.

SAS operations in Iraq sometimes ran into difficulties. On one occa-sion, a three-man SAS team was captured by Iraqis. Two of the team managed to escape, while the third was beat up and tortured. Of the two who got away, however, only one trekked to safety in Syria; the other died of exposure (it was fiercely cold in Iraq). Later, from the man who reached Syria, the TACC planners learned the location of the torture site. That night, a pair of 2,000-pound bombs were dropped through its roof.

★ Some weeks after the SAS first went out to hunt Scuds, Major General Wayne Downing's U.S. Special Operations force began to share those duties. This operation caused surprising friction with Horner's TACC team. The problem, in Horner's view, was their go-it-alone attitude and their emphasis on secrecy and rank:

> When a U.S. special forces colonel would come into our head-quarters to brief an upcoming mission, he would have great difficulty discussing its details with anyone of subordinate rank. That's fine unless you want to get the job done. The people who make decisions in air operations are often the majors and captains. You have to trust them.
>
> On one occasion, their secrecy nearly led to the shoot-down of some Special Operations helicopters, who neither informed the TACC of their operation or followed the rules laid out in the Air Tasking Order. Once they were in Iraq, they were detected by AWACS, then locked onto by eager F-15s. Luckily, Mike Reavy, the senior director on duty, denied permission to fire while he desperately tried to confirm whether the target was hostile. At the last moment, the Special Operations liaison realized the helicopters were his, thus avoiding a terrible blue-on-blue engagement.
>
> On the ground, there is no better military force than U.S. special forces, but I pray they can lighten up a little and coordinate in the manner of the SAS.

Another group of troopers who were vital to the war on Scuds got no medals and very little appreciation—the men and women of Space Command.

Throughout the Cold War, U.S. deterrence strategy had relied on detecting an attack on the United States in sufficient time to launch retaliatory strikes. A cornerstone of this strategy was the Defense Support Program (DSP) satellites, huge cylinder-shaped objects in geosynchronous orbits. Each DSP had an infrared telescope that kept track of hot spots on earth. If the hot spot started moving across the earth's surface, the satellite reported the event to the command center in Cheyenne Mountain in Colorado Springs. There, the men and women of the U.S. Space Command would evaluate the event to see if it was a threat to North America. Though the DSP had not been built to fight theater war, and was sensitive only to the high-intensity rocket plumes made by ICBMs, the wizards of space altered the computers in August 1990 to sort out the DSP data more finely. The Iraqi test firings in December proved this would work.

Of almost equal importance for Horner's people was knowledge of launch site locations.

In the Cold War, once you knew an attack was coming from Russia, you had about all the information you needed, and this was about all DSPs would tell you. DSPs were not designed to project the accuracy required to attack a launch site with iron bombs. This was a serious deficiency that could never be totally overcome. Nevertheless, the contractor, TRW, and the military wizards of space had vastly improved the design by the time the guns started to shoot, and the DSP was able to give some rough idea of launch points.

These modifications helped, but DSP's greatest contribution to the war was to provide warnings of attack, so civil defense agencies could be alerted.

Those in the TACC can never forget those chilling words, "Scud Alert!" In the early days of the war, the words ignited near panic; until the Patriots proved their worth, almost everyone donned chemical-biological protection gear and headed for a deep underground bunker.

The "Scud Alert" warning also initiated actions in the air defense cell. First, the Army troops would inform their Patriot batteries; civil defense agencies would also be notified, so they could warn civilians to take cover. Then the AWACS display would light up, showing the approximate launch point, missile flight path, and probable impact zone. This information would be relayed automatically throughout the command-and-control network, so F-15 or F-16 pilots could be vectored toward the mobile launchers. At the affected Patriot batteries, systems would be checked to make sure they were ready for computer-initiated firing.

Since to the DSP's sensors B-52 strikes initially looked very much like a Scud launch, there was a quick check with the AWACS display to discover if the Scud attack was genuine. Once that was determined, Horner would watch CNN for a real-time live report.

Though most Scuds did little damage, there were still bad moments. One that fell in Israel caused a large number of injuries, another destroyed the school attended by General Behery's children, and another fell in the street outside RSAF headquarters (it was immediately attacked by souvenir hunters). A piece of molten metal from this Scud (or from the Patriot that intercepted it) burned a hole through the roof of the RAF administration building and dropped sizzling onto a desk where a pair of Brits were having a late-night cup of tea. Finally, and tragically, in the waning moments of the war, during a period when the Patriot battery defending the city was off-line, a Scud slammed into a warehouse in Dhahran where U.S. Army transportation troops were sleeping. Over twenty-five troops were killed and nearly a hundred injured—the largest numbers of allied casualties from a single Gulf War event. In fact, Scuds killed more U.S. troops than were killed in any single engagement during the eight months of war on the sea, six weeks of war in the air, and four days of war on the ground (a total of about seventy-five soldiers were killed by the Iraqis, and another seventy-five were killed by blue-on-blue).

The failure to stop the Scud threat was Chuck Horner's greatest Gulf War failure, the one area where airpower could not secure and maintain the military initiative.

COLLATERAL DAMAGE

A major and largely unsung obsession shared by Chuck Horner, his planners, the Coalition pilots, and the President of the United States, was to prevent needless civilian casualties—collateral damage, in the military euphemism. Military targets and military personnel were fair game, but ordinary Iraqis were not responsible for the criminal acts of their rulers. They had a right to live in safety, as far as humanly possible.

Chuck Horner will never forget George Bush's anguish in August at Camp David as he contemplated the deaths that would follow the decisions he'd been forced to make—an anguish, Horner is convinced, that was the right response to the actions he was taking. Horner himself has felt similar pain many times. The needless death of civilians had to be avoided.

On the whole, Coalition airmen successfully followed this course. On two occasions, they failed:

The first, simply, was a tragic mistake. During an RAF strike on a bridge, the guidance system of a laser-guided bomb failed, and the bomb fell into a nearby marketplace, killing or injuring several Iraqi civilians. Since the target was legitimate, and reasonable measures had been taken during an attack on a legitimate target, no blame could be attached to this tragedy.

The second was more complicated—the attack on the Al-Firdus command-and-control bunker.

In the planning for the offensive air campaign, a master target list had been created. The list included thirty-three targets designated as command-and-control centers, though what exactly they commanded and controlled was not totally clear. Number thirty on the list was the Al-Firdus bunker in Baghdad, which was initially scheduled to be struck on day three of the war, a day when many targets were scheduled to be hit. (Day-three targets tended to be the leftovers, after the really important targets were struck on the first two and a half days). In the event, Al-Firdus and the other thirty-two bunkers slipped in priority, as the demands of Scud-hunting, more time-sensitive targets, and weather were met.

Still, in the eyes of the Black Hole planners, Al-Firdus remained a legitimate target of some importance to Saddam's war machine. It was definitely constructed to house military command and control, and it was camouflaged, barb-wired, and guarded (though in truth, hardly anything in Iraq was not camouflaged, barb-wired, and guarded). What Black Hole planners did not know was that hundreds of Iraqi civilians were using the bunker as an air raid shelter.

At last, after nearly four weeks of war, Al-Firdus made it to the top of the list. Planners proposed it for the night of 13–14 February; it was approved as legitimate by the lawyer in the plans shop who watched over the legal aspects of target selection (he could and did veto targets), and then it was approved by Schwarzkopf in the evening briefing.

Chuck Horner reflects:

> *In retrospect, I should have asked harder questions. For one, if we could wait almost a month to strike this bunker, what made it so important now? For another, how was the bunker actually being used to command Iraqi military forces? Since the real reason we were attacking the bunker was almost certainly the availability of*

F-117 sorties (we've got lots to spend; if we don't use them, they're wasted), I doubt that anyone could have given me a good answer to those questions. In the absence of a satisfactory answer, I could have erased that target from the list, and hundreds of Iraqi lives could have been saved and a terrible tragedy avoided. But all of that is hindsight. The reality is F-117s hit the Al-Firdus bunker, and we killed several hundred people.

However, the questions I failed to ask aren't the only questions that need asking here. For instance, why use the bunker as an air raid shelter? To the Black Hole planners and the F-117 pilots flying the missions, it is inconceivable that any Iraqi in Baghdad would want to be anywhere but in his own home during air attacks. American bombs did not hit family homes. Pilots were painstakingly careful to bomb only militarily significant targets. Their bombing was accurate.

Of course, it wasn't only American bombs that were falling out of the sky; thousands of artillery shells and hundreds of surface-to-air missiles were thrown up each night. All of that lethal stuff had to fall back to earth. In that case, maybe it made sense to seek shelter.

And yet, other questions remain.

When the other bunkers were struck, no civilian casualties were reported. Why did Al-Firdus and not the other thirty-two bunkers contain civilians? Did the local commander, in a goodwill gesture, invite locals into his bunker? Or did he suck up to his friends and superiors by offering them shelter not available to the average Iraqi? Who knows . . . except maybe Saddam?

There is one certainty in war: you will always face uncertainty. The enemy does his best to hide the answers to any question you might ask of him. He tries to tell you that he possesses nothing of value. If Saddam had announced that the Al-Firdus bunker was an air raid shelter, and not a command-and-control center, if he had painted a red crescent or red cross on the roof, would we have believed him? We would probably have asked more questions, but it's likely that the bunker would still have been hit (though if we had known the truth, that target would not have appeared in the Air Tasking Order).

The bottom line in war is you are always operating with half the story.

My first knowledge of the tragedy came from CNN, with pictures of bodies being carried from the smoking shelter. In a way, I was glad we had to endure those terrible scenes. Too often, we look on war as a game or a noble adventure. Certainly war can pursue noble objectives—stopping the murder, rape, and torture in Kuwait being a prime example. Certainly men and women undergoing the most stressful battlefield conditions rise to unheard-of selflessness. But war is still, when you get to the bottom line, killing, maiming, and wanton destruction—humans at their lowest, trying to impose their will on others. War may be necessary, but it must always be detested.

During the 1700 changeover briefing, I told the troops in the TACC: "Nobody needs to feel bad about the bunker incident in Baghdad, but we all should feel bad about the loss of life, anybody's life, because every life is precious. It doesn't matter whether it's an Iraqi soldier or a kid in a bunker in Baghdad, we should feel bad about the loss of one of God's creatures. On the other hand, from a professional standpoint, we have nothing to be ashamed of. The mission was planned and executed flawlessly. The intelligence was as good as there is available. As for the people who don't understand that war is groping in the dark trying to do dastardly things so the war will be over with, well, I don't have much time for them. You would sure think modern, educated people would understand that truth, but many choose not to, so to hell with them. We'll have a lot of 'weak willies' to worry about now. They worry about whether they'll get up in the morning, so to hell with them. You just continue what you're doing, because what you're doing is right and you're doing it very well. We've got to get Kuwait back to the Kuwaitis."

Maybe if I'd had more time to think about it, I wouldn't have made such a hard-assed speech; but I was worried that people would be overconcerned about the political cost of civilian casualties and try to shut down the air campaign. I was not wrong to worry.

Targeting in the Baghdad area all but stopped, and General Schwarzkopf began to anguish over every target we nominated, denying approval of most of them. Okay, this change was not in fact hard to accept. Most of the known high-value targets had already been destroyed or heavily damaged, and by then our main thrust had turned to destroying tanks, artillery, and lines of communication in the KTO. But a notion sticks in my throat that someone above the CINC had issued guidance based on fear of public opinion polls. This is not a fact, it's a suspicion, and yes, civilian policy-makers must guide the warriors; but it sends trembles through me. War is political. So be it.

We eventually went back to Baghdad.

The lesson must be that war is not antiseptic, that innocent lives will be lost, that commanders in arms will kill one another. It is important that leaders at all levels do their utmost to minimize death and suffering. It must be an obsession with the commanders and planners, and of everyone who has a finger on the trigger. On the other hand, survival on the battlefield and success in war require decisive action in an ill-defined environment while using the most lethal weapons ever devised. That's the rub. When the laser-guided bomb slips its release hooks, someone is going to die.

Let the deaths of American, Saudi, and British troops, let the deaths of Iraqi civilians, remind each of us that war is a hateful thing.

10

LOST AND FOUND

In combat operations, aircraft will be shot down; and in any air operation, equipment can fail. When an aircraft is shot down or its engine fails behind enemy lines, surviving crew are perilously exposed—and the people they've just bombed are hardly in a welcoming mood. This means, simply, that these crews expect a chance to come home before anyone can give them the welcome "they deserve." That chance for rescue is a fundamental covenant between combat aircrews and their commanders. Aircrews' confidence in that covenant is a function of the actual numbers rescued.

In Desert Storm, the numbers rescued, as compared with the numbers downed, was very low: Eighteen men and one woman became prisoners of war as a result of aircraft shoot-downs. Seven combat search-and-rescue (CSAR) missions were launched, resulting in three saves. That's one saved for every six lost. Not an inspiring record.

It is therefore no surprise that the confidence of aircrews in the fundamental covenant was not high.

To discover the reason for the scarcity of CSAR missions in Desert Storm, one has to go back a few years.

In military doctrine, the rescue of soldiers, sailors, and airmen was originally a service responsibility—that is, the Air Force was responsible for organizing, equipping, and training the forces needed to pick up pilots who were shot down. For years, the Air Force did just that—its Air Rescue Service trained Pararescue Jumpers (PJs), enlisted men ready to parachute into enemy territory, perform emergency medical treatment on downed pilots, and fight off the enemy while the rescued airman was being winched up to a helicopter overhead. During Vietnam, PJs became the most decorated heroes of the war. Pilots admired no one more highly.

In 1983, the Air Rescue Units were transferred en masse to the newly created Special Operations Forces Command. Since the air movement of Special Operations soldiers to and from behind enemy lines is the same function as combat search-and-rescue, this change made great sense. There is one important difference, however, between SOF operations and air rescue. In SOF operations, there is some control over timing. This difference had serious consequences.

Meanwhile, the assets the Air Force had acquired to take people to and from behind enemy lines were placed under SOF command (or CINCSOF—before Goldwater-Nichols, air rescue forces had been assigned to Military Airlift Command). Among these were various helicopters and the HC-130 command-and-control aircraft. This version of the Hercules transport provided a platform for an on-scene director to orchestrate the rescue. Vietnam-era MH-53 Jolly Green Giant helicopters were now called Pave Low IIIs, and equipped with devices that permitted low-altitude flight at night. Later, a newer and smaller rescue helicopter was introduced for the SOF, the MH-60G Pave Hawk; it was also equipped for flying at treetop level at night. Though PJs were disappearing, new enlisted crews, called "Special Tactics Personnel," were being trained to ride the SOF-penetrating helicopters. STPs performed the same functions as Vietnam-era PJs, and trained just as hard.

The monkey wrench in the works was the change in command lines that accompanied the 1983 changeover. The new SOF airmen now worked for an Army colonel whose primary focus was on glamorous missions behind enemy lines. He wanted *his* "air force" available to support *his* missions behind enemy lines and not tied up chasing after downed aircrews.

Some basic presuppositions made matters even worse: In their own private view, special forces fight alone, in isolation from other land, sea, air, and space forces. Therefore, for the most part SOF airmen trained for terrain-hugging night flights, which was considered the safest way to enter enemy airspace. In consequence, they felt they were ill-trained to conduct air rescue operations in daylight.

During the Gulf War, as it turned out, SOF airmen operating in Kuwait and southeastern Iraq* owed their survival in enemy airspace, not to their night training, but to the grounding of Iraqi fighters by Coalition airpower and to the vastness of the desert, which was so large and

---

*In the west, SOF forces had pretty much a free ride, as did the British SAS.

inhospitable that Iraqi air defense forces could not cover all of it. And when Iraqi ground forces did locate Special Operations units, these units as often as not had to be picked up and returned to safety during daylight hours—SOF bias notwithstanding.

Meanwhile, reflecting post–Goldwater-Nichols realities, the CENTCOM air force was *not* the USAF; it was the USAF plus sizable numbers of aircraft from the Army, Navy, and Marine Corps, plus thousands of aircraft from other nations operating under the command of the Joint/Combined Force Air Component Commander, Chuck Horner. In other words, the individual service responsibility to conduct search-and-rescue had grown to include a great deal more than the U.S. Air Force. To handle this new situation, General Schwarzkopf set up a unique combat search-and-rescue organization. While retaining command of CSAR plans and operations in his own staff, the CINC placed his subordinate commander, Air Force Lieutenant Colonel Joe Stillwell, and his rescue cell in Horner's Tactical Air Control Center. The TACC would likely be the first to learn when an aircraft was shot down and if the aircrew was alive; in the TACC, the CSAR cell could maintain contact with rescue forces in Iraq using the AWACS aircraft to relay commands or information; and the TACC controlled the air-to-air, air-to-ground, and Wild Weasel defense suppression forces needed to protect CSAR forces during a rescue. Finally, pilots orbiting overhead could best determine if a helicopter could survive local enemy defenses and make their pickup.

These sensible command-and-control procedures did not sit well with Colonel Jessie Johnson, the Special Operations commander. To Johnson, it appeared that the CSAR commander worked for Horner (a situation Johnson did not like). Stillwell did not work for Horner. He worked for Schwarzkopf.

For obvious reasons, Schwarzkopf tasked rescues in northern Iraq to the air forces operating out of Incirlik, Turkey.

The mission of combat search-and-rescue in central and southern Iraq and Kuwait went to Jessie Johnson. Colonel Johnson's MH-53 and MH-60 helicopters were based at King Fahd Air Base in eastern Saudi Arabia, where all SOF aircraft were based. When possible, however, they were placed on alert at forward operating locations at airfields along the Iraqi border, such as those near King Khalid Military City, and the towns of Rafha, ArAr, and Al Jouf, where A-10s were also operating in their Scud-hunting mission in the western Iraqi desert.

Unfortunately, for reasons already stated, the air rescue mission was never a top special forces priority. Thus, while the CSAR missions were directed and controlled by the joint recovery coordination cell in the TACC, the SOCCENT commander retained final mission approval and refused to okay a CSAF launch until a survivor could be confirmed on the ground. Yet, as always, the SOF airmen of the Air Force Special Operations command were eager and ready to rescue downed airmen anytime anywhere.*

The opportunity came early to test this system. On January 21, 1991, a Navy F-14 pilot, Lieutenant Devon Jones, was picked up in a daring rescue.

Jones's F-14, call sign Sate 46, was flying over western Iraq looking for Iraqi fighters to shoot down, when an Iraqi SAM slammed into the jet and forced him to eject. Jones came down in the desert, which proved to be blessedly empty of Iraqis. He immediately took out his survival knife and hacked a hole in the hard ground big enough to crouch in. Then he hunkered down on top of his parachute and pulled a scraggly bush over his head. Since he knew the shoot-down had been reported to the AWACS, all he had to do was wait for rescue or capture, whichever came first.

Hundred of miles away, Captain Paul Johnson and his wingman, Captain Randy Goff, were flying up from King Fahd Air Base to King Khalid Military City in their A-10 Warthogs, call signs Sandy 57 and 58. When they landed, they'd sit ground-alert for combat search-and-rescue tasking—not a happy prospect. Their day promised to be wasted on the ground while their squadron buddies were shooting up the Iraqi army in Kuwait.

The day turned out to be more interesting than they expected.

On a routine check-in with AWACS, Johnson and Goff found that they had new "tasking": They were to head north to help two other A-10s and a super Jolly Green Giant MH-53J (call sign Moccasin 05) find a downed F-14 pilot somewhere west of Baghdad. That was a big "somewhere," and it was a long way north of the Saudi border—and a lot farther north than A-10s usually flew. (Up there, their primary fear

---

*In fairness to the Special Operations commanders, the paucity of CSAR missions can't be blamed entirely on them. First, the density of Iraqi air defenses has to be taken into account. Flying a helicopter into a near-certain shoot-down obviously made no sense. Second, several pilots were captured shortly after parachuting over the Iraqi Army units they'd just attacked. Third— and most important—very few aircraft were actually lost in combat. Thus, little CSAR was actually needed.

was to run into a MiG when no F-15s were around. On the other hand, they had little to fear from AAA and SAMs, since the desert was pretty barren.)

Before they headed north into "Indian country," they pressed west along the border looking for a tanker to fill their fuel tanks. Though the weather was terrible and thunderstorms were all around, they spotted a KC-10 tanker in a clear spot and picked up their gas.

Meanwhile, since the other searchers had so far had no luck, AWACS sent the two Sandys off to check out a suspected Scud hiding place, which turned out to be Bedouin tents. An hour and a half later, after reporting to AWACS, "No luck on the Scuds," they got vectors to a tanker for another refueling.

Next, they headed north to a new search area, over a hundred miles west of Baghdad. Though fatigue had started to set in, Johnson and Goff *really* wanted to find and rescue the downed pilot. As they flew deeper into Iraq, Johnson repeatedly tried to contact Slate 46 on the rescue frequency. Just as he was beginning to think he was on a wild-goose chase, he heard Jones calling him with his survival radio. The signal was weak, but still strong enough for the A-10 pilots to take a radio bearing with their direction-finding needles.

On the other hand, they had to wonder if Jones had been captured and an English-speaking Iraqi was leading them into a trap. Better to be sorry than safe, however, in this case. When guys were on the ground, you had to take risks.

As they flew deeper and deeper into bad-guy territory, the radio signal grew louder and louder, telling them they were on the right track. The original searchers had been looking too far to the south.

Now the A-10s were over the downed F-14 pilot, and it was time to hang it all out: they popped down under some clouds on the deck to eyeball Jones's actual position. The big, ugly Warthogs screaming over his hideout proved to be quite a shock to the Navy pilot, but he still had enough presence of mind to call them on the radio.

The A-10s deliberately did not orbit the site, lest they give away the location to Iraqis in the area. But Johnson did let Jones know that he had seen his location and memorized the surrounding terrain features.

Meanwhile, they had a problem. The Sandys were again nearly out of gas. It would be their third in-flight refueling of the day. As they flew away, they promised Jones they'd be back after they filled up.

No problem, the Navy pilot thought. He'd already been hiding for six hours; occasional Iraqi army trucks had passed by on a nearby road, and so far he hadn't lost his cool. Now that the A-10s had his position, rescue couldn't be far away. He knew those A-10s would not let him down.

As it happened, they almost did.

Heading south, Johnson and Goff ran into headwinds. These—and their gritty determination to find Jones—had left them too low on gas to make it back to Saudi Arabia and a tanker aircraft (for obvious reasons, tankers stayed on the Saudi side of the border). When AWACS put them in contact with a tanker, Johnson asked it to fly north to rendezvous with him; the tanker pilot refused. The rules said no tankers in Iraq, and this tanker pilot was going to follow the rules.

Now desperate, Johnson pointed out to the tanker pilot that he just might fly over to him and transfer a full load of 30mm ammunition into his KC-135. Of course, he wouldn't do such a thing—and actually he couldn't. He didn't have enough gas to fly that far south. For whatever reason—fear, or more likely conscience—the tanker pilot headed across the border and into Iraq for a rendezvous with the nearly empty A-10s. Either way, just then he became a hero to the A-10 drivers.

Though by this time Moccasin 05 (the Jolly Green Giant rescue heli-copter, flown by Captain Tom Trask) had returned to its forward oper-ating base at ArAr just south of the Iraqi border, its crew had not totally given up the search, and they were monitoring their radio when Sandy 57 made contact with Jones, and later with the tanker. While the A-10s sucked gas out of the KC-135, they launched and headed north. Soon they were joined by the two A-10s.

On the flight north, AWACS controllers vectored them around Iraqi SAM sites in their path. Before long, they were talking to Jones.

The Moccasin 05 crew were going over rescue procedures with the Navy pilot when Johnson and Goff spotted an Iraqi radio direction-finding truck racing toward the pilot's hiding place; and as Sandy's 57 and 58 turned their attention to the Iraqi truck, Moccasin 05 swooped down on the pilot, his arms waving like mad. The A-10s rolled in and strafed the Iraqis with their 30mm cannons, and, in Jones's words, "the truck vaporized." It had been close.

As Johnson pulled off the burning truck, Jones was jumping out of his hole in the desert less than a football field away and running to the wait-ing helicopter. It was a sight Johnson would never forget.

Though many people deserved praise that day, in the end it was the determination and guts of Captains Johnson and Goff that made the mission successful. Nearly nine hours after they'd climbed into them, the two exhausted pilots climbed down from their A-10s.

Months later, their country would reward Paul Johnson and Randy Goff for their efforts on what had started out as a boring day sitting combat search-and-rescue alert. Johnson received the Air Force Cross, the Air Force's second-highest medal, and Randy Goff was awarded the Distinguished Flying Cross.

The Jones rescue was difficult, but it worked. Too many CSAR missions did not come off so well. The most notable of these failures occurred on the night of January 19, when an F-15E hunting Scuds was shot down by an SA-2 missile.

THE ODYSSEY OF TOM GRIFFITH

Tom Griffith was a weapons systems officer, assigned to the 4th Tactical Fighter Wing, flying F-15Es, and first deployed in the rushed chaos of early August to Thumrait Air Base in Oman.

Still locked in his memory is the anxiety of mobility processing, when no one knew where they were being sent or what to expect when they got there. This was swiftly followed by the greater anxiety of imminent war, when he was handed a real gas mask and a real atropine injection pen (which protected against nerve gas).

In Oman, he endured the hot August days and nights, putting up tents in a dust storm, eating MREs until the kitchen tent was set up, sitting alert in a jet loaded with wall-to-wall cluster bomb units. August became September, and he endured that, too.

But when September became October, he was needed back home at Seymour Johnson AFB. So he left Thumrait and went home to train new crew members and spend Christmas with his wife and four young children. Or so he thought.

In December, when the wing was moved up to Al Kharj and a second squadron of F-15Es was deployed into the theater, Tom was at the top of the list to rejoin the unit. Later in December, the call came.

Leaving quickly, he discovered, was a hell of a lot easier than leaving slowly. In August, he just said goodbye and raced off. This time there were days to take last looks at his wife and children. This time there were hundreds of awkward moments when "we don't talk about it," until the actual leave-taking finally brought painful release.

Al Kharj—known to Americans as Al's Garage—was a desolate place. The recently erected neat and orderly tent city did not improve its charm. But when Griffith arrived, he at least had the advantage of experience. The truly new guys, fresh from warm beds, Little League baseball with their kids, and Friday-night beer call, had to endure the barbs and hazing of the old heads, who'd suffered through the desert summer and fall. But not Tom Griffith.

Then December became January, and Griffith, like every aircrew member facing his first combat sortie, had to come to grips with a question that lay heavy in his heart. It was not, *Am I going to die?* but much more terrible, *How am I going to do? Will I screw the pooch? Christ, I hope I don't screw up!*

On Tom's first mission, he and his pilot, Colonel Dave Eberly, the wing DO, hit a radio transmission tower used by the Iraqi air defense system. It wasn't pretty, but the strike went okay, and the Iraqi bullets missed them. Other F-15Es hit a nearby airfield, and he watched the seeming miracle of their escape from the waves of tracers thrown against them. Though the naysayers had predicted drastic losses, all the F-15Es came home that night.

After that the confidence swelled their hearts. "Hot shit! We did it! Everybody came back!"

Relief and confidence made everyone bolder . . . which instantly evaporated when one of the jets was lost following an attack on Basra. He was shaken again when a Wild Weasel tasked to support Griffith's second mission was unable to find the tanker. It tried to land at fog-shrouded King Khalid Military City, but ran out of fuel and ideas. The crew ejected safely.

Though the losses put a chill in the aircrews, their worst fears had still not been realized. Thus, when a rushed, all-out strike was called against the Scuds in western Iraq, Griffith took in stride the inevitable confusion that accompanied this last-minute change in the ATO, and went about the job of planning his attack while briefing with Dave Eberly.

As usual when higher headquarters threw planning changes at operational people, confusion reigned. This wasn't helped when the WSOs feverishly crammed in last-minute target and route studies, which made the crews late getting to their jets. After all, it was their *reputations* on the line. They had to find the target and put them on it.

The pilots only had to work their machines.

That is, a pilot only had to get off the runway without breaking anything, lift the gear handle, avoid hitting the KC-135 during refueling rendezvous, hang on to the boom while gas was pumped, then follow the WSO's orders and put the jet into a small piece of sky at a speed and heading that would enable the bombs to hit their mark. Once that was done, he could fly back to a tanker, and then home.

During most of the mission, the WSO had it easy. That meant he could do busywork checking out systems or helping with the tanker join-up (if the pilot gave him control of the radar). Later he'd feed the route coordinates into the navigation system, which gave the pilot steering orders in the form of a small circle on his HUD. The hard part came when he took control of the radar and searched ever-smaller pieces of landscape below. When he'd found the target area, he'd work out where the bombs must impact by making a radar picture of the area (this looked like a fuzzy black-and-white photograph), and comparing that with the materials he had studied before takeoff or with drawings or pictures he'd clipped to his kneeboard. Then he would delicately manipulate the tracking handle to place the crosshairs of his radar display directly over the spot representing the target's location.

No debate. There wasn't time. The success of the mission, the payoff for this flight into harm's way, came down to how well the WSO operated his radar, made sense out of the information displayed on his cathode ray tubes, and placed hair-thin bars that showed the pilot how to place the aircraft into that point in the sky that was the right place for releasing the bombs.

In the F-15E, the glory or failure went to the WSO, and it was pass/fail. Either you hit the target, or you didn't. That night, Tom Griffith never got to try.

Things started to go bad as Eberly and Griffith's F-15, Buick 04, was finishing with the air-to-air refueling and the flight was sitting in formation with the KC-135s, waiting for their EF-111 electronic jamming and F-4G Wild Weasel SAM attack support aircraft to arrive. But these aircraft called in miles out from the rendezvous: "We're going to be late" (again, the cost of last-minute changes to the ATO). This put the F-15 flight leader in a bind. He had to leave the tanker now if he expected to make the time over target listed in the ATO. If he was early or late, he would risk interfering with other aircraft. If he went in without the protection of the EF-111s and F-4Gs, he'd risk sending the F-15Es naked into the target. It was a tough call, but he made the best choice he could. The flight left the tanker at the appointed time, and he radioed his EF-111 and F-4G helpers to refuel and join them in the target area as soon as they could catch up.

Sometime later, Buick 04 was somewhere near the Syrian border, just seconds away from weapons release, their F-15 speeding as fast as they could push it. At over 600 miles an hour, time went quickly, especially for someone trying to build a radar picture of an ill-defined target; the tension was building. As Griffith fine-tuned his radar picture, gently moving the crosshairs fractions of an inch, the steering commands in Eberly's HUD offset ever so slightly, and Eberly smoothly brought his aircraft to the new heading. All of this had been practiced hundreds of times before—except for one never-trained-for factor: Hundreds of people on the ground, equipped with a vast array of weapons, were intent on killing them. They pursued this purpose with passionate intensity.

The F-15E's warning receiver started to chatter, then displayed the symbols that told both crew members they were being tracked by surface-to-air missile-guidance radars. Griffith tore himself away from his radar and activated the switch that fired an explosive squib on the belly of the jet. This caused thousands of chaff filaments to blossom in the air and—it was hoped—blind and confuse the radar operators on the ground.

Whoosh, whoosh. A pair of guided missiles, probably Vietnam-vintage SA-2s, streaked toward their jet and exploded below and to their left. Putting aside the attack, Griffith dispensed more chaff, and Eberly turned the jet to avoid more missiles. Suddenly there was a flash, and the jet shuddered as if it had struck a wall of water. Surprisingly, they heard no noise.

A microsecond later, a grim but bemused Tom Griffith wondered if it wouldn't have been better to wait for the EF-111 and F-4G support. A microsecond after that, he moved his right foot to a switch on the cockpit floor that would transmit to the rest of the flight the news that Buick 04 had been hit and would probably abort the attack. But to his sudden amazement, he failed to reach the switch; his feet were lifting off the floor and his ejection seat was traveling up the steel rails that held it in the cockpit. Eberly was ejecting them!

How Eberly accomplished that will probably never be known, for he had suffered a neck wound and lost consciousness. He did not wake up until he was on the ground.

Now Griffith was falling through the night sky, with no sense of up or down, only that he was cold and falling and still in his ejection seat. His mind raced through his emergency training procedures, trying to recall how to free himself from his seat and get his parachute deployed. But then, just as his mind filled with the terrible image of his mangled body in the desert, still attached to the seat, all the magic worked, and at the proper altitude, the tiny explosive charges fired according to schedule and Tom found himself floating beneath his open parachute. Now he knew where the ground was. It was the place where the angry red tracers were coming from, all arcing up toward him. Images of hundreds of bullets striking his parachute flashed across his mind, swiftly followed by the more frightening thoughts of red-hot projectiles ripping into his flesh. Just then, he involuntarily clamped his flight boots together to give some protection to his more precious parts. That lasted until he realized that the explosion of one projectile would remove everything from his navel down, so he might as well be comfortable during the ride to earth.

Always thinking, Tom dug his survival radio out of his vest and, tearing off a glove, set out to flip the switches that would let him broadcast to the others. However, before he could complete the procedure, he was distracted by a large explosion on the ground beneath him. His aircraft, he imagined. Then it hit him that unless he could maneuver his parachute, he was likely to descend into the burning wreckage, not a happy thought. Meanwhile, he discovered that his radio was useless. His cold, numb fingers could not operate the switches. As he was trying to slip it back into its pocket in his survival vest, he hit the ground like a two-hundred-pound bag of fertilizer thrown from the roof of a two-story building.

The impact twisted his left knee. Worse, he was near the fire of his burning jet, its light a beacon to the Iraqis, who would surely come looking for him. Worse still, bombs began exploding nearby, shaking the earth under his feet and filling the air overhead with deadly pieces of red-hot steel.

At that point his survival training took over, and he grabbed a small packet of essential items, called a "dash pack," from his survival kit. It contained items like a radio and water, and it was small and light enough to be easily portable if an aircrew member had to run from the spot where his parachute might mark his location to enemy soldiers. With his dash pack under his arm, his sore knees sending bolts of pain up his leg, and gallons of adrenaline pouring into his arteries, Griffith stumbled away from the blazing wreckage of his jet.

The terrain quickly became a series of gullies in the hard-packed gravel desert. As soon as he felt hidden in darkness, he sat down and took stock—survival training 101. Aside from the sore knee and pounding heart, he was in pretty good shape, except for one small fact: he was hundreds of miles inside enemy territory, on foot.

Now the guns and the bombs had quit their chorus, and it was quiet. The lights of trucks headed his way as the Iraqis made their way through the desert toward the fire of the crashed F-15E. With no time to worry about his missing front-seater, Griffith began a rapid withdrawal, trying to put as many gullies as possible between himself and the plane wreckage. A plan started to come. He'd walk to nearby Syria and turn himself in to the police or army. Then he reviewed the ATO's survival procedures. It was time for him to broadcast in the blind on his survival radio. He keyed the mike and sent a mayday call. To his surprise, he was answered by the familiar voice of Dave Eberly. The conversation that followed was comically inane:

Griffith to Eberly: "Is that you?"

Eberly to Griffith: "Yes, is that you?" (An answer probably given with the quiet confidence that there weren't many other Americans wandering about the western Iraqi desert that particular night.)

Griffith to Eberly: "Yes, it's me. Where are you?"

Eberly to Griffith: "I don't know. Where are you?"

Griffith to Eberly: "I have no idea."

Now that each knew the other was alive, they started working out how to solve the problems confronting them. They quickly discovered that they were both near a dirt road and a parallel power line and that they were close to each other: they could both see the same Iraqi truck go by.

They started toward other in the pitch-black darkness, until suddenly they walked into each other.

It was a good moment. There weren't many of them that night.

The two musketeers headed west, following a small compass Griffith dug out of a pocket of his survival vest. Later, as dawn started to gray the desert, they looked for a low spot where they could hide for the day. Once they'd found what seemed to be a suitable hideout, they settled down, and Eberly tried to raise help on his survival radio. Meanwhile, Griffith went through his pockets and culled out anything of value to the enemy. As he buried them in a shallow hole, he mused: *Will some desert-dweller, maybe two thousand years from now, dig up my radio frequency card, authenticator code tables, and target drawing, and draw scholarly conclusions about mankind's follies centuries ago?*

By then, the sun was high enough to tell them something about their surroundings, and much to their alarm, they found they'd been trying to hide in a shallow depression on some sort of rock-strewn farmer's field. "Where will we hide?" they asked themselves. "And now it's getting light." But nearby, a hill rose up sharply, maybe three hundred feet, with large rocks on its crest, big enough for two men to hide behind.

Fortunately, fog came with the rising sun, and Eberly and Griffith were able to creep up to the crest and hide among the boulders.

As far as they could tell, the desert was peaceful. No Iraqi army patrols were beating the bushes trying to capture them. What's more, the hill provided a good line of sight to look for rescue aircraft and for radio. Here would be a good place to wait for rescue, they decided.

Most of the rest of the day was divided between attempts at sleep and radio calls for help. Two obsessions dominated their minds: *Gee, I hope we get out of here.* And *I wonder when they are going to come and rescue us?*

★ Efforts in that direction were under way . . . but there was no rush.

Though other aircraft in the area had reported the shoot-down and (from "initial voice contact") likely ejection of Eberly and Griffith, the CSAR cell in the TACC was stymied until they had received confirmation that the two airmen were alive and their exact location was known—the launch criteria the SOF commander had established for his rescue assets.

In point of fact, the SOF criteria were not always enforced. A day earlier, a Rafha-based MH-53 had conducted an unsuccessful search for a downed F-16 pilot in southern Iraq. And two days after the Griffith and Eberly shoot-down, Captain Trask and his MH-53 had joined in the search for Lieutenant Devon Jones without certain knowledge of the F-14 pilot's location or condition.

So why did the search for the F-15E crew not start immediately? Possibly because their condition and location had not been determined, and possibly because the enemy defenses in this corner of Iraq were considered too severe to risk a rescue attempt. In all fairness, enemy defenses there *were* heavy. This part of Iraq was known as "Sam's Town," after a country-and-western casino in Las Vegas, so named because of the aggressive SAM sites in the area. Yet, when later in the war numerous Special Operations Scud-hunting teams were flown into western Iraq, non-SOF airmen concluded that the rescue assets they relied on were more interested in supporting Special Operations missions than saving their lives.

Whatever the reason, during the following days, three CSAR sorties were flown—to no avail. They went south of Griffith and Eberly. After that, the two men were on their own.

★ After they'd settled in on top of the hill, Griffith used a piece of Eberly's parachute to clean and bandage his pilot's neck wound. Later, they could hear the seemingly endless thunder of bombs dropped by B-52s on a target far to the south. Eberly urgently tried to reach the big bombers with his radio, but to no avail. After nightfall, they managed to contact an F-15C fighter patrolling overhead, who disappeared to the south without recontacting them. This was standard procedure. Because of the Iraqi direction-finding trucks, lengthy conversations were avoided. Shortly thereafter, the F-15C pilot relayed their general location to AWACS on secure (encrypted) radio.

After that, it was another day of waiting. Yet they knew they couldn't stay where they were much longer. Though they could survive for a while without food, they were running short of water, and would have to move before they became too dehydrated to travel. They considered several plans—like stealing an Iraqi car, or highjacking one at gunpoint, and driving into Syria—but none seemed really workable.

Later, they listened on their survival radio to the pickup of Devon Jones. This was exciting—and painful—to hear.

They kept asking themselves questions: "Is this place too hot for the rescue birds? Where are we going to find water? How long will it take to walk to Syria?" And the most dreaded of all: "Does anyone know we are here?"

Late in the afternoon of the second day, they ripped up the remainder of Eberly's parachute and fashioned what might pass from a distance as Bedouin robes and headdresses. After sunset, they started walking toward Syria.

Soon, the lights of two towns appeared in the distance. From where they stood, they guessed that one was in Iraq and the other in Syria.

Meanwhile, though they tried to walk carefully in the inky darkness, they found themselves stumbling inside a circle of tents. They were in the middle of a Bedouin encampment, where maybe a dozen medium-size but very hostile dogs were doing their best to sound the alarm. For some reason, they failed to wake their Arab masters (no one appeared, or even called out), but they succeeded in thoroughly frightening Griffith and Eberly, both of whom grabbed their 9mm side arms thinking they might somehow shoot one of the beasts quietly and scare off the others. Then it came to them that the dogs seemed all snarl and bark, and the two pilgrims wandered off into the safety of the night.

After walking for several hours, the pair were crossing one of the many dirt roads that paralleled the border, when a truck roared up out of the night. Eberly and Griffith dropped to the ground, but on the flat featureless surface of the desert, they were still exposed. As it neared them, the truck slowed, but the driver either did not see them or was alone and in no mood to be a hero for Saddam. The truck resumed its speed and drove off.

Shortly, Tom raised another F-15 combat air patrol aircraft on his radio. Easily convinced that they were the crew of Buick 04, the fighter, call sign Mobile 41, did not ask them to authenticate. He told them to wait while he flew south, but promised to be back shortly. He never returned. When it hit them that he wasn't coming back, their frustrations rose to an all-time high and their spirits dropped to an all-time low.

About two in the morning, they made out the dim outline of a building ahead of them. It was not far away, and there were no lights. No one appeared to be around. When Eberly, now desperately in need of water, announced that he was going to see if he could find something to drink, Griffith cautioned against it. He'd remembered a survival training dictum about avoiding buildings. Besides, he explained, they must be close to Syria. In fact, maybe they *were* in Syria and just needed to go a little farther to be sure.

But Eberly's thirst proved too desperate for such cautious considerations, and he approached the building.* Since Griffith didn't want to

---

*Eberly became dangerously dehydrated during the escape and evasion, and later during his capture (when Iraqi doctors didn't understand his condition, much less how to treat it). After his return, his blood chemistry was seriously out of balance (a hospital stay cured it).

risk separation in the dark, he followed close behind. Suddenly, gunfire erupted from the top of the building. Someone had obviously been on guard—and doing a good job at it. Then maybe ten other troops came rushing out of the building, all firing wildly in the air or else in the general direction of the two airmen. If they were trying to scare the two Americans, they did an excellent job.

Both raised their hands and shouted, "Don't shoot! We are friends!" *Who knows?* they thought. *These guys might be Syrian.*

That hope was dashed when they were hustled inside the building and into a small room with a prominent picture of Saddam Hussein on the wall. This was a bad moment for the two American airmen.

The room was packed. In addition to the Americans, there was a flock of seventeen-year-old Iraqi privates, commanded by an Iraqi second lieutenant who appeared to be perhaps twenty-one. Though the Iraqi troops were greatly aroused by their find, they made no move to harm their captives, who, by this time, had concluded they'd run into an Iraqi border patrol guard post about a mile short of their destination. (After the war, Tom Griffith learned that it was fortunate they hadn't reached the border area. It had been mined.)

After a time, the Iraqis handcuffed the Americans, loaded them into a white Toyota pickup, and delivered them to a larger fort nearby, where they were met by a first lieutenant. Like the border troops, he and his soldiers showed no hatred and treated the two Americans in a civilized manner. Though they did their best to ask questions, they had little success, as the Iraqis spoke no English and the F-15 crew spoke no Arabic.

The Iraqis then delivered Griffith and Eberly to a larger office, where they were met by an Iraqi captain. Also present were a group of officers, one of whom spoke broken English. "I am a doctor," he explained, then examined Eberly's neck wound.

After conducting an inventory of the Americans' survival equipment (it had been taken from them when they were captured) and writing down their names, the Iraqis made some halfhearted attempts at interrogation. Questions like "How far and how fast can your aircraft fly?" brought truthful but useless answers, like "Well, it depends."

By 4:00 A.M., Griffith and Eberly had been fed and given water. Then they were handcuffed again and placed facedown on the back of a flatbed truck, which carried them to the outskirts of a nearby town. There they stopped at a modest house surrounded by a brick wall, the home of a general, their guards explained. An Iraqi captain and two guards led them past the general's white 1975 Chevy Impala and inside. Soon the three Iraqis showed them into the general's office, seated them on a sofa, then waited with them for the general. A few minutes later, the general, in his bathrobe, greeted them. Like their previous captors, he treated them civilly; when they asked if they could get some sleep, he had them taken to a room with two cots. There they were allowed to rest for the next four or five hours.

Now that they were alone, they took the opportunity to put a story together for serious interrogations. In order to keep the Iraqis from probing the defensive strengths and weaknesses of the F-15E, they decided to deny they'd been shot down; it would be easy to claim an electrical fire was the culprit. In any case, they were far from certain about what had actually bagged them (though it was likely a surface-to-air missile).

As they waited in the general's home, they were visited by a number of curious and not unfriendly guards. One who was especially friendly had studied petroleum engineering and spoke good English. "This is a terrible war," he confided earnestly. "Don't you agree?" And, "What do you think is going to happen? Something bad, no?"

But then a heavyset guard appeared, with a far more hostile attitude. "We are going to ask you a lot of questions," he announced, "and you must cooperate," implying by his tone serious penalties for noncooperation. As he warmed to his task, his comments grew more and more argumentative: "Why did you start the war?" Or, "You are all going to perish." Or, "You are all helping Israel."

Later that day, they were handcuffed and blindfolded, led outside, and loaded into the backseat of a six-passenger pickup truck. When the truck started up, their blindfolds were removed and they were taken into town. There the streets were lined with civilians chanting Arabic curses. They both bore up well under this (*After all,* they thought, *words can't hurt us, especially if the only ones we can understand are "Saddam! Saddam!"*), until a young man hurled a rock through the truck window. Then it became *Oh shit, I'm scared! Get us out of here, Lord!*

Somehow that demonstration ended without serious consequences, and they were taken back to the general's house for phase one of their interrogation.

In the beginning, the questions were simple: "Are you able to evade a missile?" And they answered in kind, "Well, that depends."

But the easy part of their captivity soon proved to be over. They were cuffed, blindfolded, loaded back into a truck, and driven off. The setting sun behind them told them they were headed east, toward Baghdad. They traveled all night, were handed off from one military unit to another. Near morning, Tom Griffith was able to sneak a peek: a road announced in English, "Baghdad 20 km."

When they reached their first place of confinement in the capital (where it was, they never learned), they were split up. From then on, the interrogation was conducted by professionals.

The next days were not pleasant. Though the questioners were well-versed in technical details—"What was the dispense rate you had set in your ALE-40 chaff dispenser?"—they hadn't the faintest notion of how American culture worked or how Americans looked at life. One day, the interrogator sat down and announced smugly that George Bush had died, expecting Griffith to break down in tears. Instead, he feigned anguish: "Oh, Christ, that means Dan Quayle is president!"

As the days passed, Griffith was moved from cell to cell and from jail to jail. He quickly lost track of where he was and where he'd been, until one day he was moved to Baath Party headquarters and confined in the cell next to CBS News reporter Bob Simon, who had been picked up on the Iraqi side of the lines, where he'd been trying to scoop the press pool. This had not been a smart place to get caught, since the Iraqis were now convinced that he was a spy and were preparing to execute him—a fact that did not thrill Tom Griffith. Could it mean he was on "death row"?

Meanwhile, by February 25 the Black Hole had picked the last targets in Baghdad, and the Baath Party headquarters became one of the few that were acceptable to Schwarzkopf after the Al-Firdus bunker tragedy. During this strike, a bomb fell short of its aim point and blew in the walls of the prisoners' cells.

"Oh Christ, I'm going to die in prison!" Griffith cried out to himself, certain that the bombs would set the building on fire.

Three other bombs struck farther away, on the other end of the building, destroying nearby cells (which, fortunately, were empty). Doors were also blown open, temporarily freeing a few POWs, who immediately—and unsuccessfully—went combing the rubble for cell keys that would let them free the others.

Since the building was now a total loss, the inmates were rounded up and sent to military facilities, where they were housed in groups instead of single cells. Tom Griffith was locked up with Jeff "Sly" Fox, who had been captured on February 18.

"How's the ground war going?" Griffith asked.

"It hasn't started yet," Fox answered.

"Ohhhhhh!" Griffith groaned, with a despairing look.

"Hey," Fox replied, "don't worry. The air war is going great. It's not going to be much longer until we get out of here!"

Welcome words indeed. Griffith had by now lost twenty-five pounds. All the old heads in prison were suffering from dysentery, and there was no way to keep clean.

Two days later, it was strangely quiet outside the cells. They could hear no bombers flying overhead. No AAA guns were popping off at F-117s. At first, the POWs thought this was because of weather aborts; but in the morning, the blue sky and warm sunshine made it clear that the bombing had stopped for some other reason. Each POW prayed it was for the right reason: that the war was over.

Very shortly after that, the prisoners were given soap and wash water, there was more and better food, and a barber came around to give them a shave—an Iraqi shave, dry with a rusty razor. (*No wonder so many Iraqis wear beards,* Tom Griffith told himself.)

"I think you will be going home soon," an Iraqi officer announced on the fourth of March.

Is this a trick to get our hopes up? Griffith wondered.

But later that day, a bus arrived for Griffith and his fellow prisoners— two special forces troopers, the Army drivers, Specialists Melissa Rathburn-Healy and David Locket, who'd been captured during the battle of Al-Khafji, and two other aircrews. Soon afterward, a representative of the International Red Cross conducted them to the Nova Hotel, where the international press was waiting. After politely thanking them for bringing the captives to safety, the Red Cross representative firmly sent the Iraqis packing (thereby making himself an instant hero in the eyes of the now-former POWs), and the Americans were asked to identify by name any others in captivity (the sins of Vietnam were not going to be repeated).

Then for Tom Griffith it was a bus trip to Jordan, a flight to Oman, and the hospital ship *Mercy* off the coast of Bahrain. Dave Eberly went from Baghdad to Riyadh, and then to the *Mercy* for a longer stay.

On the *Mercy,* Griffith's first priority was a phone call to his wife in North Carolina. Though he woke her up at 4:00 A.M., she didn't seem to mind. Tom was safe and coming home!

────────

★ Meanwhile, the failure to rescue Eberly and Griffith did not improve the already strained relations between aircrews and the Special Operations force units tasked to rescue them. The memory still burned after the war, as is evident from this comment about the Griffith and Eberly tale from a 4th Wing F-15E pilot: "Our DO and his backseater were on the ground for three and one-half days in western Iraq. Nobody'd go in and pick them up, and they eventually became prisoners of war. Before the war, the Special Operations guys came down to talk to us. 'No sweat,' they said, 'we'll come get you anywhere you are.' That, from my perspective, was a big lie. After my guys were on the ground for three and one-half days, and they didn't go pick them up, we basically decided that if anybody went down, they were on their own. Nobody was going to come and get you."

Chuck Horner concludes:

The combat search-and-rescue mission involves lots of heartbreaking decisions. In Vietnam, we tried so hard to rescue all downed pilots that on some occasions we lost more aircraft and aircrews than were saved. CSAR is not a no-risk situation. It requires rescue crews that take risks that are far beyond those normally expected in combat operations. Sometimes you have bad luck, as was the case when a U.S. Army helicopter carrying Major (Dr.) Rhonda Cornum was shot down during an attempted battlefield rescue of a downed A-10 pilot, killing three crew members and leading to the capture of the survivors. Sometimes you have good luck, as was the case with Devon Jones.

The good luck, I hardly have to say, is not the product of luck. It comes from trained aircrews keeping their cool and evading capture. And it takes commanders who are hard-hearted enough to leave a downed airman to the mercies of the enemy when it is likely that more men and women will be killed or captured.

In Desert Storm, there was a failure to fully coordinate these aspects of the CSAR mission. While there were at times brilliant rescues, the aircrews were far from confident in the system. The next Chuck Horner to fight an air war had better pay close attention to the way he (or she) organizes and controls the employment of his or her combat search-and-rescue efforts.

11

PUNCH AND COUNTERPUNCH

At this point, the focus began to shift from pure air superiority, but it is important to repeat this fundamental: airpower is not discrete, it flows. While it is useful to talk about the discrete elements of airpower (such as gaining control of the air, battlefield interdiction, or preparing the battlefield—that is, limiting the enemy's ability to harm friendly forces), such talk has limits. One element does not stop and another one start. There may be greater or lesser intensity directed toward one or the other of them, but during any slice of time, all will be working.

In Desert Storm, once air superiority was assured, greater attention was given to battlefield interdiction and to preparing the battlefield—but all the while, air superiority was never ignored.

★ Battlefield interdiction—isolating the battlefield—is a classic role of airpower, and was a natural goal for General Schwarzkopf to set for Chuck Horner.

In the case of Desert Storm, battlefield interdiction meant preventing the resupply of Iraqi forces in occupied Kuwait and southern Iraq. If the enemy was denied access to resupplies of food, water, gasoline, ammunition, and medical supplies, in time he would be rendered helpless. The length of time this form of interdiction warfare took to become effective was the big question.

Answering it depended on the answers to many other questions. How well is the enemy supplied when combat begins? What is the tempo of combat and the demands that tempo will make on his store of supplies? How effective is aerial interdiction on resupply throughput? And so on. During the war in Vietnam, efforts to isolate the Vietcong and the North Vietnamese regular army in South Vietnam failed, both because of the inefficient use of airpower and because of the crude, yet determined, supply system of North Vietnamese forces.

That failure was not repeated in the Gulf conflict.

In order to attain classic battlefield interdiction, General Schwarzkopf expected Chuck Horner to bomb the bridges on the roads and railroads running from Baghdad to Basra and on to Kuwait City. Trucks and military convoys (and indeed any likely vehicles) were to be targeted by fighter-bombers patrolling the desert south of the Iraqi capital. Iraqi aircraft would not be allowed to fly; and whenever they attempted to, they would be discovered by AWACS radar and immediately attacked by Coalition fighter pilots.

However, because of the limitations of classic battlefield interdiction, American planners began to look at new—and potentially quicker—ways to isolate the battlefield. They came to ask: "Can we paralyze the enemy by isolating his fielded forces from their sources of information and from their command and control?" In other words, "Can we practice information warfare against the Iraqi army of occupation?"

In the Iraqi dictatorship, with its fears, suspicions, and terrors, independence of thought or action is instantly uprooted and punished. A military commander who shows independence, no matter how successful, becomes a threat to Saddam Hussein and his few close advisers. Success itself is a threat, since it encourages independence and popularity. Thus, battle plans are scripted with the oversight and approval of Saddam, and deviation from the script is not allowed.

This raised a question in the minds of the air planners: "What if we can isolate the Iraqi ground forces from their supreme leader in Baghdad? Would they become paralyzed? Would the deployed forces in the field freeze in place, awaiting capture, rather than maneuver about the battlefield and oppose Coalition liberation forces?"

Because modern military command and control is accomplished primarily via electronic media—telephones, radios, and computer networks, connected by satellite, microwave nets, telephone lines, and high-data-rate fiber-optic cables—Horner's planners targeted the connecting links. Thus, Coalition bombers attacked telephone exchange buildings, satellite ground stations, bridges carrying fiber-optic and wire bundles, and cables buried in the desert. Even had there been ASAT missiles available, individual satellites would not have been targeted, since both sides in the conflict used the same satellites.

To stop the radio and television broadcasts that connected Saddam with his army and his people, transmission towers were bombed, but this effort was only partially successful. The problem was in stopping low-powered radio broadcasts emanating from more or less primitive stations scattered throughout the countryside.

Interestingly, the Iraqis themselves put very tight limits on their own radio transmissions, in the apparent belief that the Americans would either listen in on them or target the radio emitter locations. Though this successfully denied intelligence to the Coalition, it also put a chokehold on command and control of their deployed forces.

A telling consequence of the information war (as reported after the war by Iraqi POWs) proved to be the inability of Iraqi headquarters in Baghdad to provide intelligence to the Iraqi Army leadership in the field about Coalition ground force deployments and maneuvers.

It is hard to tell whether this incapacity was a Coalition success or an Iraqi failure. . . . A similar answer, it turns out, has to be given to the larger question: How successful was the air campaign in denying Iraqi command and control of their forces? There's just no way to know for sure.

For starters, no one has any idea how much Saddam even *conferred* with his generals, yet he was certainly able to convey to his Third Corps commander enough command information to initiate the invasion of Saudi Arabia in late January 1991 (the Battle of Khafji). Even so, the Coalition information and command-and-control advantage (thanks in large measure to the targeting of airpower by the Joint STARS aircraft) allowed a single brigade under the command of Khaled Bin Sultan to rout three Iraqi divisions.

The Iraqi failure at Al-Khafji raises larger questions for Chuck Horner:

> *Did we really want Saddam isolated from the battle? Given his lack of military experience, poor judgment, and micromanaging leadership style, perhaps we should have facilitated his presence on the battlefield in every way possible. Of course, that's not the American way. We like to see others the way we look at ourselves, so cutting Saddam off from his forces in the field seemed the proper thing to do.*
>
> *But this was not our worst mistake. That mistake was never*

asking ourselves "So what?" That is, we had no very good ideas about what to do after we'd succeeded in cutting Saddam off from his forces in the field. Therefore, we continued to plan and conduct a ground campaign that did not fully exploit the success we'd achieved in denying the enemy the capacity to command his forces.

Thus, our fear of Iraqi reconnaissance aircraft caused us to delay moving the U.S. corps into their jump-off positions for the ground war until after the air war began. This caution proved unnecessary, and ignoring it could have speeded up our attack and made the war more efficient. Far more telling, however: when the battle for Al-Khafji made it apparent how thoroughly airpower could destroy Iraqi forces in the attack, why didn't the Coalition leaders alter their ground campaign plans? And, for that matter, why didn't the Iraqis alter their strategy after their ground forces proved to be helpless in the face of the aerial onslaught?

Though I cannot answer for the Coalition leadership, the Iraqis in February did in fact alter their strategy: they sought to end the war, offering to withdraw from Kuwait and renounce their claims to sovereignty there. (Their offer, of course, proved to be too little and too late.)

Meanwhile, the campaign to prevent the resupply of logistics to the battlefield proved to be very effective. The Iraqi Army had serious problems providing units in the field with sufficient food and water. On the other hand, efforts to deny resupply of ammunition had little or no impact, as the defeated army surrendered before expending large amounts of ammunition. The joke was, "Come to Kuwait if you want to buy an AK-47. They are like new, shot once, and dropped once." In this war, we stopped ammunition from reaching the soldiers, but they had all they needed. After enduring six weeks of aerial bombardment, their strongest motive was surrender, not dying for Saddam.

In other words, perhaps our information-warfare attacks proved far more effective than Coalition leaders realized. And perhaps the Iraqi Army failed to maneuver in the face of our ground onslaught because our campaign to deny them intelligence had a far greater impact than we comprehended at the time. Certainly, despite our apparent success with the more traditional means to isolate the battlefield, we need to study this new form of warfare

in far more detail to determine which works best—the classical or
the new method of interdiction . . . or both together.

Isolating the battlefield, as General Schwarzkopf conceived it, had
one other—perhaps surprising—goal. Not only did he intend to prevent
food, ammunition, water, communications, or reinforcements from
reaching the enemy; he also intended to prevent the Iraqi army occupying Kuwait from getting out. Or, in the words of Colin Powell, "We are
going to cut off the head of the snake, and then we are going to kill it."

On the whole, airpower succeeded in that aim . . . at least in the open
country, where roads and bridges were exposed. Airpower so successfully
dropped the bridges across the rivers of southern Iraq that, years after the
war, it was difficult to travel by car to the countryside. Where airpower
did not succeed was in preventing the Iraqis from hiding many of their
tanks and armored personnel carriers in the cities of southern Iraq. The
only way to hit these from the air would have exposed the populations
of the cities to widespread aerial attacks, and the Americans and their
Coalition partners were not willing to do that. Attacking the cities from
the ground was, of course, another option, but few Coalition leaders
were eager to take that step when their stated goal was to eject the Iraqis
from Kuwait.

KILLING TANKS AND ARTILLERY

From one point of view, battlefield interdiction is an accessory to battlefield preparation. Putting a wall between an enemy and his sources of sus-
tenance and information obviously seriously restricts his ability to inflict
harm on friendly ground forces. Though a number of other elements
also fall under the overall rubric of preparing the battlefield, only one of
these truly mattered to General Schwarzkopf: "Kill the tanks and artillery." His reasons for this were simple, and doctrinally correct: tanks
and artillery were the Iraqis' likely means to inflict harm on friendly
ground forces.

It was for this reason that plans called for half of the enemy tanks and
artillery pieces to be destroyed by airpower before Coalition soldiers and
marines crossed into Kuwait and Iraq. From the opening moments of the
war, the Air Tasking Order called for strikes against the Iraqi Army in the
KTO.

In the west, in front of VIIth Corps, the killing effort was more or less equally divided between tanks and artillery, with perhaps a slight tilt in the direction of the modern T-72 tanks of the Republican Guard. In the east, on the other hand, Walt Boomer wanted emphasis placed on Iraqi artillery. Once the ground war started, he believed he could handle the tanks he would be facing (which were for the most part obsolete), but the artillery would cause problems, especially when he was passing his force through the extensive minefields that lay ahead of him.

Despite the priority of this mission in the mind of the CINC, killing Iraqi tanks and artillery got off to a slow start. In the early moments of the war, when most aircraft were directed to gaining control of the air, only a few sorties were available for tasking against KTO-based targets, and bad weather made it difficult for KTO-bound pilots to find Iraqi tanks and artillery without unnecessarily exposing their aircraft to enemy AAA and shoulder-fired SAMS. Worse, pilots had difficulty hitting their targets when they found them, since they were not used to initiating attacks at 10,000 feet or above. At those altitudes, strong winds often made a pilot's roll-in unpredictable; it was a struggle to place his aircraft at the right position and speed for the weapons release.

> *Combat was proving a far cry from the shine-your-ass gunnery meets we had held in the United States, where the pilots were not being shot at, where they had been briefed on the winds affecting their bombing passes, where they were flying on familiar training ranges against familiar targets, and where they could press their attacks so close to the target that there was little opportunity for a bent fin or maladjusted release rack to make a bomb errant. In the meets, you expected the bombs to go inside the open turrets of the tanks; in Iraq you could hardly see where the tanks might be on the desert floor below.*

Worst of all, after battling the weather, dodging enemy AAA fire, and straining to find their targets, attacking aircrews were often sent to the wrong place. Because target coordinates were derived from overhead photography that was hours and days old by the time it was received in Riyadh, all too often planes were sent out to kill tanks and artillery in locations the enemy had long since left. Though there were several efforts to speed the information flow, none of these really worked.

The solution, as we've already seen, was Killer Scouts—F-16s orbiting thirty-by-thirty-mile sectors of the battlefield and searching for dug-in tanks and artillery. When they found them, they'd direct the oncoming streams of fighter-bombers to their targets.

★ A second addition to tank- and artillery-killing efficiency occurred in late January. By then, control of the air had been assured and the fixed targets in Iraq had been (for the most part) hit, thus allowing more and more F-111F and F-15E* sorties to be tasked against Iraqi Army targets. The tank plinking tactics developed in the Night Camel exercises were now put to the test in the real world. The results were remarkable. On February 11, aircrews claimed 96 armored vehicles—tanks, APCs and artillery; 22 of these were killed by "plinkers." On the twelfth, film showed 155 killed; of these 93 were plinked by laser-guided 500-pound bombs. On the fourteenth, 214 were killed, and of these, 129 were "plinked." The totals grew daily (except for those days when bad weather shrouded the battlefield).

Dollar for dollar, this was the way to kill tanks. If a single F-111F carried eight 500-pound laser-guided bombs at $3,000 each, then for less than $50,000 (which included most of the other costs of a sortie) eight tanks could be destroyed. In the U.S. Army, each tank costs in the neighborhood of $1,000,000. The Russian tanks used by the Iraqi Army cost about half that. So less than $50,000 worth of air offense killed over one hundred times as much ground offense.

COUNTERPUNCH

Not much has been said in favor of Saddam Hussein as a strategist, yet in fact his original strategy for the Gulf War was simple yet brilliant—at least on the face of it. The Iraqi dictator had paid close attention to the lessons of Vietnam. If the United States can lose a war once, he reasoned, they can lose a war twice, and he nominated Iraq for the honor of inflicting that loss. "What led to the defeat?" he asked himself. Casualties on the battlefield produced discontent on the home front. Battlefield car-

---

*Because of the limited number of laser pods, only a few F-15Es were available for tank plinking. The targeting pods were brand new, and not all of them had been delivered, so some of the F-15Es dropped bombs on targets that the leader had designated with his pod.

nage translated into television images that so horrified the folks back home that the President of the United States was driven from office, and the Americans left the field of battle undefeated, yet beaten.

With all that in mind, Saddam planned for enduring a short air campaign and a fierce land battle. His troops constructed formidable defensive positions, with minefields, fire trenches, and presurveyed fields of fire for his artillery. When the war came to Kuwait and southern Iraq, perhaps his poorly trained infantry divisions would die in staggering numbers; but in doing so, they would inflict thousands of casualties and deaths on the Americans. Once the Coalition forces had been weakened, they could then be defeated or brutalized by his heavy armor and Republican Guard divisions. And even if all these plans failed and he did not win on the battlefield, the television coverage of the bloodshed would ensure his victory in the streets of Chicago, New York, Los Angeles, and Washington.

Unfortunately for Saddam's brilliant strategy, things didn't work out the way he planned.

The war started and the air came, but the air did not cease (as Saddam said it would), and the ground forces failed to take the bait. Unexpectedly, the Iraqi army was being destroyed from the air. They were totally naked to Chuck Horner's armada and had no clue about how to fight back.

Saddam had to do something to regain the initiative and resurrect his failing strategy. Otherwise his defeat would be absolute, and his regime might be lost.

★ The first such attempt occurred during the mad rush of Iraqi jets to sanctuary in Iran toward the end of January.

One day, enemy fighters took to the air out of an airfield in eastern Iraq, and AWACS controllers vectored nearby USAF F-15s in CAP orbit toward the fleeing Iraqis. Nothing unusual. But as the air-to-air jets screamed north, a pair of bomb-laden Iraqi Mirage aircraft took off and headed south. Though the AWACS crew spotted this new threat, they could not recall the F-15s, who had their hands full chasing their prey to the north.

Next in line were two F-14s at a CAP point in the northern part of the Arabian Gulf. Because the F-14s were controlled by a Navy Aegis cruiser that would not release them to AWACS (possibly because the Aegis controller feared leaving the Navy naked to the Iraqi bombers that were headed in their general direction), the AWACS controller was unable to vector these interceptors onto the Mirages.

Meanwhile, the Mirages were now flying down the coast of Saudi Arabia, approaching the huge oil refinery south of Dhahran. Saddam surely hoped that by bombing the oil fields, he would bring pain to Saudi Arabia, the same way Coalition air was bringing pain to him. For example, the pumping stations in the refineries have huge one-of-a-kind valves that would take years to obtain. If the Mirages had been able to hit the maze of pipes in the refinery, they could have put the refinery out of action for a very long time.

Unfortunately for the Iraqis, the airborne shield protecting the Saudis was both thicker and tougher than they'd imagined. Waiting next in line to shoot them down were two Royal Saudi Air Force F-15s, USMC Hawk antiaircraft missile sites, Royal Saudi Air Defense Hawk missile sites, and U.S. Army Patriot missile sites. All of them were closely following AWACS data, and waiting for orders to engage the bandits.

The first of these was Captain Shamrani, the RSAF flight leader. Shamrani took a single vector from the AWACS controller, selected afterburner, and threw his jet into a hard, descending right-hand turn. This screaming dive ended in a roll-out over the water just off the coast. Now headed south, he quickly spotted the Iraqi Mirages racing desperately toward their target. Then training took over, and he locked onto the Iraqi wingman, selected the middle position on his weapons switch, and listened to the warbling tone of his AIM-9L heat-seeking missile, which told him that the IR seeker in the missile had seen the target and was locked on. In scarcely a second, he identified the Mirage to AWACS and received permission to fire. His voice was excited but clear when he sent "Fox Two, kill" over the radio.

After easily avoiding the Mirage blowing up ahead of him, Shamrani rolled his jet sharply to the right to line up on the Iraqi leader.

Seemingly unaware of his wingman's demise or of the deadly threat behind him, the Iraqi leader drove on toward his target. This time there was no need to identify the target or request clearance to fire. Once he had his missile tone, Shamrani pressed the red button on top of his control stick and hit the toggle switch on the throttle to tell his wingman, AWACS, and anyone else listening in, "Fox Two, kill."

Scratch one Iraqi hope.

But they were not finished yet. Far from it.

Saddam's most impressive attempt to regain the initiative and make his strategy work occurred late in January 1991, when he invaded Saudi Arabia.

His thinking was this: Air was killing him; and Coalition ground forces were surprisingly reluctant to impale themselves on his defenses. So, he thought, *I'll bring the battle to them. If I invade Saudi Arabia, the Coalition will have to counterattack. If that jump-starts the ground war, and the Americans rush into my defenses, then I "win"* . . . insofar as American soldiers would die in great numbers. (It should be noted that at that point Gary Luck's deception operation had lots of radio traffic coming out of an area just south of Al-Khafji, leaving the Iraqis under the impression that the XVIIIth Airborne Corps was poised to attack from there. In fact, the corps was already in transit west to their actual attack locations.) *If my invasion succeeds,* Saddam continued, *then I "win," because I can attack into the Egyptians and Syrians near KKMC. That should inflict chaos on some of the Americans' Arab lackeys. And who knows where that will lead?*

The downside for Saddam was to continue to be destroyed from the air and certain defeat. His next decision was a no-brainer.

★ As a side note: because Saddam's hopes for his invasion of Saudi Arabia were so resoundingly dashed, several commentators have imagined that the Iraqis could not have been *really* serious about it—that, in other words, the invasion was not an invasion but a "probe."

For their "probe," they used three divisions, one armor and two mechanized infantry, including their 5th Mechanized division, one of their finest armor units (it was considered just below the Republican Guard).* Though exact numbers are not available, in all probability these three divisions contained something in the neighborhood of 20,000 troops (and perhaps as many as 40,000), a sizable force.

Meanwhile, Saddam himself thought the probe—or invasion—was of no small importance. After learning that his troops had entered the town, he announced that the attack was "the beginning and omen of the thundering storm that will blow on the Arabian Desert."

Chuck Horner will take up the story from here.

---

*It was almost entirely destroyed; only 20 percent made it back.

AL-KHAFJI

The town of Al-Khafji lies on the coast of the Arabian Gulf in the eastern province of Saudi Arabia, approximately ten kilometers south of the Kuwaiti border on the highway connecting Dhahran and Kuwait City. With no more than ten to fifteen thousand inhabitants, it can't be called big; nor does it have any real reason for existence other than as home for civil administration and a place to buy supplies. In this respect, it is not unlike many small rural towns in our own desert Southwest. On the north side of town, there is a modest desalinization plant. On the south is a modest oil-storage area. If you want a *real* oil-storage area, fly over Ras Turnira south of Al-Khafji, where you can see hundreds of giant oil-storage tanks. All in all, this little desert outpost has nothing very spectacular to offer—other than that the most important ground battle of the Gulf War was fought there.

Though the battle of Al-Khafji started in the late afternoon of 29 January 1991 and ended midday on the thirty-first, the lead-up to the battle started several months earlier.

Late one night in early August, Prince Khaled, John Yeosock, and I were having a war council. It had been a terrible day of rumors and fears—twenty-seven Iraqi divisions were poised on the border, and we had no means to stop them. Our discussion involved strategies for using the 82d Airborne Division, the Saudi National Guard, and airpower to stem the Iraqi attack, should it occur. During the meeting, Khaled kept making the point that his orders from the King were to make certain that no part—not one inch—of Saudi soil would fall to the invader. That included the town of Al-Khafji.

Unfortunately, not only was the town well within the range of Iraqi artillery, but we did not have the means to prevent its capture. Fortunately, Khaled sensibly realized that the town was a liability; and it was agreed that it should be evacuated. In that way, we would be able to create the free-fire zone that would allow us to attack the Iraqi invaders with air and artillery without the extensive coordination needed to protect friendly civilians and military. It was a tough decision, for Khaled, in effect, had to reject the guidance he had received.

He did the right thing, and from that time on, Al-Khafji became little more than a ghost town.

Not totally, however.

The town was located in the area of responsibility of the commander of the Eastern Area Command, Major General Sultan Sultan Adi al-Mutairi. After the evacuation, General Sultan placed screening forces near the town, as well as a small troop in the town itself, to protect property until the crisis was over. He also had a significant force approximately fifty kilometers south of Al-Khafji.

Most of Sultan's forces were Royal Saudi Land Force mechanized infantry and Saudi National Guard mechanized forces. Also under his command were mechanized forces from Qatar, and infantry from Oman, the United Arab Republic, Kuwait, Morocco, and Senegal. Rounding out this force was a sizable force of Saudi marines.

To the west of Sultan was the area of responsibility of Walt Boomer's United States Marine Corps—two divisions, augmented by a division of British armor (later replaced by the U.S. Army Tiger Brigade).

Very significantly for what was to come later, in November Boomer had concluded that he could not support offensive operations into Kuwait with the logistics setup created for the defense of Saudi Arabia (though Walt Boomer is a genius, he has to be a little crazy). At any rate, he built his logistics stockpiles just south of the Kuwaiti border, *north* of his own defenses. In effect, he took a big risk on the supposition that we would be ordered to attack into Kuwait after the first of the year, and the now heavily dug-in Iraqis would not be coming south into Saudi Arabia. He was half right.

★ To fully understand the Battle of Khafji, we need to understand that it was not a single battle but four. Let me explain:

Battle One was the battle for the town itself—the fight the world watched on CNN.

Battle Two was the skillful and desperate struggle by the U.S. Marines to protect their naked storage depots out in the desert. (As it happened, the Iraqis did not know they were there. If they had, they would likely have put real punch into an attack in that direction, and quite possibly have damaged the allied cause.)

Battle Three was our air attacks on the Iraqi divisions forming up to attack Khafji. Overhead, Joint STARS watched these movements and directed hundreds of sorties against them: tank-killing A-10s with Mavericks; the AC-130 on the coast highway, killing a vehicle every ten to thirty seconds; B-52s bombing the "Kuwaiti National Forest" (so called

by the pilots because in that part of the desert the Kuwaitis had been trying to grow scraggly trees that could live on the brackish water under the
sand), where the Iraqis had been forming up—and trying to hide—for the
attack; F-16s and F/A-18s dropping cluster bombs on the lead and tail vehicles of convoys so the burning vehicles blocked the road and trapped
all the rest of the tanks, trucks, and artillery pieces; AV-8s and AH-1s
strafing the Iraqis as they fled back across the border.

Battle Four was the battle that never happened—the movement of
the Iraqis to position for another attack elsewhere, such as down the
Wadi al Batin against the Egyptians and Syrians near KKMC. If the Iraqis
had succeeded in engaging the Egyptians and/or the Syrians, it would
have given us—to put it mildly—major headaches. Because the Iraqis, the
Egyptians, and the Syrians often used the same equipment—Russian
tanks versus Russian tanks—we would have had a very difficult time deciding which one to kill. And because there were few English-speaking
FACs, we would have had a very difficult time sorting out the good guys
from the bad guys. The possible results: lots of casualties and Iraqi forces
astride the Tapline Road, the single highway connecting the coast and the
west. Its possession would have allowed the enemy to prevent movement
west of the U.S. VIIth and XVIIIth Corps to their attack positions.

To make matters more complicated, we were at that point very unsure
about how well the Arab forces would fight when the crunch came.

In the event, the Saudis did extremely well at Khafji, and later during
what has been misnamed the Hundred-Hour War. But it was their country and their king. Would the Egyptians and Syrians be similarly motivated? No one knew.

In hindsight, Battle Four may have been the one Saddam should have
put all his chips on (though, in fact, if he'd tried it, he still didn't have a
chance because of the battlefield situational awareness Joint STARS gave
us). A dug-in army is tough to kill; an army on the roads is a piece of
cake.

To summarize: Battle Three was the key to winning Battles One and
Two, and to never having to fight Battle Four.

★ As early as the twenty-fifth of January, we began to see glimmers that
told us something was up.

First, Brigadier General Jack Leide, the CENTCOM J-2, warned of activity by the Iraqi IIId Corps commander, Lieutenant General Salah Abud

Mahmud. (We would get to know him better in March, when he showed up at Safwan to surrender the Iraqi Army.)

About the same time, the Kuwaiti resistance leader, Colonel Ahmed Al-Rahamani, hiding in Kuwait City with a suitcase satellite telephone, phoned the TACC and relayed to the Kuwaiti Air Force duty officer, Colonel Samdam, that some generals were meeting in Kuwait City in an hour.* Based on the address provided by Colonel Rahamani, Chris Christon used aerial photographs of the neighborhood to pinpoint the meeting's location. Christon and Buster Glosson immediately examined further evidence provided by CENTCOM, the Kuwaiti resistance, and our own intelligence; and when they were satisfied that this was a valid target, they tasked some of Tom Lennon's F-111s to pay a call. Soon, four 2,000-pound laser-guided bombs were knocking on the door. A moment later, a massive ball of fire consumed the house and a flock of Mercedes-Benzes parked in the nearby parking lot. I never learned who was at the meeting or what they were planning.

Then, on the twenty-ninth of January, Chris Christon informed me that several FROG (Free Over Ground Rocket) units had deployed into Kuwait, in his view a tip-off that the Iraqis would attack sometime during the next two weeks. He was the only one I know who even came close to predicting the attack (though he missed the date). That night, Iraqi lead elements entered Al-Khafji.

Despite the hints, we were surprised.

Suddenly, thousands of Iraqi soldiers, thinking the night had made them invisible, began to move out of their dug-in defensive positions and mass for the attack.

Because of all the unforeseeable possibilities, an army in transit is an army ill at ease. Units can take the wrong road and arrive at the wrong place, vehicles can break down and fail to arrive in time to support the attack, weather can turn order into confusion. But never before had an army moving to the attack faced what this army was about to face. Because it was moving, it could be seen on the Joint STARS radar. Because it could be seen, it could be targeted and attacked. And because it was out in the open, jammed on narrow roads without shelter or camouflage, it was going to die. The Iraqi generals trusted that darkness would hide their movement, but the reality of modern technology left them naked to

---

*We have seen this incident earlier in a slightly different context.

massive doses of death, destruction, and terror from the air. It was any ground commander's worst nightmare.

As the convoys started their march south to the Saudi border, Joint STARS picked them up. Within moments A-10, F-16, B-52, AC-130, AV-8, and F/A-18 aircraft were diverted from other targets to attack the moving Iraqi Army, and the battle grew in intensity as more and more tanks, APCs, and trucks took to the highways leading to Al-Khafji.

Moments later, the large and orderly movement of Iraqi forces into Saudi Arabia had been turned into chaos. A-10s had bottled whole convoys of tanks on roads by killing the lead and the trailing vehicles; they then methodically set each vehicle in between on fire—and lit up two- to five-mile stretches of road like day. As Maverick missiles turned the stalled vehicles into fiery infernos, Iraqi soldiers ran into the desert to save their lives.

The Iraqi Army had been intent on surprise, and they had achieved it; but surprise did them no good. The ground commander had launched his attack against Saudi Arabia and was preparing to reinforce his attack when he ran up against a menace that was not in his script—hundreds of aircraft dropping thousands of lethal munitions on his forces.

On the ground, Battles One and Two erupted almost simultaneously.

To the west of the road to Khafji, the lead elements of the mechanized division the Iraqis had placed on their right flank to screen their main attack ran into company-size Marine elements near the huge storage area just south of the Kuwait border. Instantly concluding that the attack was directed at the thousands of tons of food, fuel, ammunitions, and petroleum stored in the open desert, the Marines sent armored personnel carriers, aided by close air support aircraft, against the Iraqi units and beat them back decisively. Though the fighting was fierce (several Marines were killed), it was not sustained, as the Iraqis had no intention of making this (Battle Two) the decisive battle.

To the east, Battle One got under way when the lead elements of the Iraqi main force (an armored and a mechanized division) entered Al-Khafji.

The problem faced by the Eastern Area commander, General Sultan, was figuring out how to engage and defeat this unknown-size second battle force (and recall that the Iraqi Army had been often portrayed as battle-tested, hard, and experienced, while his own modest force had never experienced combat).

Meanwhile, Battle Three had already started when Jim Crigger, on his own hook, started diverting air into Kuwait. Since the Iraqis would move only at night, this battle had to be conducted at night; and since the weather started to close in on the twenty-ninth, our air attacks had to be conducted at low altitude under the clouds rather than at the far-preferred medium altitudes.

On the ground, close support of EAC forces became the responsibility of the USMC Direct Air Support Center at Walt Boomer's headquarters, while in the air, the C-130 Airborne Direct Air Support Center command-and-control aircraft was used for this purpose. The TACC flowed or diverted air to the DASC or into Kuwait as fast as it could be targeted. The pace of the air battle was once again dictated by the pace of the tactical air control system's management of the air.

Later that night, the USMC launched a night-capable TV-equipped drone. As the unmanned aircraft crossed the border, it transmitted pictures of dozens of Iraqi armored personnel carriers lined up behind the earthen berm that marked the border between Saudi Arabia and Kuwait.

When the pictures showed up in my headquarters, I began to understand the warnings we had been receiving during the past few days.

Next, a team of B-52s and A-10s were tasked to bomb the "Kuwaiti National Forest" just north of the Kuwait border. The B-52 strike (filmed by the A-10s) went in first. As the bombs walked through the rows of trees, armored vehicles moved in all directions, fleeing for their lives. Moments later, the A-10s began their attack, carefully picking which target to destroy.

Later, as I watched the film, I noted that the A-10 guys preferred to lock onto and destroy the tanks and APCs that continued to move. Perhaps, I mused, the Warthog drivers thought that was the sporting thing to do—to shoot fleeing vehicles rather than the sitting ducks whose crews had fled on foot. But then I noticed more A-10s arriving to clean up the sitting ducks, and that theory flew out the window. Blazing fuel and exploding ammunitions turned night into day.

Early in the morning of 30 January, Major General Sultan took a force of Saudi and Qatari armored vehicles to the west side of Khafji. When he found Iraqi armor there, he engaged it, destroying some tanks and APCs and capturing an Iraqi officer and several dozen troops (even then the Iraqis were anxious to surrender). Questioning of the captives revealed that two Iraqi battalions were in the town. This information, coupled with earlier reports that more than fifty armored vehicles were also heading toward Khafji, led General Sultan to withdraw until close air support could be secured and a more comprehensive plan of attack could be drawn up.

As daylight broke, the pace of all three battles slowed down. The Iraqis stopped moving; the Saudis withdrew; the USMC began to convoy forces into the desert to the west of Khafji; and our air attacks in Kuwait, while hardly slow or routine, lacked the intensity that occurred every night when the F-117s hit Baghdad, and the Scud hunt and Scud-launching heated up.

Late that afternoon, I was in the TACC with Lieutenant General Ahmed Al Behery, the Royal Saudi Air Force commander, watching the battle over Kuwait unfold. The phone was handed to Behery, who said a few words on channel two (Arabic), then handed the phone to me: "Chuck, it's Khaled."

"Khaled, hello, where are you?" I asked.

"Chuck, this is Khaled," he answered; and then, forcefully, "I'm at Khafji. And I need air."

"Khaled, how in the hell did you get to Khafji?"

"Chuck," he replied, "we have a battle up here, and I need air, lots of air. I need B-52s."

When a ground general says he needs B-52s, you know he's in trouble. You know he wants an instant solution to a severe problem. As he spoke those words, I glanced up at the AWACS display, which showed flight after flight heading toward southern Kuwait.

"You're going to get lots of air, Khaled," I replied in my best bedside manner.

"No, Chuck, you don't understand. I need *air!*" Khaled pleaded, with all the intensity and sincerity his voice could produce.

I whipped out the line airmen have used for decades. "Trust me, Khaled, you're going to get more air than you ever knew existed."

"No, Chuck, I need *air,*" he repeated.

As a matter of fact, his anxiety had more behind it than I thought. He did need air.

Though it was true that all available air was being funneled to defeat the Iraqi attack, I was unaware that we had no way to control close air support sorties at Al-Khafji, since, as I learned later, the Marine air controllers who should have been doing that were just then trapped and hiding in the town. The USMC had two ANGLICO (air and naval gunfire liaison company—Marine for forward air controller) teams of five men whose job was to contact the USMC DASC and coordinate and control CAS or artillery fire. These two teams were hiding on a rooftop in Al-Khafji.

Hundreds of sorties were arriving over Khafji, but when they were unable to contact any controlling agency or forward air controller, they just moved north a few miles and continued to pummel the Iraqi forces trying to reinforce the lead elements in Saudi Arabia.

The Marines' inability to control close air support at Khafji did not please Khaled. Other Marines to the west could have been sent east to handle that. But this did not happen, in Khaled's view, for the following reasons:

1. The Marines feared they'd hit the Saudi forces—liaison between Marines and Saudis being at best limited.
2. They felt their air was best employed as a combined arms element with their own ground forces and should not be deployed to the east where few of their organic forces were engaged.
3. And anyhow, they were in a big fight out to the west against a mechanized division, and needed all the air they could get.

While I'm sure all of these to some small extent guided Walt Boomer's decision, the single most important factor remained: the Marines assigned to provide command and control for close air support to the Saudis were just then surrounded by hundreds of armed Iraqis.

I am absolutely certain that Walt Boomer would have given Khaled all the CAS his team could use; unfortunately, the means for Khaled to request and execute close air support was at that time avoiding capture.

After I had once again assured Khaled that he would get more air support than he could imagine, I learned how he'd come to be in Khafji in the first place. When word of the Iraqi invasion broke, he was on his way to Dhahran to give a medal to Captain Shamrani, the RSAF F-15 pilot who'd shot down the two Iraqi Mirages. He'd immediately had his aircraft diverted and joined Major General Sultan.

As he was speaking, other thoughts were running through my mind.

From early August, Khaled had been emphasizing his long-held resolve that when it came down to the crunch, Saudi blood must be the first spilled in the defense of the Kingdom. It was a matter of honor that Saudi military forces do more than their share in defense of their land. Yes, he appreciated the support of the Coalition. Yes, he appreciated the almost overwhelming force from the United States. But when the war was over, it must be clear to all that the Saudis had performed on the battlefield in a manner that brought honor and pride to King and country. Until the Iraqi invasion of the Kingdom at the end of January, the war had been all airpower, and the blood spilled had been United States, Italian, and British blood—which is not to say that the RSAF had proved wanting. The RSAF had performed magnificently, but no Saudi aircraft had yet been lost. Now it looked as though Khaled's long-held resolve was about to be fulfilled, and if he wasn't careful, it might well be his own royal blood.

I wanted to tell Khaled to be careful; he was far more important as a live leader then a dead hero. But there was also a sixteen-year-old kid in me that couldn't resist adding to my promises of air support:

"Oh, Khaled," I said just before we said goodbye.

"Yes, Chuck."

"Just keep one thing in mind. I'm asking you to trust me while my ass is in a bunker in Riyadh and yours is in on the battlefield of Al-Khafji."

★ In fact, even after all my hopeful words, I don't think Khaled fully trusted me; and later he called Brigadier General Ahmed Sudairy to demand air from him. However, Sudairy could tell him only what I had already said, that hundreds of sorties were being sent to the battle (again, we did not know how much air was used to intercept the Iraqi advance and how much was being used by the DASC for CAS in Khafji and in the desert).

Meanwhile, as the sun went down on the evening of the thirtieth, Battles One, Two, and Three began seriously heating up. Not to fear, we had a pair of golden arrows in our quiver—Joint STARS and AC-130 gunships.

Joint STARS could look hundreds of miles into enemy territory and detect and identify individual vehicles—that is, it could distinguish cars, trucks, APCs, and tanks. J-STARS was a *new* system, never tested in battle, and Khafji was its first use in combat.

On the other hand, the AC-130 gunship system had been around since Vietnam. Though it was old, it was still deadly: its night-vision sights made it a fearsome nighttime threat, and its side-firing 105mm howitzer could pump out three to five shots a minute. In Grenada, AC-130 gunships had picked off the Cuban snipers hiding around the airfield and allowed the first elements of the XVIIIth Corps to advance from what had been a death trap. On the night of the thirtieth, this same aircraft was killing every Iraqi vehicle they saw venturing on the coastal highway into Saudi Arabia.

If I'd been the Iraqi commander that night, one question would have kept coming up: "How do they know?"

Every time Iraqi vehicles began to march south, A-10s, FA-18Bs, or even the odd Pave TAC F-111 or F-15E would show up, and all hell would break loose. Every time I tried to move my force to the battles in Saudi Arabia, the commander must have been thinking, my troops come under attack, and then abandon their tanks and APCs on the sand. Would it never cease?

The onslaught from the air that night *was* ceaseless. The fires flaming the skies of the coast road marked the trail of an army defeated before it ever reached the battle. By the morning of the thirty-first, the Iraqi Army along the coast highway was in disarray.

But it didn't all go our way.

Early on the morning of the thirty-first, the AWACS controller called the AC-130 pummeling the coast highway: "Dawn approaching, you'd better go home." (In daylight, the enemy could spot the lumbering aircraft and shoot it down with a heat-seeking missile.)

"I can't go right now," the pilot answered, "I have too many targets left on the road." It was his last transmission. Thirty seconds later, the AC-130 disappeared from the AWACS radar screen; the plane had crashed into the sea, killing all fourteen crewmen aboard. In the predawn light, an Iraqi soldier had fired a heat-seeking antiaircraft missile into the AC-130's port engine. This was our single biggest loss of airmen during the entire war.

★ By midday of the thirty-first, the battles for Khafji were over. The remaining Iraqis in the desert and in town were stranded. Saudi and Qatari forces had attacked and performed flawlessly with grit and determination, and Khaled had proved he could lead under fire (I think even he had had doubts about this prior to the battle). The results to the bean counters must have been wonderful—hundreds of pieces of armor destroyed in Kuwait and Saudi Arabia, and almost five hundred Iraqi prisoners taken (a clue that we needed to prepare for an onslaught of POWs).

This victory did not come free. Approximately fifty Islamic soldiers from the Saudi Northern Area corps were killed or wounded.

The most important outcome of the battle is that the Iraqis were now left without options to take the initiative offensively. Specifically, Battle Four was never fought. The Iraqis could no longer muster forces to attack the Egyptians and Syrians in the Northern Area command.

What had the Iraqis hoped to gain by the Al-Khafji incursion? Did they expect to draw the Coalition ground forces into an attack before the Iraqi forces were further decimated by our airpower? It didn't happen. Did they expect to inflict casualties on the Coalition forces, take prisoners, and make headlines in the United States? It didn't happen. Did they want to show the Arabian and other Islamic forces up as soft, ill-trained, or even cowardly? It didn't happen. Was Khafji part of a larger scheme, the first phase of an overall plan to go on the initiative against other Coalition forces? It never happened. Those Iraqi hopes and plans died on the way to battle under a twenty-four-hour nonstop pounding from above.

Colonel Dave Schulte, the BCE commander in the TACC, summed up the lessons learned from Khafji (my comments follow, in parentheses):

1. The Iraqis couldn't mass forces due to Blue Air; therefore they must mass air defenses first. (They tried, but we would not permit it.)
2. Iraqi battlefield intelligence was poor because they failed to predict our response. (That is why controlling air and space is so important. Imagine the consequences if the Iraqis had known about Walt Boomer's exposed logistic bases. Imagine the impact if they had been able to bring artillery to bear on the Tapline Road.)
3. The Iraqis had good command and control of their forces. This was evident during execution of the attack and retreat. (Okay. But we would do our best to destroy that command control before our ground attack started.)
4. The Iraqis fought well. (And yet they were already surrendering in large numbers, disillusioned, ashamed, tired of war, worn out

from constant air attack. Their motivation to surrender was to increase as the bombardment continued.)

The Iraqi IIId Corps commander summed it up another way. When he saw what was happening to his forces in Kuwait and Saudi Arabia, he called Saddam and asked for permission to break off the attack on Al-Khafji and begin a withdrawal.

"No, continue the attack," Saddam replied. "I want you to make this the mother of all battles!"

To which the IIId Corps Commander replied, "Sir, the mother is killing her children," and hung up. He then ordered his remaining forces to withdraw.

And this is what I said at the January 31 1700 meeting in the TACC:

"The effort last night went very well. Though there was a lot of confusion, you have to live with that. Still, there's no doubt about it, the Saudis inflicted a tremendous defeat on Saddam at Khafji. The word I got was they captured 200 [it was actually 463] and killed over 10 [actually 32], and I think the Saudis lost one guy [actually 18 KIA and 32 WIA]. That's a very important victory.

"Unfortunately, our press will make it look like we somehow bungled it; but that's all right.

"I don't know what's going to happen tonight. People are concerned about another attack in the Khafji area. It is probably likely. We also have to beware of another attack in the border area. That could be a disaster.

"The Scuds continue to be a problem, and weather is going to complicate the search tonight. But we'll work on that.

"We're not getting a lot of feedback on the Republican Guard. But the only reason I could think of for him to do the attacks at Khafji and in the Marine sector was because he felt a compulsion to force the action. He feels that we are hurting him, and that he's got to step up the pace or the train is going to leave the station, and he's not going to be on board. Of course we would like to see that happen. We would like to destroy him at our own pace; but he may not allow us to do that. So we have got to be prepared to manage chaos, we've got to keep the units informed, and we have got to be able to react without jerking the flying units around too much. It's

going to be a lot of pain for everybody if we change or divert
flights and we get into changing ordnances and all that. We will do
our best to keep that from happening. But you've got to convey to
the units down in the field that this could invoke some very quiet
changes this evening. We could have—like Khafji—a lot of serious
battles go on that we don't anticipate right now.

"Another thing—get the word out—the people at KKMC, and
to a lesser extent at Dhahran and Riyadh, need to be prepared to
respond to a chemical attack, because that's one of the tricks left
in his bag. I don't know whether he can do it or not. I don't think
he can; but we can never allow him to have the initiative. So any-
thing he does, we have to be able to counter and then just stick it
right up his nose. I think the team that worked the Khafji problem
last night [Colonel Joe Bob Phillips and his team from Nellis AFB]
did a magnificent job.

"We are in the work phase of the war now. Shooting down the
MiGs is pretty much over with; all the glorious laser-guided bombs
and telephone exchanges, that's all history. Now it's digging him
out of the ground and stomping his military forces in the field into
the dirt. There is no turning back for him. The battle of Khafji
proved that. So let's just get on with it; and let's be home before Ra-
madan, so the people in this country can celebrate their holy days
without a bunch of Americans, French, Italians, Brits, and Cana-
dians hanging around."

To which Lt. General Behery added "and Iraqis," as the meeting broke
up.

★ Tom Clancy resumes the story.

BRIDGES

After the battle of Khafji, an even greater emphasis was put on efforts to
isolate the battlefield by shutting down the transportation system. Iraq
had an excellent road system, with more than 50,000 military trucks
and nearly 200,000 commercial vehicles capable of hauling supplies to
the army of occupation in the KTO. Since it would clearly take a very
long time to shut down transportation by attacking individual vehicles

(there were simply too many of them), Horner and his planners had to try something else. They'd hit the roads and bridges.

Fortunately for Coalition planners, the major road and railroad lines paralleled the Tigris and Euphrates Rivers south of the Iraqi capital, and major road and rail bridges could be found at key cities along each route. For example, five major roads and the railroad to Basra all converged and crossed various waterways at the town of An Nasiriyah in southern Iraq.

The problem for planners was that finding suitable roads to target grew harder as one got closer to the KTO. Since craters could be rapidly repaired or bypassed on roads south and west of Basra, bombing them had little effect. As a result, planners placed most of the targeting effort on crossings over waterways and rivers. In essence, it became a bridge-busting campaign.

Where possible, laser-guided bombs were used to drop individual concrete spans over major highways—and the films from these attacks gave Schwarzkopf some of his best television one-liners: "Now you are going to see the luckiest man alive," he intoned as a vehicle barely cleared a targeted bridge microseconds ahead of the spectacular blast of a laser-guided bomb.

Early in January, the CENTAF intelligence staff had identified 579 highway, 155 railroad, and 17 inland waterway targets. Since laser-guided bombs made "one bomb one target" practical, it was estimated that fewer than 1,000 bombs, or about 200 to 300 sorties, would be needed to accomplish the mission.

In the event, "one bomb one target" wasn't far off the mark. And so the single-track rail line between Baghdad and Basra was cut by destroying bridges at As Samawah, Saquash, and Basra. These bridges were not repaired during the war, and no goods moved by rail.

But no one had considered the Iraqis' ingenuity in repairing or bypassing damaged road bridges. (They seemed to have on hand an inexhaustible supply of pontoon bridges.) As a result, nearly 5,000 weapons and 1,000 sorties were needed to close down the Iraqi vehicle-transportation system.

Yet even before the Iraqi make-dos began to frustrate Chuck Horner's planners and airmen, Coalition mistakes limited bridge-busting success. F-111Fs, Tornadoes, and F-15Es would easily place a single 2,000-pound LGB on a bridge span, yet the next day photography showed traffic moving over the bridge.

The problem: bomb fuses had been set to allow the bomb a chance to penetrate fixed structures before exploding. Though this was fine for a hangar or a hardened bunker, it meant that bombs were punching round holes in the roadway and exploding under the span—and scarcely denting the overall bridge structure. The fix was to reduce the delay on the bomb fuse, which let the weapon explode on impact with the road surface.

Next came the pontoon bridges. A bridge span would be dropped, and the next day the Iraqis would float a pontoon bridge across the waterway. A sortie launched against the new pontoon bridge would destroy or scatter tens of pontoon boats and splinter the roadway they supported, and within hours new pontoons were in place and the crossing was back in business. In some marshy or low-water areas, the Iraqis simply used bulldozers to push dirt into the waterway and bypass busted bridges. When Horner bombed the dirt, they bulldozed more dirt.

Finally tiring of all this, Coalition planners set up "bridge patrols." F-16s by day and F-111s and F-15Es at night would fly visual reconnaissance missions along specified river segments, destroying any bridges, bridging materials, or ferryboats that they found.

Shutting down the Iraqi lines of communication turned into a full-time job, but the Coalition air forces got the job done.

★ Once the bridges and ferries had been severed, Coalition aircraft were tasked to attack the vehicles in the resulting jam-up at the closed crossings. This mission initially yielded good results, but in time the Iraqis gave up trying to resupply their army from Baghdad and tried to sneak supplies over the desert from Basra; or else supplies were shifted as best they could manage among units in the KTO. Neither did them any good. During the day, A-10s, F-18s, AV-8s, Jaguars, and F-16s were on the lookout for any movement on the desert, while at night, A-10s with IR Maverick missiles were on watch. And always there was Joint STARS. One Iraqi truck unit reported that out of eighty vehicles, only ten remained after the war; and prisoners told stories of men who refused resupply missions. Air not only choked off supplies into the KTO, it allowed only a trickle of supplies to units deployed throughout the desert.

The measure of interdiction effectiveness is the effect on throughput measured in metric tons per day (T/D). Chris Christon's intelligence section estimated prewar Iraqi throughput for rail, highway, and boat at more than 200,000 T/D. By the first week in February, this had been cut in half. At the end of the war, throughput was estimated to be 20,000 tons per day.

To really understand what this means, one needs to ask what the Iraqi army of occupation actually needed to sustain itself. That answer depends: if they were on the attack (as they were during the battle of Khafji) or fighting (as they were during the Coalition invasion of the last few days of the war), then they needed substantial quantities of supplies. But if they were simply sitting in the desert doing very little more than moving tanks and artillery around (as they were doing for the five weeks before the ground attack), they needed considerably less. Coalition intelligence estimated that when Iraqi forces in the KTO were engaged in battle, they required a minimum of 45,000 to 50,000 tons per day of supplies, while sustaining the Iraqi Army when it was not fighting required 10,000 to 20,000 tons per day.

In other words, by the time the ground war began in late February, the Iraqi resupply system could barely meet the subsistence needs of its army—food, water, and medical supplies.

Air interdiction not only prevented the Iraqis from meeting the needs of their army, it limited their ability to take advantage of the significant amounts of supplies they had deployed to the field before the war began.

For instance, the air attacks forced the Iraqis to disperse ammunition storage areas throughout the desert. In that way, a single bomb would destroy only a small part of the ammunition stored at an artillery position, but the gunners had to travel long distances to obtain shells. And travel in the desert under the ever-present umbrella of Coalition aircraft was hazardous to the health.

Supply shortages took other tolls. For example, low-priority infantry units had very little to eat, with some receiving food supplies no more than once every three or four days. When the war came, several units surrendered because they were hungry.

Perhaps most tellingly, when the Iraqi generals were ordered to travel from Basra to Safwan for the cease-fire talks (a distance of thirty miles), they requested permission to make the trip by helicopter, because the road was impassable.

★ Meanwhile, there were losses. Though these were surprisingly few, any loss hurt.

On the night of 18 January, an A-6 went missing. The crew were never recovered. An A-10 was shot down on the twenty-third of January, and its pilot was captured. Early in the predawn hours of 3 February, an electrical generator failure caused a B-52 from the 430th Bomb Wing to crash into the sea while landing at Diego Garcia. When the pilot activated the wing flaps on his final approach, the electrical demand caused a massive loss of electrical power, which led to the loss of fuel to the engines. Fortunately, three of the crew ejected and were safely rescued.

TANTRUMS

Not all Iraqi sallies in the direction of regaining the military initiative took a conventional form, and some were until that time unique—deliberate assaults on the environment of Kuwait and the region. Though calling these actions "military" is stretching the term quite a lot, there may in fact have been some small military utility.

Was military gain the prime motive for the Iraqi desecration of the environment? Hardly. The motive was pure and simple revenge. "You're hurting me. I'll hurt you back. You're going to undo my theft of Kuwait. Then I'll turn Kuwait into a wasteland and leave you with nothing there you'd want." Saddam Hussein made threats like these openly and often. He tried to carry them out.

On 25 January, the Iraqis opened the pipelines that carried crude oil from the huge storage tanks south of Kuwait City out to tanker terminals just offshore. Thousands of tons of oil were now gushing into the waters of the Arabian Gulf, polluting beaches, killing waterfowl. Since there was some likelihood that the oil would float down the Gulf and eventually clog up the desalinization plants on the east coast of Saudi Arabia, this particular act of environmental terrorism may have given Saddam a small military victory. The Saudis depended on those plants for much of their water. But again, was military gain his aim? Not likely. He was just plain being ornery.

Moments after oil started spewing into the Gulf, CENTCOM intelligence had located and debriefed the engineers who'd operated the Kuwaiti oil-storage area before the war. From them came estimates of the amounts of oil that could be dumped (a lot!) and suggestions for ending the dumping. It quickly became clear that the situation was more serious than anyone had realized. Already the spill was many times greater than had been released by the Exxon Valdez tanker accident in Alaska. Something had to be done, and soon, and air was the only force available to do it. Chuck Horner immediately had his targeteers working on the problem. The strategy they came up with was straightforward. They would torch off the oil slick and shut down the pipelines the Iraqis had opened.

Needless to say, the subject came up at General Schwarzkopf's 1900 meeting. Schwarzkopf asked Horner two questions: "What is required?" and "When can we do it?"

The plan devised by Buster Glosson's Black Hole wizards called for USMC AV-8s to drop phosphorus flares into the oil slick and ignite the floating crude oil (the flares were normally used to light up the battlefield at night for close air support). Then F-111s would strike the two valves that controlled the outflow of oil. Their destruction would cause the pipeline to switch into its failsafe position, and various manifold controls would seal it off, making it inoperable. Though the pipeline could be repaired, such repairs were considered beyond the abilities of the Iraqi Army.

The AV-8 mission was fairly simple, and did not involve significant enemy defenses; but the F-111s were dropping their bombs from medium altitude in daylight, to ensure they could visually find their aim point in an area very well defended by optically aimed guns and heat-seeking missiles. It would not be easy.

"We can accomplish both missions tomorrow," Horner told Schwarzkopf.

"I'll get back to you," the CINC replied.

All the next day, they waited, but no word came out of the CINC's staff. Torching the slick was itself environmentally risky. Would a sea of fire spread to shore, where tons of black goo had already washed up? Wouldn't nature's own—admittedly slow—cleanup process be ultimately better than a big, soot-producing burn? Though Horner doesn't know this for sure, such questions were doubtless being asked in Washington. The answer: a "go ahead" for the mission to set the slick on fire never came.

However, early on the afternoon of the twenty-sixth, the "go ahead" came to the TACC for the F-111 strike. The time on target was for three and a half hours later.

Now the pressure was on Tom Lennon and his Aardvark pilots of the 48th TFW (P). The weapons, GBU-15s, had small wings, which allowed them to glide to their target from some distance away. Their guidance was provided by a radio control signal generated from another F-111 (its WSO received a television picture from a TV camera located in the bomb's nose). As the bomb flew closer, the ground image grew larger, and the WSO could fine-tune the placement of the crosshairs with a small control stick in his cockpit—all this while the bomb was flying at nearly ten miles a minute, leaving no room for error during the final seconds of flight. Meanwhile, the F-111 pilot would put the aircraft on autopilot, watch the television screen to judge how well his WSO was doing, and hope he didn't spot antiaircraft fire or missiles. During the final microseconds of the bomb's flight, the target image would swell to take over the entire screen. Then the screen would grow dark picoseconds before 2,000 pounds of tritonal in the warhead went off. All in all, a very tricky operation requiring a great deal of training, planning, and skill.

This particular mission involved four F-111Fs fragged to deliver two GBU-15s. The number three and four aircraft carried the bombs, while the number one and two aircraft carried the radio relay pods that received and transmitted the radio signals to and from the bomb.

As it turned out, when the first bomb was released and the number one WSO began fine-tuning its heading, for some reason his radio relay got interrupted and he lost contact with the bomb. Instantly, he mashed the radio button and called out that he had to abort the drop—but fortunately, the number two WSO had been monitoring the drop and immediately transmitted "I've got it," and proceeded to guide the bomb to the exact place where the first valve was buried.

Except for the hitch, the mission went as planned—two bombs dropped, two valves destroyed, the oil pipeline shut down . . . and a very happy Norman Schwarzkopf and Chuck Horner.

★ We have already mentioned Iraqi fire trenches—ditches dug in the desert and hooked up to existing crude-oil pipelines and pumping stations. When the invasion came, they were to be filled with oil and set on fire.

Though of all the Iraqi assaults on the environment, this one offered the greatest potential military usefulness, it remained an assault on the environment, or, as Chuck Horner puts it, "I will admit that war is not the place to preach ecological chastity, yet only a criminal or fool goes around pumping crude oil about the landscape."

At any rate, fire trenches were part of the extensive defense system near the Saudi–Kuwaiti border. The plan was to force Coalition ground troops to penetrate and be channeled through as many casualty-producing hazards as possible before they engaged the Republican Guard and selected armor units. As they were slowed and channeled, Iraqi heavy artillery was scheduled to make mincemeat of them.

Though the trenches themselves may have been intended as a surprise, the Coalition's control of air and space ended that hope, and taking the trenches out of action actually proved to be fairly easy. Sometimes the oil in the ditches could be ignited simply by having Warthogs strafe them. Keeping them from being resupplied with fuel, however, proved to be a little harder. Each set of trenches was fed by buried pipelines from a common pumping station, usually five or so lines to a station. The pumping stations were then connected to a major east–west oil line to the north.

The pipelines and pumping stations were attacked in mid-February— far enough ahead of "G day" (which was still undetermined) to allow other countermeasures if these attacks failed, but close enough to prevent repair.

A dozen F-117 aircraft were given the job; and it must have seemed like a milk run next to the missions over Baghdad. Ten of them would hit the fire-trench pumping stations, while the final two would drop the master oil pipeline.

This mission also went without a hitch.

As it turned out, the Iraqi Army was so physically and psychologically beat up when the ground war started that their minefields and trench lines proved to be of little value in stopping the Coalition advance.

The ultimate Iraqi environmental madness, the setting on fire of Kuwait's oil fields on or about the twenty-third of February, still burns in Chuck Horner's memory:

> *I have never seen anything so senseless, so evil, so offensive to mankind. Picture if you can dense, black, oily, greasy smoke boiling into the air from a thousand fires. The desert sand is awash with black oil topped with violent red and orange flame balls. Bright orange flames spew upward at each wellhead, with ugly rivers of burning oil spilling into low ground and creating lakes that belong in hell. Angry pillars of dense black smoke rise upward*

until they are caught by the winds aloft—some days at a few hundred feet, other days at thousands of feet—and then driven by the winds for thousands of miles. As you fly over the area, you gaze down on a solid mass of foul-smelling smoke stretching downwind as far as you can see. When you break out under the overcast, you are inside a dark wilderness.

In Riyadh and Abu Dhabi the sky has a greasy overcast and the air smells of soot. Airplanes flying over Kuwait come back with oily soot all over them, and their canopies have to be cleaned so the pilots can see.

After the war Kuwait City looked like a biblical wasteland. The concrete block houses were all burned out, with black smoke smudge over every window. Everything else was stained with greasy black soot. White cats were black. White cars were charcoal-colored.

What can I say, except to condemn the Iraqis who planned and perpetrated this outrage on our planet? How evil can you get?

Though I'm sure Iraqi citizens who lost loved ones to our bombs have felt similar outrage, to an objective viewer the Iraqi revenge on Kuwait—the Iraqi outrage to the world's environment—can never be forgotten, and it must not go unpunished. We must find ways to prevent similar despoliation in future armed conflicts.

12

A DAY IN THE WAR

CHUCK HORNER

3 February 1991

0300   I go to bed, extremely tired but feeling good. The war is going well.

0345   I wake up to Scud sirens going off in Riyadh. I lie there and think, *Should I get up, put on chem protection, and go to the shelter in the basement? Well, assuming the Scud is aimed at the RSAF building next door: since it will be coming from the north, and since my bedroom is facing south toward the RSAF headquarters, and since I am on the top floor, and since the Scud will have a parabolic not a vertical descent, then the Scud is liable to come through my room en route to the RSAF headquarters, and I will be killed. The RSAF headquarters, on the other hand, will suffer little damage, since most of the blast will be confined to my room.*

Better yet, the Patriot at Riyadh Air Base, about half a mile to my north, may hit the missile before it gets to me, which means only debris will hit me.

About then, I hear the sonic booms of two Patriot missiles taking off to the north, followed by the pop of the intercept.

Now I am going back to sleep. I always do after Scud alarms. I guess staying in bed is more attractive than making sure I save my life.

★ 0415   The phone beside the bed goes off, and I answer, "General Horner, how may I help you?" (Old habits drilled into me at the fraternity house in Iowa City die hard.) BeBe Bell, General Schwarzkopf's executive officer, is on the other end.

"General Schwarzkopf wants to talk to General Yeosock," he says. Though Yeosock usually sleeps at ARCENT headquarters in Eskan Village south of town, he had a late night at MODA and stopped here for rest.

"Okay, hold on, I'll get him," I answer. "By the way, how are things going?"

"Don't ask," BeBe says.

So I slide out of bed and go to John's door about thirty feet away. I knock, open it a crack, and hear snoring. "John, it's Bee Bee on the phone. The CINC wants to talk with"—thinking "at"—"you."

John wakes up immediately, sits up on the edge of the bed, and says, "Thanks, I'll take it in the living room."

As I turn, I hear John light up a cigar.

I stop in the head and relieve myself, then shuffle back to my room. When I get there, the phone is still resting on the table by my bed, and I can hear Schwarzkopf talking—yelling—at John. I wonder why he bothered to use the phone. All he had to do was open a window at MODA (about one and a half miles to our south) and we all could have heard him. I put the receiver on the hook, but I can still hear John answering the CINC's questions in the living room.

I fall asleep admiring John's resilience and patience.

★ 0530   My alarm goes off, and I can hear someone making coffee in the kitchen—either John or his aide, Major Fong. My new aide, Major Mark (Hoot) Gibson, is down in the UAE flying combat missions.*

I'm glad John has stayed over; I don't often have a chance to talk with him.

I hit the shower and shave there, then I'm into my desert fatigues in an instant. They are draped over a chair by the door, and I don't change them that often. Everyone else is just as grimy, and it is a pain in the ear to put all the stuff I need into the pockets of the new uniform—billfold, security badges, handkerchief, atropine syringe—all the stuff you carry around when you are involved in a war.

---

*My former aide, Little Grr Hartinger, had orders to Ramstein, Germany, a couple of months before the invasion of Kuwait. When we deployed in August, he was waiting for his PCS date, which came in September. Though he wanted to stay, we weren't sure how long we would be in Saudi Arabia, and I had already selected Hoot to replace him.

★ 0550   As John and I drink coffee and listen to the CNN news, he goes over the latest CINC tirade. It seems that late last night, after John had left for home, Freddie Franks had sent in a message that pissed Schwarzkopf off. John explains both sides of the problem and how he is going to take care of it.

It seems to me that John has two problem children, Fred and the CINC, and as a result, he isn't having much fun.

★ As far as I can remember it, the crisis that night had to do with Fred's attempts to get the reserve force assigned to him (the First Cavalry Division—the force that was to be kept available during the opening of the ground war if anything went wrong). Fred felt that he needed the reserve from the start, to ensure that the main attack went well. The CINC wanted to keep it under his command until he knew that the attack on Fred's right flank (the Northern Area Corps—the Egyptians and Syrians) was going okay; then he would give it to Fred to reinforce the main attack. Schwarzkopf was worried that an Iraqi counterattack into the Egyptians and Syrians could create problems that the reserve had to fix, in which case Fred would have to go it alone with his VIIth Corps and the British (that in fact should have been enough).

I'm guessing at this, but I suspect that Fred sent out a message to Third Army (Yeosock, his immediate boss) explaining that he needed the reserve forces assigned to him immediately—a perfectly reasonable request. Unfortunately, VIIth Corps messages too often had information addressees that included the Department of the Army, the Joint Chiefs, the commanders in Europe—a whole host of people who would like to second-guess Schwarzkopf.

In other words, it wasn't Fred's reasonable request that sent Schwarzkopf through the roof; it was the broadcast to the whole world of his case, when in fact the CINC had already told him that he would give him the reserve when he wanted him to have it.

★ It's always good to talk with John, even when cigar smoke, like now, hangs from the ceiling down to maybe a foot off the floor. We don't see everything the same way, but our perceptions and views are complementary. I have it easier than John does. My problems are shot-down planes, which targets to hit next, getting the ATO out on time, and the evening meeting with Schwarzkopf.

John's biggest problem is the wunderkinds—people like Gus Pagonis, the Army's logistics wizard, or Fred Franks, a genius at fighting armor (and there are others). All are superstars, the best at their professional role. Each appears to think that his is the most important role in the war, that he is the one person who'll be responsible for winning the war, and they each play a key role. Major General Gus Pagonis was a special challenge. On the one hand, he was everywhere, solving huge problems—working miracles moving the two corps to the west, while keeping them resupplied with food, water, and fuel. On the other hand, he had an ego as large as George Patton's. If anything he was involved with was going good, he made sure the CINC knew it; and if anything was going bad, he told John just before the CINC found out and called.

After we talk for a time, I lie on my back under the blue haze with a bowl of cold cereal on my chest. John is in a chair, and we both watch some heroic reporter on TV describe his narrow escape from last night's Scud attack. God, what guts!

Shortly after 0600, we both leave.

★ 0605   I am ashamed to admit it, but I am wearing a bulletproof vest and carry a 9mm pistol under my fatigue jacket.

It is cold and clear as I walk the dark path from my apartment building past the small shops that had housed the barber, cleaners, and recreation services before the fighting started seemingly years ago. As I reach the hole in the ten-foot-tall cinder-block wall that divides the USMTM compound from RSAF headquarters, I speak to the guards so they won't shoot me in the dark. By now we have an RSAF and USAF military policeman at every checkpoint. That way, each side knows what is going on. (For the most part, our two peoples have been working well together and bonding.)

A path has been worn in the desert sand from the hole in the wall to the covered car-parking area behind the RSAF headquarters. Because the dining hall vents are located nearby, you can smell the pleasant odor of food. Meanwhile, cats are busy rummaging through the dumpster for the remains of last night's dinner. Hope they like chicken and rice. They don't have much other choice.

★ 0610   I walk upstairs. After I enter the building, the mosque is on my right. Early prayer is in session, but attendance is low, since most are at their duty stations. You can tell how many are at prayer by counting the boots and dividing by two.

I walk down the pink and green marbled hall and take the elevator up to the third floor and my office. The night clerk tells me that there is nothing hot on my desk. Whatever else is there, George Gitchell, my chief of staff, will want to see first, so he can make sure it is thoroughly staffed before I sign or okay it. I go into my office, hoping a letter from Mary Jo came in during the night. But no such luck. You live for mail from home, and sending letters without postage is truly one of the most appreciated perks in this war.

I take off the fatigue jacket, pistol, and bulletproof vest and stow them in my desk. Then I pick up the "Read File," go to the stairwell, and descend the four flights to the basement.

★ 0625　 I walk down the basement corridor—bare cement with guard posts roughly every hundred yards—past the computer room. Things are quiet there for now. A few airmen are sitting at consoles typing in the routine events that appear in the ATO; technicians are working on terminals that need fixing. After that comes a room that is used in peacetime as the RSAF command post but has now become the area where they do administrative communications with their bases. Next there's a small makeshift plywood and curtained shelter in the hall where the airlifters have a small office that's used to coordinate the TACC with the Airlift TACC, which is still upstairs in tents on the parking lot. There just isn't enough room to collocate them together. Upstairs, they plan and publish the ATO for airlift—primarily those C-130s that are now busy moving the XVIIIth and VIIth Corps to the west, landing on desert strips and highway—an untold story.

I enter the TACC and stop at the Air Rescue Coordination Center to check on downed pilots. No bad news. In fact, the news is almost good: an A-10 pilot previously listed as MIA has turned up in Iraq, as shown on CNN. It's not good that he's a POW, but it's better than being MIA.

I stop to talk with people along the way to my place, to see how things are going. Nothing much to report.

When I reach the commander's table at the front of the room facing the big-screen display, Tom Olsen is sitting in my chair, and Mike Reavy and Charley Harr are to his left. They are probably discussing a request to divert an F-16 package to another target.

I stop by Intel, but there is nothing exciting on their displays. I don't stay long there, as they are working feverishly to finish some viewgraphs they will use in the changeover briefing at 0700.

Meanwhile, the room is full, because both shifts are there. People are explaining what has been going on and what needs to be taken care of as the day progresses. The night-shift people, who will be back in eleven-plus hours, are looking forward to getting out of the basement and into the open air and riding the bus back to Eskan Village and bed. They will probably stop for breakfast at either the RSAF or the village mess hall before they turn in.

Before I take my place, I look over the "doofer book"—the log—a plain notebook with a green hard cover that is always left on the commander's table. The only thing I find is a debrief from the F-16 LANTIRN pilots who were orbiting eastern Iraq when the Scuds were shot at Riyadh last night. There had been a low overcast, and the missile came roaring up out of it about fifteen miles to their south. Though they tried to work down through the weather to look for the mobile launcher, the cloud bases were too low for them to muck around under. They never have much time, since the Iraqis pack up their launchers and get the hell out within ten minutes of their shoot. It is frustrating for all of us.

★ 0700   By now all the national leaders have wandered into the TACC and are sitting around the small table behind my chair.

The U.S. Navy is represented by Rear Admiral (lower half) Connie Lautenbager and Captain Lyle Bien (called Ho Chi Minh by all), the USMC is represented by Colonel Joe Robbin, the Army BCE cell is fully manned, and of course there are too many Air Force people to name.

It is very crowded, with the generals and colonels getting seats on a first-come, first-seated basis. I face the room, and the formal briefings begin. From the get-go, I've tried to make sure they all feel they can speak up at any time. There is no limit to the good ideas a group harbors; the problem is to get everyone to speak up and share their views. At the same time, we don't want rambling conversations. The briefings have to be over fast so people can get to work or go home, as the case may be.

The weather briefing is short. It's either going to be good or not so good. But we will go regardless, changing targets based on what we can get. The weather briefer is usually a young lieutenant or captain, and he gets a lot of barbs thrown his way. If he has no sense of humor, he is dead meat. It helps to loosen up the room.

In their formal briefing, Intel gives BDA from yesterday, unusual events, thoughts about Iraqi air defenses or Scuds, or whatever is the hottest button. We might even get some news about events outside the war zone, such as peace initiatives by Iraqi foreign minister Tarik Aziz in Russia. (Question: How did he get out of Baghdad? Answer: He took a car to Iran and caught a commercial flight.) Sometimes the national leaders will ask questions, but not wishing to seem impolite or ungrateful, they leave the barbs at the briefers to me.

Next comes a run-through of logistics and communications, paying special attention to munitions and fuel reserves, aircraft status, and unusual transportation problems. Rider and Summers have done such a good job that they anticipate and fix problems before they become serious. It also sure helps to be fighting a war on top of most of the world's oil supply and to have giant refineries operating near the bases.

Though the B-52s at Jeddah are eating munitions at a fantastic rate, Jeddah is fortunately a large port, so we are able to truck the munitions quickly from the port to the build-and-storage areas. Rapidly generating the thousands of tons of bombs needed to support a high-tempo operation is no small thing. Even getting rid of the dunnage that the bombs came packed in is a major undertaking. And then specialized machines are needed to lift the bomb bodies and attach the fins and lugs. If you get careless, then you don't live to tell about it, and you'll probably take many of your friends along with you. Once the munitions have been built up, you have to deliver them to the aircraft and load them on the racks attached to the jets. About an hour before takeoff, the weapons troops place fuses and safety wires in each bomb.

★ 0730   The formal briefings are finished, and now all at the head table swivel their chairs and face the back of the room for Chris Christon's more speculative Intel briefing. This is where Chris sticks his neck out in a thoughtful, considered way, and it is understood that he does not have all the answers, and won't need an excuse if he is wrong. He also has a second, unofficial job—to keep General Horner awake, for I am now fighting off sleep with a vengeance. I make notes, just to keep my eyes open, but have trouble maintaining focus.

After he finishes (and it may be five or thirty minutes, depending), all feel free to challenge him, argue, or comment. Here we do our brainstorming. Obviously the junior officers are reluctant to speak, but if there is a burning idea they speak up; and if what Chris or someone else has said doesn't convince them, the bullshit flag is thrown.

Now it is somewhere near 0800, and I open the discussion to the national leaders, the top representatives from the Army, Navy, USMC, and Special Ops, and my own staff leaders. Some talk a little, some say nothing, and some have long but insightful comments. Anyone who gets long-winded, we joke into brevity. When I sense all have had their say, I wrap up the meeting with some nonthreatening (but sometimes negative) feedback and thoughts about where we need to go. When I have to threaten, I do it in private and give the individual a chance to explain.

By about 0815 to 0830 the meeting is over, and the night shift heads out.

★ 0830   Down the street, the CENTCOM staff is coming up to speed, which means that the phones will occasionally ring with their questions. Though I leave these matters to the TACC directors or my generals, I do want to know what questions are being asked, as the subject will likely come up in the CINC evening meeting, which means I have to be on top of it.

This is also a good time to chat with the national leaders, since they tend to leave during the day to visit their forces, or perhaps to escort some bigwig from their home country or grab a nap.

Tom Olsen has gone to bed. He is tireless, but getting on in years, and the night shift is a strain for him.

★ 0900   I go for a cup of coffee at the snack bar just off the right-hand side of the TACC toward the rear, over by airspace management. The cookies are abundant, and I take too many for my own good. The American people have kept us in goodies at a staggering rate. No wonder morale is so high. We know that our people at home are pulling for us and proud of us . . . so unlike Vietnam, so different.

I take my coffee and chat with the AWACS and Patriot teams, then pass by the Scud warning lady (since it's daytime, she won't have anything to do and can safely read her mystery or romance novels), the airspace management team, the duty officers on my left, the admin section on my right, and out the rear door. On good days, I make it without spilling any coffee.

Now I stroll down the hall past the ATO room, which is going full speed in mass confusion, and into the Black Hole for the daily strategy meeting. I will take what comes out of this to Schwarzkopf that night. Inside the Black Hole, Glosson, Tolin, and Deptula are drinking coffee and arguing about how the war is going and what we ought to do next. Though doctrine writers wax eloquently about this level of strategic thinking, as always it is coming down to people who don't have a clear understanding of what exactly needs to be done yet are far from blind, since they have intelligence not available to others, etc.

For my part, during the run-up to the war, I had read all I could about Saddam and the history and culture of Iraq. Dick Hallion, the USAF historian, had flooded my office with books on these subjects, which I'd devoured, sometimes reading more than one a day. It's funny how focused you get when final exams are approaching. This is the final exam of my military career.

As soon as I wander in, Dave Deptula, Buster Glosson, or Tony Tolin goes to the wall where a map of Iraq is stuck with colored pins indicating various category targets (blue might represent air defense; red, leadership; orange, NBC facilities; and green, Scud-related targets), and we discuss what needs to be done two days from now. (Sometimes when I am busy with a crisis, they do this without me; sometimes Buster comes down to the TACC and kneels beside my chair, and we go over what he is thinking.)

After we discuss the so-called strategic targets I move to the next room, where Bill Welch and Sam Baptiste will be dealing with long lists of targets nominated by our land force brethren. Fred Franks's VIIth Corps worked this list hard, both because they believed it was their duty and responsibility and because they believed air would be wasted going after targets that didn't matter to the real war if they didn't. XVIIIth's list was much shorter. Gary Luck had fewer Iraqis in front of him, and he would not get into the heavy stuff until his divisions had wheeled to the right along the rivers and attacked toward Basra. I also believed that he figured we knew how to do what was best and if he needed help he could count on us. In fact, I never got the impression he felt he was going to need any significant help. Walt Boomer's list was not as short as Luck's but much shorter than Fred's, perhaps because he figured he had his own Marine Air Force at his fingertips if he needed it. That was true in some ways, because the Harriers were thought of as CAS aircraft and really couldn't go very deep, due to range and vulnerability considerations. On top of that, the Marines will be loyal to one another in ways the Army and Air Force may not. (Neither Walt nor I have this attitude, but it may have influenced his iron majors and kept them from submitting long lists of targets in order to make sure they got their fair share of airpower, whatever that is or was.) The Northern Area and Eastern Area lists were submitted by Colonel Ayed al-Jeaid, the RSAF representative working in the C31C at MODA.

In fact, few specific targets came out of any of those lists, partly because we had adopted the kill box and level of effort concepts for attacking targets in the KTO, but mostly because Schwarzkopf really called the tune on this part of the ATO. Thus at the evening CINC meetings, the KTO targets would be briefed as 200 sorties against Iraqi divisions in this area and 150 sorties against divisions in that area. And every day, a Republican Guard division would be the "target du jour," and we would devote a great deal of effort to it. So every day we would work up a target list and present it to him; but each night he would to some extent redistribute the air level of effort. Though he was just doing his "land component commander" thing (as was his right and duty), in truth which targets we hit didn't really matter, since we were going to get them all before we started the ground war.

★ The air-superiority efforts (under Glenn Profitt) are planned in the next room of the Black Hole, but I don't have to spend much time there after the first days of the war. By now, the folks there mostly make sure the CAPs are in the right place at the right time, with emphasis on MiGs fleeing to Iran. They also frag the Wild Weasels, EF-111s, and EA-6Bs for support jamming; but that is easy, as our flights in the KTO consume most of the current effort, and about all they have to do is make sure there is coverage. Still, a few special flights require detailed support planning, such as the B-52 raid on the industrial complex north of Baghdad, or F-16s going after a nuclear R & D facility, but for the most part their work has become routine.

On my way out of the Black Hole, I pass the Scud cell, which is now empty. About all we can do is chase Scuds in real time with SAS and special forces on the ground and F-15E/F-16C LANTIRN-equipped patrols in the air. So planning consists of fragging the jets to provide coverage throughout the night, making sure we have maximum coverage at the most likely times for Scud launches. Because we have no idea where the Scuds are hiding, we have to dedicate significant resources—forty-eight jets—to work the problem.

If we were in the same boat today, I suspect we would use more human intelligence assets on the ground (such as paid Bedouin spies wandering around in places that are too hot for westerners), and better technical solutions (such as Joint STARS with automatic target recognition programs in their onboard computers, which would mean that controllers on the Joint STARS would not have to dig the target out of the maze on their scopes).

The automatic target recognition program would work like this: When the Joint STARS radar picked up a stationary Scud (using its synthetic aperture radar mode, SAR) or a transporter erector launcher (TEL) in transit (using its moving target indicator mode, MTI), the computer would recognize the target as a Scud or a TEL and alert the controller, who would then arrange for the target to be entered into the command-and-control system, and struck.

Between 1000 and 1100, I come out of the Black Hole and stick my head in the weather shop across the hall to get a detailed feeling about the weather over Iraq and our bases over the next few days. When you have a good sense of what might happen, then you better understand what people are telling you about what is happening. That is why you want to be close to the action, listen to what Intel and weather and logistics all tell you, and get a broad idea of how they reached their current solutions. So, for example, I would give the weather guys points of interest to look out for, as I described for them what I thought we would be doing the next few days. That way, they knew where to concentrate their attention when they looked over meteorological events.

After the weather shop, I hit the Marines and Navy rooms. These are built out of plywood and located in a dead-end hall next to the weather shop and across from the Black Hole. Now I am hungry and in a cookie hunt, and these guys always have some really good ones squirreled away. The Marines and Navy guys feel like part of the team and understand airpower, since most are pilots or weapons systems officers (or Naval flight officers, as the Navy calls them). I don't spend long there, because I want to get upstairs, either to clean up my desk or get a nap.

★ 1100   In my office three people are waiting to see me—Colonel Randy Randolph, my chief medical officer; Colonel Chaplain Hanson; and Colonel George Giddens, the "Mayor" of Riyadh for U.S. forces.

The doctor, Randy Randolph, wants to talk about inoculations for anthrax and botulism. He tells me what he thinks we should do with our limited number of injections and what the CENTCOM SG has put out for guidance. I go along with his advice, because he has his head on straight about everything else (from where to locate hospitals to which doctors and nurses to put in charge).

Colonel Chaplain Hanson, a Mormon, wants to know how I'm holding up, but I would rather learn his views about how everyone else is holding up. There are no surprises: we are pleased with the success we've had, but we are sick and tired of killing and having our guys shot down, and are all very tired and want to go home. It is good to meet with him, and he knows that I appreciate just talking about how God might be looking at what we are doing and about what he might want us to do—not that I believed we were any more important in God's eyes than a sparrow. Nonetheless, these higher-level questions do rumble around in your mind, and this guy gets training, time, and money to think about such things.

Last is George Giddens. Schwarzkopf instituted a "Mayor" wherever Americans were stationed, so the locals could have a single contact point where they could address concerns and get problems solved. When Schwarzkopf asked the Air Force to appoint the Mayor of Riyadh, George got the job. He is responsible for the care and feeding of U.S. residents in his city, and he works with the local Saudi civil and military chiefs; he has done a wonderful job.

George is here today because he is having a problem with some of the residents at Eskan Village and is going to take action. (I don't remember what the problem was—probably something like our guys were giving the Saudi guards on the gate a hard time, or else our guards were giving the Saudis delivering food and water a hard time, since anybody in Arab dress was looked on as a terrorist.) Since some of the troublemakers are Army guys, he wants me to know what he's doing in case I want him to back off. As usual, he is thoroughly on top of things and will get the problem solved. It is a great comfort to have such a mature, thoughtful, yet disciplined Mayor running things in my name. If he were less capable, I might find myself caught up in his job. Even though it is important to the war effort that the various staffs and troops about town have hot food to eat and a decent place to stay, I really shouldn't have to get into the hows and whens of any of that.

★ 1145   In the small dressing room next to the bathroom Tom Olsen and I share behind our office, there is a stuffed couch that looks like the finest king-size bed right about now. I sneak in for a quick nap, while

George Gitchell sits outside the door and screens calls and callers. In seconds I'm into a deep sleep, but I will wake up according to an internal alarm clock in my brain. I have always been able to wake up after whatever time I choose—fifteen minutes, thirty minutes, an hour, or 6:00 A.M. the next day. As it is, I will sleep between half an hour and an hour. After I wake up, I will go downstairs to lunch with the troops—another chance to find out what is going on and what they are thinking or worrying about.

★ 1300   Up with cold water in the face and a tooth-brushing to remove the remainders of the owl who slept in my mouth. I head downstairs to the Saudi cafeteria. The cook is an American Muslim who now lives in Riyadh after retiring from the USAF. Guess what fills my plate? You got it—grilled chicken, steamed rice with gravy, and boiled vegetables. It is tasty, but always the same. There is a salad of finely chopped, dark green lettuce mixed with finely chopped vegetables that might be green and red peppers, or might be stems of some exotic plant. Not so good, but keeps you regular. Dessert is usually a cake with crushed pistachio nuts on top. Water and a Diet Coke on the side.

I walk past the cash registers. The food's on the house, thanks to the Kingdom of Saudi Arabia. Now I search for a place to sit. I've got two criteria: (1) an empty chair, and (2) the people around it still have lots of food on their plates. Otherwise, when the general sits down, they will blush and mutter, "Got to go now." No one wants to sit with me.

I like to hit different groups—sometimes lower-grade airmen; sometimes Saudis (they freak out when I sit down, but then get over their fear because they are curious); sometimes foreign officers or enlisted men; and sometimes my own longtime Ninth Air Force staff. I will get different information from each group. The longtime companions are the most open. They tell me what they *really* like and don't like. They are my "emperor has no clothes" meter, and I try to hit them whenever possible for a reality check. The foreign officers and men tend to give me different angles on what we are doing and why we are doing it. Sometimes they give me information that can be useful in planning future operations, but often they are so indirect that I miss what they are trying to tell me. The GIs are full of questions and are an excellent source of the rumors that fill the air, most of which they believe. In some ways they represent all of America—filled with wonder about what we are doing and certain that very simple answers will handle the complex problems we face. Though most of them seem amazed that the general is sitting with them, after they get over their initial shyness, they open up in a hurry. Like all Americans, they stand in awe of no one for any length of time. I love their self-assurance, the absence of fear—they'll ask me anything that's on their minds. I love it that they think they are as good as I am. These qualities are perhaps our greatest strength as a nation. We really believe in ourselves—not in the sense that we arrogantly think we know everything, but that we are as good as the next person, and if we don't know the answer to a problem that plagues us, we are capable of understanding a good one when we get it.

★ 1345   Lunch is over, and I go back downstairs to the TACC, stopping by the computer room to check how the ATO is coming. I always have one question: "Are we going to get it to the units on time?" The answer is always "yes"; the reality is usually no. Colonel Rich Bennet, the one responsible for getting the ATO published after the Black Hole guys give him the master target list and packages, is pulling his hair out, because Buster wants to make last-minute changes that will screw the whole thing up. People are busy fat-fingering in the 100,000 details that go into any ATO—takeoff time, tanker orbit points, munitions, call signs, code words, IFF squawks, no-fly zones, fly zones, coordinating points, lines on the ground, air routes in the air. I get out of there quickly, as people are very busy and working at a frantic pace, and I hate computers.

★ 1400   I sag back into my chair in the Current Operations section of the TACC, watching the AWACS picture—yellow icons streaming into and out of Iraq. One of our aircraft has been lost, and Jim Crigger has just filled me in on what they appeared to be doing and what caused the shoot-down. As always, I hate these moments.

As I sit there, weary, I let the noise and chaos of the TACC voices, announcements, reports wash over me—the sights and sounds of my war, not the war I experienced in Vietnam. There the action was intense—sweat running into your eyes from under your helmet, your head twisting and turning, trying to see everything, from the MiG closing on your rear to the SAM trying to hit you in the face. But there you were better-rested than here, and when you got down from your mission, you were through for the day. You could go to the bar and get mindlessly drunk and fall asleep, until the next morning's briefing started you on another day of boredom punctuated by an hour or so of sheer-ass terror. In this war, there is little boredom and almost no terror, except maybe the fear of screwing up and getting someone killed.

Meanwhile, it is important for me to sit and listen when the troops talk at me about what they are doing and what is important to them. Moreover, their energy is contagious, their intelligence brilliant. It's exciting to listen to them when they come up to Crigger or Volmer with suggestions about making this or that mission more effective or making up for the bad weather over target XYZ by going to target ABC. (Colonel Al Volmer was one of the four colonels who ran the war from the TACC.) Crigger or Volmer listen to what they have to say, then tell them how to implement their brainchild without screwing up the bigger picture.

People visiting the TACC stop by, and we chat. Later, the BCE team chief and some of his people gather around the table behind my chair and they talk about the ground war, which is bound to unfold soon. Joe Bob Phillips has come in early, and I give him a task to solve, usually about finding Scuds or avoiding friendly casualties.

It's hard to describe the tension, boredom, highs and lows that occurred in that room. When CNN went off the air on the first night, we were sky-high. The tension of anticipating everything that could have gone wrong that night was erased. But then there were the moments when someone was shot down, and we watched the futile efforts to pick up the survivor. There were also the long hours of routine, coffee breath, and sand in the eyes. I often pressed a can of cold Diet Coke into my eyes to make the swelling go down. Sometimes the pain and irritation would make me tear up so much that I couldn't read reports or pay attention to the unfolding battle. There was also the anxious excitement when "Scud ALERT" was screamed out, especially during the first few days of missile attack, before we became overconfident that they wouldn't hit us. Blind trust. There was the preparation, about 2100 or 2200 each night, when we tried to anticipate what was going to happen that evening— usually Scuds or Al-Khafji type things. There were good times, stopping by the coffeepots to tell war stories about the good old days. There were times when you wanted to cry, as when Lieutenant Colonel Donnie Holland was shot down at Basra and there were no beacons, meaning that in all likelihood he was dead. Holland had been my executive officer when I was the two-star planner at headquarters Tactical Air Command.

When he wanted to get into the F-15E, I arranged it; and he was a first-rate weapons system officer. That night he was flying with a flight surgeon who was dual-rated as a pilot, and they flew into the ground. Though we gave the Iraqis credit for shooting them down, Donnie was in the rear cockpit because the doctor's work in the hospital kept him from getting as much flying time as the other pilots. So Holland, the old head WSO, was crewed with the doctor/pilot who was low on flying time.

There was lots of shared joy and shared pain, often with people who'd been strangers until we came together for the war. There was lots of serious talk and some joking around, especially with the guys who were old Ninth Air Force friends or other longtime acquaintances like John Corder. It really was a living organism; it reacted to stimuli—pain, joy, and loneliness. Too often, we in the military draw our little boxes that explain how we are organized, who commands whom, who stands where on the command food chain. That's all fine and rational and necessary, but in reality, while we try to create these hierarchies with the power to command others to go out and risk their lives in battle, we are actually a team of fallible humans who do our best to find the best course of action. But then people have to put on G suits and try. If they succeed, we all bask in the glory. If they fail, we try to learn why and perhaps have another collective go at it again. If they are wounded, captured, or killed, then the guy in the G suit suddenly gets the whole enchilada, and those of us who are ancillary to that event are left with feelings of pain and sorrow, and a somewhat guilty sense of relief that it wasn't us who paid that price. Fortunately, I had been shot at and had taken pretty extreme risks, which gave me a fairly good understanding of the folks who strapped on the jets and headed for danger. In my view, anyone who sends others off, perhaps to die, needs that kind of understanding. As much as this thing we call command and control is about modern computers, communications, planning tools, and satellite photography, it is also about people wandering around in partial ignorance, trying to do good by doing evil, and feeling—sometimes all at once—joy-pain-fear-uncertainty-fatigue-love-and-grief.

★ 1600   I have appointments with the press—first with a newspaper writer, and then with TV people. The newswoman meets me in a trailer in the parking lot out back; the air conditioner hum keeps out the noise of planes and people. As she takes out her tape recorder, I sneak a peek at her legs. It's been over six months, and I am no priest. She asks me about how the war is going, what is the matter with BDA, and when the ground war will start. I want to answer "Good," "Nothing," and "You have me confused with somebody who gives a shit"; but instead I try to be as open as I can.

My PA, Major Oscar Seara, is with me. At 1645, he steers the lady to the gate and me to the Airlift TACC tent, closer to the building. Here the camera and mikes are set up, and I meet ABC's Sam Donaldson (or someone of that ilk). This is a love-in. The war is going well, and they need about three minutes with me on camera so they can give their audience an orgasm. The lady reporter had asked some difficult questions because she had done her homework and wanted to write an insightful piece. How can you get real information from two-minute TV slices? On the other hand, the TV reporter is real good at stroking people's egos, and I like having mine stroked in front of millions of people.

★ 1730   I finally get out of there and reenter the RSAF Headquarters at the door near the mosque. The turnout is better than it had been this morning. The wail of the prayers and the sun dropping low in the horizon put me in an oriental mood, so I guess it's time to drop in on Behery. I visit him at his office because this honors him, it's a nicer place than mine, and his staff will serve *gaua* and tea.

Anytime we are together, I do my best to pick his brain about today's problems and crises. I want to know his thoughts about how things are going and what we ought to do. But he is operating on a very different plane. He wants to give me instruction about his land, his culture, his religion, and his people. His words are often about the tenth century, and I am thinking in the twentieth. And yet this is not wasted time.

Even though our backgrounds are vastly different, we have a real and very deep friendship. It's hard to find words to describe it. In many ways, I guess, I look up to him much like an older brother. He is always courteous, always thoughtful, yet sometimes he is wary of Americans, especially of our willingness to move mountains no matter who lives in their shadow. He is thoughtful, where I am anxious to get going. He weighs risks, where I look for opportunities. He thinks about consequences, where I don't often give a damn.

I can tell you this. With westerners, I have friends—good friends—people I like to sit and talk with, people I like to fly with and drink with;

but they are just that, friends. When an Arab allows you to be his friend, your heart leaps against your breastbone and you feel a rush of joy. This is not corny; it's true. I guess we in the West give our friendship so freely that it has little value. An Arab gives his friendship so warily that once you are accepted, you realize how deeply you have to appreciate it. I am poor at describing this, but good at feeling it.

★ 1800   I'm back in my office, boning up for the coming staff meetings, shift change, and the follies at MODA with Schwarzkopf. After that I read the "Read File" (even though George Gitchell and Tom Olsen have taken care of all the routine stuff that I would normally have to bother with in peacetime). I also read the Army and Navy messages, so I know what they are thinking and are worried about. I can read very quickly; I go through a three-inch-thick folder in twenty minutes.

Then it's time to write Mary Jo, which I do in about ten minutes. Not much I can tell her, except how much I truly miss her and that I will be a much better husband when I come home (this will last about a month).

By 1855, I'm finished with the paperwork and have had some private time to sit and think. Do not discount the value of calm private reflection as you prepare for a frenzied evening of meetings and Iraqi tricks.

★ 1900   I'm back in the TACC and all are assembled for the changeover meeting. We start on time. (It's important to start meetings promptly. That way, people will make every effort to be on time; and anyhow, it's the polite thing to do.)

Except that the briefers are different, this changeover is not much different from the one in the morning. This time, the Intel people discuss the Iraqi transportation system and which bridges we should strike. The BCE briefs the Army situation. Not much there except for complaints from a corps commander that we are not hitting his nominated targets and therefore he will lose the war. YGBSM.* Chris Christon gives his spiel, and there is more discussion with the national leaders around the table. I end the meeting with as much guidance as I feel safe to give. Most of it is very general, as I am looking for what they think, not what I think. I want people offering up their own insights, not guessing at mine, and then offering that up as their own.

The day shift clears out by 2000, and the night shift moves into action,

---

*You got to be s——ing me.

Reavy and Harr get spun up; Crigger and Volmer get ready to take off. Joe Bob Phillips has his tactics team formed and around the map table behind my chair. They are talking about what-ifs we may face tonight, primarily Scuds.

★ 2030   I meet Buster upstairs by the front door. He is always running late, getting the master target list built and ready for the evening briefing at MODA. And as always, he comes racing up the stairs, with maybe Tolin or Deptula chasing after him with last-minute bits of information.

Now the second most important meeting of the day occurs. I sit in the front of the car with my driver, and Buster sits in the back with his notes and charts. As we drive to MODA, we plan the strategy for the meeting. The goal is to get through it with our air campaign intact and the CINC pleased—knowing that he will change the Army-nominated targets all around. We do not wish to incur his withering temper (which we've managed to avoid since the war started). Though we are not trying to be cunning or manipulative, there is no reason not to make a successful sales pitch. Buster is a master at thinking on his feet, and I reserve for myself the role of peacemaker. E.g., the CINC questions some assumption or decision of Buster's, and I jump in with, "You're exactly right; we will take a closer look at it, and I will let you know." We even plant a few questionable items in the briefing so other items look more acceptable. In some ways, we have it tough, because we are the only game in town. When the land forces start doing something besides moving west and talking about getting ready, then sitting in this meeting will be pure joy. We'll be home free, knowing we'd done our job as advertised, and they will be subject to the CINC's judgment that they are screwing up.

We arrive at MODA in time for Buster to rush downstairs to set up his charts, and I drop by to talk with some of the CENTCOM staff— sometimes with Bob Johnston, the harried chief of staff; sometimes with Cal Waller, who is full of himself; sometimes with Brigadier General Jack Leide, CENTCOM J-2 (Intelligence), who is really helping us; sometimes with the RSAF chief in the C3IC, Colonel Ayed Al-Jeaid, who is my conduit into Khaled and one of the sharpest men I have ever worked with.

Five minutes before nine, I wander into what the CINC calls the war room. It's a conference room with maps and telephones that holds about twelve people at a table in front. For the CENTCOM staff and key onlookers, there are built-in tables, raised up amphitheater-style about the sides and back of the room. I sit to the left of the CINC. Usually Sir Peter de la Billiere or Bob Johnston is to *my* left, and then Stan Arthur's and Walt Boomer's representatives. On my right beyond Schwarzkopf are Cal Waller, John Yeosock, and the Frenchman, Lieutenant General Michel Roquejeoffre, with his interpreter kneeling at his side. Buster Glosson sits in the back.

The CINC usually strides in on time. He may be in a good mood. He may be in a foul mood. For me it is not important what mood he is in. My job is to sell him another day of airpower the day after tomorrow, and that is what I am focused on. After the CINC sits down, the rest of us take our seats, and the usual briefings follow.

Often Jack Leide takes some hits. His job is to provide estimates of what is going on in Baghdad. But since no one knows that for sure, his opinions are always open to criticism—especially when these differ from the CINC's reading of the tea leaves. Moreover, the CINC often wants answers that are simply not available. So when he asks, and Jack can't answer (nobody could, except the enemy), he gets a needle from Schwarzkopf (who thinks that will make Jack work harder—an impossibility, as he is working as hard as he can). Despite the needles, he is bulletproof and barely flinches when he's roared at. The man has style.

There also may be briefings about such things as how the army is doing on its march to the west. Interesting, but not very important to me. I make sure I say nothing, but look intelligent, interested, and respectful. A J-3 staffer briefs the air war, and does a pretty good job at it. He should, since my people gave him everything he is briefing and made sure he didn't say the wrong things or otherwise light a fuse under the CINC. (The good thing about his temper: people listen when you tell them how to avoid it, and they are grateful. Of course, the bad thing about it is that most will not tell him anything substantial. Why get chewed out when you'll all be going home in a couple of months? Best to hang in there silent.) I avoid his temper because it might force him to make a bad decision that I would have to live with or somehow get changed. This is serious business—but then, it should be, and we are big boys.

Finally, Buster gets up and briefs the forthcoming air campaign. This goes well, because that is the way it should go. A lot of thought and effort have gone into our planning and presentation. If either Buster or I sense we are heading toward a possible train wreck, we avoid it by softening the briefing.

Toward the end, we come to the KTO targeting. At this point, Buster takes out a notebook; we know we are going to get new guidance. Without any bluster (other than to ask who was the dumb SOB who nominated these targets, at which John Yeosock winces), the CINC turns to a map on his right and points to the Iraqi divisions he wants struck. Not a problem, as they are all in the same general locale, and the flyers are going to strike what is hot anyway, based on Killer Scouts, Joint STARS, or newer intelligence.

The meeting finishes with a swing around the table, to give each of the top commanders a chance to speak. And then Schwarzkopf does some schmoozing with the foreign officers—a reinforcing-the-Coalition sort of thing.

If I need to discuss anything with him, I will ask for time in his office after the meeting. If it is a small matter, we take care of it in quiet whispers right there. This drives the staff crazy, because they want in on what I am telling him; but I have learned never to talk to him in front of anyone, as it forces him to agree, or worse, disagree. Once it is public, you have great difficulty walking the cat back.

After the meeting breaks up, Buster often stays behind to work with the CENTCOM staffers. He has spies in place there gathering information that will concern tomorrow night's presentation. This is serious business, and we take it seriously.

★ 2230   Back in the TACC. Deptula is already working the changes from the CENTCOM meeting. He probably had them reworked before the meeting took place, as we have become good at anticipating the CINC, and feed in those decisions we want changed, so the ones we don't want changed will not suffer.

Now it's fun time. The Iraqis are on the move, relocating their vehicles, scaring the Army strung out along Tapline Road, or shooting Scuds. The place heats up.

Event One: Joint STARS reports a small column of twenty armored vehicles moving in the vicinity of Jabar airfield in south central Kuwait. Solution: divert a flight of IR Maverick A-10s. They work with Joint STARS, find the column, and hit the lead and tail vehicle. Once these are ablaze, the column is halted, and F/A-18s, F-16s, and more A-10s finish off the survivors.

Event Two: We get reports that the Iraqis are attacking in the vicinity of Listening Post 11.

"Intel, what do you have?"

"Nothing."

"No signals?"

"No."

"AWACS, do you see anything [such as helicopters]?"

"No."

Twenty minutes of "What the hell is going on?" follow, until we realize that it is some of our troops who went sight-seeing into Kuwait to check out the wire and mine fields and decided to come home another way (which is code for they got scared and lost, but managed to find a way out).

Event Three: Intel shows a Scud en route to western launch boxes. "Get F-15Es on that."

They attack four large vehicles with 500-pound bombs and CBUs, and the targets blaze in the night sky. It all probably means that four Jordanian families have lost their fuel-truck-driving fathers on the highway between Baghdad and Amman. Sorry, but they need to stay off the road. It's dangerous out there.

Event Four: AWACS calls out that an Iraqi helicopter is in the west near the Saudi border and headed west. Two F-15Cs call tally and are cleared to fire by AWACS, since there is no friendly traffic fragged for that area.

Reavy is skeptical, because the Iraqis have pretty much shown good sense about where and when they fly. Thinking it is probably a Special Ops mission, he calls the Special Ops liaison and tells him to get his ass into the TACC (Special Ops had a little private room of their own just outside the TACC).

When the guy comes out, he says the helicopters are not his, and they can die as far as he cares.

Mike Reavy still thinks something is wrong here and tells the major to get his ass back into his secret room to check.

He comes out minutes later, pale as a ghost. They *are* Special Ops choppers, inbound to a drop zone.

Event Five: The young lady on my left has stopped reading her romance novel and announces a Scud attack in a very loud but controlled voice. The room stirs, but holds off a response. I pick up the master attack list and look at the clock: 1235. Then I scan the TOT listings. Sure enough, there is a flight of three B-52s dropping on the Tawalkana Republican Guard. At 1236, there they are on the AWACS display.

Fifty seconds later, the same young lady in the same very loud but controlled voice announces, "Disregard the Scud alert. False alarm." (The DSP IR satellites had seen the intense heat across the earth made by a string of bombs and duly reported it to the ground station in Colorado. However, when the watts per steradian did not match the Scud profile loaded into the computer, the event was reported as an "anomaly," which is space-geek talk for "hell if I know.")

In between events, I read my mail, lots of it, and I love it all—from Mary Jo, from friends, from people I've never met and probably never will. It is a lifesaver for all of us and a great source of energy.

★ It is now 0200 in the morning, and Tom is fully in charge. Things have quieted down, and I am very, very tired. I've already fallen asleep twice in my chair, but this is not an uncommon sight when things are slowing down and you have someone next to you who can fill in if needed. It's not like guard duty.

It's time to haul my tail upstairs, put on the pistola and bulletproof vest, and head back out through the wall, talking calmly to all the guard posts en route. I do not want to get killed in this war.

The apartment is dark, but I don't bother to turn on the lights or hang up my uniform. I just place it over the chair and crash into the bed. Fortunately, there will be a clean bed and fresh underwear, thanks to the house boy, Chris from Sri Lanka. He is never there when I come and go, but he always picks up after me and keeps the laundry clean and ready.

I will change fatigues in the morning, so I'll get up a little earlier than usual. But then, since John is not sleeping here tonight, at least the phone won't be ringing. I am asleep in seconds.

13

THE TEN PERCENT WAR

In February 1991, during the waning moments of the war, a debate went on in the White House about choosing a moment to cease hostilities. As Colin Powell reports in his autobiography, the debate ended when John Sununu suggested 0500 on February 28. That way the "war" would have lasted a hundred hours and could be plausibly named "The Hundred-Hour War." And so it came about. It was a brilliant idea. The name had PR pizzazz.

There was only one problem: the war did not last one hundred hours. The duration of the war—from mid-January to the end of February—was closer to a thousand hours. Sununu and the others in the White House were thinking of the ground war, of course—an easy misconception, but maddening to Coalition airmen, who bore such a large part of the burden of winning this war. To them, the ground effort was not a Hundred-Hour War, it was a Ten Percent War.

This is not to say that the ground war was a waste or unnecessary—far from it—and as January turned into February, and February wore on, Coalition air devoted an ever-greater portion of their effort to preparing for it. The ground invasion of Kuwait was to come soon, everyone knew, but when? When was G day?

The decision to start the ground war was based on the answers to three questions:

1. Were the Iraqis beaten down enough to allow Coalition ground forces to attack with a minimum of casualties?
2. Would the weather be favorable enough to allow air support?
3. Were Coalition troops trained and logistically ready, and at their assigned starting-out locations?

We'll look at the answers to these questions over the course of this chapter.

BEATING DOWN THE IRAQIS

The answer to question one depended on three factors. First: battlefield preparation. How successful was Coalition airpower in reducing Iraqi armor and artillery? Second: The choice of which Iraqi units to hit, how hard, and when. (These two issues were related, but they were kept separate at CENTCOM and CENTAF, because of the understandable interest of Coalition ground units in the condition of the Iraqi units they themselves would be facing.) Third: PSYOPS. How successful were Coalition psychological-warfare efforts in undermining the morale of Iraqi ground forces? An army that has no taste to fight is an army that is beaten—even if they are equipped with state-of-the-art equipment in pristine shape.

★ Though air attacks had hurt Iraqi forces in the KTO before the beginning of February, the Iraqis were still a reasonably effective fighting force. February ruined them. The following summary is based on a Chris Christon report from February 10, 1991.

In his view, initial attacks—primarily directed against the air defense system, Scud sites, infrastructure, leadership, and weapons research, development, and production facilities—had had no major impact on the Iraqi Army. Commanders and their staffs had proved very flexible in handling the difficulties that Coalition air attacks had imposed on their operations. For example, when air attacks cut telephone lines, the Iraqis used message carriers on motorcycles. When air disrupted their command-and-control networks (as part of the destruction of the centralized air defense system), the Iraqis developed work-arounds; and their command-and-control network remained effective, secure, and capable of supporting major military operations.

On the front lines, they had adjusted their routines around the timing of air attacks, and for the first part of the war, the Iraqi Army found sanctuary at night. They were able to do this because the most capable Coalition systems for night attack—F-117s, F-111s, and LANTIRN-equipped F-15Es and F-16s—were tied up chasing Scuds or hitting fixed targets outside the KTO, which left the job of hitting the Iraqi Army at night mostly to A-10s, A-6s, and B-52s hitting area targets.

All this changed in February, when most of the air effort was devoted to shaping the battlefield. For example, of the 986 bombing sorties scheduled for February 11, 933 of them were tasked to that mission. And here is how shaping-the-battlefield sorties were allocated by corps during the period from February 10 through February 12:

SAMPLE SORTIE ALLOCATIONS* (IN PERCENTS)

	XVIIIth Airborne Corps	VIIth Corps	NAC	USMC	EAC	RG
February 10	1	13	24	33	1	28
February 11	2	22	20	33	2	21
February 12	2	17	16	31	2	32

Note: Daily Sorties Flown—Feb 10: 957; Feb 11: 933; Feb. 12: 952.

By mid-February, the total air campaign was well under way. Now the sorties against front-line forces were flying night and day. Now attacks on the Iraqi transportation system were starting to have effect, and enemy reports of food and water shortages began to filter into the intelligence system. Now the war was almost as boring as an airline schedule—except that it wasn't passengers that were being delivered.

What gave interest to this sea of monotony were the Scuds at night, combat losses, and the weather, which was a constant problem, as waves of low pressure swept down across Baghdad toward Basra.

Meanwhile, the tank plinkers were bagging up to 150 tanks per night, which was the best news Chuck Horner could give General Schwarzkopf, who was by then engrossed with the details of the ground offensive plan. This last was in turn good news to Horner, because, first, it meant they

---

*The numbers refer to sorties flown against units in front of XVIIIth Airborne Corps (including French forces), VIIth Corps, Northern Area Corps (Egyptians and Syrians), the U.S. Marines, and Eastern Area Corps (Arabs, primarily Saudis), except that the final listing is for sorties flown against the Republican Guard.

were closer to going home, and, second, it meant that the CINC pretty much stayed out of Horner's business, except for his nightly reorganizing of the target list of Iraqi Army units.

The question remained: "When will the ground war start?" Part of the answer depended on accurate knowledge of BDA—bomb damage assessment. But here there was controversy. "Have we destroyed a third of the Iraqi tanks? Half? A quarter?" The desired number was 50 percent, but how close or how far Horner's pilots were to attaining that number was a matter of dispute, according to the estimating body.

A comparison of estimates gives insight into the confusion, the interagency bickering, and, in Horner's words, "the slavish desire to count beans rather than estimate combat power" that surrounded what some call the great Battle Damage Assessment War. On February 23, in an effort to determine when to start the ground war, various intelligence agencies reported the following:

NUMBERS (PERCENT) OF REPORTED IRAQI EQUIPMENT LOSSES

Organization Reporting	Tanks	Armored Personnel Carriers	Artillery
JCS/ CENTCOM	1,688 (39)	929 (32)	1,452 (47)
Central Intelligence Agency	524 (12)	245 (9)	255 (8)
Defense Intelligence Agency	685 (16)	373 (13)	622 (20)

Chuck Horner comments:

Needless to say, such wide variance was not only fiercely debated between Washington and the theater, it turned into an ugly game of intelligence analysts' one-upmanship. After the war, it was learned that JCS/CENTCOM numbers had been not too far off the mark. Based on this more accurate database, it appears that on or about February 23, the Iraqis had actually lost 48% of their tanks,

30% of their armored personnel carriers, and 59% of their artillery pieces.

In the final analysis, the BDA controversy had nothing to do with the actual success achieved. For in the end it was not the intelligence agencies that would tell Generals Schwarzkopf and Khaled when to start the ground war, it was their gut feelings. Call it intuition, experience, judgment, whatever you like, that is what the commanders were stuck with when they made their life-or-death decision. The decision to send soldiers forward was the province of the commanders, Schwarzkopf and Khaled. That is where it belonged, and they got it right. If they had believed the BDA estimates from Washington, we would have delayed the ground war until after Ramadan. If they had believed their own intelligence count, they might have waited a little longer than they did and perhaps have given Saddam time to put together a diplomatic way to extract his army from the hell of the KTO. But they didn't do either. In the end, they did what commanders are trained to do. They took the information available, judged it against standards of common sense, swallowed hard, and ordered the troops forward into uncertainty.

In the absolutely final analysis, the ability of Coalition ground forces to defeat the Iraqi Army so rapidly and thoroughly may have had little to do with destroying tanks and artillery. There is powerful evidence from the 88,000 POWs that air's most significant impact on Iraqi fighting strength was the destruction of morale.

Morale was undermined in several ways. The isolation of the battlefield denied the Iraqi soldier food and water, but he was at the same time worn down by the incessant air attacks, and by the PSYOPS campaign that held out hope in the form of surrender. He was also effectively disarmed, because by the time the ground war started, he and his companions feared going near their vehicles—APCs, tanks, and artillery pieces, which air attacks had made death traps.

So as the ground attack was sweeping the remnants of the Iraqi Army aside, intelligence analysts were still hunched over their overhead photographs of Iraq and Kuwait, trying to count individual tanks and artillery pieces; for these "accountants of war" had no other way to understand airpower, no other way to measure what had happened during the revolution in military actions that was Desert Storm.

There was a second (and related) controversy in February—the prioritization of which units got bombed, when, and how much.

The problem was complex. In order to make a correct determination, the status of particular Iraqi units had to be known with some accuracy. All of them had been bombed for weeks now, some more than others, and many had been seriously degraded. In some cases, Horner's intelligence people knew the exact condition of a particular unit—often the units were severely debilitated by desertions and destroyed equipment. In other cases, it was anybody's guess. (It's doubtful that the Iraqi corps commanders had anything like a clear idea of the condition of their assigned forces.) Either way, the status of individual units often changed daily, just as the status of particular locations changed daily, as individual units moved back and forth, here and there (the Iraqi Army, Fred Franks has pointed out, was not skilled at maneuvering, but annoyingly they could and did shift unit locations).

Just as in the BDA controversy, the various intelligence sources could not agree on the status of individual Iraqi divisions in the KTO. So the question remained: how much more work had to be done before a ground offensive could begin?

★ Meanwhile, each of the ground force corps commanders believed he alone was responsible for success. This is not a criticism. A prudent commander takes nothing for granted; after all, the lives of his troops are at stake. So each corps commander planned his war—his narrow slice of the battlefield—as if it was the only game in town. He didn't worry about adjacent ground battles as long as the adjacent commander was doing his job, and no one's flanks were exposed.

Yet for Horner, demands on air now came from three to five directions (not including Schwarzkopf and Khaled). It was his responsibility, when building each day's tasking order, to service each corps commander's needs in accordance with the overall guidance set forth by Schwarzkopf and Khaled.

Someone had to decide who got the most, who got the next most, and so on. Someone had to set target priorities, had to make a sequential listing of the Iraqi divisions that were to be bombed each day. In an ideal world this should have been a simple task. Of the approximately forty Iraqi divisions deployed in the desert, some were more important than others by virtue of their equipment, their location, or their current strength.*

Their location proved to be the real thorn in Chuck Horner's side. Each ground commander thought the Iraqis in his own battle space were the most important Iraqis. Though each corps commander was aware of the CINC's guidance and general battle plan, each still had to win "his war" on his own.

In practical terms, things worked this way:

Walt Boomer in the east coordinated his offensive plan with the Islamic corps on his right, the Eastern Area Command, and with the one on his left, the Northern Area Command. For his part, Boomer was generally confident that the targets of immediate concern to him would be serviced, because USMC aircraft were collocated with him and had limited range. Boomer's enemy was going to get bombed, simply because the basing and design of Marine air vehicles, such as the AV-8B Harrier, left little other choice. This was in itself fine, until we consider that Boomer faced the largest number of Iraqis, but with aircraft that were the least capable in payload, range, and use of precision munitions.

Fred Franks's VIIth Corps (including a British division), to the left of the Northern Area Corps, was designated the main attack, because their job was to outflank Kuwait and plunge into the Republican Guard and Iraqi heavy armored divisions. Franks justifiably wanted most of the air to go against these well-equipped divisions, for there the fighting should be the fiercest.

Though the other U.S. and Islamic corps commanders doubtless agreed with him, the lives of their troops were as valuable as the lives of VIIth Corps and British troops; and therefore, they were not about to be submissive when it came time to argue for air. Gary Luck's XVIIIth Airborne Corps and the French forces in the far west had the big job of driving farther north into Iraq than the other corps, and then swinging to the

*It should not be forgotten that someone did set target priorities—Norman Schwarzkopf. And in the final analysis, targets were chosen by the airmen in the air, by the Killer Scouts and the controllers in J-STARS. But saying this does not deny the legitimate concerns of the corps commanders, or the problems these concerns gave to Chuck Horner.

right and fighting farther east. Though they had the fewest enemies per mile of travel, they had the most miles of travel. Like the other commanders, Luck wanted his share of the air.

On top of all of this, John Yeosock's Third Army headquarters oversaw Franks's and Luck's planning efforts, with Yeosock's G-3, Brigadier General Steve Arnold, being the man in the middle between the corps commanders and Schwarzkopf. Arnold's job was to argue Franks's and Luck's case against the requirements of the two Islamic corps, represented by C3IC's Paul Schwartz and Abdullah al-Shaikh, and Schwarzkopf's other component commander, Walt Boomer.

In point of fact, John Yeosock should have been the man to work the problem out, but he did not command the two Islamic corps (who were under Khaled) or the USMC ground forces (the U.S. ground component commander was Schwarzkopf, remember). There is no doubt in my mind that John Yeosock would have been a superb ground commander, and there is no doubt in my mind that Walt Boomer could have worked for John with the same respect and loyalty he showed the CINC. Finally, there is no doubt in my mind that Paul Schwartz and al-Shaikh at C3IC could have worked with John Yeosock. Yet this was not to be. So we remained in some ways a debating society for air until the evening meeting with Schwarzkopf, when he would decide how much air would be tasked against which Iraqi division two days hence.

The debate was a waste, and never-ending, because some corps commanders were never satisfied with what they were getting and could never accept some kind of rational harmonizing of their needs with those of the other commanders. More important, they could never accept that the Air Force was not under their control. We wanted to service their genuine needs, but we stopped being a branch of the Army fifty years ago. What they could—and should—have done was send in their target nominations and accept whatever they got. If they had a specific need, all they had to do was tell the BCE, and if it made sense they would have gotten it. On the other hand, since the CINC made the final decisions about targets, it was all a tempest in a helmet.

On February 4, an attempt was made to end the logjam among corps commanders. The DCINC, Cal Waller, would develop the prioritized target list, a list that would take into account the needs of all ground components.

The idea was that he would draw up the list of targets. Then the combined Coalition staff in the Black Hole would apply air expertise to determine what could and could not be hit. Then the list would return to the DCINC for approval, after which point the ATO would be cut.

Brigadier General Mike Hall, Horner's liaison with Cal Waller for this program, would work up a seventy-two-hour rolling target list, based on the requirements of the combined divisions, as modified by their corps headquarters, as modified by the Third U.S. Army, C3IC, and the USMC component. Thus, on a normal day, Waller's prioritized list would send about 1,000 sorties to strike Iraqi Army units. Buster Glosson's targeteers would meanwhile continue to work up targets outside the KTO, and these would be serviced by sorties taken off the top, usually by F-117s, F-111s, and half the F-15Es (the rest continued to hunt Scuds).

This should have worked, but it didn't, and Chuck Horner never expected it would, since he never imagined that Waller would be able to bring into harmony the various corps demands.

Soon after the system was set up, Colonel Clint Williams, Waller's point man on the effort, relayed to the duty officer in the TACC that the DCINC was unable to come up with a list.

Colonel Dave Schulte, the head of the BCE, was tasked with finding out what was holding things up, and he immediately set out to find out how the ARCENT target list was built. Colonel Schulte spent five hours with the ARCENT Deep Operations shop, where he learned that the VIIth and XVIIIth Corps representatives received and worked their target inputs differently, primarily because each used different software to track Iraqi forces and analyze the target nominations.

But the real problem remained. The representatives from each corps—usually majors—were unable to stop fighting among themselves over air. Each thought he was responsible for grabbing as much for his corps as he could (it was thought of as a zero-sum game), and Waller wasn't strong enough to bring sense and system to the situation, or to get the majors organized and working in harmony. That's why I offered to let Waller build the list in the first place. Because I felt he couldn't do it, and Baptiste and Welch were doing fine as it was, especially since Schwarzkopf made the final decisions anyway.

Meanwhile, a Captain Simms had done what he could to bring order to the building of the priority lists, and had tried to come up with a fair and reasonable way to allocate target selection. His system was to rotate the nominations from each corps on a 5-3-2-2 weighted basis. That is, each list had five ARCENT targets first, followed by three VIIth Corps targets, and two each XVIIIth Airborne Corps Northern Area Command targets. The next five would come from the ARCENT list, and so on. Any priority among targets was made by the unit nominating it.

At least it was a list. If the Army was happy with it, then I was happy with it. But they weren't. The corps commanders wouldn't accept Simms's system of priorities.

The target priority controversy continued after the war. Various war councils were held, lessons learned were published, and a variety of doctrinal documents were drafted. The goal of these councils was to increase the voice of the ground commanders over where, when, and how air was used. Their basic premise was that the joint force air component commander would misuse his office, ground would not control the air, and air would not be used properly. It made little difference that Desert Storm was a success by most every measure. That aberration was simply the result of the friendship and trust between Yeosock, Boomer, Arthur, and Horner.

Well, let me tell you, this doctrinal bickering is horse manure. First of all, in Desert Storm we had one ground commander for each of the two forces, and they approved every target. Their names were Schwarzkopf and Khaled, and they trusted their air component to organize a daily air campaign, which they reviewed as land component commanders, and then as CINCs either changed or approved. Though all the subordinate ground commanders had their say in the process, they had to understand that they were not in charge of the air effort—or, for that matter, of the ground effort. They could not own the air, and it stuck in their craw.

Secondly, all subordinates in a war must understand that no joint force commander wants to lose. He hopes to use air, land, sea, and space assets in a way that will bring victory on the battlefield. So back in the Pentagon, quit writing doctrine that is a compro-

mise between the way each separate service wants to fight wars, be-
cause they don't fight wars. Unified commanders and their allied
commanders (in Desert Storm, Schwarzkopf and Khaled) are in
charge. If we follow the doctrines of compromise published by the
services and the Joint Staff, we will end up with "war fought by
committee"—a sure loser.

I thank God Schwarzkopf was in charge in the Gulf, because
there was no wondering about which service doctrine was going to
prevail. There no component would dominate the planning. This
was not Vietnam, where the Pentagon warriors dictated targets,
tactics, and procedures. We were a team with one vision of what
needed to be done. It is true that we had to muddle along as we fig-
ured it out (as was the case in identifying Iraqi Army target prior-
ities); but I knew we would get the job done, however we decided
to do it, because the CINCs were in charge, and the components
respected and trusted each other.

PSYCHOLOGICAL WARFARE

Psychological warfare has been an element in all combat, and its importance in warfare will inevitably grow, as skill grows in influencing the
moods, motives, and will of others. The range of psychological influence
has also grown with the range of media influence. Vietnam was not lost
on the streets of American cities, but it's hard to find another war whose
outcome was so affected by television (it's doubtful, by the way, that the
North Vietnamese leadership were aware that their actions would have
that effect).

The Gulf crisis saw a new growth in psychological warfare—PSY-
OPS—which was in part due to the presence of television cameras in
Baghdad and on the Coalition battlefield.

The power of live video broadcast to a worldwide audience was not
lost on the Iraqis. So, for example, images of Saddam kindly patting a
hostage boy on the head were part of an (inept) attempt to influence the
world at large of the benevolence of the Iraqi leader and the justice of his
cause. It failed miserably.

The Coalition achieved greater success by targeting its message to the
Iraqi Army. But it wasn't easy.

In the beginning, Central Command planners had a hard time putting a psychological-warfare plan together. Though this was historically the responsibility of the Army component, in recent times (such as during the operations in Panama and Grenada), the primary responsibility has gone specifically to Special Operations forces. When the Gulf crisis broke, Central Command, lacking expertise to plan a PSYOPS campaign, requested help from the Commander in Chief Special Operations Command (collocated with CENTCOM, as it happened, at MacDill AFB).

The plan that resulted was useful in identifying targets for PSYOPS efforts, but was an overly "Ameri-centric" view of influencing Arabs. Next, in Riyadh, Schwarzkopf asked John Yeosock to prepare a comprehensive (and less *American*) PSYOPS campaign. This was completed and published in November, and was meant to guide Coalition efforts to influence Iraq's leaders, its people, and most of all its forces in the field. The message was simple: "What you are doing in Kuwait is evil and against your religious beliefs. Get out or die."

Meanwhile, Khaled bin Sultan became interested in the efforts to prepare leaflets and radio and television broadcasts, and to exploit enemy deserters. With his help, the message was made more subtle and complex. Where the American aim had been intimidation, he wanted to emphasize cooperation. In his view, Iraqi soldiers would respond positively to messages like "We know you didn't want to invade Kuwait, and we, your brothers, will right this wrong. Please don't oppose us. Join us instead."

In essence, the enemy was hit with two different messages: The Schwarzkopf tough message showed a B-52 saying, "Desert Storm is coming to your area. Flee immediately." The Khaled message showed Coalition soldiers sitting around a campfire, eating roast lamb, drinking tea, and saying, "Come and join us; we are your friends. This leaflet will be your ticket to safety." Both had an impact.

The PSYOPS message was primarily delivered by air. During Desert Shield, Volant Solo aircraft and selected ground radio stations beamed the Voice of America service in Arabic. These broadcasts continued throughout the bombing campaign and the ground war. After the war began, C-130s, B-52s, and F-16s dropped leaflets on the Iraqi Army. Schwarzkopf personally devised a plan whereby air-dropped leaflets would inform a targeted Iraqi division that they were going to be bombed by B-52s the next day. And so it would happen; the next day hundreds of 500-pound bombs would rain on the division. Afterward, more leaflets would be dropped, advising the Iraqis to flee, as more strikes were planned for their area. And the next day, the unit would be hit again.

Debriefings of Iraqi POWs indicated that this operation significantly affected the troops' morale and was an important factor in their decision to surrender or desert.

★ Because psychological warfare is more art than science, it is very difficult to judge the effectiveness of a PSYOPS campaign.

It is clear that no one in the target audience was missed. Nearly thirty million leaflets were dropped in the KTO, and the world saw Iraqi soldiers surrendering by the thousands, clutching the white leaflets that guaranteed their safe treatment. Radio broadcasts probably also had an effect, as a third of the POWs stated in their debriefings that these affected their decision to surrender.

Nevertheless, a study of PSYOPS after the war concluded that it was not so much the leaflets and the broadcasts as the incessant aerial attacks, the unrelenting presence of Coalition aircraft over the battlefield day and night, that changed people from fighters to quitters. Airpower sent a message to Iraqi soldiers that they had no refuge from attack from above. The noise of jet engines throughout the night, the inability to travel safely, the devastating and sudden attack from an unseen B-52 or F-111 laser-guided bomb drove them into a helpless, hopeless state. The leaflet offered hope of survival. The brutal, unrelenting air campaign made the message on the leaflet count.

However we explain it, nearly 80,000 out of an estimated 200,000 Iraqis in the KTO surrendered, and most of the remaining 120,000 took to their heels when Coalition tanks appeared on the scene.

★ During February, desertion became the number one problem for the Iraqi generals. In some Iraqi divisions, hundreds—even thousands—of troops simply went home. After the Battle of Khafji, the IIId Corps lost at least a further 10 percent of its troops to desertions, and the rate of desertion was accelerating as air continued to pound them. There were even desertions in the pampered, privileged Republican Guard.

Not only were the trigger-pullers walking off the battlefield, but other vital functions were suffering. The logistical resupply of the army was not adequate, and there were shortages of food and water. Essential maintenance was being ignored, and as a result, many of the vehicles, radars, heavy guns, and other machines of war were inoperable or impaired. The lack of maintenance on their fleet of vehicles, combined with air attacks on everything that moved, had reduced the Iraqi logistics teams to using Kuwaiti garbage trucks to carry supplies to their troops dug in on the desert. The trends for Iraq were all bad.

As February wore on, Joint STARS picked up more and more movement at night. Convoys of up to fifty vehicles were trying to evade the ever-present aircraft overhead. Though the darkness of night gave them some shielding, their best ally turned out to be the waves of drizzly weather that passed through the KTO every few days. Unfortunately for the Iraqis, the F-16 pilots developed attack options with the moving target indicator displays on their radar, and took away the Iraqi weather advantage.

At that point, the national community (the intelligence people who didn't deploy to the war) estimated that the Iraqis could no longer meet the logistic requirements that ground combat would impose. While they were believed to have plenty of ammunition, they would run out of food and fuel.

To the Iraqi generals in Kuwait, withdrawal doubtless seemed the best course; but it was too late for that, unless they could find a way to get the aircraft off their backs.

Schwarzkopf's dilemma remained "When do we cross the border? When do we start losing Coalition ground forces to save Kuwait?" To which Chuck Horner added, "When can we get this over with and stop the loss of Coalition airmen's lives, losses that started on January 17? Too often, these deaths were overlooked by the media and others whose eyes saw only ground combat, as if that were the only game in town."

MISSION CREEP

As the war went on, the effectiveness of the Iraqi Air Force continued to decline, even as Iraqi aircraft played no part in the defense of the homeland, after their futile attempts during the first few days of the war. The aircraft lost were invariably parked in shelters or fleeing to Iran, and the losses did not always come from Coalition guns and missiles. On February 7, twelve Iraqi jets made a run for Iran. Three of these were shot down by F-15s, and six crashed in Iran, either because they were unable to land safely or because they ran out of fuel. The fear factor must have been very high among Iraqi pilots.

To offset the failure of their most effective air defense systems, fighter aircraft and radar-guided surface-to-air missile, the Iraqis bolstered defenses in the KTO with short-range, optically aimed heat-seeking surface-to-air missiles, such as the SA-16 or some variant of this Russian-built weapon.

The increased battlefield defenses proved especially dangerous to USAF A-10s. The Warthogs were descendants of World War II P-47 Jugs, as well as the Vietnam-era Thuds that Chuck Horner had flown. They were tough, heavily armored (for aircraft), and very survivable, but slow; and they were used primarily for attacks against enemy armor in close support of friendly ground troops. For that purpose they packed quite a large punch, primarily a 30mm Gatling gun in the nose, one round from which could destroy a tank over a mile away (the Warthog was designed around this gun, which is as big as a Volkswagen, when you include the ammunition drum). It also carried the IR Maverick missile, as well as regular bombs.

The Warthogs were especially vulnerable to short-range SAMs, because they took such a long time to zoom back to the safety of medium altitude after a bombing, strafing, or missile-diving attack.

The good news was that intelligence estimates placed only about two hundred of these missiles in Iraqi hands. Thus, one strategy Horner considered—and instantly discarded—was to deliberately expose his aircraft, in order to "run them out of bullets." *Not a smart idea,* he told himself. *There have to be other ways to defeat heat-seekers.*

★ At the start of the war, the A-10s were used in the role for which they were designed, attacking enemy armor in close proximity to friendly forces. Warthog pilots described the first day of the war as a "turkey shoot." Because Sandy Sharpe and Dave Sawyer, the A-10 wing commanders, kept their aircraft above 10,000 feet, they were able to inflict great violence on front-line Iraqi divisions without unnecessarily exposing the aircraft to enemy defenses (though two aircraft were hit by small-arms fire, the damage was negligible).

The picture got complicated after the opening days of the war, when bad weather over the KTO gave the Iraqis time to dig in deeper.

By the time the weather cleared, later in January, the Iraqis had gone to ground and the impact on them of the high-flying A-10s was far less devastating than before. Consequently, on the thirty-first of January, it was decided that the Warthogs could initiate their attacks from 4,000 to

7,000 feet. In that way, the pilots would be closer to their targets and could more easily spot the dug-in and camouflaged tanks, APCs, and artillery pieces. It also put the aircraft closer to the Iraqis, so they could more accurately aim their guns and heat-seeking missiles.

Despite the increased risk, the A-10s were getting the job done very well, and this encouraged their commanders to task them against other targets, such as SAM sites, fixed structures, and logistical storage areas. The commanders in the TACC, and even at the wing, did not realize that they were all in the process of "mission creep." As a result, they were putting this aircraft and their pilots in needless jeopardy.

For a time, everything went along just fine. The lower altitude allowed the A-10 pilots to find their targets more easily than before, and the tank kills rose. Meanwhile, the defensive threat seemed pretty much unchanged, as the pilots followed the daily directives Sandy Sharpe and Dave Sawyer gave them both verbally and in the pilots' "Read File." Then came A-10 successes hunting Scuds in Iraq and as a "Wart Weasel," and mission creep went into high gear.

Soon, TACC commanders were sending A-10s against targets deep in the KTO, and the command element aboard the ABCCC EC-130 began to divert the A-10s deeper and deeper into Kuwait and Iraq.

Though the A-10 pilots questioned this ever-increasing tasking of the A-10 deeper into harm's way, headquarters ignored their fears (though the two wing commanders did manage to work with the Black Hole and choke off the truly insane mission creep jobs, such as a proposal to bomb an SA-2 storage site near Basra).

Now that A-10s were flying deep behind the lines, battle damage to the aircraft began to mount, and some serious hits were tearing off major portions of the aircraft structure. The pilots were attacking the Tawalkana and Medina divisions of the Republican Guard at 4,000 feet above the ground and sixty to seventy miles north of the border and safety. On the fifteenth of February, the Republican Guard stopped taking it lying down and launched eight SAMs, which knocked down two aircraft and extensively damaged Dave Sawyer's jet.

Sawyer climbed out over the hostile desert at a sizzling 200 knots, with thousands of holes in his engines and tail, and the top of his right empennage blown off. Just as he crossed the last Iraqis, some fifteen miles north of the border and safety, he looked down to see a flight of faster F-16s working over a huddled third-string Iraqi infantry division that Saddam had staked out to absorb our ground offensive's first blow.

A lonely moment. Also an angry one. Somebody had badly screwed up priorities.

We had a problem. Our most effective tank killer was being shot up at an alarming rate. In fact, before February 15, we had lost only one A-10 (on February 2 to an IR SAM), while suffering a little over twenty-five other aircraft shot down. Still, before February 15, the large number of battle-damaged A-10s was wearing on my mind. Thirty or forty had been hit, yet had survived and limped home for repairs—a tribute to their rugged design and safety features. But a lot of hits was a lot of hits. Too many hits.

On the fifteenth, when I walked into the TACC, I learned that two A-10s were down and three damaged, with one of these losing much of its tail. The airplanes were too valuable in a variety of roles, from Scud-hunting to close air support, to have them grounded by battle damage. There was a strong possibility that the Iraqis would run me out of airplanes before they ran out of SAMs.

With a heavy heart, I told the battle staff we were going to pull the A-10s back and use them only against the Iraqi divisions near the border. The Republican Guard and other armored divisions being held in reserve would now be off-limits to the A-10s, until later in the war, when the Iraqis had run out of heat-seeking missiles. Though I was worried that my decision would sting the egos of the Warthog drivers (a fate they sure didn't deserve, since they were excelling at everything they'd been tasked to do), I just couldn't stand by and watch them take hits and now losses.

But Dave Sawyer wrote me the next day, the sixteenth, and (without really meaning to) relieved my worries. "Your guidance to limit A-10s to southern areas is appropriate and timely," he wrote. (That's military for "Thank you, boss. We were being given more than our share of pain and suffering.") He went on to relate the specific procedures he and Sandy Sharpe had worked out:

"We have prohibited daytime strafe for the present, except in true close air support, search and rescue, or troops in contact situations. With the OA-10 forward air control spotters, flight leads using binoculars, or a high (relative) speed recce pass in the 4–7,000 foot range, we should be able to determine worthwhile armor targets, then stand off and kill them with Mavericks. We'll save the gun (and our aircraft) for the ground offensive. The OA-

10s and our two night A-10 squadrons have yet to receive battle damage. There's safety in altitude and darkness. When the ground war starts, we'll strafe up a storm and get in as close as we need to to get the job done. No A-10 pilot should ever have to buy a drink at any Army bar in the future. Until G day, request you task A-10s only in air interdiction kill boxes you've now limited us to. If you need us to go to deeper AI targets, we plan to impose a 10,000-foot above-the-ground minimum altitude there, and employ only free-fall ordnance and Mavericks. We'll promptly exit any AI area in which we get an IR or radar SAM launch."

It wasn't a case of the A-10s failing to do the job, it was rather a matter of building on the strengths of our overall force. We would use the strengths of the F-16s, with their speed and auto-mated bombing systems, to attack the heavily defended divisions deep in the KTO, while the more capable close-in capabilities of the A-10's 30mm cannon would be reserved for the more heavily dug-in, but more lightly defended, Iraqis just across the Saudi bor-der.

Later—after the results of the war were compiled—the superior survivability of the Warthogs was amply demonstrated. Of the U.S. aircraft tasked to carry the mail against the Iraqi Army, only the F-16s and USMC F/A-18s exceeded the A-10s in fewest losses per 1,000 sorties.

There is a story about a young fighter pilot who walks into a sa-loon in some faraway place and sits down at a table with a tough old veteran, deep in thought and drink.

"What is the secret to life and success in flying fighters?" the youngster asks the old hero.

And the steely-eyed, well-worn fighter pilot sings out, "More whiskey, more women, and faster airplanes."

Well, in this war the Warthogs had a lot of success, but they sure didn't have much whiskey, women, or a fast airplane; they did it with brains and courage.

APPROACHING G DAY

Since the Schwarzkopf plan for the ground offensive involved a massive, surprise flanking attack (which was to be anchored by a direct assault into Kuwait), the ground forces slated for the flanking attack had to secretly relocate to assembly areas west of their original positions. The secrecy was crucial to the plan, and the CINC had been adamant about maintaining it. As we have already seen, he had refused to let the Army start its movements until the air war started, lest the Iraqi Air Force discover his preparation for the "end run" of their defenses.

For Gary Luck's XVIIIth Airborne Corps, this directive proved to be a big problem, for they had the farthest to go—over 400 miles, with nearly 15,000 troops and their equipment—at the same time that Fred Franks's VIIth Corps was making its own way west over the same, two-lane Tapline Road. Despite the obstacles, Luck and his two heavy division commanders, Major Generals McCaffery and Peay, worked out how to make this difficult movement.

Luck had one serious advantage over Franks's heavily armored corps, in that his own corps was more easily transported by air. In fact, the 82d Airborne and to some extent the 101st Air Assault division were designed for air transport.

Enter the USAF's General Ed Tenoso and his fleet of C-130s.

Up until the move west, the C-130s' main task had been in high-priority cargo-moving—supporting all the Coalition forces (though with emphasis on United States forces). Where they went and what they moved was decided by Major General Dane Starling, Schwarzkopf's J-4, or logistician.

Early in Desert Shield, Bill Rider, the CENTAF logistician, and his director of transportation, Bob Edminsten, had set up a C-130 airline in the theater. The C-130s flew regular, scheduled passenger flights, called Star routes, and cargo flights, called Camel routes. Starling determined what had priority on these flights, and Tenoso's airlifters put that in the Air Tasking Order.

This "airline" was already a vast operation before the move west, but the effort associated with that move was simply staggering (and largely unsung), with a big C-130 landing every five to ten minutes, every hour of the day, every day of the week, for two weeks after the start of the war on the seventeenth of January, hauling the vast army to faraway places like Rafhah, hundreds of miles up the Tapline Road—a nose-to-tail stream of C-130s.

★ As the armies completed their moves to the west, and the forces south of Kuwait came up on line, weather became the enemy.

Chuck Horner now takes up the story:

★ As February wound down, General Schwarzkopf was under great pressure from Washington to initiate the ground attack before the Iraqi Army was able to negotiate a surrender that would allow them to leave Kuwait with their remaining tanks and guns. The date Schwarzkopf selected for G day was the twenty-fourth of February.

A few days before the big moment, we had had our final war council before the ground war. Generals Franks, Luck, and Boomer had come to Riyadh to brief their final schemes of maneuver to Schwarzkopf, while the Egyptian, Syrian, Saudi, and Gulf Cooperation Council forces were doing the same with Khaled. For all the others, this meeting had to be a high-anxiety affair (*they* were, after all, on the line), but for me it was a relief. For once, someone else was briefing the CINC, and the airmen were (sort of) getting the day off after being the only show in town for thirty-seven days.

So when the war council started, I relaxed in my chair, wondering how well plans would be executed, and how many men would die bravely, needlessly, or because of our failures of leadership. All three U.S. generals were calm and deliberate. No surprises.

Then the weatherman got up and briefed the weather forecast for the night of February 23–24, and it was going to be terrible—rain, fog, winds, and cold temperatures. Cloud bases would be touching the ground, so visibility for the troops would be measured in yards, not miles. That in itself would not be so bad, as enemy troops would suffer the same limitations. In fact, that would cause them far greater problems, since they had to see attacking troops in order to direct their fires. But the bad weather would cause us one problem: it would keep our aircraft and helicopters from providing close air support to attacking forces. Not only would they be denied the power of massed aircraft striking at enemy strong points in their path, but if they chanced to be pinned down in a minefield by Iraqi artillery, they would find themselves in a seriously bad way. This situation, predictably, left the CINC visibly anguished.

Though he was under intense pressure to start the ground war, his obligation to the troops not to spend their lives needlessly always came first with him, and he was prepared to delay the ground attack, no matter how great the pressure from Washington. Still, this decision, if he had to make it, would not come easy (it would have left him naked to Washington's slings and arrows). So when the CENTCOM weatherman briefed rain, fog, and misery, Schwarzkopf's shoulders slumped, and he placed his huge head in his hands.

Meanwhile, my own weatherman, Colonel Jerry Riley, had already given me a preview of the likely weather on the night of the twenty-third and twenty-fourth. Riley was a spectacular weather "guesser," both as a scientist and as a seer, reading tea leaves. He not only brilliantly grasped the scientific data sent by satellites and aircraft over the battle space and from meteorological stations all around the world, but he had a record of accurate "gut guesses" as well. Before Schwarzkopf's high council, Riley assured me that the CENTCOM forecaster's reading of the tea leaves of isobars, low-pressure areas, upper winds aloft, and frontal passages was wrong. As Riley read them, the worst the weather would throw at us that night would be cloud bases one to two thousand feet above the ground, with visibility of three miles in light rain and fog. I believed him. He had been forecasting the weather over Iraq and Kuwait for the previous five-plus weeks with uncanny accuracy. Though we had faced abysmal weather (it had been one of the wettest, coldest winters on record in the region), time and time again he had figured out the weather we would encounter—where, when, and how severe—well enough to let us plan our air campaign. Though the weather was going to be far from ideal on G day, he assured me that it would be good enough for our jets to slip under the clouds and hit the targets the ground forces needed hit.

So there I was, with positive weather information that I believed; and there was Norman Schwarzkopf, actually suffering over the negative report from his own weather guy. And just then I did something I'd never imagined I would do. I put my right arm around his shoulders and whispered in his ear: "Boss, I have a weatherman who's been calling the weather accurately for the past six weeks, and he tells me that the weather is not going to be all that bad. The worst we'll see, he tells me, is a couple of thousand feet of ceiling and a few miles of visibility. We can handle that. I promise you we can provide the close air support your guys are going to need. Trust me on this one, boss. The weather is going to be okay."

I don't know whether or not he believed me, but a burden seemed to lift, and we continued the meeting.

Later, he ordered the ground war to go as scheduled.

And when the troops began their attack of Kuwait and Iraq, they did it in the worst damned weather we encountered during the entire war, with rain, fog, low ceilings, and blowing mud.

Because our troops were ready, and the Iraqis debilitated, we began a ground offensive that turned out to be over more quickly, with fewer casualties, than anyone had ever dreamed. So in the end my weatherman wasn't wrong—the weather was good enough to start the ground war. He just got the numbers wrong, as the weather was for the most part ghastly—zero ceiling, zero visibility.

THE GROUND WAR

At four o'clock on the morning of February 24, 1991, the ground war to free Kuwait began.

That night I had checked into the TACC early. The weather reports were horrible—cold, fog, rain, and drizzle, with blowing winds.

As morning approached and we waited for progress reports from the BCE, the room was filled with tension, even dread. Yet we were also relieved. For airmen, this moment marked the last spurt in a long and difficult struggle. And we were quite simply exhausted.

I tried to imagine what the Marines were going through as they picked their way through the barbed wire and minefields, always waiting for an artillery barrage to rain down on them, which they could only take or retreat.

I knew that the Marines and the Eastern Area Corps were going to give us our best clue about what was really going on. Out to the west, it was going to be more difficult to track the XVIIIth Airborne Corps and French Army, as they became strung out over miles of desert. Though they did not have to confront the massed defensive works that faced Walt Boomer, Gary Luck had problems of his own. Primarily, he had to take his forces and their logistics tails deep into Iraq before the Iraqis discovered they were there, and then he had to place his forces in position to cut off retreat of the forces facing Fred Franks's VIIth Corps, the British, and the Northern Area Corps (Franks's main attack was scheduled for launch on the twenty-fifth).

We were, of course, also aware that the Iraqi Army had crumbled, and that Saddam had desperately tried to escape the battlefield and occupied Kuwait. Hours before the attack, the Russians had delivered a desperate message to Washington, promising unconditional Iraqi withdrawal from

Kuwait, if they were allowed a twenty-one-day cease-fire. No way. Because we wanted their army destroyed, we would not permit them to leave with their equipment, so our response was: "You have twenty-four hours to clear out, not three weeks."

As early as February 20, Army Apaches flying strikes against Iraqi targets in southern Kuwait had reported that the noise of their helicopters had brought Iraqi soldiers streaming out of their bunkers to surrender. These prisoners reported that whole units were prepared to surrender en masse, and were just waiting for our attacking army. Even so, there was plenty of Iraqi Army left to inflict casualties on Coalition ground forces.

No one can overstate the courage of those first ground forces as they carefully picked their way into Kuwait and Iraq in the cold wet darkness of that opening night of the ground campaign.

★ The opening reports were confused. The lousy weather added to the natural confusion, and the troops in the attack had better things to do than send messages to higher headquarters.

Later, reports began to dribble in, and the lines on the maps began to move; but there were no reports of engagements, only the slow, agonizing movement as the two corps in the east moved into occupied Kuwait. Best of all, there were no reports of our losses.

By midmorning, CENTCOM started to send us information: the Marines were through the wire and mine fields and moving ahead at speeds five to ten times greater than expected, there were very few casualties, and the Iraqis were surrendering in such numbers that the advancing infantrymen were having trouble handling them.

Meanwhile, aircraft were streaming over the battlefield, hitting the armored and Republican Guard divisions, as they were, we thought, preparing to maneuver for a counterattack. Though our air attacks were severely hampered by the weather, we dropped thousands of bombs on enemy encampments, trying to obstruct their movement in any way possible. Joint STARS had very few meaningful reports of movement. The Iraqi Army was frozen in place.

By noon, it looked like a rout. Though there had been some sharp engagements, our worst fears were not being realized. Iraqi artillery positions had been found unoccupied, and when Iraqi armored vehicles attempted to engage the Marines, they were quickly silenced. The Eastern Area Corps on Walt Boomer's right flank were advancing apace, rolling up Iraqi defensive positions designed to repel the mythical amphibious landing.

When it became obvious that the Marines were advancing much faster than anticipated, I knew that Schwarzkopf's plans for the main attack would be disrupted.

The original plan called for Walt Boomer and the two Islamic corps to initiate an attack into the teeth of the Iraqi defenses, leading Saddam to think that theirs was the main attack. In the far west, Gary Luck would race north and then swing east behind the Iraqi Army, cutting off their escape. Twenty-four hours after the first units had crossed into Kuwait and caused the Iraqis to react to this three-corps attack in the east, VIIth Corps would launch a devastating blow into the flanks of the Republican Guard and armored divisions (for the most part located near the northwest of Kuwait) as they maneuvered to their left to engage the fake main attack.

But the Iraqis refused to act as predicted. As the attack in the east raced north, the Republican Guard and armored divisions stayed put, probably in the belief that if they moved, they would suffer air attacks like those at Al-Khafji.

Meanwhile, as the Marines and the Northern Area Corps moved forward, their own left flank became increasingly exposed to the Iraqi armor located west of Kuwait City.

The only solution was to push up the launch of VIIth Corps. In that way, the Republican Guard and other Iraqi armor would stay pinned, but the flanks of the Marines and the NAC would be protected.

When I heard that the CINC was contemplating this move, I thought to myself, *It needs to be done, but it is sure going to cause problems for Fred Franks.* The coordinated movement toward a common goal of a large mass of people and equipment is difficult, no matter whether it's third-graders on a field trip or an army corps about to violently encounter a large enemy force. And keep in mind the weather, with visibility in feet and yards, as blowing sand mixed with rain and fog to produce blowing mud.

CENTCOM kept us informed about the traffic between Schwarzkopf and Fred Franks, as they discussed changing the launch of VIIth Corps' attack. I could imagine the confusion this introduced into the carefully planned operation. Nonetheless, the order went out for the VIIth Corps to move up the attack, and the race was on.

Iraqi Effectiveness

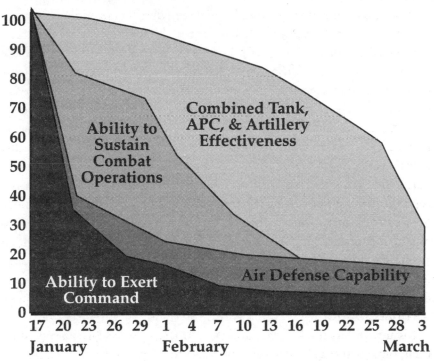

Jack Ryan Enterprises, by
Laura DeNinno

Soon, all five corps were in Iraq and Kuwait. The weather was getting better, but there were few requests for close air support. The fighters were ranging ahead of our forces on the ground.

★ Earlier, during the "air-only war," we had done everything in our power to minimize aircraft losses. Thus, my orders then had stated, "No enemy target is worth one of our aircraft. If you can't hit it today, because of weather or enemy defenses, go somewhere else and we will come back tomorrow." But now the orders were just the reverse: "You have a sacred duty to help the men on the ground. If they need you, you go, even if it means that you may stand a good chance of being shot down or losing your life. . . . Now is the time for you to risk your jet, to risk your life, because they are down there engaged in combat and are for sure risking *their* lives."

At the same time, we had to make sure that our close air support did not endanger the lives of the ground troops. From the start of the war, I had agonized about air-delivered weapons falling on friendly forces.

Modern air war was so deadly that even the slightest mistake was catastrophic. In other wars, if you bombed a friendly position or vehicle, someone might be killed or wounded. In this war, if we mistakenly unleashed our deadly guided weapons or fragmentation bombs on a friendly position, everyone in the vicinity of the attack would be killed. Airpower had grown too deadly for the mistakes one expects in the fog of war. I knew such mistakes would happen; they always do; and they had—during the battle of Al-Khafji, an A-10's errant Maverick missile and bombs from A-6s had killed Marines and Saudis on the ground—but I wanted to make sure we had done everything within our power to prevent more.

Thus, I gave an "if in doubt, don't" order. And I had challenged everyone on the staff, especially the tactics team headed by Lieutenant Colonel Joe Bob Phillips, to figure out ways to avoid hitting Coalition ground forces, and a number of measures, rules, and guidance had been worked out between the Black Hole planners and the BCE.

The factor that drives our approach to close air support is not what one might think. Though bombing or strafing of enemy positions is certainly important, the chief aim of CAS is to *avoid* bombing and strafing our own forces. We do this by establishing boundaries, using ground references to guide our operations.

The first such boundary is usually called the Front Line of Own Troops, or FLOT (though there are other names for it, such as FEBA, Forward Edge of the Battle Area). Whatever it's called, the concept is simple: Your guys are behind a line (the FLOT), and ahead of them is a no-man's-land or else enemy. You don't drop bombs behind the FLOT.

A second line is called the Fire Support Coordination Line, or FSCL, pronounced "fissile." Between the FLOT and the FSCL are enemy ground forces opposing your own ground forces. If you drop a bomb in this region, you stand a good chance of killing an enemy soldier.

The complication comes because of the fluid nature of warfare. That is, the close air support pilot wants to make sure there are systems and procedures that let him avoid hitting friendly soldiers who have advanced since the FLOT/FSCL lines were determined. Thus the role of forward air controllers, and the rule "When air operates in close proximity to friendly ground forces, it must be under the control of a forward air controller." A FAC is an airman who is in contact both with the ground commander and with the CAS aircraft, so he understands what the ground commander wants done and can convey that to the pilot, while making sure the pilot does not mistakenly attack friendly ground forces.

This rule always applies—except during emergencies, as when the guy on the ground is being overrun and says, "To hell with it, my only hope is for air to bomb my position. Maybe the enemy soldier with the knife at my throat will get hit instead of me."

The area between the FLOT and FSCL defines close proximity, meaning that if you are attacking a ground target between these two lines, you are doing close air support and are by definition in close proximity. On the other side of the FSCL, any military target could be hit.

The FSCL is usually placed where it makes sense. For example, in a static situation where neither side is moving on the ground, a good place to put it is somewhere near the outer range of friendly artillery along some clearly recognizable feature, like a line of hills. If the ground forces are in the defense and expecting to fall back, you want the FSCL quite close to the FLOT, so you can attack the enemy ground forces with the least restrictions as they mass for the attack. If friendly ground forces are attacking and moving forward, then the FSCL should be reasonably far out, because of the greater risk of hitting your own troops as they overrun the enemy.

To accommodate the rapid advance we expected during ground operations, the land forces and airmen had arranged a whole series of "on-call preplanned FSCLs"—lines on maps that could be activated as the attacks progressed. Thus, if one corps didn't move forward as fast as expected, its FSCL would remain close to the Saudi border. If, on the other hand, the adjacent corps moved faster than anticipated, its commander could push to the next preplanned FSCL (or at least the segment in front of his FLOT).

During the nine hundred hours of war that preceded the ground offensive in Desert Storm, the FSCL was the border between Saudi Arabia and Iraq-occupied Kuwait.

First, there were no friendly ground forces north of that line (except for a few Special Air Service and U.S. Special Forces hunting Scuds, and we had special measures in place to protect them). Second, there was a bulldozed berm marking the frontiers between Saudi Arabia and its neighbors to the north. Every pilot could easily see if he was over friendly forces or the enemy.

Who decides where to put these lines?

Since the FLOT is determined by the actual placement of friendly forces, you simply find out where your own guys are and draw a line on the maps.

Placing the FSCL, however, is much more difficult. As I pointed out earlier, a number of factors are involved: Are you on the offense, defense, or holding ground? Are the friendly ground forces using weapons that must be deconflicted with the air strike? You don't want a midair collision between an Army artillery round or rocket and your fighter-bomber. One must also consider the terrain—that is, the pilot needs some ground reference for his lines (this last requirement will in fact soon pass away, with the introduction of moving map displays and Global Positioning System satellite navigation systems and displays).

In practice, the ground commander defines the FSCL relative to his needs and his position on the battlefield, but—and this is a big but—he must coordinate with the air commander who is providing the close air support sorties.

Why must the Army coordinate with the Air Force? Because the FSCL limits the airman's flexibility in killing the enemy. If a fighter pilot flying between the FLOT and the FSCL spots an enemy tank, he cannot attack it unless he is cleared and controlled by a forward air controller.

★ During the Gulf War, the placing of the FSCL caused a number of problems.

At the opening of ground operations on February 24, when the BCE ground representatives posted the FSCL in the TACC, it became instantly clear that the Army units were not talking to each other: their FSCLs looked like teeth on a saw blade. (For obvious reasons, the line has to be reasonably neat and uncomplicated.) So the FSCL would be drawn ahead of one corps. Then, when it reached the boundary with the adjacent corps, it would drop or advance tens of miles.

Now, this was serious business. Even in the best of situations, the FAC might miscommunicate the relative positions of the target and friendly forces. Visual identification of the enemy target was not always possible, as friendly vehicles became covered with desert mud and dust. Engagements became fierce and confused, as pilots dodged ground fire while trying to locate targets hidden by the smoke and dust of the battlefield.

Fortunately, we were able to work out the sawtooth FSCL problem.

The BCE got in touch with Third Army headquarters and made them see the light.

We encountered a worse problem toward the end of the war.

When I came to work on the last morning (after finally getting a full night's sleep; I'd left the night before around 2200) and reviewed the ground situation, I noticed to my amazement that during the night, the FSCL had been drawn well north of the Tigris River, in a straight line running east to west. This made no sense.

First of all, we had no forces north of the river and very few north of the major highway south of the river. In other words, the river made an excellent FSCL boundary.

Second of all—and far worse—this FSCL placement ruled out the independent operations of air to halt the Iraqi tanks that had crossed the river and were fleeing north. Our planes could fly over them, but could not bomb them without permission and control from a FAC.

When I asked the BCE duty officer who in the hell had placed the FSCL that far north of the river and why, there was a long and sheepish silence. "It was General Schwarzkopf," he answered finally.

So I said to my own duty officer, "Get General Schwarzkopf on the phone. He's done a dumb thing and needs to be told. He's letting the Iraqis escape the noose he himself built when he sent XVIIIth Corps around from the west."

But then it got very quiet, and the Army duty officer said, "Please wait a minute, sir." And I knew something was up. I waited while he called Third Army headquarters to let them know that I was angry, and why.

It turned out that the CINC had not actually drawn that FSCL. Rather, Third Army headquarters had indicated to my duty officer that he had. Though my duty officer would have protested the stupid placement at any other time, since the war was almost over, and since the CINC apparently wanted it, my colonel had gone along with the change. In reality, Schwarzkopf knew nothing about it, and would have probably objected if he had.

When I challenged all this (even to the point of risking exposure to Schwarzkopf's wrath), then the jig was up, and the Army had to come clean. The FSCL was immediately renegotiated and placed on the river, but too late to hit a great many fleeing Iraqi tanks that had poured through the open door we'd given them.

To this day, I do not know why anyone wanted the FSCL so far north.

My theory at the time was that the 101st Air Assault wanted to use their Apache gunships to attack the enemy, and if the FSCL was on the river they would have to coordinate their actions with the TACC (or else they might have been mistaken for Iraqi helicopters by our fighters).

In fact, all they needed to do was let us know their desires, and we could have easily coordinated operations. But joint operations require give-and-take, and often the land, sea, or air unit will cut corners rather than take the time to coordinate and cooperate. In this case, taking time to work with the TACC was apparently considered too difficult, when it was easier to bluster a FSCL well north of the river. Well, it worked for the Iraqis and not our side.

★ As the army drove forward, stories began to come into the TACC from our tactical air control parties with the Army battalions, divisions, and corps. Some were funny, some showed the tragic stupidity of men at war, and some were heroic.

One forward air controller reported that his battalion commander provided him with a lightly skinned M-113 armored personnel carrier while he himself and his operations officers mounted the attack in more survivable Bradley fighting vehicles. Well, as they moved into Iraq, the team suddenly discovered their maps were next to useless in the trackless desert, but the FAC's Global Positioning Satellite receiver was invaluable. Rather than risking the loss of their Air Force guest in his M-113, the two Bradleys closed to positions on either side of the M-113 as they roared through the desert. If they encountered enemy fire, the Bradleys were likely to absorb the first round. Meanwhile, the Air Force "fly boy" would periodically use his GPS receiver to find their location, write the coordinates on a piece of cardboard, and stick his head up through the observers' hatch in the M-113 to show the commander and his operations officer their position.

On another occasion, two battalions were advancing line abreast through the Iraqi desert, when Iraqi long-range artillery in one sector began to fire on the U.S. troops in the adjacent sector. Since the artillery was inside the FSCL, air could not be tasked to hit the artillery without the close control of the FACs. When his Army counterparts told the FAC under fire the location of the enemy artillery, he called his fellow FAC miles away to coordinate an attack, and the second FAC diverted fighter-bombers from their preplanned targets and directed them against the artillery several kilometers away. The fighters spotted the guns and silenced them with bombing and strafing attacks.

One of the most poignant of these stories came from a FAC with VIIth Corps, also in an M-113 armored vehicle. His unit had progressed rapidly into Iraq and already overrun a lot of Iraqis, most of whom had surrendered without firing a round when they came upon a prepared defensive position consisting of fortified rifle and machine-gun positions. As they proceeded slowly into the apparently abandoned complex, the FAC noticed movement in a nearby trench. Suddenly, a few Iraqi soldiers leapt out of the trenches, threw down their weapons, and started running toward the American vehicles with their hands over their heads. Just as suddenly, an Iraqi machine gun a little farther away opened up on the surrendering Iraqis, cutting them down from behind. At that point, the FAC, seeing one of the Iraqis writhing on the ground, called for his Army driver to move ahead. Disregarding his own safety, the FAC climbed out of the forward hatch of his vehicle, picked up the wounded and badly bleeding Iraqi, and, shielding him with his own body, carried him back to the vehicle. After the driver had pulled back to safety, the FAC did what he could to prevent shock and stop the loss of blood, but it looked very likely that the Iraqi had had it. His flesh had been torn from his arms and legs, and he'd lost a lot of blood. As the army driver rushed them to a forward medical aid station, in a weak voice, but in clear English, the Iraqi explained that he was a doctor who'd trained in America before he was drafted. When the U.S. army doctors at the aid station heard that one of their own was wounded, even though he was an Iraqi, they took heroic measures to save his life; and they were successful.

BLUE-ON-BLUE

Friendly fire—blue-on-blue, fratricide, whatever you wish to call it—has been around as long as war. During the Gulf war, we put greater efforts than ever before into reducing this tragedy. Though we tried hard, and can take satisfaction from our efforts, it was a battle we did not win. The blue-on-blue statistics from the Gulf war are shocking. After-action reports of U.S. Army deaths indicate that about half of their losses were caused by friendly fire, and over 70 percent of U.S. army tanks and APCs that were hit were hit by friendly ground fire.

In the Gulf, the majority of friendly-fire incidents occurred ground-to-ground; that is, people on the ground were hit by fire from ground-bound platforms.

On the other hand, there were no air-to-air blue-on-blue incidents—the result of stringent rules of engagement, modern technology, aircrew discipline . . . and luck.

Here is a story to illustrate all that:

Captain Gentner Drummond was an F-15C pilot assigned to Boomer McBroom's 1st Tactical Fighter Wing at Dhahran, and he looked every inch like the central casting dream of a fighter pilot—tall, slim, handsome, steely-eyed, with a soft Oklahoma drawl. Of course, his name, "Gentner," was a negative. It should have been Spike or Rip or Killer.

At any rate, this misnamed, but highly talented, fighter pilot was leading an element on MiG CAP south of Baghdad the first night of the war, when AWACS called out a bandit—high-speed, low-level, headed south out of the Baghdad area.

Gentner came hard left and rolled out on the vector he got from AWACS. He then pointed his antenna down and got an immediate lock on a target heading south 1,000 feet above ground level at very high speed. He began pushing the buttons on his stick and throttles that would identify the target and tell him whether or not it was friendly, and if friendly, what type of aircraft.

In the meantime, AWACS was calling for him to shoot.

Gentner knew that the AWACS controller had access to intelligence information from the Rivet Joint Aircraft that would confirm that the aircraft was Iraqi. Still, there was room for doubt.

As the F-15 pilot streaked through the night at 30,000 feet, he worked his system on the target. Time was running out. In a few moments, he'd be inside R minimum, which is the closest in range he could get to the target and still use his AIM-7 missile. There was still no ID.

Meanwhile, the AWACS controller was ordering Gentner to shoot.

He decided not to. He wanted to be sure in his own mind, and he figured that his altitude advantage would allow him to perform a stern conversion. That way he could get a better ID of the target, and then down it if it was an Iraqi.

Pulling his Eagle around hard left and down, he screamed into the night and pulled up alongside a Saudi Tornado on his way home from a successful strike deep into Iraq.

For this act of restraint, Gentner received a Distinguished Flying

Cross—that is, he received it for *not* shooting down an aircraft. His composure under the most extreme stress, his use of logic and judgment, and his concern for human life prevented what could easily have been a tragic mistake.

In fact, his was not the only such story, yet it is typical of the stress our aircrews had to endure, as well as the high standards of conduct expected of them.

★ Unfortunately, our record in air-to-ground combat was not perfect.

More than twenty friendly ground forces, U.S., Saudi, and British, were killed by weapons delivered from the air.

Thus, during the confusion at the Battle of Al-Khafji, a USAF A-10's Maverick hit a U.S. Marine armored vehicle, a Marine A-6 bombed a Marine convoy, a Marine gunship attacked a Saudi National Guard armored car, and an unknown aircraft strafed Saudi troops who had wandered into a free-fire zone. Later in the war, a pair of Air Force A-10s attacked two British armored personnel carriers, Army Apaches destroyed two Army APCs, and our airmen destroyed two more British armored vehicles.

Lives were lost in each of these tragic events.

Though all were great tragedies, when placed against the total of air-to-ground attacks, their numbers were quite small—especially compared with other wars. Moreover, we must also weigh in the lives of friendly ground forces saved because air attacks on the Iraqis were so devastating. Of course, no saving of friendly lives makes any loss of friendly life "acceptable" to a commander. Mistakes happen, to be sure, but every effort should be made to prevent needless killings.

★ The officer I tapped to work the fratricide-prevention problem was Lieutenant Colonel Joe Bob Phillips and his fighter Weapons Tactics Team. Joe Bob and his team of eight fighter weapons school instructors had arrived early in February, after General "Tiny" (six feet four and three hundred pounds) West, the commander of the Fighter Weapons School at Nellis, had offered them, both to augment our staff in Riyadh and to capture Gulf war experiences. They'd come not as experts—"We'll tell you how to win this one"—but as field hands. After the war, they could go home to train others, using what we had learned in the only school for combat—war.

With typical fighter-pilot confidence and enthusiasm, Joe Bob and his team went to work. They had a big question to answer: if we had four incidents at Al-Khafji, how many would we face when five corps were unleashed on the Iraqis?

Here are some quotes from Joe Bob's notes: "Working the CAS problem hard. Basically, the mechanics of generating the flow and communication are OK. We're working backups for traffic jams. We have a shortage of airborne FACs and need tighter rules for TICs [troops in combat] situations. Seems that we have forgotten the need for fighter pilots to have guidance on ordnance type and distances from friendly forces, unwise delivery modes, etc. for TIC contact. Also, have only twelve OA-10s [airborne FAC aircraft] in theater—not enough to provide coverage for a hooba of this size. We are working out procedure and agreements with the corps commanders to keep the Killer Scouts employed both inside and outside the FSCL. Inside the FSCL, the attack aircraft must be under control of a forward air controller and prevent attacks on friendly forces and to hit the targets the Army wants hit. Outside the FSCL, the attacking aircraft is cleared to strike without any additional control. He may use J-STARS or Killer Scout, but a FAC is not required."

By mid-February, these efforts were starting to make sense. As previously mentioned, we developed preplanned FSCLs, so that no matter how fast the ground war went, we could stay ahead of it. The more than 2,000 U.S. Air Force people assigned to work forward air control with the ground forces (except for the British and Marines, who provided their own FACs) would be adequate for that job, and our shortage of airborne forward air controls would be augmented by the Killer Scouts. Using AWACS, Joint STARS, and airborne command-and-control aircraft of the USAF and USMC, we were able to meter the flow and provide the needed control that would let us put bombs on target in a timely fashion, while avoiding friendly forces. Though it was a huge and complex undertaking, Joe Bob stuck to it, in spite of occasional abuse from me.

These are from his notes for February 19: "Have been continuing to work the CAS issue hard over the past several days. General Horner has thrown us out a couple of times. I think we are getting closer to understanding his approach. The closest analogy I can come up with is Force Protection. Only, the protected force is super-large and undisciplined, and both sides look the same. Our job is to anticipate what the enemy will throw at the force and come up with a plan and ROE [rules of engagement] to maximize enemy kills while preventing fratricide. VID [visual identification] is out. Assuming that the Army knows where its forces are is out. Earlier approved concepts of providing CAS for an advancing friendly force are out, because they emphasized a superior force attacking a retreating enemy. Kill zones are okay, when the friendlies are in dire straits and need air at any cost. 'Figure it out, shithead, that's your job' is a phrase I'm getting accustomed to from General Horner."

When Joe Bob's plan was published, it provided guidance to FACs, Scouts, Planners, and Air Tasking Order writers. Its basic messages were: "If in doubt, don't. Service CAS requests first. Don't even assume things will be easy or go as planned." And for the most part, they worked.

AND THEN THERE WERE NONE

As the days of the ground war continued, the attitude in the TACC grew ever more relieved. Spirits were high. At each shift change, you could hear the upbeat buzz as the guys related how well the troops in the sand of Kuwait and Iraq were doing. Most important, there were few reports of casualties, and incredible reports of Iraqis surrendering in such numbers that our forces could only give them food and water and tell them where they needed to go to be picked up.

To be sure, we had problems—placement of the FSCL, the weather, friendly-fire incidents, and trying to keep track of all that was going on the battlefield, with its hellish oil fires and rainy weather—but the good news continued.

By February 26, Walt Boomer was a few miles south of the major highway intersection west of Kuwait City; Gary Luck had turned the corner and was racing down the Iraqi highway south of the Euphrates; and Fred Franks was advancing toward the Republican Guard, his ultimate target.

At that point, the Iraqis totally lost heart and started to evacuate occupied Kuwait, but airpower halted the caravan of Iraqi Army and plunderers fleeing toward Basra. This event was later called by the media "The Highway of Death." There were certainly a lot of dead vehicles, but not so many dead Iraqis. They'd already learned to scamper off into the desert when our aircraft started to attack. Nevertheless, some people back home wrongly chose to believe we were cruelly and unusually punishing our already whipped foes.

Meanwhile, numerous tank engagements shredded the myth of Iraqi Army "battle hardness." Fred Franks's VIIth Corps slammed into the heavy divisions of the Republican Guard and other Iraqi armor. And always POWs, and more POWs.

It wasn't all easy. An A-10 was shot down; and an Army helicopter attempting to rescue the pilot was itself shot down, killing several of the crew, with the rest being taken prisoner. Even though it was absolutely clear that the Iraqis were thoroughly defeated, they still remained dangerous, simply because they remain armed, and were frightened and disorganized, in many cases an armed rabble.

By February 27, talk had turned toward terminating the hostilities. Kuwait was free. We were not interested in governing Iraq. So the question became "How do we stop the killing?"

I knew we were close to answering that question when General Schwarzkopf asked me how much notification I would need to turn off our attacks. He was trying to come up with a plan for stopping the war. He knew Washington was going to be asking him very soon, "When can you stop? How long will it take to turn off the ground fires and air fires?"

"I figure two hours," I said, "will be enough to get the word to the pilots before they take off, or drop off a tanker, en route to their targets.

"Once there's a cessation of hostilities," I went on to explain, "we will still maintain fighter patrols over the country, in case the Iraqis attempt a sneak punch with their remaining fighters or bombers. We'll also keep aircraft on the ground loaded with bombs and missiles, in case the cease-fire fails and Iraqi ground forces threaten Coalition ground forces."

But I knew this was just playing it safe. In reality, all that was left to do was begin the talks at Safwan that would make the end official.

After Schwarzkopf's call, I sat in the now very hushed TACC as the duty officers busied themselves reading books or trying to figure how to get back home. There was still flying to do over Iraq, but it was routine. There were still a few engagements on the ground as the Iraqis stumbled into our ground forces and a firefight broke out. We still shot down a few Iraqis who thought it was okay to attack their insurgents in the south and north. But in our hearts, the war was over. We knew it was time to stop the insanity.

14

SHOCK AND AWE

The war to liberate Kuwait ended on February 28, 1991. To be sure, conflict in the region did not cease; armed revolts broke out throughout Iraq. Nonetheless, the purpose of the Coalition forces had been achieved. Kuwait was free. But what did we learn from all this? Chuck Horner continues:

★ As Coalition forces packed up their kits and headed home, historians began analyzing and comparing—and some comparisons are enlightening; see the accompanying charts—while military staffs began compiling studies (in militarese, these are often referred to as "Lessons Learned"). A problem quickly became apparent: This war was so different from—and in many ways so much more successful than—any other example of armed conflict, it offered advocates of practically any point of view an opening to make a favorable case. In the United States, the Joint Chiefs of Staff and each of the service departments published "Lessons Learned" documents that were in fact advertisements for individual programs, requirements, or services. This is not to say they were totally dishonest. Some of them actually uncovered areas that needed to be fixed.

Still, the so-called "studies" tended to be self-supporting rather than critical of the agency that sponsored the work. And too many of the books, articles, studies, and official documents misstated the facts, with the aim of salvaging a weapon system, military doctrine, or reputation whose worth could not otherwise be supported. They were public relations documents, not clear-eyed, honest appraisals, and they were aimed at influencing the soon-to-come budget reductions and debates over each service's roles and missions.

Since the various conclusions tended to be contradictory, there were inevitable battles. The pie was finite.

U.S. Bomb Tonnage Used per Month by Conflict

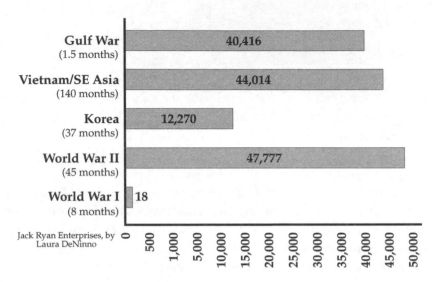

Jack Ryan Enterprises, by
Laura DeNinno

U.S. Aircraft Combat Losses/Sorties by Conflict

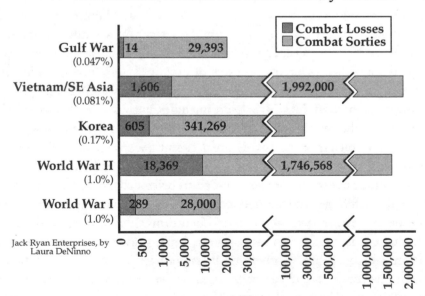

Jack Ryan Enterprises, by
Laura DeNinno

These battles were best summed up in the debate over whether or not the Gulf War was a "revolution in military affairs," or RMA, as it was expressed in the acronym-happy Pentagon.

The RMA debate divided those who wished to continue business as usual from those who believed that war had changed so fundamentally that new organizations, strategies, doctrines, and military forces were needed. The former tended to come from the land services. They took it as an article of faith that war was a matter of meeting the enemy army, navy, and/or air force on the battlefield, and inflicting such damage that he could no longer resist the will of the dominant military force. The goal was to destroy the enemy military so greatly that resistance was impossible or futile.

The revolutionaries—often air, sea, and space advocates—tended to talk about asymmetric warfare. In asymmetric warfare, an apparently weak nation (call it nation A) will refuse to engage its stronger enemy (nation B) in the areas of its strength, and instead will attack where B is most vulnerable. Thus, if B has a large land army, A will avoid ground combat, and perhaps use computer attacks against B's national infrastructure to weaken it, while inflicting large numbers of casualties on B's army with weapons of mass destruction. In asymmetric warfare, A's forces may not even engage B's in direct battle. For example, A might try to isolate B's economy or to debilitate its political leadership to the point where A's will could be imposed, while B's military forces remained relatively intact.

In fact, both schools have missed the point of the Gulf War. Desert Storm was not about a revolution in military affairs, it was a demonstration of the revolution that had already occurred in technology. The RMA has not happened to any great extent because neither the United States military nor its counterparts around the world have been able to fully exploit the technological revolution revealed during the Gulf War.

The Gulf War demonstrated the possibilities available to a nation that decides to revolutionize its military operations. If used effectively, precision weapons, Stealth aircraft, space reconnaissance, and rapid communications would so change military affairs that today's military leaders would no longer recognize the military in which they served. Certainly, Schwarzkopf, Yeosock, Boomer, Arthur, and I did not fully understand how to exploit these revolutionary capabilities. Yet we perceived the clues and (within our own limitations) tried our best to use the resources available, to free Kuwait as soon as possible, while keeping the loss of life at a minimum.

Since this book is about airpower, what is the future of air, looked at from the light of the coming revolution? The best way to get a handle on that, I think, is to examine how we dealt with the new technologies during the war, and then to use that as an entry into the coming revolution in military affairs. Parts of this story will be familiar, but not from this angle.

★ The Coalition strategy was simple—to gain control of the air, use airpower to isolate and debilitate the Iraqi army, and then use ground forces to drive them from Kuwait. The war in Vietnam did not have air superiority as a pressing goal; the result was a drawn-out conflict with thousands of aircraft shot down. I could never forget that lesson. Therefore, the first step, gaining control of the air, was key.

For this, I had advantages no other commander in history had enjoyed. For starters, a U.S. Navy analysis of Iraqi air defenses provided a system-wide understanding of the role of each element that had been designed to protect Iraq from air attack. The point to pay attention to is the *system,* not the elements. No longer would I have to bomb every enemy airfield, or shoot down every enemy fighter, or destroy every enemy surface-to-air missile site. If I could isolate and destroy the heart and brain of the Iraqi air defenses, then the arms and legs could not function, and attacking them would only use precious resources that would be better used in attacks on other target sets.

The analysis of the system told the air planners what nodes should be attacked, in what sequence, and when the attacks should be repeated. These attacks would be conducted with such ferocity and accuracy that the air defenders would be shocked into a state of awe and helplessness. The tools, Stealth and precision, would exploit the opportunities revealed by the complete knowledge of the Iraqi air defense system.

And so it happened.

Because the planners who devised this brilliant takeover of Iraqi airspace had available to them the knowledge of Iraq's air defense system as a living organism, they knew precisely where to inflict wounds, and they had the means to conduct the attacks at low risk and with great precision. The result was the imposition of a regime of shock and awe so great that the Iraqi military situation became hopeless soon after the opening minutes of the war.

"Shock and Awe" (sometimes also called "Rapid Dominance")—a relatively simple concept—is one of the foundations of an understanding of the coming revolution in military affairs.

In war, the goal is to make the enemy accede to your will, to make him do what you want him to do. Traditionally, you accomplish this by destroying his means to resist, as we did with Germany in World War II, but that is not the only way. For example, why not catch his attention in such a way that he is *unwilling* to resist you? In World War II, Japan was worn down as Germany was, but not to the point of total surrender. Then a pair of A-bombs induced such shock into the nation, causing the enemy to hold us in such awe, that they surrendered rather than conduct a bloody defense of the home islands.

In the Gulf in February 1991, Iraqi soldiers were in a state of shock and awe, and surrendered.

★ Today, a B-2 carries sixteen precision bombs (the F-117 carries two) and can strike with the same impunity as the smaller Stealth aircraft. Each of these sixteen precision munitions are guided by signals from global positioning satellites; they can be programmed in the air to strike any target; and unlike the laser-guided bombs of the Gulf War, they can operate effectively in any weather, day or night.

Imagine the impact of a flight of four unstoppable B-2s arriving over an enemy capital and releasing sixty-four 2,000-pound guided bombs on sixty-four targets the enemy deems vital. Instantly, the enemy leader could be denied control of his military forces, his people, and his own governing apparatus. A second wave of four aircraft could then inject shock into another key sector of the enemy's controlling system.

What is required to exploit this revolutionary technology?

First, we must think in terms of what Admiral Bill Owens, a former Vice Chairman of the Joint Chiefs of Staff, called "systems of systems." That is, we must think of an enemy not as an army, navy, and/or air force, but as a system much like the human body. For example, if we wish someone to miss when they shoot at us, we could blind them temporarily with a bright flash of light. If they are chasing us, we might disable the nerves that operate their leg muscles. In other words, we must analyze the weakness and strengths of the adversary and apply our force quickly and precisely. The first trick is knowing what we wish to achieve, the second is knowing how to apply our forces, and the easiest trick is to apply the force.

The kind of knowledge I'm talking about requires a break from traditional methods of evaluating our enemies. In the past, we counted ships, planes, and tanks; and then, to impose our will, we destroyed as many of them as possible. Now we must learn how to look at an enemy through his own eyes, so we can attack him where *he knows* he will feel pain. This will require training not only in how we fight, but more important, in how we think and plan for war. We must have new ways to conduct intelligence analysis.

★ We can learn from the battle for Al-Khafji.

There, once again, the revolutionary technology available to Coalition forces was not known or appreciated by the Iraqis who planned the attack.

On January 25, a prototype Joint STARS aircraft used its revolutionary technology to report in real time the movement of Iraqi forces massing for the attack. The Joint STARS radar discovered and identified military vehicles as they left the protection of their bunkers and moved toward their assembly areas, mistakenly thinking that night and weather made them immune to detection and air attack. They soon learned otherwise.

Their forces were decimated long before they were able to conduct their attack. In the nights and days that followed, the Iraqis gamely attempted to continue their attack, but any movement brought an immediate Coalition air response. As one captured Iraqi said after the battle, "My division lost more vehicles in thirty minutes of air attack than we did in six years of war with the Iranians."

Though the Coalition response was confused, poorly coordinated, and slow to recognize the enemy plan, Coalition forces fought with great courage and dedication, and a force of about 5,000 soldiers defeated an invading heavy armor force that may have had 25,000 to 35,000 soldiers.

There has to be a reason for this success other than the élan and excellence of the Coalition ground forces, and that reason has to be the revolutionary nature of Coalition technology, especially the technology of the Coalition air forces.

Armies depend on movement. They use it to create surprise and to provide protection (by denying certainty of their location and strength). They move to place themselves beyond the reach of their opponent army's weapons. They rely on vehicles for heavy firepower, armored protection, supplies, engineering support, and face-to-face meetings between command echelons.

Yet at Khafji, the Iraqis found that to move was to be discovered, to be discovered was to be attacked, and to be attacked was to die, if you stayed in your vehicle (no matter how much armor plating protected you). They quickly found that when they saw or heard aircraft, their best course was to abandon their vehicle. "In the Iran–Iraq War," a captured Iraqi general reported, "my tank was my friend, because I could sleep my soldiers in it and keep them safe from Iranian artillery. In this war, my tank was my enemy," because it was constantly attacked by aircraft day and night. If his soldiers slept in their tanks, they were sure to die.

This fact did not impact on our planning as forcefully as it should have. During the Gulf War, we had almost unrestricted information about the size and location of the enemy forces but failed to appreciate all his real strengths and weaknesses. We could count his tanks and locate them daily with overhead intelligence, Joint STARS, or Killer Scouts, but we missed the implications of the Iraqi soldiers' terror of sleeping in their tanks. Our reconnaissance pictures showed us parked tanks with new slit trenches nearby. Those who measure effectiveness by the number of tanks destroyed fail to understand that sleeping away from your tank means that you are highly unlikely to get the first shot off if you are suddenly attacked, and are therefore likely to lose the engagement.

★ The aircraft and weapons of today are far more capable than those used in the Gulf War. With more modern computers and improved radar, the Joint STARS aircraft now has a far greater capacity to detect and identify moving vehicles. GPS bombs can now be dropped in any weather. The wide-area munitions, such as the sensor fused weapon, permit aerial attack of massed armor columns, with tens to hundreds of submunitions homing in on individual vehicles.

What does the denial of movement mean for battlefields of the future?

Certainly it means that you have to control the air if you want to maneuver your forces. It also means that you should no longer prepare your ground forces to fight force-on-force against a slow-maneuvering enemy. Given that our control of the air puts severe limits on an enemy's ability to survive the lethal battlefield of the future, expect him to feature small, fast, stealthy movement, and expect him to collapse into urban areas, jungle, or mountainous terrain and to avoid combat in the wide-open spaces.

Meanwhile, if our own ground forces continue to follow current doctrine, our enemy army can expect to find large, massed U.S. ground forces opposing him, but with our mobility and capacity to maneuver hampered by our own ponderous logistical tail. As a result, he will attempt to employ his own form of airpower—guided missiles, ballistic and cruise—to weaken or even defeat this easy target.

This means that the intelligent commander of the future will configure his land forces to mass and disperse quickly. He will reduce the size of his force while increasing the lethality of his firepower. He will select transportation systems that can rapidly move his forces about the battle space with minimum fuel (to reduce the logistics tail). He will be hard to find, yet able quickly to exploit the advantages his superior surveillance of the battlefield affords him.

To bring all of this about will mean that land forces' equipment, organizations, tactics, and strategy at the operational level of war will change drastically.

So the question is not whether or not there has been a revolution. There has certainly been a revolution in military technology, but not in how the military fight, or plan to fight.

★ Let's look at how some of these technological changes affect the individual fighting man.

In the Gulf War, close air support relied on visual acquisition of the target by the pilot in the fighter aircraft, who was guided to his target by voice directions from a forward air controller located on the battlefield. The procedure was cumbersome and imperfect, and too often pilots misidentified the target and attacked Coalition ground forces. Fortunately, such mistakes happened more rarely than in wars in the past; unfortunately, the mistakes were far more devastating than they were in past wars.

Using present technology, however, we can virtually eliminate such mistakes.

For example, our soldiers in Bosnia are now equipped with small Global Positioning Satellite receivers that are coupled with a small laser range finder and radio transmitter. When the soldier sees a target threatening him—say, a tank or a sniper—he simply points his aiming device at it and initiates laser ranging. The device knows where it is in the GPS coordinate system, knows the heading and distance to the target, and relays that information to a nearby F-16 equipped with an improved data modem. The information from the ground is received in the form of a data burst, which is not audible to the pilot but is translated into words that appear on his heads-up display which describe the target and its GPS coordinates. The fighter pilot can either slave his radar crosshairs onto the target; or, when he's in the clear, superimpose the target on the ground with the target designation box and gunsight on his heads-up display; or insert the target's coordinates into a GPS-guided precision weapon. In effect, we are giving the individual soldier a 2,000-pound hand grenade.

This raises questions about how the land and air arms of our military services are developing tactical doctrine to exploit this unique capability. How are they exercising to develop procedures for the soldier to call upon air, and how are we examining command-and-control measures to make sure the weapons are used on the highest-priority targets? These questions will be increasingly important, as potential enemies study the Gulf War and conclude that the best way to avoid destruction from U.S. airpower is to hug their opposite U.S. land force member as closely as possible.

CONTROL

Control is the goal of most warfare. When we are unable to achieve our political ends through persuasion or threat, then physical attack, with the goal of controlling the behavior of our enemy, looks increasingly attractive.

In the past, achieving control has required the physical dominance of one side over the other. Today, new technology provides other means of control. For example, with information technology, we can dominate his senses, reasoning, or mental faculties.

During the Gulf War, the vast majority of the Iraqi army who had not already deserted, surrendered to Coalition land forces. Both the surrenders and the desertions came about because Iraqi soldiers had been dominated by the psychological campaign we had waged. This campaign came with both a stick and a carrot.

The stick: We fatigued and terrified them with unwavering air attack. They knew no peace; they were always in danger; they could not easily be resupplied with food and water; and communications between levels of command were close to impossible.

The carrot: The Arab elements of the Coalition understood which arguments would sway the Iraqis away from their own leadership. Saddam had insisted that Kuwait was part of Iraq, and that it was right and just to return it to the fold, while at the same time he exploited the normal dislike Iraqis felt for Kuwaitis. By way of contrast (and with the help of our Arab allies), we played on their faith in Islam and Arab brotherhood. We told them they were Muslims and Arabs, just as the Kuwaitis were Muslims and Arabs, and it was sinful to make war on brothers of the same faith. While they did not like the Kuwaitis, they felt guilty about the evils the occupation was bringing to Kuwait City. While they were loyal to their families in Iraq, they had no loyalty to Saddam.

For those themes to take root, we needed to control the environment. The air attacks did that.

The Iraqi soldier became fearful. Often, our advancing ground forces found vehicles, tanks, and artillery positions abandoned and filled with blowing sand. With Iraqi soldiers hiding in their bunkers and wondering when the next B-52 strike or A-10 attack would kill them, leaflet, radio, and television messages telling them to give up this unholy occupation of Kuwait easily took root.

Soon, those who could, went home. Those who couldn't desert, waited for the chance to surrender.

By the time Coalition ground forces moved into the Iraqi lines, we had clearly established control over most of the Iraqi army, as was evident by the surrender of nearly 88,000 Iraqi soldiers. Most had not fired a shot.

★ Control can also be exerted on the environment.

For example, during the Gulf War, we made extensive use of electronic countermeasures (ECM) and anti-radiation missiles to exert control over Iraqi air defense radar sensors. The ECM hindered the effectiveness of individual radars and confused the long-range search radars used to cue the short-range, and more accurate, radars used to control guided antiaircraft missiles.

This war also featured a new and highly successful form of control, Stealth. The F-117 proved to be the only aircraft we could send into the air defense cauldron of Baghdad and be certain it would survive, and it could do that with unprecedented efficiency—that is, it did not require large support forces of air-to-air escort, ECM support jamming aircraft, and Wild Weasels carrying anti-radiation missiles, while its laser-guided bombs made it truly efficient in terms of targets destroyed per sortie.

The secret of Stealth: it controls its environment.

The F-117 can go anywhere its pilot commands, and it cannot be sensed by the enemy except visually, meaning that it flies only at night and/or during adverse weather. Though an enemy may be aware that an F-117 is present (he can, after all, see or hear bombs exploding), he cannot locate it with enough accuracy to shoot it down.

Stealth and supercruise will give the F-22 even greater control of the environment. With supercruise, F-22s will fly at supersonic speeds without using afterburner. Thus they can cruise at speeds above Mach 1 with their engines at fairly economical fuel flows. Flying that fast cuts down an enemy's time for action once he detects you—and with Stealth, he will detect you very late in the game. Supercruise and Stealth also collapse the envelope for the employment of his weapons. An air-to-air missile shot from a tail aspect at a supersonic jet has a very small effective range, since the missile has to spend all its energy catching up.

With these advantages, F-22s will almost certainly achieve air superiority over enemy aircraft, and in turn this will permit the entire spectrum of the joint force's non-Stealth aircraft to operate unhindered by enemy defenses.

★ Another good way to control the environment is by using information warfare—the current hot topic in military circles, and for good reason.

Everyone talks about weirdo, geek computer hackers who break into heavily protected bank or military computer systems. But imagine using hacker skills for military purposes. For instance, imagine the military value of taking an enemy's command-and-control system, and inserting a depiction of forces you want him to see, instead of the real-world situation. How about entering his air defense system and letting him "see" false attacks to the west, while your real attack comes from the east? Why not lead him to believe that your ground forces are located where they are not, so he will exhaust his artillery ammunition pounding barren land, while your force escapes unharmed? Or even make him believe the forces arrayed against him are so vast and dominating that he will sue for peace before the battle begins?

Information warfare can be conducted at all levels of conflict, and includes a defensive side as well.

Of all the nations of the world, the United States is the most vulnerable to computer attacks. We use computers everywhere. Our telephones are now simple computer entry pads. Our wristwatches are computers. We plan our days, operate our automobiles, and communicate with computers. Our military equipment is so advanced largely because computers aim our guns, fly our planes, and operate our ships.

Therefore, even as we do our best to control the inputs to an enemy's computers and knowledge system, we must also protect the integrity of the knowledge systems we are using to prosecute the battle.

Most easily understood is the need to protect our own computer databases from corruption or other manipulation. Though private industry and the military have been working this problem for years, the threat has grown at a pace equal only to the raging change in computer capabilities worldwide. There are no longer "have" and "have not" nations when it comes to the capacity to access and manipulate computer databases and programs.

Meanwhile, most current users are in a state of denial about the vulnerability of their data systems, simply because they have some small protection—and the alternative is too terrible to contemplate.

For example, the banking industry loses millions of dollars each year to computer crime. They can afford to overlook that loss. But what if computer criminals learned how to attack the customer trust and confidence on which their industry is built and relies? Could they afford to overlook that? Other financial markets, such as stock exchanges, suffer the same vulnerability.

The military operates under far different expectations. Where the financial industry likes to operate in a precise world, down to the fourth decimal point, the military is used to operating in the fog of war, a world of uncertainty, and at levels of efficiency that might reach 5 or 10 percent—that is, a soldier has less than one chance in ten of hitting the enemy when he fires his rifle. Such levels of uncertainty mean that we in the military so overload our capacity to conduct warfare that a hacker who steals our secrets, inserts misleading information, or injects confusion will not cripple a military operation, only lower its efficiency.

Still, if the opposing military forces are somewhat close to parity, then computer attacks might spell the difference between victory and defeat in battle.

This is the good news. The bad news is that the U.S. military has an extensive capacity to fool itself.

We can talk ourselves into believing our own lies.

Imagine the situation I described earlier: We have entered the computer system associated with the enemy's command and control for air defense, and have depicted a mythical raid in the western part of his country, while our Stealth bombers are in the east. Believing what he sees on his displays, he sends his interceptor forces to the west.

In the meantime, another echelon of U.S. command is secretly pirating the enemy air defense command-and-control data and feeding this information to our air defense units. However, owing to the classification of the computer insertion activity, some good guys don't know what the other good guys are doing. As a result, the intelligence gatherers believe we are *really* attacking to the west. As a result, when our attacking force returns to friendly territory after their unopposed attacks, they are engaged by their own friendly air defenses, who have concluded that they are enemy attackers.

This example is simplistic, yet it illustrates how complicated new forms of warfare can become, and how dangerous can be the failure to work as one force, one team. Control must be all-encompassing in every aspect of the conflict, and it must be coordinated both offensively and defensively. Modern warfare's widespread communications, computer-assisted information systems, and surveillance of the battle space will dictate that the dominant forces have full knowledge of the battle and control of its environment.

They also mean that the victor will be the combatant who can act with the greatest speed.

SPEED

In future wars, the warring parties may not be equal in size or firepower, yet one side's numerical advantages may be offset by a smaller opponent who acts rapidly, decisively, and accurately. Because any nation or group participating in organized warfare can now access computers, space systems, and commercial communications, any warring party can now act rapidly, decisively, and accurately. They can review and analyze data, decide to act, and then commit with such speed that their opponent is reacting to these actions rather than initiating actions that facilitate his own advantages.

This is the advantage of surprise and initiative: long prized by United States military doctrine, and exemplified by the German *blitzkrieg* of

World War II—but a difficult goal for the regimented military mind and ponderous ground armies.

In the future, rapid movement over strategic distances will be required if our military power is to be deployed in time to prevent a crisis from escalating to war or to halt an invasion. This is why American military forces so highly value our vast strategic fleet of airlift aircraft. Going one step further, imagine conventional-tipped intercontinental ballistic missiles, based in the United States but capable of delivering a crippling blow within thirty minutes anywhere in the world. Surely, in that future, the words of warning delivered by the United States ambassador to a dictator marshaling his forces on his neighbor's border would be more carefully evaluated than was the case in 1990.

The essence of modern airpower is rapidity. It is truly the forte of the B-2. Though based in Missouri, it can reach anywhere on the globe in hours, with little preparation or support.

★ For the United States military, "rapidity" has strategic as well as tactical implications.

The United States is blessed with good strategic location, safely tucked as it is between two large oceans on its east and west, and two friendly nations to its north and south. While it is subject to attack from the sea, air, and space, such attacks can be contained, given an adequate navy, air force, and ballistic missile defenses. Since naval, air, and space forces are highly mobile, they can be sized and operated both for domestic defense and warfare throughout the world. U.S. land forces, on the other hand, must expect to engage in faraway parts of the world and not in homeland defense, but their mobility is limited, and it takes time.

Thus, in conflicts far from our shores, the maritime, air, and space forces will either already be on scene or will quickly arrive on scene; the limiting factor will be the arrival of ground forces. Space is on scene at any given time, based on the orbital characteristics of the system. Airpower can arrive in minutes or hours, depending on basing. Sea power may be on scene, or can arrive in days, depending on the location of the ships. But the ever-increasing CONUS basing of land forces means that they will take weeks or months to arrive in strength in a conflict region far from the United States.

It follows that if we are to use military force to deter or resolve conflict in its earliest stages, then we must exploit the rapid strategic mobility of space, air, and naval forces. And if we are to advance the capability of our military forces to deter or resolve conflict, we must increase the rapidity of the land forces' strategic mobility.

Since we are seldom able to predict the outbreak of hostilities, it is vital that the United States have forces that can reach the scene of conflict as quickly as possible, and then move quickly within a battle space.

★ Any future enemy will surely have precision attack weapons that exploit standoff. This means that our military forces must be able to hide or disguise themselves (control the environment) and to rapidly relocate (to areas where enemy weapons are not aimed). This also means that air weapons systems must have longer range, to allow them to be based under our own defensive umbrellas or at airfields or on ships beyond the reach of enemy missiles. This also means that land forces must be able to mass and disperse rapidly in order to accumulate the decisive power needed to win a battle, while denying enemy standoff weapons large, lucrative targets. Tactical mobility is achieved in the air by high-performance aircraft, at sea by long-endurance powerful turbine engines, and on land by high-speed vehicles and by forces that are not tied to large logistic support lines.

While military forces throughout the world are seeking these capabilities—long range, high speed, and freedom from encumbering supply trains—they are not always training and organizing to exploit the advantages of rapid thinking and acting.

BRILLIANCE

This brings me to the last of the elements needed to attain victory in the future—the "brilliance" with which we employ advanced technology. Brilliance is a code word for initiative, and is therefore nothing more than the decisions produced by humans in a decentralized environment.

This is a revolution, not because it is new but because we live in an age when all the natural tendencies drive us toward centralization.

So, for example, the revolution in computers and communications means that information can be transferred on an unprecedented scale from the battle back to some headquarters. From this, some conclude an increased value in centralized analysis and decision making. Why not, they claim, watch over the battle in the calm, cool environment of some headquarters that is close to the President and far from the agony of war?

Wrong!

This is the false trail that (at least in part) led to our failures in Vietnam, where targets were picked in the White House by leaders with immense knowledge of the politics of the war and little comprehension of battle. We must accept the reality that the closer we come to the battle, the more we are likely to know what it takes to fight effectively.

Though each succeeding higher headquarters will—rightly—have a role in determining goals and objectives, we must keep in mind that those who are closest to the action are the most important participants in the action. They are the ones the so-called higher echelons are there to support.

SPACE

Any discussion of Desert Storm cannot ignore the immense contribution made by our space forces. Even less will we be able to ignore their contributions in the future. In Desert Storm, the primary role of space was to provide knowledge. Space, of course, has many other military uses.

Space operations fall into one of two areas—information or combat. Information operations provide data, either as a medium (such as communications satellites) or as a source (such as ballistic missile launch warning, imagery, GPS navigation, and time data). Combat operations include weapons that pass through space (Scuds and ICBMs arrive through space), weapons that defend against such weapons (either lasers, target trackers,* or kinetic impact devices), and weapons that shoot down satellites (in the 1980s, the USAF shot down a satellite using a missile launched from an F-15).

The Air Force has been an able steward of space. The ballistic missile programs of the fifties, sixties, and seventies have matured into the space lift of today, and now upward of 95 percent of our military space assets and operations are acquired and operated by USAF programs and organizations. Blue suits dominate the military cooperative programs with NASA and the National Reconnaissance Office, and Patrick, Vanden-

---

Target trackers accurately track single or multiple warheads in space so other systems can use this targeting information.

berg, and Falcon Air Force Bases have become the core of our military space launch and on-orbit operations.

This situation is not without problems. For starters, our reliance and ability to exploit space grew from support of Cold War deterrence operations. Some of these mind-sets still remain. Second, space is often seen as a subset of air operations.

In fact, as Desert Storm has shown, space has become a pervasive influence in almost every aspect of military operations.

Take GPS.

The GPS system not only tells everyone where they are, it provides everyone the same time (which is vital to such things as the synchronization of encrypting devices on radios), and it is everywhere accessible to all.

Take reconnaissance.

We can watch the enemy nation and adjacent seas anytime in any condition.

Take global broadcast.

We can beam two hundred channels to our forces deployed in any country. The Army can watch updates of battle maps; the Air Force can get target information; the Navy can get weather reports; the chaplain can air his message for the day; and the commander can brief the troops on the upcoming offensive. Anything that is classified will require a decoder box for that channel; no problem.

In other words, space has become too big, too important, to be treated as a subset of air operations or of the Cold War.

Airmen now face a difficult choice: either to define space as air operations at a higher altitude, or to develop doctrine that describes space operations in terms as different from air as air is from land or sea. For the time being, the Air Force has crafted a course of action that defines itself as an "air and space" force that could become the "space and air" force. But that may not be enough.

Our space force is the servant to all our military services. The Army and Marine Corps rely more heavily on global positioning satellite information than do their comrades in the air or on the sea. The Navy requires satellite communications to coordinate the activities of their far-flung fleets. As a result, the land and sea forces are deeply concerned that they rely almost exclusively on the USAF to satisfy their space needs. The problem here is that the Air Force has its own needs (many of which have little to do with space), and these needs have to be funded. As long as each service is funded at an artificial rate almost equal to one-third of the defense budget, the Air Force will be hard-pressed to fill its core air responsibilities while growing its role in space.

All of this means that our space force may need to become a military entity in its own right, equal and apart from our air, land, and maritime forces. At some point the nation must ask itself if we should artificially limit our space and air capabilities with the present budgeting methodology, when both are growing in importance to our defense strategy.

CINCSPACE

I have a particular interest in space because, after the war, from 1992 to my retirement in 1994, I was commander of the U.S. space forces.

Space people are *interesting*. By that I mean that most of them don't seem very much like most of us—not *X-Files* different, but definitely leaning toward strange.

For one thing, you'd think space people would be the most flexible, daring, and future-oriented individuals you're likely to meet. In fact, that is not usually the case. Most of them are incredibly cautious. Many bad things can go wrong in their world; and when they do, the results can be catastrophic. Even a little glitch can be a big problem when the glitch is 22,500 miles above the surface of the Earth. Each space launch is a unique event (just as it was forty years ago). Every time space folks put a satellite on tons of explosive fuel, their memories retain the scars of huge explosions on the launch pad or shortly after liftoff. We all saw the Challenger tragedy on our television sets.

In other words, space folks are the most conservative group you will find. They make Swiss bankers look like druggy surfers. They agonize over every aspect of their trade. The design and construction of satellites can take many years. There are inevitable delays—often measured in years. *Nothing* is left to chance.

Once the bird is in orbit and functioning, it is turned over to the satellite flyers, men and women who work in windowless rooms in front of flickering computer screens. They are backed up by the men and women stationed around the globe (usually at lonely, faraway locations such as island atolls and Arctic wastelands) who operate the radio net that communicates with the orbiting vehicles.

In the control rooms, you'll find computer geeks, people who are among the most highly trained, motivated, educated, disciplined, and competent professionals in our military.

When you enter the room, you notice the hush. The hum of air conditioners is about the only sound present, until you begin to realize there's also a click, click, click of computer keys. That's the noise the space pilots make when they fly their vehicles.

Occasionally, there'll be an anomaly that the operator cannot fix—say, an overheating transmitter as the sun bakes the side of the bird facing its rays. The operator desperately tries to coax the bird to turn so more heat-dissipating material will protect the affected part, but to no avail. When the operator finally realizes he (or she) can't resolve the anomaly on his (or her) own and turns to the supervisor on duty for help, they don't yell "Help" or "Mayday" or "SOS"; they look up from their screens and wave their hand to beckon their leader to their station. The expert then quietly rises from his/her own computer station, walks to the unhappy operator, and bends down to look at the flashing red numbers to which the operator is pointing on the computer screen. These are code for the problem occurring halfway around the world and thousands of miles out in space. The supervisor reaches over and moves the computer keyboard where he or she can tap the "backspace" key to clear the command column, then types in a series of numbers and letters to command the bird to take healing action. Both watch the numbers on the reporting display change as the action takes effect and the bird is saved. Then both go back to their normal work.

The battle was fought without anyone speaking a word. Welcome to the silent world of space.

Is it surprising that such people have made little impact on the guys with guns and bayonets, or that the warriors have had little understanding of how space can support their operations?

When I arrived at SPACECOM, I very quickly found the reason for this. It was fear. The space people were afraid that the mean, ugly warriors would laugh at them for being geeks, and the warriors were afraid the space geeks would laugh at them for being stupid. I knew I had to do something.

First, I accused the space people of doing "a war dance in their own tepees." That is, they were busy creating systems to support military operations, but they were not out marketing their wares, for fear they'd get laughed at or rejected. Then I publicly announced that I was Geek Number One and that I was going to learn all I could about their black art. Since I had some experience getting shot at, I figured this was one geek the warriors would not reject. Then I started marketing the wares space could provide the warriors.

At the same time, I made sure that the often hobby-shop efforts of the space people actually related to the needs of the folks pulling triggers in anger.

Soon it became fun for everyone, as the warriors began to realize more and more the immense contributions space systems and products could make to their efforts; and the space geeks began to gain confidence, not only because of the excellence of their work, but because national heroes thought highly of them and their work.

We are not there yet, but I long for the day when a space geek walks into a fighter pilot bar and announces, "You boys better get out of here. I've had a bad day flying my satellite, I intend to get drunk, and if that happens I may get mean and hurt one of you." At that point, the space pilots will have earned their spurs. "Every man a tiger" applies to *all* the skies, those above the air included.

These are some of the first things I learned as Geek Number One:

To start with, keep in mind that when you enter space, nothing is there. That's good if you want to fly without drag, or if you want to use a laser without the attenuation problems one gets in air, or if you want to see without clouds or dust getting in the way. But living and breathing don't come as easily as down here.

So why go there? Because you can do a lot of things you can't do on Earth. Satellites offer a very convenient platform.

How do satellites work?

Imagine a big cannon. Shoot a projectile out of it at, say, a forty-five-degree angle; the projectile makes an arc and hits some distance away. Shoot the projectile with greater velocity; the projectile makes a longer arc and falls farther away. If you keep increasing the velocity, eventually the projectile falls completely around the Earth, and it has become a satellite. It is now in orbit.

An infinite variety of orbits are possible, and various orbits have various useful purposes.

For example, if you place a satellite at approximately 22,300 miles above the equator and set it in motion with a speed that matches the

Earth's rotation, then it just sits there (at least from the point of view of the Earth). Looked at from below, it's stationary—or geosynchronous (GEO), to use the technical term—with a little less than half the world in its field of view (the exceptions are the polar areas). That means it can receive line-of-sight signals from Earth and beam them back to a receiver located anywhere else in the world that is in its field of view. Hooking these two stations up would mean a lot of copper wire; plus, you can send transmissions to intermediate stations in between. Best of all, you can send the radio beam to another satellite, also hovering over the equator, and that one can send it to another. Either of these can send the message down to a station within its field of view. In that way, you can contact anyplace on Earth (except at its very top and very bottom).

This orbit is best for communication satellites. It is also the home of our Cold War infrared satellites, such as the ones that detected the ballistic missiles launched at Riyadh or Israel.

If you want your satellite to listen to radio broadcasts from some station on Earth—say, KRNT radio in Des Moines, Iowa—it turns out that GEO may not provide a view of an area you want covered. That means you want your satellite to be closer to the station. The problem is that a GEO orbit is the only place in which the satellite will stand still over the surface of the earth; and besides, since you don't care to listen to ABC in Perth, Australia, on the other side of the world, you want your orbiting satellite to float over Des Moines and whiz by Perth. That means you'll want to create an egg-shaped orbital path, with the Earth located at the bottom of the small part of the oval. In that way, your satellite will spend most of its time looking down on Iowa and very little time looking down on down-under. This kind of elliptical orbit is called a "Monayia" orbit (the word is Russian; I don't know what it means).

If you want to use a satellite to look closely at the surface of the earth, then you'll want to fly it as close to it as you can get, because the closer you are, the better you can see things. So you put your satellite in as low an orbit as possible. The problem now is that if you get too low, you start scraping air, and your bird slows down and eventually falls to earth. This orbit is called Low Earth Orbit, or LEO (about 60 to 300 miles up).

If you want to listen instead of look, then you might go higher, so your satellite has more of the Earth's surface in its field of view. This is called Medium Earth Orbit, or MEO (anything between LEO and GEO). Hence, the space geeks talk about LEO and MEO, GEO and Monaiya.

And if you learn to say "anomaly" when something is screwing up, and "effemerius" when you mean speed, altitude, and heading, then you're well on your way to becoming a true space cadet.

★ As CINCSPACE, I had three jobs.

First, I was CINC NORAD. There, it was my responsibility to maintain the air sovereignty of the United States and Canada. Though watching over sovereignty involved keeping track of what flew over our nations from outside our borders, the real job was to evaluate the indications of a ballistic missile attack on the United States and Canada, in order to advise the President and the Prime Minister, so the President could order the nuclear response that would end the world. NORAD handled this warning and evaluation (rather than, say, CINCSTRAT, who would order the attack, should that come) to keep the evaluator separate from the trigger-puller. Of course, the biggest tip-off would have been the radar and IR satellite detection of an ICBM attack.

Second, I was CINCSPACE. There, I commanded components from Army, Navy, and Air Force (of which Air Force Space Command was the largest).

AGENCY	PERSONNEL	BUDGET FY98
US Space Cmd	786	$18.2 million
AF Space Cmd	37,625	$1.7 billion
Navy Space Cmd	562	$70 million
Army Space Cmd	652	$51 million

As CINCSPACE, I evaluated and influenced the space programs of the various services. I also validated the requirements documents used by the services to support the funding of their programs and made sure that the service programs coordinated with, and supported, the efforts of the sister services. I provided space services to the regional CINCS through the components. So, for example, I made sure the AFSPACE flyers of the comm satellites positioned their birds to support the needs of a CINC—say, the CINC Korea (technically, the commander combined forces Korea), who had a special need and had been authorized access to the satellite by the JCS and DISA (Defense Information Systems Agency, which handles long-haul communication and tries to make the services' programs interoperable or joint). I worked with other space agencies, not the least of which was the National Reconnaissance Office (which is responsible for acquiring and operating space vehicles that provide national intelligence, and is headed by an Assistant Secretary of the Air Force). This made sure that the services' interests were represented in the national community requirements documents. In the past, this had been a big problem, as the NRO mainly responded to the Cold War and did not like to get close to regional conflicts. Though that changed after Desert Storm, I still had problems with the CIA, who wanted the Cold War to remain, so they could do business as usual.

Third, I commanded AFSPACE, the Air Force space component, by far the largest of the three service components working for CINC Space. My job there was to make sure operations went as planned and that satellites were maintained and controlled. I also operated ground stations around the world that collected intelligence, talked to satellites, tracked objects in space, launched satellites, or operated the bases that controlled civilian and NRO-launched satellites. I was additionally responsible for recovery of the space shuttle, should there be a problem. If launches or landings went as advertised, then NASA did the job. But if things went bad, then the job was mine. This is because I had the rescue helicopters and military crews capable of reaching and recovering survivors.

As the commander of AFSPACE, I supervised the staff that built the requirements documents that led to new space systems. I managed the funds needed to operate the space networks, maintained the bases, and had a full staff, like any large component.

And finally, I was responsible for the creation of a pair of institutions of which I remain particularly proud, Fourteenth Air Force and the Space Weapons Center.

Fourteenth AF has assigned to it all the space assets of the USAF and serves as a space component in the event of war.

Its assets include both launch complexes at Vandenburg AFB, California, and Patrick AFB at Cape Canaveral, Florida; Falcon AFB (now Schriever, named after General Bernard A. Schriever, who was the genius behind our development of ICBMs, as well as the engines we use to put satellites into orbit—Atlas, Titan, and Delta) east of Colorado Springs, where the actual flying of satellites is managed; and units around the world that make up the AFCN (Air Force Control Network).

Until Fourteenth AF came into existence, there was no specific space component responsible for war-fighting. Space "products" were simply delivered haphazardly.*

As I said earlier, the space folks didn't know war, and the warriors did not know space. Therefore the spacers had capabilities that could help the troops with guns, but since they had no idea what the armed mob did, they could not tell them what they had to offer. On the other hand, the armed mob had no idea what was available. Keep in mind, as well, that most of space is highly classified, owing to its long association with the Cold War and national agencies. Is it surprising that the left hand hardly ever knew what the right hand was doing?

The Space Warfare Center was set up to allow a group of people (half of whom were space warriors and half of whom were air warriors) to think about space war and to exercise space war in the same manner that the Fighter Weapons Center had done since the 1960s. They would then bring space to unified command exercises in Korea or the Middle East, or to service war games such as Blue Flag and Red Flag.

My role at Space was to bring as much war-fighting awareness to the space people, to organize them to respond to the needs of people in combat or crisis management. I pushed for systems that would pay off in regional war and tried to kill everything that addressed only Cold War requirements, such as low data rate communications satellites (satellites that could withstand a nuclear burst in space and thus maintain CINC-STRAT's command-and-control communications, so his airborne bombers could execute their missions).

Most of all, I worked on the awareness, attitude, and motivation of the space people. In other words, lots of Bill Creech—Pride, Product, Professionalism, Initiative.

★ I couldn't close out any discussion of space without a discussion of space exploration. This may seem like a long way from Iraq and Desert Storm, but it's all on the same continuum of what man can dream and achieve.

People talk about space as the last frontier. It's right that they should. Oh, there are people who oppose it, mostly among those who call themselves intellectuals and opinion makers. Their objections take two forms.

Fourteenth AF has a proud World War II heritage. It was the numbered air force in China; and the Flying Tigers (23d Wing) was one of its first units after it was formed.

First, these people want to see space free from human contamination. "Why subject humans to the intolerable risk of space travel, when robots do a better job?" True, space is not safe, but that's not the point. The point is that men and women will go where men and women want to go.

Second, they want to keep space free from the contamination of weapons. "Why not keep the contagion localized?" Their argument is stronger here, but they may as well try to keep their daughters virgins. Weapons are already in space. See above.

In the sixteenth century, there were Europeans who argued against exploring and settling the new continents to the West. They are now forgotten.

There seems to be enough water on Mars to support life—if not Martian life, then the earthly kind. Let's go there. Let's mine the asteroids. Let's go to Titan and gaze meditatively at Saturn's rings. And why stop there?

As we fly beyond earthly bonds, let's face it, we're likely to get into fights. We're contentious. Sure, there's a possibility that sanity will prevail (and I pray that it will), but, humans being humans, don't count on it.

But so what?

Humankind needs expanding frontiers. We are a curious, questioning, outward-going (in every sense), contentious, competitive bunch. We don't like confinement—even when the boundaries of our confinement are as wide as the world that gave us birth.

Man will not be contained.

So let him soar!

BUILDING COALITIONS

When we talk about "Lessons Learned," there is one that hasn't been emphasized enough in the literature I've read about the Gulf War, and I want to underline it here, at the end of this book. Desert Storm was an international team effort. It couldn't possibly have worked as well as it did—or maybe even worked at all—if all the nations hadn't cooperated, paid respect to one another, and shouldered equal portions of the burden. This was not an American war. It was a Coalition war. And we'd better remember how we did it if we're to be successful in the wars of the future.

The same thought occurred to Chuck Horner on a day in mid-February 1991, a time when the air war was on autopilot. The planes took off in the morning and sallied forth to bomb the Iraqi Army. They returned to bases in Saudi Arabia to load more bombs, then continued the pounding of Saddam's helpless troops—now little more than an armed rabble, hunkering down anywhere that offered safety from the aerial onslaught.

Among Coalition airmen, everyone was tired, worn down, fatigued, for this was the hard part of war—the unnecessary part. The outcome of the war had been decided, yet the killing went on. Even after his losses of the first month of the war, and even after days upon days of mind-numbing bombing attacks, the contest of wills between the Coalition and the Iraqi leader continued. Saddam Hussein still held on to the notion that he could somehow win this conflict and keep his stolen treasure, Kuwait.

In mid-February, a new addition to the Coalition air force arrived, when Korea sent four C-130 transports to help move the armies to the west for the ground offensive. The day they landed at their new home at Al-Ain Air Base in the United Arab Emirates, Chuck Horner greeted the *senior representative of the Republic of Korea Air Force, Major General Lee. Lee would go on to command the ROKAF, become the chairman of their military forces, and eventually become the Secretary of Defense of his country; but that day he was another member of the Coalition, an equal.*

At their initial meeting, Horner was surprised at Lee's quiet, humble, and somewhat abashed tone.

At that point, Horner was totally unaware that the ROKAF had never engaged in foreign deployed operations—operations the USAF takes for granted. Thus they were not equipped with the kits of aircraft spare parts, maps, radio navigation charts, tents, fuel bladders, and bags of individual equipment (such as helmets and chemical weapons protection gear) that are everyday life to an American C-130 squadron. They had simply loaded up their transports with maintenance personnel and whatever spare tires and maintenance equipment they could carry, and had flown off to the unknown. The possibility that they might get shot down and die was of little concern. The questions General Lee faced were far more troubling: How would he feed and house his men? Where would they get fuel and supplies to maintain their jets? Most of all—as newcomers to a war that was well into its fourth week—would they be accepted? The honor of an entire nation rested on his troubled shoulders.

He had no doubt that his men would work tirelessly to do whatever was asked of them. He knew that they would risk their lives to fly missions in support of the Coalition ground forces as they advanced into occupied Kuwait and Iraq. But he also knew that without a helping hand, he would fail, and his aircraft would sit on the ground, idle, even a burden, while others fought and died. Despite this profound unease, he was too proud to beg.

As they talked, Horner began to realize how truly worried and anxious the Korean was—even as he himself knew for certain that most of General Lee's worries were groundless.

And at that moment, he had a small revelation. It hit Horner as it had never hit him before what the Coalition was all about. Let him tell you his ideas on that.

★ When I met General Lee, my first thoughts were *Gee, another nation is joining us, and we can sure use their transports. Our airlifters are worn out moving the armies to the west.* But when I met him, I was struck with his apologetic, almost embarrassed, manner. He was worried that he might not have the wherewithal to accomplish his mission. I quickly put those fears to rest with a warm handshake, and with assurances that whatever his people needed would be provided: housing and meals courtesy of the UAE Air Force hosts, spare parts and command and control from his USAF counterparts, and lots of productive work from everybody. *We're all partners in the war to free Kuwait,* I concluded.

After my assurances, a huge wave of relief came over him, and in a moment, he and I became friends.

Up until that instant, I had almost taken the Coalition for granted.

It was then that I began to comprehend the nature of this Coalition, its uniqueness in history, and its importance as a defining aspect to future warfare. It was then that I began to treasure the—what was the right word? Brotherhood? Fellowship? The precise term didn't come easy; we were in a new world here—which I had been too busy to comprehend since those early days of August.

For the first time I realized that this coalition was far different from the joining of forces that had occurred in World Wars I and II . . . that we were a team, not the augmented American force of the Korean War and our ill-fated attempt to fight as a coalition in Vietnam . . . that we Americans were in a position of leadership—yet were truly not in charge . . . that the other national leaders on the team were aware that we were big, had all the nicest equipment, and could be painfully self-assured and arrogant; yet that equality with us was their right and privilege—even though they could never ask for, much less demand, that status, because to do so would be an admission that we were in fact in charge.

General Lee had hit me right between the eyes. He'd made me awaken to the sacrifice it must have been for the other members—especially those from outside NATO—to trust the Americans. And suddenly I began to actually identify with my fellow airmen from this rainbow of nations, joined under a common command in a common purpose.

★ Later that week, I ran into Colonel Mohammed Al-Ayeesh in the Black Hole. This Saudi fighter pilot and Major Turki bin Bandar (called Little Turki) had been the first foreign officers to join the Black Hole planning group in September.*

Al-Ayeesh is now a major general and the commander at Khamis. Turki is a colonel and graduated at the top of his class at the USMC Command and Staff course in 1997.

In September, we had had no foreign officers assisting our planning for offensive air operations, and that had troubled me. Yet I knew that if I asked permission from Schwarzkopf, he would be concerned about security leaks and deny my request. Still, in the belief that it was better to seek forgiveness than to live a life of indecision, I'd gone to General Behery.

"Ahmed," I said, "you must know we are planning offensive operations against the Iraqis."

With a smile, he assured me he was well aware that all those Americans shuttling to and from the large conference room next to both our offices must have been involved in something beyond the defense of Saudi Arabia.

I then explained that I did not want to commit his nation to a war in Iraq, but we both knew that such a thing would be required if Saddam did not terminate the occupation of Kuwait.

He agreed.

Then I took a deep breath, prayed that Schwarzkopf would not kill me when he found out, and asked if General Behery had a couple of bright young officers who could participate in our planning efforts. If we were to be a true coalition, we needed representation from the other nations that would join in the fight to free Kuwait. I assured him that this did not constitute a formal agreement by his government, and added that, though I fully expected them to keep him informed, anyone he gave me would be sworn to secrecy.

He nodded. Then we turned our conversation to other matters.

Later that day, Ayeesh and Little Turki reported to my office, and I took them to the Black Hole to meet their new boss, Buster Glosson.

★ When I ran into Ayeesh that day in February, I asked him about those opening days back in September, and especially about how the Americans had accepted his presence. I wanted to understand how we treated Coalition members from other nations.

Breaking into a huge smile, his eyes sparkling, he asked me, "You really want to know?" When I nodded, yes, he bluntly told me, "They treated me like a dumb officer. The moment I walked in, they shunted me to the side.

"General Glosson was a great boss," he went on to explain, "and he treated us with respect; but we didn't work with him. We had to work with our counterparts in your air force; and with them I was reluctant to speak, and they were not interested in what some Arab who had never been to war had to offer."

By February, of course, the two Saudis had become full partners in the Black Hole team, but I realized what a high hill they'd had to climb to overcome the inherent prejudices of the Americans.

I thought back then to the beginning of the war, when Sheikh Mohammed from the United Arab Emirates had flown to Riyadh with his two planners in order to ensure that the largely American staff accepted them. I recalled the first time I had met Colonels Khalid and Faris as they and the Sheikh had nervously ridden down the elevator with me to go meet Buster.* Because their Chief of Staff had trusted them to ensure that their fledgling air force was well represented in our councils of power, they were proud, almost arrogant; yet they were also afraid. You could see it in their eyes as they entered this den of Americans—violent, self-assured people who liked to call Arabs "ragheads" behind their backs, and whose movies about terrorism always seemed to feature bad guys who looked very much like they did.

It was Ayeesh who made me ponder the importance of this coalition and how hard it is was to form it and sustain it.

★ What set this coalition apart from other military associations of states was not the nobility of their cause. Certainly the mission of the Allies who liberated occupied nations in World War II was measurably more important on that scale. What set this coalition apart was the attitude of the Americans.

It all started with the President. George Bush instinctively knew the role he had to play, and it was far from the interventionist role that had characterized the attitude of his predecessors in Vietnam. It was not his role to dictate the contribution of others, to tell them how they would fit into an American war. Rather, George Bush's experience as head of the CIA and Ambassador to China and the United Nations had taught him that Americans did not have all the answers and that others could contribute more than just the lives of their fighting men. For that reason, he had sent Dick Cheney to Jeddah in August to ask King Fahd what he

---

*Khalid is now Brigadier General Khalid, commander of the UAEAF; and Faris was recently reassigned from Commander of the UAEAF Academy to England for advanced studies.

thought we should do after the invasion of Kuwait. And as the days dragged on, the Coalition grew stronger, not weaker, despite the difficulties that countries of such diverse cultures and interests experienced working side by side. In large measure, that was because the American President did not throw his weight around. He listened and sought counsel from the others.

As a result, the men and women from other Coalition states did not receive secret phone calls from their capitals warning them to watch the Americans, telling them to be careful lest the United States military lead them down the path taken in Vietnam.

The Americans needed this Coalition as much as those fighting to defend their countries in the Gulf needed us.

At the end of the Cold War, there remained a single superpower, the United States. How long she will remain so, only God knows, but for now we are it. This is a very dangerous thing. Our economy dominates the economies of other nations. Or as the Saudis (whose riyal is tied to the dollar) say, "When America gets a cold, we get pneumonia." If the President of the United States decides to bomb another nation, who can stop him? Sure, other nations can condemn our actions, and Russia retains the means to rain thousands of nuclear weapons on North America. But the size, economic strength, and military power of the United States is without equal.

Therefore, it is incumbent on the American president to walk carefully and to think before acting, as unintended consequences of military action—no matter how noble the cause—can have far-reaching effect.

This is why the Gulf Coalition and the way it was formed and maintained is so important. The cause was noble—to free Kuwait. The Americans were needed, because of their military power and leadership roles in organizations such as the United Nations. But the Americans needed the other Coalition partners: to provide bases and ports for access; to provide soldiers, sailors, and airmen to confront a huge Iraqi military machine fighting on their own soil; but most of all, to provide counsel and legitimacy for a superpower that, left to its own devices, could fall into a pit of quicksand like Vietnam.

Because of the divergent cultures, self-interests, and experiences of its partners, the Coalition was hugely difficult to form and maintain. The biggest divergence was between Americans and Arabs.

The four-decade-plus existence of NATO provided common experience for American, Canadian, French, Italian, and English members of the Coalition. And for airmen, integration was further eased because they all spoke English and (as noted earlier) flight operations are task-organized. Thus, they could fight in the same piece of sky and work as one, using the common Air Tasking Order as guidance while retaining prerogatives appropriate to their national identities.

By way of contrast, the Gulf Cooperation Council nations did not share an experience like those from NATO. More important, they did not have the combat experience of Korea, Vietnam, and the Cold War. Thus, they entered the fight as an equal partner who did not feel equal. More important still, their air forces were young. If it was troubling to a young USAF pilot to wonder how he would do his first time in combat, consider how troubling it must have been to an Arab fighter pilot to wonder how he would do his first time in combat.

In fact, the Arabs had nothing to worry about on that score.

Let's look at the record.

In their brief combat in a life-or-death losing cause, the Kuwaiti Air Force did very well. When the Iraqis came across the border that night long ago in August, the air force of Kuwait rose to meet them.

A key ingredient of the Iraqi plan had been to capture the emir of Kuwait and his family, so the invaders could establish a puppet government and legitimize their theft of the nation and its people. In advance of the attacking tanks, Iraqi special forces, some of Saddam's best-trained, best-equipped, and most loyal troops, were flying in helicopters to Kuwait City to surround the royal palace, overwhelm the royal guard, and capture the emir.

It didn't happen. KAF fighter aircraft and surface-to-air missiles shot down thirty-three of the Iraqi vanguard.

Though the fight was over quickly, and Kuwaiti air bases were overrun by tanks early the next morning, the KAF had bought the time the emir needed to flee to Saudi Arabia. Having saved their emir, the KAF fighters had to turn themselves and flee to Saudi Arabia. While they were bitterly ashamed of their defeat, they had fought well and now only wanted another chance to avenge the unholy occupation of their land and to liberate their wives and children in occupied Kuwait. Men like Lieutenant Colonel Al-Samdan, who represented his nation in the TACC, had only one fear—that the Coalition would not go to war, that Kuwait would not be freed, and that they could never go home to their families.

For the other GCC nations, the choices were less clear.

The year before, Bahrain had received brand-new F-16s, the world's premium multirole aircraft, after its pilots and ground crews had operated F-5 fighters for years. Though F-16s are easy jets to fly and maintain, it is difficult to maximize the full capabilities of this amazing aircraft's avionics suite. In the USAF, years of training are required before pilots are capable of using the F-16 to its fullest. The Bahrainis didn't have a year, and they didn't have homegrown leaders who had fought in Vietnam to guide them.

But they did have "Saint"—the call sign used by an American who had left the USAF and taken a job in Bahrain as an instructor pilot. I cannot use his real name. A typical fighter pilot, Saint loved flying more than anything else. So when the chance came to fly with the Bahrainis—to fly daily, with no paperwork other than filling out grade sheets—he jumped at it.

When Iraq invaded Kuwait, the emir offered his nation's squadrons of F-5s and F-16s to the task of aiding Kuwait, and he asked Saint to help.

This request meant problems for Saint. As an American citizen and not a member of our military forces, it was legally forbidden for him to take part in another nation's combat operations. So when the Iraqis threatened Bahrain, he should have joined those who fled the region. Instead, he stayed on where he was needed, training pilots.

After the war began, Major Hamad, the commander of the Bahraini Air Force, was faced with a dilemma: His air force was eager to enter the war; his pilots were well trained; he had some of the best-maintained jets in the world; but he had no one with combat experience—no one with the self-confidence that combat instills. He didn't have to look far for a solution.

He went to Saint and asked him to help get them started, and Saint was not only delighted to help, he was overjoyed at the chance to return to combat, and honored that Hamad had asked him.

Saint flew the first Bahraini combat mission as leader. He flew the next one as number three. Then, as the Bahrainis gained combat experience, he flew as number four.

He did this fully aware that flying combat for Bahrain was putting him into a legal no-man's-land. At worst, if he was shot down, he had no status as a prisoner of war and could be executed as a spy. He could also lose his citizenship, as our State Department takes a very dim view of

Americans running around the world fighting for other people. But he was a fighter pilot, and such insignificant details couldn't keep him from strapping on his G suit.

Saint flew as many missions as he could, but reckoning had to come, and finally, friends in the American embassy warned him that the State Department had heard rumors about his activities and were preparing to investigate.

Though his combat missions had to stop, Saint's experience and example had made a significant contribution to the Bahraini pilots' self-confidence. Day in and out, they flew combat air patrols and bombed targets in Kuwait.

Were they afraid? Certainly. Was it a huge challenge? Yes. But they did everything asked of them with professionalism and pride.

After the war, I visited Sheik Isa Air Base and pinned air medals on the chests of twenty-two extremely proud Bahraini fighter pilots. In the back of the room stood Saint. He had no medals on his chest, yet there was just as much pride on his beaming face.

Bahrain may have had the smallest air forces to fly combat in the Gulf War, but their record in the war was second to none.

★ The United Arab Emirates received new Mirage fighters in late 1990. So getting them into the war was a very near thing.

When Saddam Hussein invaded Kuwait, Sheikh Zayed had been the first Arab leader to ask for American military assistance. We had deployed two KC-135 tanker aircraft to conduct air refueling exercises with UAEAF aircraft flying defensive air patrols in the Arabian Gulf. Later, Sheikh Zayed's pilots and their new French fighters joined the Coalition air forces working to free Kuwait. The only problem: his pilots were not trained to operate the new jets, let alone fly them into combat.

Many people believe Arabs are lazy. I can tell you that when the temperature is over 120 degrees Fahrenheit, no one wants to engage in physical labor out-of-doors. Nonetheless, these men from the UAE had no other options. They *worked*. They put in eighteen-hour days, in ground school and in the air, learning how to fly their new jets, learning how to use their electronic warfare systems, radar, missiles and bombs, and honing combat skills in air-to-air and air-to-ground combat.

Young Colonel Abdullah led their first combat sorties. Though these didn't go perfectly, the pilots got the job done; they got better; and day after day, they joined the stream of Coalition fighters coming out of the air bases in the UAE and going forward to free Kuwait.

★ Perhaps the biggest hurdle Coalition airmen had to overcome was the fear of failure.

Even Saudi pilots had to face such fears—though they are among the most experienced in the world. Their commanding general Behery, for example, had flown an F-86 on the national acrobatic team, and their Ambassador to the United States, Bandar bin Sultan, had been a skilled F-5 and F-15 pilot before his King assigned him to duties in Washington.

Even so, young Saudi pilots still had to confront the fear that every fighter pilot faces on his first combat sortie. And for the Saudis, the stakes were higher than normal. After all, the Iraqis were on *their* border.

The following story of one young Saudi pilot on his first combat mission is not atypical.

SOMETIMES IT TAKES A HERO

Imagine you are a young man who has caught the bug to fly.

Though you live in a nation that has not known war since its birth in the early days of the century, you join your country's air force, and they send you off to fly the most wonderful airplanes, sleek F-5s and the awkward but powerful high-tech Tornado. You love the freedom of flight, and you are good at it, so there is the pride that comes from competence, and you are proud to serve your king and country.

It is not all easy. Some of your mates do not survive the hazards of flying fighters. You are often away from home, attending schools in the United States. And because you are a Type A personality, you put in more hours around the squadron than do some of the others. Still, it is an idyllic existence—until Saddam Hussein decides to rape Kuwait and threaten the safety of your nation, family, and home.

"Errr," you think, "maybe being in the Air Force has some drawbacks. . . . Oh what the heck, we've been training for this for years. . . . Still, I wonder if I can hack it?"

Lieutenant Colonel Sultan Farhan Al-Milhim—our young aggressive Tornado pilot—loved flying, his country, his family, his base commander General Turki (who was his role model), and his God. Everything else was down in the noise level.

After the dust settled in August, the Royal Saudi Air Force got back into a training routine. Flying out of Dhahran's King Abdullah Aziz Air Base, Sultan prepared to repel the Iraqi Army if it came across the border from occupied Kuwait.

Later, he planned strikes into Iraq. His target was an airfield, and his sortie on the war's first night would be part of a major effort involving RSAF Tornadoes, U.S. Navy F-14s, and USAF Wild Weasels.

Early in January, with things heating up, the overall mission commander for the target Sultan had called a meeting of all the flight leaders aboard the aircraft carrier USS *Kennedy*. The mission commander was responsible for making sure all the planning bugs were worked out and that everyone understood what needed to be done for a successful strike. Once the mission was initiated, the mission commander could call a change or abort—depending on weather, enemy defenses, or the condition of the target.

The meeting went well; the U.S. Navy F-14 WSO mission commander and the Saudi Tornado pilot strike leader were on the same wavelength. Because the plans had meshed so quickly, Sultan was able to slip out to take care of the real reason he'd wanted to visit the carrier: to watch takeoffs and landings—among the most difficult operations performed by any fighter pilot. Though he'd love the challenge of trying that himself, he knew he'd never have the chance. His country didn't have a carrier.

On January 16, with no inkling yet that war was only moments away, Lieutenant Colonel Sultan put in a long day at work, mostly going over maps and tactics the squadron aircrews would use to attack a variety of targets in Iraq. He worked well past midnight and then headed for home, a lonely place now, as his wife and children had gone to Jeddah to escape the threat of Iraqi Scuds.

On the way home, he stopped at a small restaurant in El-Kobar, a nearby town, for a bite to eat. At home, he called his wife to reassure her that all was well, turned on CNN, and slipped off his flying boots.

The phone rang. It was his squadron commander. "Sultan?"

"Yes," he answered. (*Who else would be here?* he asked himself.)

"I want you to come back here," the squadron commander said.

"Why?" Lieutenant Colonel Sultan asked. "Is there anything wrong?"

"You need to come back. Something has come up."

"What kind of thing?"

"Maybe we are going to war."

"Are you serious? You're not joking?"

"No, come to the squadron."

The young pilot quickly put his boots back on, turned off the television, and ran to his car. On the way to the base, he drove slowly, thinking about what might be ahead, and as a devout Muslim, his thoughts soon turned to prayer—a prayer shared by all the aircrews that night . . . not for the protection of his life or forgiveness for the horrible acts he was about to do. It was the universal fighter-pilot prayer: "Please God, don't let me make a mistake."

At the base, everything was quiet. He wondered where everyone had gone, but then he noticed lights in the mission planning room. When he got there, the room was crowded. Everybody was there, from General Turki, the base commander, on down; and everybody was talking, trying to brief Turki on the details of the mission they'd been tasked to fly.

Sultan walked across the room to the general, saluted, and asked, "What is going on?"

His squadron commander answered, "We are going to war."

Sultan then asked, "Is it real?"

The general slowly and sadly answered, "Yes, this is real."

The aircrews were now assembled, and now it was time for the mission commanders—like Sultan—to lead them. The young lieutenant colonel was one of the oldest fliers in this young squadron in this young Air Force, and now it was time for him to take charge.

Sultan walked to the mission planning table, where the crews were poring over maps and intelligence plots of Iraqi air defense guns and surface-to-air missile sites. At that point, Lieutenant Mohammed Raja, Sultan's weapons system officer, gave him some disturbing yet exciting news: "Colonel Sultan, sir, I think it's our time!"

Sultan looked at him. "Are you sure?" he asked, and Mohammed nodded yes.

As they turned to leave, General Turki stopped them. All the pilots at Dhahran's King Abdullah Aziz Air Base respected Turki. Not only was he a superb aviator, he listened when they needed to get anything off their chests, he chewed them out when they made a mistake, and he praised them when they shined. Because the aircrews loved their commander, they wanted to please him; and because he was one of them, he loved them in return.

Now they had to go on the RSAF mission of war.

Colonel Assura, the chief of logistics, who was standing beside Turki, took Sultan's hand. "I wish you good luck," he said.

Then Turki put an arm around him. "Just go for it," he said. "Good luck. I wish I was with you."

Moments later, Sultan had assembled the crews in the personal equipment shop. There they donned their survival vests and G suits. Once they were suited up and gathered close around him, he could sense their eagerness and fear. "I know you are used to having a briefing before we fly," he told them. "Tonight this is war. We will fly off the plan. Don't change anything. We have been planning this strike for six months. Just follow the plan and you'll be all right."

Though he was the oldest man there and was doing all he could to calm them, in his heart Sultan himself was deeply troubled. Most were his students. They hung on his words. But this night would see the birth of a combat air force. After tonight, they would be the old heads, the veterans—but first they had to make it through the night. This was a first time for everything—first time into combat, first time to carry and drop the huge JP-233 runway-busting munitions, and the first time someone would make a concentrated effort to kill them.

The bus ride to the aircraft shelters was deathly quiet. Each man was locked in his own thoughts. For his part, Sultan wondered why they were fighting this war. He thought about the Iraqis, brother Arabs, united in Islam, who had savagely violated Kuwait, also brothers. He thought about an old adage: If someone points a gun at you, and you think he'll shoot, then you must kill him. Well, the Iraqis were pointing their gun at Saudi Arabia, so he and his WSO Mohammed had killing work to do.

At the aircraft, number 760, the crew chief was busy pulling off the dust covers. Sultan did not do a preflight, since the crew chief had already done that, and he appreciated Sultan's trust and confidence. As he swung his right leg into the cockpit, a warrant officer on the ground crew asked if they could write a message on the bomb load slung under the fighter's belly. With a grin, Sultan told them to write whatever they wanted to, then went through the time-honored procedures of strapping the jet to his body. He never learned what message he carried to Iraq, because he was too engrossed with engine start and system check to find out.

Because Sultan had skipped the preflight, he and Mohammed reached the runway first. Though they rolled into their takeoff position eight minutes behind schedule, they knew they could make up the time because slack had been built into the inflight refueling delay. The engine run-up was good, and the afterburners lit off, blasting the night's silence and darkness with a roar and yellow-blue flames. As they rolled down the runway, however, Sultan realized he had never flown so heavily loaded and had not computed the takeoff data, check speed, nosewheel liftoff speed, takeoff speed, and distance.

"What's the takeoff speed?" he asked Mohammed on the intercom.

"I don't know," Mohammed replied. In true WSO fashion, the backseater had no intention of doing the pilot's job for him, even if it meant he might wind up in a ball of blazing twisted metal off the end of the runway.

"Okay," Sultan told Mohammed, "I'll take her to the end of the runway, and then if we can't get off, I'll eject and take you with me, okay?"

Mohammed did not answer, as the fighter was now going over 150 miles per hour.

Aware that the heavy bomb dispenser fastened under the aircraft required added speed for a safe takeoff, Sultan watched until the "3,000 Feet Remaining" sign flashed by, then tenderly pressed the front part of the control stick, and the nose of the Tornado started to fly off the runway. As the last of the runway flashed by, the jet was waddling into the darkness.

Sultan had never flown in worse weather—thunderstorms, rain, and lightning buffeted the jet as they searched the night sky for their RSAF KC-130 tanker aircraft; yet when they reached the air refueling contact point over northern Saudi Arabia, they were now only four minutes behind schedule . . . only, there was no tanker. They had to refuel or they could not get to the target and make it back home.

This really must be war, Sultan thought, *because things are rapidly getting all screwed up.*

Breaking radio silence, he called the "Camel" aircraft, asking for his position ("Camel" was the call sign used by Saudi pilots for their refuelers).

His tanker answered that he was a hundred miles to the south, too far for Sultan to make a rendezvous, refuel, and make it to the target on time. In other words, Sultan and Mohammed were out of the show their very first try at combat.

Just then, another Camel aircraft called, its pilot a longtime flying buddy of Sultan's. "Sultan, is that you? Do you need gas? I'm at the refueling track at the next block altitude, sixteen thousand feet."

In their excitement, Sultan and his KC-130 pilot friend were talking in Arabic instead of the more correct English, until someone else came up on frequency to tell them to keep quiet (they were supposed to be comm out). Sultan then climbed up 4,000 feet and put his Tornado behind this new tanker. Now he had to get hooked up to the basket trailing a hundred feet behind the KC-130. During daylight and in good weather, this was a demanding task. At night and in thunderstorms with a heavily loaded jet, it proved close to impossible.

Sultan called his tanker friend: "If you really want to help me, climb another four thousand feet so we can get on top of this weather."

"I can't," Camel replied. "There are aircraft above us." (He had read the Air Tasking Order, good man.)

Always the fighter pilot, Sultan simply hooked up and said, "Then keep your eyes open and give me high flow." (That meant pump the gas at maximum pressure, so the receiver aircraft would fill its tanks in the minimum time.)

As they bounced through the night sky, riding the tops of angry clouds, desperately hanging on to the hose of a pirated tanker, risking collision with other aircraft scheduled to use that same piece of sky, Sultan asked Mohammed to let him know exactly when they had enough fuel to get to the target and back. Though they were now eight minutes late and still short on gas, Mohammed advised Sultan that they could do that.

Sultan thanked the tanker and backed off, then rolled the fighter onto its back and split "S"s down into the inky blackness. Because of their high-speed descent, and because the tanker had dropped them off at the north end of the refueling track, they were able to save six minutes. Now they needed only to fly faster and make their appointed time over target.

Leveling off at 3,000 feet, Sultan checked out the terrain-following radar and its connections with the jet's autopilot. Since everything was working, he selected 1,500 feet, soon followed by 1,000 feet; and then, swallowing hard, he flipped the switch that caused the fighter to drop to 200 feet above the ground.

This was another first—the first time this crew had operated this close to the ground using the terrain-following system.

Mohammed extinguished the aircraft's exterior lights, and now, the only light came from the eerie glow of the cockpit displays.

Meanwhile, Sultan watched his moving map display, which showed them where they were located at any given time. He watched with fascination as the Saudi border with Iraq began to approach. *This looks like the real thing,* he thought, *ten miles to the border. Perhaps they'll call us back. Surely they will call this off.*

When they flashed across the border at 200 feet above the desert, Sultan sadly concluded, "Well, so it's war!" and armed up his weapons dispenser.

On the radio, two squadron mates called that they were three minutes behind and low on fuel. Sultan ordered them home, as they could not possibly catch up, and they must not be late. Meaning: Sultan and Mohammed were now alone.

Mohammed then said to his pilot, "We're on track and on time."

Sultan looked ahead, but saw nothing except darkness. At thirty-five miles out, he concluded they were headed for the wrong target, or else nothing was there. At twenty-five miles, the supporting Wild Weasel launched a high-speed antiradiation missile at a SAM radar, and suddenly night turned to day, as thousands of tracers lit the night sky.

In his surprise, Sultan cried out, "My God, look at this, Mohammed!"

But Mohammed, ever the quiet one, had nothing to say about the show. And anyhow, he had more important things to do than gawk at fireworks; he had the exacting work of putting the crosshairs on the target.

At fifteen miles, Sultan asked his mate if he was happy with the target. Meaning, is the radar picture good enough for an accurate release of their weapons?

"See that big fire?" Mohammed answered, meaning the SAMs and tracers rising from the airfield ahead. "That's it."

It's a beautiful thing when your WSO is cool, while you are thinking you'll never see your wife and children again.

Sultan then realized that it was time to pay more attention to what he'd been sent out to do. At the same instant, it occurred to him that he was likely to die. Thinking he'd better let Mohammed have a vote, he asked, "Mohammed, we can turn back. It's up to you. Will you go with me?"

The taciturn Mohammed replied simply, "I'll go."

Then Sultan repeated the Islamic prayer uttered by those about to die.

As they neared the target, Mohammed got a perfect placement of the crosshairs on the runway that was their target.

Meanwhile, Sultan had grown concerned that the terrain-following autopilot might give a fly-up command because of all the debris being thrown up in front of them. He toggled off the automatic flight system and began to hand-fly the aircraft, easing it down to below 100 feet.

His preplanned attack had him flying across the runway, so bombing errors would be canceled out by the long string of bomblets carried in the JP-233 dispenser. However, since the other Tornadoes tasked to cut the runway would not be coming, he made an instant decision to fly down the runway to ensure it was rendered inoperable for its entire length. Even though this change in plan would expose their aircraft to the maximum gauntlet of enemy fire, he knew he had to do what he had to do.

Slamming his jet around in the night at hundreds of miles per hour, only tens of feet above the ground, he lined up on the long runway now located somewhere in the holocaust of bullets and rockets shooting into the sky. He pressed down with his right thumb on the red button on top of the stick, and the fire-control computer initiated the process that would dispense the runway-cratering bomb over the target.

The jet flashed into the bright streaks from the bullets and rockets meant to kill them, and Sultan spent his longest six seconds, flying down the Iraqi runway.

Then they were streaking back into the darkness and Sultan was about to sigh with relief, when he heard a loud thump, and the aircraft made a shudder. He froze, certain they had been hit by the antiaircraft fire. He nervously checked his dials and lights to see where the problem was. *Are we on fire? Are we streaming precious fuel? Is this the end just when I've cheated death?*

He shouted to Mohammed on the interphone, "We've been hit!"

"No, no," Mohammed answered with his usual cool, "that's just the empty weapons dispenser." The dispenser automatically jettisoned when all the bombs were gone. Then he implored his fearless leader, "Please turn back, or else we are going to Baghdad!"

Filled with relief, the pilot pulled his aircraft around to a southerly heading and climbed away from the place of terror and death toward home.

As they crossed the border into the safety of the Kingdom, Sultan and Mohammed were filled with pride—and with gratitude that they hadn't screwed up. A month earlier, Sultan had gotten into trouble for doing an aileron roll during a night flight. But now as they crossed the border, he made a series of celebratory rolls to the right and then to the left. They were both alive!

At home in the shelter, the crew debriefed to a wildly enthusiastic ground crew. They had successfully brought off a lot of firsts for their young air force.

The next day, I reported the success of their mission success on world-wide news. Their attack had been so precise, I said, that you couldn't have placed their munitions more accurately if you had driven them out to the runway in a pickup truck.

Meanwhile, after the laughter and crying, General Turki sent Sultan and Mohammed home and told them to take the next day off, which they did; but these combat veterans quickly discovered that in war you don't relax, except through exhaustion. After they returned to the flying schedule, they flew thirty missions.

Let me add that after his first experience of low-level ground fire, Sultan demanded that they stop flying low-altitude bomb runs, and Turki backed him up. This paid off, for the only Saudi Tornado lost in the war ran out of fuel trying to land in fog at the King Khalid Military City forward operating base (where there was no approach control capable of handling such emergencies).

Some jobs require heroes. Someone has to set the records for others to follow. The hero is afraid, sure: afraid of enemy fire, afraid of being killed, but most of all afraid of screwing up and letting his mates down, afraid of failure. In spite of their fear, Captain Sultan and Lieutenant Mohammed fought the people like me at headquarters who failed to give them adequate warning, fought the weather that dark and stormy night, fought the disruptions that left them the sole aircraft to attack the target, and fought the Iraqis, who had not yet learned to fear and respect our Coalition airpower. They fought and won.

Thank God for heroes.

BUILDING COALITIONS

The key ingredients to forming and maintaining a military coalition are common purpose, political leadership, and military forces that can work together.

The common purpose removes the tendency to define national interests, as in, "What's in this for me?"

The coalition that fought in the Gulf had one common purpose, to liberate occupied Kuwait. Sure, there were other national interests at stake. For the Europeans, it was access to affordable oil. To the Arabs, it was national survival. Nevertheless, the overarching purpose, the one used to goad the United Nations into action, was to stop the rape, murder, and robbery of one nation by another.

It's easy enough to say that we need to have a common purpose. The trick is to understand and articulate it. Or, as General George Marshall said, "The hardest thing to do is define the political objectives of war. Once that is done, a lieutenant can lay out an appropriate military strategy."

★ The political leadership President Bush provided the Desert Storm Coalition was critical to its success. Because he listened to and consulted with the political leaders of the Coalition nations, they were confident that their views and concerns were being considered as the Americans formulated policy and actions. The outgrowth of this trust at the top was trust at the military levels below. And so as the military leaders met, there were no hidden agendas. Certainly there are already enough honest differences between air, land, sea, and space approaches to war; suspicions of national agendas could only have made it far more difficult to plan and execute military operations.

For our part, we among the military worked hard to respect the rights of other sovereign nations. Where a nation had concerns and sensitivities, we modified our rules of engagement, our proposed operations, or our tactics to accommodate them.

We also worked hard to develop interpersonal relationships with our Coalition partners. This was not easy, as rank, egos, and the size of each nation's military contribution could cause divisiveness.

For airmen, fortunately, rank had little importance, and all spoke the common language of aviation, English. But egos were inevitably a problem, especially for United States personnel who have been taught to swagger from the first day of pilot training and have been brought up in a nation that has little experience of international tact. The size of a nation's contribution could also have led military leaders to conclude that one nation had more combat expertise than another. Yet superior equipment and more personnel did not automatically translate to wisdom. All had to listen to the others, and where there was honest difference of opinion, it had to be resolved by hard-fought, respectful, but honest debate.

Here the United States military was at a disadvantage, as we are so certain of ourselves. Since we are usually the biggest player, without meaning to, we tend to intimidate our partners. Sure, the others want Americans to lead, but they resent it that we act as though we are in charge.

★ Being in a coalition means doing business the hard way. It takes time and patience. Ego has to be set aside, as the lives of men and women hang in the balance. You won't have all the answers, and mistakes will be made. But if you build a relationship of trust and openness, respect and acceptance, then you can work through the difficult times.

The immediate success of the Gulf War was the liberation of Kuwait. Perhaps the more enduring success was the working together of the Coalition nations.

In the future, the United States will face many national security challenges that will require military operations ranging from humanitarian aid to war. We already see the United States in a NATO-led coalition doing housekeeping (technically termed "out-of-area operations") in the former Yugoslavia. It is likely that similar combined military operations will be the pattern for the future—ad hoc coalitions that provide room for many nations to be united in a common cause, with the United States providing leadership but not necessarily in charge.

We were lucky in the Gulf. We had a history of working with the Gulf nations and our NATO partners. But how will we prepare for the future?

Coalition operations are not easy. Command arrangements can be difficult. So can communications (radio equipment is often incompatible, even when the language is common). Intelligence must be shared (the United States often classifies for "U.S. eyes only" even the most obvious details about an enemy). Yet the last remaining superpower needs international partners. We not only gain valuable insights from our compatriots about what needs to be done and how to do it, but we are inhibited from making stupid mistakes. Our combined efforts gain legitimacy because they come from many nations, not just one. Therefore, we need to prepare in peacetime to undertake combined operations during a crisis.

This has begun to happen. Already, United States military forces train with the men and women of other nations. Blue Flag exercises at Hurlburt Field bring together the Gulf War nations to plan and execute air operations, should they be needed in that part of the world. As our focus turns from the Cold War to a more complex new world of ethnic violence, proliferating weapons of mass destruction, and peacekeeping operations, U.S. forces in Europe work with new partners from Poland, the Czech Republic, Ukraine, and Russia.

Annually, our airmen, sailors, soldiers, and marines deploy to Korea, the Middle East, and Africa to train alongside our friends around the world, and our sale of American equipment to other nations ensures we will be capable of operating side by side.

The only question that remains is this: Will our future political leadership have the wisdom and training to form a coalition like the magnificent team that fought in the Gulf? Or will we repeat the mistakes of Vietnam?

ACKNOWLEDGMENTS

Thanks to all the men and women who flew over the Gulf and performed such magnificent feats, as well as those who supported them on the ground and on the water. Thanks, too, to G. P. Putnam's Sons, for letting me do these four books on command—it's been a real learning experience. And thanks to you, Chuck—the right man in the right place at the right time.

Tom Clancy

The folks who deserve acknowledgments from me are Tom Clancy, who collaborated with me and got me hooked up with William Morris, who didn't want me but learned to love me. To John Gresham, who got me started with lots of clerical help and shared enthusiasms. And to Tony Koltz, who asked the right questions, told me how sorry a writer I am, and procrastinated sufficiently to mean I am working on this four years after I was ready to go.

Chuck Horner

BIBLIOGRAPHY

Atkinson, Rick. *Crusade: The Untold Story of the Persian Gulf War.* Boston: Houghton Mifflin Co., 1993.

Cohen, Eliot A., dir. *The Gulf War Air Power Survey.* Washington: Office of the Secretary of the Air Force, 1993. Five Volumes and a Summary Report.

Coyne, James P. *Airpower in the Gulf.* Arlington, Virginia: The Air Force Association, 1992.

Creech, Bill. *The Five Pillars of TQM: How to Make Total Quality Management Work for You.* New York: Truman Talley Books/Dutton, 1994.

Gordon, Michael R., and Gen. (Ret.) Bernard E. Trainor. *The Generals' War: The Inside Story of the Conflict in the Gulf.* Boston/New York: Little, Brown Co., 1995.

Hallion, Richard P. *Storm Over Iraq: Air Power and the Gulf War.* Washington: Smithsonian, 1992.

Khaled bin Sultan. *Desert Warrior: A Personal View of the Gulf War by the Joint Forces Commander.* New York: HarperCollins, 1995.

Kitfield, James. *Prodigal Soldiers: How the Generation of Officers Born of Vietnam Revolutionized the American Style of War.* New York: Simon & Schuster, 1995.

Levins, John. *Days of Fear: The Inside Story of the Iraqi Invasion and Occupation of Kuwait.* London: Motivate Publishing, 1997.

McMaster, H. R. *Dereliction of Duty: Lyndon Johnson, Robert McNamara, The Joint Chiefs of Staff, and the Lies That Led to Vietnam.* New York: Harper-Collins, 1997.

Powell, Colin L. *My American Journey.* New York: Random House, 1995.

Schwarzkopf, Gen. (Ret.) H. Norman. *It Doesn't Take a Hero: The Autobiography.* New York: Bantam, 1992.

Tennant, Lt.-Col. J. E. *In The Clouds Above Baghdad: The Air War in Mesopotamia 1916–1918.* Nashville: The Battery Press, 1992. Originally published 1920.

Ullman, Harlan, and James P. Wade et al. *Shock and Awe: Achieving Rapid Dominance.* Washington: The Center for Advanced Concepts and Technology, 1996.

INDEX

Numbers in italics indicate illustrations